The Two Traditions
The Art of Storytelling
Amongst French Newfoundlanders

The Two Traditions
The Art of Storytelling Amongst French Newfoundlanders

Gerald Thomas

BREAKWATER

Breakwater
100 Water Street
P.O. Box 2188
St. John's, Newfoundland, Canada
A1C 6E6

The Publisher gratefully acknowledges the financial assistance of the Canada Council.

The Publisher acknowledges the financial assistance of the Aid to Scholorly Publications Programmme which is jointly administered with the Social Science Federation of Canada and is funded by the Social Sciences and Humanities Research Council of Canada.

Cover photograph courtesy of Scott Jamieson.

Canadian Cataloguing in Publication Data
Thomas, Gerald, 1940 -

The two traditions

Translation of: Les deux traditions.
Includes bibliographical references and index.
ISBN 1-55081-055-3

1. Tales — Newfoundland — History and criticism.
2. Canadians, French-speaking — Newfoundland —
Folklore. * 3. Tales - Newfoundland.
4. Storytellers — Newfoundland. I. Title.

GR113.5.N49T5613 1992   398.2'09718   C92-098681-1

This is the author's revision and translation of *Les Deux Traditions: le conte populaire chez les Franco-Terreneuviens*, published in 1983 by Les Éditions Bellarmin, Montreal.
[ISBN 2-89007-519-2]

Table Of Contents

To Luc Lacourcière (1910-1989)

Acknowledgements

Every author knows that the completion of a book is subject to the inescapable factor of time. It is all the more inescapable when the author, enmeshed in University teaching and research, has little to spare. I am therefore extremely grateful to the President and the Board of Regents of Memorial University of Newfoundland for granting me sabbatical leave from the beginning of September 1980 to the end of August 1981, in which period the major part of this book was written.

I am equally indebted to the Social Sciences and Humanities Research Council of Canada which awarded me a Leave Fellowship for this period. The award greatly facilitated my task. Publication of the French edition of this study was supported by a grant to Editions Bellarmin of Montreal by the Canadian Federation of the Humanities; this same organization awarded the author, in 1984-85, a grant to facilitate translation of the work into English. This generous support is hereby duly acknowledged.

It has long been one of my aims to give back to French Newfoundlanders, albeit in a form different from that in which they so generously gave it to me, a significant part of their cultural heritage. It was in order to stress their ethnic background that I originally wrote the book in French, although it is not my mother tongue. I recognise here my debt to colleagues in the Department of French and Spanish, especially Professor Mireille Thomas, and the then French Assistants Anne Thareau and Nadine Renault, who between them corrected the inaccuracies in my French. I also thank Marie-Annick Desplanques who reviewed my French translations. I particularly wish to thank Vivian Labrie of the *Institut québécois de recherche sur la culture* who read with a critical eye a significant portion of the manuscript. The present edition owes its lack of gallicisms and general stylistic infelicities to the editorial help of Richard E. Buehler, Generalist, of Memorial's Department of English. My appreciation of his care is great.

This study is the result of ten years of research and fifteen years of collaboration, both as student and colleague, with Professor Emeritus Herbert Halpert. Without wishing to lay at his door the faults that may be found in the following pages, I would nonetheless point to him as the fountainhead of such merits as the book may claim. My studies in folklore were done under his direction and I expect to carry the imprint of his thinking to my grave. The thought, needless to say, is a happy one.

The debt I owe Luc Lacourcière is much harder to specify, since I never studied with him. I do know, however, that from my first contact with him in 1967, I was drawn to that subtle mixture of the great scholar and compassionate friend. He would not, I trust, be offended at my considering him a spiritual father. At another level, he always encouraged me in my work, which was pursued at times in quite difficult circumstances. It is for these reasons that I dedicate this book to him.

My original intention had been to devote this book to the study of the storytelling art of a gifted narrator from Mainland, Mrs. Elizabeth Barter. Her daughter Geraldine, who began working with me in 1973 and was forging for herself a promising career as a folklorist, was suddenly afflicted, in the summer of 1979, with a serious illness, the effects of which still linger. In deference to her mother's wishes the project has been set aside, but with the hope that she will eventually continue her work. Her devotion to the study of her own culture and the invaluable assistance she afforded me deserve a special word of gratitude.

I will never be able to thank too strongly the persons who provided me with the great bulk of this book's subject matter, Mrs. Blanche Ozon and Mrs. Angela Kerfont of Cape St. George, and Mr. Emile Benoit of Black Duck Brook, the former representing storytellers of the private or family tradition, the latter those of the public tradition. Their contributions to this study have been invaluable, as the reader will quickly realise. It is with great sorrow that I must record the deaths of all three storytellers since the French edition appeared in 1983: Mrs. Blanche Ozon, on July 23, 1984; Mrs. Angela Kerfont, on November 11, 1991; and my truest of true friends, Emile Benoit, on September 2, 1992. They are all three greatly missed.

I would never have been able to appreciate the value of the three storytellers, however, had it not been for the many other French Newfoundlanders who, in different ways, provided me with the abundant data that justified the founding in 1975 of the Centre d'Etudes Franco-Terreneuviennes, which is devoted to the study of their traditional culture. By this book, I hope to demonstrate my gratitude.

Centre d'Etudes Franco-Terreneuviennes,
Department of Folklore,
Memorial University of Newfoundland,
St. John's, Newfoundland,
March 1993.

Introduction

From the end of the eighteenth century and throughout the nineteenth, a handful of French people, some from Acadia, some from Brittany, Normandy or the islands of St. Pierre and Miquelon, settled along Newfoundland's West Coast. The Acadians, coming mainly from Cape Breton Island, chose to settle the fertile lands bordering the interior of Bay St. George and the Codroy Valley; farmers for the most part, they wanted to reestablish themselves in the wake of the tragic events of 1755, in a region free of constraints. Their descendants share the same land today with Scots, Irish, English, and a small number of Micmacs.

That they were able to start their lives anew in and around the present towns of Stephenville and St. George's was in large part due to the lack of any effective government in the region. Furthermore, the coastline from Cape Ray in the south to Cape Norman in the north offered a succession of harbours to French fishermen alone, England having granted a monopoly to France in the 1713 Treaty of Utrecht. This was, until 1904 when French rights came to an end, the so-called "French Shore." Along this stretch of coast French fishermen set up installations which enabled them to carry on a fruitful in-shore fishery. They readily tolerated the Acadian settlers they encountered, for while the Acadians' presence was, strictly speaking, illegal, they did not interfere with the fishery and were moreover able to offer the French certain services. The fishermen arrived in the springtime, caught, cleaned, salted and dried their catch, transporting it to France at the end of the autumn.

The various French installations, the most important of which were controlled by merchants from St. Pierre (or by French interests with St. Pierre branches) for most of the nineteenth century, offered the fishermen a hard life; indeed, most of the "fishermen" were young lads whose first year or two were largely spent cleaning and "making" the fish on the shore. They were most often peasants from the hinterland of Breton fishing ports like St. Malo or St. Brieuc, or Norman ports such as Granville.

They were prompted by reasons both material and romantic to sign up for work in conditions so difficult that some of them would eventually desert, seeking refuge in the then uninhabited woods of the Port-au-Port Peninsula. The deserters were never very numerous, but they eventually managed to found families through unions with the daughters of legitimate residents (whose role was to oversee the fishing installations in winter) or with Acadian girls from the St. George's region. Later, some families whose heads had completed their service in St. Pierre, left to return to the peninsula, where the men had worked for so long and which they

11

knew so well. Thus were founded the present villages of Cape St. George, Degras, Mainland, Winterhouses and Black Duck Brook, where the French are still in the majority.

Between 1904, when the French finally renounced their rights to the Newfoundland coast, and 1940, the different French communities, Acadian and metropolitan alike, slowly but surely grew. While the influence of English became more pervasive, for by force of circumstance it was the language of the Church, of schools and of business, the relative isolation of the French, especially of those living at the peninsula's western extremities, prevented an effective linguistic and cultural assimilation.

The establishment of an American Air Force base at Stephenville in 1940 was to have a disastrous effect on the Acadians, who gave up their farm lands to make way for runways and buildings. They were not only dispersed again but worse, they were submerged in a flood of English speakers, American, Canadian or Newfoundlander. But at the same time the base offered to the French, men and women alike, the possibility of paid work. This was an irresistible temptation with, as its consequence, the immersion of many French speakers in what was, officially at least, a uniquely anglophone workplace. The demands of employment contributed to a growing assimilation far more radically than did the combined weight of Church and State.

There followed a period of approximately twenty-five years in which even the peninsular French, though physically distant from the centre of anglophone influence, seemed on the point of giving up their cultural heritage. While it is true that the ethnomusicologist Kenneth Peacock uncovered a rich folksong tradition there in the course of his fieldwork in the late 1950s, in point of fact he recorded few singers, and most of the French songs he later published were from the repertoire of one singer, a woman then in her fifties.[1] Whole families gave up the use of French, and a passing visitor in this period predicted the disappearance of the French language there within twenty years.

Such was not to be the case, however. Twenty-five years later, French culture on the peninsula was enjoying exceptional good health. In the early 70s French Newfoundlanders, inspired in part by some innate feelings, in part by the federal government's policy of the day promoting bilingualism and biculturalism, were beginning to take renewed interest in their culture.

It was at that point I began my research on the folklore of the peninsular French. Having completed an M.A. in Folklore in 1970, I was looking for a topic for doctoral research. My supervisor, Professor Herbert Halpert, directed me towards the island's French minority, on the grounds that at that time I was the only scholar in Newfoundland able to ally a knowledge of French with training in folklore. In this regard Halpert was supported by his friend Luc Lacourcière, who encouraged me to work in one of the very few French-speaking regions of Eastern Canada where he had not himself undertaken folklore fieldwork.

Under Halpert's wing I had been trained as a folklorist convinced that my role was not simply to collect folklore, but to do so in such a way as to be able to explain the way folklore functioned among those who used it. To do this, one had to observe the human and physical context in minute detail, to be, in a word, a "contextualist-functionalist."

I chose to work on the peninsula, rather than among the Acadians, because I believed that its relative isolation would have helped maintain certain traditions which were vanishing elsewhere before the rising tide of modern technology. I also knew that ten years earlier, Kenneth Peacock had vaunted the region's rich traditions.

My particular interest was in folktales, but the methodology I expected to adopt, one which required in-depth and long-term fieldwork, supplemented by several short field trips, was aimed at acquiring a very broad overview of the traditional life and culture of my future informants, so that I might place the tales collected in the widest possible context.

Thus it was that I spent a period of eight months in Cape St. George, sharing the daily life of informants who soon became friends. In the course of my stay I began to see life from their point of view and to assimilate their life-style as far as was possible. To this lengthy stay I added several visits, some of only a few days' duration, others of a few weeks, to the villages of Mainland and Black Duck Brook. Once a year I took the students enrolled in my course on the traditional culture of French Newfoundlanders at Memorial University on a field trip to one of these communities.

In November 1975, a most illustrious "student" joined my merry band of budding folklorists: Luc Lacourcière, who, after a little ceremony at the University in the course of which he was awarded an honorary doctorate, was able to fulfill his dream of doing some fieldwork among French Newfoundlanders. He is still remembered there, if only for the trick he played on me, letting me think that during my absence, one of my best storytellers, a woman, had remembered a fine version of the tale-type AT 950, which she promptly proceeded to tell me. In fact, Lacourcière had told her the story shortly before my return, and put her up to the deception....

By the end of 1977 I had finally completed and defended my dissertation. I continued (and indeed continue) making field trips to the peninsula, but I needed a period of reflection, the better to digest and assimilate the fruits of my earlier research. I wanted to take up certain ideas that had been little developed in my dissertation. This book is the result of my reflection.

From my earliest recordings of folktales from the French of the peninsula, I had been struck by the fact that the people telling me folktales claimed not to be storytellers. On the other hand, they provided me with names of people, living or dead, who were, from their point of view, authentic storytellers. When they described old-time *veillées* (social evenings) in which these authentic narrators had performed, they spoke of them in terms which indeed seemed to give validity to the distinction. While drafting my dissertation, it seemed clear to me that there existed, or had existed, two narrative traditions, the one a private or family tradition to which I had had access, the other a public tradition which seemed to have disappeared.

This observation raised two questions: how to identify the factors which distinguished the two narrative traditions, and how to explain the decay of an oral narrative tradition which still had, as my research had demonstrated, many male and female practitioners?

It was in the context of my interviews with the two women representing the private or family tradition in this book, Mrs. Blanche Ozon and Mrs. Angela Kerfont of Cape St. George, that I was to find a partial solution to the two problems. I was in the habit of letting the tape-recorder run throughout recording sessions with all my informants. This method allowed me to gather all kinds of interesting remarks which very often helped clarify my understanding of my informants' lives, and which, when the conversation turned to stories, provided me with useful insights into my informants' attitudes towards storytelling.

Among storytellers of the private or family tradition, at least, there was to be found a distinct dislike of long stories and of the repetitive character of *Märchen*.[2] On the other hand, I could see the real pleasure felt by many people as they watched soap operas on television. As incongruous as it may seem, I compared soap operas to folktales, concluding that the folktale tradition suffered directly from competition with television.

Based on my informants' remarks on the attractions of television, on their criticisms of some features of folktales, and on their comments on the style of storytellers from the older public tradition, I was able to acquire a sense of the similarities and differences between the two traditions. It was essentially a matter of style and interpretation in narrative performance. I had reached this stage of my thinking when I completed my dissertation.

In the ensuing period of reflection, I focused more and more on the criteria of excellence governing folktale narration in Franco-Newfoundland tradition, as I had been able to define them in light of my fieldwork findings. It was obvious that if I wanted to confirm them, I should have to study and observe a storyteller from the public tradition. It is true that I had met a narrator from that tradition, and he had convinced me my notions were not erroneous; but he was a person who had set aside tale-telling and was only rarely willing to share his time with me. What I lacked, therefore, was adequate comparative matter.

And then, in 1978, I met Emile Benoit. A virtuoso of the fiddle, composer, raconteur, a "character," Emile Benoit did not have a reputation as a storyteller in the public tradition. But we quickly became friends, and I was able to spend a great deal of time with him. He told me *Märchen*, anecdotes, legends, personal experience stories. If he did not have a reputation as a storyteller, it was because he had chosen consciously and deliberately to express himself through his musical talents. But by his own admission, he could have been a storyteller; he had the talent. Observing him tell folktales to audiences of different kinds or to me alone, I realised that he seemed to embody all the qualities usually attributed to storytellers in the public tradition.

I was at last able to compare at first hand the characteristic features of performance style in both traditions, with the aim of sketching the broad lines of community aesthetics, at least as far as the narrative tradition of the pre-technological era on the peninsula was concerned. As was noted earlier, I had been led to focus on this question because all my informants, wittingly or otherwise, commented on stories and storytellers in ways which implied a value system. They appreciated, they criticised, they passed judgements. They were making, in other words, aesthetic judgements.

These preoccupations happened to coincide with new directions a growing number of American folklorists had begun taking in the preceding dozen or so years. Motivated by a desire to redefine the discipline, based in part on contextualist thinking initiated by Herbert Halpert in the late 1930s, and in part on concepts drawn from the related disciplines of anthropology and linguistics, scholars began looking at folklore in context. The clearest expression of this tendency was offered in a series of essays edited by Dan Ben-Amos and Kenneth S. Goldstein, of the University of Pennsylvania, in their *Folklore. Performance and Communication* (The Hague: Mouton, 1975).

Their Introduction clearly expounds the theoretical evolution leading to a perception of the contextual approach to folklore as focusing upon "...these situations in which the relationship of performance obtains between speakers and listeners. It concentrates on those utterances which transform the roles of speaker and listener to those of performer and audience."(p. 4) While they insist on the importance of textual authenticity (a question to be taken up later in this introduction), the authors stress the need, in contextual studies of folklore, of supplementary documentation: "...they require proxemic, kinesic, paralinguistic, interactional descriptions, all of which might provide clues to the principles underlining the communicative processes of folklore and its performing attributes."(p. 5)

The accent is placed, then, on the concept of folklore as *performance*, and just as in the theatre the informed spectator will take heed of the actor's interpretation of the text, so will he take note of how the actor uses the tricks of his trade—his gestures, gesticulations, body movement, in brief, the actor's dramatic artistry. Moreover, just as the text is not all-important in the theatre (in the sense that we attend the performance of a play by Shakespeare not for the novelty of its lines but rather for the actors' interpretation of it), so is the text of a folktale, its plot, relatively less important for the tale's audience. The storyteller is judged for his overall narration and not simply for his fidelity to the plot, although I do not wish to imply that this fidelity is not important.

The contextualist's approach is different from that of a folklorist whose bias is literary, comparative, structural or otherwise oriented, in that he feels an absolute necessity to recreate, as far as is possible, the complete narrative event, including the pauses, hesitations, corrections, interruptions, asides, even the telephone calls which may intrude. The telling of a tale is not an isolated phenomenon, but a synchronic manifestation of a diachronic event which exists in variable physical and human contexts. To grasp the character of the phenomenon it is important to describe, in as much detail and with as much precision as possible, the event itself and other representations of the same kind. This is what I have attempted to do in my analyses of the recording sessions made with storytellers from both traditions. Such a tentative approach can only be incomplete, given the vast breadth of detail involved.

Indeed, the problems raised by simply attempting to write down a purely oral form of dialectal French are themselves great, though not insoluble. But given the demands of the methodology adopted, I have tried to reproduce a faithful approximation of my informants' speech, in a readable form, giving in parentheses details which may clarify non-verbal features of the narrative event.

Although this study was the first devoted to the French folklore of Newfoundland and although it takes as its starting point a relatively novel approach to the description of a francophone narrative tradition in North America, it can be placed in a lineage going back to the researches undertaken by the Louisiana native Alcée Fortier, at the end of the last century. Taking Quebec, the core of the French presence in North America, as a reference point, one can distinguish two chief lines of research upon the folktale. In Quebec, Marius Barbeau and his collaborators, E.-Z. Massicotte, Evelyn Bolduc and Adélard Lambert, laid solid foundations with their series of *Contes populaires français* published in the *Journal of American Folklore* between 1916 and 1950. Luc Lacourcière, and the founding in 1944 of the *Archives de Folklore*, both supported by Barbeau, added an enormous quantity of data, in breadth as well as in depth, to material collected before 1940. Lacourcière's work, the summation of which will be his *Catalogue raisonné du conte populaire français en Amérique du Nord*, will incorporate almost all of the major and minor collections of French folktales, and will undoubtedly prove to be this century's major monument to French-Canadian and Franco-American folklore.

In addition to Quebec scholars such as Carmen Roy, Jean-Claude Dupont, Conrad Laforte and others trained largely by Lacourcière, whose work has been devoted primarily to the folklore and folktales of Quebec, there is a second line of descent from Lacourcière. He trained or influenced most of the folklorists who have studied enclavic French folklore in North America, from Joseph-Médard Carrière in Missouri to Fr. Anselme Chiasson, one of the pioneers in Acadian folklore, to Catherine Jolicoeur and Lauraine Léger in New Brunswick and Georges Arsenault in Prince Edward Island, from Germain Lemieux who has single-handedly exploited the riches of Ontario's French narrative tradition, through New England to Louisiana and Corinne Saucier, Calvin Claudel and Elizabeth Brandon; these and

15

many others have been influenced by Lacourcière to a greater or lesser extent.[3] His support of my research amongst French Newfoundlanders was decisive. He made me feel that I was part of an old and noble family. When I collected some new version of a folktale, my first thought was often to wonder what Luc Lacourcière would say of it.

I cannot say to what extent he influenced my preference for seeking *Märchen* in the course of my fieldwork, but the vast majority of tales which follow are readily classified according to the major tools of folktale scholarship, Antti Aarne and Stith Thompson's *The Types of the Folktale*, Paul Delarue and Marie-Louise Tenèze's *Le Conte populaire français* and, for the details, Stith Thompson's *Motif-Index of Folk-Literature*. Each tale is identified as far as possible according to this triple reference (motif Z71.1), with a commentary noting interesting details about the tale or its performance. This technical aspect is completed by a bibliography in which the reader will find, among other things, a selection of works on the French folktale in France and North America, and titles in the theoretical literature which have influenced me to a greater or lesser extent.

This study has as its aim, therefore, the examination, from a novel point of view, of the narrative tradition of Newfoundland's French enclave on the Port-au-Port Peninsula. This introduction anticipates the main thrust of the book by noting the salient features of the history of French Newfoundlanders, by outlining the theoretical basis of the study, and by providing the broad lines of the methodology employed. I have proposed that the two narrative traditions can be distinguished by an analysis of features of style and performance, taking into account the influence exercised upon these traditions by various factors of social change, notably television. I have alluded to the essential role of the storytellers themselves. In conclusion, I must mention another aim which has guided my thinking throughout the preparation of the book.

It is a question of the responsibility I feel to French Newfoundlanders. One cannot spend so much time with a group of people and not begin to identify with them. Coming as I do from an ethnic minority, I have always felt most strongly something that was but rarely articulated by my friends on the peninsula—a feeling of hope in their future as French Newfoundlanders, in spite of the historical and socio-economic realities of their status as a tiny minority. More than anything else, this book is a way of giving back to French Newfoundlanders a part of what they gave me so freely and so generously. I hope it will contribute to the strengthening of their identity, belittled for so long but now seemingly on the threshold of a new flowering.

NOTES

1. *Songs of the Newfoundland Outports* (3 vols., Ottawa: National Museum of Canada, 1965). Peacock included some forty French songs in his collection, most of them from the repertoire of Mrs. Joséphine Costard (Josie Lacosta) of Red Brook (parish of Cape St. George). In August 1981, at the age of 77, she came to St. John's to take part in a provincial folk festival. She sang a dozen songs for me, which were added to the fifty or more she had sung for me since 1973. Mrs. Costard was also a talented storyteller. She died in February 1982.

2. In accordance with standard Anglo-American scholarly usage I use the German term *Märchen* to refer to what is more commonly, though incorrectly, known in English as *"Fairy Tale"*, or a *conte merveilleux* in French. For a European perspective on the choice of terms, I refer the reader to the Danish scholar Bengt Holbek's *Interpretation of Fairy Tales. Danish Folklore in a European Perspective*, Helsinki: Suomalainen Tiedeakatemia, 1987: FF Communications No. 239. See particularly pp. 449-453, Terminology, and footnote 1, p. 611.

3. See *The Bibliography* for details of their work.

16

BRITTANY

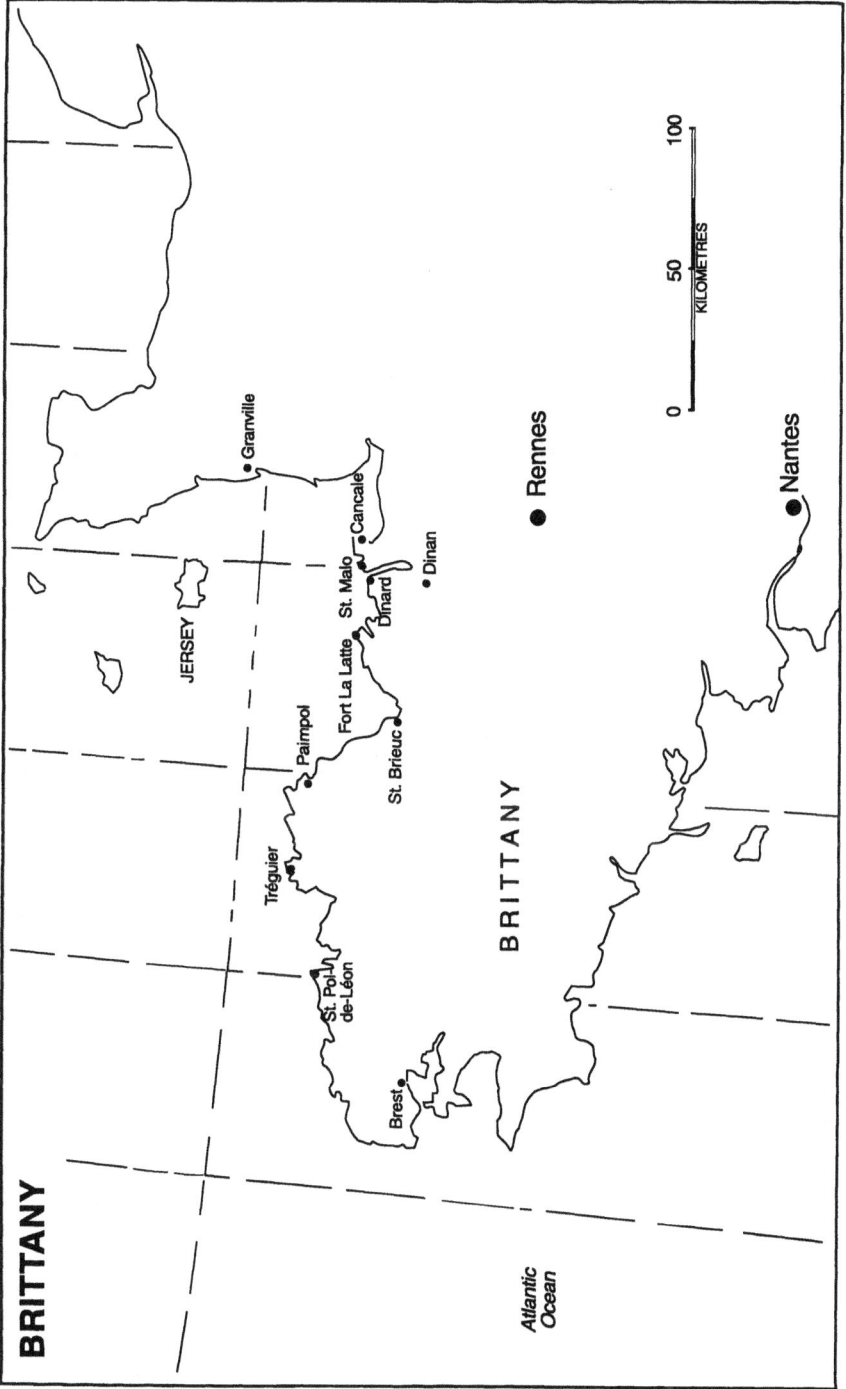

Granville

Cancale

St. Malo

Dinard

Dinan

Fort La Latte

Paimpol

St. Brieuc

Tréguier

JERSEY

St. Pol-
de-Léon

Brest

BRITTANY

Atlantic
Ocean

● Rennes

● Nantes

0   50   100
KILOMETRES

17

THE ATLANTIC PROVINCES OF CANADA

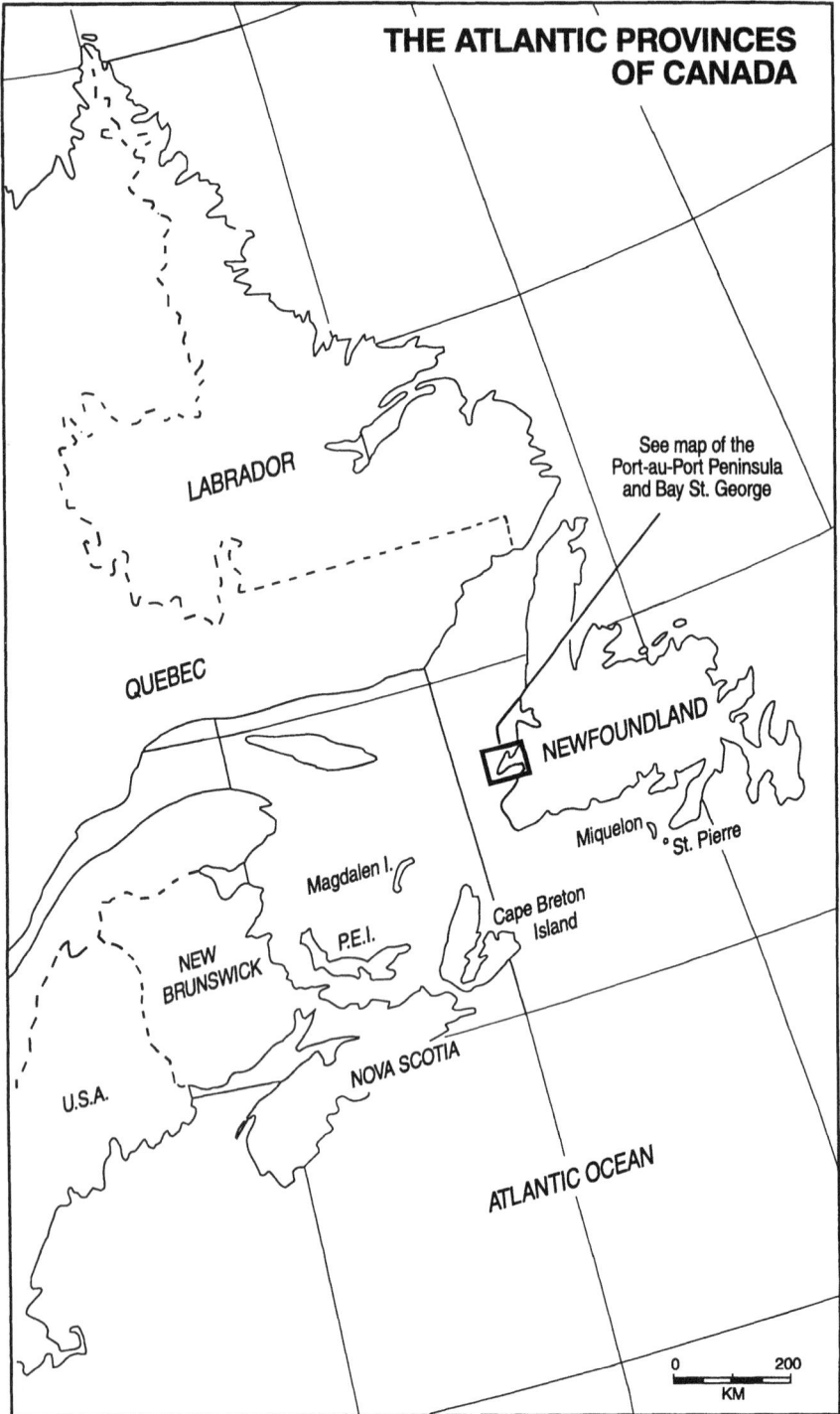

LABRADOR

QUEBEC

See map of the
Port-au-Port Peninsula
and Bay St. George

NEWFOUNDLAND

Miquelon

°St. Pierre

Magdalen I.

NEW
BRUNSWICK

P.E.I.

Cape Breton
Island

U.S.A.

NOVA SCOTIA

ATLANTIC OCEAN

0   200

KM

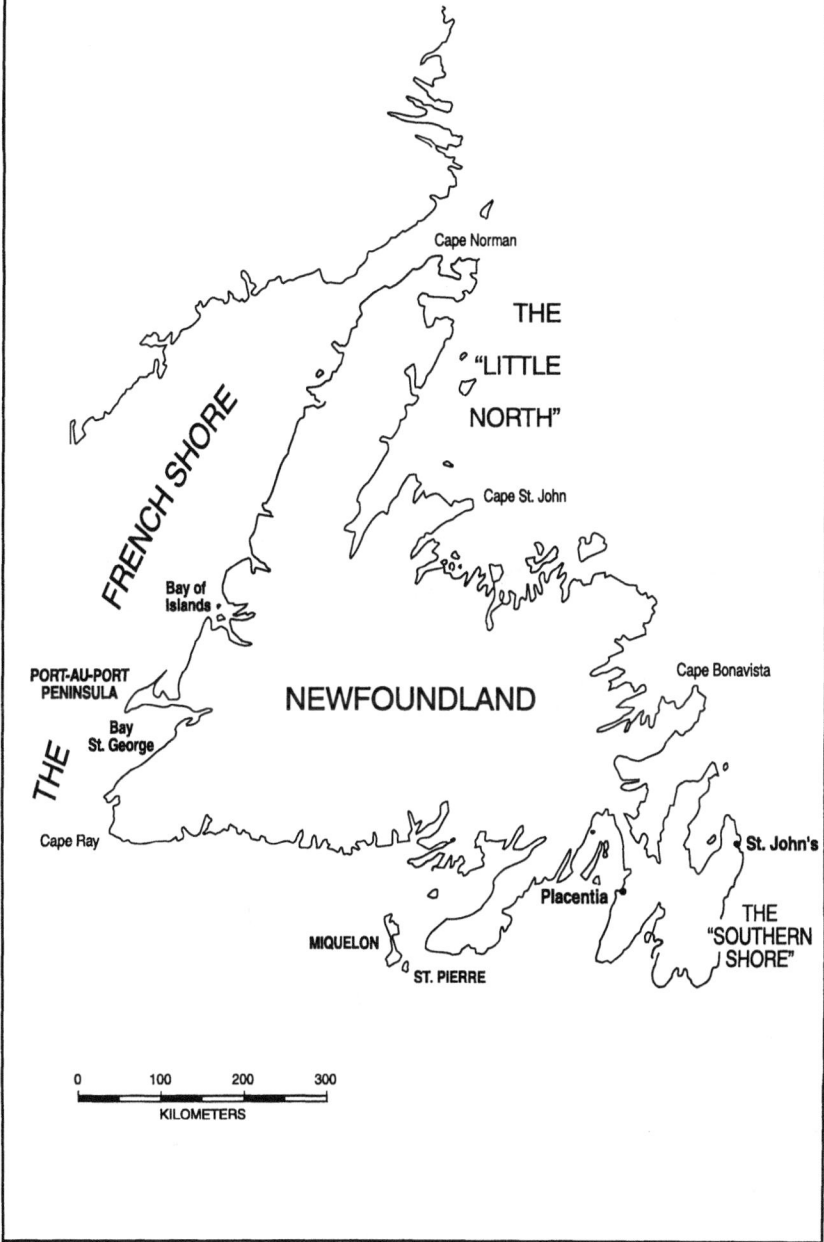

NEWFOUNDLAND

Cape Norman

THE "LITTLE NORTH"

FRENCH SHORE

Cape St. John

Bay of Islands

PORT-AU-PORT PENINSULA

NEWFOUNDLAND

Cape Bonavista

THE

Bay St. George

Cape Ray

St. John's

MIQUELON

ST. PIERRE

Placentia

THE "SOUTHERN SHORE"

```
0    100    200    300
KILOMETERS
```

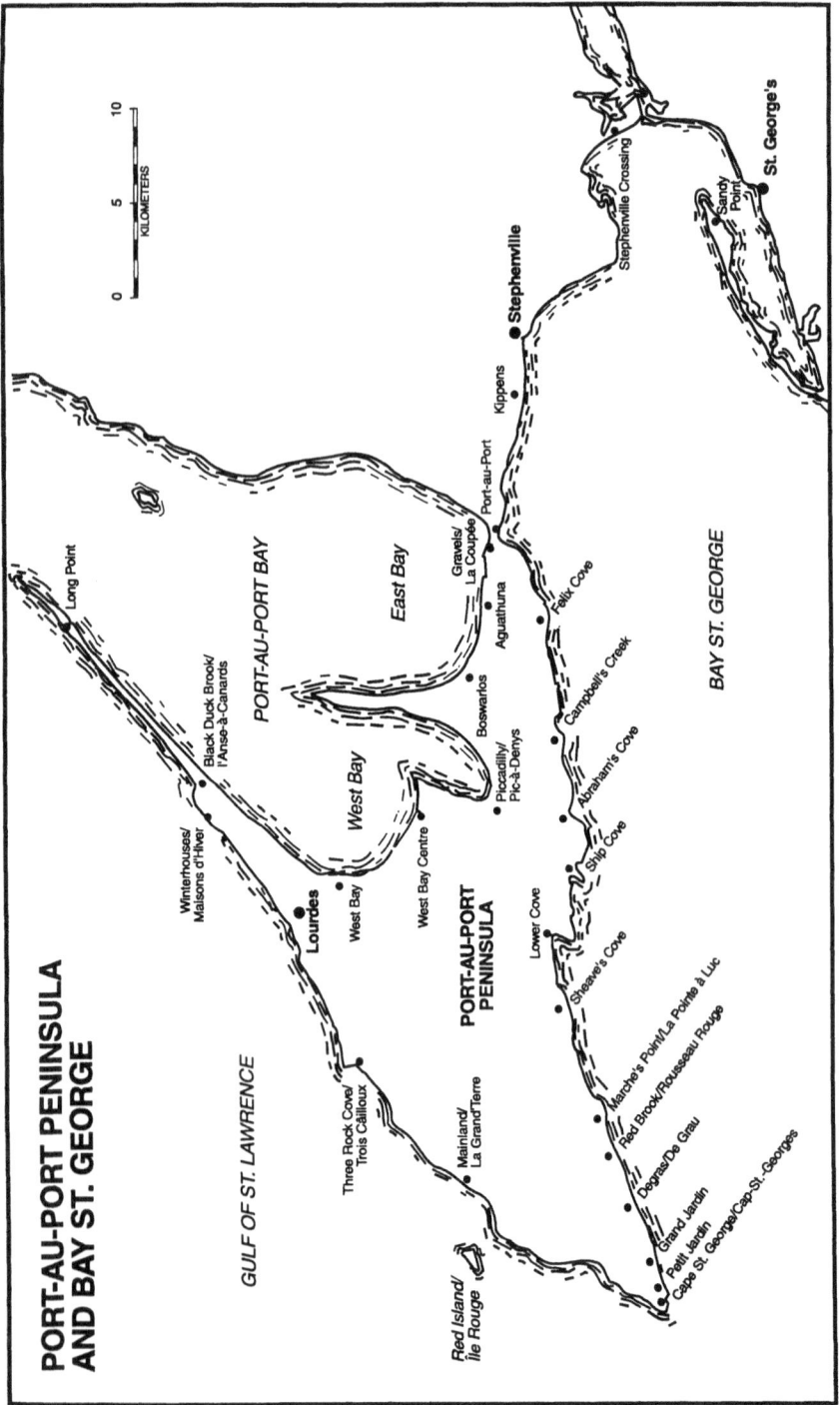

PORT-AU-PORT PENINSULA
AND BAY ST. GEORGE

0 5 10
KILOMETERS

GULF OF ST. LAWRENCE

PORT-AU-PORT BAY

East Bay

West Bay

PORT-AU-PORT
PENINSULA

BAY ST. GEORGE

Long Point

Black Duck Brook/
l'Anse-à-Canards

Winterhouses/
Maisons d'Hiver

Lourdes

West Bay

West Bay Centre

Gravels/
La Coupée

Aguathuna

Boswarlos

Piccadilly/
Pic-à-Denys

Port-au-Port

Kippens

Stephenville

Stephenville Crossing

St. George's

Sandy Point

Felix Cove

Campbell's Creek

Abraham's Cove

Ship Cove

Sheaver's Cove

Lower Cove

Marche's Point/La Pointe à Luc

Red Brook/Rousseau Rouge

Degras/De Grau

Grand Jardin

Petit Jardin

Cape St. George/Cap-St.-Georges

Red Island/
Île Rouge

Three Rock Cove/
Trois Cailloux

Mainland/
La Grand'Terre

I
THE FRENCH SHORE

Origins and Evolution of Franco-Newfoundland Communities

The aim of the present study is the analysis of a narrative tradition which is in many ways unique. I noted in the Introduction that bilingualism is a striking feature of Franco-Newfoundland culture. This is not of course a rare phenomenon in Canada, nor indeed in other countries; but no study in the field of folklore, in Canada at any rate, recognizes this fact. The great francophone research centres in Canada have largely set aside French folklore expressed in English, to concentrate uniquely on its French language forms.

Nowhere else in Canada are French minorities as small as in Newfoundland. The most recently consulted statistics suggest it makes up less than one percent of the population of the Province of Newfoundland.[1] Surrounded by anglophones and strongly influenced by their presence, French Newfoundlanders have necessarily been subjected to linguistic and cultural pressures. It would be dishonest to claim that Franco-Newfoundland communities constitute a cultural enclave free of all English influence, and that they have maintained their traditions through the medium of French alone. This study will prove the contrary, while demonstrating that Franco-Newfoundland culture is indeed fundamentally French.

In order then to appreciate in a general way what constitutes the originality of Newfoundland's West Coast French population, and more specifically the role of its narrative tradition, it is important to provide a broad outline of the history of its establishment. I will therefore provide the historical and socio-economic context in which may be placed the narrators and their stories, for the factors which were to enable the creation of a French enclave in Newfoundland also contributed to the maintenance of the *Märchen* and the folktale in general.

France and the French Shore to 1800

Links between France and Newfoundland, forged by sailors and fishermen, go back to Newfoundland's discovery by John Cabot, in 1497. According to the American historian Samuel Eliot Morison, the first authentic documents attesting to the presence of a French vessel on the Grand Banks go back to 1504, when a certain Jean Denys of Harfleur was fishing between Cape Bonavista and the Strait of Belle Isle; in 1506, Thomas Aubert of Dieppe fished there in the *Pensée*. As early as 1529, Norman merchants were exporting to England cod caught in Newfoundland waters. In 1542, no less than sixty vessels set sail from Rouen on the same day, bound for the Grand Banks.[2]

A significant Breton presence should be noted among the early fishers of these northern seas, a presence which became predominant in the nineteenth century with the founding of the French communities of the Port-au-Port Peninsula.[3] Jacques Cartier, himself a Breton, born in St. Malo in 1491, was the first to sail down the west coast of the island. Moreover, a curious coincidence links Cartier to the modern French communities on the Peninsula.

During his 1534 voyage of discovery in the Gulf of St. Lawrence, Cartier discovered an island which he named, after the colour of its rocks, Red Island, and about two and a half kilometres from it, the imposing cliffs of a cape which he called *Cap de Latte*, recalling *Fort la Latte* near St. Malo.[4] The cape, now known as Cape St. George, gave its name to the nearby village, one of whose earliest inhabitants, settled there as early as 1837, was a certain Guillaume or Djillaume Robin, a deserter from the French fishery and like Cartier, a native of St. Malo.

Cape St. George and the village of Mainland, which was to grow opposite Red Island, are French communities whose early inhabitants were in large part from Brittany. The Breton presence is also attested in the villages of Black Duck Brook, Winterhouses and Degras; a French geographer working at Cape St.George in about 1950 claims to have heard the Breton language spoken by certain old men who have since died.[5] As we shall see shortly, family names in the region include typically Breton forms.

Between Cartier's voyages and the end of the eighteenth century, the French presence on the West Coast does not seem to have led to any permanent settlement. Until the Treaty of Utrecht in 1713, France was, for all practical purposes, mistress of a major part of the Newfoundland coast with, as capital of its colony, the town of *Plaisance* or Placentia, situated in the bay of the same name. English colonies of the period were limited geographically to the eastern coast of the island of Newfoundland, between Cape Bonavista and what is known as the Southern Shore, the east coast of the Avalon Peninsula (see map). But the Treaty of Utrecht, which brought an end to the War of Spanish Succession, the chief protagonists in which were England and France, took away from France not only her colony of Acadia, but also her Newfoundland possessions. France lost everything but her fishing and drying rights; and between 1713 and 1904, the limits of the French Shore were constantly diminishing. During the nineteenth century, the period of greatest interest to us as far as the contemporary French enclave is concerned, the French Shore extended from Cape Ray in the south to Cape Norman in the north.

The French Shore Fishery After 1815

It was not for purely economic reasons that France clung so tenaciously to her rights in Newfoundland. Before the end of the Napoleonic Wars in 1815, part of the importance of the Shore fishery, compared to that carried out on the Grand Banks, lay in the fact that it required considerable manpower, making of it a breeding-ground for future sailors. Charles de la Morandière, historian of the French fishery in North America, explains the value of the French Shore fishery:

The numerous and diverse operations [of the shore-based fishery] obliged the owners and captains to take a large number of men either for shore work or as mates to the fishermen. In order to be a shore worker there was no need to be a born sailor nor a sailor by profession. A young country lad, provided he was of sound constitution, quickly proved entirely satisfactory...even if he had never before seen the sea. Similarly, all that was needed to work alongside the experienced sailor in charge of the actual fishing, to help trim the boat and even to use a jigger, was good will and a little dexterity. According to Pléville Le Pelley, a beginner could catch as many cod with a jigger as an experienced fisherman. In two or three seasons, a lad of sixteen to eighteen soon got the hang of fishing, got to know the sea and ships, and even if he did not turn into a first-class seaman, could be drafted into the

[French] Royal Navy.... The wet fishery was less interesting in this respect because apart from the fact that the vessels had crews of no more than fifteen to twenty men—and not the eighty or hundred or even the 130 to 150 men aboard the cod-fishing boats headed for the shore fishery—they required sailors who were also skilled fishermen.[6]

I will return shortly to one of the consequences of this practice.

It is nonetheless certain that an economic motive prompted France to insist on her rights. The northern part of the French Shore, called "The Little North" (*Le Petit Nord*) between Cape St. John and Cape Norman, was a most fruitful fishery which was in the hands of St. Malo fishermen. Cod was plentiful, of a uniform size, smaller than the cod taken on the Grand Banks. It was a fish ideally suited for export to the West Indies.

If the *Petit Nord* fishery was controlled by St. Malo fishermen, it was St. Pierre merchants who, after 1816, acquired the monopoly of rights on that part of the coast between Cape Norman and Cape Ray. Links between the islands of St. Pierre and Miquelon and the West Coast of Newfoundland were forged after the repossession of the archipelago by the French in 1816, from whom the English had taken it in 1793. This St. Pierre interest in the West Coast was of an essentially practical nature.

Every five years, fishing boats leaving France—from Brittany and Normandy especially—took part in a lottery, the purpose of which was the allocation of harbours on the French Shore. St. Pierre merchants complained of the difficulty they had in taking part in the lottery, and consequently were granted certain bases on the southern part of the coast, notably at Codroy, Bay St. George, Port-au-Port and Red Island. Metropolitan interests acquired part of this monopoly, on condition that they make use of local manpower. If, during the nineteenth century, the French fishery on Newfoundland's West Coast became less and less important, Red Island remained a centre of St. Pierre exploitation until 1904, and served as a springboard for most of the French who were to settle on the Port-au-Port Peninsula.

In 1870 a French captain noted the presence on Red Island of a doctor, a surgeon, and 120 men. The following year, 132 men were counted. Toward the end of the century, at a time when the declining cod-fishery was being replaced by the lobster fishery, the number of active fishermen continued to fall. There were five St. Pierre lobster 'factories' on the French Shore in 1898, with a total complement of 133 men. In 1901 there were only 87 fishermen on the length of the coast, and, despite a bonus of 50 francs paid to every man who agreed to fish cod, 77 engaged in the lobster fishery.[7]

This brief summary of the history of the French Shore provides a context within which to place the beginnings of present-day French communities. If I have emphasized the French presence, it has been to underline the Breton and St. Pierre influence on the Port-au-Port Peninsula.[8] In passing, it is important to dispel a widely held notion in Canada that all French Newfoundlanders are Acadians. On the other hand, there is indeed an Acadian enclave in Newfoundland, quite close to the French enclave with which, by the force of circumstances, it has intermingled from the very beginning.

The Acadians in Newfoundland

Let us now trace the evolution of the two groups. I shall first consider the Acadians, and if I pass rather more rapidly over them than the peninsular French, it is because the latter are the bearers of the traditions I shall be examining.

Readers may recall that in 1755 the English, having acquired Acadia in 1713, decided, for reasons not to be discussed here, to dispossess the Acadians of their lands. This was the time of the "grand dérangement", the "great trouble." Expelled from their young land, numerous Acadians settled in Louisiana; others were returned to France; yet others escaped the English, hiding in the woods until they found new lands to settle. It was thus that the Acadian centres of the modern maritime provinces of Nova Scotia, New Brunswick and Prince Edward Island were formed.

In the midst of this confusion a small number of Acadian families settled in Newfoundland, in the interior of Bay St. George, close to the modern towns of Stephenville and St. George's. Documents attest to the presence of at least two families in the region as early as 1770.[9] But more solid facts are not recorded until the early decades of the nineteenth century. Thus, Charles de la Morandière, working with French naval documents, informs us that in 1821 there were thirteen families at St. George's Harbour and five at 'Grand Barachois' (present area of Stephenville Crossing). The officer's report consulted by de la Morandière tells us further that some forty years earlier, in about 1780, only two families were in the area, one at each location.[10] But the report did not indicate their nationality.

By 1830, the population on the French Shore had increased considerably. Here is an extract from a letter written by a French naval officer to the Governor of St. Pierre, which I borrow from Charles de la Morandière:

In Bay St. George (a little further to the north) he wrote, there is a population of some 2,000 souls, which can be divided into four parts, to wit: 400 English, 1,200 Acadians, French and Indians 400. The most industrious of these are undoubtedly the first and the last. The other two are lazy wretches who live from hand to mouth. Although work is a vital necessity for them, hunger alone impels them to it.[11]

According to de la Morandière, other reports drawn up between 1830 and 1850 bear witness to the alleged laziness of the French element in the region. He clearly distinguishes between the Acadians on the one hand and the French from France on the other. The former "...were drawn to this land by the absence of law and order. There are no taxes, no police, no laws there! The St. John's government took not the least interest in the people under its administration in the region, to which it sent its representative at long intervals only."[12]

As for the French, known pejoratively as "Jacotars," "...these were in general fishermen wanting to avoid military service, and who were more than happy to live in a land where police were virtually unknown. There were, however, a few good individuals among these Frenchmen; they were the fishermen left to winter there by the merchants, in order to protect their establishments."[13] But contrary to what happened on the peninsula, where the French found French-speaking spouses with whom they could establish homes, the Bay St. George French most frequently ended up with English wives; assimilation, always dangerous for the area's French speakers, make its insidious effects felt early on.

The Acadians entering the region at this period were less subject to assimilation, because they frequently arrived with their families. Thanks to the research of Thomas W. White (Leblanc), it is known that between 1825 and 1860 there was a regular Acadian immigration, and we even have precise details as to their place of origin and subsequent family history.

They were for the most part from the Cape Breton villages of Margaree and Cheticamp. From 1847, members of the Aucoin family settled at Stephenville, St. George's and Codroy. Benoits from Arichat appeared in about 1850 and in 1855 a Bourgeois, born in France and married to an Acadian, settled at St. George's. The first Cormiers reached Sandy Point, opposite St. George's, in 1847, followed in the same year by a Doucet or Doucette, who went to Port-au-Port. The Gallant family was in Stephenville in 1846; the Gaudets in 1855. From 1830 a Jesseau (Jessôme, Jesso) family, from Bras d'Or in Cape Breton Island, had settled at St. George's, later moving to the peninsula. A branch of the Lejeune family also arrived in 1830, a year which brought a family of Pierrots; for reasons unknown they changed the family name to Alexandre.

Between 1847 and 1855 various branches of the Leblanc family, from Margaree, settled in the region; some of these had lived in the Magdalen Islands before settling for good in St. George's. Between 1846 and 1860, another branch of the same family settled in Stephenville where its members, who had brought with them cattle and equipment, became prosperous farmers. Other Acadians reached Newfoundland in the fifties, notably branches of the Longuépée, Chevarie, Chiasson (written Chaisson in Newfoundland), Poirier, Deveau, Muise and Madore families, as well as more Aucoins, Gallants and Cormiers.[14]

These are typical Acadian family names.[15] If there were metropolitan Frenchmen in the area, they must have been few in number and quickly assimilated. The Acadians alone were able to maintain their identity, at least until the arrival of American armed forces in Stephenville in 1940. On the other hand we are certain, despite the almost complete lack of documents (and the available documents are not always easy to interpret) that the French villages of the Port-au-Port Peninsula were founded in large part by settlers from France, in which the Breton input was not insignificant.

The French and Breton Contribution

There is indeed evidence from oral and family tradition supporting the little available written documentation. Let us recall, first of all, the state of the French Shore fishery in the nineteenth century. As I noted earlier, St. Pierre merchants had been allocated certain harbours between Cape Ray and Cape Norman from which they fished, the best known of which were at Codroy, Bay St. George, Port-au-Port and Red Island. At the same time, a condition had been imposed on the merchants that they use St. Pierre-based manpower. This manpower included not only St. Pierre-born fishermen, but also a considerable number of fisherman or *graviers* (shoreworkers, working on the *grave* or shore), who came directly from France to work, or seek work, with companies based in St. Pierre.

During the nineteenth century most of these transient fishermen were from Brittany. The reason for this is simple: prior to this period, agricultural technology in the hinterlands of the French fishing ports most active in the Newfoundland shore fishery was poor: Granville in Normandy, St. Malo and St. Brieuc in Brittany, St. Jean-de-Luz in the Basque Country. After 1815, better technology enabled Norman peasants to achieve a more satisfactory agricultural production, diverting them from the sea. For other reasons, Basque fishermen also neglected the Newfoundland fishery. On the other hand, Brittany had not yet benefited from improved agricultural technology and, in consequence, merchants were obliged to recruit more and more Bretons for shore work. Throughout the nineteenth century, young Bretons not only set out from Brittany, but also from Norman ports, especially Granville.[16]

Thanks to the fieldwork and research of the great Breton folklorist Paul Sébillot (1846-1918), we possess precise data which would have otherwise been most difficult to obtain:

Almost all the Bretons fishing in Newfoundland are from the bays of St. Malo and St. Brieuc. They spend half the year on board ships taking them to the fishing grounds; the other half of the year, more or less at the end of autumn, during the winter and at the beginning of spring, they remain in their native villages where they practice an inshore fishery from small boats and also small-scale farming. There are even some Newfoundlanders [i.e. Bretons who fish in Newfoundland] who live quite far from the sea, only becoming sailors during the Banks season, when they work from St. Pierre schooners. They are in fact peasant-sailors ....[17]

Sébillot seems to disregard the shore fishery and the importance of these "peasant sailors" in his research, but in acknowledging that they passed through St. Pierre in search of work, he does confirm my point.

Sébillot gives details, too, on the provenance of the Bretons:

It is they [the peasant-sailors] who, in order to be taken on by the captains, make their way to the Newfoundlanders' Fair, also called the Sailors' Fair, held on the first Monday of December in the Old Town [of St. Malo]. It rarely begins before 10 a.m. and does not go on after 4 p.m. All the lads, some 2,000 in all, come in carriages with their families. They come from Cancale and St. Coulomb; but most of all from the towns and villages of the cantons of Châteauneuf, Pleudihen, Pleugueneuc and Dol. As all these lads are destined for the St. Pierre schooners, it is naturally the skippers of these vessels who come to the fair to sign them on. As for the crews headed for the Banks fishery, they are made up of professional fishermen, and it is not rare for whole crews to come from the same village.[18]

Sébillot's writings, which emphasize the distinction between professional fishermen and peasant sailors of the shore fishery, are also important because they echo the oral testimonies gathered in French villages on the Port-au-Port Peninsula.

While most French Newfoundlanders cannot name the place of origin of their first ancestor to settle on the peninsula, some have retained precise place-names. If the town of St. Malo often appears in these reminiscences, it is doubtless because so many fishermen signed on there for the shore fishery based in St. Pierre. Moreover, most villages and cantons named by Sébillot are in the St. Malo hinterland. La Roche, probably the village of Roche-Derrien, not far from St. Brieuc, the other Breton port which fitted for Newfoundland, is another name which often appears in the recollections of older men.

I have collected from a French Newfoundland woman a sadly fragmentary memory of a custom which, despite its lack of detail, seems very similar to a custom observed by Sébillot, "Drowning Carnival":

One year when the Newfoundland fishermen were twenty days late departing, they drowned Carnival. On a cart taken at the Dinan Gate, they had set up a huge mannequin stuffed with straw, and were singing to the accompaniment of the accordeon, their favourite instrument:

> Mardi Gras, ne t'en vas pas,
> J'f'rons des crêpes et t'en mangeras
> [Jack o'Lent, don't you take off,
> Pancakes we'll make, you'll have a scoff][19]

And then, all together:

> Mardi Gras s'en est allé,
> J'f'rons des crêpes sur n'un gal'tier.
> [Jack o'Lent has gone away,
> We'll cook pancakes in a pan today.]

Then, with loud shouts, they took up their victim and threw it in the sea, where it drifted off. The "Straw Man" had made the wind change, they said, and the sailors were able to sail that very day.[20]

This description is close enough to one collected in Newfoundland to suggest a kinship between the two.

The Breton origins of numerous French Newfoundlanders is proved by linguistic evidence. The French geographer Pierre Biays, who visited Cape St. George in 1951, met old Frenchmen who spoke Breton together.[21] Twenty years later it was no longer possible to hear this Celtic tongue spoken; only a few deformed and scarcely recognizable words remained in their children's memories.

Yet family names on the peninsula are also eloquent. Bozec, Cornic (or LeCornic, today, Cornect), Carrautret (or Karotret, pronounced Cowtrett, extinct now in the area), Lagatdu, Kerfont or Karfont, Tallec (written Tallack), Scardin (or Scardon, Secardon), Robin (often written today as Robia or Rubia and pronounced in the English fashion), Rivolan, Huon and still others are either typically Breton names or common in the region of St. Malo and its hinterland. Oral evidence frequently tells us that the first bearers of these names were Breton speakers.

Other names found on the peninsula and associated with the western provinces of France include Chrétien (Christian), Dubé, Dubois, Félix, Formanger, Lecoure, Lecointe (often written Lecountre or Lecointre), Leroy, Louvelle (or Nouvelle), Lemoine, Lainey, Marche, Renouf, Retieffe, Rouzes, Savidon and Simon. There are families in the villages of Black Duck Brook, Winterhouses, Mainland and Cape St. George which have more or less acknowledged ties with contemporary St. Pierre families, such as the Briands, Morazés, Ozons, Poiriers and Simons.

It is immediately evident that these family names are quite different from those of the Acadians. It is true that over the years there has been a mingling of the two traditions, with Acadians settling on the peninsula and Frenchmen moving to the Stephenville area; but the distinction between the two groups holds true, since the "French from France" distinguish themselves from the "Stephenville French," that is, the Acadians.

Looking at the list of French family names, one notices a certain number of changes in their spelling. This is due in part to the absence of a literate tradition, in part to the effects of assimilation. The Acadians, for example, who have been most susceptible to the pressures exercised by a predominantly anglophone culture, have straightforwardly anglicized many family names. Thus Leblanc becomes White; Benoit (without the circumflex accent in Newfoundland), Bennett; Aucoin, O'Quinn; Lejeune, Young; Alexandre, Alexander. But some families had more urgent reasons to disguise their identities. We know that most of the first French settlers on the peninsula had deserted from the French fishery, and had a real fear of being captured by the authorities and sent back to France.

A family by the name of Rioux, from Mainland, was known formerly as Boloche, according to oral testimony. Even today the name Leboloch exists in St. Pierre.[22] It is likely that the name change was prompted by the desire to conceal the bearer's identity. One old lady told how, when she was about six years old, she saw a squad of armed French sailors come ashore from a warship. They asked her if she knew where certain men were to be found; she did not, but learned subsequently that the men being pursued had deserted and hidden in the woods behind Mainland until the sailors left. This took place in 1900.

It has been my aim to establish the places of origin of French Newfoundlanders, and without being able to provide very precise details, it is possible to say that most Acadians came from Cape Breton Island, and that most of the peninsular French have more or less strong ties with Brittany and, directly or indirectly, with St. Pierre. But it is even more important to ask why a number of French fishermen should choose to start a new life in an isolated and inhospitable part of Newfoundland, rather than return to France. Once again, I shall make use of the little available documentation and oral tradition in considering this question.

Living Conditions of the French Fisherman

Oral testimony is categorical. Among the first Frenchmen to settle on the peninsula many, if not all, had deserted from the French shore fishery. De la Morandière has drawn our attention to the presence of a few deserters in the St. George's area; these would have been quickly absorbed by their Acadian cousins or by the Anglo-Irish settlers. It is curious to note that few informants can say why their ancestors deserted. It is implicitly suggested that the fishermen's living conditions prompted desertion; but the deserters themselves were, it seems, disinclined to say anything at all about their lives before deserting, except among themselves.

What then were the conditions prompting them to start their lives anew? Firstly, it should be remembered that most of the men involved in the shore fishery were not professionals. They were, to use Paul Sébillot's term, "peasant-sailors" or better, peasant-fishermen, people who, for different reasons, did not earn a good living from the land and sought to add to their means by engaging in the fishery.[23] Without backgrounds in the fishery, they were most often obliged to do the shore work.

These shore workers were often quite young. As noted earlier, the shore fishery required much greater manpower than the Banks fishery, and in the nineteenth century it was attracting fewer and fewer experienced fishermen. 'Boys' and novices were always in demand.[24] The age limit had been set, at the beginning of the century, at sixteen, but there is good reason to believe that 'boys' often began their new careers as young as twelve or thirteen years old. The prestige associated with the seaman or sailor's life, as well as economic needs, prompted numerous young Bretons to engage in an occupation the realities of which they ignored totally.

Once at sea, however, reality made itself felt. In so far as they were extra, non-working passengers, the future shore workers were allotted the worst bunks for the four week passage, and they lived in unhealthy and uncomfortable conditions. After reaching St. Pierre they had to go ashore, then board ship once more to head for the 'factories' awaiting them on the French Shore, for a stay of about six months, involving for them little but long hours of exhausting work. Contrary to what happened at Codroy, St. George's and Port-au-Port, the shore workers on Red Island had no possibility of any social life, however ordinary. For in the first three places villages were beginning to grow, whereas at Red Island there was no local population, and presumably this situation contributed to the rather high number of desertions which occurred on the peninsula. One should note moreover that Red Island was the busiest of these shore bases during the nineteenth century.

Red Island is a rock of conical formation rising to a height of 89 m. (292 ft.), situated some two to three kilometres off the western end of the Port-au-Port Peninsula, opposite the present-day community of Mainland. During the nineteenth century, Red Island was the site of a very active fishing establishment. A quite remarkable document portrays the place as it was in about 1860. It is a chapter from a book by the diplomat-author Count Arthur de Gobineau who, on a mission to Newfoundland, visited the island. Here is his description of the shore workers' lodgings:

At the foot of the cliff a row of huts made of branches, containing only cots and hammocks, serve as dormitories for the fishermen. They are not merely humble, they are utterly wretched; and it is hard to imagine, in such a wet and foggy climate, in which the damp is often icy-cold, how anyone can without objection tolerate such an improvised type of shelter.[25]

Let us not forget, however, that Gobineau was representing his country and its commercial interests. He was not going to paint too disagreeable a picture of the French fishing stations. Despite his evocation of the conditions of such quarters, he adds:

Experience however does seem to prove that no harm results from such conditions and that the fishing crews enjoy the most flourishing health. Always in the open air, always active, the men have no time to be bored, their blood circulates briskly, and they are not prone to colds which, contrary to what one might expect, are quite rare in the area. While they are always more or less wet, they are none the worse for it. There are blessings in every profession.[26]

28

Perhaps one should not be surprised at such a point of view, coming as it does from the author of an *Essay on the Inequality of Human Races*. Gobineau continues with his description of the island:

The shore was covered, in a manner as little gratifying to one's sight as to one's sense of smell, with a layer of bloody cod remains; the shingle covered with heads and guts as abundantly as other places are with marine plants thrown up by the sea. A few steps further on, the near vertical cliff face rises up. The establishment proper is on top of it. A stairway made of planks has been constructed, as straight as a ladder, to the right of which are wooden rails; up and down these are hauled, by means of a capstan placed on top of the hill, all the burdens needing to be moved.

After clambering up a goodly number of steps we found ourselves amidst the stores, all made with planks, the manager's and doctor's quarters, in the centre finally of an intelligent and successful enterprise.[27]

This then is a good illustration of a double standard: the shore workers below, on the beach, in cabins made of branches, surrounded by rotting fish guts; the management, and the fish, comfortably installed in plank-constructed stores.

In fact, Gobineau has a poor opinion of the shore workers:

At sea, these people are passengers only. They are crowded together as tightly as is useful in every corner of the ship. They are not particular and settle for little. Once they reach the shore, they are disembarked and sail no more for the rest of the season; their duties are limited to receiving the fish brought in by the fishermen, splitting and gutting it, extracting the livers for their oil, spreading the fish between layers of salt, and finally subjecting it to the different phases of its drying on the beaches.[28]

Gobineau would have us believe that the shore workers led a life of undemanding simplicity, humble and satisfied with their modest lot. He even goes so far as to condemn them. Contrasting the fisherman with the shore worker, Gobineau notes that if the former has some measure of pride,

The shore worker has nothing like it. He is a pariah. He means nothing to anybody. Beside him, the lowest of sailors becomes a person of rank. If he drowns, he does so obscurely, without even the honour of being partly to blame. It is the others, as they founder, who take him down with them. He ekes out a wretched existence, sustaining it only with great difficulty. And finally, he spends the greatest part of his time and his days on the fishing stage, a rough introduction to purgatory.[29]

What is this purgatory Gobineau speaks of? His description is eloquent:

A fishing stage...is a big hut built on piles half in the water and half on land; made with planks and logs, it is designed to allow the easy circulation of air. Some large ships' sails cover it.

A part of the floor, especially that lying over the water, is open; and here are placed kinds of benches on which the cod are split. The stench on the stage is indescribable. It is the most horrible charnel-house imaginable. The air is constantly filled with ammoniacal vapours. Half rotted or totally decomposed fish guts accumulating in the water finally lie inside the room itself and as the workers are not particularly sensitive people, they rarely give a thought to ridding themselves of this disgusting refuse.[30]

Despite this revolting atmosphere, as Gobineau describes it, the shore workers are in no danger, other than of cutting themselves with their knives:

Suppurating sores are frequent amongst them and have serious consequences, sometimes resulting in the need for amputation.[31]

But Gobineau seems to scorn such dangers; he notes the presence of a doctor and emphasizes just how much the shore workers' health is to be envied. Charles de la Morandière, however, taking up the same question some one hundred years later, does not treat it so lightly. He discusses at length the problems of recruiting doctors for service on the French Shore, their duties and their efficiency. While various ministerial edicts of the period required the presence of doctors on board vessels and on shore bases, the law was not always obeyed. Quoting a report made by a Captain Mer of the French naval station in Newfoundland, de la Morandière notes that:

Captain Mer tells how the fishing admiral came for him, bringing a fisherman whose hand was in a very bad state. In fact it was in such a bad state that a finger had to be amputated. He was a master-capliner.

I asked the fishing admiral why no doctor was available. He replied: the owners could not get one. Which means, quite simply: the owners did not want the expense.[32]

During the nineteenth century, other French naval officers commented on the absence of doctors. In 1872, a report cited by de la Morandière noted that cases of scurvy, lung infections and typhoid fever were almost always fatal for want of adequate treatment, and because of the lack of basic care, normally harmless cuts might lead to amputation.[33]

In addition to the effects of a wretched and unhealthy environment, of thankless and exhausting labour, the shore workers also had to bear in mind the likelihood of military service at the end of their time on the French Shore. Indeed, it should be recalled that the Seaboard Conscription founded by Colbert in 1670 allowed non-professional fishermen to go to the Newfoundland fishery on condition that they sign up for a mandatory five-year term in the navy. A number of oral testimonies collected from French Newfoundlanders suggest that some deserters from the fishery deserted specifically to avoid this military service.

The causes of desertion were to be found then in large part in the shore workers' living conditions. Young men were obliged to work for six months or more on an isolated coast, without diversions of any kind, with conditions as unsanitary and as improvised as were the habitations they had to occupy. They were daily menaced by the consequences of untended cuts and by the diverse sicknesses which were rife. They then had the certainty, after four or five years of shore work, of having to spend a similar period in the French navy.

We are not certain of the precise number of deserters who settled on the Port-au-Port Peninsula. From a study of the distribution of French family names we can place at about fifty the number of deserters who settled there in the period 1816-1904. This is apart from what we believe to have been a small number of individuals who settled in English communities along the Northern Peninsula (the "Petit Nord" coast).

The First Homes

These deserters were usually bachelors. To make homes they needed wives. These were found without too much difficulty in the small number of families which came straight from St. Pierre to settle on the peninsula. Finally, the peninsular French could go from time to time to the Acadian villages where they might find eventual spouses. Among the ancestors of Emile Benoit, the man who represents in this work the public folktale tradition, are both "French from France" and "French from Stephenville," that is, Acadians. In principle, once they had completed their time in the fishery, the fishermen who had come to Newfoundland through St. Pierre had to return to France. Some preferred to go back to Newfoundland, but to do so they at times had to have recourse to secret flight. The moving testimony of an old Franco-Newfoundland fisherman supports this statement. Mr. Frank Woods, born Francis Dubois in St. Pierre in 1893, told how his father, a pilot at St. Pierre, upon completing his service, was required to return to France (he was a native of St. Malo). He and all his family took flight one stormy night, pursued by French vessels, managing eventually to reach the West Coast of Newfoundland where they settled in the Bay of Islands. Frank Woods was six years old at the time, but well remembers the dramatic nature of the event. Later, the family moved to the Port-au-Port Peninsula. Charles de la Morandière notes that among others a family of Poiriers escaped from St. Pierre, seeking refuge in the Magdalen Islands in 1819.[34] One should emphasize that those who left St. Pierre for the peninsula were already familiar with its waters, having worked there for so long.

There was another source of French blood on the peninsula. Agreements reached between France and England in 1884 and 1885 confirmed the right of the French to allow whole families to winter in the vicinity of French fishing installations, in order to watch over the facilities and keep them in good repair. These agreements simply confirmed what was already a well established practice.[35] One must conclude that it was the presence of these families on the otherwise "uninhabited" peninsula, which allowed for the eventual establishment of true communities. The present-day village of Winterhouses no doubt indicates the dwelling place of former caretakers. The agreement probably explains, too, some of the ties between Newfoundland and St. Pierre families, ties which, not infrequently, have been maintained to this day.

It was from this small number of deserters from France or St. Pierre, and the few French families whose presence was sanctioned, that were founded the villages of Cape St. George, Degras, Mainland, Winterhouses and Black Duck Brook. Following the establishment at St. George's, in the seventies, of a religious authority (which naturally exercised secular powers, too), several Acadian families left the Stephenville and St. George's region to resettle on the peninsula, where they might at least share a common language and culture with the French who were already there. The Acadians brought with them a few Micmac Indians, descendants of those who had come to Newfoundland at the time of the Placentia colony. It is known that the two groups often intermarried, and there are at least three families on the peninsula to whom oral tradition attributes Micmac blood. And finally, there came English and Scottish settlers to the area, although the peninsular French seem generally to have shunned intermarriage with anglophones until a fairly recent period.[36]

The Evolution of French-speaking Communities
Having considered the origins of French Communities in the region, it is now time to examine some of the stages of their evolution. One needs to see how the first families managed to survive and prosper so well that today the French-speaking villages of the peninsula include over 1,500 inhabitants whose mother tongue is French even if they are, with few exceptions, bilingual.

Unfortunately, few documents exist describing the life of the early settlers on the peninsula. One can of course make use of reports prepared by French naval officers and, after 1857, of censuses made in the area; but one must sometimes beware of figures, the interpretation of which is not always safe.

One must first ask how the earliest settlers nourished themselves. Charles de la Morandière provides useful information regarding the provenance of some foodstuffs. Quoting a Mr. Carpon, a surgeon who had made several passages to the French Shore fishery, and who gave an account of his experiences in a book published in 1852, de la Morandière tells us:

The ship carefully carries many young cabbages planted in earth-filled baskets. These baskets are suspended beneath the tops so that the sea rime does not damage the vegetables so conserved, and which grow perfectly well there. In this way all the cabbage stalks and their roots are preserved, the leaves having served to make soup for part of the crossing. Upon arriving in Newfoundland these are planted, along with potatoes. Turnips, peas, lettuces, chervil, spinach, cress, swedes and radishes are planted, and it is a pleasure to see them grow so quickly. These labours are performed under the direction of the surgeon.

The first deserters and other settlers no doubt took advantage of such gardens planted with vegetables brought from France. But life must have been hard in the first winters, even if the inhabitants could catch fish, rabbits and birds taken with snares, and pick berries. It was not an extravagant diet. Their dwellings, until they were able to acquire carpenter's tools, were as unpretentious as the shacks made of branches described by Gobineau. Yet, at the time when the first census was taken on the French Shore, each community recorded seems to have been well stocked with life's necessities.[38] But before taking a closer look at questions of a material nature noted in the census figures, concerning the number of animals, fish catches, buildings and the like, it is useful to consider briefly the question of population.

The 1857 census, the first to include data on the Port-au-Port Peninsula, indicates a total of 39 inhabitants in 'Port a Port Bay West and Bay East.' Of these, 26 were born in Newfoundland, the remainder in British colonies, no doubt Nova Scotia and New Brunswick. No mention is made of any French presence. Of course, the 1857 census did not cover the whole peninsula; yet we know that the principal French villages already existed, without counting the French working on Red Island, of whom there were well over 100 at the time. The French geographer Pierre Biays, however, notes the arrival, in 1837, of a Guillaume Robin from La Roche, one of the very first Frenchmen to settle at Cape St. George. One may surmise, if Biays' information was correct, that Guillaume Robin did not spend twenty years in total isolation.

It is of little use to detail here the growth of each French village year by year, and we shall only provide the main features of the evolution of Cape St. George, Mainland, and to a lesser degree, Black Duck Brook.[40] Cape St. George and Black Duck Brook appear for the first time in the 1874 census, while Mainland is not recognized until 1884, ten years later.

The 1874 census joins Black Duck Brook to 'Port-au-Port Bay,' the total population of which is 127. As in the 1857 census, Newfoundland and British colonies are the only sources of ethnic origin mentioned. On the other hand, Cape St. George, where only 21 souls are noted, indicates two persons born in 'Foreign or other countries,' and one may conclude that the foreign countries include France. Ten years later, in 1884, the census does not mention Cape St. George but talks of Green Gardens, which has a population of 147.

These figures underscore the difficulty of interpreting censuses in the region. Until 1921, communities are very poorly defined. It seems likely that the 1884 census included the present village of Cape St. George, designated as "Green Gardens," as well as the neighbouring villages of Degras and Red Brook. It is even more interesting to note that in a total of 147 inhabitants, only four people are given as being born in a foreign country. One must suspect that this figure and others like it are not exact. It was obviously not to the advantage of deserters to admit they were French, as they justifiably feared capture by French authorities and a return to France, as the oral testimony noted earlier telling of a manhunt at Mainland in 1900 reminds us.

In 1884 Mainland had a population of 29, two of whom admitted being born in a foreign country. The 29 persons were spread among five families. Black Duck Brook then counted 86 inhabitants, one of whom admitted to foreign birth.[41] It seems obvious that somebody was hiding the truth. Oral testimony claims today that the majority of families at Cape St. George, at Mainland and Black Duck Brook, descend from French or St. Pierre ancestors. One must conclude that in the years prior to 1904, only a few old men admitted their true origins. With the departure of the French companies from the West Coast after 1904, the figures begin to indicate a growing number of foreigners. The last settler at Cape St. George, a deserter from the French fishery, apparently came there in about 1895.[42]

Material Life

Let us now examine the material situation of the French population of the period. In 1884 the French villages on the peninsula possessed a variety of domestic animals which would have produced fresh and, after the purchase of bulk salt, salt meat. In 1884 the five Mainland families shared 14 cows and 31 sheep. These animals would have provided milk, butter and wool which was made into clothing. In Cape St. George at the same date there were 12 milch cows, 89 sheep and two pigs. One must assume that the settlers had bought their livestock from the St. George's Acadians.

These were fishing villages. At Cape St. George in 1884, 1503 quintals of cod were salted and 41 kegs of herring produced. Mainland, a smaller village, had produced 195 quintals of cod, four kegs of herring and nine of caplin.

The study of successive censuses shows a slow but steady growth in the population of each village, given the variation in defining the communities. In 1891, Mainland had a population of 33, rising to 110 in 1911, at which date eleven people admitted to having been born in a foreign country. Cape St. George in the same period passed from 147 in 1884 to 75 in 1891, and 99 in 1901. The figure is different again in 1911, but the variations are due in the main to changes in the boundaries of census sub-divisions. Thus one may conclude that the figure of 147 given for Cape St. George in 1884 also included the populations of Little Gardens, Green Gardens and Big Gardens, Cape St. George, Degras and Red Brook. The three first named "villages" are all part of the present community of Cape St. George but they appear at different dates as independent villages. With these divisions in mind, the total population of Cape St. George in 1911 was 203, 243 if one adds the village of Red Brook. This total was spread among 35 families.

The first school noted in a census is listed in 1901, at Red Brook. Before 1901, the educational level of the inhabitants was not very high, and those who went to school stayed for a minimum period of time. Teaching was in English, although intended for children who did not know that language. Oral testimony suggests that the only French people in the area with any real education had acquired their learning in France or St. Pierre, before coming to Newfoundland. The first school at Mainland is noted in 1921, while there was a school for the Black Duck Brook population by 1901.

Spiritual Life

As for the spiritual life of the peninsular French, it left much to be desired. That is not to say they were wanting in faith or piety, on the contrary, but there was a lack of priests and churches. Without exception, the French population seems to have been Catholic. Yet there was no church at Cape St. George before 1921 (at any rate, the 1911 census does not mention one) and it was only in 1975 that Mainland began to receive a weekly visit to its recently constructed chapel, of an English priest from Lourdes.

Strictly speaking, the religious history of the region only begins in 1850 when a Quebec priest, Fr. Alexis Bélanger (1808-1868), set foot at Sandy Point (on the 7th of September). His mission was one of extreme difficulty. His parish was vast, effectively covering the whole of the West Coast and, given the absence of roads, every journey was made on foot or by boat. Fr. Bélanger, who had already worked in the Magdalen Islands, had no language problems of course with the French and

Acadians. In the Codroy Valley he even managed to bring in, once a year, a Gaelic-speaking priest who was able to minister more readily to the spiritual needs of the Scots.

On Fr. Bélanger's death in 1868, the fate of the French took an important turn. His replacement, Mgr. Thomas Sears (later the first bishop of the diocese of St. George's) did herculean labours in the region, building roads, churches, and schools, but making English more and more the language of the church. Despite the subsequent presence here and there of a few French-speaking priests, English was nonetheless the language of both religious and lay instruction.[43]

Once again, oral testimony speaks eloquently, at least on the peninsula. Prayers recited by informants in French were often so garbled as to be scarcely recognizable: for lack of French-speaking priests and instruction in French, prayers had only been transmitted orally. The peninsula French would dearly love to be served today by a French-speaking priest.

The Period of Assimilation: The English Influence

If the first decades of the nineteenth century can be considered as a period of foundation, and those of the end of the nineteenth century and the beginning of the twentieth century as one of consolidation for the French villages in the area, 1940 inaugurates a time of rupture and assimilation. It is true that the 1930s was a baleful period in the economic life of the French, but the Great Depression was the same for everybody. The only notorious and traumatic event before 1940 was the resettlement of the village of Clam Bank Cove by English and Irish fishermen transplanted from Fortune Bay, in southeastern Newfoundland.

This establishment of an anglophone village in the heart of a French community took place in 1935-36, under the charge of an Irish priest, Fr. O'Reilly. It is ironic that the only village on the peninsula with a categorically French name (at least on official maps) owes its name to an anglophone priest. This later implantation had the effect of sowing discord between French and English settlers; the latter brought with them different values from those held by the former. The new village of Lourdes (as Fr. O'Reilly had rebaptized Clam Bank Cove) subsequently prospered, to become by the 1960s, the largest population centre on the peninsula.

The older French settlers found themselves relegated to an inferior position, both economically and socially; the new village physically severed ties between Mainland on the one hand, Black Duck Brook and Winterhouses on the other; and schools serving this area of the peninsula were centralized in Lourdes, consequently imposing an almost totally English language educational system on it. I visited the town in 1970 to exchange views on the teaching of French there, and the then high school principal said that he was obliged to ask the few French students in the upper classes to help him with French pronunciation. The students themselves were frustrated because their pronunciation was different from the one proposed by the teachers, which further contributed to the devaluation of French in the eyes of both sides.

But let us go back to 1940. This year saw the creation of an American Air Force Base at Stephenville. In fact, the American government had purchased the necessary land in 1939, following agreements between the U.S.A. and Great Britain. At the time, the region's inhabitants considered the construction of the Ernest Harmon Air Force Base to be a great benefit. And not without cause. Faced with a choice between the sometimes precarious life of a fisherman and that of an employee paid regularly in cash, many of the French decided to seek work on the base.

Work was not lacking. Between 1940 and 1966, when the base was closed down, several thousand non-military personnel were employed. At the high point of the base's construction, between 1,500 and 2,000 civilians found work there, and as time passed they occupied posts of considerable responsibility. If the French did not hold management jobs, they contributed much to the general manpower, putting to good use their natural gifts as carpenters or plumbers—and receiving, when necessary, appropriate training. For the first time, the region's inhabitants had easy access to the benefits of the great American economy, and quite naturally, acquired a taste for it. But on the cultural level, there were unforeseen consequences.

Firstly, the Acadians, for whom the Stephenville area had provided fertile land, saw the land swept clean to make way for runways. Some stayed to work for the Americans, others went into business, in the hotel trade, for example. Others simply left, some moving to the peninsula, others seeking land further out from Stephenville, at Kippens and other places. For those who remained in the town, there was the possibility of a better material life, but at the price of being swallowed up not only by the Americans, their language and culture, but also by the numerous outsiders, almost always anglophones, who came to Stephenville with the hope of making their fortunes. Acadian culture was submerged.

On the peninsula, life was less influenced by the American base than was Stephenville, quite simply because of its isolation. But the American presence nonetheless made itself felt. Many men and women found employment on the base, contributing thereby to a rupture in their traditional life style. Men left the fishery and all found themselves subject to the pressures of a vibrant culture, access to which required a good knowledge of the English language. If the Church and the schools had been unable to impose the use of English, the economic prosperity surrounding the American presence almost succeeded in doing so. Between 1940 and the 1960s, many families turned their backs on their language, believing that adoption of English language and culture would enable them to bestow a brighter future on their children. It is for this reason that some visitors to villages on the peninsula in the late sixties concluded that within twenty years the use of French would have died out there.[44]

Factors other than the American presence helped accelerate the process of assimilation during this period. By the end of the war, passable roads served all the peninsula's communities, and even if most of these were not paved until the 1970s, they helped bring out of isolation any who were ready to travel in search of work. On the other hand, it should be noted that French communities on the peninsula remain badly serviced. In 1985, Mainland, Winterhouses and Black Duck Brook were still waiting for paved roads.[45] Apart from Cape St. George, these communities form the nucleus of the French population on the peninsula, and it is not difficult to recognize, behind excuses of an economic nature, a certain lack of concern for the welfare of the French villages. This at least is the feeling of the French themselves, who publicly protested the state of their roads.

The Influence of Modern Technology and the Mass Media

The coming of electricity to the peninsula in the early 1960s brought with it a new element of cultural disruption: television. Its effect was to turn people away from traditional forms of entertainment, such as the *veillée*. It would of course be wrong to refuse anyone the advantages of modern technology and to regret the near passing of a particular way of life. As was the case elsewhere, French Newfoundlanders took to television with pleasure but without always realizing that it indirectly represented a new threat to the survival of their language and culture for, until 1974, television was entirely in English. The effects of television will be discussed in the next chapter; it suffices to emphasize here that some programmes had a crucial influence on viewers, an influence which in turn seemed to give the coup de grâce to the folktale as the chief form of entertainment.

35

The sixties brought more than electricity to the French of Newfoundland. The upgrading of highways allowed easier access to work available in Stephenville and even further afield. But in 1966 the American base finally closed down, putting an end, in one fell swoop, to the principal source of prosperity. At this period the traditional occupation, the fishery, to which the newly unemployed might have returned, was suffering from the effects of over-exploitation. Bay St. George, which for generations had provided an abundance of cod and lobster, seemed on the point of depletion. Almost overnight people had to rely on social security programmes in a milieu in which most French Newfoundlanders had previously been able to earn an adequate living.

Other factors of a cultural nature were added to the influences of economic depression. Ever since Confederation in 1949, and even well before, the government of Newfoundland had attempted to apply a policy of assimilation towards the French. It was an undeclared policy, of course, the chief instrument of which was the Church, which controlled education in the area. Attempts were made to impose the use of English through both lay and religious education. This "positive" aspect of assimilation was reinforced by another negative one, which was quite simply a lack of concern for the interests of the French.

This negligence, demoralizing to the French, was buttressed by a disdainful attitude towards them on the part of anglophones on the West Coast and elsewhere. The most commonly used pejorative term aimed at the French—"Jacotar" or "Jackytar"—had been used since the early years of the nineteenth century to designate the descendants of mixed French-Micmac unions.[46] In using the term, people made fun of the accent of the French when they spoke English, and of other qualities unkindly attributed to them such as laziness or immorality.

This was the low point of their misfortune. Some French people even began scorning their language and culture. And then, all at once it seemed, the French took a new and apparently spontaneous interest in their future as French people. Several mutually reinforcing factors contributed to this renaissance.

The French Newfoundland Renaissance

Firstly, the end of the sixties witnessed the creation, by the Federal government of the day, of the Commission on Bilingualism and Biculturalism. In 1971 I accompanied three members of the commission on a visit, made at my suggestion, to the West Coast. Knowing, from census returns, that there were francophones in Newfoundland, the commission members had gone to St. John's, hoping to find them there. Doubts and disappointment were dispelled by their findings on the West Coast, which prompted them to recommend, in their 1975 report, the establishment there of a federal bilingual district.

While this recommendation was never followed through, it was nonetheless a sign of growing activity and interest in the fate of French Newfoundlanders. Already, in 1971, supported by the Secretary of State's Social Animation division, French Newfoundlanders had founded the *Association des Terre-Neuviens Français* at Cape St. George. In 1974, the French were provided with a French language television station, by satellite relay from Montreal. In September 1975 a bilingual school was established at Cape St. George, which offered the French, for the first time ever, education in their mother tongue. And since 1970 my own research in the traditional culture of French Newfoundlanders has not only established the existence of a very rich folklore, it has also helped French Newfoundlanders give new value to their language and traditions.

Yet the future of the West Coast's ethnic French group is by no means assured. It has been calculated that there are no more than 3,000 people in the area who usually speak French in the home.[47] While this figure is undoubtedly the largest ever in the history of the French in the region, it is nonetheless true that they remain, will always remain, a minority. And one may always be tempted to see the new cultural contributions I have mentioned as efforts of superficial value.

Hope resides in the fact that despite all the pressures to which the French have been subjected, they have nonetheless been able to sustain their language and culture. It is my intention to demonstrate the richness of these by examining an aspect of traditional life which has long been one of the chief vehicles of Franco-Newfoundland language and culture: the tradition of the folktale or *Märchen*, through which I hope to illustrate a very human, joyous, indomitable temperament.

NOTES

1. According to the 1971 census Newfoundland, with a total population of 522,105, included 15,410 of French origin, 9,860 speaking French (bilingual and unilingual), and 2,295 for whom French was the everyday tongue. It may be assumed that the last figure includes the French of Labrador, of Quebec origin. Source: Census of Canada, 1971.

2. See Samuel Eliot Morison, *The European Discovery of America: The Northern Voyages*, New York: Oxford University Press, 1971, 270-273.

3. The name 'Port-au-Port' seems to be a relatively recent deformation of an earlier *Port-à-Port*; it appears thus on eighteenth and nineteenth century French maps. But the name derives perhaps from an even earlier Basque denomination, 'Opoportu.'

4. Morison, *op. cit.*, 359.

5. See Pierre Biays, "Un village terreneuvien: Cap-St-Georges," *Cahiers de Géographie* I (1952), 5-29.

6. Charles de la Morandière, *Histoire de la pêche française de la morue dans l'Amérique septentrionale*, 3 vols., Paris: Maisonneuve & Larose, 1962, 1966. See vol. II, 519-520.

7. A more detailed description of these questions is in de la Morandière, vol. III, 1351-1353.

8. Modern Newfoundland maps do not carry the French forms of the names of the peninsula's francophone villages, with the exception of Degras (or De Grau). If Cape St. George, so named by the English according to Samuel Eliot Morison, is easily rendered in French as Cap-St-Georges, its most usual appellation is quite simply "Le Cap" or "The Cape." Degras, shown on official maps at the location of Rousseau Rouge (Red Brook), is a name found elsewhere in Newfoundland (Cape Degrat, Quirpon I.) and also in Nova Scotia (Petit Degrat). The meaning of the word seems to be 'a secondary fishing station.' La Grand'Terre (Mainland) owes its name to its position relative to Red Island; the name is also found in Brittany in a similar situation. Trois Câilloux (Three Rock Cove) indicates the presence of three rocks emerging from the sea, near the shore. Lourdes was named by an Anglo-Irish priest who brought the first English settlers there from the Fortune Bay area in the mid 1930s; he had earlier made a pilgrimage to Lourdes, in France. Maisons-d'Hiver (Winterhouses) seems to owe its origin to the period of the French fishery when wintering fishermen left their bases at l'Anse-à-Canards or la Barre (The Bar) for better winter shelter. L'Anse-à-Canards (Black Duck Brook) owes its name to the presence, it is said, of a kind of wild duck (*anas rubripes*).

9. Oral communication from Fr. R. T. White, priest at Stephenville Crossing and the St. George's diocesan historian.

10. De la Morandière, vol. III, 1175.

11. *Ibid.*, 1179.

12. *Ibid.*

13. *Ibid.*

14. Thomas W. White, "Les Acadiens de Terre-Neuve," *L'Evangéline* (Moncton), nos. of 26 & 28 February, 4, 11, 18 & 25 March, 1, 8, 15 April and 6 May 1948.

15. See in particular Geneviève Massignon, *Les Parlers français d'Acadie*, 2 vols., Paris: Klincksieck, 1962, vol. I, 42-75, in which the author presents the 76 most common Acadian family names and details about the origins of each family. For the origins of French and Breton family names, see Albert Dauzat, *Dictionnaire des noms de famille et prénoms de France*, Paris: Larousse, 1951.

16. See de la Morandière, vol. III, 1064-1065.

17. Paul Sébillot, *Le folk-lore des pêcheurs*, Paris: Maisonneuve, 1901, and reprint, Paris: Maisonneuve & Larose, 1968; coll. *Littératures populaires de toutes les nations*, vol. XLIII, 299-300.

18. *Ibid.*, 300-301.

19. This rough rhyme is offered to give the spirit of the original. I have translated 'Mardi-Gras' as 'Jack o'Lent' as "In parts of Cornwall a straw figure dressed in cast-off clothes and called Jack o'Lent was formerly carried round and then burned at the beginning of Lent." (Elizabeth Mary Wright, *Rustic Speech and Folk-Lore*, London, 1913, p. 291). The custom seems related to the one described by Sébillot.

20. Sébillot, *op. cit.*, 301-302.

21. See Biays, *op. cit.*, 16.

22. See Melville Bell Grosvenor, "White Mist Cruises to Wreck-Haunted St. Pierre and Miquelon," *National Geographic* CXXXII, 3 (Sept. 1967), 378-419.

23. For a description of nineteenth century Brittany see Yann Brékilien, *La vie quotidienne des paysans bretons (au XIXe siècle)*, Paris: Hachette, 1966.

24. The term 'mousse' (boy) refers, in the French fishery, to a beginner or apprentice, the legal minimum age for which was 16. A novice was generally a boy with at least two years' experience.

25. Count Arthur de Gobineau, *Voyage à Terre-Neuve*, Paris: Hachette, 1861; reprint, Montreal: Editions du Jour, 1972, p. 140. All quotations are from the 1972 edition.

26. *Ibid.*, 140.

27. *Ibid.*, 140-141.

28. *Ibid.*, 141.

29. *Ibid.*, 142.

30. *Ibid.*, 142-143.

31. *Ibid.*, 143.

32. De la Morandière, vol. III, 1282. 'Capitaine prud'homme' (fishing admiral), is a term replacing, after 1815, the earlier 'amiral', as in English usage in Newfoundland. The title was given to the oldest captain in a harbour, and he had the same functions as the earlier admiral save that he did not distribute beach areas, which was decided by the drawing of lots. 'Maître capelanier' ('master capliner') was a term applied, on the French Shore, to those fishermen whose role was solely to catch caplin for bait, in boats called 'capelanières'.

33. According to de la Morandière, *ibid.*

34. De la Morandière, vol. III, 1282.

35. From de la Morandière, vol. III, 1201, 1204.

36. On this point see Nicole Lamarre, "Kinship and Inheritance Patterns in a French Newfoundland Village," *Recherches sociologiques* 12, 3 (1971), 345-359.

37. De la Morandière, vol. III, 1048, from M. Carpon, *Voyage à Terre-Neuve*, Paris & Caen, 1852.

38. Towards the middle of the nineteenth century, political and economic questions had prompted the government of Newfoundland to insist on its rights to jurisdiction over the French Shore. The debate was only concluded in 1904 when, by the terms of the 'Entente cordiale,' France gave up all its rights. De la Morandière deals with this question at some length in vol. III of his *Histoire*.

39. Biays, *op. cit.*, 15. Biays, who must have interviewed one of the first Robin's descendants, notes that he was from La Roche-Derrien, near St. Brieuc, a Breton port which equipped ships for the Newfoundland fishery. Biays was at Cape St. George in 1951. The grandson of the first Robin, also named Guillaume, to whom I spoke frequently from 1970 on, claims his grandfather was from St. Malo. St. Malo was, of course, the point of departure for Newfoundland for many fishermen leaving to work on the French Shore; but this town was not necessarily their place of birth or habitual dwelling.

40. Students registered in my course on the *Traditional Culture of French Newfoundlanders* have made analyses of censuses for the area which concerns us here. A critical and descriptive summary of these is to be found in Geraldine Barter, *A Critically Annotated Bibliography of Works Published and Unpublished Relating to the Culture of French Newfoundlanders*, St. John's: Centre d'Etudes Franco-Terreneuviennes, Memorial University of Newfoundland, 1977.

41. These figures come from the following studies: for Cape St. George, Ruth King, "Communities of the Cape St. George Area of the Port-au-Port Peninsula: 1874-1911"; for Mainland, Robert Wayne Barbour, "The Community of Mainland, 1884-1921: A Factual Report"; for Black Duck Brook, Catherine Hanlon, "Census of Black Duck Brook (1874-1921)." For further details, see Barter, *Bibliography*. These studies may be consulted at C.E.F.T.

42. According to Biays, *op. cit.*, 15, it was a man by the name of Yves Lemoine. It should be emphasized that serious analysis of parish records remains to be done; it will certainly provide further details.

43. From R. P. Michael Brosnan, *Pioneer History of the St. George's Diocese, Newfoundland*, Toronto: Mission Press, 1948.

44. John T. Stoker, "Spoken French in Newfoundland," *Culture* 25 (1964), 349-359.

45. By 1990, the communities had succeeded in acquiring paved roads, within the villages and linking them; but the dream of a paved road between Mainland and Cape St. George, the two most dynamic of French villages, has still to come true. Such a road would cut the present circuitous sixty-five kilometre drive to one of ten kilometres or less.

46. To my knowledge no adequate etymology of this term has been proposed. 'Jackytar' or 'Jacotar' is a still current slur aimed at French Newfoundlanders. Folk etymologies derive it from 'Jacques à terre' ('Jack ashore') with the meaning of a deserter. Patrice Brasseur and Jean-Paul Chauveau's recent *Dictionnaire des régionalismes de Saint-Pierre et Miquelon* (Tübingen: Niemeyer, 1990), proposes, without supporting evidence, the English 'jack tar' as the origin of the epithet. For other current nicknames in Franco-Newfoundland tradition, see my article "Some Examples of *Blason Populaire* from the French Tradition of Western Newfoundland," *R L S Regional Language Studies... Newfoundland*, No. 7 (June 1976), 29-33.

47. A figure moreover much disputed; the 1991 census claimed as few as 955 French speakers in the Bay St. George region. See Bertrand Bissuel, "Déchiffrer le fait français," *Le Gaboteur* Vol. 9, No. 9 (5 March 1993), p. 3.

II

The Two Traditions

For French Newfoundlanders the golden age of the folktale, if indeed there was a golden age, must have spanned the period between the founding of the first francophone communities in the nineteenth century, and the early nineteen-forties. Until 1940, daily routine was tied to the seasons and saw little variation. Most men, young and old alike, were fishermen who sold their catches to local merchants; they were more precisely fishermen who had been forced into a barter system, for they were rarely paid in cash.

With the beginnings of the logging industry at the turn of the century, a number of Frenchmen sought employment in the camps, a custom which has continued to this day, and which allowed them to earn small amounts of money. Some signed on for the Banks fishery, and a handful of hardy souls ventured as far afield as the Caribbean, on board schooners plying the salt fish trade. But most Frenchmen stayed at home throughout the year, supplementing the fruits of their fishing with the meagre produce of subsistance farming.

Women raised their families, looked after the home, often fished with their husbands in their dories, took care of their vegetable gardens and the needs of their animals. They sheared sheep, washed, carded, spun and knitted their wool. It was a hard but full life.[1]

The *Veillée*

The *veillée* was simply a gathering of adult couples at a private home with, most often, a storyteller present. The storyteller would be invited for the evening and if he accepted, the invitation was extended to neighbours and friends. But even without a formal invitation people would come, as long as they did not live too far from the home in question. There might be no more than one or two couples present, or as many as a dozen.

The visitors arrived at the house at about seven in the evening. Until 9 o'clock card games were often played, and this would be followed by a supper or "lunch" prepared by the hostess: a dish of beans, bread and jam, biscuits, tea or, less frequently, a home-made wine.

After the meal, it was time for stories. If no acknowledged storyteller was present, everyone would be asked to sing a song, tell a story, a joke, ask a *devinaille* or riddle;[2] but the "classic" *veillée* was the one at which one well-known storyteller was present, there specifically to tell folktales. His speciality was the *Märchen* (or fairy tale), some of which might last for three hours or more; there is evidence that certain tales were so long it took two consecutive evenings to tell them. Thus, a *veillée* might well continue until two or three o'clock in the morning.

The *veillée* was the principal context in which the well-known storyteller, the public storyteller so to speak, performed, since he told his tales to an audience drawn from several homes. Moreover, the public storyteller was usually a man, although many women also had extensive repertoires. We may note in passing that studies or collections of *Märchen* have most often been drawn from the repertoires of public storytellers.[3]

The *veillée* was usually held in the kitchen, the most important room in the house, where most domestic activities took place. The hostess would busy herself feeding wood into the stove, which warmed the room lit by a kerosene lamp standing on a shelf above the table. The audience would be seated on benches or wooden chairs, facing the evening's narrator. The children, whose presence was generally accepted as long as they stayed quiet, lay on the floor, hidden in the shadows cast by the lamp. There they listened, learning the tales they heard, until they fell asleep.[4]

The *Veillée* in Decline

After 1940 the *veillée*, as I have just described it, began losing its importance due to changes taking place in the region. The arrival of the Americans in Stephenville at this time, and the work provided by the construction of an Air Force base there, attracted many French people. They found work readily. They put to good use their skill and experience as carpenters; and numerous secondary positions—as cooks, maintenance and service workers—offered further possibilities for paid work.

The air base naturally drew more men than women to it. And since the best storytellers in the Newfoundland French tradition were men, their absence had an important effect on the *veillée*. Firstly, the fewer storytellers there were, the less there were public *veillées*; but more importantly, wives whose husbands were away from home did not care to go to *veillées* alone. It was therefore a period of disruption in the tradition, and while one cannot go so far as to say that the *veillée* disappeared at this point, it is nonetheless certain it suffered a severe blow.

The American base lasted longer than the war which had brought it into being, only closing down permanently in 1966. At its height, the base employed between 1,500 and 2,000 civilians working full-time; in the fifties, any of the French who wanted work there could find it. There was, therefore, a social disruption which influenced everything, not just the *veillée*; and by the beginning of the sixties, other innovations were beginning to make themselves felt.

The French had had battery-powered radios well before the war, and some of them had probably seen movies, thanks to portable, dynamo-generated equipment (although I know French Newfoundlanders who claim never to have seen a film before 1964).[5] All the same, such things would not have interfered greatly with the custom of the *veillée*. The chief reason the public *veillée* disappeared was undoubtedly the electrification of the French communities at the beginning of the sixties.

Television, and to a lesser but equally important extent the record-player and the tape-recorder, came at the same time as electric lighting, and when I talked about *veillées* with my informants, almost all of them pointed at the television set. They did not need prompting from me to say that television had given the death blow to the public *veillée*. Later, I shall examine in more detail the influence of television on the tale tradition; we should, nonetheless, take note here that when I began my field work in 1970, some informants had not told any tales for at least ten years.

The general influence of television and, to a lesser degree, of film and radio, had been to destroy the element of participation at the personal level, a feature so characteristic of the *veillée* and the storytelling context. At the same time, entertainment became more private, more closed. One remained seated in front of the television looking at the picture, rather than participating with one's friends in the interaction between narrator and audience. One should also take into account the enduring novelty of television, and its educational value. A whole new world became visually accessible to people for whom the attraction of books had never been very great, for the very good reason that, given the educational attainments of most French Newfoundlanders, extensive reading would have been more tiresome than enjoyable.

Other forms of entertainment became available to French Newfoundlanders in the sixties, for it was in that period that the former country paths were transformed into paved roads. It was now possible to go elsewhere, to visit one's friends in other communities, to "go in", to Stephenville, to go and enjoy oneself in the taverns and bars which began springing up in neighbouring villages. All this, combined with the pressures towards assimilation which were at their strongest during and after the war, served to erode old customs.

The effect of such social change on storytellers was predictable. Used as they were to demonstrating their talents at *veillées*, they soon became aware that their profession was no longer held in much esteem. They therefore stopped performing their art and, little by little, forgot their tales. A casual visitor might well have concluded that the folktale tradition was dead.[6]

Maintenance of the Narrative Tradition

Such was not the case. This book bears witness to the fact that, while one part of the narrative tradition seems to have disappeared, the other has stayed alive. One can still find numerous storytellers, or at least numerous people who are able to tell stories. I shall return to this distinction in a while, but let us first look at the reasons prompting such a distinction. We know that not every home had a television set. People who did not have one would have sought, from time to time, entertainment of a more traditional kind. Others, after the novelty of television had worn off, certainly preferred stories and songs or traditional music to the unidirectional television set. Yet others quite simply maintained a part of the narrative tradition which, to the outsider's eye, was never very obvious. It is what I call the private or family tradition of folktale telling.

The Private or Family Tradition

I must admit that the early months of my field work among French Newfoundlanders, in 1970 and 1971, were rather discouraging. With one exception, I met nobody who was a reputed storyteller, or who was willing to tell tales. There was one exception, however: a relatively young man told me a few fine versions of *Märchen*, but had no real desire to be interviewed.

As time passed, and particularly during an eight month stay at Cape St. George, I slowly realized that once I had been accepted by various families, I was able to gain admission to a side of the narrative tradition that only a lengthy stay in the field would permit. I learned that many people knew tales, that they told them quite frequently, save when outsiders were present.

I learned, in fact, that if the tradition of the public storyteller and the *veillée* represented the visible side of narrative tradition, and this tradition was indeed in the process of disappearing, there nonetheless existed another, hidden side to it, with the same kitchen context, the same winter nights, but one in which the audience differed to a certain extent from that of the public tradition. We were dealing here with a family *veillée* in fact, where the mother, a few older relatives, sometimes the father, would entertain the children with tales learned in the *veillées*. Or, and such was the case of the two ladies who appear in this book, it was the occasional get-together of two old friends who would entertain themselves in the course of an evening with their favourite stories.

As my field work progressed in depth, I came to realize that most of the people who told tales to family or friends often had quite broad repertoires, and the versions were not necessarily fragmentary but, quite the contrary, rich, long and, according to other participants, complete. Yet none of my informants, male or female, called themselves a storyteller. This was a title they reserved for those accustomed and reputed to tell tales, and tell them well, in public.

This distinction, which I have already referred to, is important because it eventually allowed me to work my way into hitherto unsuspected corners of the narrative tradition. Once I had made the distinction between public and private or family storytellers, I felt obliged to make a detailed examination of the causes of such a distinction, which emanated from the French themselves.[7]

While making the distinction, I was ever conscious of doing my field work at a moment in history marked by important cultural and socio-economic changes. The public storyteller was no longer active because he was no longer needed. My analysis of the private tradition showed numerous differences of interpretation, of presentation, of style, of performance, of points of view between the tradition I was able to observe and the public tradition which, for a long time, I was only able to know through hearsay. I realized that a crucial evolution was taking place in the field of what we may call the Franco-Newfoundland narrative aesthetic.

My research set as its aim to isolate, as far as was possible, the constituents of this aesthetic, taking up at the same time the causes of change and, consequently, the new aesthetic. I make no claim to having isolated all the factors involved, but believe that those which I have identified are valuable, allowing me not only to cast some light on the evolution of a particular tradition in a specific region, but also to suggest possibly fruitful research directions elsewhere in the world.

A very large part of my comments and conclusions are due to the two women who represent the private or family tradition in this book, Mrs. Blanche Ozon and Mrs. Angela Kerfont, both of Cape St. George. Together, they told me some twenty tales, *Märchen* and others. But more than that, they managed to draw my attention, consciously or unconsciously, to numerous factors which illustrate the evolution of a tradition.

Bilingualism

English language and culture have always been a reality for French Newfoundlanders. Theirs is a culture which is now, more than ever, bilingual. This mixed culture is very much in evidence when Mrs. Ozon and Mrs. Kerfont are together. The former rarely spoke English, and her tales were always in French. Mrs. Kerfont, on the other hand, who was quite at home with French, always told her tales in English. I shall examine this peculiarity in more detail when I describe my folktale sessions with the two women, only noting here that it is characteristic of numerous Franco-Newfoundland homes.[8] It may well be typical of other Canadian provinces with French majorities or minorities, but I am not aware of it.

Neither Mrs. Ozon nor Mrs. Kerfont thought of themselves as storytellers in the public tradition. Indirectly they criticized their own storytelling style, and were always quick to draw attention to aspects of the older story tradition which they disliked. Indirectly, too, they drew my attention to the role of interaction in a private context. Even in the very middle of narrations they displayed a lively repartee. And they, more than anything else, focussed my attention on the influence of television.

These questions, and others which I have only touched upon here, allowed me better to grasp the nature of the private tradition. As far as the public tradition was concerned, on the other hand, all I had at my disposal were the remarks and comments about narrators in *veillées* made by former participants in the tradition. Such remarks were more than valuable; their authors served as windows on the past. But comments alone could not ultimately replace the direct observation of a public storyteller. As I have already noted, it was impossible to take part in a public *veillée*, because they no longer took place; the few public narrators still living no longer cared to tell tales. After all, they had once stood in the limelight, but now were without a stage. What good would it do to try and restore to life what was now dead and gone? To be sure, it sometimes happened that such and such a storyteller might fleetingly reacquire a taste for tales; but it was usually without conviction.

The Public Tradition

Then, in March 1978, I began a series of recordings with Emile Benoit. During my stay at Cape St. George in 1972-73, and subsequently during my numerous visits to Mainland, I had frequently heard about Mr. Benoit. He had long enjoyed in the area a reputation as a fiddler who combined with his musical talents that of a comical raconteur. He had, at the age of 61, begun a new career as a professional musician, first by taking part in folk festivals, then by playing in clubs and bars in St. John's and elsewhere. Thought of as an outstanding representative of traditional Franco-Newfoundland music, he guested on several radio and television programs, on both English and French networks. In 1979, he cut his first record, *Emile's Dream.*[9]

Yet Emile Benoit is not at all typical of Franco-Newfoundland musical tradition. This is not because of his lively and engaging style, but because Emile Benoit is a composer of fiddle tunes; in the course of his life he claims to have composed well over a hundred jigs and reels. His originality does not end there. Much of his talent, and it is never so evident as when he is playing in a club, lies in the introductions to each of his compositions. He always has a personal experience to relate which he recounts with such art and enthusiasm that his audience is unfailingly convulsed with laughter during his monologues, as they are prompted to dance or tap their feet while he plays his tunes.

But if Emile Benoit, at the age of 78 (he was born in 1913), has managed to carve out a career as a musician-storyteller for himself, there is a side to his talent which remains concealed from the public at large. Emile Benoit is also a great storyteller in the old public tradition. Obviously, he cannot narrate an hour-long story in a bar, given the limitations of a professional engagement; but in other contexts, anything is possible.

I have been a close friend of Emile Benoit since 1978 and have frequently been able to observe his storytelling talent. I was able to confirm my ideas on the two traditions, for Emile Benoit has clearly illustrated what other informants had told me about the style and performance of storytellers in the public tradition. I may add that only in one respect does he differ from the old public storytellers: he is first and foremost a musician, and admits having forsaken tales; his repertoire of *Märchen*, for example, is not large, at least not in my experience. I shall return to this matter later, in the two chapters about him.

Characteristic Features of the Two Traditions

It remains for me to define in detail the characteristic features of the public and private or family traditions, and to outline the constituents of the community's narrative aesthetics. In the chapters devoted to Mrs. Ozon and Mrs. Kerfont, we shall see to what extent they represent the latter tradition, and how far Mr. Benoit represents the former. Five broad areas can be identified, the elements of which may be contrasted with each other and which will allow us to distinguish the two traditions of the public and private storyteller. These areas include: the context (physical and human), repertoire, function, (textual) style, and performance.[10]

45

Context

As I have already indicated, the physical context of the public *veillée* was the same as that of the private or family *veillée*: the kitchen. The difference lay in the human context. In a public *veillée*, the well-known storyteller was the centre of attention; everything revolved around him. The audience was often large, made up of husbands and wives and young unmarried adults. If the host and his wife had any children, their presence would be tolerated. From the start of the story, the listeners would be as attentive as if they were at the theatre, and the parallel is deliberate: they were present at a kind of play, in which all the parts were performed by the same actor. Given the numerous dramatic or comic elements in the performance one could expect predictable reactions from the audience. But above all, if the storyteller was a virtuoso, the audience would refrain from behaviour which might in any way be considered disrespectful.

The private or family *veillée* was quite different. While there might well be a large number of people present, given the large families, with children spaced evenly over a twenty or so year period, and without forgetting the grandparents, the evening was quite lacking in formality. There would be comings and goings from one room to another, all kinds of interruptions. There might well be a nucleus of serious listeners, but there would be as many who paid only fleeting attention to the storyteller. If a tale was being told to infants, they would likely ask questions, and one might notice the smiles of older people at the children's reactions.

If, on the other hand, the *veillée* included no more than two or three people the same lack of formality characterized their behaviour. There would be a succession of comments, questions, pauses, laughs, comings and goings. A private or family *veillée* became even less formal when the conversation turned from *Märchen* to other, less structured types of narrative. If a *Märchen* was told in such a *veillée*, its relative length naturally imposed on the audience a certain effort of attention. But when one started telling jokes laughter would ring out, and if talk turned to ghost or devil legends, reactions would become more nervous and agitated.

Repertoire

In other words, repertoires in the respective *veillées* were not exactly the same. In the public *veillée*, the great storytellers were tellers of *Märchen*. People wanted to hear the adventures of the brothers Tom, Bill and Jack, about seven-headed monsters, old witches, giants, talking animals, beautiful princesses and impossible tasks. And since the storytellers' repertoires were nonetheless limited, and since they often had their own, personal versions of the same tale, audiences perhaps paid as much or even more attention to the storytellers' performances as to the actual stories. The tales were known, having been told and heard so often. The pleasure to be derived from the *veillée* came less from the originality of a tale as from its interpretation.

To be sure, public storytellers did not restrict themselves to *Märchen*. All sorts of traditional themes might be treated; but from my analysis of the body of narratives associated with the *veillée*, I can assert, as one might well imagine, that the place of honour fell to the *Märchen*, followed by the romantic tale, which differed from the *Märchen* mainly by the absence of marvelous or magical elements. Thereafter, humorous tales were greatly appreciated, especially those dealing with dupes, fools and married couples. And for these tales too, it should be emphasized, the audience was as appreciative of the storyteller's performance as it was of the tales themselves.

In the private or family *veillée*, one could hear the same *Märchen*, romantic or humorous tales, as in the public gathering. But as I have already noted, there was no rigidity of narrative content in the course of a private or family *veillée*. One might go from a *Märchen* to an item of gossip, from a religious legend to a personal

46

experience, from talk about the weather to an example of *blason populaire*. And quite the opposite of the public *veillée*, everybody had the opportunity of slipping a word in. Moreover, the private of family *veillée* was not limited to storytelling. Someone might sing a humorous song, another might intone a love song, yet another a dramatic ballad. Riddles might be asked, or some old-timer might play a few airs on the fiddle, or a jig on the harmonica. In short, an absence of formality characterized the private of family *veillée*. Whether the audience was large or not, everyone was entitled to contribute to the evening's enjoyment, indeed, everyone was responsible for it.

Function of *Veillées*

The differences between the two traditions in terms of the human context on the one hand and of repertoire and behaviour on the other, suggest that the two kinds of *veillée* had different functions. To be sure, they coincide in certain ways: in both cases we are dealing with a gathering of people, formal or informal, with the aim of enjoying themselves. But other functions set them apart.

Consciously or not, participants in public *veillées* were sharing an aesthetic experience. That was where one learned to appreciate narrative art. It is not without reason that my informants said they were not storytellers; storytellers for them told their tales in public. This indicates that they must have acquired, during their lifetimes, notions of what separated a good storyteller from a bad one. It is not surprising that when one questions people about former storytellers, the same names recur. It is a pity that, generally speaking, my informants were not able to articulate precisely their criteria of excellence. But I shall return to this question shortly.

While it was in the family *veillée* that children acquired the primary components of their aesthetic formation—the subject matter of the folktale as a genre—it was in the public *veillée* that they learned to appreciate the interpretive possibilities of storytelling. Narrative aesthetics were therefore received and traditional; as long as society did not evolve too rapidly, they varied but little. But when the socio-economic changes of the post-war period made themselves felt, aesthetic criteria were overturned.

This aesthetic function, which seems so obvious in the context of the *veillée*, may explain why "tradition" so often appears to be very conservative. As a child, one learns by example, receiving from one's elders, by their conscious or unconscious actions, notions of what is good, and what is not good. And if a society is deprived of the possibility of continuous and advanced intellectual development, it only has example to follow, and no desire for change. As outlined in the preceding chapter, the history of the Franco-Newfoundland populations has followed this course: a long period of stability marked, on account of its status as an ethnic minority, by an educational system which ignored, or feigned ignorance of, the linguistic realities. Then the war, the development of mass media and new possibilities in the economic realm all helped to upset the status quo.

In the family *veillée*, the aesthetic function played a minimal role. To be sure, the very fact of employing certain traditional genres introduced young people to the subject matter of tales, and this introduction had a didactic function. Once familiar with the subject matter, young participants were ready for the aesthetic experience of the public *veillée*. It is now time to take a closer look at the elements which allow the elaboration of the folktale aesthetics of French Newfoundlanders.

Aesthetics: Style and Performance

I am making a somewhat artificial distinction between (textual) style and performance, the last two criteria which allow us to set the two traditions apart, for both are combined at the moment of a tale's narration. If the storyteller may himself be aware of the different components of style and performance, if he can manipulate them at will, it is nonetheless true that they are parts of a whole. Having made this point, let us look more closely at the two most important features of folktale narration which allow us to distinguish the public from the private or family storyteller.

When I talk of style in relation to the narration of a tale, I am in fact talking about a certain number of formal elements which can be grasped through textual analysis. Storyteller and audience are quite aware of some of these elements, while others do not seem to have any particular significance. The first element which should interest us is the structure of the *Märchen*.

In Western tale tradition, and even in other areas of our experience, we perceive a predilection for triple repetition.[11] We have only to think of the international tale-type AT 303, *The Twins or Blood-Brothers*. We find the three brothers, three dogs, the brothers' horses, the three life tokens and thrice repeated events or actions. At one moment or another most storytellers focus the collector's attention on this triple repetition. On the other hand, in the private tradition, storytellers tend to simplify this linear structure, by eliminating or abbreviating one or two of the repetitive elements. One of my female storytellers repeated over and over that she no longer cared for this kind of tale precisely because "Everything goes in threes."

Triple repetition at the level of narrative elements is repeated at the level of detail. Thus it is that the brothers Tom, Bill and Jack, in the tale *The Twins or Blood-Brothers*, each has a dog, and each dog has a name. In the public tradition, storytellers faithfully used each name at the proper moment. The dogs are variously called Brise-Fer (Iron-Breaker), Brûle-Fer (Iron-Burner) or Passe-Partout (Pass-Any-where). The names are so well known to French Newfoundlanders that a rather clumsy child may be nicknamed "Un vrai petit Brise-Fer" (A real little Iron-Breaker). In the same vein, the classic, almost formulaic description of the old witch who turns Tom and Bill into stone will be repeated at the appropriate moment: "Worm in the ground" says the storyteller, "dust on my hands, an old woman comes out, her hair and her beard dragging on the ground!" In the public tradition, the storyteller will repeat the whole sentence, word for word, each time one of the brothers confronts the witch. In the private or family tradition, the storyteller may omit the phrase after the first encounter, or even not use it at all.

The omission of these stereotyped words and phrases is characteristic of the general lack of attention paid to detail in the private tradition. One can easily multiply the number of examples of such omissions through the textual analysis of tales in the private or family tradition, in contrast to the often very detailed texts of the public storyteller.

A consequence of the public storyteller's faithfulness to the structure and detail of *Märchen*, and of the folktale in general, is that in the public tradition, tales were often very, very long. Many informants mentioned that "in the old days" such and such an old fellow used to tell stories that lasted from two to three hours, and some spoke of storytellers who needed two consecutive evenings to finish a tale. The storyteller who could tell very long tales was generally much admired. One of the criteria of excellence in the public tradition then was the length of the story, assuming other requirements were met, of course. It is certain that Emile Benoit, the public storyteller in this collection, knows how to fill out his stories, to the point that he told me at least two tales which lasted about seventy-five minutes each. He was quite surprised to learn there were still people who liked long stories, and at one particular moment he told me that had he known of my taste, he could have lengthened such and such a tale.

For it must be admitted that nowadays, and perhaps in the past, even when the public tradition was still vigorous, stories in the private or family tradition were usually quite short. Narrators are moreover quite aware of this difference between the two traditions. To be sure, they may sometimes attribute the brevity of their narrations to their not having told tales for several years, or to a failing memory;[12] and that is no doubt frequently the case.

But it should not be forgotten that if the private or family tradition has survived despite the demise of the public tradition, its practitioners must have gone on telling stories between the end of the public *veillée* and the arrival of an interested researcher. They did not resurrect a tradition just to please an outsider. One must therefore seek other explanations for the difference in tale length in the two traditions. From my observation of dozens of private storytellers whom I know, I can affirm not only their omission of all kinds of details in their tales, but that very often they do so consciously. It is quite rare to find a private storyteller who will tell a tale lasting more than half an hour. Many storytellers in this tradition, moreover, give evidence of a real aversion for very long tales. This aversion, and the word is not too strong, is due in part to the influence of television. Before going on to the final aspects of style and performance which characterize the two traditions, it is important to pause a moment and take a closer look at this influence.[13]

The Influence of Television

Television came to French Newfoundlanders, as we know, in the early sixties. Ten years later, in 1970, and in subsequent years, I was frequently struck, in day to day conversations, by allusions to certain television programs, and in particular to serialized melodramas. Furthermore, in the course of some of my interviews I became aware that at about 3.30 p.m. storytellers tended to quicken the pace of their narrations. I was given to understand that they did not want to miss the next episode of the serial, the soap opera which began at 4 p.m., which was referred to as the "four o'clock story."

I began to pay a good deal more attention to this kind of serial than hitherto. Comparing it to *Märchen*, I discovered similarities and differences which, in their respective ways, all helped make the telling of folktales much less attractive to numerous storytellers than had formerly been the case. First of all, let us consider the similarities.

The most important similarity between the two genres is in their theme. Many storytellers, female in particular on the Port-au-Port Peninsula, tended to emphasize the romantic aspect of tales. One such narrator spoke from time to time of her taste for tales in which the hero and heroine succeed in overcoming all manner of obstacles and in becoming united. This feeling was so strong that she spoke of the time she was courting her fiancé, and of their subsequent marriage, in terms of a folktale: "Then all, all that came about eh, it all came about eh, y'know? It all came true at the end of the story, it all came true eh—it all came true at the end of the story eh."[14]

The storyteller was referring to events in her own life, from her own personal experience. Concern with the drama of personal relationships is typical of female Franco-Newfoundland storytellers. And, as Horace Newcomb has observed, "Soap opera content is confined almost exclusively to a consideration of vital human problems. But they are not dealt with as universals, as the old verities. Instead, they are focussed upon and magnified to an overwhelmingly individual point."[15] If this element is present in tales, and emphasized by female narrators, if not by the males, in serials it is magnified to such an extent that other human concerns appear only fleetingly in them. Serials therefore exercise a disproportionate influence on viewers, giving them a diet rich in personal conflict, whereas tales offer only a diluted and relatively impersonal dose, for folktale heroes and heroines are stereotypes, and show little character development. This diet seems to have helped turn many French Newfoundlanders away from the oral folktale, in favour of the visual, televised story.

49

There are other, more technical similarities between the folktale and the serial. Folklorists have long recognized the merits of Axel Olrik's observation that there are never more than two characters active at a given moment in a folktale episode.[16] As Newcomb states, "In the soaps...it is rare that more than three characters appear in a single shot, and in most cases we see only two characters. In these scenes it is also rare that we are offered more than a head-and-shoulders close-up."[17] Apart from the fact that the storyteller plays all the parts, the audience will pay most attention to the upper half of the storyteller's body.

This preoccupation with the face, in serials as in folktales, is due to the emphasis on dialogue. The soap opera is a dialogic drama with little physical action. On the television set, moreover, bodily movement of the soap operas' characters often seems awkward and stiff.[18] Male and female narrators in the private or family tradition both exercise restraint, too, when representing violent physical action, whereas in the public tradition storytellers were unbridled in their movements.

The unnatural character of physical movement in soap operas needs to be underscored. In the days before television came to the peninsula—that is to say before the early sixties—at a time when the *veillée* was the chief form of public entertainment and when the gifted storyteller was the star in a kitchen packed with people eager to hear him, physical action, a sometimes exaggerated bodily movement, was part and parcel of the storyteller's style. He jumped around, gesticulated, imitated, mimed. This excessive physical activity is still associated with the "old Frenchmen." A child or adult too prone today to exuberant gesticulation will be mockingly referred to as "an old Frenchman." It is not a compliment.

It does seem likely that the somewhat restrained and static style of soap opera actors has been a negative influence on the unbridled style so characteristic of older storytellers. To be sure, the few remaining narrators in the public tradition uphold the old style, on the rare occasions when they practice their art; but people make fun of them. Most contemporary storytellers, almost always women and representatives of the private or family tradition, are also fervent soap opera fans, as are moreover their eventual audiences. They admire the actors playing their favorite soap opera characters and knowingly or otherwise may imitate their style and relatively static acting.

There is a final parallel between the televised serial and the folktale. It is the physical context in which the tale narration and the soap opera action take place. The storyteller practiced his art in the *veillée*, in a kitchen, that is, in a familiar and physically restricted milieu. In soap operas, the action almost always takes place in a house or building, even when allusions are made to events happening outside. This familiar context is important on the technical level, from the audience's point of view. The viewer is not provided with vertical or panoramic shots in soap opera. Most often he sees the actors' faces, just as a storyteller's audience watches his face. The televised serial imitates the reality of a traditional narrative.

Differences Between the Two Genres

If the similarities between soap opera and folktale link the two genres in a positive fashion, the differences serve only to emphasize the powerful attraction of the soap opera. The most obvious difference is in the structure of each genre. A tale's development is perfectly predictable. The triple repetition of events is so characteristic that even if a listener has never heard such and such a tale before, he knows what to expect: three brothers, three tasks, the failure of the first two, the success of the third, and so on. There is very little suspense in folktales.

It is certainly true that formulaic-like actions and situations are not lacking in soap operas; but they are not of the same kinds as repetition in tales. In soap operas one encounters the same motifs of marital infidelity and intrigue, as well as certain character-types. But the problems raised by the highly emotional interaction of the actors are so personal, in that an audience may readily identify with them, that one tends not to notice the repetition of conflict and intrigue. Moreover, the soap opera does undergo real evolution. The scenario is organic, changing from day to day, from month to month, from year to year, allowing the growth and development of characters.

It is this development—of characters and situations—which guarantees the soap opera its constant suspense, compared to the folktale which is repetitive and lacks character development. And unlike the soap opera, the folktale (which has a clearly indicated beginning and end) is a discreet unit of narrative entertainment. The soap opera evolves over an unlimited period of time, it is always "to be continued." It has organic evolution, and its repetition is not obvious, as is that in the folktale. If one may ultimately guess that such and such an affair will come to naught or will end in tragedy, its detailed development is not predictable, and suspense is kept at a very high level, especially by the Friday cliff-hanger. Suspense engendered by soap operas seems to have had the greatest effect of all on storytellers and their audiences, perhaps because soap operas seem to more accurately reflect the uncertainties of life.

Another factor which seems to contribute to the popularity of soap operas is time. Soap operas come on at set and predictable times and are of a fixed length— half an hour, an hour, an hour and a half in general. The viewer may, if he so desires, plan his day around the soap opera. *Veillées*, on the other hand, did not take place at regular intervals and their length was not predictable. Moreover, storytelling was mainly a winter activity, while the soap opera is on television from Monday to Friday, all year long. The *veillée* was far more susceptible to vagaries of the weather, the availability of the storyteller, or other requirements. The soap opera has no seasonal routine. It is more convenient to be able to call up one's favorite program at a specific time at the touch of a button. Television, more than any other modern commodity, has contributed to the decline of the folktale.

Formulas

In the public tradition, the storyteller made especial use of opening and closing formulas. Of course, these served as audible signs signaling the beginning or the end of a tale; but they had, or have, a real effect on the audience: a smile of recognition betraying an expected pleasure. Opening formulas vary little in Franco-Newfoundland tradition. The most common one, "Once there was a time," some-times becomes "Once there was a time, and a good time it was," and occasionally one meets "Well, once there was a time, and to tell you once, it's not in my time and it's not in your time—it's in olden times—there was a man and a woman." The most usual closing formula, "And if they're not dead, they're livin yet," is sometimes preceded by an innocuous addition, "And when I passed by they gave me a cup of tea." But this addition may undergo numerous variations which at times betray a very personal device of the storyteller. We shall see this later, when we look at the style of our public storyteller, Emile Benoit.

These formulas are characteristic of the public tradition, but in the private or family tradition they may be deformed or quite simply omitted. Omission is also apparent with internal formulas, that is, stereotyped expressions within an oral text. Most of these formulaic expressions serve to indicate, quickly and conventionally, the passing of time. One in particular takes its effect from the triple repetition of a verb: "He walked, he walked, he walked a long time." Repetition heightens the meaning of the word or phrase in question and in oral discourse it is used so often it becomes a striking stylistic device. To suggest the passing of a long period of time, a phrase very frequently used is "In a story it goes quick." And I have even recorded a rhymed formula:

51

Marche aujourd'hui, marche demain,
A force de marcher on fait beaucoup de chemin
(Walk today, walk tomorrow, the more you walk,
the further you go.)

If the public storyteller was faithful in his use of these formulas, the private storyteller was not under the same obligation; he leaves them out or changes them. He may even go so far as to parody them:

Walk today, walk tomorrow,
If you don't fall with your nose in the shit
The further you'll go.

Or, "By dint of walking, stuff your nose in the shit." And given the different attitudes of young and old towards folktales, it is not surprising to learn that in the private or family tradition the narrator often feels obliged to excuse some impossible motif with the phrase "It's a story!" right in the middle of his tale. This does not seem to have been part of the public storyteller's language.[19]

Rhythm of Narration

In specifying the differences between the two traditions, I have so far dwelt on formal aspects of style which can be grasped through textual analysis. Other stylistic traits which require our attention are rarely indicated in texts, because of the difficulty posed by their transcription.

Narrators of both traditions try to reproduce the rhythm of natural conversational speech, and to exploit the dramatic potential of voice, by lowering it, for example, before a violent or striking event. But important differences between the two traditions are to be observed. Narration in the private or family tradition is usually full of hesitations, corrections and non-dramatic pauses. Faulty memory quite probably contributes to the presence of these features, but the frequent intrusion of phrases such as "No—er—I'm ahead of my story" followed by a rearrangement of the motif sequence, interrupts the normally fluent flow of a narration. In the public tradition such interruptions were not normal and would have reflected badly on the storyteller's reputation. The private storyteller does not have to fulfil the same obligations.

Macaronic Speech

In so far as a mixed linguistic context can at times be disconcerting, macaronic speech may also impede the easy progress of a narration. Macaronic speech is not a necessary characteristic of the two styles, but its very existence typifies reality for an ethnic minority. French Newfoundlanders, as we have seen, have long been subjected to assimilative pressures from the English majority, and a mixed linguistic context is characteristic nowadays. This mixture is nowhere more apparent than with our two female storytellers, Mrs. Ozon and Mrs. Kerfont, for the listener is plunged into a conversation in two languages, English and French. Contemporary storytellers especially show the pervasive influence of linguistic assimilation, since they no longer have complete command of their language. They look for a word in one language, a phrase in the other, and this contributes to multiple breaks in speech flow. One may assume that the further back in the past one might go, the fewer macaronic intrusions into conversations there would be.

The Storyteller as Actor

We now take up the last stylistic feature distinguishing the two traditions, a feature I have already alluded to. It is an aspect of what may be called the storyteller's acting style or his performance and, more particularly, his use of body movement. In the public style the storyteller was uninhibited in his use of gesture and gesticulation. Numerous testimonies emphasize the vigorous use of the body made by old storytellers of the public style. They waved their arms about, their hands were never still, they contorted their bodies, they illustrated facial elasticity to the full. The audience, sitting around the storyteller, on the floor or on chairs, were always liable to be stepped on if, in his excitement, he jumped up the better to describe the combat between the hero and the seven-headed monster. The listener had to watch out for the storyteller's gestures and gesticulations.

Aesthetics of Franco-Newfoundland Narrative Tradition

Here then are the broad lines of Franco-Newfoundland narrative aesthetics. The public tradition required the presence, in the usual kitchen context, of a renowned storyteller. The large audience could expect a wide repertoire of *Märchen*, the performance of which would illustrate the community's standards of excellence, simultaneously offering the most widely enjoyed type of entertainment.

Given that most people taking part in a *veillée* had already heard the tales told there in the informal context of the private or family tradition, it is evident that they expected more than the simple telling of a tale. They expected a story interpretation which adhered faithfully to the norms of the public tradition.

The storyteller had to prove his mastery of an inherited style. As far as a tale text was concerned, he would have scrupulously respected the use of formulaic expressions, opening and closing formulas, stereotyped phrases; in the often triple repetition of an event, he would have repeated almost word for word the elements of the narrative motif. In brief, he would have told his tale with all possible exactness, faithful to the text as he had received it. To his textual fidelity he would have added a theatrical interpretation characterized by much bodily and gesticulatory movement, from a wink to a jump carrying him half way across the room.

His mastery of the text, combined with his physical actions, made of his narration a vigorous performance, lively and rich with an almost ritualistic language. But just as the gifted actor will not play a given part exactly like his peers, the renowned storyteller also had his own genius, which direct and continuous observation alone would allow us to uncover. I shall try to evoke in a subsequent chapter the genius of one of the few living storytellers who may be thought of as typical of the public tradition: Emile Benoit.

Parallel to this acknowledged and esteemed tradition there existed another, recognized but thought of differently: the private or family tradition. It was an "amateur" tradition in that its representatives did not think of themselves as storytellers in the public sense of the word; they told stories to children, to the close family or, in certain cases, when a few old friends gathered together to recapture the pleasures of a distant youth.

In the family tradition storytelling did not function simply as a way of entertaining the young and not so young; it also introduced young people to the narratives which were an important part of their cultural heritage; material which, in the proper context, would provide them with the high point of their artistic experience. But the private or family tradition was more preoccupied with the content of tales than with their artistic interpretation; storytellers in this tradition were in no way obliged to follow the rules governing the performances of their public counterparts. It was therefore an informal and unrestrained tradition which

both entertained and taught a certain body of material; again, generically speaking, narrations in family or private gatherings could be enormously varied.

In order to establish the existence of two narrative traditions among French Newfoundlanders I have raised questions of context, repertoire, function, style and performance, noting in passing external influences that have had a powerful effect on the evolution of the two traditions.[20] My observations and analysis have allowed me too to outline the aesthetics of folktale narration in the public tradition, and to suggest directions contemporary aesthetics seem to be taking, very largely those of generalized North American popular taste.

But these considerations, based on the analysis of a long period of observation and a rich harvest of tales, have so far been presented in a necessarily rather abstract manner. There remains now the agreeable task of filling out these abstract thoughts with concrete illustrations, by introducing the chosen representatives of each tradition to the reader. Obviously, without a very broad sampling of storytellers it will be difficult to illustrate in depth each and every abstraction; that would be an enormous task, going far beyond the limits of this book.[21] I do believe, however, that through my two storytellers, Mrs. Blanche Ozon and Mrs. Angela Kerfont, through the personality of Emile Benoit and the richness of his artistic interpretations, I can provide eloquent testimony which others may one day confirm or modify. I shall first introduce the representatives of the private or family tradition, Mmes Ozon and Kerfont. They will illustrate a still vital tradition, although not readily accessible to those unwilling to devote considerable time to its investigation. I shall then move to the public tradition, in the person of Mr. Emile Benoit. With his biography I shall portray the man, and through the analysis of his tales, his art and talent.

NOTES

1. The daily life of French Newfoundlanders is described in several studies made by my students. See Barter, *Bibliography*, for further details.

2. One will note the way fiction may reflect life; in some tales to be found later in this book, the ending is preceded by a meal, following which the guests must take turns telling a story or singing a song.

3. A selection of books or articles on French folktales (from France and Canada) can be found in the *Bibliography*.

4. On this point see Geraldine Barter, "The Folktale and Children in the Tradition of French Newfoundlanders," *Canadian Folklore canadien* I, 1-2 (1979), 5-11.

5. See Michael Taft, "The Itinerant Movie-Man and His Impact on the Folk Culture of the Outports of Newfoundland," *Culture & Tradition* I (1976), 107-119.

6. "...There seem to be little or no trace of folk-songs or folk-tales, arts or crafts." J.T. Stoker, "Spoken French in Newfoundland," *Culture* XXV (1964), 349-359; see page 358.

7. "The two traditions" is a phrase which has already been used by folklorists, but in connection with folksong. I am thinking in particular of a paper read by Edward D. Ives at the second annual meeting of the Folklore Studies Association of Canada in Fredericton in 1977, and subsequently published: "Lumbercamp Singing and the Two Traditions," *Canadian Folk Music Journal* V (1977), 17-23. Ives also distinguishes between a public tradition dominated by men, and a private tradition dominated by women. He deals with the context of folksong in the American north-east and the Maritimes.

8. This phenomenon has been little studied by Canadian folklorists; Newfoundland and its west coast must be a fruitful area, for apart from my own observations, Margaret Bennett has also looked at the question of bilingualism, indeed of trilingualism, in her article "Scottish Gaelic, English and French: Some Aspects of the Macaronic Tradition of the Codroy Valley, Newfoundland," *RLS Regional Language Studies ....Newfoundland* No. 4 (May 1972), 25-30.

9. Quay CS 7932, 1979.

10. On this point see my article "The Folktale and Folktale Style in the Tradition of French Newfoundlanders," *Canadian Folklore canadien* I, 1-2 (1979), 71-78.

11. One may read with pleasure Alan Dundes' essay entitled "The Number Three in American Culture" in his book *Interpreting Folklore*, Bloomington & London: Indiana University Press, 1980, 134-159.

12. Vivian Labrie has studied the mechanisms of story recall in her article "Le Sabre de Lumière et de Vertu de Sagesse: Anatomie d'une Remémoration," *Canadian Folklore canadien* I, 1-2 (1979), 37-70.

13. I have examined this question in greater detail in the following article: "Other Worlds: The Folktale and Soap Opera in Newfoundland's French Tradition," *Folklore Studies in Honour of Herbert Halpert*, ed. K.S. Goldstein & N.V. Rosenberg, St. John's: Memorial University of Newfoundland, 1980, 343-351.

14. Gerald Thomas, "Stories, Storytelling and Storytellers in Newfoundland's French Tradition: A Study of the Narrative Art of Four French Newfoundlanders." Ph.D. dissertation, Memorial University of Newfoundland, 1977, 845 p. See p. 132.

15. *TV: The Most Popular Art*, New York: Doubleday/Anchor, 1974, 171.

16. "Epic Laws in Folk Narrative," *The Study of Folklore*, ed. Alan Dundes, Englewood Cliffs, New Jersey: Prentice-Hall, Inc., 1965, 129-141 (reprint and translation of the 1909 original).

17. *TV: The Most Popular Art*, p. 168. I underline my debt to Newcomb, who drew my attention to many points which I had overlooked.

18. The reader will recognize that these and subsequent observations were made at a period before the proliferation of soap operas, before the lengthening of episodes, and before the investment of large sums of money allowing a more highly developed vehicle to emerge.

19. The importance of formulas in tales has long been recognized. A few useful references include: Johannes Bolte & Georg Polívka, *Anmerkungen zu den Kinder- und Hausmärchen der Brüder Grimm* (5 vols., Hildesheim, 1963; reprint of the first edition, Leipzig, 1913-32); see vol. IV, 1-40; for examples of French language formulas see George Laport, *Les contes populaires wallons* (FF Communications No. 101, Helsinki, 1932), 6-9 (Laport also provides interesting details on a public storyteller from his area); Elsie Clews Parsons, *Folk-Tales of Andros Islands*, Bahamas, New York, 1918; Memoirs of the American Folklore Society, vol. XIII, x-xii; and Daniel J. Crowley, *I Could Talk Old-Story Good: Creativity in Bahamian Folklore*, Berkeley & Los Angeles, 1966, University of California Publications, Folklore Studies 17, "Opening and Closing Formulae," p. 32 ff. For the use of formulas in an Amerindian tradition, see Melville Jacobs, *The Content and Style of an Oral Literature: Clackamas Chinook Myths and Tales*, Chicago & London: The University of Chicago Press, 1959, 212-215.

20. The notions of "style" and "performance" have concerned a growing number of folklorists in recent years, especially in the U.S.A. My thinking has been influenced by the reading of certain articles or books, but derives above all from a lengthy reflection based on continuous participant-observation of narrative contexts in Franco-Newfoundland tradition. For practical purposes, I provide here a selection of titles which have been particularly useful: William Hugh Jansen, "Classifying Performance in the Study of Verbal Folklore," *Studies in Folklore, in Honor of Distinguished Service Professor Stith Thompson.*, ed. W. Edson Richmond, Bloomington: Indiana University Publications, Folklore Series 9, 1957, 110-118; Dell Hymes, "Introduction: Toward Ethnographies of Communication," *The Ethnography of Communication*, ed. John J. Gumperz & Dell Hymes, *American Anthropologist* 66, 6 (1964), 1-34; Dan Ben-Amos, "Toward a Definition of Folklore in Context," *Toward New Perspectives in Folklore*, ed. Américo Paredes & Richard Bauman, *Journal of American Folklore* 84 (1971), 3-15, and published in a special volume, Austin, 1972; Richard Bauman & Joel

Scherzer, *Explorations in the Ethnography of Speaking*, New York: Cambridge University Press, 1974; Erving Goffman, *The Presentation of Self in Everyday Life*, New York: Doubleday/Anchor Books, 1959; Richard Bauman, "Verbal Art as Performance," *American Anthropologist* 77 (1975), 290-311; Dan Ben-Amos & Kenneth S. Goldstein, eds., *Folklore. Performance and Communication*, The Hague: Mouton, 1975; Barbara Babcock-Abrahams, "The Story in the Story: Metanarration in Folk Narrative," *Studia Fennica* 20, *Folk Narrative Research*, Helsinki, 1976, 177-184; John Ball, "Style in the Folktale," *Folk-Lore* LXV (1954), 170-172; Melville Jacobs, *The Content and Style of an Oral Literature*, Chicago: The University of Chicago Press, 1959; Ruth Finnegan, *Limba Stories and Storytelling*, Oxford: The Clarendon Press, 1967; Richard M. Dorson, *Negro Folktales in Michigan*, Cambridge: Harvard University Press, 1956; and his article "Oral Styles of American Folk Narrators," *Folklore in Action: Essays in Honor of MacEdward Leach*, ed. Horace P. Beck, Philadelphia: The American Folklore Society, Inc., 1962, 77-100. Of equal interest is the article by Istvan Sandor, "Dramaturgy of Tale-Telling," *Acta Ethnographica* XVI, Budapest, 1967, 305-338; see also K. Haiding, *Von der Gebärdensprache der Märchenerzähler*, Helsinki, FF Communications No. 155, 1955, and the works of Francis C. Hayes: "Gestos o Ademanes Folkloricos," *Folklore Americas* XI, 2 (1951), 15-21; "Guia por el que recoge ademanes o gestos," *Folklore Americas* XIX, 1 (1959), 1-6; and "Gestures: A Working Bibliography," *Southern Folklore Quarterly* XXI, 4 (1957), 218-317. I will not provide here a sampling of works relating to the question of popular aesthetics. I only note that my thinking in this area has been influenced by Herbert Halpert who, almost forty years ago, was already asking his informants about the qualities making a good narration or what made so-and-so a good storyteller. I owe him much more than a series of references.

21. Let it be stressed here that such data have been collected. Tales from many dozens of Franco-Newfoundland storytellers, mostly of the private or family tradition, are stored, classified and catalogued in the Centre d'Etudes Franco-Terreneuviennes of Memorial's Department of Folklore.

III

The Private or Family Tradition:
Blanche Ozon and Angela Kerfont

In chapter II I drew the reader's attention to the central feature of the Franco-New-foundland narrative tradition: the existence of two parallel traditions. The one, which I term public, is characterized by known and reputed storytellers; the other, the private or family tradition, is distinguished by male or female storytellers not recognized as such outside of a very closed circle. The two types may tell the same folktales, the same stories and anecdotes, but the first adhere to a style marked by a certain rigour, while the latter are not constrained to conform to any style at all. This chapter will introduce the reader to two storytellers from the private or family tradition: Mrs. Blanche Ozon and Mrs. Angèle (Angela) Kerfont, both of Cape St. George.

I shall reserve a description of the two ladies' style and performance for the next chapter, providing here brief biographies of the two storytellers and an evocation of the quite singular context of the interviews I had with them. Such a description is necessary because it raises the question of *coaxing*,[1] an almost obliga-tory prelude to the narration of a tale in the private or family tradition: one had to coax stories out of representatives of this tradition. Such was not the case for the public storyteller during the period in which his art was fully appreciated. But coaxing is not only symptomatic of a personal reticence on the part of certain storytellers: by dint of coaxing the two women, and especially Mrs. Kerfont, I was able to bring out a number of important factors contributing to the decline of the *Märchen* and of the folktale in general in Franco-Newfoundland tradition. I dare say that these are factors which have influenced narrative tradition everywhere in the western world.

Biographical Notes

The biographical notes on the two ladies provided here are not cumbersome; they have both led routine lives, quite typical of French Newfoundland women of their generation. I provide them however neither as a scholarly necessity nor out of simple politeness; among other things, these notes will help us understand the unusual context in which they told me their tales: Mrs. Ozon only used French, while Mrs. Kerfont preferred English, only infrequently making use of French. I shall discuss this macaronic context later, for it reflects a state which, for French New-foundlanders, must have become increasingly common with the passage of time. But this same context also provides us with some interesting insights into the personality and temperament of a storyteller.

Mrs. Blanche Ozon

Mrs. Blanche Ozon, a native of Cape St. George and at whose home my interviews with the two ladies were made, was born on October 13, 1907. Her parents, Adolphe Simon and Joséphine Renouf, had nine children in all, but at the age of thirteen she lost her father, who drowned while fishing. Adolphe Simon was a son of the first Simon to live at the Cape, and family tradition has it that the first Simon was born in France. He would have deserted the French fishery about the middle of the nineteenth century. It is sometimes claimed that the first Renouf to settle at the Cape was in fact the very first Frenchman to settle there, while others in the community claim a certain Guillaume Robin was the first. In fact we do not know the truth, which would be difficult to establish in any case. It is enough to say that Blanche Ozon is a descendant of one of the first Frenchmen to settle at the Cape.

At the age of eighteen she married Jean Ozon whose father, Pierre, born in St. Malo, Brittany, came to Newfoundland after a stay in St. Pierre, where there are Ozons to this day. Another branch of the Ozon family settled at St. George's. Mrs. Ozon had but one child, a daughter; the name will disappear from the Cape with them, for she has been a widow for many years.

Mrs. Angela Kerfont

Mrs. Angela Kerfont was born at Lourdes (at the time, Clam Bank Cove) on August 5, 1915. Her mother was Maggie Chaisson from Cape St. George; a first marriage took her to Lourdes. At the death of her first husband, she married a second time, to Albert Marche of Lourdes, Angela's father. At the age of twenty-two, Angela (or Angèle) married a widower, Joe Kerfont, and came to live at the Cape. It seems that in her youth she had spoken French with her mother, but used English more commonly. After her marriage to Joe Kerfont, French became her daily language.

In marrying Joe Kerfont, Angela assumed responsibility for her husband's seven children by his first wife. She gave him ten more. Having taken up certain maternal functions when she was herself a girl and, having subsequently helped raise some of her grandchildren, she could say with a certain pride that "I reared up t'ree families, me—almost four!" She too has been a widow for several years.

Meetings

In the period in which I interviewed the two ladies, the winter of 1972-73, Mrs. Ozon was sixty-five years old. Short, plumpish, with greying black hair, her piercing eyes betrayed a sometimes peppery temperament, to which she added, if need be, a biting tongue. Her voice was hoarse and when she laughed, it often ended in a harrowing cough. She sometimes seemed to be on the verge of sleep, but her darting eyes proclaimed an alert wakefulness.

Mrs. Kerfont, barely more than five feet tall, seems smaller than her friend. This petiteness emphasizes her impish proclivities. Her eyes sometimes failed to mask a malicious gleam, and her tongue was just as sharp as her friend's; this combination of qualities shared by both ladies provoked a constant round of teasing between the two, which amused me but seemed to exasperate Mrs. Ozon.

This teasing occasionally had bothersome consequences and the two ladies would not see one another for a few weeks. By way of contrast, let us note that Mrs. Kerfont seemed more dynamic than her friend, and her dynamism was reflected in her speech. Her talk was less measured and more staccato than Mrs. Ozon's; her voice grating and nasal, and remarkably deep for such a small person. But these qualities added a certain flavour to our storytelling sessions, as we shall see.

I first met Mrs. Ozon shortly after arriving at Cape St. George in early October 1972. My hosts, Mr. and Mrs. Henri Simon, had to visit a sick relative in Halifax. Mrs. Ozon, an aunt of Mr. Simon, had come to spend a week at the house in order to look after the three boarders and Mr. and Mrs. Simon's youngest son. During the week I made one recording with Mrs. Ozon; she spoke mostly about her youth, giving no hint that she knew any stories. I was left with the impression of a friendly and voluble woman whose potential as an informant was slight, at least as far as my main interest at the time, folktales, was concerned.

And then, two months later, on the ninth of December to be precise, I was talking with Mrs. Ozon's nephew Robert Simon, in the kitchen of Henri Simon's home, where we were both lodging. Robert Simon had been playing cards the evening before at his aunt Blanche's home, which was nearby. During our conversation he alluded to what seemed to me to be a fool tale motif. Intrigued, I pursued the matter and learned, to my considerable surprise, that at the end of the card game Mrs. Ozon and her friend Mrs. Kerfont had told a few humorous tales. Robert Simon was able to recall the occasional motif, but not being in any way a storyteller himself, his accounts were not clear enough to allow a provisional identification of the tales.

I asked him more questions and finally learned that the two women frequently spent evenings together; they passed the time playing cards, singing songs, and telling stories. This last activity interested me most particularly, the more so because after two months at Cape St. George I had not yet succeeded in recording a francophone storyteller. This in spite of the hopes raised in 1971 when I had met and recorded an excellent teller of folktales, Mr. Cyril Robin.[2]

Robert Simon insisted, however, that I say nothing to the two women when I met them of how I had learned they told stories to each other, and that I not allude to the storytelling session in which he had participated. He felt they would be angry with him for passing the information to an outsider. He added, in passing, that they were both somewhat irascible and he derived some amusement from telling me about their occasional tiffs, for which they were noted in the community.

Indeed, the two frequently were not on speaking terms, on account of some trifling disagreement, although the duration of such silences was rarely excessive. Unfortunately, one of these disagreements occurred shortly after my interviews with them, and by the time they were friends again I was already busy with other storytellers. This is why I have somewhat fewer biographical details on them than I would have liked, for I had been hoping to learn more about each one when I knew them better.

To get interview time, I decided to take advantage of my acquaintance with Mrs. Ozon, made during her stay at the Simons'. I knew she was in the habit of going to the Saturday night dance at the "Salon du Cap" and hoped that her friend Mrs. Kerfont might accompany her. The following Saturday night I went there with Robert Simon.

Halfway between the entrance and the bar, we noticed Mrs. Ozon sitting at a table with another lady. As I had hoped, it was Mrs. Kerfont. I went to the bar for a beer, stopping to greet Mrs. Ozon on my way back; she warmly returned my greeting. Mrs. Ozon introduced me to her friend, and I offered them a drink, which they accepted. Later on in the evening, I went to sit with them. They were both in good humour, glad to have had a few dances. I told them how much I was enjoying the evening, and from these general remarks I gradually directed the conversation towards the subject of stories and storytellers.

When I uttered the word *conte* (story), they looked at each other and started to laugh. I mentioned the titles of stories Robert Simon had heard from them, and while they guessed my source, they did not seem to mind. Little encouragement was needed for them to agree to an interview, which we set for the afternoon of December 21, 1972, at Mrs. Ozon's home.

It had seemed to me, during my conversation with the two women at the "Salon du Cap", that Mrs. Kerfont had not understood my French as well as did Mrs. Ozon; and indeed, part of our conversation had been in English. On the other hand, I knew

Mrs. Kerfont spoke French, because Mrs. Ozon used it exclusively, and Mrs. Kerfont sometimes replied to her in the same tongue. It seemed obvious to me that, like many French Newfoundlanders, Mrs. Kerfont did not readily understand the standard French which I spoke. But I was beginning to master Newfoundland French, which would be essential to the success of my fieldwork.

The Storytelling Sessions

Thus it was that I found myself, on a cold December afternoon, seated in Mrs. Ozon's kitchen, in what I hoped would be a more natural narrative context than those I had so far experienced. But I was also penetrating a world which, linguistically speaking, must have seemed very strange to anyone living in a monoglot environment, although such a world is typically Franco-Newfoundland. For it is a bilingual environment in which most people speak French and English, if they are of French descent.

Mrs. Ozon hardly ever used a word of English, while Mrs. Kerfont mostly spoke English, but used French words and phrases; both ladies understood each other perfectly. Being bilingual myself, I obviously had no great problem following their conversation, but the difficulties encountered by a monoglot person in such a context would certainly be tremendous. I shall take up this question in more detail later, when I consider their respective narrative styles.

The Physical Context

The three storytelling sessions took place in Mrs. Ozon's kitchen. I shall sketch the room in some detail in order to evoke a narrative context typical of the private tradition. The kind of intimate *veillée* shared by Mrs. Ozon and Mrs. Kerfont is far more prevalent than is assumed; major surveys have tended, quite naturally, to focus on well-known storytellers of the public tradition. Short of living and working in a particular milieu for some considerable time, one may barely suspect the existence of this other tradition.

From my experience at Mrs. Ozon's home, the two ladies were accustomed, while spending an evening together, to sit in the same place in the kitchen, and to follow a predictable routine. The house itself was a small rectangular structure suiting the needs of a widow living alone. At the entrance there was a small porch or *tambour*, where coats were hung and shoes left, and where, for want of a bathroom, stood a slop-pail.

From the porch one went immediately into the kitchen, the main part of the home. To the left stood a big Waterloo stove and beside it, in the corner, a day bed. Opposite the stove stood a small table, with one side against the wall, around which were three wooden chairs. One of these was a rocking-chair or *chaise à barcer*, facing the door. This is where Mrs. Ozon was usually installed, allowing her to identify visitors as they came in.

Next to her, with her back to the stove, sat Mrs. Kerfont, on a straight-backed chair furnished with a cushion. She was most often kneeling on the chair, turned towards Mrs. Ozon when telling a story, rather than towards me, sitting at the third side of the table, facing the two ladies. The tape-recorder was in front of me and to the side, so that it was inconspicuous.

At my back was the entrance to Mrs. Ozon's bedroom, a long curtain serving as a door. I could glimpse the big bed where the two women sometimes passed the night together. Behind Mrs. Ozon was a small pantry and a sink. Various objects adorned the walls: a cross made out of match-sticks; a portrait of the Madonna in a plastic frame; a photo of Queen Elizabeth, and another of Newfoundland's former premier, Joseph R. Smallwood. To me the most interesting was an old photograph of Mrs. Ozon's parents, in a fine wooden frame. The floor was covered with linoleum, as it was in most Franco-Newfoundland houses. Unhappily, a short time after my departure from the Cape, the house and all its contents were destroyed in a fire.

The stove, the sole means of heating the house, produced an intense heat. When she was baking bread, as she did once while I was present, the heat was almost unbearable. It added to the thirst-inducing business of storytelling, and after the first session, to which I had come empty-handed, I brought a case of beer, which encouraged conversation and relieved the thirst occasioned by the great heat.

I recorded Mrs. Ozon and Mrs. Kerfont on three occasions: the afternoon of December 21, 1972, and the evenings of the 3rd and 19th of January 1973. In all I made seven hours of recordings, the greatest part of which took place in the two evening sessions, which began at about 8 p.m. After the last recording, I made a brief visit to St. John's, expecting to continue with the interviews on my return. Unfortunately, however, when I returned the two women had had a temporary falling out, and by the time they had made up their differences I was busy with other informants. I recorded them no more.

It was in this context, then, that my interviews in Mrs. Ozon's home took place. But it is one thing to gain access to a storyteller's home, and quite another to get him (or her) to tell stories. I earlier made use of the term 'coaxing' to indicate a characteristic feature of the private or family tradition. We are dealing here with the almost inevitable need to convince an unenthusiastic narrator to tell a story. In the course of fieldwork which has been going on now for over twenty years, I have almost always had to persuade storytellers of the private or family tradition to begin narrating. This is, perhaps, not a definitive characteristic of a private or family storyteller; yet the only exceptions to the rule I know are storytellers from the public tradition.

Logically, I should perhaps describe the coaxing of the storyteller in the section devoted to the analysis of style and performance, but I take it up here as it leads directly to the kinds of pressures which have had a harmful influence on the Franco-Newfoundland storytelling tradition. So before considering the tale performance proper, let us examine the causes and functions of coaxing. We shall see that some characteristic features of the *Märchen* are no longer appreciated, at least in the private or family tradition, and that a new aesthetic is in the process of being forged, partly attributable to the influence of television. I shall now provide concrete examples to illustrate the theory presented in the preceding chapter.

Coaxing

The first recording session began without Mrs. Kerfont, who arrived some five minutes after Mrs. Ozon had begun telling a fool tale. Mrs. Ozon, who had invited me in the first place, was not overly reluctant to tell me a story, but betrayed some nervousness when faced with the tape-recorder. She was also waiting for the *truck à huile*, the oil-truck, to come by, as her supply of fuel was dwindling. During her narration she was constantly looking out of the window at the road. To put her at ease, I simply asked her the source of her story; she replied that she had it from her late husband, and immediately began the story, but not without this remark: "M'en vas commencer, bien j'vous dis pas si j'peux finir"—'I'll start it, but I can't say if I can finish it'—either because she could not recall the tale in its entirety, or on account of her worrying about the arrival of the oil-truck. In order to stop it, one had to go on the road and signal to its driver. At any event, my impression was of a storyteller who wanted to finish her story as soon as possible.

The coaxing proper began with the arrival of Mrs. Kerfont and Mrs. Ozon's granddaughter, Monica Chaisson, who was making a fleeting visit. It was quite evident that Mrs. Kerfont was nervous about my presence, for her only contact with me before had been in the very different atmosphere of the Salon du Cap. At first, she would not hear tell of stories.

The first stage of the coaxing began when Monica Chaisson mentioned the name of a story, which was taken up by Mrs. Ozon:

B.O.: "The Hound Dog."

M.C.: It's a real nice story.

A.K.: I don't tell stories.

G.T.: That's not true now—you say you don't tell stories—I know you *do* tell stories!

B.O.: A sait conter des contes—a veut pas! Alle est gênée, hein? (She can tell stories—[but] she doesn't want to! She's embarrassed, eh?)

G.T.: Tell, tell me the other thing about Jean-le-Sot, the different way that Blanche says it now—you said there's another way to say that now.

A.K.: Yes, there's a couple o ways...now I hear them saying eh?

G.T.: Which, which...

B.O.: Tu vas n'en conter ton *way* asteure (You're going to tell it your way now).

A.K.: I don—I forgot it!

M.C.: Ha ha!

A.K.: In aute conte (another story)—goes different ways that story, it goes three or four ways that story y'know.

B.O.: Alle a son *cheque* dans la poche, in deblâme pour aller à la boutique, mais tu vas pas tu sais (She's got her cheque in her pocket, it's an excuse to go to the store, but you're not going, you know).

A.K.: I'm goin to the store, yes!

B.O.: Pas asteure (Not now).

A.K.: I'll go to the store by n by.

B.O.: Oh!

It is difficult to evoke in print the lively exchange between the two ladies. The conversation was fast, especially when Mrs. Ozon was teasing Mrs. Kerfont about her cheque. Mrs. Kerfont at first claims not to tell stories, but then admits there are other versions of Mrs. Ozon's story (during the narration of which she had arrived). At the same time, she betrays her anxiety by insisting that she must go to the store, even though she had come to the house specifically to tell stories. This initial skirmish confirmed she knew stories, but also showed she was not yet ready to tell any.

Mrs. Ozon, who had carefully pointed out that her friend was embarrassed, then began reassuring her, telling her what she knew about me—that she had seen photographs of my family, which I immediately produced, thereby allowing Mrs. Kerfont to feel more at ease, as she complimented me on my children. I was then able to bring the subject of our conversation back to stories, and asked Mrs. Kerfont from whom she had heard the versions of the Jean-le-Sot (Foolish Jack) tale she knew.

She started praising Mrs. Olive Marche, a storyteller I had not met but who enjoyed an excellent reputation at Cape St. George and who must have been of the public tradition:

G.T.: Where did you hear those stories about Jean?

A.K.: Adolphe Marche's wife, that's the one!

B.O.: J'ai dit çui-là tantôt là, eh? (The one I told just now, eh?)

G.T.: From Olive!

B.O.: Olive.

A.K.: Oh ouais! I'm tellin' you she knows some, she knows some—that's her all that—stories there?

G.T.: Yeah?

A.K.: That's how come I learned that!

G.T.: When did she tell you those stories?

A.K.: When she was stayin up here, eh?

G.T.: Oh yeah? In the *veillées*?

A.K.: Oh oui! We used to go up there an we used to come home—well—some nights—almos daylight there tellin stories.

B.O.: Tiens (Here).

G.T.: Merci Blanche (Thanks Blanche).

A.K.: Tell stories. Moi aussi tu sais (Me too you know).

B.O.: Tire ta capote, eh? (Take your coat off, eh?)

A.K.: My God, c'est—c'est toi! (My God, it's—it's you!)

G.T.: Merci (Thanks).

B.O.: J'devras aller à la boutique (I should go to the store).

A.K.: I got... my nails... all browned an I don like that.

Mrs. Kerfont now affirms twice that she knows stories and lets us know indirectly how much she likes them. But she is still reluctant to begin telling stories, and when Mrs. Ozon serves us a cup of tea, she uses the moment to change the subject, by drawing our attention to her tobacco-stained fingernails.

It was Mrs. Ozon who took up the task of persuading her friend to tell a story, by recalling motifs from the fool tale she had told me earlier. She was quite aware that Mrs. Kerfont would be the star of our storytelling sessions, and the fact was confirmed when, at the end of the recordings, Mrs. Ozon had told seven and a half stories, Mrs. Kerfont fourteen and a half. Mrs. Ozon's initiative led to the final stage of the coaxing process, culminating in the first telling of a story by her friend. I furnish the whole conversation, as it characterizes the general model of coaxing with the two ladies:

G.T.: Blanche said that you, you know some—some fairy stories, is that what you call them?

A.K.: Yeah, but fairy tale, eh?

G.T.: Fairy tale.

B.O.: Des contes que j'avons conté l'aute soir, eh? Tu n'en as conté l'aute souère (Stories we told the other night, eh? You told some the other night).

A.K.: Bien, goddam!

G.T.: What one was that?

A.K.: Ah?

G.T.: What one was that that you told the other night? Fairy tale?

B.O.: Ah ha ha!

A.K.: Le diabe là! (The devil there!)

B.O.: Oui, le conte de... (Yes, the story of...)

A.K.:	That's too long there!
G.T.:	No! Do you know what? I have yet to hear somebody tell me a nice, a nice long story, you know?
B.O.:	Dis-lui çui-là que tu nous a conté l'aute souère là pour la—les trois frères, eh? Qu'avont té—pis les deux autes frères qu'étiont—dans la chambre en-haut—ç'ta-ti des frères ou des soeurs? Trois soeurs? Cui-là qu'alliont à la fotaine là—pis qui vnait back—pis trouva comme in chien... (Tell him the one you told us the other night there for the—the three brothers, eh? Who had been—then the other two brothers who were—up in the bedroom—was it brothers or sisters? Three sisters? The one where they went to the fountain there—then came back—and found a kind of a dog...)
A.K.:	Oh, that's a fox, a fox...
B.O.:	In ptit ernard (A little fox).
A.K.:	Ouais! (Yes!) T'ree sheeps!
B.O.:	Three sheep! Oui ça, c'est in beau conte eh? Comment qu'est-ce qu'i va? (Yes that, that's a nice story eh? How does it go?)
A.K.:	Oh my geewhiz!
B.O.:	Bien oui! My God! T'es pas gênée avec Mr. Davies—Davies! Ha ha! (But yes! My God! You're not embarrassed with Mr. Davies—Davies! Ha ha!)
G.T.:	Gerald.
B.O.:	T'es pas gênée avec Gerald—parce que lui, c'est pareil comme nous autes (You're not embarrassed with Gerald—because he, he's just like us).
A.K.:	Yeah, but—er—it's 'ard, eh, me I don know—I knows it all right, like me an you...
B.O.:	Bien, c'est mignon ça! (Well, that's nice!)
A.K.:	Yeah, but I can tell it good to you!
B.O.:	C'est ça qu'i veut! (That's what he wants!)
G.T.:	Why can't you tell it good to me? I'm no different from you!
B.O.:	Allons y pâsser in papier pis s'assire à la porte! (Give him a paper and sit by the door!)
G.T.:	Just because I come from a different place it doesn't mean it's any different.
B.O.:	Viens t'assire ici, tchiens! Sus la grande chaise. Conte-y in conte, pitchié! (Come and sit here, there! On the big chair. Tell him a story, for pity's sake!)
A.K.:	Oh my God, j'ai peur! Ho ho! (Oh my God, I'm afraid! Ho ho!)
B.O.:	Tu sais, oui, tu n'l'as conté l'aute souère! Tu peux l'conter à M—tu peux le conter à Gerald (You know, yes, you told it the other night! You can tell it to Mr—you can tell it to Gerald).
A.K.:	It goes three times over.
G.T.:	Eh?
A.K.:	It goes three times over.
G.T.:	That's all right.
A.K.:	That's so long!

This lengthy quotation is important because it summarizes, so to speak, the whole process of coaxing. The interviewer raises the question of storytelling almost inadvertently; Mrs. Ozon alludes to a specific occasion on which a tale was told; Mrs. Kerfont reacts with an oath (because a secret of sorts has been divulged to the interviewer, thereby removing her argument that she did not know any tales), and the interviewer grasps the opportunity to pursue the idea.

Mrs. Ozon makes fun of her friend's embarrassment and Mrs. Kerfont, recognizing her awkward position, makes a final assault upon the interviewer, calling him a devil; but she does so with a smile on her face. Her defences are in ruins, and she falls back upon her ultimate weapons: the quite significant ones of the length and repetition of folktales.

When she expresses her fears concerning the length of the story she has in mind, she receives indirect praise, and Mrs. Ozon clumsily refers to some of the tale's motifs. This of course prompts Mrs. Kerfont to recall details from the story, and to feel obliged to tell it properly. She has a feeling for what is appropriate in a story and what is not, and will not allow Mrs. Ozon's inaccuracies to go uncorrected. Mrs. Ozon and I make light of her alleged lack of acquaintanceship with the interviewer, and of her claims that the story in question is both too long and too repetitive.

Excuses and Praise

In different manners, the process of coaxing preceded the telling of almost all the stories told by the two women, and especially those told by Mrs. Kerfont. To complete the picture it should also be noted that at the end of a story, the storyteller excused herself and her audience praised her. A few examples will illustrate this typical feature of performance in the private tradition, typical even when taking into account that the interviewer was nonetheless an outsider. I shall return shortly to this question; let us only note here that in my experience in the region, both the coaxing which precedes a tale and the excuses and praise which follow it are quite characteristic and seem to fulfill two functions.

Firstly, the narrator prepares the audience for a narration which will probably not fit the criteria of the public tradition, and then excuses himself for errors he has perceived in his narration, compared to one performed in the public tradition. On the other hand, the audience, by denying perceived errors and by praising the performance, encourages the storyteller to begin another story.

At the end of the first tale told by Mrs. Kerfont, the following conversation took place:

A.K.:   I can't tell it to my likin at all!

B.O.:   C'est mignon, ça! (That was nice!)

A.K.:   I gets confused, eh?

G.T.:   C'était bon! J'ai beaucoup aimé ça! (It was good! I really liked it!)

B.O.:   Pas d'danger! (For sure!)

G.T.:   Eh? Oh oui! J'ai jamais entendu cette histoire-là (Eh? Oh yes! I've never heard that story before).

A.K.:   Non? (No?)

G.T.:   Jamais, non. Mais... elle est bonne! (Never, no. But... it's a good one!)

B.O.:   C'est eune belle histoire. (It's a beautiful story).

This very brief exchange was followed by a period of insignificant conversation which led to another round of coaxing and the telling of a new story. Mrs. Kerfont had been assured that she was appreciated, despite her doubts. It is not always necessary to furnish direct or open praise. In the following quotation, the interviewer uses the storyteller's confusion, not to fill in the gaps in her narrative but, through his intonation, to convince her of his enthusiasm for her narration:

A.K.: ... so e'd never return eh?—"Mes amis, ej la prends par la friggin du cou et, ej zig! Coupe, coupe d'Dieu prends ça!" ("Boys, I grab her by her frigging neck and zig! Cut, cut, take that by God!)

B.O.: Ah ha ha ha!

G.T.: What happened when he picked up all the bones then?

A.K.: E pick up all de bones—e knowed it was is sister's own eh? E knowed it was is sister in de pot.

G.T.: Now what was the big white sheet that came down on him?

A.K.: God knows!

At this stage of the interview it was obvious that Mrs. Kerfont was beginning to feel at ease with me, for her replies to my questions were made as spontaneously as her conversations with Mrs. Ozon. Yet the same procedure had to be followed. The next example records a conversation taking us from the end of one story to the beginning of another, with the praise, excuses and coaxing characteristic of the transitional period between two tales:

A.K.: .... An then—if they're not dead—they might be livin yet.

G.T.: I've never heard that one before!

A.K.: Non? (No?)

G.T.: (to B.O.) No. You heard that one before? No? Never?

A.K.: By gee, I knows some nice ones me, I knowed some nice ones. Tut tut! So far, so far, so long eh?

B.O.: Oui, oui, trop long, t'as oublié (Yes, yes, too long, you've forgotten).

A.K.: Oublié (Forgotten).

G.T.: What about, er... you said er... "The Three Gold Mountains."

A.K.: That's—there's a giant in that too.

G.T.: A giant in that one as well.

A.K.: Hm.

G.T.: Did Olive tell you that one as well?

A.K.: That one there...

G.T.: That one—"The Twenty-Four Robbers," yes... Tell that one about three mountains an the giant, then.

A.K.: By God, that's not short either, that.

B.O.: Ha ha!

A.K.: I don't forgets any—I forgets some.

G.T.: You remember em—an I'll tell you some—short ones! If I can remember them!

A.K.: Yeah!... I forgets how it goes now... If I can remember... One time there was a man an a woman, an they ad three sons, Jack an Bill an Tom...

To bring the subject of coaxing to a close, one can assert that it is an integral part of the private or family tradition on the Port-au-Port Peninsula. Of course, one might attribute its necessity to the fact that I was an outsider, that I spoke a brand of French different from that spoken locally, and that I always had a tape-recorder over my shoulder. But I emphasize it, because all the evidence suggests that in the

Franco-Newfoundland public tradition a renowned storyteller would tell his stories willingly, without coaxing.

Indeed, it seems that the extrovert alone does not need encouragement to sing a song, to dance or tell a story in informal contexts. There is an obvious parallel here between the extrovert in a party, where it is difficult to get the first couple to dance, and the renowned storyteller of the *veillée*. Neither the one nor the other need coaxing: both perform on demand. I would argue that coaxing is an important and perhaps normal part of the informal storytelling session. Other researchers will have to do in-depth fieldwork in order to confirm or refute this assertion.

As I noted earlier, my main reason for dealing with the rôle of coaxing is that my exchanges with Mrs. Kerfont will lead her to clarify the causes of the breakdown of the tale tradition. Of all the storytellers, male or female, that I interviewed, none was as clear on the subject as Mrs. Kerfont. If she seemed to be talking about two different subjects—the length and repetitive nature of tales on the one hand, television on the other—, they are intimately connected. It is the moment therefore to consider Mrs. Kerfont's views on stories and on television.

The Length of Tales

Time and time again Mrs. Kerfont drew my attention to the excessive length of tales:

G.T.: Is it a long story?

A.K.: Oh, it's a long story that, mignon.... oh, da's a long story dat... Oui, ça c'est trop long qu'ej laime pas (Yes, that's too long, I don't like that).

And again:

G.T.: "La vieille sorciaise et la pelote de laine" (The Old Witch and the Ball of Wool), that's a right long story, you said?

A.K.: Oh my God yes, too long.

Before her telling of another story, Mrs. Kerfont insisted: "That one there, I don't think I'm gonna tell it, it's too long." She never did tell another story she entitled "The Blue Bull" and when I asked her a direct question about the length of tales, she replied quite unambiguously:

A.K.: That story was difficult too—I didn't remember who told that story—it was a long story too.

G.T.: Don't you like telling long stories?

A.K.: Not too much!

Mrs. Kerfont flatly refused to tell one particular story, saying, at the end of our talk about the story in question: "Oh, but I'll never tell you dat, me, it's too long!" Before or after each narration, Mrs. Kerfont commented on the tale's length, expressing an implicit or explicit dislike of long stories.

Repetition in Tales

Her aversion for stories which, for her, were excessively long, was equalled only by her aversion for the structure of *Märchen*. The triple repetition of events or episodes in stories was summarized by her in the phrase: "Everything goes in threes." A few examples will illustrate the seriousness of her negative feelings about the phenomenon:

G.T.: Is that a long story too?

A.K.: Oh yes, I guess—on de first it's not too long as on de last—it goes about t'ree times over eh? It goes t'ree times over again, anyway.

Mrs. Ozon, for her part, could see no inconvenience in the triple repetition of events in a story, but her question to her friend provoked a vehement reply:

A.K.: It goes t'ree times over, eh?

B.O.:   Tchelle diffarence? (So what?)

A.K.:   Moi j'hais ça (Me I hate that).

Hate is indeed a strong word to use concerning a story, but Mrs. Kerfont also used it in English, in a similar context: "Now—I hates goin over an over, me...". That length and repetition are the two factors which, more than any other, contribute to her aversion to telling *Märchen*, becomes evident in the following exchange:

A.K.:   Oh my God, j'ai peur! Ho ho!... It goes three times over—it goes three times over for that.

G.T.:   That's all right.

A.K.:   That's so long!

In reality, one can surmise that lengthiness is less bothersome in stories for Mrs. Kerfont than repetition. For it is the repetitive description of events which produces the impression of excessive length, rather than the actual length of a tale. Some of her stories were no more or no less long than others in which triple repetition played a part. But in the few stories in which repetition was not glaringly evident, the storyteller's pleasure was obvious, as the following conversation suggests:

A.K.:   I'll never forget dat story ["The Woman Who Had a Foal"].

B.O.:   Oh.

A.K.:   No sir. Dat one dere I wouldn't ferget. I like it eh?

G.T.:   What do you like about that?

A.K.:   I like dat story eh?

G.T.:   Yeah.

A.K.:   So I wouldn't ferget it.

G.T.:   Why is it so nice for you?

A.K.:   I like it again eh.

G.T.:   Yeah.

A.K.:   Easy to tell eh.

G.T.:   Yeah, oh yeah.

A.K.:   Yeah.

G.T.:   Hm... It's a long story so when you've got to say things three times you don't like...

A.K.:   I don't like it.

G.T.:   Why not?

A.K.:   It's too long eh? No, I don't like—t'ree times over I don't like it...

In this story, there had in fact been a thrice-repeated motif, but only one. This unique repetition obviously did not bother Mrs. Kerfont, for whom the simplicity of the narrative thread seems to be an important criterion.

The Influence of Television

I earlier noted that a second factor, tied to the questions of length and repetition in stories, had also influenced the tale tradition. This factor is, of course, television. The first time I noticed the influence of television as a possible cause of a dislike of tales was towards the end of a recording session with Mrs. Ozon and Mrs. Kerfont. The session had taken place in the afternoon, beginning at about 2.15. I was coaxing the two ladies to tell one last tale:

G.T.:   One more, one more before I go now?

B.O.:   Conte-lé (Tell it).

A.K.: Oh yeah, but de story soon to be on too, dere you know [pointing to the television].

All: [Laughter]

B.O.: Coutez-vous ça? (Do you listen to that?)

G.T.: Quoi? (What?)

B.O.: Le conte de quatre heures là, "The Edge of Night" la? (The four o'clock story there, "The Edge of Night" there?)

G.T.: Non (No).

B.O.: Coutez pas ça (You don't listen to it).

A.K.: C'est beau ça (It's really nice, that).

G.T.: Oh oui, parfois, parfois, oui oui (Oh yes, sometimes, sometimes, yes yes).

B.O.: Belle histoire ça (It's a beautiful story).

G.T.: Oui, c'est à quatre heures (Yes, it's at four o'clock).

B.O.: Ouais (Yes).

G.T.: Oui. Contez-moi une histoire maintenant pis après vous allez regarder "The Edge of Night." (Yes. Tell me a story now, then after you'll watch "The Edge of Night").

B.O.: Débrouille-toi! (Get on with it!)

A.K.: I tells you I can't.

B.O.: Conte-le in morceau dans in jusque les quatre heures va venir ben tu vas t'couper là. Ha ha! (Tell him a piece of one until four o'clock then you can cut off there. Ha ha!)

This conversation requires comment because it implies several revealing facts about cultural change. Linguistically, one first notes that Mrs. Ozon talks about the televised serial in terms of a *conte*, a folktale: "le conte de quatre heures," 'the four o'clock story'. Among French Newfoundlanders, the term *conte* is most usually reserved for what folklorists term *Märchen* (Fairy-tale, Wonder Tale, Folktale Proper). Secondly, she asked me if I *listened* to the serial and not if I *watched* it (the usual word in Newfoundland French for *to watch* (television) being *veiller*). Normally, of course, one listens to a story. One may therefore assume there is a close parallel between the oral folktale and the televised serial. Mrs. Kerfont also used the term *beau* (beautiful) to describe the serial, thereby implying an aesthetic judgement; tales and serials are *beau*, they have an attraction for storytellers and audiences. There is no point in repeating here the detailed analysis of the influence of television on the tale tradition, or the relationship between folktale and serial I made in the last chapter; it will be enough to say that it was based on Mrs. Kerfont and Mrs. Ozon's remarks that I began to consider the question.

It is because television is a rather recent innovation on the Port-au-Port Peninsula, only appearing at the beginning of the nineteen-sixties, that it is still possible to record the quite extensive repertoires of people of all ages. If the erosion of the public tradition was begun by such factors as the coming of radio in the nineteen-thirties, social and economic pressures brought about by the 1939-45 war, it was television which gave the death-blow to the public *veillée* and, by depriving him of his favourite stage, to the public storyteller.

This chapter has introduced our two private or family tradition storytellers, and examined the reasons for the necessity of coaxing: among others, the now inordinate length of stories and their repetitive structure, next to which one can place television, which is convenient, full of suspense, and seems to promote a high

69

degree of personal involvement in people, in particular where the soap opera is concerned.

The next chapter will look at two aspects of the private storytelling tradition among French Newfoundlanders. The first concerns the rôle of metanarrative devices, of the interaction between storyteller and audience, clearly illustrated by the example of Mrs. Ozon and Mrs. Kerfont. The second aspect of the private tradition to be considered is the narrative style of the two women, and I shall pay particular attention to the use they make of formulaic or stereotyped language on the one hand, and of macaronic speech on the other. Together with remarks on their speed of delivery, their physical movement or gesture and vocabulary, these features may be considered typical of a storyteller and his performance in the private or family tradition.

NOTES

1. On the question of "coaxing," which I first discussed in my 1977 doctoral dissertation, it is interesting to note that the same problem arises in the context of folksong. See I. Sheldon Posen, "'Just One More Before You go': Singing and Coaxing in an Irish/Québécois Community," paper read at the Annual Meeting of the Folklore Studies Association of Canada, Saskatoon, 1979, and summarized in the *FSAC Bulletin* II, 4 (1979), 16.

   The reader might be tempted to suggest that the coaxing so characteristic of my interviews with Mrs. Ozon and Mrs. Kerfont was due to the presence of the collector, the outsider. While this may well have had some influence on Mrs. Kerfont, I was to learn from many people that coaxing was quite typical in private or family contexts even when there were no outsiders present.

2. I have published two folktales collected from Mr. Robin; they can be found in the following articles: "Contexte, fonction et style d'un genre de littérature orale: *Le Rouban d'Varture*, un conte merveilleux franco-terreneuvien," *Nord 7, Contes et Légendes* (1977), 65-83, and "'Le Conte de la Main Coupée': Conte Franco-Terreneuvien de Cap-St.-Georges," *The Livyere* I, 2 (1981), 6-8.

IV

The Private or Family Tradition: Performance and Style

The preceding chapter introduced Mrs. Blanche Ozon and her friend Mrs. Angela Kerfont. While both were good storytellers, the latter's lack of enthusiasm for storytelling prompted me to discuss the role of coaxing, necessary to persuade her to narrate. This discussion led to an examination of those factors which seem to have had an important negative influence on the storytelling tradition: the length and structure of tales, and television.

Much of the development of the preceding chapter would not have been possible without the unique narrative context in which I recorded the two ladies. They were in the habit of getting together for private *veillées* and I was able to participate in three such sessions. I was fortunate enough to observe, in circumstances as natural as an outsider might desire, what I dare say is the characteristic behaviour of participants in such intimate traditional narrative sessions.

Stylistic Elements in the Storytellers' Performances

Consequently, while paying some attention to such aspects of the two ladies' performances as speed of delivery, emotional involvement and gesticulation, I shall concentrate on the unique qualities of their performance: metanarrative devices,[1] the interplay which took place between them, and some characteristic features of their narrative style. In this latter aspect, emphasis will be given to their use of formulaic speech and, especially, what I term the "macaronic context," in which the one used French almost exclusively, the other English with a little French.[2]

Speed of Delivery

Neither Mrs. Ozon nor Mrs. Kerfont are storytellers of the calibre of Emile Benoit, the public storyteller to be considered in the next chapter, but they do not claim to be. In fact, they do not consider themselves storytellers at all, reserving this title for representatives of the public tradition. Mrs. Ozon, whose narrative delivery tended to be uniformly rapid, created the impression of an overly thoughtful storyteller. She punctuated her phrases with frequent short pauses, as if she were looking for the next motif, unsure of her narrative skill.

Moreover, she herself asserted she was not a storyteller, and had never wanted to learn stories: "J'sais pas les *stories* là. Non, j'les sais pas. Non, j'sais pas ça, moi. J'ai jamais su çte conte, j'ai jamais voulu apprende des contes" (I don't know those stories. No, I don't know them. No, I don't know it, me. I never knew that story, I never wanted to learn stories). But of course she can tell stories, although without the conscious mastery of the renowned narrator. She is a storyteller from the private tradition, not the public one. At moments of high emotion in a tale, she seems carried away; and the consequently rather excessive speed of delivery diminishes the dramatic effect that a more varied intonation pattern would have given to her narrative.

Mrs. Ozon is what the Swedish folklorist Carl von Sydow would have called a "passive tradition bearer"[3] in the sense that, not considering herself a storyteller, she does not seek to pass on her knowledge, which is nonetheless important. The tempo of her narratives is partly dictated by the metronomic accompaniment of her knitting needles, because she knitted assiduously at each session. Knitting also limited the amount of gesture and gesticulation she could permit herself while telling a story. She always tended, too, to be a rather poker-faced narrator except at moments of hearty laughter. These few negative features combine to suggest that her narrations were barely more than half-remembered recitations, a sure sign of the passive narrator. Let it be emphasized, however, that these comments in no way detract from Mrs. Ozon's qualities as a private storyteller; in many ways, she is a typical representative of this tradition.

Mrs. Kerfont, while not a narrator in the public tradition, is nonetheless an active bearer of the Franco-Newfoundland narrative tradition. She monopolized, so to speak, our storytelling sessions. What distinguishes her from her friend is her present lack of enthusiasm for stories, as was noted earlier.

But while apparently having a much larger repertoire than Mrs. Ozon, she shares most of her performance characteristics. She speaks rapidly, with relatively little variation in her intonation, and her voice often does not reflect the emotion of narrative episodes; this she sometimes successfully portrays, however, by purely stylistic devices. Like Mrs. Ozon, her narratives tend to be staccato, because of the frequent short pauses with which she punctuates them. These characteristics were more evident in our first recording session, however, and as time progressed, she overcame the anxiety which probably contributed to her nervous delivery. She then allowed herself a more generous elasticity of speed of delivery and intonation, thereby rendering her narration more dramatically interesting.

Gesture and Gesticulation

Like Mrs. Ozon, on the other hand, she never allowed herself any freedom of gesture and gesticulation. The reasons for this lie, no doubt, partly in her nervousness before me and my tape-recorder, and partly in her fear of embarrassment. She was certainly aware, as were all my informants, that spectacular gesticulation was a characteristic of the old, public French storyteller. She curbed her instinct to gesture for fear of being mocked, as would most French Newfoundlanders of her generation.

While it is possible that I never saw the real Mrs. Kerfont performing, because I was an outsider, one may conclude that the outline of her style, as I have presented it, is both valid and accurate. This is because the two women were always together when I visited Mrs. Ozon at home, and because Mrs. Kerfont, in particular, almost always spoke to her friend, rather than to me. Although I was present at the sessions, my presence was not a real inhibiting agent.

Metanarrative Devices

This very natural context furnished me with an unique opportunity to observe the two storytellers at work, so to speak. When they were in the mood to narrate, they seemed almost to forget I was there, and at the very least not to think of me as an outsider. I was thus able to observe the interaction which took place between them, and the metanarrative devices which were part of it; this enabled me thereafter to offer the reader a view of the dynamics of a storytelling session in the private tradition.

I have already remarked that in the public tradition, interaction between storyteller and audience was limited to exclamations, interjections and explanations. The storyteller manipulated his audience, and respectful of the storyteller's rôle, the audience was careful not to make any undesirable interruptions. In the less formal context of a *veillée* in the private or family tradition, everything suggests that the audience was allowed to behave differently. The example of Mrs. Ozon and Mrs. Kerfont seems to confirm this point of view.

Exclamations

There are a variety of metanarrative devices, the simplest of which is the exclamation. Mrs. Ozon and Mrs. Kerfont punctuated moments of tension, of high emotion, of pathos or humour in each other's stories with a wide range of exclamations and interjections: "Oh my God!", "Oh no!", "Phew!", "Yes!" and "Yes indeed! (Oui dame!)", together with laughter, are scattered throughout the tale transcriptions. These metanarrative devices are both the most frequent and most spontaneous such effects, in no way hindering the tale's progress. They are numerous and, generally speaking, typical of the two traditions.

Cooperation

On the other hand, other kinds of metanarrative devices such as cooperation, explanations, justifications and teases are more common in the private tradition. Cooperation helps resolve certain problems encountered by the storyteller—one of the ladies, for example, will remind the other of a forgotten detail or a whole episode of a tale, or will help solve a linguistic problem; on one specific occasion, Mrs. Kerfont took over entirely the telling of a tale. Here are some typical examples of cooperation:

B.O.: Pis asteure, il ava dit, hein, quand qu'il alliont la tuer d'y arracher les deux yeux d'la téte pis y apporter pour, pour *proof* hein? (Then he'd said now, eh, when they were going to kill her, to pluck both eyes out of her head to bring as, as proof eh?)

A.K.: Ptit Golo (Little Golo).

B.O.: C'est Golo qu'était son nom hein? (It's Golo was his name, eh?)

A.K.: Oh ouais, ça tait son nom (Oh yes, that was his name).

B.O.: Cte gars-là. (That fellow).

A.K.: Golo, Golo, ouais (Golo, Golo, yes).

B.O.: Quand qu'il arriviont pour tuer sa femme... (When they were coming to kill his wife...)

In this example, Mrs. Kerfont reminded her friend of the name of a villain.

In another case, Mrs. Ozon specifies a motif for Mrs. Kerfont:

A.K.: So anyhow—wait now, I kinda fergets there... Ah yes—no, I fergets there, look!

B.O.: Elle a-ti pas été dans la chambe qu'i ava trouvé çte beau prince? (Didn't she go into the room where she'd found that handsome prince?)

A.K.: Ah oui! (Ah yes!) She went in—it was a castle then.

B.O.: Oui (Yes).

In the following example the storyteller, Mrs. Kerfont, hesitates over a word and appeals to Mrs. Ozon and myself:

A.K.: ...He says, "In de bottom a de, de, is—dey had a big, big well dere, y'know—used to support all de town eh? An in dat well e—was, a, a, ah, comment ça? (What is it?)

B.O.:   Garnouille? (A frog?)

A.K.:   Oh no no no, no... in crapaud? (A toad?)

G.T.:   Crapaud? (Toad?)

A.K.:   In crapaud... (A toad...)

G.T.:   Eh? A toad.

A.K.:   Yeah, I spose.

G.T.:   Toad, yeah, un crapaud.

A.K. &
B.O.:   Ouais (Yes).

A.K.:   Well da's it. Dat, dat now used to suck all de water. An de wheat dere I guess was de, de a souris blanche (a white mouse) fer to eat de, de, de—machine là (—thing there).

G.T.:   Hm?

A.K.:   Des racines là (The roots there).

B.O.:   Oh! oh!

A.K.:   De roots.

G.T.:   The roots?

A.K.:   Yeah, uh well now, he had it all een—knowed it all...

Several examples of these minor lexical problems appear in Mrs. Kerfont's narrations, usually told in English, whereas Mrs. Ozon, who always narrated in French, has hardly any.

I note this final example of cooperation in which Mrs. Ozon, quite entangled in her narration, gives up her rôle as storyteller to her friend, in the very middle of the story:

B.O.:   Ca fa s'couche avec eune jambe en bas du lit hein. A dit "Quoi-ç-qu'est la cause de ça" a dit, "t'es pas capabe de t'coucher dans l'lit?"—"Bien" i dit, "c'est d'même qu'ej couche" (So he goes to bed with one leg hanging out eh. She says "Why is that" she says, "can't you sleep in the bed?"—"Well" he says, "that's the way I sleep").

A.K.:   Poor way!

B.O.:   "Troisième soirée à souère" a dit— ("The third night tonight" she says—).

A.K.:   Ah ha ha ha!

B.O.:   "Tu t'couches avec eune jambe en bas du lit." Ca fa i dit, "C'est okay" i dit, "dors." Quand qu'alle était endormie, il *ertourne* encore don hein. Ca fa il a pas ervenu. Mais asteure moi ej sais pas là là. Ej sais pas ça hein ("You sleep with one leg hanging out of the bed." So he says, "That's okay" he says, "sleep." When she was asleep, he *goes back* again eh? So he didn't come back. But now I don't know that, me. I don't know it eh).

A.K.:   Il a ervenu lui. (He came back him).

B.O.:   Mais anyway l'endemain, le lendemain matin don quand son père se lève il a té en jardin... (But anyway the next day, the next morning when his father gets up he went in the garden...).

A.K.:   No no, wait now. It was an ole witch in dere y'know. Er...

B.O.:   Ej sais pas (I don't know).

A.K.:   Well yes now, when—de two o dem when dey went wit deir dogs eh? So anyhow when ah, when ah... When she come she said "Oh my God, I'm frighten your dog" she said, "tie your dog!" —"My dog is not cross," he said...

And thus Mrs. Kerfont continues to the end of the story.

Explanations

Explanations in tales are frequently of a linguistic nature, as in the earlier example of the toad. Occasionally the narrator addresses me directly, as when Mrs. Ozon asked me if I knew what a *noix* (walnut) was, glossing it with the term *noisette* (hazelnut). At one point I had myself asked a question about the meaning of an expression I did not know, and the two ladies gave me two explanations, one in French, the other in English:

A.K.: ...Ah! well her, she couldn eat! Alle a trapé eune venette! (She got frightened!)

B.O.: Phew!

G.T.: Quoi-ç-qu'alle a attrapé? (What did she catch?)

A.K.: Eune venette (A fright).

G.T.: Qu'est-ce que c'est ça?

B.O.: Eune peur (A fright).

A.K.: She was frightened, eh?

G.T.: Yeah—ah oui (—oh yes!)

A.K.: An... ha ha! eune venette! (A fright!)

G.T.: Je connaissais pas ça!

B.O.: J'appelons ça eune venette, nous autes! (We call that a *venette*, us!)

G.T.: Oui (Yes).

What should be remembered here is that neither my various interruptions nor those made by both women interfered in any way with the progress of the narration. Such interruptions would not, however, have been well received in the context of the public *veillée*.

Justifications

Justifications in the telling of a tale quite often appear as formulaic statements, uttered by the storyteller when an implausible motif has drawn mocking laughter from the audience:

B.O.: "Comment qu'tu dmandes pour ta vache?"—"Ben" i dit, "ej la vends cinq sous l'poil" ("How much do you want for your cow?"—"Well" he says, "I'm selling her at five cents the hair").

A.K.: Ha ha ha!

B.O.: C'est in conte! (It's a story!)

Mrs. Kerfont herself used the formula while telling a tale in English, in circumstances identical to the above:

A.K.: "Well" she said, "get in that an I'll put you under my tongue". There...

B.O.: Ha ha ha!

A.K.: C'est in conte! She says, "There, she wouldn find you eh?" Okay...

This apparently trivial formula underlines the importance of studying metanarrative devices, because it conceals and contains at least three levels of interpretation. Firstly, it betrays a very significant change in the attitude of people towards folktales. Formerly, and particularly in the public tradition, no one would have questioned the storyteller's seriousness by making fun of a time-honoured motif. Nowadays young, and even not-so-young French Newfoundlanders are indifferent or disrespectful towards *Märchen*. This is not because of what the great French folklorist Paul Delarue considered to be a very French penchant for the rational;[4] it is rather due to new tastes in entertainment, in part from the influence of television, as I suggested in the preceding chapter.

Secondly, the formula lets us see the gulf separating the two narrative traditions. Even today, in the rare cases when one can watch a public storyteller performing, one would not make fun of him with interjected remarks. "It's a story" was not a formula often used by public storytellers.

Thirdly, the mocking interruption made by Mrs. Ozon had a certain piquancy. Mrs. Kerfont had already made fun of her: Mrs. Ozon was now getting her own back. This under-current of mockery, ever present in my sessions with the two women, brings me quite naturally to a consideration of what I have termed "the teasing reprimand."

The Teasing Reprimand

During my interviews with the two storytellers, I was myself the occasional object of always unmalicious reprimands. They criticized one another so frequently, on the other hand, that one can consider this kind of metanarrative device to be quite typical of the context. Mrs. Kerfont first reprimanded me while telling a story; she interrupted herself while in full flight in order to urge me to drink my bottle of beer as fast as she was doing:

A.K.: ...So she passed him the note. Drink! Oh nom de Dieu drink! (Oh, in the name of God, drink!)

G.T.: Mais je bois dans la bouteille! (But I'm drinking from the bottle!)

A.K.: Eune pile! (Some lot!) Look at mine, almost all gone!

G.T.: Ah!

A.K.: Ah!... Then he passed him the note...

That I attempt to loosen her tongue by offering her a drink was quite acceptable to her, what was not acceptable was that I drink more slowly than her. In passing, let it be emphasized that the reprimand was indeed a tease, for Mrs. Kerfont was pretending to be angry; the offences which brought forth the reprimands were always trivial, and the exchanges always prompted bursts of laughter.

The second time I was criticized by Mrs. Kerfont was also in the course of a narration: I had thought she was coming to the end of her tale, but was mistaken. I winked at Mrs. Ozon, who well knew my interruption was intended to encourage Mrs. Kerfont to finish her tale anyway. Always alert, Mrs. Kerfont again reproached me for emptying my bottle too slowly:

A.K.: That's the witch she made into her.

B.O.: Oh my God!

G.T.: That's the end of the story?

A.K.: It's not the end of the story.

G.T.: It's not?

A.K.: No.

G.T.: No.

A.K.: No.

G.T.: What happened then?

A.K.: Tiens, maudit gars, he winks! (Look, the damned fellow, he winks!)

B.O.: Ah ha ha ha ha ha ha!

A.K.: I boit pas là (He's not drinking there).

G.T.: Si si, je bois (Yes yes, I'm drinking).

A.K.: Ah, gardez, i boit pas vous autes! (Ah, look, you guys, he's not drinking!) Look at me! I'm almost two bottles gone! J'vais m'jaguer! (I'm going to get drunk!)

G.T.: What's the end of the story?

A.K.: Anyway, well, the old woman...

It was Mrs. Kerfont, moreover, whose tongue was the sharpest. At one point, she interrupted Mrs. Ozon in the middle of a story to reproach her for talking with her hand in front of her mouth:

B.O.: ...Tire sa calotte, i fait bien noir— (Takes his hat off, it's really dark—)

A.K.: Tire tes doigts d'ta djeule! Tire tes doigts d'ta djeule! (Take your fingers out of your mouth! Take your fingers out of your mouth!)

B.O.: Oh toi, t'es folle! (Oh you, you're crazy!)

A.K.: Ha ha!

B.O.: Là anyway, la troisième soirée... (There, anyway, the third night...)

Given that, of the two ladies, it was Mrs. Kerfont who spoke an often macaronic language, interspersing French words, phrases and expressions in her English speech, it is not surprising that Mrs. Ozon occasionally took revenge by making fun of her friend when she mixed up the two languages:

G.T.: Well, how does it go on from there?

A.K.: Well yes. They was jealous of the other—she was so pretty her, eh? She was pretty, her. An she was, three an they were ugly as the devils. An now they used to put her... all... cendres, eh? A la place eh? Assez, tu sais! (...cinders, eh? on the floor eh? That's enough, you know!)

B.O.: Ah ha ha!

Once, Mrs. Ozon made a comment, in French, to describe a character in a story Mrs. Kerfont was telling; but she did so with a little malicious gleam in her eye, glad, noting another macaronic form in Mrs. Kerfont's narration, to have paid her in kind:

A.K.: An her, she wasn dancin at all, the ugly one! Blank!

B.O.: Trop vilaine! (Too ugly!)

A.K.: Trop vilaine!... Gardez-la! (Too ugly!... Look at her!) After, anyhow...

Mrs. Kerfont's "Gardez-la!" was aimed at Mrs. Ozon, thereby indicating she knew she was being teased.

Sexual Allusion

To the foreign ear, there is no doubt that the most striking feature encountered was their use of sexual allusions. We are not dealing with vulgar or obscene language, however, far from it; it is rather a question of tone or attitude. None of the tales they told me were bawdy. It is interesting to note, in passing, that while some folklorists have been studying bawdy or saucy stories for many years, they have tended to neglect the part played by allusion and euphemism in folktales. Yet, however much disguised, the mild sexual allusion often gives rise to an interesting tension and provokes laughter from the narrator and audience alike. In company with the other devices of which I have been speaking, it adds a new dimension to our perception of the folktale.

It is pointless to dwell on the importance of laughter as a means of putting someone at ease. Mrs. Ozon used an allusion to encourage her friend to tell her first story to me:

G.T.: Well when you tell me some more times, I mean you'll get used and you won't bother about me then.

B.O.: Non! (No!)

G.T.: Right?

A.K.: Right.

B.O.: C'est l'premier coup qu'est l'pire! Oh ho ho! (It's the first time that's the worst! Oh ho ho!)

The allusion, which made us all laugh, succeeded in relaxing Mrs. Kerfont who shortly thereafter began her first narration in front of a tape-recorder.

It was again Mrs. Ozon, with the same aim of persuading her friend to tell another story, who shortly provided another allusion:

G.T.: Come on now, tell that story!

B.O.: Bien, tu sais... (Well, you know...)

A.K.: It's not long, it's only a short piece.

G.T.: Okay, that's all right.

B.O.: C'est meilleur qu'—in ptit morceau c'est meilleur qu'arien! Ha ha! (It's better than—a little piece is better than none at all!)

Mrs. Ozon did not monopolize the allusions. She was describing the meeting of two young people:

B.O.: "Ah" i dit, "moi j'as rien vu." Là anyway i s'faisont l'amour... ("Ah" he says, "me I didn't see anything." So anyway they make love...)

A.K.: Uh dame, c'est bon ça! (Ah yes, that's good!)

B.O.: Ouais, faisont l'amour. (Yes, they make love).

Mrs. Kerfont did not hesitate to chip in which her remark, putting a smile on every face.

During the telling of a tale by Mrs. Kerfont, Mrs. Ozon intervened twice, first to express her appreciation of the hero's action, secondly to sympathize with his frustrated desire:

A.K.: The room come full o lights—an he look in the corner—beautiful lady! "Tom" she says, "come on, we'll have a good time tonight, me n you" she says. Well my God! He was tired, mais i l'a garâchée toute en grand! (but he threw it over him!)

B.O.: Ha ha ha ha! I guess!

A.K.: He trow the blanket over him an he took her! An he was just gonna give her a kiss, alle a rentré d'dans ielle, la vieille là (...she came in her, the old woman there).

B.O.: Oh!

It sometimes happens, as in the following example, that the allusion comes from the storyteller herself, a personal inspiration owing nothing to any interruption from her audience:

A.K.: When she got a-ways down the yard, the ball o wool come out of her arms, eh? An it fell, an it started to roll eh? An it fell in a hole eh?... That's a thought!

B.O.: Ah ha ha ha!

Mrs. Ozon's laughter allowed for no ambiguity, and emphasized the underlying tension expressed through these metanarrative devices.

In the following case, it was a chuckle in Mrs. Kerfont's voice which made the phrase "man in de night" take on added significance, much appreciated by Mrs. Ozon:

A.K.: "Now" he says, "what do you want me to be" he says, "dog in de day and man in de night, or man in de day an dog in de night?"— "Oh" she says, "I radder for you to be dog in de day" she says, "man in de night."

B.O.: Ha ha ha!

The subtle use of intonation was the means of insinuating a double-entendre into the flow of narrative:

A.K.: "She wants you to sleep with her foal."—"Well me, I likes foals so much" she says, "I'll like it."

B.O.: Ha ha ha!

Mrs. Ozon alertly picked up the significance of the phrase "I'll like it."

A final example of such allusion has Mrs. Ozon commenting overtly about her expectations, as projected through the heroine of the tale:

A.K.: Oh! She got in de bed a nice bed an eh, gosh, by an by she look is a young prince comin den, murder!

B.O.: [Whistles] Woh, what a night! Ha!

A.K.: He jumped in dere wit her too y'know!

B.O.: Ha ha! I guess!

It is difficult to say whether the various kinds of interplay I have described are necessarily typical of all narrative contexts, or even, indeed, of the Franco-New-foundland narrative context. But in the public context, one may assume that a good storyteller would not have neglected the dramatic effect of allusion, sexual or otherwise. The *Märchen* might well entertain children, but it was a genre intended for adults. The presence of a handful of children at a *veillée* might well have obliged the storyteller to be rather more circumspect in his speech; allusion allowed him to indicate to the adults what he did not wish to say in words. Far from being simple, natural and direct, oral narratives were characterized by a dynamism due in part at least to metanarrative devices, the interaction between storyteller and audience. If some devices were less common in the public tradition, a more formal context, others must have played an important part, depending on the narrator's taste and art.

In the private or family tradition, the constraints imposed on the audience's behaviour in the public *veillée* are not and were not in effect; and the private storyteller does not follow the same rules either. But the same dynamism is evident, and levels of interaction are accentuated by the constant round of metanarrative devices such as laughter, exclamations, interjections, cooperation, explanation, teases and sexual allusions.

Formulaic Speech

Thus far in this chapter attention has been focussed on aspects of the narrative performance of Mrs. Ozon and Mrs. Kerfont, stressing the importance of metanarrative devices. It is time now to turn to two other questions, to wit their use of formulaic speech, and what I earlier called the "macaronic context." In passing, I shall also examine some stylistic features relevant to the dynamics of the text.

Opening Formulas

Neither Mrs. Ozon nor Mrs. Kerfont make great use of formulaic expressions. In the public tradition, no tale would have been complete without an opening and a closing formula. Apart from the formulas' function as a "key" or linguistic signal—announcing on the one hand the beginning of a tale and on the other its conclusion—storytellers and audiences alike seem to have considered them integral parts of a well told tale. The opening formula always produced a lively response from the audience: the well-known phrase announced an entertainment which could last for several hours. Thus it was that "Il y avait une fois, par une bonne fois" ("Once there was a time, and a good time it was"), or some variation on this theme, was an indispensable introduction to a successfully told *Märchen*.

The numerous Franco-Newfoundland storytellers kind enough to tell me their stories over the last twenty years have all been, with rare exceptions, from the private or family tradition. While a few of them used the various formulas regularly, the majority used them only rarely and often in incomplete form. The storytelling tradition has suffered so much in the last twenty-five years or more that even the few public storytellers who can be persuaded to narrate do not always follow the rule. My informants nonetheless all agreed that in former times formulas were indispensable.

Mrs. Ozon and Mrs. Kerfont are quite typical of the private storyteller. It is true that they both use stereotyped expressions which serve as opening or closing formulas. Mrs. Ozon began almost all her tales with a phrase such as: "C'ta in homme et eune femme" (There was a man and a woman), or "Bien, ça ç'ta in homme et eune femme" (Well, it was a man and a woman), or "Bien, y avait in homme et eune femme" (Well, there was a man and a woman). To this introductory sentence she sometimes added the number of children the couple had: "Il aviont in garçon" (They had a son), "Il aviont ç'ptit-là hein" (They had this little one eh), "Il aviont in ptit garçon" (They had a little boy) or once, "I viviont tout seuls, eh, tous les deux" (They lived alone eh, the two of them).

Mrs. Kerfont makes use of similar formulas, except that they are in English: "One time dere was a man an a woman, dey ad t'ree sons—Jack an Bill an Tom"; "One time there was a king an a queen"; "Well one time it was a man an a woman, they ad—t'ree daughters." Almost all her tales begin in this way, varying only in the addition of a "Well" at the beginning of the sentence. But neither of the two ladies began a tale with a formula like the following one, used by Mrs. Joséphine Costard (Lacosta) of Red Brook (Rousseau Rouge), a well-known singer before her death and a storyteller in the private tradition: "Bien, y a eune fois, et pour vous dire eune fois, c'est pas dans mon temps ni c'est pas dans vote temps, mais c'est dans le vieux temps, hein? Y avait in, in homme et pis eune femme don"[5] (Well, there was a time, and to tell you what time, it's not in my time and it's not in your time, but it's in the old time, eh? There was a, a man and a woman now).

Internal Formulas

As far as the "internal formulas" or stereotypical expressions found in the body of the text are concerned, they are few and far between in Mrs. Ozon and Mrs. Kerfont's tales. In general, phrases marking the passage of time are very common in Franco-Newfoundland narrative tradition. Many narrators will say "Dans in conte ça passe vite" (In a story it goes fast) when, for example, they wish to move from the hero's birth to the beginning of his adventures. Similarly, when the hero has to go on a long journey, the distance covered is indicated to the listener by the triple repetition of verbs of motion; it will be said, for example, that "Il a marché, il a marché, il a marché in grand boute" (He walked, he walked, he walked for a long time).

Repetition

If the two ladies do not seem to use the first expression noted above, they do make use, from time to time, of the triple repetition of verbs. Mrs. Ozon did so three times in seven tales: "Anyway, i marchont, pis i marchont, i marchont anyway" (Anyway, they walk, and they walk, they walk anyway); "Anyway i marchont, pis i marchont, i marchont anyway;" and "Ca fa anyway, i marche anyway, i marche et i marche pour des jours et des nuits" (So anyway he walks anyway, he walks and he walks for days and nights). But most often repetition is double rather than triple, a sign of the weakening tradition; this is especially true in Mrs.Kerfont's case: "So he travelled an travelled"; "They travelled les gars (They travelled, boys), they travelled a long while." Once she used the formulaic "three days and three nights", which serves to abbreviate narrative repetition: "Anyhow he travelled three days and three nights too."[6]

Other internal formulas are typical less of the old tale tradition than of a tradition in transition, and function to justify the narration of an episode which nowadays is too unlikely and lends itself to easy mockery: "C'est in conte hein" (It's a story eh) and "C'est d'même qu'i conte eh?" (That's the way it's told, eh?) are phrases used by both women, and also by numerous other storytellers of the present-day private or family tradition. Such phrases probably did not occur in narrations in the public tradition; the implausible was accepted in the context of the *Märchen*.

Closing Formulas

Neither Mrs. Ozon nor Mrs. Kerfont maintained the closing formula in their tales as well as some other private storytellers nor, with greater reason, as well as public storytellers. Mrs. Ozon never once used the time-honoured Franco-Newfoundland formula: "S'i sont pas morts, i vivont encore", "If they're not dead, they're living yet." Generally, if she made use of any kind of terminal phrase it was no more than a simple "Pis c'est ça! C'est fini" (So that's it! It's finished) or "Pis ça a fini là" (So it finished there) or "Tout fini—c'est tout qu'ej sais" (It's all over—that's all I know).

Such a lack of closing formulas on Mrs. Ozon's part demonstrates on the one hand that she is indeed a storyteller from the private tradition, and on the other hand that she does not have mastery of her tales. This is an observation, of course, which she herself had confirmed—that she had never wanted to learn tales. But the memory of better developed tales remained in her mind for she often added, at the end of a narration, that her version was 'pas l'ptit quart" (not the little quarter) or "pas l'ptit quart d'la motché" (not the little quarter of the half). That is to say she knew her versions were not complete, while unable to recall the remainder.

Mrs. Kerfont once made use of the following innocuous formula to end a tale: "So c'est fini, c'est fini là" (So it's finished, it's finished there). But a more gifted storyteller than her friend, she sometimes used variants of the standard closing formula "If they're not dead, they're living yet." Let it be noted, however, that her use of the formula was hardly consistent, its form changing from tale to tale: "An then—if they're not dead—they might be livin yet"; "So dey're not dead, dey're livin"; "An dame, dey're livin yet"; "An if dey're not dead, dey're livin"; and finally, "An dey're not livin". Occasionally, she omitted the formula altogether.

Mrs. Ozon and Mrs. Kerfont, like most storytellers, male or female, in the private or family tradition, limit themselves in their use of formulas which seem to have been typical of narrations in the public tradition. It may be assumed that for them, as for other representatives of their tradition, fidelity to some aspects of style is not as important a criterion as it was for public storytellers. For them, the main thing in the telling of a tale is the thematic action. On the other hand, given the general erosion of the Franco-Newfoundland tale tradition, the phenomenon can be seen as a sign of a declining artistic tradition.

The Macaronic Context

I said earlier that in addition to formulaic speech, another question would be of concern to us: the "macaronic context." Firstly, we should note that after the passing awkwardness of the first recording session, I was able to observe the interaction taking place between the two women without anyone being embarrassed. I was able to record local bilingualism in its most natural manifestation. It is a mark of English influence on the Port-au-Port Peninsula that almost all francophones can communicate in English, with more or less confidence. So much cannot be said for anglophones in the area although some, for different reasons, have acquired the use of French; but they are not numerous.

Generally speaking, older people use French when they have the choice; younger people, on the other hand, even when they speak French fluently, most frequently choose English, even in a family context. It is not unusual to hear both languages used simultaneously in a conversation; and most French Newfoundlanders, at ease in both languages, use both indifferently. This bilingualism may be attributed to numerous factors: school, the Church, the media, and the region's socio-economic structure. There are exceptions to this rule, but bilingualism is an inescapable fact.

Mrs. Ozon, for example, speaks English only when she has to, that is, when speaking to a monoglot anglophone. Mrs. Kerfont, born of mixed parentage, spoke little French before her marriage, at which time French became her daily language. Although she learned her stories in French, she tells them in English. She speaks both languages fluently, but seems to prefer English. The consequence of almost universal bilingualism is the penetration of one language by the other. This question has been studied elsewhere; I shall confine myself here to a consideration of linguistic intrusion in folktales.

Macaronic Speech

My use of the term "macaronic speech" incorporates several phenomena, but in essence I give it the following meanings: firstly, the use, in one language, of words borrowed from the other language. It also includes the intercalation of expressions or whole sentences from one language in the context of a narration in the other language; and finally, in a very broad sense, a macaronic context in which at least two people are speaking to each other, one in one language, and one in the other. For whoever is unaccustomed to the macaronic context, it is a curious experience and at first, somewhat disconcerting; but it is also a frequently encountered context among French Newfoundlanders. As it is therefore a characteristic situation, it merits careful examination.

Anglicisms

Mrs. Ozon and Mrs. Kerfont use isolated English or French words in their speech. Mrs. Ozon perhaps incorporates rather more anglicisms in her speech than does Mrs. Kerfont gallicisms in hers. Anglicisms used by Mrs. Ozon are widespread among French speakers in the region.

Anglicisms include verbs, with English pronunciation, to which appropriate French endings are added. However, in order to facilitate pronunciation for the French reader, I have transcribed such words in a way which permits application of the rules of French pronunciation, when it corresponds to English sounds. This occurs especially if the English verb, left in its English form, would give the wrong pronunciation. If there is any possible ambiguity, I add the proper English infinitive in parentheses. Here are a few examples from Mrs. Ozon's speech: *i maillndiont* (to mind); *i wonderiont* (to wonder); *i draillviont back* (to drive back); *feedait* (to feed); *j'feele pas* (to feel); *souter* (to suit); *banishé* (to banish); *stanner* (to stand, tolerate).

Nouns borrowed from English generally designate objects or translate concepts which did not exist at the time of the arrival of the first French settlers, or which were not commonly used at the time: *le truck à huile* (the oil truck); *le power* (electricity, power); *le mail, le mailman, le bus*. Other words of a non-technical nature have also been adopted by the French. Some, such as *in puttin* (a pudding) often

82

have a French equivalent, but they are used because they better reflect a regional cultural reality, a characteristic local dish in the case of *puttin*. Some words seem to suggest or betray a formerly widespread attitude among the French: the social superiority of the English majority. One speaks of the *alphabet*, pronounced in the English manner; *eune djob* (a job), which is more important than *in ouvrage* (work, a piece of work) because it is paid; *in visitor* rather than *un visiteur*, especially when the visitor was English, and to whom evidence of faultless courtesy had to be offered.

Apart from these isolated words (which, with all the anglicisms noted, only comprise approximately one percent of the average Franco-Newfoundlander's vocabulary), one also comes across a variety of harmless oaths scattered throughout the conversations: *By geewhiz Chris'*, *Goddam!*, *Oh My God!*. This is not an exhaustive list, but Mrs. Ozon did not use many more during our recording sessions.

Gallicisms

Mrs. Kerfont's English was quite free of purely lexical gallicisms. I noted less than half a dozen isolated French words in her stories. On the other hand, entirely French phrases and sentences were scattered throughout her tales. They seem to be of three kinds: those in which she cannot remember the English words or phrases; those which she uses when the emotion engendered in her story causes her to revert to the use of her mother tongue; and finally, those which she recalls, consciously or otherwise, from the original French narration as she had learned it.

Occasionally, simple lexical lacunae prompt Mrs. Kerfont to use French in her tales:

A.K.: She made the soup herself eh? She knowed what she put in, eh? But after the soup was cooked, well, des *garnouilles* and all kinds o beasts to be seen eh?

Having temporarily forgotten the English word *frog*, she used the local word *garnouille*.

At times it is difficult to know if she has forgotten a word or the whole motif:

A.K.: So anyhow, the girl takes the stick an she strucked on the rock, oh my God! She got a suit the colour o the sun! An a—what she had? A—a little waggon—by God!—c'est pas des chouals, c'est pas des chouals. My gosh j'sais pas ça (It's not horses, it's not horses. My gosh I don't know that). Well I put it for a horse anyhow, I forgets it.

This kind of problem encountered by the storyteller may lead, as I noted earlier, to interaction between her and her audience. In the following extract, Mrs. Ozon and I help Mrs. Kerfont find the words she needs (some quotations have been used previously, to illustrate other points):

A.K.: He says, "in de bottom a de, de, i's"—dey had a big, big well, dere, y'know—used to support all de town eh? An in dat well e—was a, a, ah, comment ça? (What's that?)

B.O.: Garnouille?

A.K.: Oh non non non... in crapaud?

G.T.: Crapaud?

A.K.: In crapaud...

G.T.: Eh? A toad.

A.K.: Yeah, I spose.

G.T.: Toad, yeah, in crapaud.

A.K. &
B.O.: Ouais.

A.K.: Well da's it. Dat, dat now used to suck all de water. An de, de, de wheat dere I guess was de, de a souris blanche fer to eat de, de, de... machine là.

G.T.: Hm?

A.K.: Des racines là.

B.O.: Oh oh!

A.K.: De roots.

G.T.: The roots?

A.K.: Yeah.

When Mrs. Kerfont is lost in this way, she returns to the use of French, consciously moreover:

A.K.: "Yes" he said, "you got horses an ploughs, plough up your wheat good" he said, "c'est eune souris blanche hein?" I've got to French it. "I's eune souris blanche" he said...

Mrs. Kerfont is well aware of the humour inherent in such linguistic confusion, as the following exchange indicates; but she also justifies herself, a point I shall take up shortly:

G.T.: Well how does it go from there?

A.K.: Well yes. They was jealous of the other—she was so pretty her. An she ad three an they was ugly as the devils. An now they used to put her... all... cendres, eh? A la place eh? (all...ashes, eh? On the floor eh?) [to B.O., who was smiling hugely at her] Assez, tu sais! (That's enough, you know!)

B.O.: Ah ha ha!

A.K.: In French it goes better eh? It goes—it's a French story.

B.O.: Moi j'sais pas ça mignonne! (Me I don't know that my dear!)

A.K.: Ah! Tu sais! (Ah! You know it!)

Return to the Mother Tongue
The second kind of macaronic intrusion includes the use of French when Mrs. Kerfont is carried away by the strong emotions provoked by the action in the story. She goes back to her mother tongue:

A.K.: When the dog he made a spring at her, she says, alle a garâché toute en grand là! (She threw everything down, there!) I'm French an English to it, me y'know.

This explanation was addressed to me rather than to Mrs. Ozon who, quite naturally, had no problem following such macaronic speech. The emotion in Mrs. Kerfont's voice occasionally appears on the printed page, with her oaths and onomatopaea:

A.K.: "What!" e said, "you cooked de little girl for me for my dinner?" She said "Yes, to ave peace wit you" she said. "I sent de boy wit it to bring it to you, fer you to eat so e'd never return eh?"—"Mes amis, ej la prends par la friggin du cou et, ej zig! Coupe, coupe d'Dieu prends ca!" Pis c'est tout (My friends, I grab her by the frigging neck and zig! "Cut, cut by God, take that!" And that's all). Da's all it is là.

The use of French, of course, the use of her mother tongue, reflects the heightened emotion felt by Mrs. Kerfont at the climax of her narration. Here are three further examples illustrating the same point, the use of French at moments of tension.

84

A.K.:   ... They'd be around you, but they won't hurt you. C'tait ielle, la vache! I should tell it just the same.

The *vache* or cow of whom she speaks is the old witch or *vieille sorciaise*, the villain in the tale.

In the following example, a letter falls into the hands of the hero, Jack, which reveals proof of a plot to him. The tale context prompts Mrs. Kerfont to use the expression *attraper eune venette*, to get a fright:

A.K.:   Okay. They was at the table, so Jack hauled his plate, eh? It fell on his lap. Il a regardé (He looked at it). There was him, then the queen, then his daughter, eh? He read it—he passed it to the queen. Ah! Well her, she couldn't eat! Alle a attrapé eune venette! (She got a fright!)

The final example presents one of the three brothers flinging himself at a beautiful girl, after the old witch has forbidden him to leave his bed. The two most tense moments are uttered in French:

A.K.:   Well my God! He was tired, mais i l'a garâchée toute en grand! (...but he threw it over him!)

B.O.:   Ha ha ha ha! I guess!

A.K.:   He trow the blankets over him an he took her! An he was just gonna give her a kiss, alle a rentré d'dans ielle, la vieille là! (...she came in her, the old woman there!)

One may assume here that the fact of reverting to French, the language of the original narrations for Mrs. Kerfont (as we shall soon see), is a sign that English is a superimposed language. Not only does she use French at moments of tension, as I noted earlier, but certain key words in the stories are also in French:

A.K.:   Jack set out. He was only small him—tout ptit, tout ptit (right small, right small). Well, he told his mother an father...

Jack, the usual hero of Franco-Newfoundland tales, be they told in English or French, is always *tout ptit*, always "right small." This description is classic; the Franco-Newfoundland storyteller's vocabulary, moreover, avoids the use of adjectives save for cliché descriptions applied to typical characters in the tales. It is a dynamic vocabulary, as we shall shortly see.

The *vieille sorciaise* or old witch (a term also used to mean a mid-wife) is often the villain in the Franco-Newfoundland folktale. Mrs. Kerfont used both forms at the same time, either because she wished to translate the French term for me or because, as I have already suggested, she deliberately wanted to use the classic term:

A.K.:   She looked in the hole an saw a vieille sorciaise là. Ha ha ha! An ole witch there...

A characteristic expression, rendered with difficulty in English, is used by Mrs. Kerfont, while telling a story. Faced with Mrs. Ozon's reaction, she feels obliged to justify her usage:

A.K.:   ..."An when you talk, you'll say "prout-prout ma mère"! ("fart-fart my mother"—English lacks the onomatopaeic effect of the French)

B.O.:   [claps her hands] Ha ha ha!

A.K.:   An er... dat's de way we heard it now—don't come tell me that!

Mrs. Kerfont's justification tells us she had learned the story from a French-speaking narrator; in her telling of the tale, she recalls the striking expression from the French narration.

Such expressions are indeed stereotypical, and lend themselves to use in the original language, as in the following case:

A.K.:   "You're gonna drive de fire an me I'll be gone to de store." Okay. Now e
         was, im, e was makin fire im. A dit "Ti-Frère, Ti-Frère" a dit, "tu m'brûles,
         tu m'brûles!" (She says "Little Brother, Little Brother" she says,
         "you're burning me, you're burning me!) Da's from de story, eh? E look
         aroun, e couldn see er eh? A dit "Ti-Frère a dit, "tu m'brûles!" (She says
         "Little Brother" she says, "you're burning me!") E heist up de cover to
         see what was in dere—all cooked.

Once again, Mrs. Kerfont explains her use of French in the middle of a narration:
"Da's from de story, eh?" That is how it was in the original French version.

A final example, in the form of a proverbial comparison, underlines the tenacity
of the mother tongue and the memory of certain key words in the original French
version:

A.K.:   He wouldn't look at the other one at all. The other one was vilaine comme
         in diabe! (...ugly as a devil!)

The True Macaronic or Bilingual Context

In the following passage, Mrs. Kerfont speaks explicitly about her use of French, but
at the same time, through her conversation with Mrs. Ozon, she illustrates the third
type of macaronic speech, what I have termed the "macaronic context." Both
speakers use a different language, one from the other, but with perfect comprehension:

A.K.:   Oh gosh, go on! Tell a few words to it dere Saint Zenevieve dere. Come
         on. C'est beau ça, me, I likes French stories. My gosh!

G.T.:   Hm.

A.K.:   I likes dat me—come on!

G.T.:   But you heard all those stories in French, that you told me?

A.K.:   It's all French stories I knows eh?

G.T.:   But they were told to you in French.

A.K.:   Told to me in French, I larn quicker French stories dan I larns English.

G.T.:   But you tell them in English.

A.K.:   I tells them in English eh? It goes good in French though. Come on!

B.O.:   T'es folle! (You're crazy!)

A.K.:   My God, a hard tête (a hard head)! Here, come on.

B.O.:   J'feele pas, j'feele pas pour conter in conte (I don't feel, I don't feel like
         tellng a story).

A.K.:   Feel, feel, tu feeles, feel in conte (Feel, feel, you feel, feel like a story).

B.O.:   J'feele à dormir (I feel like sleeping).

A.K.:   Well yeah, you talk see. Like dat you, you, you'd be all right eh? Come on
         mignonne, chante, chante, chante! (Come on my dear, sing, sing, sing!)
         Ha ha ha! Come on!

B.O.:   Ej sais pas ça moi (I don't know that, me).

That both ladies are bilingual also explains how Mrs. Kerfont can pass from
one language to the other in the middle of a sentence. In the preceding passage, she
does so in order to tease her friend who has no desire to tell a story, pleading
sleepiness as the reason.

As far as her use of English in storytelling is concerned, Mrs. Kerfont took up
the same argument as she had earlier:

A.K.:   I can't larn English stories, eh?

B.O.: Non.

A.K.: No sir, I larn quicker French stories.

G.T.: Yeah?

A.K.: Dan I larn....

B.O.: Que des contes anglais (Than English stories).

A.K.: I, I talk, tell em in English, eh?

And finally, Mrs. Kerfont explains her preference for English:

A.K.: If I could talk good French, it'd be some nice. But me, French stories, sometimes I don't tell it in English.

B.O.: C'est funny.

A.K.: Oh, I can tell it in French too, eh?

B.O.: Mais oui.

A.K.: Some words I can't pronounce in English, I says it in French.

Like many French Newfoundlanders, Mrs. Kerfont claims her French is not "good" and it is, perhaps, less fluent than Mrs. Ozon's. The ease with which many French Newfoundlanders express themselves in French varies considerably, and it is perhaps for this reason that the macaronic context is so widespread.

In its different forms macaronic speech is without a doubt characteristic of French Newfoundlanders. It is symptomatic of a culture which has been subjected to considerable linguistic, social, economic and cultural pressure. Some would see in macaronic discourse supplementary proof of the erosion of the integrity of the Newfoundland French dialect, its presence in folktales a disturbing element in the smooth narrative flow, provoking confusion in the minds of the listeners, and creating the need for interruptions, explanations, and justifications. Together with the other pressures that have influenced the folktale tradition on the Port-au-Port Peninsula, macaronic speech would simply be seen as another factor in the decline of an old tradition.

Tenacity of the Private or Family Tradition

It is clear that I do not share this point of view. In one way, macaronic speech is a sign of successful adaptation to a world which at present seems to be constantly changing. And if, at the level of folktales, our two storytellers no longer seem to have the same taste for the genre as they formerly did, due in large part to the influences of television and its soap operas, macaronic speech can be seen as nothing more than a metanarrative device which, far from contributing to the decline of the folktale, gives it a real dynamism. Whoever has the good fortune to take part in a storytelling session with Mrs. Ozon and Mrs. Kerfont will not fail to be struck by the vitality of their performance.

Despite televised serials, despite the length and repetition of folktales, despite the need to coax the ladies to tell stories, despite the influence of English, despite all these apparently negative factors, Mrs. Ozon and Mrs. Kerfont still tell their stories, and tell them very well, as representatives of the private or family tradition.

As was said earlier, access to the private tradition is not easy. One might assume, as some have done, that the folktale tradition is dead among French Newfoundlanders. In order to penetrate the intimate world of the private or family tradition, one has to spend a long time in its broad environment. Only after a long stay among French Newfoundlanders is it possible to discover the richness of their folktales. People have been claiming for over one hundred and fifty years that *Märchen* will disappear with the present generation; I would claim, on the other hand, that an in-depth and thorough exploration will demonstrate that even if the public tale tradition is dead for all practical purposes, the private tradition is alive and well. Mrs. Ozon and Mrs. Kerfont represent the visible tip of the iceberg, so to speak.

This chapter has explored one part of the two Franco-Newfoundland tale traditions. It has attempted to demonstrate, through the example of two storytellers from the private tradition, that while this tradition differs in many ways from its public counterpart, it is nonetheless a less visible but parallel continuation of the public tradition. It is time now to examine the public tradition, through the example of Emile Benoit.

NOTES

1. I made an initial presentation of this phenomenon in an article entitled "Effets réciproques entre conteur et assistance dans un contexte narratif franco-terreneuvien," *Culture & Tradition* V (1980), 33-42.
2. See, on this point, the article by Margaret Bennett (note 8, ch. II).
3. *Selected Papers on Folklore Published on the Occasion of his 70th Birthday* (Copenhagen, 1948), p. 15.
4. *Le Conte populaire français*, Paris: Ed. Erasme, 1957, p. 46.
5. For a sample of Mrs. Costard's narrative art, see my article: "'Le Conte du Renard Rouge': Conte merveilleux franco-terreneuvien," *The Livyere*, No. 1 (Summer 1981), 8-11.
6. Compare Melville Jacobs' remarks on "Devices Which Date," *The Content and Style of an Oral Literature*, 230-232.

Angela KERFONT and
Blanche OZON,
Cape St. George, 1981.
Photo: Les Terre-Neuviens Français

Angela KERFONT,
Cape St. George, 1981.
Photo: Les Terre-Neuviens
Français

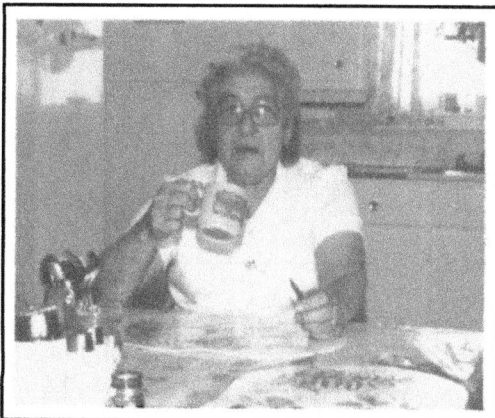

Blanche OZON,
Cape St. George, 1981.
Photo: Les Terre-Neuviens
Français

Emile BENOIT at Cape St. George, 1945.
Photo: Unknown

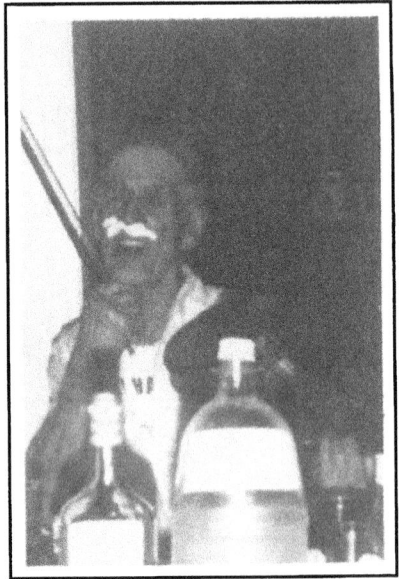

Emile with his paper moustache and fiddle, March 1983.
Photo: Clara Murphy

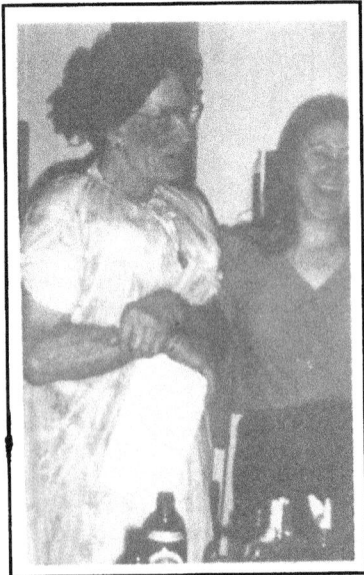

Bessie Benoit introducing "Emile's sister Emily from St. John's,"
March 1983.
Photo: Clara Murphy

Emile will do anything, anywhere, at any time. He rolls up a plastic bag and sticks it up one nostril. March 1984.
Photo: Barry W. Rowe

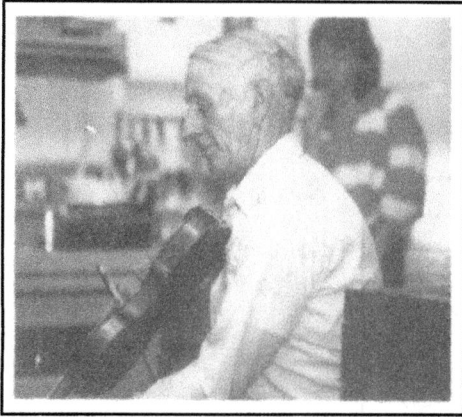

Emile BENOIT at the fiddle in his kitchen, Black Duck Brook, March 1986.
Photo: Susan Dean

Emile BENOIT singing, Black Duck Brook, March 1986.
Photo: Elaine Pelley

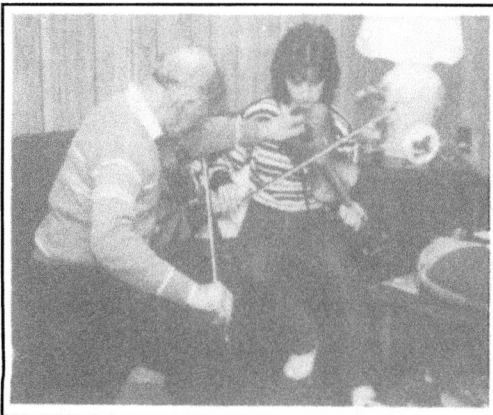

Emile BENOIT fine tuning daughter Roberta's fiddle, Black Duck Brook, March 1986.
Photo: Susan Dean

Emile BENOIT,
Black Duck Brook.
February 1983,
Photo: Gerald Thomas

Emile BENOIT
playing the fiddle,
Black Duck Brook,
April 1977.
Photo: Elizabeth Cahill

Emile BENOIT,
the pensive fiddler,
St. John's, August 1982.
Photo: Scott Jamieson

V

The Public Tradition:
Emile Benoit, The Man

The keystone of my argument, as outlined in Chapter II, is the existence of two parallel narrative traditions among French Newfoundlanders. In the two preceding chapters, I attempted to illustrate the private or family tradition through an examination of the narrative context of two female storytellers, Mrs. Blanche Ozon and Mrs. Angela Kerfont who, while not known as storytellers, carry on a covert tradition, so to speak. They, like many others, tell their stories in a private context, access to which is denied to most people. It is now time to turn to the other side of the narrative coin, that of the public tradition, and I have chosen as its representative the quite remarkable Mr. Emile Benoit, a native of L'Anse-à-Canards (Black Duck Brook), on the Port-au-Port Peninsula.

When discussing the two traditions in Chapter II, I noted that the days of the public tradition seemed to be over. Social and economic evolution and, especially, technological innovations, have all contributed to the upsetting of the traditional way of life of French Newfoundlanders. And in this changing society, old forms of entertainment have suffered the most from the new technology. Instead of going to *veillées* at one's neighbours' during the long, cold winter nights, French Newfoundlanders stay at home to watch television, or spend a few hours with their friends at a club or bar. The advent of television in the sixties was the final blow for the public storyteller: he no longer had a stage on which to perform.

By what right then may Emile Benoit be spoken of as a public storyteller? In a general way the answer to this question is not complicated, but it becomes a little confusing on account of Emile Benoit's personality, as we shall shortly see. For, if the public *veillée* is for all practical purposes a thing of the past, such is not the case for the storytellers whose reputations were made in them. Former public storytellers are still alive, and quite young French Newfoundlanders remember having seen, when they were very small, such and such a storyteller performing. Making fun of a young man by calling him an "old Frenchman", on account of excessive gesticulation, is a tease which finds its mark; for many young people have experienced the performances of old storytellers. Storytelling, in public at least, is an art little appreciated today faced with the competition offered by television. Who would wish to tell stories to an audience that is going to condescendingly make fun of the storyteller?

Emile Benoit owes his reputation not to his talents as a storyteller, but to his much better known gifts as a musician: he is a highly talented fiddler-composer. In fact, he is not reputed as a storyteller at all, and French Newfoundlanders whom one might ask for the names of famous public storytellers associated with the *veillées* would probably not mention Emile Benoit's name. It would seem to be a strange paradox, then, to choose to illustrate the public storytelling tradition a man who has never enjoyed a storyteller's reputation.

How then may I justify my choice? As he will tell us himself, Emile Benoit could have become a public storyteller. If he did not, it is because he recognized at an early age that he wanted to devote himself to his first love, the fiddle. His is a talent that has been recognized only within the last few years outside his immediate environment, the Port-au-Port Peninsula. After playing for over fifty years at community dances, weddings, family or village get-togethers, Emile Benoit has now embarked on a career as a semi-professional musician. At folk festivals, on radio and television, in the context of other public performances, he is finding new audiences which greatly appreciate not only the numerous jigs and reels of his own composition, but also his gifts as a comic and a raconteur. His first record, entitled *Emile's Dream*, appeared in 1979 and concretized his success.[1]

This fully deserved success is due not only to his gifts as a fiddler-composer but also, as I noted earlier, to his talents as a comic and a raconteur. When Emile Benoit is on stage, he usually introduces each tune with an *histouère* or story, an aetiological narrative outlining the circumstances of its composition. These *histouères* vary in length from two to fifteen minutes, depending on the mood of his audience; and it is during these narrations that one begins to divine his storytelling talents. Like any accomplished artist, he knows how to move his audience. Through his physical play, his timing, his dramatic sense, through the intrinsic interest of his subject matter, Emile Benoit gives evidence of a storytelling talent which, according to the many testimonies furnished by French Newfoundlanders, places him squarely within the tradition of the old public storytellers.

For this fact alone, one might wish to take a close look at Mr. Benoit as a representative of the Franco-Newfoundland public storytelling tradition. But we need not restrict ourselves to his dramatic skills, for he has an important repertoire of *Märchen* and other traditional narrative genres. Emile Benoit was telling folktales from the age of seventeen, having learned them in his childhood at *veillées*; but, as he remarked to me one day: "J'arais, m'aras ieu toutes ces contes-là, mais dame, ois-tu? Mais mon intérêt était plus dans le, dans ma musique, que les contes. J'avais le violon eune tapée dans l'idée vous savez" (I would have, I would have had all those stories, but well, you see? But my interest was more in the, in my music than in stories. I had the fiddle in my mind a lot, you know).

Who then is Emile Benoit, a man who, without having been a public storyteller, nonetheless embodies the qualities, the talents and performance style of old French storytellers and who, perhaps better than anyone else today, can illustrate the public storytelling tradition? In the next chapter we shall consider Emile Benoit the storyteller; but we must first sketch a portrait of Mr. Benoit, one which will be drawn for the most part in his own words.

Biographical Notes

Emile Joseph Benoit was born on March 24, 1913, at L'Anse-à-Canards (Black Duck Brook), on the Port-au-Port Peninsula. His father Amédée was also born there, in 1888, the son of Henri Benoit whose father, Emile's great-grandfather, was born in France. According to family tradition, this first Benoit came as a fisherman to Newfoundland from St. Malo, in Brittany. As a young man, he worked as a *gravier* or shoreworker not far from the location of Emile's present home. The French "aviont eune grosse factrie là—c'est encore là, la, la fondation des fac, d'la factrie" (had a big factory there—it's still there, the, the foundation of the fac, of the factory). It is not known if this first Benoit had then deserted from the fishery, as did several

Frenchmen at that period, or if, as seems most likely, he stayed at Black Duck Brook to oversee the various fishing installations—first on a temporary basis, but subsequently in a permanent role. In any case, the Benoits of Black Duck Brook have a long history in the community, owning considerable land there.

On his mother's side, Emile Benoit is of Acadian descent. His mother, Adeline Duffenais, came from Chéticamp, on Cape Breton Island, according to Emile.If the name, often anglicized to Duffney, does not seem widespread in Acadia, it is quite common on the peninsula. But Emile had little to say on that side of his family, save to remark that "...mon grand-père Duffenais—il avait dit euh, une génération allemand—dans lui" (My grandfather Duffenais—he said he had, er, a German generation—in him).[2] Emile's mother had eight children in all, five daughters and three sons; Emile was the third child and first son. She had lost two children, and Emile tells how his parents almost lost him, too. According to him,

I wasn't big. And er, he, the doctor told my father, he said "To save that little child" he said, he said, "you'll have to" he said "cut the wool, the wool from off a sheep"—and that's in March now—"and don't wash the wool—leave it—like it is—and then pack your baby up in it" he said "and leave him in it" he said "for eighteen days." Only that on me. And er he says, "Maybe you'll save him." Anyway they packed me up in the wool and then they kept me under the stove—one of those big stoves, the Waterloo ones. And they kept me there for eighteen days, kept the fire in—to keep the same heat you know then er—I—I revived.[3]

There was a school at Black Duck Brook when Emile was a young boy, and he went to it long enough to finish three years of schooling. He remembers his teacher: "La maîtresse d'école que j'avais—c'est eune, eune Dubordieu—a tait mariée avec in Duffenais. Ouais. Et pis a parlait anglais (The teacher I had—she was a, a Dubordieu—she was married to a Duffenais. Yes. And she spoke English). Emile spoke only French before going to school: "C'est là que j'ai appris à parler—commencé à parler anglais" (That's where I learned to speak—started to speak English).

In fact, his teacher had not herself benefited from a great education. Mrs. Isabell Duffenais, née Dubordieu, was born in 1887 at Freshwater, Conception Bay. Her father, Summerest Dubordieu, moved to Port-au-Port to be a customs officer, and in 1903 Mrs. Duffenais completed her studies there, becoming shortly after the school mistress at Black Duck Brook. At the age of ninety-two she was able to recall her experiences at the school, if not a certain Emile Benoit:

Everybody spoke French, you know, and I can't speak French. I don't think the people liked the teachers very much because they spoke English.... The children were all good in school, when they came. They didn't have to come you know, it wasn't compulsory then and it wasn't in my time either. The children would come to school and I had to teach them English, some couldn't speak English very well.[4]

So Emile Benoit learned his English from an east coast Newfoundlander, and did his three years of schooling, like most French Newfoundlanders in those days, and even today in some cases, in a foreign language.

Later on in her account, Mrs. Duffenais was to note that after the age of fourteen or fifteen young people stopped coming to school. The boys went fishing, the girls sought work. But many young French Newfoundlanders left school well before that age. Emile Benoit, as we know, was one such; he explained his reasons to me:

G.T.: Why did you leave school after grade three?

E.B.: Well, it was a hard time to live—and er, me, I was the, the eldest [boy] in the family.

G.T.: Hm.

E.B.: So my father, well, he was the mailman—and that took er—three to four days in the winter to—to do the *mail*, because he had to go from, to Clam Bank Cove, right down to the end of the Bar.

G.T.: Yes.

E.B.: To *Long Point* they call it (About 20 km in distance).

G.T.: Yes yes.

E.B.: So it took three-four days in the winter because of the banks of snow, banks of snow and it was, by horse and you couldn't do it in a day—it was impossible.

G.T.: Had to get down to dig, to shovel—

E.B.: Wood had to be cut.

G.T.: Yes.

E.B.: The—animals had to be looked after—

G.T.: Yes.

E.B.: That we had. So like that I couldn't go to school—we would have lost everything.

G.T.: Yes yes.

E.B.: Like that I didn't get any school.*

Emile Benoit, Fisherman

The domestic tasks which kept Emile at home while his father was away allowed him to discover a side of his character which his lack of education was to prevent him developing. By dint of looking after animals he discovered in himself a talent about which we shall speak shortly, and which would have made of him, in other circumstances, a doctor. But first of all he had to enter the profession which had drawn the French to the then inhospitable vicinity of the peninsula: the fishery. I asked Emile how old he was when he began a man's work, and as we shall see, his description of his experiences is such as one would expect of any good storyteller.

G.T.: The, the first thing you did was to go fishing with your father?

E.B.: Yes.

G.T.: How old were you—twelve?

E.B.: Er...no—I was er, I was nine at that time.

G.T.: Nine.

E.B.: When I went the first time.

G.T.: That was er....

E.B.: Ah—I was trying to jig cod but I couldn't. But—so he was catching some—so I don't know what he was doing to do that. But er—oh, he caught a lot of fish and I couldn't catch one. Well, that was all right. "Well" he says, "makes no difference" he says, "it seems to me"—he said that to me now—I haven't forgotten—he says "It makes no difference" he says, "perhaps the Good Lord" he says, "perhaps he's going to give you one like that" he says, "it's hard to say." Y'know? Anyway—he was rowing—me I was rowing too, but a small pair of oars, I wasn't putting any strength to it but enough for sure, I, I—anyway—he says er, he catches a fish and throws it over the side and a, a fish, it, it floats and me I was, I was rowing—behind and so he was rowing—in front eh? So I had my back to him. He says "Look at it, look at it, look at it on—"—I look, look at the fish, floating! *Holy Jaze* I jump—I jump into the sea, me!

G.T.:	Heh!
E.B.:	I caught the fish!
G.T.:	Heh!
E.B.:	He hooked me y'know! Heh! He hooked me by the bottom of my pants and hauled me back in. But I had the fish! Ooh! I was soaked! With my head it was under water and all. But I had the fish.
G.T.:	Yes.
E.B.:	"There, do you see? I told you" he said. "God would give you a fish." And wasn't I proud Gerald, I've never forgotten that now, look.*

This experience, still fresh in his memory after almost seventy years, shows us not only a nine year old boy's innocence, but the love between father and son. Emile often spoke about his parents, always with the greatest affection and respect. But at the same time, his recounting of the event demonstrates his ability to evoke, through lively conversation and straightforward description, the reality of the personal experience. And to that must be added the gestures and gesticulations he used to describe the events of which he speaks. His arms, his head, his whole body move to link the word to the action. And, being a humble man, the sparkle in his eyes betrays the pleasure he feels faced with his own innocence. Children about him today are always treated with great tolerance and real affection.

It was not long before Emile Benoit was a tried and tested fisherman: "...J'avons commencé la pêche moi pis mon frère Joe [Joachim]—euh, tout seuls, moi et lui, j'avais tchinze ans et lui avait treize ans—il allait sus quatorze ans...." (We started fishing, me and my brother Joe—er, all alone, me and him, I was fifteen and he was thirteen—going on fourteen...). At the age of fifteen, Emile knew his business so well he was able to instruct a younger brother in the art. It was only at the end of 1980 that Emile officially retired from the life of a fisherman, which he had been for almost sixty years, but he had already begun a new career, that of musician.

Emile in the Woods

Contrary to the custom of most French Newfoundlanders, Emile Benoit did very little winter work in the woods:

E.B.:	...That—er, no, I was, I worked in the woods—I was one, once—when I was a widower—I worked there for five months. I was a cookee—in the woods.
G.T.:	Where was that?
E.B.:	At Camp Fifteen—they call it—down at *Black Duck*.
G.T.:	Ah yes.
E.B.:	*Black Duck Siding*.
G.T.:	Yes.
E.B.:	Yes. I was gone there five months. And I had my sisters here staying with, with my children, looking after them, like that.
G.T.:	Were you well paid?
E.B.:	Oh well, I er, worked five months—and I came home with six hundred dollars.
G.T.:	Six hundred dollars.
E.B.:	Yes, for five months.
G.T.:	That wasn't too bad for those days.
E.B.:	Oh yes, but y'know I didn't go anywhere or anything, I....

G.T.: No no.

E.B.: I saved my money.*

This episode in his life is unique for him, but his warmest memory concerns the Saturday night concerts:

G.T.: Saturday nights, what did you do on Saturday nights?

E.B.: They played the fiddle and they had concerts, had *concerts* there.

G.T.: Yeah.

E.B.: We had it at the end of the *bunkhouse* and we put blankets—in front.

G.T.: Yeah.

E.B.: And then to—we—we fixed it up with a, a rope and then—we hauled on the rope to—close the blankets, I hauled on the rope to open the blankets—when the—oh I had fun.

G.T.: You always had your fiddle with you.

E.B.: Oh yes yes yes. We did foolish little things amongst ourselves y'know, but they were really fine concerts y'know.

G.T.: Yes.

E.B.: No fear! What we did by ourselves y'know.

G.T.: Did people tell stories on those concerts?

E.B.: Uh no, no, oh no, no no. We came, finish—pass....

G.T.: Songs and....

E.B.: Yeah, yeah—and talk like other people and er, you know, perform like other people.

G.T.: Yes yes.

E.B.: And so on.... Oh! We had a good time! People still talk about it, old people y'know.

G.T.: Yeah.

E.B.: Yeah. We had fun. Oh, they had fun, them—but me, that's my pleasure, me now.

G.T.: Yes yes.

E.B.: That did me good, me.*

This evocation is interesting for several reasons. Quite apart from what we learn about the entertainment of men in the woods—concerts in a makeshift theatre, in which everyone took part—, Emile indirectly draws our attention to an aspect of his dramatic talent—his imitations which, drawing not only on his vocal range but also on his precision with gesture, made of him a man gifted to "...talk like other people... and... perform like other people." And, of course, he always had his fiddle with him. We shall return to his love of music shortly, taking up here his greatest ambition in life, to be a doctor.

Emile Benoit, Doctor

Emile evoked for me his interest in medicine, firstly with regard to animals, then with regard to people:

G.T.: ...When did you start er, say, what, working with animals there, fixing animals?

E.B.: Oh well, that was—in my father's time.

94

G.T.: Your father taught you that?

E.B.: Well he—not everything—not everything—no, not everything. Er—he did—he fixed animals, he marked them and so on.

G.T.: Yes.

E.B.: Me well when I got, I got married, I started—doing that, the same *job* too.

G.T.: Hm.

E.B.: I didn't go looking for him—I did it myself.

G.T.: Yes.

E.B.: And then all at once there was a, my grandmother had a, a cow—er, she was going to have a calf—and the cow was sick and her side was all—sticking out d'you see?

G.T.: Hm.

E.B.: And then there was my uncle Lecoure, Job Lecoure—he was a, he had a—doctor's book—but now I couldn't see that book, me—because you had to be—you had to be married for that, see. You couldn't see that in those days.

G.T.: No.

E.B.: No—they kept it to themselves all that. Well that cow couldn't have her calf because her side was out—and the old woman started—*smoothing* it—and she wanted to have the calf. Well er—old Tacannou him, he—he thought he was something too—but e didn't come give me a hand—and I.... Well, that's why she wanted—and it turned out it was a heifer.

G.T.: Yes.

E.B.: Yeah. That was a big *job*. But those were my, my, was my big enterprise.

G.T.: And.....

E.B.: Then after that—

G.T.: How old were you when you did that?

E.B.: I was twenty-two.

G.T.: Twenty-two.... And after that you did all sorts of things with animals.

E.B.: After that—all sorts of things.*

Emile had however already acquired something of the reputation of a healer before acting as a vet, and giving evidence of a true scientific sense of self-experimentation, had cured himself of tuberculosis:

G.T.: What kind of illnesses did people have most often, that you could cure?

E.B.: Well there were, there was a lot of consumptive people and all sorts of things like that... and er—

G.T.: What did you give them?

E.B.: Well—they didn't want to take it me I, I was T.B. too and I cured myself.

G.T.: Yes.

E.B.: And my father and mother didn't tell me to do it but er I knew I had T.B. Well, I caught a, er, a pleurisy—and then er, I knew I had T.B.

G.T.: Yes.

E.B.: Well there—I was by the barrel on the shore there and I—I was fishing at that time there and so I, I was keeping all the cod livers.

G.T.: Yes.

E.B.: And we would put them in, in barrels we call them—

G.T.: Hm.

E.B.: Barrels, something like that—and we'd let that melt in the sun then we'd take it, we'd draw the oil off the top there and well you had—twenty-five cents a, a, a gallon.

G.T.: Yes.

E.B.: At that time. Er, it, it was a lot.

G.T.: Hm.

E.B.: Well—that's good. That—that winter it—the time I was attacked by T.B.—it was in March—when I was a young fellow—I was seven, seven, seventeen at that time—oh er, lots of things happened to me when I was sixteen and seventeen and eighteen—

G.T.: Yes.

E.B.: I did a lot of things and a lot of things happened to me, it, it was a *blockade* you call it, er.... That's good. So. I said I've got T.B. I go down to the shore—er—and I look in the barrel and it was—Gerald—it's black, black, like—like ink.

G.T.: Hm.

E.B.: There—and the flies on it! It was—full of flies. That's true—what I'm saying there, there, there's not a word of a lie in it.

G.T.: No.

E.B.: That's true, it's the whole truth I'm saying there.

G.T.: Hm hm.

E.B.: I looked at that. *Lovely!* Heh! Die! Ha ha! Like they say, eh? *Live or die.*

G.T.: Right.

E.B.: I get my bottle—I had a bottle like that here I had, my son—

G.T.: Yes.

E.B.: Three quarts—a *t'ree half-pint* they call it.

G.T.: Hm.

E.B.: So I push the flies aside and dip it in—just enough to get the oil there. And it was like coal tar eh?

G.T.: Yes yes.

E.B.: And it was emptying, emptying, it starts filling up, filling up and all at once hullo! The bottle's full. So I come back home and put it under the window—straight like that. And the next morning—I got up—the bottle here—was—all that there underneath there—half the bottle—it was all white like a—it wasn't white—it was a kind of yellow, something like that eh?

G.T.: Hm.

E.B.: And the rest of it there—it was, t'was black ink. Coal, heh! There! I take a little spoonful like that there—and I empty it—and I swallow it.

G.T.: The black or— the, the clear?

E.B.: The black!

G.T.: You—you—

E.B.: I didn't stir it or anyting, I left it—

G.T.:   No!

E.B.:   Like that, I took the black.

G.T.:   Hm.

E.B.:   Well, my friend—I burnt all my mouth inside—it's like I took a mouthful of acid. Aie! All day long it came back you know, the er, the smell eh?

G.T.:   Hm.

E.B.:   Ah, my dear man, ah it was—you need, you need a stomach to take something like that—euh... nobody else who, who would attack it—no, no. Try it, no, no, they couldn't. And I did that for nine mornings—seven mornings—and the seventh morning—I was eating my breakfast—and I was sitting like this here—sitting at the table—and I did like this here [he pinches the skin on his wrist]—it—it was—it was *oily*, oily, it was, the, the back of my hand there—eh?

G.T.:   Yes yes.

E.B.:   Then—a *spell*—say, you would have said a string of—blubber eh, by the, by the smell there.

G.T.:   Yes.

E.B.:   So I lift up my shirt like that—and pick up a small er, piece of, of wood lying on the floor—and I do that like that—and when I got there—it was as thick as that—across my hand here [mimes scraping a piece of wood across his arm, which accumulates a thick layer of oil].

G.T.:   Yes.

E.B.:   Blubber eh? It's like the colour of ink it was—under the oil there.

G.T.:   Yes yes.

E.B.:   Now do you understand that?

G.T.:   Yes yes.

E.B.:   Yes.

G.T.:   Yes.

E.B.:   There. I took that for nine days—nine mornings—if my mother was alive—she's not alive, she's gone—but if she was alive—she could tell you—she could tell you. And I was wearing woolen underwear—

G.T.:   Hm.

E.B.:   Because the doctor er, had told my father—to put wool on me—er, not to put cotton on me—never! I've never used wool for the rest of my days.

G.T.:   Hm.

E.B.:   ... Anyway that's fine. The ninth day—yeah—and nobody told me, no one in the world—told me to do that—the ninth day, I tell my mother—I say—"Today—I'm going now" I say "to purge myself." I'm going to take a packet of—of—salts eh, the, the, the, *Epsom Salts* they call them.

G.T.:   Yeah.

E.B.:   It's for animals, it's not for people—but it used to come in small packets, I think it was an ounce each.

G.T.:   Yes yes.

E.B.:   Per packet—an ounce. So—I take two, two... Well, that's fine. So there I take my purge—now here's how, how I did it.

G.T.:   Hm.

E.B.: I take my packet of *salt*, I take two *pill*, the, the *Dr. Chase Kidney Liver Pills* they called them in those days. They came in little barrels there.

G.T.: Yes.

E.B.: I take two—and I left that for—about five hours—then I take the packet of *salt*—and I pack it over with a glass of water. There. The next morning— no, not the next morning, it wasn't too long—but my friend—er, Gerald— it's frightening what came out of me—it's frightening. And if I hadn't done that—I would have died—it would have killed me.

G.T.: What came out?

E.B.: Dirt and, and all, all, all kinds of stuff me, I can't tell you—I can't—but there was no blood though. But the rest—oh! it was frightful!

G.T.: Hm.

E.B.: There. So I tell my mother now—she's going to boil some water—and we had those big barrels y'know, they'd hold er like thirteen to fifteen gallons, fourteen gallons, something like that, y'know, big barrels.

G.T.: Yes yes.

E.B.: We had them to, to get washed in eh?

G.T.: Yes yes.

E.B.: It was galvanized eh? Anyway that's good. Boils the water—then she puts a little bit of mustard in it, mustard heh!—dry mustard.

G.T.: Hm.

E.B.: A little spoonful of dry mustard... And there I heave myself in—I take my clothes off—and get into it—well, with some soap—cod oil now—we didn't have soap, no *t'ilet soap*, the, the, the toilet there, nah! No—we— had it with, with ashes and some, some, some cod oil and you boiled that together with a stick of, of, of *gellac—Gillett Lye* you call it.

G.T.: Hm.

E.B.: There was a lion on it eh—hm. And that, that cooked the, the—then you washed with that. Ho! Hah hah! And the girls who were—you should see them heh heh heh! That's good—there. There! My mom looks at my clothes, she says "My dear child" she says—she says "you're going to burn that!" She says, "That," she says, "never, never," she says, "am I going—to get the smell out of it." Now she had to knit in those days, knit woolen underwear eh.

G.T.: Hm.

E.B.: It was hard, y'know eh, there! Well that's that. What to do eh? Well she burns my clothes—in little pieces—because if she had thrown the whole suit in—well the house would have caught fire.

G.T.: Oui.

E.B.: That's good. There. Gerald—I wash myself properly—it took two barrels of water—after I was washed—there was a good finger like that—on top—it was the same *stuff* I showed you there—hah?

G.T.: Blubber.

E.B.: Yes. Blubber—eh—on the water, floating on the water eh? It was still that.

G.T.: That came out of your body.

E.B.: Came out of my body—the luck of God—out—out of my body—and I could wash the rest after the purge eh?

G.T.: Hm.

E.B.: Y'know eh? It was all there eh? And nobody told me eh? What to do eh?

G.T.: Hm. It cured you.

E.B.: Eh?

G.T.: It cured you.

E.B.: Well yes—then—I was *a'right* after.

G.T.: Yes.

E.B.: Yeah.

G.T.: Unbelievable eh.

E.B.: Yeah, it's hard to believe—but it's true.*

This long extract is important because it allows the better to see certain aspects of Emile Benoit's character. Firstly, he is a resolute and tenacious person. After deciding upon a drastic remedy, which others, as we shall see, would refuse, he followed his idea through to its conclusion. His description of it is quite clear, and also illustrates the firmness of his belief as to the cure's efficacy.

At the same time, Emile's description of his treatment of what he considered to be a serious illness is not without humour. While telling me about his trip to the cod liver oil barrel with its fly-covered surface, he was smiling. The text does not show us the expression of disgust on his face when, flicking his hand from side to side, he mimes his effort to clear away the flies. Later, recalling his mother's words about his oil-soaked clothing, he subtly evoked the sense of despair she must have shown—not only because of the unpleasant smell permeating his clothes, but also because of the extra work it meant for her, since she had to knit new underwear for Emile. The guilty look on Emile's face had to be seen to be appreciated. It was a very refined humour Emile directed towards himself. He is indeed a very humble man.

But above and beyond these characteristics—of resolution and humour—we also face a gifted raconteur. Emile recounts a personal experience, an account poignant in the variety of emotions he evokes, and in the energy of his narrative flow. As we shall see, it is in the telling of his personal experiences that Emile reaches the heights of the raconteur's art. If, in a completely informal narrative such as the one he has just related, the spontaneity of the account leads us to believe that he was recalling an outstanding experience for the first time in many years, this apparent spontaneity is also characteristic of his narratives in formal circumstances. When he is on stage, Emile Benoit introduces one of his own tunes with a tale that is fresh and full of verve—even if he has told it on many previous occasions. We shall take up these comments again in the next chapter.

It was noted earlier that the cure Emile had concocted for himself was not to everybody's taste. He tells how his first wife reacted to it:

G.T.: And you had people die who had T.B.

E.B.: Yeah—my wife had T.B. and I told her—"Do what I did" and I told her "You're going—"

G.T.: She didn't want—

E.B.: I gave her a spoonful she took a little drop, *holy Moses!* She started crying she said "I'm going to die" she said "because I can't take it." There.

G.T.: Hm.

99

E.B.: So I said "Yes, me too," I said.

G.T.: How old was she when she died?

E.B.: She was er—as good as say thirty, twenty, twenty-nine, let's say twenty-nine going on thirty.

G.T.: Hm.

E.B.: Well she died. And if she'd listened to me—and taken it—

G.T.: Hm.

E.B.: And had the *pluck* there—but she didn't have the *pluck* but that's it.*

Happily, Emile was to be successful in other areas of medicine:

E.B.: There was my brother there, he came here once with his, his jaw broken in two places.

G.T.: Yes.

E.B.: His nose split, his mouth split—

G.T.: Joachim there?

E.B.: Joachim.

G.T.: Yes.

E.B.: And look at the work I did on that eh.

G.T.: You did all that?

E.B.: It's me who did that.

G.T.: How did you do it?

E.B.: Well I put his, his jaw together—

G.T.: Yes.

E.B.: Bandaged it an everything eh?

G.T.: He couldn't eat for a while.

E.B.: Oh no—he—he only had a—a soup, I made soup for him.

G.T.: Hm.

E.B.: Yeah, oh yeah.

G.T.: How did he do that? How did he do that?

E.B.: He did that, he banged into, into a plank, and the horse *kicked* him in—

G.T.: Oh my God! Yes.

E.B.: Starting here.

G.T.: Yes.

E.B.: His nose cut there. I looked after it right, a good *job*.*

On another occasion, Emile, by administering first aid to his uncle, saved him from serious consequences:

E.B.: Now my uncle Jean he had a, a cartridge—which went off in his hand, it smashed up his hand—he was y'know eh, and he was unwrapping the cap because it had—it hadn't gone off I'll say eh.

G.T.: Hm hm.

E.B.: And when he was hauling it off that made it fire—but there was no shot in it.

G.T.: Hm.

E.B.: But it went off and tore his hand right up, his thumb here was fallen right back there—

G.T.: Hm.

E.B.: All the skin was gone off and everything. I went to get him down at the   Bar—

G.T.: Hm.

E.B.: With my horse—and I brought him here. Then I, I had some, some, some, some *salt* and I had some salt—I put all that in boiling water—then I made him—*soak* his hand in it.

G.T.: Yes.

E.B.: Cold sweat was running down his face.

G.T.: Yes.

E.B.: Ah! my friend it wasn't pretty. There were my two, two sisters, Bernadette and Marie, she's alive her—Bernadette is dead—and they looked at it and they fainted.

G.T.: Hm.

E.B.: They couldn't *face* it.

G.T.: And you sewed it up after.

E.B.: I didn't sew it, no.

G.T.: No?

E.B.: No no. I washed it—all right clean—

G.T.: Yes.

E.B.: Then I put his thumb together—and I had to wash it, I—I looked over him for eleven days—but now I couldn't do anything—and it was coming time to fish and everything—

G.T.: Yes.

E.B.: I had to earn my living too, me.

G.T.: Yes yes, yes yes.

E.B.: Then I took him to the hospital. And then er—I went with him, the doctor looked at his hand and asked how long it had been. Well it had been eleven days. That day—I took him to the *Crossing*. The, the old man said more than once, "You saved my life you" he said. Ha! He would never forget it, he said.

G.T.: Yes yes.

E.B.: Had—saved my—had saved his life.

G.T.: Hm.

E.B.: So the doctor looked at his hand. Well he said, he said, "Did you do that?" And I said to him "Yes, I did." But he says "There's no doctor or anyone," he said, "who can do better than you have."

G.T.: Well! That's a nice compliment, eh?

E.B.: He said, "There's no gangrene in it, *no gangarene in it*, nothin."

G.T.: Hm hm.

E.B.: "*It's natural.*" Well there they kept him in hospital and they cut a few pieces from his buttocks and they—

G.T.: Yes.

E.B.: Filled in his hand d'you see.

101

G.T.:   Yes.

E.B.:   Well now I couldn't do that.

G.T.:   No no.

E.B.:   But er—I—I saved him.

G.T.:   My God!

E.B.:   Ah!?

G.T.:   Yes yes.

E.B.:   If it hadn't been for me he would have died. Gangrene would have set in and he would have died.*

Broken bones, tooth-pulling, were all part of Emile Benoit's practice. But he could also play the shrewd psychologist, as this last example illustrates:

E.B.:   I had my sister—er, I was getting dressed that evening—

G.T.:   You, you delivered a child.

E.B.:   Oh yes.

G.T.:   Who was that for? Which child did you deliver? Was it—

E.B.:   Oh—yes yes, it was my sister.

G.T.:   Your sister.

E.B.:   My sister—I didn't deliver it—I didn't deliver the child—but er, I set him on his way.

G.T.:   Yes yes.

E.B.:   She couldn't bear her child, she was two days and two nights in, in agony, suffering.

G.T.:   Yes. Yes.

E.B.:   Eh? And I went, she, she asked for me because—I'm her godfather—

G.T.:   Hm.

E.B.:   With that—and her brother.

G.T.:   But you could have—....

E.B.:   Anyway I went, er, and I said to her, I said, "If you stay there—they'll sleep later on," I said, "but—you'll be gone."

G.T.:   Yes yes.

E.B.:   But I tell her, "You're going to have to move from there,"—I said, "if you want to have your baby."

G.T.:   Hm.

E.B.:   "No," she said, "I can't."—"Well," I said, "If she won't—if she won't listen to me I'm going. I'm going home, I'm going home."

G.T.:   Yes.

E.B.:   I tell her, "You're not going far." But she says, "What must I do?" But I tell her, "You've got to get up from there." So I get the blanket and put it on the floor. There. I say, "Come on."—"No no, I can't." So I say, "Come on!" I say, "You can or you can't—that's it!" And then I say, "The good Lord suffered for us too—and they took him—" Well I said, "Do it to him he said and take her too. That's all."

G.T.:   Hm.

E.B.: Now mom heard it, the shouts, "Ho-ah-ta-qua-qua-qua-qua-qua-qua!"—but she gets down, lies down. So I get—she was lying down face up, the girl there, on the floor—under the blanket. And then Gerald, she goes as true as the Good Lord—I started pressing on her stomach there eh—

G.T.: Yes,

E.B.: And I press—and I waited—quat! She went down—he went, he went down, eh—

G.T.: Yes yes.

E.B.: So I leave her then. For the labour—I wasn't a *busynose* at all me.

G.T.: No no.

E.B.: I go down and—in front of the mirror. And when I was in front of the mirror to put my *neck-tie* straight, I had to go, me—running around ah ah! I was a widower eh, was a widower.

G.T.: Yes yes.

E.B.: "Wah!" Her! Already!

G.T.: Yes.

E.B.: So I said you've got to think—er already, the time to come down stairs—

G.T.: Yes.

E.B.: And straighten my *neck-tie*—after three or four minutes there—

G.T.: What you did was, you turned the baby around.

E.B.: Yes yes yes, there, he was, he was sideways.*

I have provided these quite long accounts of Emile Benoit's role as a doctor not only to illustrate his narrative liveliness or to underline his pride in his achievements in this domain, but also to demonstrate how serious he is on the subject. When recounting the words of the doctor about his treatment of his uncle Jean's injured hand, he was obviously proud. For his greatest ambition had always been to be a doctor. His success in healing men, women or animals only confirms his point of view that if he had had the opportunity to pursue his studies, he could have fulfilled his ambition:

E.B.: Well. If I had been educated, Gerald, I would have been—a doctor.

G.T.: Or, oh yes.

E.B.: I would have been—*surgery* or—

G.T.: That's what you would—

E.B.: I would have been a den, a dentist, or I'd have been something.

G.T.: That's what you would have liked to do.

E.B.: Oh yes, it's in my heart, that.

G.T.: Yes yes, yes yes yes, yes. To heal people.

E.B.: You could cut yourself in half, it's no difference to me, that. I would, I would sew it together again.

G.T.: You would—you would have liked to be that—a doctor.

E.B.: Oh yes! That's what I'd have liked to be!

G.T.: Yes yes.

E.B.: Oh that's what I'd have liked to be. Yes yes yes. I would have liked, it was my heart, that.

G.T.: Yes yes yes, yes yes yes.

103

E.B.: I really, I really liked that.*

His Faith

It is evident to what degree Emile wanted, and still wants, to achieve his ambition. This desire to help his fellow creatures is the pragmatic side of a positive philosophy inspired by his faith. Emile is a practicing Catholic of deep faith who believes, as the following passage will show, that one's devotion can be rewarded during one's life:

E.B.: Well Gerald, I'm going, I'm going to tell you a little story there—about my life's intention—er, I've played a lot of times for nothing—and my intent was all for, the Church eh, the Church—in my—in the religion that I belong to. Er—my Church. Well, I used to play—really tired—and play and play and play, play, play. But that didn't matter—I did it for my Church. But playing for the others there they had—lovers, girls and *so on* we'd talk now and again but I couldn't have, I had to play, me, and play and play and play and then I had to walk six or seven miles—in the mud and everything—well, I said, "Well, it's for the Church."

G.T.: Hm.

E.B.: Then all at once—there were three or four churches they had to build and then tear down again—and all at once, hey, a church has to be built—that I worked for so much—Gerald—and all at once a man comes up to me and he says, "You want a *job* on the church? Come and work on it."

G.T.: Hm.

E.B.: And they were crawling about like worms looking for work on it—me I didn't go looking for work—they came looking for me.

G.T.: Hm.

E.B.: The church, go on, work for the church. And I worked, I went.

G.T.: Hm.

E.B.: And after that my *luck* changed after that—nah!*

As this conversation gives us to understand, Emile Benoit's life was not always an easy one. On a purely personal level, he had the misfortune to lose his first wife. Married at the age of twenty-one, nine years later he was a widower. His late wife had given him five children, four of whom were to survive. But even helped by his sisters, he led a hard life. And then, after seven years of widowerhood, Emile married his present wife, Rita Collier, who gave him nine children. Rita is a great source of comfort and support for Emile who, while constantly teasing her, as is his nature, finds in her the touchstone of his security as well as a source of musical inspiration.

Emile Benoit, Musician

It is a fact that music is of primary importance to Emile Benoit, and has been so since his childhood. And as I have already said, he fashions his personal experiences into preludes to the performance of his compositions. Emile was twelve years old when he acquired his first real fiddle. But his love of the instrument precedes its acquisition by three or four years. In the following account, Emile relates, in English, how he first acquired a taste for the idea of the fiddle, if not for the instrument itself:

E.B.: Well—when I started playin de fiddle, I never, I had never seen a fiddle like dat [pointing to his own], never seen it, never seen it in my life. But her father used to, his father, my grandfather you would say, he was a fiddler, he was a "Scotchman," played scotch. So he could euh, e, e, when

104

his father died he was only four or, four years old. So he could hear, euh, euh, he couldn remember too much of his father. Four years old eh. But he used to take two little sticks an take it—he used to sing dat, "Taratata-la taratata-da-tara-ta-ta-taratata-taratata-taratata-taratata." Dat's ow e used to sing now, y'know? But I didn, I didn't find it nice. D'you find it pretty? So all right, went on like dat. [...] So anyhow, heh heh! I had de, de, de, de sticks. See father played de sticks. I said, "Could you make me a fiddle?"—"Oh no," e said, "I can't make a fiddle but I could make you," e says, "something," e said. So e took a piece a, a little piece a board, was about three inches wide I spose, he took is pocket knife an e start, y'know, makin a fiddle. So all right, now we had a, dem times, it's still euh, still on de market. Sewing thread. Coarse thread. We used to patch clothes with that, y'know, eh? Still euh, still here yet. But he, you get dat for eight cents a roll eh, de big rolls, dey was, euh, a tousand feet in it or something like that. Well, he made it now, he made four little gap dere an four dere an took your tread an, he showed me for the first time, how to do it. First time. Là. Dey made a little bow, too. De bow was about dat long I spose [about eight inches]. So all right. So now, I start. Start wid dat now. An I used to sing an I used to play but t'was, t'wasn't a song like dis [bows his fiddle]. T'was someting like dat y'know [scrapes the bow over the strings behind the fiddle's bridge]. I knew I used to go like dis now. Once when I used to play [makes chin music and scrapes his bow over the strings]. An de firs ting one string gone. So anyway, "Mom, could I get another piece a tread? Where I broke a string?" Heh! An I put that, that's another, oh, she'd say, "Yes"—on the first time, yes but after a while she use, Mom start to get! Ah, heh! An so, I, dere was no money dem times t'was all trade y'know. You hadda bring a, you had to bring a cow to get it roll a, to get a roll a, a reel de tread. All trade, no money. She said, "Oh well, spare de tread," she said. "Yes but," I said euh, "I broke a string." Ha ha! Well I kept goin like dat, kept my, done dat for two years. Playing on dat little bow dere. But I, I couldn't play no, no reel or nothing but I was practicing all de time, eh [bows a few notes, beats time with his feet]. Practicing de feet an singin an, y'know, an I was practicing. So all right. So I had a, an uncle called John, Jean, Jean-Pierre his name was. John-Peter.

Emile must have really liked his cardboard, cotton and kindling fiddle, to practice in this way for two years. What is striking to the spectator during this narration is Emile's animation, his imitations (of the voice of the little boy he once was, the voice of his mother), and the spontaneity of his performance. He speaks quickly, occasionally gets muddled, but creates the impression he is reliving a nearly sixty year old experience. But let us take up his account once more, when his uncle Jean-Pierre Duffenais enters the scene:

E.B.: Yeah. So good enough. I said, "Uncle, you should try to make me a fiddle!" But him he, he used to drink so much y'know. Drunk all the time, all de time. Never got married, he was eighty-two when, an when he died he died drunk. He was drink all de time, all his life. "Well," he said, euh, "maybe sometime," he said. But he got a, a new head y'know, from an old violin from somewhere or whatever in de back. But he made de top, somehow, an he stuck, an stuck it on an he got some catgut string an put it on e, e made, he made a little bow too, the bow, the same bout dat long I spose. So he brought it but dis used to sound, y'know, not like dis but euh, y'know, not too bad, not too bad. So I said now, yes but I tried. Same like a, y'know, was euh nothing dere. But de swing was there all right, but I didn't know where to put de fingers for to bring in de—so I said euh, "You show me, euh, how you"—he could play a small little bit y'know. "You play like dis now." [Emile plays] An den he'd play like dat now, euh, y'know. So I got dat from him. [Plays again] An dat looked, while he was doing dat, my inside—was going like dat now. Yeah. [Taps his feet] You know, two feet to get it, get de fiddle, to get de fiddle. Could—aïe? What a tease. How many times teased about dat, eh. If I could see my, my family wid a nature like dat dere eh? How proud would I be eh? So anyhow, I, I got! He, euh, passed us de, de, de, de fiddle an I played it just as good as him now. Played just as good as him. "Now," I said, "I wants, euh, de fast, fast reel dere." Now he could play dis one day euh, "De Devil Amongst de Tailors." So he passed de fiddle, I played it too. Now so, "Good enough, Uncle," I said. So I start. Well, I played—all dat afternoon, I played all night, didn't go to bed at all—an, euh, well I played till part of a next day. Nothing to eat, oh I was starved. Well I, I practiced dem now and on de last mon ptit garçon, hold on now! I was comin around! Tcheeh! An after dat psshut! I had it made. Suppose I never seen my uncle John anymore, ha ha! I had it—and I start from dat.

It is difficult not to be carried away by Emile Benoit's liveliness and enthusiasm in the course of this narration. And he is moved by the same spirit today as he was some sixty or more years ago. At the age of twelve and a half, Emile obtains his first real fiddle and five years later gives his first public performance, playing at a wedding. His father drove him to it in a *cabarois*, a one-horse carriage. From that moment, Emile never ceased playing at dances, weddings and 'times' or parties.

His professional career only began in 1973, however, when, at the age of sixty, Emile took part in a fiddlers' contest at Stephenville. He won the second prize, but his greatest pleasure was to hear the winner, in a short speech, talk about Emile Benoit. This contest led him to St. John's, and once he was known to the organizers of folk festivals, he began to travel widely. In 1975 he played at Ottawa, at the Mariposa festival the following year, in 1977 at a festival in Boston. This was the period, moreover, at which folk festivals began proliferating in Newfoundland in general, and at St. John's in particular, stressing a renewed interest in traditional music.[5] He began appearing as a guest on television programs, firstly in broadcasts devoted to traditional music, but subsequently in programs viewed nationally such as "Ninety Minutes Live," whose host, Peter Gzowski, introduced Emile to a multitude of English Canadians, leading to a series of public engagements from one end of the country to the other. He did numerous radio programs on both French and English networks, and for the last few years has accepted occasional gigs in bars, especially on the Port-au-Port Peninsula, at Corner Brook, and in St. John's. In 1980, Emile was the only Newfoundlander to be engaged for the "Pistroli en Atlantique," a show bringing together French musicians of a traditional bent who gave a series of concerts in the Atlantic provinces. He quickly became the star of the tour.

His greatest success, in his own eyes, was the 1979 launching of his first 33 r.p.m. record entitled *Emile's Dream*, produced by a young Newfoundland musician, Kelly Russell. In a sense, the record put his work in concrete form, but Emile Benoit's influence on traditional music in Newfoundland goes far beyond this success. Since 1970 there has been a veritable tidal wave of renewed interest in traditional music on the part of young Newfoundland musicians. Different groups, such as *Figgy Duff*, *The Wonderful Grand Band*, *Tickle Harbour*, *Three Turn Tune* and *The Barkin' Kettle*, some of which have endured and some dispersed, but all of which brought together exceptionally talented musicians, have been influenced, in one way or another, by Emile Benoit. Some admire his compositions, borrowing and adapting them to their own style; others have imitated his style, the secret of which he never hesitates to reveal. He is admired and loved by many musicians and traditional music enthusiasts.

Humour and Spirituality

If Emile Benoit has attracted such a throng of admirers, it is of course in part thanks to his musical and narrative talent—and, one might be tempted to say, his talent as a clown. Formerly, before he became known to a wider public, it was not rare for some of his peers to label him a "fool" or a "clown." Emile gave support to this attitude through his continual play when he had an audience; he never stopped playing the fool. I asked him the following questions:

G.T.: And if I'm not mistaken, Emile, one of the greatest pleasures in your life is to make people laugh.

E.B.: Oh yes, yeah, oh yes, that's true—that's true.

G.T.: You've always been like that.

E.B.: I—make people laugh and try to make people happy. That's er, that's my life, that.

G.T.: Yeah. And you'll do anything to do it.

E.B.: Yeah, yeah, yeah, I—I'd throw myself in the sea if it would make you, make you laugh enough.*

It is clear Emile takes his clownishness very seriously. From conviction he set himself the task of contributing to people's happiness. If his success in his artistic activities has been spectacular, we also know of his life's humanitarian bent in other fields: we can recall his work as an unofficial doctor when the nearest doctor was some forty miles away from his home, and when roads were neither safe nor easy. On a more spiritual level, we may also remember his devotion to the Church. And it is now we begin to see Emile Benoit's true face. He is a man of deep spirituality, a spirituality which he expresses most often through what he does best: playing music and telling stories.

Emile combines his spirituality and talent in his performances. We have already noted how he often precedes his musical interpretations with a story in which he explains, with all the art at his disposal, how he came to name the composition which follows. As an example, let us take his views on the devil, a being who looms large in the folklore of French Newfoundlanders and who serves as a link between official and folk religion. While we were chatting together one day, Emile began talking to me about the devil without any prompting on my part:

E.B.: And everything you heard, t'was with the devil. You know, I think about that, me—a lot, Gerald. I've heard it said, that's in my time y'know—

G.T.: Hm.

E.B.: The more you name the devil's name, the closer he comes.

G.T.: Hm.

E.B.: Now you take all the, the, the apostles there are today. But it's not often they're going to say—the devil. Perhaps they'll say the, *the Evil eh, Evil Spirit eh?*

G.T.: Hm.

E.B.: But it's not often—but in those days—but by the gee you can't break wind but you were going to the devil! But the devil will get you! The devil was there and, the devil is after you—and they used to see all sorts of things, all sorts of, of, of—er—y'know I often think to myself d'you see, er, er, I, I've got no learning—

107

G.T.: Hm-hm.

E.B.: But learning doesn't count—what comes into your mind there. Eh?

G.T.: That's right, yes.

E.B.: He was, he was named enough—that they'd say—just about take them over.

G.T.: Yeah.

E.B.: Yeah! But now they leave alone. There's nothing now.

G.T.: Yeah.

E.B.: You don't hear people saying but I saw this last night, I saw that last night. You don't hear anything. Eh?

G.T.: Yes.

E.B.: They've left him alone. You know—I say that to Rita too, now and again—we shouldn't er—name the name of, of that man.

G.T.: Yeah.

E.B.: We should never name his name at all.

G.T.: Yes yes.

E.B.: No, we should leave him alone. There.

G.T.: Yes yes.

E.B.: Now that's what I think there.

G.T.: Yes yes, I understand.

E.B.: You know what I mean eh. We should leave alone. Like that well he'll leave us alone too—he'll stay clear of us.*

In recalling the past, the time of his parents, and in underlining the importance people attached to the devil, Emile is not exaggerating the deep belief which moved, and which still moves, his peers. The folklore of French Newfoundlanders is full of references and allusions to the devil's works. While this may seem picturesque to cynics whose education has not led them to a better understanding of different life styles, it is nonetheless true that Emile's words are based on shared experiences sometimes hard to explain in the context of small isolated communities. French Newfoundlanders, heirs to a rich French tradition, had a world view which allowed them to explain phenomena that science tends to eschew. They had a belief system which let their society function harmoniously.

All was not of course dark in this system. While collecting supernatural personal experience stories from French Newfoundlanders, the folklorist will encounter as many humorous as frightening ones. Today, one is less likely to collect frightening accounts told with earnest conviction, for people fear being made fun of. And it is here precisely that Emile shows the difference between himself and most French Newfoundlanders. Not only is he not afraid to speak his mind, he will also do so in public, in front of an audience, and with as much conviction as any man can invest in the expression of a deeply felt belief.

Thus it is that the *Skeleton Reel*, one of his favourite compositions, is preceded by the recounting of the experience which prompted him to so name the composition. As we shall see, his narration is frank, sincere, serious—and also demonstrates his storytelling talent:

Dis here, dis is a true story. Dere's no lie about it, dere's nothing. But I don't hope you gets scared! It's not everybody can see, an can hear, but I was one of dem dat heard an I seen. So good enough! I was seventeen years old around, going on eighteen, I was goin on.... Dat happened in March, on de twenty-fourth of March,

108

dat was my birthday. It just happened a few days before dat. So I had a girlfriend, I used to go every Saturday an, euh, I used to stay dere to her home dat night. Next day, used to go to mass. After mass, I spend de afternoon wit her an we had to come for ten o'clock. Dere was no such a ting one, two, three o'clock in de morning, we had to be home ten o'clock. So Sunday, I, dat special Sunday. So I left dere nine o'clock. Used to take me an hour to come home, so I'd be home for ten. Da's my father's rule, a regulation, eh? So, good enough, I go, I go that night. I used to go before dat too, but, euh, I'm sayin da's, euh, dis special night. So good enough, walkin down, walk, walk, I used to smoke eh, eh? I used to roll a cigarette now n den, light it, smoke. And it was a beautiful night, beautiful evening. So by n by, when I got to de graveyard, pass de graveyard, cos, when I used to pass de graveyard, I always make de sign of de cross an ask God to rest the souls in peace. Don't matter who, what kind of religion it is, I don't care. When I sees bodies layin down dere, cold, I cross myself, an ask God to rest them in peace. So, I pass. Notting happened, an when I travelled past the graveyard, *tchiens*! I looked along side a me, here a *squelette*! A skeleton, a man but wit no flesh on, only de bone! Just de bone! Okay, I was walkin, I was lookin at it, side by side like me n you dere, walkin, I was lookin at im but I wasn't frightened. No. Not a bit frightened in de world. So I walk a little ways, then I turn around, then I spoke to him. I said, "What do you want?" Didn' answer. I said, "If you are under the protection of God," I said, "answer!" I said, "An I'll do, do what I can do for you." He wouldn' answer! An I said, "If you're, if you're under the protection of the Devil," I said, "go on!" I says, "In de name a God!" An when I said dat, shhht! he'd gone! It's so funny, eh? Now you hear me tellin dat, you tink it's a joke, eh? Yeah, people tink it's a joke, dey, some people believe, but light, eh? Light. Eh? But *c'est ça*, it's de truth, I wasn't drunk or notting. I was a sober man. And if I hadda seen it only once well, I'd say, well, it's my imagination an all dat. An I wasn't frightened an dat, I was frightened me, frightened to see ghosts or anyting like dat! Oooh! Always scared I would see a ghost. But dat time I wasn't frightened! I walk a little ways again, here's de same ting happened again. So I say de same ting. Gone again! An I walked like dat for say about a mile. An de first ting, shhht! Gone! Don't see im no more. So I walked, walk, walk. Nice ways! I said gone. Look, don't see im no more. An de first ting I seed someting like dat, you know, like a shadow. An I turned around like dat. I'm sure he was twenty, twenty-five feet high an he was about de width of dat wall to here dere. Standin up! An de arms by de sides, an de bones eh? De finger, fingers about dat long, an de teeth. I could see de teeth [Emile roars ferociously]. I fell down y'know, I got such a fright, it gave me such a shock, dat I lost, euh, I faint, I spose, or whatever. I don't know. But I fell back, an it happened I fell on a stick wit a big stick in de beach. At de top a de beach. An I fell, I spose, my back side fell down and I lost senses. But I don't know how long I was dere. I can't say. If it was fifteen minutes or half an hour, I don't know. An by n by, I come to. An when I come to, I was soakin, soakin wet. Same ting as if you took a bucket a water an trow it over me. Or trew me in de brook an hauled me out of it an put me dere. Soul of God! I was soaked, soaked, soaked... an den I look round. An I look an look. I never lost my senses, because my remember was dere, I know what I'd seen! So I looked an looked. Notting to see, notting to see, notting, notting, *notting*! *Là*! Then I tried to get up. I fall down again. I tried to get up. Fall down again. I tried dat about seven times. By n by, den I used to rub my legs back an forth like dat, y'know? For to try to—I knows dat my leg was dead. De blood wasn't circulating into it. I know dat! But after a while, Jeez I got up. So good enough. I got up an I fall down again. But den, move, move a little while, move, move, move. Hah! I manage! But den I went to de house—I'd say about euh, a hundred and fifty yard, or someting like dat. I'll say about dat. And euh, good enough. I never seen notting. Not a ting—took all my time to get dere for dey—had a kind of a ro—a rise to walk up, you see? Oh, I suffered to get there, bye. Jeez! I was all in.An when I put my foot on de platform for to go in de house, for to open de door, I looked in de carner over dere, here e was again! Standin dere to de carner, de same, de same ting as I had seen im before! Small y'know? E's about my size, eh. He was dere! Right to de carner. So anyway, e didn frighten me at all! No! Didn frighten me den! No. I opened de door an I got in. An as soon as I got in, my fadder an mother were just gettin ready for to say de rosary. Now. Cos dey, dey say de rosary every night, every night, every night. So—dey jumped up. Dey said, "What is wrong wit you? What you done? What happened, are you sick?" Okay—oh, I say I'm not gonna—hear my father yet. He used to call Mommy—*Adéline*, eh? "*Adéline, Adéline, et what—quoi-ç-qu'i y a de lui et quoi-ç-qu'i y a de wrong*?" Hah. So I never said nutting because my fadder didn' believe in dat, him! He didn' believe, "I don't believe for ghosts an skeletons. Eh. It's only your imagination." Hah! Yes! Imagination! Yeah, but I didn wanna say anyting. He asked me what was wrong, I said, "I never done nutting wrong." No, I never done nutting wrong. So I went to bed—but I never slept dat night! Stayed awake all night! It was de same like I used to see it but I didn *see* it. I didn see de skeleton. But it seemed, y'know? Dat de, de, de fright started to come back, come back, yeah! An nex day, an look! It was over two years after, I couldn go out in de night alone. I hadda go to—if I go to see Mary—I could euh,—I was home before dark. He wouldn catch me now in de dark.... But went on like dat an euh—when I was twenty-two, I got married—an den I had dat in my mind all de time, all de time, all de time. So I composed a reel. An—I said I'm gonna call dat de *Skeleton Reel*, because, I said—dat reel—would be so—so true—dat I said dat, dat de story will go forever—so an it goes like dis... [Emile plays the composition].[6]

Emile realizes that many listeners will treat his account as a joke; but I have observed him frequently, in front of very varied audiences, telling the same story; and each telling is marked by the very same details, the same liveliness, the same sincerity. For Emile believes firmly in the reality of his experience and cares nothing for Doubting Thomases.

In the next chapter, I shall attempt to detail the characteristics which help shape Emile Benoit the storyteller. For the moment, let us recall the question asked at the beginning of this chapter: Who then is Emile Benoit? It is evident that the portrait I have painted of him here cannot show everything; and for this reason I have tried to underline especially certain features which, as much from his point of view as from my own, seem to explain his chosen rôle in life. Motivated on the one hand by a deep religious belief, prompted by his faith to do good for people, he is, on the other hand, a many-gifted man.

His seriousness appears throughout his narratives, especially those dealing with his ambitions in the field of medicine. It is true, his situation in life never let him achieve his ambition, and so he did what was most accessible to him—first aid, for man and beast alike. He worked hard throughout his life, as a fisherman, as a doctor-cum-dentist, as a blacksmith, as a vet, as a cook in the lumber camps, and always as a good husband and father. Yet by none of these occupations is he identified by his peers.

Emile Benoit is known for his music, for his fiddle, and for his style. Indeed, as I have already suggested, some would call him a clown, fit only to amuse. It is a judgement which is valid for two reasons. Emile chose to present his clown-like side to the world. He loves making people laugh and he does it very, very well. If some people sometimes speak disdainfully of him, it is because they have yielded to electronic temptation, blindly rejecting the enriching qualities of their own tradition, qualities embodied in Emile Benoit.

This apparent distinction in his character is not in fact a reality. Gifted as he is, Emile has made his desires and ambitions real through his music and stories, through his artistic gifts. For him, pleasing people, prompting laughter in an ever widening audience, is a God-given gift. It serves his faith, a faith that none can question, by bringing a little happiness to friends and strangers. Yet he is very modest; he knows there are other, more accomplished fiddlers than he; but, and here his humanity appears most clearly, he recognizes that each individual has a gift and that each must do the best he can with it. It remains for us to examine how Emile has made the best of what fate has given him.

NOTES

1. In 1980, Emile was the subject of two film portraits: *Emile Benoit, Fiddler* (28 mins., col.) and *Ça vient du tchoeur: Emile Benoit, musicien et raconteur franco-ter-reneuvien* (29 mins., col.), both productions of the Memorial University of Newfoundland Educational Television Centre, produced by Fred Hollingshurst; I was happy to be able to contribute to their making. In August 1982, his second record appeared, entitled *Ca Vient du Tchoeur/It Comes from the Heart* (PIP 7311), a bilingual production including not only his original compositions but also the narratives explaining the circumstances of each composition.

2. I am grateful to Mr. Alan Stride of Ottawa, whose research into his own genealogy led him to suggest, with documentary evidence in support, that the original form of the name Duffenais, Duffney, is the French surname Dauphinée. Further, the name is recorded in Lunenburg Co., Nova Scotia, which was populated in part by German-speaking settlers; this would account for Emile's assertion about his grandfather Duffenais' 'génération allemand" (Correspondence from Allan Stride, November 1st, 1990). I have provided an extensive treatment of French and Acadian names in Newfoundland in "Some Acadian Family Names in Western Newfoundland," *Onomastica Canadiana* 62 (Dec. 1982), 23-34, and "French Family Names on the Port-au-Port Peninsula, Newfoundland," *Onomastica Canadiana* 68, 1 (June 1986), 21-33.

3. Given the bilingual nature of the subject matter of this study, I feel it is important to provide the original French versions of tales and quotations. Short quotations in French are maintained in the text, with parenthetical translations immediately following; with the exception of this extract, which is the first provided in Ch. XIII, lengthy quotations have been translated immediately, and are signaled by an asterisk indicating that the original French texts can be found in chapter XIII. Italicized words in the translated versions were English in the original, except in a few cases where they indicate emphasis on the part of the speaker.

4. Gary Joseph Duffenais, "Education on the Port-au-Port Peninsula since 1904. The personal experiences of three generations of teachers," MUNFLA 79-673 (1979), 4. The author is Mrs. Isabell Duffenais' grandson.

5. See my article, "Contemporary Traditional Music in Newfoundland," *Bulletin, Canadian Folk Music Society* XV, 3 (1981), 3-6.

6. See the penultimate narration in his repertoire for another version of this personal experience story.

VI

It Comes from the Heart:
Emile Benoit and the Public Folktale Tradition

In the last chapter I provided a broad outline of the character of Emile Benoit, our representative of the Franco-Newfoundland public folktale tradition. If, paradoxically, he has never enjoyed the reputation of a public storyteller among his peers, it is because of his predilection for the fiddle; yet by his style and performance, Emile Benoit is also a storyteller who fits, better than anyone else nowadays, the image of the old storyteller of public tradition.

We have come to know a man of multiple talents, both practical and artistic, who is motivated by deep faith and who has chosen, as his aim in life, to "faire rire le monde et pis assayer d'mette le monde hereux"—"to make people laugh and try to make people happy". If Emile Benoit has succeeded in his aim, his success is certainly due in the first instance to his musical gifts, both as a composer and performer. But a part of his success is also due to his talent as a storyteller: on a public stage he enlivens his audience with the stories preceding his compositions and by the verve and dramatic art with which he performs them. On a practical level, of course, he rarely has the opportunity to tell a *Märchen* in public because of its length; obviously then, outside the rather limited context of his neighbourhood, few can begin to divine his talent in that domain. Yet he has been and remains a storyteller who fits squarely into the public tradition, and who embodies best of all today the narrative and stylistic qualities of old French storytellers.

This chapter will first describe, again in his own words, Emile Benoit's experience with the Franco-Newfoundland folktale tradition. He will speak of *veillées* in former times and of his apprenticeship as a storyteller, at the same time evoking for us some old storytellers and their influences upon him. He will broach the question of motivation, which will lead us in turn to certain critical features of the storyteller's performance. To complete the survey, I shall add a few details of a technical nature about Emile Benoit's narrative style, from both a textual and dramatic perspective.

The Storyteller's Apprenticeship

The seasoned folklorist knows that an innocuous question may often prompt an unexpected answer, or at the very least details hitherto unremarked by him. I wanted to know at what periods of the year *veillées* took place during his youth:

G.T.: It was, er, what time in the year that—they started—going to *veillées*?

E.B.: Oh—when it came around to, to October, November, it started... yeah.

G.T.: And it went on until, until when, until April?

E.B.: Oh it went on until April, yes, yeah. Now at Lent well, there was nothing like that d'you see, we gave it up altogether for Lent.

G.T.: Yes.

E.B.: Nobody danced, it, it—there was nothing, nothing moved at all.

G.T.: Yes yes.

E.B.: But now when—Easter came, ah well yes, then then—*gee!* Then the guns were firing, big-et-di-bang! It was just like a wedding.

G.T.: Yes yes.

E.B.: Oh it, it, it was fun. They'd fire a shot here, then you'd hear a shot over there and another shot there and er—it was like a war my friend. Heh!

G.T.: Heh! Yeah.

E.B.: Everybody had a barrel of wine or something like that or a barrel of beer made and that made it...

G.T.: It was a bigger holiday in those days than now.

E.B.: Oh yes—now well they go to clubs and *so on*—but in those days well we stayed at home—we went visiting our neighbours, go here and there you know, and then...

G.T.: And when they, say there would have been a *veillée*, here tonight, what time would people come—to start?

E.B.: Oh-it was—it was before night here.

G.T.: Yes.

E.B.: Yeah. They'd come about six o'clock, five o'clock—they'd drink and dance—but now—it's got to be ten or eleven o'clock at night before people start moving.

G.T.: Yes yes.

E.B.: But now in my time it was all—it went on till the next morning.

G.T.: Yes. And the people, they'd play card games or...

E.B.: Oh yes yes. Yeah, yeah. You had to go drinking like that having, having a time like that, they played cards—oh yes.*

While replying to my first question, Emile Benoit underlined the changes which have taken place over a generation. Today, people do not observe Lent as assiduously as before; social upheaval brought about by the coming of the Air Force base to Stephenville in 1940 firstly, compounded by Confederation in 1949, electrification from the sixties on, paved roads, all these contributed to the creation of a broader perspective on life, while at the same time destroying, in part at least, the quite tightly knit structure of a formerly small rural society.

If *veillées* "went on till the next morning" it was partly because children in those days were less motivated to go to school; they stayed up until they fell asleep, and their parents were not so obligated to rise early in the morning to send their children off to school. We may also note that whereas *veillées* sometimes began as early as five or six o'clock in the evening in the past, they now begin at a much later hour. The pace of life has changed completely.

There was a much greater freedom of action in Franco-Newfoundland communities of former times; people were not slaves to the clock. Emile points out as much, while talking about his apprenticeship as a storyteller:

G.T.: When you were a lad—were there lots of *veillées*?

E.B.: Oh yes, yes—well—once a week—and sometimes twice a week. *veillées* —oh yes.

G.T.: In the winter.

E.B.: In the winter, yes.

G.T.: Yes.

E.B.: And sometimes travellers—they came from Mainland, there were some from the Cape and they travelled, they got the idea to come by the house and then er, the, the old man loved stories. And so there he—er, he got them to tell stories. Well now me I was a child—I listened—and then I picked them up. But there were—I knew lots of stories—loads of stories— but I've forgotten loads too, you know—because...

G.T.: People used to tell...

E.B.: Didn't, didn't, didn't—keep up the, the, the practice, keep up the practice—but it, it...

G.T.: When there er, when there was a *veillée*, how many people would there have been er—in the house?

E.B.: Oh—the family.

G.T.: The family.

E.B.: The family, oh yes.

G.T.: And...

E.B.: It was pretty rare there were others, others who came you know because they were all busy here and there, they had *veillées* you know—in—from place to place—they went now perhaps to er, we'll say to my, to my uncle's or something like that. Well they wanted to go there—there'd be about twenty or thirty of them—and they were there just as well say every night.

G.T.: Yes.

E.B.: Then after a bit they'd change places, then they'd go to a—to another house and then—they'd, they'd play music and...*

Several points in this conversation are worth remark. Firstly, Emile specifies that in his childhood and youth, he heard and learned the tales that were told at home and at his uncle's home and elsewhere. It is certain that in Franco-Newfoundland tradition, many storytellers learned a large part of their repertoires before they were twenty. If he forgot some subsequently, it is because by the time he was twelve he was becoming more and more interested in music. And finally, we should take note that certain homes—his uncle's, for example—were landmarks for travellers from other French communities in the region. There was exchanged the latest news, and there people amused themselves—telling stories, singing songs, making music. Moreover, Emile seems to be carrying on the tradition established by his uncle, for at certain times of the year the same atmosphere prevails, with the same crowd of people, busy night and day amusing themselves in his home. It is the rare visitor who does not stop at Emile Benoit's home, be he politician or priest, folklorist or musician eager to learn.

Of course, Emile has not forgotten all the stories he learned in his youth, and this led me to ask him why he had remembered some at the expense of others:

G.T.: You told me there that you'd forgotten lots of stories.

E.B.: Oh yes, I've forgotten a lot.

G.T.:	I know because the practice has gone—but you—you've remembered—certain stories. Why have you remembered, say, the *Black Mountain* or er, or the, the *Seven Headed Monster*, those stories rather than other stories? Why did you keep those stories in your mind?
E.B.:	Because I told them a bit more often than the others, you know.
G.T.:	Yes yes, but—when, when do you tell them? When do you tell them?
E.B.:	Well, when I go like that you know—from a—or clear—of company that comes and they ask me to tell them a story—travellers sometimes—like you and *so on.*
G.T.:	Yes yes, yes yes. But before there, when there weren't many people like me who came....
E.B.:	Oh well yes, well yeah.
G.T.:	...from St. John's or anywhere but—when there were only French people around.
E.B.:	Oh well, we, we had, had a drop to drink and er, all at once well, one says, "Go on, give us it, come on, a little story, come on!" Well then that's it, well, "Give us the *Seven Headed Monster*, give it to us, let her come...."
G.T.:	They asked for stories—by name.
E.B.:	Oh yeah yeah, yeah yeah, oh! yeah, yeah. Yes.*

Now if Emile was asked for a particular tale, by its usual title, there must have been very good reasons. Indeed, the two tales named in our exchange are among the best loved of *Märchen* in French tradition as a whole, for reasons we shall see later. And it is also evident that if he was asked for a story by name, the story was already well known to the audience. One must therefore seek an explanation of the popularity of a given tale not only in its matter, in its content, but elsewhere: in the storyteller's performance of it.

The Old-Timers' Style

It has already been noted more than once that contemporary generations tend to make fun of individuals given to excessive gesticulation—*gibas* or *magies*—comparing them to the *vieux Français d'avant* or 'old-time Frenchmen.' I often asked Emile to speak about the old Frenchmen, and without always specifying tales, he gave me an idea of the atmosphere which reigned in the *veillées*, be they formal or informal:

G.T.:	And er, so at that time there, there were people who, who were known as good storytellers?
E.B.:	Oh yes, oh yes, yes yes.
G.T.:	Tell me the names of....
E.B.:	Well there was one whose name was er—Jack Tourout.
G.T.:	Yes.
E.B.:	Then there was another whose name was er, er... Narcisse Chaisson—he was a really good storyteller too—and then er, and his brother er, Julien, Julien, Jules they called him, Julien Chaisson—he was a good storyteller too. Yes er, French and English. Oh it was, it was a fine company—they didn't understand half of what he was saying you know but well, it, it went good, it sounded good and that's it.
G.T.:	Who, who didn't understand the half?
E.B.:	Er, well, the er....
G.T.:	The people?

E.B.: The people, yes, us, me and my brother were at his er, er, what d'you call him er, call him—Julien, Julien Chaisson. He had a, a jug of, of—of beer made—and er, he gave us each a drop—but him he was already feeling it—*spree.* Well we asked him to sing a song—er, he starts. There, he's singing. Ah! He was there jumping from side to side in the, on the floor, we we almost died me and my brother, my brother Joachim, well, well, well, well—it wasn't too hard to understand, in his heart, his love and then, that's it—but the rest it's not, there was no, no way to understand anything at all—but gee—it went good!

G.T.: Er....

E.B.: So then we ask, he said he wanted English songs? Yeah! I know English songs! I guess! he said. So there he was singing there too—and it was "all my love," "*my heart and my love*" an "*broke my heart*"—stuff like that, y'know! Bits and pieces—but it was fun though!

G.T.: Yes yes.

E.B.: Oh it, it made us laugh, y'know, a real pleasure y'know! It was *fun.**

Emile's pleasure as he recalls such moments is obvious, but what is important is the clue he furnishes to the source of his pleasure: it came as much from the singer's gesticulations, as much from the macaronic clownishness of a half-English, half-French song, as from anything else.

One did not have to be a good storyteller or a good singer, at least to amuse Emile and his peers. Later, he would recall other old Frenchmen whose performances had impressed him:

E.B.: ...Here! Drink! They used to drink, they used to drink beer and things like that, they, they....

G.T.: Did they sing the, the "Marseillaise"?

E.B.: Oh yes, yes.

G.T.: "Allons enfants de la patrie."

E.B.: Yes.

G.T.: Can you sing that?

E.B.: Old, old Scardin there, him, he used to sing that, him.

G.T.: Yes.

E.B.: Yeah yeah. But the others, they couldn't, they weren't singers.

G.T.: No.

E.B.: Old, old Lecore there. Job Lecore he couldn't sing, neh!

G.T.: No.

E.B.: There was, he used to sing one in English—"*She be down*" he said, "*she*" there was no "a" [she, in Newfoundland French] in it at all him, it was all "*she*". And old Tacannou it was all "i" [he, in Newfoundland French]—"i", "i".

G.T.: Ha ha ha!

E.B.: And old Lecore, "*she*"—it was all "she"! "*She be dere, she be, she be come*" er, oh yeah. He used to sing there er, "*She be down the numbornal* [?], *she be down the numbornal*" and then he, he, he'd say a few words with that then they'd dance, see.

G.T.: Yes yes!

E.B.: Don't wipe, you! The big—heh heh! We had fun though!

117

G.T.: Yeah.

E.B.: I watched that, me—but you know, I enjoyed it, me?

G.T.: Yes yes, yeah, yeah.

E.B.: And in those days there was nothing to see—but I liked that.*

The old Frenchmen amused themselves by playing the fool, singing, dancing, talking nonsense. Their manner impressed the young Emile, who discovered a great deal of pleasure in it, in both the general atmosphere and the unbridled gesticulation. His elders' actions provided him with a model which, at the time, represented a more widely appreciated form of behaviour:

G.T.: Tell me if er I'm right, when I, if I think that—when people were telling stories, the people there didn't say anything.

E.B.: Oh no!

G.T.: They listened.

E.B.: They lis—they laughed for sure, if it was er... yes.

G.T.: Yes yes.

E.B.: Yeah.

G.T: But—were there storytellers if, you'd make fun of him perhaps....

E.B.: Oh yes.

G.T.: ... They would have gotten angry—or—if he was telling his story and er....

E.B.: Oh no, no no, they didn't do anything like that, no.

G.T.: No because he would have been angry.

E.B.: Oh yes yes, oh yes yes. No no. Every—anyone did anything he wanted to do, nobody made fun of him. No.*

For nowadays, an older person telling a story to young people is open to all kinds of mockery; but in the past, the good storyteller, the good singer earned the esteem of one and all.

His Motivation

It was this kind of behaviour that suggested to Emile how best to play the part which, little by little, he was creating for himself. At different times, when asking him questions about his beginnings as a musician or as a storyteller, I was struck by the strength of his motivation, which has been the real key to his life:

G.T.: How old, how old were you when you started telling stories?

E.B.: Oh, about—around seventeen.

G.T.: To people. Seventeen.

E.B.: Seventeen, I started, yes.

G.T.: And er—you were what, right small when you started hearing stories.

E.B.: Oh, yeah, twelve, something like that, around fifteen, *so on*. When I was young.

G.T.: Yes.

E.B.: I had the fiddle on my mind a lot, you know.

G.T.: Yes.

E.B.: That's what—but if it hadn't....

G.T.: More than stories.

E.B.: I would have, I'd have had all those stories, but gee—you see?

G.T.: Yes yes.

E.B.: But my interest was more in, in my music, than in stories.

G.T.: Yeah, yeah. Yeah.

E.B.: Yeah. We, we had fun.

G.T.: Yes.

E.B.: Oh it was, we had some good times. It seems to me—that we had more good times in those days than now.

G.T.: Yes yes.

E.B.: Yes—there was more, it seemed—more, more joy.*

The pleasure he felt at the *veillées* of his youth, as part of the audience or as a musician or storyteller, was evidently very strong. He was to take up the same theme again: "Et moi tu sais ben le, le plusse de mon idée moi tait euh, la carnasserie, ois-tu? Hein? Ca ç'tait—jouer d'la musique—pis amuser le monde—les faire rire—assayer d'les mette hereux—j'ai jamais été eune parsonne moi pour parler mal du monde..." (And me, you know the, most of my mind was er, playing around, you see? Eh? That was—playing music—and amusing people—making them laugh—trying to make them happy—I've never been one to speak badly about people, me...).

Here, in a single sentence, is the reason for his existence, stated indeed in a very serious way; he was to give a sense of the same feeling on another occasion, but with his characteristically modest humour:

G.T.: And if I'm not mistaken, Emile, one of the greatest pleasures in your life is to make people laugh.

E.B.: Oh yes, yeah, oh yes, that's true—that's true.

G.T.: You've always been like that.

E.B.: I—make people laugh and try to make people happy. That's er, that's my life, that.

G.T.: Yeah. And you'll do anything to do it.

E.B.: Yeah, yeah, yeah, I—I'd throw myself in the sea if it would make you, make you laugh enough.

G.T.: Heh heh!

E.B.: Yeah, yeah.

G.T.: Yeah yeah.

E.B.: And I can't, I can't—swim.*

The Tricks of His Trade

So far, Emile Benoit has provided us with a few glimpses of his contact with the *veillées* of his youth, his apprenticeship, so to speak, at the feet of old Frenchmen, while at the same time showing us what was to become his motivation as a traditional artist. During our conversations, about old-time storytellers or about his own storytelling, Emile frequently drew attention to the qualities or, to put it better, the tricks of his trade. And, need it be stressed, we are in a position to appreciate the aesthetics of storytelling in Franco-Newfoundland tradition when we know what these tricks are. The leitmotiv of his art can be summarised in one word, his *acting*:

G.T.: And how old were you when they started asking you for stories like that?

E.B.: Oh I was about seventeen—sixteen.

G.T.: They knew already that you could tell stories.

E.B.: Oh yes yes yes.

119

G.T.: Yes yes.

E.B.: And er I acted to make them laugh! Lo! Oh! Yeah.*

His experience with old Frenchmen had prompted him to juxtapose laughter with the fact of "acting."

On another occasion, Emile elaborated on the importance, to him, of the acting of old Frenchmen:

G.T.: You, when you're telling an experience or a story you, you're always—on your feet....

E.B.: Oh yes, oh yes.

G.T.: And then er....

E.B.: Yes.

G.T.: So they say the old Frenchmen were like that. Is that true?

E.B.: Oh yes that's true, oh yes.

G.T.: When you were a boy, did they tell stories like that—like the old-time Frenchmen?

E.B.: Oh yes there were, yes—you, you take someone like er, the, the, the— Julien Chaisson—I told you about him there.

G.T.: Yes.

E.B.: Him there he was, he jumped around like that too him. But er, I don't know—but it was so funny.

G.T.: Yes.*

Emile had been so impressed by Julien Chaisson's acting that, without a moment's pause, he launched into an imitation of Julien Chaisson narrating an episode from the *Story of the Black Mountain*:

E.B.: He had, he was telling there the time he told the time—the Story of the Black Mountain. But he said—when it was coming to the end there— when the, when the devil had married his, his daughter and this, this— her young man. So it was coming to the end there and—he, he, now they had to get to the Holy Land you know and euh, he says, he says, this, this here, his daughter he says got down he says off the horse and then she put her, her ear to the ground—then she says—"Father's coming." So they only had about a hundred yards to go he says to get to the Holy Land, heh! Anyway, he says, that's good. There she gets back on, she says, "Father's coming," she says, "and he's close." Well he says, "My good lord God," him now, "there," he says, "there," he says, "now she flies, there," he says, "she's going now, I guarantee you she's moving now," he says, "the belly," he says, "no more," he says, "than four inches off the ground, and she's going now, a hundred yards, hm! hm!" well, that's good, that's good, she's going, she's going, she's going, she's going, she's going, she's going. And after a while she says, "Father's getting near father's getting near." So then, well he starts giving her the whip he says under the horse's belly—ah the horse he says, "There. Well," he says, "there! Now she's going! *Now* she's going! *Now* she's going! There— now," he says, "earn your oats now," he says, "earn your oats!"— something like that—y'know. Anyway—she only four yards—"Well," she says, "Father's back there, I can see him," she says, "only four yards to go," she says, "to, to jump into the Holy Land. Only four yards—ah! My good lord God there toh! aaah, tayorh! she's going now, ah! Now there," he says, "that there, it's it's, ah! Forgive my foolishness," him he

120

says. Hah! She's moving now. *Now* she's going—four yards—well that's what made you laugh there, d'you see. Yes. It wasn't a short enough time he was going on with his four yards there before he gets there all of a sudden here's the devil who gets there and hooks the horse just as he was jumping into the Holy Land—and he was left with the horse's tail in his hand he says. Well that's what, what made you laugh.

G.T.: Yes.

E.B.: Just think now by the saints, five minutes to say that now.*

It is clear that the pleasure Emile derived from the original narration came largely from the fact that the storyteller had so successfully filled out an episode which, told by other storytellers, might have lasted no more than a dozen seconds. And the effect of the repetition, made with a progressively more excited voice, only adds to the humour of the situation. Need it be pointed out that in reality the horses would have covered the hundred *yards* much more quickly than the storyteller would have us believe. Emile had to be seen, too, during his narration, for he was wildly agitating hands and arms, his whole body, which added a whole new comic dimension to his performance.

Did Emile Benoit model himself on Julien Chaisson? I asked him the question:

G.T.: Well—when you—you started telling stories—did, did you want to tell them like him, for example?

E.B.: Oh well, a bit like him but gee, I didn't tell them exactly the same as him.

G.T.: No no.

E.B.: Because he put too much into it, him—you know.

G.T.: But you were trying to....

E.B.: Yes yes.

G.T.: Put life into it.

E.B.: Yeah yeah, oh yes, to put life into it. Oh yes, of course.

G.T.: And do you think, were there many storytellers like that?

E.B.: No—there weren't many.

G.T.: People who....

E.B.: Now there was Jack Tourout, he told—yarns too, stories—old-time stories—but well, he didn't act in the, in the story, when he was telling them. Er, Narcisse Chaisson the same—he told stories too but er...like that.*

This is an instructive conversation for two reasons: firstly because Emile insists on the importance of the narrator's acting; and secondly because he has not modelled himself blindly on anybody. He observed, noted, chose, in order to create, like any great artist, a style both traditional and individual.

Emile was to emphasize on many occasions the importance of the storyteller's acting, at one point offering me some profound comments on the art of storytelling. It is rare enough that the folklorist is privy to such remarks:

G.T.: But—I understand that you like music better than stories—but all the same you remember stories—er, what is it in stories that, that you valued?

E.B.: Aaah... well—the stories I liked, well there's lots of the devil in it, the, the, the, y'know... and when you tell stories and there's, things like that, well—it, it, it's a thrill, d'you see, that, and you're acting there.

G.T.: Yes yes.

121

E.B.:   Yeah, it, it, it, it moves you, you see.

G.T.:   Yeah.

E.B.:   Oh yeah. Apart from that—the, the—the story would, wouldn't be interesting.*

When Emile has a gig in a bar, he is often asked what he thinks is the most important aspect of his music. He always replies, "That it comes from the heart." The preceding conversation helps us the better to understand the emotion he experiences in the practice of his art: "it's a thrill," "it moves you." And without the acting, the telling of a story would not be interesting, neither for the audience nor the storyteller; a story must have "lots of the devil in it," movement and action.

How does Emile put "lots of the devil" into his narrations? He is a born comedian, with a fertile imagination. Without too much prompting from me, he recalled certain devices, some of the tricks of his trade:

E.B.:   But er me, the way I am, when I told stories, but gee, it made people laugh y'know, I had to talk like the old witch and—I had to talk like the other one, y'know, y'know, change my voice *an so on.*

G.T.:   Yes.

E.B.:   And—now in my time I—there was no television, there was no radio, there was nothing like that, but you had to make your own fun you see— I'd play the fiddle a bit and then er, after that I had to tell stories. Well then I had, some, some, some, sometimes I'd put some spun wool—on my head to make long hair, then I'd make some paper teeth, black teeth, long teeth—then I'd stick that in my mouth and er, I'd act like the old witch and er threaten the people, and they, they, they laughed then, it was fun y'know.*

Emile was always ready to disguise himself, in order to better amuse his audience, and he did not restrict such acting to the performance of a *Märchen.* He was (and still is) quite capable of dressing up for a straightforward personal experience story:

E.B.:   One time I had, I had, there was a priest, er—he'd come here—and he stutered—you know—he always went "brouou"—and well me I'd been to his home—and they'd say to me, "Do the priest there." So then I get up and I'd talk like the priest. And, and I'd preach like he would, you see, preaching to the people *an so on.* Well that made them laugh eh. Then all of a sudden there I put a cabbage on. I pull out the heart from the cabbage and stick the cabbage on my head and I've got the roots sticking up, and then I started acting like the priest there. Well they almost died, it's no use, it, it, *my*—we had some fun, we had some fun—pleasure, a great pleasure. Yeah.*

It is easy enough to see how his friends "almost died" at the spectacle of Emile, a cabbage on his head, preaching Heaven knows what Gospel like a stuttering priest.... But hidden behind such unbridled clownery, as we have seen, is a very serious soul. Emile Benoit is an artist conscious of his art, and is as well able to handle and control his story as he does his public. This is how he puts it:

G.T.:   Tell me—the stories there—I was, I've been told that stories were often quite long—eh, two or three hours sometimes. Is that true?

E.B.:   Oh yes, yes. Oh yes.

G.T.:   A story which lasted three or four hours?

E.B.:   Yes. Not four hours but er—two or three hours for sure.

G.T.:   Yes.

E.B.:	*Oh my!* Yeah. But gee, d'you see, you can make stories long there you see— you can stretch them out eh.
G.T.:	Yes yes.
E.B.:	Oh yes.
G.T.:	How do you do that?
E.B.:	Well you put little pieces in and *so on* and you—round them out here and there, oh yes.
G.T.:	Yes.
E.B.:	Oh yes, no danger—and it's better too you know.
G.T.:	Oh yes yes, yes yes.
E.B.:	And little bits with that to—to fill it out. Oh yes.
G.T.:	Yes.
E.B.:	Oh yes yes. It holds together better y'know.
G.T.:	And when you do that, you're acting there on the floor, I suppose that, that stretches it out too eh?
E.B.:	Oh yes, of course, oh yes.*

We have already seen how much Emile appreciated the art of the late Julien Chaisson, with regard to the episode from *The Black Mountain*. For the art of "stretching out" a story was obviously a necessity for the storyteller, given that one of the criteria of excellence in the narrative tradition was precisely the storyteller's competence in telling very long stories. Emile was therefore consciously seeking to satisfy this criterion, and we shall see later to what degree he has succeeded.

Thus far we have seen to what extent Emile, in his own words, fits into the Franco-Newfoundland storytelling tradition. He has spoken especially about the performer or storyteller's acting, but has also raised a few related issues, such as his apprenticeship, his motivation, his storytelling aesthetic. But one cannot expect a storyteller to cover all the details of his art, even less that he offer an analysis of the tricks of his trade in the language of folklorists. One of the folklorist's tasks is to draw the attention of the interested reader to such features of the storyteller's art, whether the latter takes them for granted or considers them to be of little importance.

Stylistic Features of his Art

I shall conclude this chapter by endeavoring to highlight features of Emile Benoit's art that he himself has not raised, features which are, however, typical of the Franco-Newfoundland public storytelling tradition. But at the same time, we shall see how, like any great artist, Emile brings to his narrations that very personal spark which gives a special hall-mark to his performances. I shall look briefly in turn at the use he makes of repetitive language, including opening and closing formulas; at his delivery, including the dramatic use he makes of his voice; and at the dynamics of his vocabulary. As a link between these essentially stylistic and textual features and dramatic aspects of performance I include a brief examination of the interaction between storyteller and audience.

Formulas

One of the most striking features to the ear of whoever listens to the narrations of a good traditional storyteller is the use he makes of formulaic language, of stereotyped forms of speech. But one must not be deceived. It is not a question of tedious usage, for repetition has several important functions in oral tradition. The type of formulaic expression, which allows moreover a certain degree of variation but which is recognized by all, is one which introduces or concludes a tale narration; the opening formula on the one hand, the closing formula on the other. These formulas function as audible signals indicating either the formal beginning or ending of a story. Once the signal has been given, the audience can permit itself to plunge into a world of wonders or, inversely, withdraw from it. In the past, at least, such was the case; nowadays, the wonders in folktales seem less attractive than those of television.

Opening Formulas

In Franco-Newfoundland tradition the choice of opening formulas is not wide and, as we have seen in the context of the private or family tradition (see chapter IV), the opening formula may be reduced to a very simple form. Generally, Emile Benoit remains true to the most usual formula: "Par eune bonne fois y avait in homme et eune femme" ("One fine time there was a man and a woman," which Emile used to illustrate, out of context, the best known formula). Variants are not numerous: "In coup par eune bonne fois—y avait eune femme et une homme—il aviont in enfant" ("One fine time, there was once a woman and a man—they had a son," (*The Seven Headed Monster*); "Bien, in coup, in coup par eune bonne fois—comme c'est toujours par eune bonne fois les temps pâssés ça ça arrivait" ("Well, once, one fine time—it's always one fine time in the old times it happened," *The Black Mountain*)— in which we may note to what extent Emile is aware of tradition; "Bien, in coup par eune bonne fois i y avait in homme et eune femme—pis il aviont in enfant" ("Well, one time, one fine time there was a man and a woman—and they had a child," *Rude People*, not itself a *Märchen*, but from time to time storytellers will use a formula to begin an anecdote). For one story only, Emile had no formula at all (*John-of-the-Woods*), but this is a special case to which I shall return in my commentary on the tale.

Once, when Emile came to St. John's, he was entertaining one of my classes with his anecdotes, personal experiences, and his music. He was on the point of telling a folktale (*The Guesser*) to my students and began in French: "Oui bien in coup y avait eune bonne fois...." (Yes well once there was a fine time...") but out of consideration for a few anglophone students who had come to see him as audits, I said "It's in English now." He began anew: "Oh yes. One upon a time there was a fella he was not too kind..." provoking, by his singular use of the English formula, a round of unrestrained laughter. But when he tells a story or anecdote in English, he usually begins, "One time it was a man an a woman....", which more or less translates the French version and which is quite typical of the usage of most French Newfoundlanders when narrating in English.

Closing Formulas

Opening formulas are less well developed than closing formulas. The latter comes, after all, at the end of a story in which the storyteller has been able, to the best of his ability, to manipulate his audience. Emile Benoit, for his part, has brought a very personal touch to the closing formula, without however departing from its traditional format. As noted elsewhere, the most usual closing formula is a variation on the theme "And if they're not dead, they're living yet." In the private or family tradition, it is sometimes abridged or omitted. On the other hand, some storytellers, in both traditions, will add a personal touch to this formula, by identifying themselves as participants in the festivities which conclude the story.

This addition is normally quite simple; having announced, for example, the union of hero and heroine, the storyteller will say: "And when I came by they gave me a cup of tea, and if they're not dead, they're living yet." Emile Benoit takes the idea of the addition and enlarges it to such a point that it may occupy a whole paragraph, and he may even go so far as to omit the usual formula, although he knows it: "There—they send for the minister, and they get married, and when they had the wedding party—but me I couldn't play, play the fiddle much in those days!

But at their wedding they were around, having, having a spree—they had *home-brew* made with spruce, heh! *Holy gee!* He had me co—'Come in!' But I was well received *though, bye*—I played for—a, a part of their dance—and everything—but I was well received. Yeah." (Conclusion of *The Seven Headed Monster*.)*

It is interesting to observe how the storyteller has integrated two aspects of his own existence into this conclusion: on the one hand, the fact of playing the fiddle at weddings, something Emile has done all his adult life—and, on the other hand, the pleasure derived from home-made beer, spruce-based home-brew. These familiar details always provoke smiles from the audience, while functioning at the same time to link the world of *Märchen* to the real world. That spruce beer was formerly indispensable at Franco-Newfoundland weddings must have marked Emile indelibly, for the same detail appears in the following formula: "And gee he had to go back home and—me I was there—it's, and it's one, one of my uncles, the one who came—when they got there well he said 'She's a beautiful woman *though, bye.* Beautiful woman.' I was there when they arrived with their, their, with the white horse—but a handsome little horse too. Yeah. Yeah and they had the devil of a wedding, *ho, holy gee!* Yeah we had some *fun!* Lots of *home-brew* there—hah hah! Yeah! It's *all right.*" (Conclusion of *The Black Mountain*.)*

A final example emphasizes how Emile identifies himself with the characters in his stories, linking once again the fictional world with the real one: "And when I got there, when I was there, it turned out just like that—but gee—between me and Wooden-Leg and the cat—we buried the giants—and er, we cleared out of there, there, heh heh! there, the smell and if they're living with the newly-weds—they're living!" (Conclusion of *Jean-of-the-Woods* or *Wooden-Leg*; see the commentary to this tale.)*

One should perhaps stress here that the success of an innovation is measured by the reaction of those to whom it is offered. From my own observations, Emile Benoit's closing formulas remain close enough to the traditional not to offend, but, stamped with the mark of his originality, they add a much appreciated piquancy. That is to say that on the occasions I have seen Emile telling stories to his peers, their reactions to these formulas were positive, ranging from smiles to laughter, from an approving nod to an appreciative dig in a neighbour's ribs.

Internal Formulas

Compared to present narrators of the private or family tradition, Emile Benoit does not feel the need to excuse the wonders he evokes in his stories. Internal formulas noticed in Mrs. Ozon and Mrs. Kerfont's tales, as in those of other male and female storytellers in the area, such as "C'est ienque in conte" ("It's only a story") or "C'est in conte" ("It's a story"), are not part of Emile Benoit's vocabulary. While telling a story, his intention is to please, to prompt laughter, and if nowadays people laugh at moments at which they would formerly have been quiet, he pays no heed.

The same is true for another formula uttered by many male and female narrators of the private or family tradition: "Dans in conte ça pâsse vite" ("In a story it goes quick")—a sure sign of a temporal transition which is sometimes a lacuna on the part of the storyteller. Once only did Emile Benoit use a phrase which might suggest the abridgment of an episode when, towards the end of his telling of *The Black Mountain*, which had already lasted over an hour, he said: "Bien ç'a té, pour finir l'histouère in ptit peu vite—ç'a té assez..." ("Well it was, to finish the story a little, a little quicker—it was quite..."). It was the same episode, as the reader may recall, which Emile had used to illustrate the narrative style of the late Julien Chaisson who, in his opinion, "put too much into it," lengthened it excessively.

Repetition

Opening or closing formulas represent the most distinctive forms of stereotyped language used by the traditional storyteller. But as we have already seen, there are other types of conventional phrases which, most often, serve to indicate the passage of time. We are dealing generally with the triple repetition of a verb of motion, such as the verb *marcher*, to walk: "Il a marché, il a marché, il a marché in bon boute" (He walked, he walked, he walked a long time"). This usage is not of course restricted to verbs, nor to verbs of motion, but the storyteller, by using this kind of repetition, underlines the duration or intensity of the event in question.

Naturally enough, Emile Benoit makes use of this convention, and the reader will notice such examples of triple repetition in all his *Märchen*. There is no point in giving examples, so common are they; but where Emile differs from traditional practice is in his intensification of the feature. For he does not limit himself to the conventional triple repetition; on the contrary, he will repeat such and such a word four, five, and even six times. The effect of this intensification is, just like his personal treatment of closing formulas, to render what is accepted and approved in a sufficiently novel way to induce in his approving audience the awareness of a striking stylistic effect. At a purely immediate level, the listener will react with a smile or a laugh, for Emile links to the repetition a rising intensity of voice. I shall return to the question of voice shortly.

Like all Franco-Newfoundland storytellers known to me, Emile punctuates his narrations with diverse phrases which serve not only to indicate a transition large or small, but also to provide him with some breathing space; sometimes carried away by the momentum of an episode, he uses this vocal pause in order to get back on his narrative track. Some of these phrases are quasi-formulaic, fixed by usage and marking the passage of time. Should the hero go on a journey (lasting, of course, three days and three nights), the daily travel will be indicated, for example, by the repetition of the verb *to walk*, until the storyteller announces: "Bientôt vlà la nuit qu'arrive" ("Soon, night falls"), or "Bientôt la nuit arrive encore" ("Soon, it's night again"). The hero beds down, and soon the storyteller tells us: "L'endemain toujours" ("So the next day anyway") or "L'endemain matin i s'erlève" ("The following morning he gets up"), or some such variation.

There is also a wide variety of short phrases, ranging from "Et euh..." ("And er...") to "Pis là ("And then") or "Ben là" ("Well then") or "Ah ouais, c'est bon" ("Ah yes, that's good"). There are others, which the reader will no doubt remark. But their effect is not only to give breathing space to the storyteller: they also serve to slow down the pace of the narration, providing the listener with a moment of calm between animated, not to say turbulent periods.

His Delivery

Before passing on to questions of greater breadth, we must conclude this brief comment on details of language in Emile Benoit's stories by focussing our attention on his narrative flow and the nature of his vocabulary. The speed of Emile's delivery varies according to the needs of the episode being related. While this may appear to be perfectly normal, it should nonetheless be stressed that most storytellers of the private or family tradition tend to speak with a somewhat monotonous delivery. This type of delivery can be attributed to various causes: sometimes, for example, the storyteller has difficulty recalling the story, and the listener has the impression of an almost mechanical, disincarnate recitation. The private or family storyteller does not command his or her stories. In the public tradition, on the other hand, the storyteller must be able to direct his audience so that it reacts as he desires. If he wants a lively audience, the storyteller will quicken the pace of his narration, slowing down if he wants to calm the audience. He takes his audience's emotions in hand.

The Dynamism of his Language

A part of his direction depends on the nature of his vocabulary. Whether or not Emile Benoit is aware of the technique in question, we are dealing in essence with the dynamics of his vocabulary. An oral "text", like any literary text, may appear slow and heavy if it is chockablock with adjectives, while their relative absence tends to reinforce the accelerated speed of delivery. Emile Benoit's vocabulary is a very vigorous one, made so by an abundance of transitive, active verbs. A rapid count of verbs scattered throughout his stories gives more than 175 active verbs, whereas there is less than half this number of adjectives.

What is more, a good number of these verbs appear only once in any given story and their use is, for this reason, all the more striking. On the other hand, most adjectives used by Emile form part of the generalized and utterly conventional corpus of French Newfoundlanders' descriptive vocabulary. They are cliché adjectives, used in folktales in stereotyped fashion. Thus, the hero of tales is always "ptit" (small) but "beau" (handsome), and sometimes "smart" (clever; fit). Depending on his deeds he may be "trisse" (sad) or "fier" (proud), but being "chanceux" (lucky), is able in the end to become "hereux" (happy) and "riche" (rich), and is thus able to repay his parents who, at the beginning of the story, were "vieux" (old) and "pauves" (poor).

It is much the same for the heroine, who is always "jeune" (young) and "belle" (beautiful), "jolie" (pretty) and "bonne" (good). Like the hero, she is often "smart" and, again like him, is "heureuse" (happy) at the end. On the other hand, the villain of the tale, whether it is a seven-headed monster, a giant, a devil or simply a wicked man, is always "mauvais" (bad), "vilain" (wicked, ugly) and, usually, very "gros" (big). As for the emotions of the tale's characters, language offers a relatively narrow choice. At awkward moments, the hero will be "chagriné" (distressed), "deconforté" (discomforted), "découragé" (discouraged), "depité" (vexed), "misérabe" (wretched) or "trisse" (sad), if he does not feel altogether "enruiné" (despairing). But he will be "consolé" (comforted), "hereux" (happy) and, in general, "meilleur" (better), when events turn to his advantage, which is quite usual.

Most storytellers of the private or family tradition use all these; the listener hardly notices them. Emile Benoit, on the other hand, gives proof of his gifts by using, at appropriate moments, a descriptive language which enriches the episode in question. This is how Emile describes the second of the three sisters who help the hero in *The Black Mountain*: "He fell, fell backwards. When he sees that. Oh she, she was ugly! Ah! Oh, big teeth coming down her chin there and black! She had white patches and, and black patches, on her—and she was bent here and there—and she—warts coming out of her nose there all pointy! Well my friend—she, she was ugly! Oh she was ugly! And her, her, her, her eyebrows there—it was all curly like, like trout hooks there. And her two eyes—blazing! Blazing! They were like candles! Oh she was ugly, ugly, ugly!"*

Combined with the proverbial comparisons and a certain amount of repetition, and a voice more and more carried away, the use of these simple adjectives has a very striking effect on the ear; and that is without taking into consideration the accompanying gesture and gesticulation. But if the listener can visualize, without too much effort on his part, a person of the most extreme ugliness, the storyteller's artistry thereupon produces a contrast which cannot fail to strike the audience, for Emile goes on with an evocation of the ugly sister's goodness. The storyteller's language is characterized, all things considered, by a consciously controlled dynamism, and he easily manipulates his audience's emotions.

Conversation in the Tales

But Emile is nowhere better in his stories than when he moves to direct conversation, either in monologue or dialogue form. As an illustration, here is an extract from *John-of-the-Woods*, in which his cat wonders about the best way he can recompense his master: "And, but, he says, 'It's, I've got to do good for—John-of-the-Woods, I've got to do something good for him sometime,' d'you see, 'and there are, there are three giants there,' he said. And he was figuring now what he was going to do—but he didn't tell John-of-the-Woods, he didn't tell, no, but he was figuring it out now, and he knew there was a, a king there, where he was living, and he had a beautiful daughter. 'Well if,' he says, 'if only,' he says, 'I could succeed there and,' he says er, 'and he could' er, John-of-the-Woods now, 'could marry the king's daughter there now,' he says, 'a beautiful girl like that,' he says, 'and if I could er, destroy the three giants me,' he says, 'if I could find a plan—a way—and, and he, and it must be, give him that as, as a surprise, something like that—how proud he would be!' he says, 'That, that, that would put joy in his heart again. Well he's been so good to me in, in my whole life. He's been so good.'"*

All at once Emile succeeds in anticipating for the audience the probable outcome of events, while at the same time practicing the art of lengthening a story, by filling it with a monologue both lively and full of noble sentiments. The reader will find, scattered throughout the texts of his stories, other examples of the same kind.

A fine example of his mastery of dialogue in tales is furnished in the following extract, taken from *The Black Mountain*: "Soon, at three o'clock—three o'clock in the morning—she started prodding him with her elbows—she says, 'Old man, old man! Old man!' There. 'Now what's the matter, you crazy old fool!' he says. She says, 'I'm sure,' she says, 'they've gone, I'm *sure* they've gone!'—'But surely you know, you told me that before but,' he says, 'I spoke to them, and I spoke to her and she—they were there! She's there, she answered me, it's her!'—'No no!' she says,—'And there's something going on there.' Well there he says, he called out, 'Jane!' he says, 'Are you asleep?'—'Ah!' she says, 'Well,' she says, 'I was asleep,' she says, 'but you woke me up!'—'Are you asleep! Crazy old fool! Look out!' he says—'If you are, you could, you can sleep—you're going to get, you're going to get my hand in your mouth,' he says. 'Ohh! You don't have to be nasty,' she says, 'because,' she says, 'I know something's going on,' but he says, 'I know' he said, she said, spoke—'you've got no—are you deaf?'—'Oh no I heard it.'—'So er, go to sleep! Crazy old fool, go to sleep!' So then hnrrr! Now she's asleep, now they're sleeping....'"*

Emile has to be seen telling this part of the story, carried away by the passion of the giant whose wife has prevented him from sleeping. His staccato phrases, words swallowed in his anger, his hand raised threateningly, all this, compared to the surly but conciliatory tone of his wife, offers a most lively and very natural dialogue. Emile succeeds in bringing the audience right into the middle of a conjugal squabble. Once again, this example is far from unique; the dramatic possibilities of conversation are frequently exploited in Emile Benoit's stories.

Interpolations

Both of the preceding samples of conversation illustrate an aspect of oral tale tradition which has been and which remains a controversial issue among folklorists. I shall discuss this question at greater length in the *Note on Text Transcriptions* which precedes the folktales, but the question raised here concerns the use of the interpolations "i dit" (he says, he said) and "a dit" (she says, she said). It is obvious that in the narration of an oral folktale, neither the storyteller nor the audience has the benefit of a printed text. But the moment the oral folktale is transferred to the printed page, certain folklorists succumb to an attack of "edititis," if it may be so called. An abundance of such interpolations, it is claimed, tire the reader's eye, and the editor avoids them so that he has a text which corresponds more closely to the norms of a literary text. I am totally opposed to this procedure, for the good reason that I am not trying to present a literary text, but as precise a representation as possible of an *oral* reality.

Emile Benoit, like all Franco-Newfoundland storytellers, makes a very frequent use of these interpolations, to the point that a sentence may be so divided a dozen or more times. To the ear, such interpolations are not a problem, but, on the contrary, serve to recall to the audience (and perhaps the storyteller himself) the actual speaker. The reader interested in oral literature and oral style prefers to see the text of an oral tale in a pure form, if not scientifically noted.

Vocal Effects

In underlining the tale's orality, I must here take up an aspect of Emile Benoit's art to which I have alluded on several occasions: the use he makes of his voice. It is here, of course, that we encounter the greatest problem in the transposition of spoken tale to written text. In literature, the author can describe the tone, accent and vocalic subtleties of his speakers before or after their conversations. The folklorist who wishes quite simply to present what was said is reticent about filling his text with too many explanatory notes, for they disturb the flow of the story. He does, of course, use traditional punctuation, specifying the special conventions he has had to adopt; but the problem remains difficult to solve.

The question is all the more difficult, and all the more important, because Emile Benoit makes the fullest use of his available vocal effects. He is a very comical imitator, and the *reader*, even assisted by parenthetical explanations, can never appreciate the immediate dramatic effect of the storyteller's transition from a deep and serious voice in one sentence to the high-pitched squeak of an old biddy in the next. Yet Emile Benoit does this kind of imitation in most of his stories, and such imitations add much to his audience's enjoyment. In the texts which follow this essay I shall try to evoke, as concisely as possible, the kind of voice used by Emile at specific moments.

Another aspect of his vocal art is his use of onomatopaea. French, like English, possesses a number of words which, in conventional fashion, express certain sounds, such as a duck's "coin-coin" (quack-quack) or a cow's "meuh" (moo). The oral storyteller is not, of course, obliged to adhere to this usage, and Emile Benoit does not. He has, therefore, numerous onomatopaeas expressing the sounds of men and beasts, which I have tried to represent in legible and accurate fashion. The intensity of the sound or onomatopaea varies, depending on the emotion of the moment, but added to this, Emile does not restrict himself to pure onomatopaea. Sometimes carried away by the emotions of what he has just been narrating, he adds to the end of his sentence a kind of commentary composed of syllables of his own devising. Some of these sounds recall onomatopaeas, while others are rather exclamations which may be transcribed either conventionally or by creating a special orthography.

However, one cannot be satisfied with a description of the kinds of vocal effects Emile brings to his tales. It is even more important to record his audience's reaction to his unbridled cries. His exclamations and onomatopaeas intensify the moment's emotion and seem to produce in his audience an emotional tension; this tension makes them all the more enthusiastic towards the story and, of course, towards the storyteller. These vocables are sometimes so unusual, so original, that one cannot refrain from chuckling. The effect is enhanced if, as is often the case, the listeners have drunk two or three bottles of beer. Need it be stressed, storytellers in the private or family tradition are almost never so unbridled: exclamations and onomatopaea, just like gesture and gesticulation, were the attributes of old Frenchmen of earlier generations.

Metanarrative Devices

Emile Benoit, an artist well aware of the tricks of his trade, is not, in fact, carried away by his narrations to the point that he seems lost in his own world. On the contrary he is very alert to his audience's reactions; should a particular device produce a happy response, he will use it again. We are entering here, then, the domain, often neglected by folklorists, of metanarration, that is to say the area of interaction taking place between storyteller and audience.

The good storyteller creates a temporary world to entertain his audience and always runs the risk, as the mere narrator of the episodes in his tale, of becoming a kind of mouthpiece detached from his audience, as is often the case with private or family storytellers. The most important function of metanarrative devices is that they enable the audience to enter more readily into the temporary world created by the storyteller. For, contrary to what happens with storytellers of the private or family tradition, the public storyteller does not tolerate a great many exchanges with his audience. We have seen, with Mrs. Ozon and Mrs. Kerfont, a very broad range of metanarrative devices, devices which, moreover, are at the very least part of the pleasure the two ladies took from their evenings together.

The most frequent device used by Emile Benoit is a remark addressed directly to the listener. Most often he will add at the end of a sentence a "ois-tu?" (d'you see?) or a "t'sais" (y'know), which serve to draw the listener deeper into the flow of his story. The listener's reaction is simple, acknowledging the remark addressed to him by a "hm" or a "yes." Without listing all the possible words or phrases addressed to the listener, I give here the most common ones used by Emile. The "Eh?" which requires an affirmation in daily conversation demands the same response in a story. On the other hand, phrases such as "mon vieux" (my old friend), "mon ami" (my friend), "mon homme" (my man), "j'te garantis" (I guarantee you) generally require no more than a nod of the head. Sometimes, in our private sessions, Emile will call me by name: "Pis là Gerald" (And then Gerald), "Là Gerald mon homme" (There Gerald my man).

From time to time Emile has a slip of the memory, a verbal lacuna, and he will ask the listener for help; on one occasion, for example, he could not remember the word "fonderie" (foundry) and asked for the correct word. But the difference between Emile's lacunae and those of Mrs. Ozon and Mrs. Kerfont is the way in which he covers up: if he cannot remember a certain detail, such as a person's name, he will add a phrase such as "i m'avont pas dit" ("they didn't tell me"), or, by the tone of the sentence, we are led to believe that "they" were none other than the hero and heroine of the story (with whom, as we have seen, Emile manages to associate himself in his closing formulas). That is to say that even in awkward moments, the public storyteller can profit from his own lapses.

Occasionally, Emile succeeds in bringing the audience in contact with him by offering an unrequested explanation. At the beginning of *The Seven-Headed Monster*, he explained to me that the hero's name is always *Jack*, and never *Jean* as one might expect in a French folktale. Further on, he felt obliged to explain to me the question of the age at which one attained one's majority: "And, the lad worked, he was working, he was working all the time—but in those days—well—you had to be twenty-one before you—you were your own man. When you were twenty-one, ah well gee, you were your own man. Well that's good. Anyway, here's his—his birthday comes up—twenty-one. Hah! Oh it's no small business, he's a man now, d'you see, oh ho! I guarantee you!".* Emile perhaps thought that in my own tradition the custom was different, and so gave me a glimpse of his. Such explanations are not numerous throughout his stories, but they serve both to instruct his audience and to make it more a part of his narration.

The penultimate type of metanarrative device is of a kind usually produced automatically. Sometimes, the storyteller coughs or sneezes, and excuses himself. Emile coughs frequently enough, and excuses himself. While his fits of coughing are in no way part of the narrative content, they are indicated quite simply because they are present. I do not go too far in my care for preciseness: storytellers are, after all, human beings, and it is not my intention to have the reader believe that every narration is a model of perfection. Moreover, the look on his face when he excuses himself is so amusing it prompts further laughter in his audience.

The last device is laughter. While entertaining his audience he laughs himself, making those who watch him laugh too. Laughter follows Emile as surely as the sun follows rain. I have already noted on several occasions some of the devices which provoke laughter in his audience, and these devices are primarily verbal in nature. In concluding this examination of Emile Benoit's art, we must take a glimpse at his body's elasticity, and the use he makes of it.

Body Movement

Emile Benoit is a veritable plastic man, an inimitable contortionist. This talent is nowhere more in evidence than when he plays some of his special pieces on the fiddle, those which lend themselves to a comic use of the instrument. One has to see him playing the fiddle behind his head, or lying on the floor, or between his legs. In one piece, in which he imitates an old musician from his community, he sits on a chair and plays, at first in a furious tempo, with his legs flying in all directions like an unhinged windmill, but slowing to a deathly tempo, to the point at which he seems likely to fall out of his chair, for he is imitating an old man victim of a sleeping sickness. With his mouth half open, his eyes half closed, he brilliantly conjures up a somnambulist fiddler—only to return to his original tempo and behaviour when somebody shouts out: "Wake up old man!"

Emile is no less vigorous when telling a story. He jumps up in order to wield the imaginary sword with which the hero will decapitate the seven-headed monster, using his whole body in a series of exuberant gesticulations. In *The Black Mountain*, the devil, trying to catch hold of the horse on which his daughter and the hero are mounted before they set foot in the Holy Land, lunges desperately forward only to tear out the horse's tail. Emile succeeds, in his movements, in translating perfectly the anger, despair and frustration of the outwitted devil.

Yet more than bodily movement, more than the unchecked gesture and gesticulation, it is Emile's face which makes the greatest contribution to his remarkable performances. His mouth and lips are of an incredible elasticity, and the absence of his dental plate (for he is toothless now), adds to this elasticity. His face can express the glaring anger of a seven-headed monster, or the nauseating manner of an old woman trying to charm a would-be suitor for her daughter's hand. At one moment he is the empty-eyed, gawking idiot boy, drooling when he talks, at the next he is the enchanted cat, giving, in magisterial fashion, a lesson in behaviour to his master. Emile can put himself easily into all the roles his stories require. Motivated by a burning desire to make people laugh, and an acute observer of people, he is able to translate these qualities into the traditional folktale genre. A master of the conventions of the Franco-Newfoundland public folktale tradition, he goes beyond the ordinary because of his particular genius, which allies the usual talents of the public storyteller to his own very personal gifts of gestural and vocal imitation. Like every good actor, Emile Benoit takes his audience in hand, and provides it with an unforgettable narrative experience.

VII

Conclusion

The Port-au-Port Peninsula, on the west coast of Newfoundland, is the refuge of the descendants of a few dozen deserters from the French fishery and other Frenchmen who settled there during the nineteenth century. Mixed together with a small number of Acadians who settled along the interior of Bay St. George at the same period, these sons and daughters of fishermen and small farmers have long suffered the fate of all ethnic islands in North America: strong pressures to assimilate to the anglophone majority; in a provincial population which in 1980 was more than 550,000, French Newfoundlanders constituted less than one percent of the total.

For a long period, peninsular French were protected from the worst ravages of assimilation thanks to their relative geographic isolation in the villages of Cape St. George, Degras, Mainland, Winterhouses and Black Duck Brook, all situated on the peninsula's periphery. Their Acadian cousins, on the other hand, were to find themselves in a less favoured environment which, after 1940, became more and more open to anglophone influences.

There is no question that geographic isolation contributed greatly to the maintenance of the language and the rich traditional culture of the peninsular French. Yet, in the forties, fifties and sixties even their identity seemed destined to disappear beneath the rising tide of English influence and the new technology which, more than Church and school, put upon them a cultural and linguistic diet that was wholly English. But in the end, such was not the case.

At the beginning of the seventies French Newfoundlanders, spontaneously at first, then with the support of government services, entered a period of rebirth. They began to acquire a new taste for their language, and to take a new pride in their origins; a pride which had very nearly been crushed, not by hammer blows but by subtle, barely seen influences.

It was at the beginning of the seventies, too, that the first in-depth scientific studies of Franco-Newfoundland culture were initiated. Apart from the short but important visits made to the area by musicologist Kenneth Peacock in 1959 and 1960, no serious research had been undertaken on the traditional culture of French Newfoundlanders.

It became very quickly evident to the author and his future co-workers that Peacock's abundant collection of folksongs was to be equalled by collections just as rich in other areas of traditional culture. My particular interest was in folktales, and after only a short period of fieldwork I was rewarded. But far from wishing to simply make a collection of tales or other folklore genres, it was my intention to try and understand the part played by folktales and other kinds of folklore in people's lives, and to do this I had to make several excursions to the area, of both short and long duration.

As a result I plunged into the daily life of the Newfoundland French rather more than a folklorist usually does. The more I came to know them, the more sensitive I grew to their hopes and fears, sympathetic to their aspirations. I undertook, therefore, not only to make a scientific study of their culture, especially their oral literature, but also to help them, to the best of my abilities, concretize their sense of identity as French Newfoundlanders. It was my aim, then, to return to them a part of their heritage which, for various reasons, seemed most in decline, and to do this in their own language, at least as far as the tales themselves were concerned. For their speech is not that of Paris nor Quebec, nor even of Acadia. It is a form of French which has been fashioned without the help of an élite over a period of more than 150 years, without any religious or lay education in the mother tongue.

At the very beginning of my research amongst French Newfoundlanders, I had been warned that they had no folklore—no folktales, legends or anecdotes. Common sense said that the warning was without foundation, but after a few weeks I was beginning to wonder if it were not true, at least as far as *Märchen* were concerned. It is true I was given the names of certain old men reputed to be storytellers, but they most often claimed to have forgotten everything, or quite simply that they no longer cared to tell stories of any kind.

However, the methodology I had adopted, that is, immersion in the community, finally produced good results. I met more and more people who, while not calling themselves storytellers, remembered folktales of all kinds and were even accustomed, from time to time, to tell them to family or close friends.

It was these first acquaintances and their stories which led me to recognize what was chosen as the title of this book: the two traditions. For those people who so generously offered versions of tales repeated over and over that they were not storytellers; and on the contrary, they persuaded me that I had to look elsewhere for real storytellers. Moreover, they indicated to me some of the characteristic features of "real storytellers."

Little by little I came to realize that there existed two narrative traditions among French Newfoundlanders: the private or family tradition and the public tradition. It was the former which had provided me with my first folktales, and I had generally collected them in their particular context—the small family group, or the informal gathering of a few old friends. In this tradition, the storytellers were not particularly rigorous in their performance of *Märchen*: they willingly abridged episodes, were not strict in their adherence to formulaic language and phrase, frequently paused and hesitated, and readily tolerated interruptions and corrections. Indeed, there was a very real interaction between storyteller and audience. Storytellers made no great play of gesture and gesticulation, which they associated with the "real storytellers" of former times. Their narrations were generally not very long, although full of verve, and they often gave the impression of wishing to tell the gist of the tale, the basic narrative events, without embroidering or otherwise lengthening it.

It was, to a degree, by comparing such performances to the remarks and comments made to me by my informants about those they thought of as real storytellers, that I was able to isolate the main features of the public tradition. Storytellers from the public tradition certainly shared the same repertoire as those of the private or family tradition, for they had taken them from the same source, but their performances were truly theatrical, dramatic.

The notion of abridging a story, for whatever reason, hardly ever entered their minds, for they adhered faithfully to the diverse narrative conventions; thus, their tales were very long, for alongside a repetitive and formulaic language, storytellers willingly inserted monologues or dialogues into the narratives, which served to lengthen the story. Storytellers added to their talk a very vigorous physical, gestural play which approached knock-about farce. They did not tolerate interruptions from, or other exchanges with the audience, unless they themselves deliberately prompted them.

On the linguistic level, the further one went back in time the more tales were told in French; but pressures to assimilate, which grew stronger and stronger during the twentieth century, led inevitably to a generalized bilingualism among French Newfoundlanders and, to a much lesser degree, among certain English speakers in the area. English became another vehicle for tales and undoubtedly permitted the transmission of new themes from one language to the other. It was, and still is, possible to take part in a macaronic tale-telling session; one person will tell a tale in English, another will tell one in French, with perfect mutual comprehension.

It was not difficult to find competent storytellers to illustrate the private or family tradition. My choice fell finally on two ladies, Mrs. Blanche Ozon and Mrs. Angela Kerfont, both of Cape St. George. They met often to spend evenings together, and had a very good repertoire of folktales. Their narrations were typical of the private or family tradition, and they illustrated perfectly the interaction which could take place among the participants of an informal *veillée*. But, and it is perhaps the overriding reason which determined my choice, they represent eminently well the mixed bilingual or macaronic tradition; both bilingual, Mrs. Ozon almost never used English, while Mrs. Kerfont made only a very rare use of French, which produced a very interesting linguistic context.

Finding a storyteller from the public tradition was a much more difficult task. It is true that a small number of public storytellers were still alive, but a changing society and their own aging had had a baleful influence upon them. They no longer cared to tell stories to people who, in general, no longer appreciated old, lengthy and repetitive tales which lacked suspense and were filled with old fashioned wonders. Actors without stage or audience, they rarely deigned to provide a sample of their art to interested but transitory visitors.

And then, in the context of a folk festival at St. John's, Newfoundland, I met Mr. Emile Benoit, of Black Duck Brook. I had known him by reputation from my earliest visits to the Port-au-Port Peninsula, where he enjoyed much fame for his gifts as a fiddler, composer and raconteur. We quickly became fast friends, and to my delight I learned that he knew some folktales and liked telling them, even though his love of music left him little time to practice his art. The more he told me his tales, the more I realized that Emile, who was uninhibited, an excellent mimic and a great comedian, mirrored almost exactly the mental image I had formed of the public storyteller. If he had not in fact acquired that particular reputation, it was because he had consciously chosen between the fiddle and folktales. If his folktale repertoire is not what one might expect from a public storyteller, then it is perhaps the only gap in his role as a storyteller. At present, he more than any other person stands in the lineage of the great Franco-Newfoundland public storytellers of yore.

One might define the two traditions in terms of a parallelism between, on the one hand, the "professionals" and on the other, the "amateurs", without any question of remuneration, of course, and taking as cultural references the actor and the theatre. Based on this analogy, it now becomes possible to outline the constituents of the Franco-Newfoundlanders' folktale aesthetic. We are not of course dealing with a codified aesthetic; few people take the trouble to analyse what they consider to be criteria of excellence in a particular domain. But that does not prevent them from entertaining the desire to compare, distinguish, to choose. When a common choice has been made with regard to cultural taste, there then exists a true community aesthetic.

The public storyteller's reputation was based on the following features: he could tell very long stories (and especially *Märchen* which, of all possible narrative genres, offered the greatest stimulus to the imagination) and was faithful to the diverse conventions of the "text"—the ordered repetition of phrases, episodes, formulas; he could fill out his tales with lively dialogue, to which he allied vigorous gesticulation. Through his own personal genius he enlivened his narratives with careful use of voice and intonation, and the subtle possibilities of facial expression. In sum, he gave dramatic performances, lively, vigorous, enthusiastic interpretations of a text which he followed closely in its broad outline, but which allowed him, as might certain theatrical texts, great freedom to improvise. Among French Newfoundlanders there was no problem distinguishing between those whose narrations adhered to these criteria and those who simply told stories. The social and economic, technological and cultural upheavals of the last four decades have profoundly changed the traditional life of French Newfoundlanders. One cannot predict the evolution of Franco-Newfoundland society which, like many rural or coastal communities in Newfoundland, risks being submerged by the uniform tide of mass popular culture. But in a relatively short period of time, we have witnessed a rebirth of interest on the part of French Newfoundlanders, young and old, in their language and culture. They have discovered a new pride in their identity as French Newfoundlanders. This book aims to contribute to this reawakening, by putting forward the notion that one need not necessarily reject one's tradition while receiving cultural elements (such as television) which seem to refute the value of former pleasures. It is still possible to appreciate the telling of a *Märchen*, while faithfully following televised serials. And, when all is said and done, knowing that one possesses a unique artistic tradition reinforces assertions of identity. French Newfoundlanders have "De quoi d'n'en ête fier"—something to be proud of.

VIII

A Note on Text Transcription

The theoretical framework of this book, as noted in the *Introduction*, is contextualism, which maintains that one cannot separate an item of folklore from its context or human and physical milieu. It is not enough to record a folkloristic "text", to study its theme or variants: comparative study is the domain, in fact, of the literary scholar, and if he tries with his analyses to uncover constants of human creativity, he does so neglecting the rôle or function of his text in its human environment. The contextualist may well consider the same questions which bother the comparatist, but he examines in greater detail the "text" in its linguistic, behavioural, communicative, expressive, dramatic and artistic context.

In preceding chapters I have dealt most particularly with the rôle of the storyteller, male or female, in their human context—the interaction which occurs between storyteller and audience—, with the nature of traditional narrative performance, with the storyteller's play and style, with his art. This is an approach consistent with the contextualist's concerns, as is evidenced by this quotation from the American folklorists Dan Ben-Amos and Kenneth S. Goldstein: "For contextual folklore studies a text is necessary but not sufficient documentation; they require proxemic, kinesic, paralinguistic, interactional descriptions, all of which might provide clues to the principles underlining the communicative processes of folklore and its performing attributes."[1]

Such a detailed description of the narrative context demands a similar treatment for the narrative text, and this entails a theoretical and methodological statement of position. The contextualist-folklorist is obliged to create for himself a system of text transcription which responds to his own theoretical exigencies, and not to those of other disciplines, however closely related to folklore they may be.

No system based on the written word can ever succeed entirely in reproducing a given oral and visual event in all its details and in all its shades of meaning. But it is nonetheless possible to refine traditional systems of transcription. After identifying non-verbal features he wishes to emphasize, the folklorist will provide the necessary indications in the form of notes or parenthetical explanations. If he does not note everything, from the slightest movement to the squeaking of a chair, it is because he has to choose; not because he considers such details to be devoid of significance, but because their significance does not justify parentheses which, by dint of commenting on everything, would conceal the essentials beneath a mass of details of variable value. The reader would not see the forest for the trees.

The problem is similar at the level of the word. The contextualist must note everything that is uttered in the course of a narration, and he must do so in a way that allows the reader to appreciate the narrator's style. One should stress, moreover, the effort required from the reader, who must recognize that he is reading the transcription of oral discourse, not the polished speech of a gifted orator. We are dealing with the transcription of an oral text and style often drawn from a tradition lacking any great *literary* culture. If the reader wishes to appreciate an oral tradition, then it is the folklorist's rôle to present the material as faithfully as possible, and not to present an edited text, pleasing to the eye, unless he openly admits to having renounced all scholarly pretensions. Noting everything in the verbal context of narration, includes, as we shall see, apparently useless repetitions and verbal tics of all kinds.

But far more serious than verbal tics is the problem of language properly speaking. Put simply, the questions can be posed thus: is the folklorist going to "translate" the storyteller's everyday, colloquial, dialectal speech into a polished, "standard" language, or is he going to try to offer an approximation of the storyteller's speech? The possibilities are numerous. On the one hand, some folklorists, worrying about the opinions of colleagues in Linguistics who maintain that to have any real value, the folklorist's transcriptions must be "normalized," normalize their texts, leaving to linguists the task of providing a phonetic transcription, the only valid procedure in the mind of many linguists, who thereby arrogate to themselves the right to dictate to their colleagues in other disciplines what is only one methodology among others. Linguists offer justification by pointing to folkloric texts which are useless to them as transcriptions.

In fact, linguists themselves are divided as to transcription protocols, and are rarely familiar with the different theories adopted by contemporary folklorists. Their darts have been aimed in the main at literary folklorists, whose interests lie in the study of folktale themes as much as anything else. It matters little at this point whether the text is normalized or not. But this aim is by no means the only one governing folklorists' research, and if on occasion, in his effort to produce a faithful rendering of the storyteller's words, he offers a transcription full of apostrophes or spellings which are hard to grasp if not downright fantastical, he is at least on the right road. The folklorist has his own interests; he does not undertake his fieldwork solely to provide colleagues in other fields with study materials.

Be that as it may, I have devised a system of transcription intended to note down Franco-Newfoundland speech. I have tried to reproduce, as faithfully as possible, the narrator's pronunciation in a way which makes it accessible to the interested reader. To this end I have allied my own knowledge of the phonetics of French and its dialects with the acute hearing of a number of French Newfoundlanders who, with adequate training, have helped me attune my ear to variations or shades of pronunciation in their speech, features which seem important and significant to them.

It must be emphasized, of course, that my transcription remains an approximation; it is not a phonetic transcription attempting to note the most minute differences. There comes a point at which neither the foreign ear, however keen it may be, nor the native speaker, can distinguish certain shades of sound. What is important is that what is retained seems important to both. This transcription also takes into account variation from one community to another and from one person to another, indeed, in the speech of a given individual. Even if I did not see any significance in idiolectal differences, and this is not always the case, the requirements of scientific accuracy alone would be enough to prescribe this kind of notation. Interested linguists will always have access to the original recordings.

I, therefore, do not normalize pronunciation, vocabulary or syntax, and try to indicate, however imperfectly, through the use of punctuation, certain features of the storyteller's intonation, rhythm or delivery. It is true that the folklorist's rules may be modified over the years or, better, refined, which should be a constant aim in the methodology of folklorists and of other scholars.

The basic principle of the orthographical system adopted in my transcriptions is the following: I have used the values of the conventional graphies of international French to render the sounds of Newfoundland French. Any word of Newfoundland French will be read as one would read a word of international French.[2] Each letter or combination of letters retains the conventional pronunciation.

The reader will quickly realise, however, that Newfoundland French is neither standard French, nor Quebec French, nor even Acadian French, with which it nonetheless shares many common features. It is a form of French which has evolved, like any form of speech free of formal codification, without constraint. It shares numerous features with popular French, that is, daily, colloquial French, which pays no heed to the grammarian's rules. Given its origins in Brittany, both in the French and Breton speaking areas, the language has features of vocabulary, pronunciation, syntax, and a system of forms which owes much to the western French provinces in general. One also finds features considered typically Acadian, quite logically, given their common origins and the contacts shared by French Newfoundlanders and Acadians since the early decades of the nineteenth century.

There is no point here in detailing features of Franco-Newfoundland phonology, which have been described elsewhere.[3] It is enough to remember the basic principle mentioned earlier. We may note simply that it includes a few sounds which are not part of international French. Apart from the aspirated *h* (the English *h*) in words such as *haut, haler, hune* (high, to haul, top), which aspiration is not noted in the transcriptions, and the short vowels *i* and *u*, which appear in a small number of Franco-Newfoundland words such as *icitte, farine, boute, toute* (here, flour, period [of time] or room, all), the only sounds which are not part of international French are the consonants noted as -tch- and -dj-, in words such as *tchurieux, tchinze, cotchille, djerre, andjille, badjette* (curieux/curious, quinze/fifteen, coquille/shell, anguille/eel, baguette/ramrod). The graphies are those used in international French for words of foreign origin such as *Tchécoslovaquie* (Czechoslovakia), *djinn* (djinni, djin). The difficulty for the inexperienced eye comes from the unusual position of certain sounds. Some are easy to recognize, as with the metathesis of the word *erligion* (religion) or the syncope of the words *ptit, pis* (petit, puis; small, and/or then). Others, brought about by the vocalisation of a consonant, produce graphies that are at first disconcerting, such as *aouère, enouoyer* or *choual* (avoir/to have, envoyer/to send, cheval/horse). But the reader will quickly become familiar with such forms for they appear often, and the word's context will generally suffice to provide its meaning. As long as the reader remembers he is dealing with what was at first a spoken text, and if he is willing to make the effort to read aloud what he sees, it will not be long before he manages to recreate a fair approximation of the original.

It is important not to normalize the graphies proposed, nor to expand the numerous contractions so typical of the spoken language, if one wishes to capture the orality of speech. For once a text has been corrected, the reader will never be able to read a "correct" form other than according to a received pronunciation or worse, a fanciful pronunciation. I have, moreover, experimented with "normalizing" a Franco-Newfoundland text and then giving it to a French Newfoundlander to read. There was hardly any similarity between the original and what my assistant read, neither to his ear nor to mine. Given that a most important aim of this book is to give back to French Newfoundlanders a sample of their culture as honestly as possible, I cannot allow myself to falsify the text more than the written language allows.

139

If other systems wish to normalize texts, it is often because their authors claim to be disheartened by the abundance of apostrophes considered necessary to indicate the dropping of a sound or a letter.[4] It is true that some transcriptions are bewildering, even when the interested reader finally masters the system. Yet a simple solution is readily available: the apostrophe is quite straightforwardly omitted except in cases where it is used conventionally, and in a few special cases.

Consequently, one will read *i* instead of *i'* (il/he, it), *çte* instead of *c'tte* (cette/this) or *çt* instead of *c't* (cet/this), *ptit* instead of *p'tit* (petit/small). I use the final mute *e* of French without replacing it by an apostrophe, because it serves to indicate that the preceding consonant is pronounced, and this avoids the necessity of using double consonants (*boute*. instead of *boutt'*, for example). When the dropping of an -*e*- brings two of the same consonants together, I do use the apostrophe to separate them, and this also indicates that both consonants are articulated: *d'dans, d'd'là* (dedans/in, inside; (de) de là/from there); they should not be read as *dedans, de de là*. The absence of the apostrophe is especially easy to appreciate when it replaces a consonant fallen from a group: *vende* (vendre/to sell), *mette* (mettre/to put), *attende* (attendre/to wait). Once again, the attentive reader will soon grow accustomed to this usage.

As already noted, I correct neither spelling "mistakes" nor "incorrect" liaison forms. If the storyteller says "les chouals" I do not write "les chevaux." If he says "un gros-t-homme" I do not write "un gros homme." French Newfoundlanders, nowadays, are no longer ashamed of their forms of speech, and I will not willingly put into their mouths sounds that they do not make, nor take out sounds that they do make. It does happen from time to time, however, that they use expressions that have no precise equivalent in international French. Instead of "Où va-t-il?" for example, a French Newfoundlander will say *Ioù-ç-qu'i va* or *Aillou-ç-qu'i va*? (Where's he going?) "Qu'est-ce que tu fais?" (What are you doing?) is *Quoi-ç-tu fais*? It is not my intention to render these forms in the standard, but to maintain them as they are.

With regard to bilingualism, the normal state of affairs for French Newfoundlanders, it is obvious that a certain number of English words have been adopted into French speech. How does one write them down? Generally, English words are pronounced according to regional English usage, with more or less "French accent." I thus maintain the usual English form of the word unless its pronunciation is markedly different from the general norm. Thus one will read *le mailman, anyway, le truck* in English fashion. A characteristic feature of the English of Newfoundland is the pronunciation of -th- (as with the article *the*, especially) as -d-. Usage varies, of course, and the reader will encounter both *de* and *the*.

Some English words have forms which lend themselves to French pronunciations, pronunciations which would, however, be incorrect. *Plane* and *job* should be read as English words, and such cases are indicated by italicised forms. Other words, notably English verbs with French endings, are rendered in a form which allows a quite precise pronunciation: *maillner* (to mind). Keeping the English form, *minder, min'er*, would give an incorrect French pronunciation. In any event, English words will be clearly shown as such.

I conclude this discussion of transcription by specifying my use of punctuation. I do not use paragraphs, which belong to literary usage. They are useful for separating well conceived units of thought, but also give a sense of order foreign to oral narration. One must become accustomed to their absence, which allows greater appreciation of the breathless continuity of an oral tale.

I do not separate words spoken by characters in a tale with a dash, nor by indenting dialogue. This is a convention of the written language, where one has time to think; the same function is served by the continuous use of the interpolated *i dit, a dit* (he says, he said, she says, she said) in oral narrations. To edit these interpolations would be to misrepresent oral style, for purely cosmetic purposes. When dialogue is in inverted commas but not separated by an interpolation, I use the dash to indicate the change in speaker.

The period is used to indicate the logical and obvious end of a sentence. Three kinds of pause should be noted, each indicated differently. The brief pause indicated by the meaning of the sentence or thought is conventionally marked by the comma. A pause which seems to mark a hesitation, a forgetting, or a forthcoming correction, but which is not very long, is indicated by the dash; a very long pause, suggesting confusion or considerable hesitation, or a moment of reflection, is indicated by points of suspension. The absence of the comma separating the same word repeated more than once is intentional, and indicates a very rapid delivery on the part of the storyteller.

The question mark indicates an interrogative intonation and not necessarily a direct question. The exclamation mark indicates an actual vocal exclamation on the part of the storyteller, an accelerated intonation and delivery usually bearing on a phrase or part of a phrase. When a word is italicised, the italic indicates that the word is heavily stressed (except in the case of anglicisms). The combination of italics and exclamation mark indicates an extremely strong stress, almost exaggeratedly so, usually accompanied by a rising intonation and much accelerated delivery. The reader will find non-verbal indications in parentheses, following the word or phrase they accompany, explanations of useful contextual details, or any other necessary explanation.

This exposition has emphasized the theoretical importance of a precise and faithful transcription, and has suggested a system of transcription which, without claiming to be perfect, takes these theoretical requirements into account.[5] I trust the reader will find it accessible even if he must, at first, take pains to become familiar with it. By remaining faithful to my theoretical and methodological principles, I have tried to clear a path for myself towards a better appreciation of the nature of the oral folktale. It is up to the reader to judge the success or failure of the attempt.

A Note To The English Translation

A Note on Text Transcription was my response to the problems faced in writing down the oral speech of French Newfoundlanders. Few French Newfoundlanders of past generations were able to read and write French, and I know of no serious attempt on the part of anyone, French or English, to devise a readable form of the Newfoundland French dialect. The Note was, of course, essential to the original French edition of this book, addressed as it was primarily to French speakers.

I have maintained it in its integrity because I have included the original French versions of folktales in an appendix. Readers interested in studying the originals, without having to resort to the French edition, will therefore find the note useful. The chief reason for providing the original French texts, however, is that my essay makes constant reference to words, phrases or sentences in the primary form. An appendix with the original texts is therefore an absolute necessity. Translations, however good, cannot serve as the primary source of study.

Owing to the bilingual character of Franco-Newfoundland culture, not all the original tales need translation. All of Mrs. Kerfont's tales, and some of Emile Benoit's, were told in English. But following such an extensive justification of my system of transcription of French tales, the reader may well ask what principles have governed the transcription of tales in English, those originally told in English and those I have translated. I have not treated both in the same way.

Broadly speaking, transcription of tales recorded in English have followed principles similar to those governing transcriptions of French tales. That is to say, I have attempted to provide a faithful approximation of the English spoken by French Newfoundlanders, not wishing to distort or "correct" a distinctive form of speech. However, my knowledge of the phonetics of English is by no means as solid as my knowledge of French phonetics, and I have not attempted to be as methodical in my representation of the English of my informants as of their French.

In reality, this is not as much a problem as might be expected. There are a number of features which I have noted consistently, and which, to my ear, seem distinctive. The average English reader will have little difficulty reading the transcriptions, and will readily accept the few conventions adopted.

Most evident among these are the rendering of the standard English -th- as -d- (e.g. de for the, dat for that) or -dd- (anodder for another) or as -t- (e.g. ting for thing, tree for three). The reader should be aware, however, that this usage will not appear to be consistent, and that both forms are attested; this reflects the variation which occurs in an individual's speech.

The reader will also note the absence, in other than standard circumstances and a few specific cases, of apostrophes. As with my French transcriptions, I have not indicated an unpronounced letter by an apostrophe, preferring to let the oral form stand, thus goin for goin', somethin for somethin'.

Spellings which may at first disconcert the reader should be interpreted according to standard English usage, giving conventional values to letters which appear in unorthodox contexts.

The only other major features of the English of French Newfoundlanders which require comment concern the syntax, which while not standard is quite readily accessible, and the "French accent" of the speakers, which is not noted in the text, for want of a system that would be legible to the average reader.

My approach to the translation of French narratives into English is slightly different from my transcription of tales told in English. While nearly twenty years of familiarity with the speech of French Newfoundlanders would allow me to attempt a translation along totally colloquial lines, my ear is far more attuned to the French Newfoundland tongue than the English. Consequently, while the English rendering of French tales is colloquial, the careful reader will note some differences between my versions of French tales and those originally told in English. The comparison can be made most specifically in the case of tales told by Emile Benoit. The major difference is that my translations include rather more standard forms of speech, which I have adopted so as to avoid any accusation of attempting to parody the English spoken by French Newfoundlanders.My work, and that of the few former students who have also focussed their interest on Franco-Newfoundland culture and language, have concentrated on the French language spoken on the Port-au-Port Peninsula, rather than the English spoken by French Newfoundlanders. The time is ripe for linguists interested in speech in Newfoundland to examine at length and in depth a Newfoundland dialect coloured by French adstrata.

NOTES

1. "Introduction," *Folklore: Performance and Communication*, Ben-Amos and Goldstein, eds., (The Hague: Mouton, 1975).

2. Amongst the numerous treatises on French pronunciation or phonology (which generally claim to represent educated Parisian French usage, or "international" or "standard" French), I have retained the following, not because I subscribe to the notion of the innate superiority of one type of speech over another, but quite simply because the French they describe serves as a useful and conventional point of reference: M. Grammont, *Traité pratique de Prononciation Française* (Paris, 1933); A. Martinet, *La prononciation du français contemporain*

(Paris, 1945); P. Fouché, *Traité de prononciation française* (Paris, 1956); and H. Van Daele, *Phonétique du Français moderne* (Paris, 1927).

3. Gerald Thomas, "The French Spoken on the Port-au-Port Peninsula of New-foundland," in *Languages in Newfoundland and Labrador* (preliminary version), ed. Harold J. Paddock, St. John's: Memorial University of Newfoundland 1977, 51-73.

4. This criticism has been directed at Germain Lemieux's remarkable collection *Les Vieux m'ont conté* (Montreal: Bellarmin, vol. 1, 1973, vol. 29, 1990). It is true that Fr. Lemieux's transcription seems awkward and hard to read, but it at least has the merit of attempting an authentic transcription. It is perhaps the best such attempt since the publication, in 1937, of Joseph-Médard Carrière's *Tales from the French Folk-Lore of Missouri* (Evanston & Chicago: Northwestern University), described by Paul Delarue as "a model to follow for the presentation of a collection of tales" (*Le Conte populaire français*, vol 1, 71).

5. The transcription protocol used here to reproduce Franco-Newfoundland speech had been conceived, though not as refined as the present system, well before the publication of Vivian Labrie's *Précis de Transcription de Documents d'Archives Orales* (Quebec: Institut Québécois de Recherche sur la Culture, 1982). It is a study which offers, among other things, a sampling of different transcription protocols adopted primarily by research centres in Canada. The author provides, moreover, one such specimen from the Centre d'Etudes Franco-Terreneuviennes, although the example had not then reached the stage of refinement claimed for the present protocol. While I agree with Vivian Labrie on many points, I differ on others. Among the diverse approaches she has examined, I cannot find one which is inspired by a theoretical position similar to my own. It is for this reason that I do not intend making any modification to the currently used protocol.

But, honour to whom honour is due: I quote the dedication Vivian Labrie wrote me on a copy of her book: "It has been said that no one can find salvation without passing through the eye of a needle, but does it really have to be the same needle...?" Debate on the transcription of oral texts remains open, and Vivian Labrie has provided the debaters with an indispensable reference tool.

IX

Technical Data

The tales told by Mrs. Ozon and Mrs. Kerfont were recorded on December 21, 1972, and January 3, 1973, at Mrs. Ozon's home in Cape St. George, Port-au-Port Peninsula, Newfoundland, on a Sony TC-222A, using Scotch 202 tapes at three and three-quarter i.p.s.

The original tapes have been stored, for purposes of conservation, in the Memorial University of Newfoundland Folklore and Language Archive (MUN-FLA), under the accession numbers 74-195/F1707, 1708, 1709, 1710 and 1711. Copies of these recordings used for transcription and study have been deposited in the archives of the Centre d'Etudes Franco-Terreneuviennes (CEFT), Coll. Gerald Thomas, Nos. 55-59 (74-195/C2337, 2338, 2339, 2340).

Tales by Emile Benoit were recorded on March 1st, 1978, in CEFT (*The Guesser*); and 19, 20 and 21 September 1980, at Emile Benoit's home at Black Duck Brook, Port-au-Port Peninsula, on a Sony TC-158 SD, using Sony C-60 tapes at one and seven-eighth i.p.s.

MUNFLA accession numbers of these tapes are 74-195/F3218; 80-201/F3532c, 3533c, 3534c, 3535c, 3536c and 3537c. At CEFT, the tape copies are accessioned as Coll. Gerald Thomas, Nos. 155 (74-195/C32l6), 174 (80-201/C4873), 175a, 175b (80-201/C4874, C4951), 176a, 176b (80-201/C4875, C4952), 177 (80-201/C4876), 178 (80-201/C4877), and 179 (80-201/C4878). The last two narrations from Mr. Benoit are from the Goldstein-Thomas collection, accession No. 78-239/F4l58c, the CEFT copy of which is C3581. The collection was made from 25 to 27 July 1978 and includes the recording series 78-239/F4158c-F4162c (C3581-C3585).

The tale "*We Three*," recorded at CEFT on August 24, 1981 on a Sony TC 110B using a Sony C-60 tape is from the Thomas collection, 81-281/F3963c, the CEFT copy of which is Thomas 186, C5308.

145

X

The Tales

See the *Note On Text Transcription* for technical aspects of the presentation of the tales.

Each text is preceded by a title, which is normally that used by the storyteller. When no title is provided, I give one in parentheses. Generally, each story begins at its real beginning; I do not provide the conversation preceding the narration. I have elsewhere indicated, on the other hand, that in the private or family tradition the narration of a tale is usually preceded and followed by a verbal prelude or post-script encouraging or praising the storyteller.

Once the story has begun, nothing has been edited. For Mrs. Ozon and Mrs. Kerfont's tales, given that they narrate the one in French, the other in English, I have not indicated, by the use of capital letters, the storyteller's name. When, in the course of a narration, one or other of the ladies, or myself, intervenes, the necessary indication is provided (A.K., B.O., G.T., etc.). The storyteller taking up her narration again, or joining conversation in the middle of a tale, is indicated by a dash. The system is the same used for Emile Benoit's tales.

The original French versions of the translated tales appear in an appendix. In the English translations, words which were originally in English appear in italics.

A *Commentary and Notes* follows each tale. The commentary draws the reader's attention to diverse features of the narration, stylistic devices and other points. The notes serve primarily to identify each tale according to the tools recognized by folktale specialists. To this end, the basic work is Antti Aarne and Stith Thompson's *The Types of the Folktale* (2nd revision, Helsinki: Suomalainen Tiedeakatemia, 1961; FF Communications No. 184). Each tale for which the authors have provided an identification is indicated in my notes by the sign AT followed by the appropriate number, as well as the general title of the tale.

Given that the catalogue of the French folktale in Canada has not yet been published (we refer to Luc Lacourcière's magnum opus, the *Catalogue du conte populaire français en Amérique du Nord*), references are also provided to the French national catalogue, Paul Delarue and Marie-Louise Tenèze's *Le Conte populaire français* (Vol. 1, Paris: Erasme, 1957; vol. 2, Paris; Maisonneuve & Larose, 1964; vol. 3, Paris: Maisonneuve & Larose, 1976; vol. 4, tome 1, Paris: Maisonneuve & Larose, 1985). These volumes, published in an order different from that proposed by *The Types of the Folktale*, cover, in the first two volumes, Tales of Magic (AT 300-749); in volume 3, Animal Tales (AT 1-299), although this volume does not follow the international classification; in volume 4, Religious Tales (AT 750-849).

147

Also provided is identification of the motifs in each tale according to Stith Thompson's *Motif-Index of Folk-Literature* (6 vols., revised edition, Bloomington & London: Indiana University Press, 1955-58). This most detailed work (often in a somewhat ambiguous English, rendering the original French translation of motifs a rather difficult task) is essential, if only because numerous folktale specialists still use it, judging by Herbert Halpert's conclusions in a paper presented at the VIth Congress of the *International Society for Folk Narrative Research* (Helsinki, 1974), entitled "Towards A Future Revision of Stith Thompson's *Motif-Index of Folk-Literature*."

It has sometimes not been possible to make a precise identification, although the tale seems to suggest one. Thus, in some instances, new numbers have been proposed which are indicated as such by a following (CEFT) (Centre d'Etudes Franco-Terreneuviennes). The indications for such additions are based on those introduced by Ernest W. Baughman in his *Type and Motif-Index of the Folktales of England and North America* (The Hague: Mouton, 1966). Baughman makes use of a combination of lower-case letters and asterisks to indicate his refinements (in relation to Thompson's *Motif-Index*); wherever a number is added to his series, the appropriate sign is maintained.It has not been my intention to furnish comparative studies in my notes, nor even comparative notes to each tale. On the other hand, useful references to the distribution of French language versions have been provided, according to *The Types of the Folktale* or *Le Conte populaire français*, or a list provided by Luc Lacourcière which is now out of date (and not complete in my copy), for versions of tales catalogued in Laval University's *Archives de Folklore*. Also provided is the number of versions collected from French Newfoundlanders, and any other useful observations.

XI

The Private or Family Tradition:
Folktales of Blanche Ozon and Angela Kerfont
Commentary and Notes

THE STORY OF JOHN AND JOHNETTE

It was a man and a woman, they lived all alone, eh, the two of them. And she wasn't all there, her, you know, understand eh? So anyway, they had a garden and they had some animals eh? Cows and they had some pigs. So anyway, he was working and her now she looked after that. So when autumn came anyway, they had a cow to be killed eh? So they killed the cow. And he says, "We've got a big cabbage garden" eh? So, he says, "We'll put a piece with each cabbage"—so, he hadn't explained to her, you know, how they were going to put a piece with each cabbage. If she understood, she didn't understand that they were going to cook a piece of—meat, with a piece of cabbage eh, a cabbage. So anyway, he says, "We're going to put a piece with each cabbage," anyway, that's how the story goes eh? So then him he goes off to work. So anyway, she wasn't all there, eh? When he'd gone, she takes the meat, cuts it up—and she goes into the garden and she put a piece with each cabbage, eh? [She laughs] So anyway, that's the way it goes. But after a while now she found it funny there was no meat cooking, y'know? Now her name was Johnette, and his name was John—it was John and Johnette eh? But he was Foolish John, we'll say. So anyway he says, "Why is it you're not cooking any meat, we've got loads of meat."—"Yes," she says, "but," she says, "didn't you tell me to put a piece with each cabbage?" [She laughs] He says, "You're not going to tell me you put a piece with each cabbage?" She says, "Yes!"—"But," he says, "that's not what I told you to do, I told you to cook a piece of meat with a cabbage," eh? She says, "I put a piece of meat with each cabbage!" They lost their meat, anyway!... So anyway, so they had a pig to kill, eh, when it was getting towards Christmas time there, well, he kills his pig. "Not now," he tells her, "Now," he says, "that's for Christmas," he says, "a piece for Christmas, and a piece for New Year's Day." Yeah. Takes off—for work. So anyway, Christmas Eve, not the eve but a couple of days before Christmas, a man comes there. So he says, "Good day, Ma'am!" She says "Good day, sir," and she says, "I don't know you." He says, "You don't know me!"—"No," she says, "I don't know you."—"But," he says, "I'm Christmas."—"Oh," she says, "I guess you've come for your piece of the pig." [She laughs] He says, "Yeah, I've come for my piece of the pig." Tuh! She gives him his piece of pig and off he goes with it. When her husband comes home in the evening, eh, "Well," she says, "John," she says, "I had a visitor." He says, "Yes?" She says, "Yes." She said. "Yes, I've seen old Christmas today." He says, "Old Christmas? It's not even Christmas yet!" Well, she says, "He came for his piece of the pig," eh! [She laughs] He says, "You didn't give him a piece of the pig?" She says, "I gave him his part," eh, "you said it was for Christmas and New Year's Day, well, I gave him his part," eh? He says, "Now there's another piece left." And he says, "Don't be giving it—away," he says, "it's for New Year's Day," eh? Yeah! So good and so good. Anyway—off he goes to work

150

again. John goes off to work. Oh! When it was coming up to New Year's Day, anyway, there, the same man comes by eh? He says, "Good day, Johnette. She says, "Good day, sir," she says, she says, "I don't know you."—"No?" he says. "But," he says, "me, I'm New Year's Day," eh? "Oh!" she says, "I guess you've come for your pig," eh? [She laughs] He says, "Yes, I've come for my piece of the pig." He says, "Me, I'm New Year's Day." She gives him the piece of pig and off he goes. Goes off with it. Anyway, when John comes home, eh? "Well," she says, "John," she says, "I had another visitor." He says, "Yes? Who was it?" She says, "New Year's Day." She says, "I gave him his piece of the pig and he took off with it." [She laughs] There he gets mad! "Well," he says, "you put all the meat with the cabbage, and you've given the whole of our pig to the same man. And now," he says, "here we are with no meat!" Eh? "Well," he says, "I'm going." And he says, "When I've found someone as foolish as you, I'll come back!" [She laughs] Okay. So off he goes. He walks and walks, a couple of days anyway, he meets two men, with a cow. And they were arguing now, eh? There was a building and there was some hay growing on it, eh? And they were wondering what they had to do to get up there now so the cow could eat the hay. And one of them says, "You're crazy, eh, me," he says, "I know!" he says. "What's the matter you're quarreling like that?"—"Well," one of them says, there's one of them who says, "Now," he says, "there's some hay there," and he says, "we'd like to have it for the cow," and he says, "now we can't figure out how to get it!"—"But," he says, "climb up and cut it then you can give it to the cow."—"No," he says, "we won't do it that way." He says, "We'll cut the cow's head off," he says, "and put the head up there!" [She laughs] "Well," he says, "I've found someone as foolish as Johnette." So he turns around, and goes back home. So anyway, he gets back home. "You're back?" He says, "I've come back and found," he says, "I've found someone as foolish as you! I've come back." And he says, "I'm not staying." He says, "I'm going." She says, "Me too, I'm going." [She laughs] So anyway, he gets dressed. And he goes out through the door, and she says, "I'm going too."—"Well," he says, "haul the door!" She hauls the door and carries it off with her! It's a story eh?... Anyway they walk, and they walk, they walk anyway. He heard a noise, he heard some people, eh, so he climbs up into a tree. The two of them. What it was, was four robbers. They'd just stolen some money, eh? And they come to the foot of the tree where they were, up in it, them. She's taken the door up with her, eh? They put their door, they make—a, a, a thing, they put the door there eh? Cooking soup. Anyway, okay. So there the robbers are, counting their money. So it went, eh, "That's my share—yours, mine." But there were four of them, eh? Said, "My share, yours, mine." And the other one said, "That's my share" he says, "And where's mine?" Well they didn't mind, they were counting, eh? So there she says, "John, my God," he says, "I want to piss!"—"Well," he says, "piss from branch to branch, so the robbers won't hear you," eh? She sits down. She pisses in the pot [she laughs], the robbers' pot. Oh, one of them says, "Listen," he says, "listen, listen!" he says—he says, "The Good Lord is sending us vinegar!" He was stirring the pot and saying that, "The Good Lord is sending us vinegar!" [She laughs] Okay. There they start counting again—"My share, mine, yours," and the other one didn't get any, eh? No, there was no share for him. So there they are quarreling. "Oh my God!" she says, "John, I want to shit!"

A.K.:   (Who has just come in) Oh my God!

—And he says, "Shit from branch to branch so the robbers can't hear you!" She aims herself, and she shits [laughing] in the pot!

A.K.:   Ha ha!

—Ha! "Oh!" he says, "look! The Good Lord is sending us mustard!" He sets to stirring the pot, stirring the shit like soup, so anyway... there they are then, there they are quarreling again and counting their money—but they couldn't count parts for four, they could only count parts for three—but him, the poor devil there, no money—he was as big a robber as they were—he wanted his part!

A.K.: Yes! I know!

—Oh, a while after, they start quarreling, by geewhiz Chris', it was hot! "Oh well," she says, "John, I can't stand it any more," she says, "I've got the door on my back, I can't hold it any more!" He says, "You didn't bring the door up?!"

A.K.: Ha ha ha!

—She says, "You told me to bring the door."—"No," he says, "I told you to shut it!"—"Well," she says, "I've got it!" [She laughs] "Well," he says, "drop it from branch to branch so the robbers can't hear you!" She gives a goddam kick to the door! [She laughs]

A.K.: Ha ha ha!

—And there the robbers were shrieking with fear, the devil was coming! But him there, who didn't get his part, stays there, eh?

A.K.: Ah!

—They'd left all the money there and they took off, afraid, eh?

A.K.: Yes!

—Anyway, they come down, John and Johnette, from up in the tree. So anyway, they thought it was the devil coming, and all the time it was the door. So anyway, he says, "What are you doing there, you!"—"Well," he says, "me, I'm eating soup," and he says, "my soup is hot."—"But," he says, "you're not smart," he says, "scrape your tongue!" He scrapes his tongue, yes, the soup's not hot, eh? He says, "What can I scrape it with, me?"—"Give me a knife! [laughter] Give me a knife, me, I'll scrape your tongue!" He picks up a big knife and him he sticks out his tongue, and the more he scraped, the more he stuck out his tongue, when it was long enough, he cuts it off!

A.K.: Oh my gosh!

—And him there screaming and taking off, they were camped further away eh? The others eh? Him he starts shouting, "Lear-la, lear-la, lear-la," he couldn't talk, eh? They said "We're going lear-la," they took off and that's it! [laughter] It's finished! [laughter].

Commentary and notes

The Story of John and Johnette, the first Mrs. Ozon told, was begun a few minutes before the arrival of Mrs. Kerfont. Mrs. Ozon seemed to feel ill at ease, so that her narration was at first somewhat stilted. Each sentence ended with an eh? as if she was seeking approval, and her anxiety was betrayed by the repetition of the phrases *So* and *So anyway (ça fa, ça fa anyway)*, and the laughter which punctuated her narration. Wishing to encourage her, I refrained from laughing out loud, but kept a smile on my face. Little by little, however, her confidence grew; she leveled an *it's a story eh?* at me, allowing her to excuse the implausibility of Johnette's action, but indicating at the same time that she had become relaxed enough to detach herself somewhat from the story. Her dialogues were lively and succinct.

The arrival of Mrs. Kerfont put her friend even more at ease, for Mrs. Kerfont did not hesitate to show her feelings. The final part of the narration was extremely lively; each gift Johnette let fall from the tree was accompanied by a laugh or a gasp from Mrs. Kerfont.

A part of Mrs. Ozon's anxiety no doubt came from the fact that, at the beginning, we were face to face, with the tape-recorder between us; after Mrs. Kerfont's arrival, and in all our subsequent sessions, I was always to the side; the two ladies addressed each other, almost oblivious to my presence. Even though Mrs. Ozon was never able to narrate with the same ease as Mrs. Kerfont, her narrations were nonetheless lively, and kept her two listeners in constant delight.

Mrs. Ozon told *The Story of John and Johnette* at her home on the afternoon of December 21, 1972. She had heard it from Mrs. Olive Marche, a noted storyteller in Cape St. George.

John and Johnette combines five international folktale types, according to the classification established by Antti Aarne and Stith Thompson in *The Types of the Folktale* (Helsinki, 1961). These are AT 1386, *Meat as Food for Cabbage*; AT 1541, *For the Long Winter*; AT 1384, *The Husband Hunts Three Persons as Stupid as his Wife*; AT 1210, *The Cow is Taken to the Roof to Graze*; and AT 1653A, *Guarding the Door*. Motifs according to Stith Thompson's *Motif-Index of Folk- Literature* (Bloomington, Indiana, 1955-58) include J1856.1, *Meat fed to cabbages*; K362.1, *For the long winter*. J1701, *Stupid wife*; H1312.1, *Quest for three persons as stupid as his wife*; J1904.1, *Cow (hog) taken to roof to graze*; K1413, *Guarding the door*, and K335.1.1.1, *Door falls on robbers from tree*.

The combination of these different tale types is quite common in Europe, where they are widespread, in a variety of combinations. Curiously, while the tradition of the foolish man (or foolish woman) is well known in France, the tale types in Mrs. Ozon's version do not seem to be widespread there. According to Stith Thompson's inventory, there was no version of AT 1386, 11 of AT 1384, 12 of AT 1210, 14 of AT 1541 and 29 of AT 1653A. These figures are not imposing, but reflect the relative lack of interest on the part of French folklorists in traditional humorous genres. In French Canada, where Luc Lacourcière and his colleagues have made such rich collections, the situation is hardly better, with one version of AT 1386, 10 of AT 1384, 7 of AT 1210, 7 of AT 1541 and 6 of AT 1653A. Even accepting that these figures for French Canada are no longer up to date (we must await the publication of the *Catalogue raisonné du conte populaire des francophones de l'Amérique du Nord* for complete information), I must assume either that these tale types are no better rooted in France than in French Canada, or that researchers have not been especially interested in them. It is of course possible that the Irish influence has had some effect in Quebec as in Newfoundland, for North American versions, as has been demonstrated for other tale types. But in Newfoundland, I know of only one other version of AT 1210 and one of AT 1653A, in French tradition.

We may conclude, as far as the quantity of fool tales collected is concerned, that most collectors have been more interested in *Märchen*, only recording humorous tales when *Märchen* have run dry. I have myself been guilty of this approach, before I became more interested in the performance of any narrative, with the aim of discovering the narrative aesthetics of French Newfoundlanders.

THE FOX

Well one time it was a man an a woman, they ad—three daughters—they ad each a sheep—so one marnin, the oldest one—she took er sheep an she went now to feed er sheep. So a voice came. It said, "Leave your sheep an go look for your fartune." An you'll find, eh? So her she takes, she leaves er sheep there an she takes off for ome. So anyhow when she got ome, she talk to er mother—"Well," she says, "now I'm goin." Okay. So she packs up her lunch an off she start. So she travelled an travelled till she come to a brook. So she was hungry, she set down an she started to eat. By n by she eard something—in the woods eh? Well, it was a fox.... "My," e said, "I guess it's a long time since I never eat, I'm starved," e said. "Should give me a piece o bread, a piece a your bread."—"No!" she said, "I haven't got too much myself!" He says, "Where you goin?"—"Well," she says, "me I'm goin," she said, "this marnin," she said, "I heard a voice, leave my sheep, go look for my fartune," she says, "an I'm goin to see if I can find it."—"Well," he says, "mother wants a sarvin girl." He says, "Come stay with us." Okay. So, he goes ahead an her behind. So when they got almos to the house, they ad a big black dog chained, eh? So when

153

the dog seen the girl e made a jump at er—if she ad got er, she would eat him up. She got frightened. So they ran home. It was an ole shack all moss, the ole woman the moss was grow on er back. God, it was enchanted, eh? Pitiful! "Mother!" e says, "I brought you a sarvin girl."—"I told you," she said, "bring me no more, they don't stay."—"Don't you fear," she says, "granmother, I'm goin a stay with you."—"Well," she says, "you'll have nothin to do, only wash the dishes, cook the meals for the dog an get water for the night." Okay. An er... so anyway, she done her work, an after, she took her dinner, she brought it to the dog, the woman had made some—piece o cake. When the dog seen er he made a spring at er, *alle a garâché toute en grand là*! [she threw everything down, there]. *Tout* [All] at once! I'm French an English to it, me y'know.

B.O.: Ha ha! Ah oui!

G.T.: That's all right.

B.O.: That's all right.

—Anyway, then she goes home, she takes her buckets o, her buckets, an she goes to the well. When she gets to the well she dip her buckets o water, well, well, what a pretty well, was all kines o roses you could mention, they was all aroun. She was sittin down there watchin them—by an by she seen a little boy comin to her—kickin a ball ahead of im. Comes up to er—she says, "What you doin there?"—"Well," she said, "I'm gettin water for my night." An e says, "Where you stays?" She says, she says, "I stays at—the ole woman down there."—"Well," she says, "that's an ole devil, that! She's goin a kill you!" He says, "At home they wants a sarvin girl cos they won't stay with us." Well, she leaves everything there an she takes off. When she got there—a *maudit* [lit. damned; here, augmentative, i.e. a great big man] big man, take her by the arm an pitch er in the room. Locks er up in the room. So anyhow, it was gone for now, that's... a long time ago—in that time now, that marnin anyway, the second oldest went to feed er sheep. So she heard a voice too—"Leave your sheep an go look for your fartune." She took off for home. "Mother," she says, "I heard the same thing this marnin," she says, "an I'm goin. Maybe," she says, "my sister she's happy an lots o money, maybe." She took off. She takes her lunch an she took off. She travelled an travelled an she got to the same place. She sit down. She was at the same place as her sister. By n by, she heard a racket again. Oh! It was that little fox! "Oh my sakes," he says, "I'm starved today," he says. "You haven't got a *crumb* to give me?" he said. "No!" she said, "I haven't got too much for myself!"

B.O.: Oh!

—*Va-t-en*! [Go on!] Okay. He says, "Where you goin?"—"Well," he says, she says, "I'm goin see if I can look for my fartune," she says. "I'm on the pint of quittin, me," she says. "Well," e says, "come an stay with us!"—"Okay," she says. So they goes—takes off. When they got almos to the dog again, when the dog seen er, e made a snap at er, well, would ave killed er. So she goes to the house. Fox, e said, "Father," e said, "I brought you a sarvin girl."—"I told you," she said, "it's no use you bring a sarvin girl here, they don't stay!"—"Don fear granmother," she said, "I'm goin a stay." She says, "You haven't got much work to do," she says, "jus wash the dishes, sweep the floor, an cook the dinner for the dog," she said. Her she couldn move, she was in her chair. Couldn move at all. She was stuck there. Okay. So anyhow she done er work, an after, she went an give her dinner to the dog, she took the basin an fritch—like a big horse—*peur à mort*! [frightened to death!] So she goes to the house, takes her two bucket an she goes to the well. She got there—the well was too down for her to reach the firs time—but the girl was there. She took her water—she set down—she's there lookin at the well. By n by she seen two little boys comin. Each a ball kickin ahead o them, till they got there. Anyhow they got there—"What you doin there?"—"Well," she says, "I'm gettin water for my night." He said er—"Where you stayin you?" She says, "I stay at that ole woman down there."—"T's that ole devil!" She said, "She's goin a kill you!" She said, "You think that?" she said. "Sure!" he said. "Your sister's home, you can see her—she's big an fat—lots a fun—you know, lots o money, lots a sport she got, come with us," she said. "Yes!" she said, an she goes with them. When they got there that big man come grab her holt an fritch in the room.

B.O.: Oh!

—When she got there, face her sister, she almos fall! Just a frame left, her sister! Right pale! She never seen the daylight since she was down there! That was a long time! See, the story eh? Her buckets o water stayed there an the ole woman stayed there.

B.O.: Oh!

—Now—I hates goin over an over, me—*taisse-toi*! [Shut up!—Mrs. Ozon is smiling as Mrs. Kerfont says she dislikes repetition] So anyhow, all that time, anyow now, this last one, the last one of all, Mary was her name, now—so anyhow this marnin she goes to see—to feed her sheep—she heard a voice sayin now—"Leave your sheep an go look for your fartune, you'll *find* it!" So she goes to the house, so, "Mother," she says, "I heard that this marnin too," she said. She says, "Maybe," she says, "my other two sisters," she said, "they're happy, lots o money, sport a lot—me I'm goin too."—"Youse gonna all leave me," she says, "an leave me all alone, old like I am."—"No fear, mother," she said, "I'm goin a come git you."—"Well I hope so," she said. So she takes her bundle an off she starts. She passes the same road—she took the same road as the other two took—come to the brook. She sit down here, she'd eat—"I'm gonna eat now." She eats. By n by she heard a shout in the thicket. She jus started to eat, she heard a racket around her—it was the fox. He said, "Good day!" he said. "My gosh," he says, 'I'm starved today," he says, "could I have a piece of—I..."—"No no," she says, "come an have dinner with me," she says. "I'm some glad," she says, "all alone sittin there," she says, "have company!" Fox sit down there—an he has dinner with her. After he says, "D'you want a drink o wine?" She says, "Yes!" Goes in the brook, passes her—tail in the brook—bring out a glass o wine! He said, "Where you goin?"—"Well," she says, "I'm goin," she says, "well me," she says, "I heard this marnin, I heard a voice—I leave my sheep go look for my fartune," she says. "I'm goin see if I can find it!"—"Well mother's sarvin girl," she said, "come with us."—"All right," she says. Took off. Him ahead an her behind. When the dog seen her, oh! in the name o God! If he could heat her, he would heat her! Oh my. Oh, gladness he was to see her! Gladness, gladness! He was lickin her an everything! Oh my God, when he got it she was there—she stayed there with the dog a spell.

B.O.: Oh! My!

—What a gladness the dog was for her! An her too, she liked the dog, eh? Little fox ran in the house. "Mother," he said, "I brought you a sarvin girl!"—"I tole you," she says, "not to bring me no more," she says, "I tole you they don stay," eh? "No fear me granmother," she said, "I'm goin a stay with you," she said. She liked the dog, eh? So anyhow—she—"You'll have nothin to do," she said, "you'll have dishes—cook dinner for the dog, an," she says, "clean the house and git the water for the night." All right. She done all her work—an then she cooked dinner an when the dinner was cooked she'd get the dinner an go to the dog an she was there God knows how long with the dog—now the dog eatin the dinner there chattin him up, eh? Then after—she goes to the house, she takes her bucket an she goes over—to the well. When she got to the well she took her water, my God, my gosh, the roses round the well was pretty, pretty! She had to stay there a spell—to watch it—it was that pretty. Ah! By an by she seen three little boys comin. Each a ball kickin ahead o them. They come there—"Good day, good day."—"What you doin there?" She said "I'm gettin water for my night!" He says, "Where you stays, you?"—"Well," she says, "I stays at the ole woman down there." She says. "That's the devil!"—"The devil?" she says, "no, a nice ole woman!" She says, "That there." He says, "Come to work with your two sisters there, they're big an fat, they got lots o fun."—"I don care me!" she says—"What they got," she says, "so long," she says, "as I'm happy there with that ole woman," she says, "an I likes there—an I'm goin there—there," she says. "I ain't goin with you," she said.... So she says—now that was the nex day now—she anyhow she takes her two buckets an she goes home. When she got ome the ole woman was lacin up her shoe. Phew!

B.O.: Ahh!

—Her shoe...

G.T.: Go on!

B.O.: Ahh!

—So anyhow, anyhow, the night comes, so they go to bed. Her room—the piece of hay come through the walls, eh? So anyhow, when she woke up in the marnin, through the night then, my God, a nice room—my God! There was red lace an ribbons an evryting was comin down. Okay. In the marnin she woked up an she heard somebody walkin eh? The ole woman was to come an wake her up!

B.O.: Oh!

—Come to wake her up! My God, my God! She gets up anyhow—hee hee! She gets up now an she er... gets her breakfast, gives the dog his breakfast, she brought it to the dog, an then she come in, she clean up her house, an she took her two buckets an she went to the well. Another two buckets o water. Now she dip her buckets o water, my God, my God, the three little boys comin again—she said, "They're comin again," she said. An er... she said, "Your sisters tellin us for you to come—to help them cook dinner."—"Cook dinner?" she said, "They can't cook it theirself?" She said, "No, they wants you to come with her too."—With them eh? "Well," she says, "I don know. I don know that," she says. "Not today. I'm not goin today, but," she said, "I'll go tomorrow," she says—"if I got time now!" she said—"If I got time!" Anyhow she goes to the house again, my God!—the ole woman walkin toward her too, nice! An then, after the night come again she goes, she goes to bed that ole woman—that was for the use of the ouse—gettin to it all the time, eh? So anyhow she cooks dinner for the dog an she gave the dog dinner an after she came out of her ouse an she went back to the well. So anyhow not long she was there to the well, they come back again. She—"Youse come back again?" she said. "Yes."—"Well I'm goin," she said, "help the granmother" she said, "I...[pause to change the tape].

G.T.: Okay—where—she'd come down to the well again an the boys had come?

—Yeah.

G.T.: Yeah.

—Well, she says, "I'm goin, but," she says, "I'm not stayin long." So anyhow she got there, she went there—a big tall man come get her by the hand to bring her—she said, "I never come here to go in the room," she said, "I come here to help my sisters cook dinner—an get them here an hurry up," she says, "because," she says, "I got lots o work to do," she said. Her two sisters come out—she—they was fallin almos apart—with the poorness!

B.O.: Oh!

—"My gosh!" she said, "That's never you, that?!" she said. There's a good chance—time you had, you—get fat." Little boys, eh? "Now," she says, "come on,"

156

she says, "get to work." So they made some soup. There were three giants there. She put—after their soup was cooked she put the giants on one side of the table an them on the other side. She asked her sisters—"Is there any pison there?"—"Oh! We don know. The day we came here, we was in the room, we never saw the night come after the day." She looked for some. She *found* some! She put some in the three giants' plate. "Now," she says, "dinner's ready, come—come an eat...." Anyhow, they was eatin, by n by one, "My gosh," he said, "I've got a bad headache!"—"Do like me," she says, "lay down," she says, "it'll pass away." By n by, another one. "Go back—go on, lay down," she says, "it'll pass away." The other one the same thing. The three of them was down, eh? They were gettin *pisened*!

B.O.: Oh ho!

—"Now," she said, "hurry up, let's clean it up. Clean it all up now. Now," she said, "hurry up n go home," she said, "youse comin?"—"We don know," she said. "Well if you don know," she said, "I'm goin!" She passed the door, an when she passed the door, the castle went—fell apart. Sisters not gone either.

B.O.: Oh!

—She goes home. She got the dinner for the dog, she goes an give the dog his dinner. She was sayin to herself, "What a sin, that dog was chained all the time. I'm goin to unchain him now for *in ptit boute* [for a little while], a spell, if she's not there. I'll chain him back." Okay, she unchained the dog—he disappeared away! Ooh! Gone. Too.

B.O.: Ha ha!

—All the afternoon she was out of doors—she said she had a sore stomach, eh? Call the dog, call the dog. No dog. She was wonderin. So anyhow—wait now, I kinda forgets there—ah yes.... No, I fergets there, look!

B.O.: Didn't she go into the room and find that handsome prince?

—Ah oui! She went in, she went in—it was a castle then.

B.O.: Yes.

—It was turned into a castle—an a beautiful castle! Anyhow, she goes in the room, the young prince sittin down smokin his pipe on the bed.

B.O.: Phew!

—That was the dog—the fox—it was the king.

B.O.: Oh no!

—An the ole lady—it was the queen. Was enchanted. Enchanted—all the town! Could see—the town—marder! An then after—now it was no use—the dog—that was her boy friend—eh?

B.O.: Yeah.

—They got married—they got married. "Now," she said, "I promised my mother," she said, "to look for her at home—I'll go an get her," eh? She says—"an I'm goin." So she—guv her a horse an carriage an she went down. "Now mother," she said, "I come for you."—"It's never *you*, Mary?" She said, "Yes." Her she had found her fartune all right!

B.O.: Ha ha! Yes sir!

—So she made her mother go back with them, they went, they went up, an stayed with them, an good enough!

B.O.: Heh heh heh!

—I can't tell it to my likin at all!

Commentary and notes

Mrs. Kerfont told *The Fox* shortly after the conclusion of the preceding tale told by Mrs. Ozon. Both Mrs. Ozon and I had to coax her a little to tell her story, but once she made up her mind, she set to without hesitation. At times rather laconic in her style, this feature is most noticeable at the beginning of a narration and in dialogues which, however, are not lacking in pungency. Mrs. Kerfont tinges both her daily conversations and those she puts into her characters' mouths with irony.

The reader will notice the relaxed atmosphere of the narration; on more than a dozen occasions, Mrs. Kerfont's remarks provoked a vocal intervention on the part of Mrs. Ozon, one at least of which in turn provoked a teasing reprimand from Mrs. Kerfont to her friend. Two important comments made by the storyteller should also be noted: the first, when she says "I'm French an English to it, me y'know", after using a few French words, underlining the bilingual character of the tradition; and the second, her remark "I hates goin over an over, me"—underlining the degree to which storytellers in the private or family tradition no longer accept repetition. More generally, the reader will recognize the importance of not ignoring such comments, at least if one is to see in narratives rather more than simple stories devoid of all context.

Towards the end of her tale, when Mrs. Kerfont thinks she has lost the narrative thread, we observe a fine example of cooperation, the metanarrative device whereby a member of the audience assists the storyteller by reminding him or her of the missing words. Such devices are scattered throughout both ladies' narrations.

At the very end of the tale, Mrs. Kerfont leaves out the closing formula, probably because she had not been able to recall the final episode without Mrs. Ozon's help; she is upset, hence her concluding remark: "I can't tell it to my likin at all!"

Mrs. Kerfont attributed her version of the tale to Mrs. Olive Marche, the same source as Mrs. Ozon's first tale.

The tale is a version of the international type AT 431, *The House in the Wood*. International motifs in the tale include P252.2, *Three Sisters*; D1890, *Magic aging*; D113.3, *Transformation: man to fox*; Q2, *Kind and unkind*; L54, *Compassionate youngest daughter*; B211.2.5, *Speaking fox*; compare B119.1, *Dog (whose skin) turns water to wine* (mead); D141, *Transformation: man to dog*; D1413.6, *Chair to which person sticks*; D477.1, *Transformation: water becomes wine*; D731, *Disenchantment by obedience and kindness*; L50, *Victorious youngest daughter*; and L162, *Lowly heroine marries prince (king)*.

The Types of the Folktale records only a single French version of this tale, and only one Franco-American version. Even if these figures are now out of date, the tale is obviously not well known in French tradition. The Archives of the Centre d'Etudes Franco-Terreneuviennes possess another version, one told in 1973 by Mrs. Josie Lacosta (Joséphine Costard) of Red Brook, though a native of Mainland. The transcription of Mrs. Costard's version was published in *The Livyere* (No. 1, Summer 1981, 8-11); it closely resembles Mrs. Kerfont's version.

THE JUNK O GOLD

One time there was a man, he ad three daughters eh, an him, he was to be out workin all, all the time, eh? Workin. So anyway...

B.O.:   The oil-truck is down—it's down in the west.

—Anyway...so anyhow, one evenin he come home from work an e ad a junk o gold eh—now he didn want to tell his daughters was his own, eh? So anyhow, he guv it to them, he said·er, dis—"Youse gonna pick up this good junk o gold," he said, "it's not belongs to me," he said, "it's belong to a man *Can't Pass*." He knows there's nobody named *Can't Pass* eh? Okay. So anyhow, passed off like that so one day, one day anyhow, he said, "I'm not goin to work tomorrow," he says, "I'm goin,"

158

he says, "in town now, to buy stuff," eh? An he was goin to take them something now, y'know, he was to treat the girls. So e asked his daughter, he says—the youngest one—he says, "Gimme my jug o gold,"—eh—*non! C'est pas d'méme que ça va!* [No! That's not the way it goes!] I'm ahead o my story...

G.T.: Well go back.

—The nex marnin when he was gone workin, eh, a man come in—man come in. "I spose," she says, "you come for your jug o gold there? What's your name?"—"My name is *Can't Pass*," e said. "Yes. You come for your jug o gold." He said, "Yes." *Alle a té pis a l'a pris, a l'a donné* [She went and took it, she gave it to him.]

B.O.: Yes?!

—*A l'a donné* in jug o gold [She gave him a jug o gold]—he took off—went right back—took off. So in the evenin now, when her father come from work, he tole dem, he says, "Tomorrow," he says, "I'm goin a go to town," he says, "an buy some stuff." He says—"I spose my jug o gold is here yet?"—"Your jug o gold!" she says. "The man came here with it, the man came here this marnin," she says, "his name's *Can't Pass*—he had come for his jug o gold—an he got it."

B.O.: Oh ho! ho ho ho ho ho!

—"What we gonna do?"—"Well," she says, "we're goin a go."—dey dress erselves up, tree o dem an dey took off. Almos dark, dey come to a place you know—in a house an were people, had to board dere—an stayed overnight, eh? For to go somewhere else eh? Because it's too far. *E* was there, him. They didn have to pay there for nothin, eh? So they told the woman, in the house—they'd put the—they'd make their bed in the same room as *him*, eh? Him now'd be sleepin in the bed eh, they'd make a feel bed before for the three of them—show the woman how it was eh? Then give—e ad the jug o gold his father—her father jug o gold. Okay. So anyhow the time come to go to bed—they goes to bed first—but the other two fall asleep but er, she stays awoke—the youngest one. So e come to bed too him. An e said eh, she told im, she said, "You're goin to wake us up early tomorrow marnin, right early, early." E said, "Yes," e says, "what's your name?"—"Well, my oldest sister, *I wants to shit*"...[laughter] an she said, "My second one, *I'm goin to shit*,"—an he says "You?"—"*I have shit, me.*"

B.O.: Ah ha ha ha! [Slaps her hand on her knee].

—All right! So anyhow, she stayed awake, she never fell asleep. By n by he falls asleep. There he was there, snorin. She gets up—he took the jug o gold an put it into his boot—she seen him y'know. She gets up, she takes the jug o gold out o the boot, *alle a chié d'dans. Alle a chié d'dans, ielle!* [she shit in it. She shit in it, her!]

B.O.: Ha ha!

—Ha ha! An she woke up her two sisters, an off they start, for home. They got home, they were the nex marnin, he came, they were jus wakin up eh? An he was rubbin his eyes—"*I wants to shit!*" Ha ha ha! The man says, "Don't you shit there!" Ha ha ha!—"*I'm goin to shit!*"—"Don't shit there," he said, "because you'll clean it!" he said. "*I have shit!*" [laughter].... Ah well, it was finish—he gets up—dey were gone—he put his hand in the boot for to get his jug o gold—t'was a jug o shit in his hand!

B.O.: Ha ha! [she joyfully claps her hands].

—He said, "They're gone with it." So that's all it is.

Commentary and notes

The beginning of this tale demonstrates that Mrs. Kerfont and Mrs. Ozon were still not completely at ease, Mrs. Ozon in particular since she was awaiting the arrival of the oil-truck with her fuel. Mrs. Kerfont, on the other hand, got a detail confused in her story. It is also interesting to note that at some moments of tension, she expresses herself in French.

As ever, Mrs. Ozon is unrestrained when her friend is talking. Her laughter is spontaneous, her gestures unbridled. It is obvious that both ladies greatly appreciated the rather coarse or shocking language in the tale, and the farcical element at its conclusion.

Mrs. Kerfont learned the tale from a Mr. Anthony Jesso, of Red Brook, who had told it in English, when Mrs. Kerfont was a girl.

By its use of equivocal names, this tale vaguely resembles AT 1541, *For the Long Winter*, but no precise identification can be provided. The tale's motifs include P252.2, *Three sisters*, and K359.2, *Thief beguiles guardian of goods by assuming equivocal name*. It is not without interest to note that it is yet again the youngest daughter who takes all the initiative, as in the *Märchen*.

THE ORPHANS

I'll give you one there before I fergits it—I forgot it, I don't think I'm gonna be able to tell it.

G.T.:   What's it about?

—That's fine eh? It's the piece of a one, eh? About a little boy an a little girl, eh? It was a woman an a man, y'know. I'm gonna try it anyway. I don know if I can tell it. Anyhow it was a man an a woman—they had a little boy an a little girl an they was stayin—right up in the country, eh? In the woods, eh? Now anyhow, they had just a little bit o flour for to make some pancakes—they was far from—the country—they were—right in the country, they was. So they had a—one cow—well the ole man says, "Tomorrow marnin," he says, "I'll have to go sell my cow." An he said, "I got to go take the shart way." The shart way—is where there's all kinds of, all kinds o beastses—but they got to make the round, an I don know what, all it takes to make the round, eh? It would take too long, so he jus—take a short cut. Like gets eat the same. All right. Nex marnin e takes his cow an e goes—e never went far into the country—the beastses got around to kill him, eat the heart, eat the cow an eat him.

B.O.:   Oh!

—E wait, e wait, she wait for her husband—she said, "Your father's eat," she said. "Well," she says, "I got a sheep lef—tomorrow," she says, "I have to go to get you to eat or we'll got nothin at all. Just a little bit more left in the barn. I'll have to go tomorrow." An she says, "I'm takin the same road."—"You're not gonna get eat," she says, "what are we goin a do the two of us here alone?" They was ony young eh? "I don't know," she said. So anyhow the nex marnin she takes her sheep an she start too. She never went far, she got heat too. There. They wait an wait for their mother an father, "Well," she says, "we're well *baisés asteure* [done for now]." Well anyhow, they was only just a little bit o flour left, they made some pancakes on the stove, "Now," she says, "we're gonna heat a couple an we're goin a sit here an have a couple to go." So it was a bit o snow, eh? So they took the package on their sleigh an off they start. They travelled, *les gars* [boys], they travelled a long while. By n by they met up with a camp. It was a camp eh? So anyhow, she was goin a go there for a spell. They was all in. When they go there anyhow, they opened the door—there was a stove in there, a table, just somebody comes here! So the little boy him he wouldn see in there, he was frighten, eh? So he said, "You go in, sleep, an me," he says, "I'll stay out an watch." So anyhow. By n by... by n by, he heared a horse, gallopin, eh? Somethin comin! Up comes a young prince—on horseback. An they were pretty, the two youngsters, oh! Her she was prettier yet! So that was his camp. While he was a going huntin. When he got there anyhow, my sake, "Where you going?" he says, "my little boy?"—"We don know," e says—"it's me an my sister,"

160

he said, "we don know where we're goin. We lost our father an mother an we're—we're alone, we're goin to God knows where."—"My gosh," he says, "you're pretty."—"You finds me pretty?" he said. "You should see my sister," he said, "she's prettier than me yet." He said, "Where is she?"—"Well she's," he said, "she's in the house sleepin—sleepin my son, she's all in." So anyhow, he said, "Us go an see." Good. She was jus gettin up, eh? Oh my geewhiz! He almos gone foolish! "Well," he said, "youse gonna come home with me." He says, "My, it's ony me an my mother alone"—the queen eh? An e says, "You're gonna stay with us." All right. He was glad. So, he told the old, he told his mother to get home—"Now," he says, "mother," he said, "I got a girl for you, company for you, an I got a boy, company for me," e says, "when I goes—huntin." She was glad too, her, she would be all alone, eh? Anyway, so anyhow, nex marnin start—with the man, eh? The little girl, she stays to the house with the woman. They used to go in the woods—an the more he was to see her, the more he was to *like* her. Oh my God, set to think when she got in age, eh? Now—they made a promise before they left home, eh, well, er, she wouldn get married unless—his word, eh, he says for her to get married, she can get married—an if she don want, well he can't get married, or she can't get married—see?

G.T.: Right.

—So, one day anyhow, he hasks the girl—in marriage eh? "Well," she said, "I can't. Because," she says, "the promise we made, me n my brother before we left home," she said, "that I wouldn be able to get married now, unless his consent, eh, without gettin his word." Okay. So anyway, he for days use to go in the woods with the prince who was *number one*, was good to im an everything, eh, but still he was good to im, eh? But that day, he was *sulkin*, he was hardly talk to him. So anyway, it got after two days... an now—wait now—oh yes! Not the first day—the second day, he told his sister, he said, he said eh, "Is er... I finds him funny," he said, "the prince. Ever since I'm here," he said, "he was good humour with me all the time, talkin, jokin, evrything eh? An," he says, "it's *two days* today—that er—he's not the same with me at all." He says, "I think," he says, "he wants us to get from here, he's tired of us there—he wants us to go."—"No," she said, "it's not that. Well", she says, "he never told you, but," she says, "I'm goin a have to tell you," she says, "he hasked me in marriage—an I said I couldn get married unless your word, eh?"—"My gosh!" he said, "you knowed yourself you should get married to—me," he said, "I don care."—"Oh well," she says, "the promise you made, eh?"—"Yes, sure, you can get married." Okay. So anyhow, that night then, eh, so he goes with her, you know, eh, an they talk—an e told er—she told im—she told im that, you know, he said—sure for to get married up. He almos come crazy! Almos come crazy! No! I don't think I'm gonna tell it—wait now. No—she, he never, he never, she—she never tole the prince at all there. So the nex marnin—they were back in the woods again. An he sat down, eh—so anyhow, they sat down the two o them. He said, he said, "Prince, er—something wrong with you," he said. "Something wrong," he said. "Is you tired of us? Tell me," he said, "if you're tired of us"—he said, "well tell me an we'll go."—"Oh no!" he says, "it's not that—it's not that," he said. "It's not that at all. No, he never told his sister, I'm ahead o my story—he says "It's not that," he says. He says, "What can it be?" he says. "Somethin?"—"Yes," he says, "somethin."—"Well, he says, "tell me. If I can't help you," he says, "I'll luv you."—"Well," he said, eh, "I'll tell you," he said. "I hasked your sister," he says "in marriage, eh, an she tole me she couldn." She says. "Why?"—"Well," he said, "that's the promise he's made when he's left home, eh."—"Yes," he said, "that's true. But," he said, "if you wants to marry her, my poor—boy," he says, "go ahead." Oh well, he, he almos come *crazy*! He said, "We're not goin in the woods, let's go back—go back to the house," he said. An he was *right lively* when he got to the house, you know, eh.... So anyhow, he goes where she was, the girl—he told her, he said, "It's okay now," he says, "he tole me I can have you." An her she was to like him too. Pretty! Oh! I never seen that, me!

B.O.:   Ah ha ha ha!

—So anyhow, they got married there—now—there's—lots, lots longer than that—but I don know, eh?

Commentary and Notes

Mrs. Kerfont, like most storytellers in the private or family tradition, is always ready to tell fragments of tales as well as complete versions. It is all the more remarkable that she can make of an episode from a longer tale a fascinating and highly tense narration. The narrative content is indeed slight, but her use of dialogue, which is both economic and dramatic, amply compensates for this lack.

Mrs. Kerfont could not recall the source of her tale, any more than she could remember it in its entirety, which was "lots, lots longer than that."

It is possible that this is a fragment from AT 450, *Little Brother and Little Sister*, but there are so few readily identifiable elements in the tale one can hardly say more. Motifs in the tale include P253, *Sister and Brother*; L162, *Lowly heroine marries prince (king)*; and compare motifs S143, *Abandonment in forest*, and S301, *Children abandoned (exposed)*.

If this fragment does indeed come from AT 450, it would be the only version of it so far recorded from French Newfoundlanders. On the other hand, according to Paul Delarue and Marie-Louise Tenèze's *Le Conte populaire français*, the tale is not well known in France either, only a dozen versions having been noted. Three versions only are known in Quebec. AT 451, *The Maiden Who Seeks her Brothers*, broadly related to AT 450, is better known both in France and Quebec (or at least in North American French tradition) and the Centre d'Etudes Franco-Terreneuviennes has two versions of it.

THE GIRL IN THE POT

One time dere was a man an a woman dey ad a little boy an a little girl an him, he use to go up in the country every marnin an she was to go up an bring his, his lunch eh? So anyhow dey was a good size, dey was a good size de little boy an little girl an dey was all time played together eh? So anyhow, now e tole is wife, "Tomorrow," e says "I'm goin," e says, "an I'm goin—an ave some meat for my dinner."—"My," she says, "I got no meat."—"You're goin to *fine* some," e says, "an be sure to ave some. If you don ave no meat you know what you're gonna get." My God, er, where to get meat, she didn know eh? But anyhow, he, he went in the woods. So she tole the little boy, she says, "You're gonna go outdoors an get me a armful a wood." An time e was gone outdoors she ad a moses big bar on de stove an time the little boy was gone outdoors she took er little girl an whacked er in the pot.

B.O.:   Oh! Oh!

—Unrigs, unrigs, unriggeds er an drag er in the pot. So anyhow de little boy come an put de wood on side de stove. Un, den er, *là*, she said er, "You're gonna drive de fire an me I'll be gone to de store." Okay. Now e was, im, e was makin fire in. *A dit, "Tit-Frère, Tit-Frère," a dit, "tu m'brûles, tu m'brûles!"* [She says, "Little Brother, Little Brother," she says, "you're burning me, you're burning me!]—Da's from de story, eh? E look aroun, e couldn see er, eh? *A dit, "Tit-Frère," a dit, "tu m'brûles!"* [She says, "Little Brother," she says, "you're burning me!] E heist up de cover to see what was in dere—all cooked.

B.O.:   Oh my!

—It's er vice e eard, see, dat see, she was cooked see. E pulled out quick an den so after brought er out. E never put er in dough. "*Là*," she said, "You're gonna go bring your, er, your father's dinner you." E says, "Where's my little sister?" She

162

says, "I don know, gone outdoors somewhere," she says. "Well," she says, "go alone." Oh, and she packs it up into a basket y'know an.... So e went, brought is father, his father's lunch, an every little bone his father use to heave out, e use to pick it up—put it back into his bag. He says, "What are you doin dat for?" E said, "Fer nutting," e says, "fer my, fer to play on my way goin ome," e said. E knowed. After is father was all finish e took all de bones an put it in is basket an takes off...wait now...wait now, wait now, wait now, no. On is way goin eh, is a big sheet, big white sheet come down on de groun eh? An e sit down dere a long spell on dat sheet eh. Den after e went an brought is father a lunch now an e—an on is way comin dat sheet come down again an nabbed im an fritch, gone wid im. So she wait for er little boy. She wait. So de ole man come down in de evenin. Come in an says, "Where's de children?" She says, "I dunno," she says. "Dat little boy is not come yet dat brought your dinner eh?" E said, "Yes, e come all alone."—"*Mais* [But]," she says, "e's not ere yet."—"Well," e says, "fine dem!" e says, "or you're gonna be killed."— "Well," she says, "I'm gonna tell you de truth. You wanted meat for your dinner, eh?" E said, "Yes."—"Well," she said, "I cooked de little girl."—"What!" e said, "You cooked de little girl for me for my dinner?" She said, "Yes, to ave peace wit you," she said. I said, she said, "I sent de, de little boy,"—I don know, I fergets is name anyway—she said, "I sent de boy wit it to bring it to, fer you to eat so e'd never return eh?"—"*Mes amis, ej la prends par la friggin du cou et ej zig! Coupe, coupe d'Dieu prends ça!*" [My friends, I grab her by her friggin neck and zig! Cut, cut by God take that!]

B.O.:   Ah ha, ha ha!

—*Pis c'est tout*. [And that's all.] Da's all it is *là*.

Commentary and Notes

It seems likely that the preceding tale brought this one to Mrs. Kerfont's mind, as both tales have two children as the central characters. This, like the preceding tale, is fragmentary.

Apart from Mrs. Ozon's predictable reactions, the reader will note in particular Mrs. Kerfont's use of French phrases at the most dramatic moments in her narration. She says moreover that they belong to the tale, "Da's from de story, eh?" One must suppose that she very clearly recalled such key phrases, while not able to remember her source for the tale.

The tale seems to be a fragment of the international tale-type AT 720, *My Mother Slew Me; My Father Ate Me. The Juniper Tree*. Motifs in the tale include P253, *Sister and brother*; G61, *Relative's flesh eaten unwittingly*; E607.1, *Bones of dead collected and buried*; N271, *Murder will out*; and Q211, *Murder punished*.

More than sixty versions of this tale have been recorded in France, a dozen in French-speaking areas of North America. The Archives of the Centre d'Etudes Franco-Terreneuviennes possess a second, equally fragmentary version, with however some important differences in it, little red shoes are offered to the child returning with the biggest bundle of firewood (this element being absent from Mrs. Kerfont's version); if one can judge by Paul Delarue and Marie-Louise Tenèze's *Le Conte populaire français* (II, 707), this motif is characteristically Breton.

It seems possible that the French words used by Mrs. Kerfont (*Ti-Frère, Ti-Frère, tu m'brûles, tu m'brûles*) may have been part of a sung refrain; in most French versions of the tale, a similar refrain occurs at the crucial moment. The version as a whole seems closer to Breton forms of the tale than to those of other French provinces. One can readily understand the importance Mrs. Kerfont attached to the phrase, which she did not translate.

THE STORY OF THE GARDENER

That was a man and a woman, they had this baby eh. They had, they were a long way from the church and they were the only people living there eh? And they couldn't find a godfather and godmother for their baby, eh. So one day, she takes her baby and packs him up anyway, the woman, and then she says, she says, "I've got to find a godmother and godfather for my baby today because it's time he was baptised." So she says, "The first person I find, I'll take for godfather and god-mother." So she takes her baby and takes off and then anyway she walks a ways and then she meets a woman, eh? She asks her if she likes her baby. She says, "I'm going to get him baptised, but I haven't got a godmother." She says, "Would you go godmother for my baby?" She says, "Yes." She says, "You go to church," she says, "I'll be there too." So then she says, "I haven't got a godfather," eh, "but," she says, "the first person I find will go godfather for my baby." So anyway she walks a ways and she meets this man eh. "Where are you going with your baby?"—"Well," she says, "I'm going to get him baptised," she says, "I found a godmother but I haven't got a godfather." She says, "Would you go godfather?" He says, "Yes, right away." He says, "You go on," he says, "we'll be there soon. I'll be there soon," he says. So there she goes to the church, eh. And then the priest he comes and then when she comes they're both there. So she baptised her baby and she goes home. He says, "Did you find a godfather and godmother?" She says, "Yes." So she didn't know who they were eh. So the baby grew up until he was old enough to go to school. So one day anyway, he was going to school and he was walking by a little brook and every time he passed by the little brook he used to play in the brook eh. Anyway that day he starts playing in the brook and then when he gets up to go, eh, well this woman comes up to him, eh. So he says, "Hello," and she says, "Hello," she says, "I guess you don't know me." He said, she says, "I'm your godmother." So anyway, she says, "Put your head in the brook," she says, "as far as your hairline," eh. She says, "Be careful not to go further." She says, "As far as your hairline, soak your hair in the water," eh. Anyway, does as his godmother tells him, eh, his head in the brook. And there, when he'd gotten up, his hair was all golden, eh. So anyway she gets a beret and puts it on his head to his hairline eh. And then she says, "Now"—she says to him, eh?—"Don't take that cap off your head until I tell you," eh. So anyway every night the little boy came home, they wanted to take his cap off but he didn't want to eh? So then, it's long too, eh? There anyway, he grows up there and when he was clear of school he says, "I'm going to look for work," eh. His father and mother were poor you know. So anyway, he walks, anyway, he walks and he walks for days and nights, eh. There anyway, he comes to a castle, a king's castle. To the door. He goes to open the door. She says, "What do you want?" He says, "I want to see the king, I want to talk to him." She tells the king, and there anyway the king tells him to come in, eh. That a little boy wanted him, eh. He says, "Tell him to come in." So he comes in and goes up to the king and he says now, "What do you want?"—"Well," he says, "me, I'm looking for a job." I says, "My father and my mother are poor and," he says, "there's only me and," he says, "I'd like to get some work to help them out."—"Well," he says, "I've got no work to give you only," he says, "a helper for my gardener." He says, "I've got a gardener and," he says, "he's by himself so," he says," you can—I'll keep you to give him a hand." So anyway the next morning—slept that night—the next morning he got up to go to his job, you know. He goes to the garden. His godmother comes. She says, "Now do as I tell you." She says, "Me, I'm your godmother." She says, "Do as I tell you," she says. She says, "You'll be okay," she says. She says, "Don't plant your flowers with the roots down. Plant your flowers with the roots up."—"But," he says, "they won't grow." She says, "Yes, they'll grow." There anyway he does as his godmother tells him. He plants his flowers, he planted his flowers with the roots up, eh? And there now the other gardener tells him, he says, "Why are you doing that?"—"Well," he says, "that's how I plant my flowers, me," he says, "with the roots up."—"But," he says, "you're crazy! Your flowers aren't going to grow," he says, "you've got the roots up."—"Uh well," he says, "that's that. That's the way it's got to be." The next morning when he gets up, and goes to his garden, the flowers are all in flower, eh?

A.K.: Oh my God!

—And the other one his flowers were *dull* y'know. So, he does that for a while. There, the other fellow was jealous, him. Anyway, he tells lies to the king and so the king calls him and says, he says, "I can't keep you." He says, "I can't do it," he says. He says, "The other gardener is supposed to be the boss." He says, "Now you've got a better garden than him, so," he says, "he's not happy." It caused a problem, that did. So he says, "I'm going to put you to take—to care for the horses." So anyway, "Happy with that?"—"Oh yeah," he says, they had, he had three horses eh. And anyway the first morning he went to f—feed his horses his godmother comes eh. And there was an old one there, an old horse. It was a misery for him to move, eh? She says to him, "Now, feed that one better than the others. So," she says, "you're going to spoil that one." Okay. She says, "Me, I'm your godmother." And so in no time at all the horses were right strong. The old horse looked as young as a, as a three year old, eh. He was feeding well you know. From time to time she came to see. So anyway—er, so the king had three daughters. So anyway they get jealous. There, the, the, the other gardener didn't want him eh. So he says to the king, he says, "Get a little cabin made for me outside and I'll go stay there, in my cabin, by myself." So he says, "I'll have my own place, be able to do what I like." Okay, builds a cabin and off he goes. To stay in, in the little cabin. So, anyway the king's three daughters there now, eh, they were up in their room there them. Anyway the first night—there he was, he was kind of in love with one of them there y'know. They weren't allowed to go to his cabin. The first night, once it was really dark, he takes off his cap and goes once around the cabin, once inside. They saw that. The oldest said, "There's something in there," she says, "I'm going to see." So yes, knocks on the door. He opens the door. He says, "Yeah? Where are you going?"—"Me," she says, "I'm coming here." He says, "Go away. I don't want you here. Your father brought me here," he says, "he's going to tell me off again and he'll send me away."—"No," she says, "We saw something," she says. She says, "It was like a light." She says, "It went once around your cabin and then went in."—"That's not true, that!" he says, "Go on, go off home. I don't want you here." She takes off anyway. That night goes by and the next the girl, the two, eh, the second one, she says, "Tonight, me, I'm going," she says, "I'm going to see who it is, to have a look." So, he goes twice around the cabin and then whish! goes inside again. Yeah, goes inside again. And she get there, knocks at the door. He says, "Where're you going?" She says, "I saw something pretty just now," she says. She says, "It looked like a light," she said, "it went twice ar, around your cabin and," she said, "it went inside."—"That's not true," he says. "I know what you're doing. You want to come in here, you want to come in here, like your sister, she came here last night," he said. "You want to come in here and make me lose my job again." He says, "Go away! Don't want you here." She takes off. So anyway, no way, eh. "Ah!" she says, "There's no way to get around him," she says, "I don't know." She says, "I'm not going again." Well the youngest said, "Tomorrow night, I'm going to go. *I bet you*," she says, "I'll find out, me. I'm going to find out what's going inside there." So the next evening, at nightfall, they were up there, eh. Takes off his cap, it's really dark....

A.K.: Take your fingers from over your mouth! Take your fingers from over your mouth!

—Oh you, you're crazy!

165

A.K.:   Ha ha ha!

—There anyway, the third night, that's the youngest eh. Goes three times around the cabin and whish! into the cabin again. She says, "I'm going." She asks him to find out what the truth is. So, yeah, knocks on the door. Opens the door. "Where are you going?" She says, "I've come."—"Well," he says, "come in."—"Well," she says, "we saw something pretty." She says, "Tonight, I've got to know the truth." She says, "There's something here." He says, "What do you think's here?"—"Well," she says, "I don't know." She says, "It went three times around your cabin and then it went inside and," she said, "it's in here."—"Ah!" he says, "I didn't see anything, me." There anyway they start making love...

A.K.:   Uh gee, that's good, that!

—Yeah, making love. There *anymore*, when it was time enough, he sends her home. He says, "Off you go. If your father finds out," he says, "he'll make me lose my job again." There anyway, she takes off home. There her sisters ask her. "Ah!" she says, "There's no way to get anywhere with him."—"But," they said, "How is it you got in and the rest of us couldn't get in?"—"Uh gee," she says, "I don't know, I can't tell you." So every night when her sisters were asleep she went, eh, to find him and—yeah. It was like that anyway until he asked her to marry him eh? So anyway she says, "Yeah. But," she says, "my parents will be against it," she says, "you, you're a gardener." There anyway he says, "The king put me to it." And he says to his daughter, "You're not marrying that gardener, not you! A girl like you," he says, "marrying a gardener! What will it look like," he says, "dishonouring my family, that's all." He kicks her out. There, she told him, she says then, "Still I'm not, I'm not going to give him up." She says, "I love him."—"Well," he says, "clear out! Don't come back anymore!" He kicks her out anyway. So anyway when the time came for the, the wedding, he didn't want to hear talk of it. No, no, it's not like that. There, the first one gets married, the oldest, she gets married to a prince. They weren't asked to the wedding—them. And the second got married. No. It's not like that. When the first one got married, eh, well they were married there, them, they are married anyway.

A.K.:   Who?

—They are married, the prince, the prince and the gardener. I made a mistake. So there anyway the oldest gets married, and they weren't asked to the wedding, eh. So he says to his wife he says, "We're going to the wedding tonight." She says, "You're crazy, you." She says, "We haven't been asked." She says, "I've been looking after my father's castle," she says, "it's not to have the same right," he says, "yeah, we're going." Anyway, he goes into his room, his godmother was there, eh. And she gives him three nuts—you know what a nut is, eh?

G.T.:   Hm.

—Hazel nut. She says, "Now in that," she says, "there's a suit in each one. And," she says, "the wedding will go for three nights, so," she says, "you'll go to the three weddings, to the three nights." And she said, "You'll have a change of clothes in each nut," eh. So anyway when it came time to get rigged up, he says, "It's time to get rigged," eh, "But," she says, "I'm not going to a wedding, not me," she says, "I haven't got a dress."—"Well," he says, "Here, crack this nut," he says, "your suit is inside." So there she cracks her nut, eh. She put it on, she saw it, the colour of the sun, eh?

A.K.:   Oh God!

—In the nut, eh? And him he cracks his and it was the same, eh? Each a suit the same colour. So, his godmother said to him, she says, "When you're ready, there'll be a horse and carriage to take you there." So they get rigged out and off they go. When they get there, well, the king, nobody knew them, eh?—"Look!"

166

A.K.:   Oh!

—That's the way they made the stories. You did that first. There anyway it goes on. So the second night when it was time they crack the second nut. Well this time, so it was a suit the colour—of the moon. So off they go but nobody knew them, eh? So when the time was over, they took off, eh? And so then a bit later on the third night, they crack the third nut and it had a suit the colour of stars. And so the third night now they each had—to tell a story....

A.K.:   Oh yeah?

—So anyway—there all the others told stories, it was only the last two left, eh. Those two, eh. So he starts telling his story, eh. When he had left home and, he said he had been to the king and had stayed there he says. "This is where I worked—do you remember," he says, "the little gardener," he says, "who planted his flowers with the roots up?—"That's not you!" he says. He says "Yeah, that's me."—"Well," he says, "you banished me from the castle," he says, "and," he says, "now I'm as good as you. I married your daughter for—happy—happiness, but," he says, "I'm just as good as you all the same." And that's the end there.

Commentary and Notes

The Gardener is a fine example of a tale told in the private or family tradition. After four tales told by Mrs. Kerfont, she insisted that her friend take her turn. Once convinced, Mrs. Ozon began a narration in which a goodly number of the metanarrative devices discussed in chapter IV make their appearance.

Mrs. Ozon notes, shortly after the transformation of the boy's hair, that "...it's long too, eh?" She wanted to focus my attention on the length of the tale she had begun, but at the same time to have me understand that very long narrations were no longer appreciated. Later, there was an exchange involving a teasing reprimand, when Mrs. Kerfont exhorted her friend to take her fingers from in front of her mouth. Still later, in a mild sexual allusion, Mrs. Kerfont loudly approved of the hero and heroine "making love," that is, kissing.

I was the recipient of an unsolicited explanation, when Mrs. Ozon glossed the word *noix*. In terms of the narrative content, it was obviously important that the meaning of the word be understood. On three occasions Mrs. Ozon made mistakes in her narration, a common enough occurrence in the private tradition, if not in the public. She did not conclude her story with a closing formula, something which is also quite characteristic of her tradition.

Alongside these somewhat negative remarks should be placed the agreeable tension which governed the whole narration. Mrs. Ozon always told her tales enthusiastically, even when she made a mistake. But both ladies went to it with a will during our recording sessions. The tales were less important than the human warmth and personal interaction which characterized our time together.

Mrs. Ozon attributed her version of the tale to her late husband Jean Ozon, whose father was from St. Malo.

Mrs. Ozon's tale is a version of the international tale-type AT 314, *The Youth Transformed to a Horse*, although in a quite abridged form. Motifs include F311.1, *Fairy Godmother*; P296, *Godparents*; D1788.1, *Magic results from contact with water*; D475.1.10, *Transformation: hair to gold*; K1816.1, *Gardener disguise*; K1816.0.3, *Menial disguise of princess's lover*; T91.6.4, *Princess falls in love with lowly boy*; T55.1, *Princess declares her love for lowly hero.*; T31.1, *Lovers' meeting: hero in service of lady's father*; L113.1.0.1, *Heroine endures hardships with menial husband*; D1868.1, *Broken down nag becomes magnificent riding horse*; B316, *Abused and pampered horses*; F821.1.5, *Dress of gold, silver, color of sun, moon and stars*; H11.1, *Recognition by telling life history*.

This tale has been collected in some forty versions in France and in more than a dozen from the French of North America. It is therefore a tale well rooted in French tradition (see Delarue & Tenèze, *Le Conte populaire français*, I, 242-263). The Centre d'Etudes Franco-Terreneuviennes has three versions in addition to Mrs. Ozon's, all three similarly abridged. It may be that future fieldwork will record more complete versions.

FIVE CENTS THE HAIR

I know he wanted to send his son to sell his cow—it was Jack, eh?

G.T.: Yes.

A.K.: Five cents the hair.

—Yeah.

G.T.: Eh?

—She wants five cents the hair.

G.T.: Yeah.

—For her cow, eh?

G.T.: Yeah.

—He meets a man, he says, "Where are you going with your cow?"—"I'm going to sell it," he says. "How much do you want for your cow?"—"Well," he says, "I'm selling her for five cents the hair."

A.K.: Ha ha ha!

—It's a story! "Well," he says, "you're asking quite a lot for your cow."—"Uh well," he says, "if I don't get five cents the hair, you don't get my cow." Anyway, he—he sets off, eh. He meets another man. Anyway he says, "Where are you going with your cow, Jack?"—"Yeah," he says, "I'm going with my cow. I'm going to sell her." He says, "What are you asking for your cow?"—"Five cents the hair."—"Uh," he says, "you're asking too much for your cow. You won't sell her."—"Well," he says, "I've got to ask what my cow's worth." He says, "If you don't give me five cents the hair," he says, "I won't sell her." Well! Anyway, he finds a third man and asks the same thing, eh? And so he asks him where he's going with his cow and he says, "I'm going to sell my cow." He says, "How much are you asking for your cow?" He says, "I'm asking five cents the hair." He says, "Well," he says, "you won't sell her."—"Well," he says, "leave it, you don't want her, leave it. Ask another price for my cow," he says, "wait." Anyway, he walks. He comes to a church. He ties up his cow outside and goes in. There anyway, he sees a statue of the Holy Virgin. He goes up to it, he says to it, "Do you want to buy my cow, you?" No answer. It was a statue, eh. He says, "I'm asking you if you want to buy my cow." And he says, "Answer! If you don't answer," he says, "you'll be sorry."

A.K.: Ha ha ha!

—Uh, so there anyway, doesn't answer. Yeah. "Well," he says, "I'll ask you for the third time. Speak," he says, "if you don't answer," he says, "you're going to give me a proper answer, or you'll be sorry." He asks her if she would buy his cow—for the third time again. No answer. He takes a stick and gives it to her. He breaks her. But that's where she's got the treasure, eh!

A.K.: Ohhh!

—And there he starts picking it up, he was saying "That's enough, that's enough, that's enough!" He says, "Not too much, not too much!"

A.K.: Ha ha ha!

—So that was funny, eh? It kept on pouring out eh?

A.K.: Well yes.

—He got a sack full of money and leaves the cow there and takes off home with the sack of money eh? He's had enough, five cents the hair!

A.K.:   Uh yeah!

Commentary and Notes

The beginning of this story illustrates well how, in the private or family tradition, a tale is often set in motion. Mrs. Ozon was asked if she knew any *Jack* tales, Jack being the usual hero of French *Märchen* in Newfoundland; by recalling the motif of the cow's price, which she associated with the name *Jack*, she was able to remember her version of the tale.

The reader will note the phrase "It's a story!" (C'est in conte!), common in the private or family tradition when a particular motif provokes laughter from the audience. Public narrators did not have to justify their stories in this way; an unlikely motif was accepted without difficulty. Mrs. Ozon could not remember the source of her tale.

Five Cents The Hair is a version of the international tale-type AT 1643, *The Broken Statue*, including motifs J1853.1, *Fool sells goods to a statue*, and J1853.1.1, *Money from broken statue*. *The Types of the Folktale* records fifteen versions of the tale for France, but seems unaware of the handful of versions held in Quebec, at Laval University's *Archives de Folklore*. The Centre d'Etudes Franco-Terreneuviennes has two other versions of the tale, in which the hero is named *Cornantchul* (indicative of their Breton origins). For a general discussion of the fool in French tradition, and references to other French versions of the tale, see *Contes de Jean-le-Sot*. (Versions collected in Angoumois and Saintonge and assembled by Mme. A. Cadet, Presentation and Commentary by Gerald Thomas, Special Number, *Société d'Etudes Folkloriques du Centre-Ouest*, 1972), 3-60.

THE LION IN THE FOREST

Well, one time there was a man and a woman. They ad three sons—Jack an Bill an Tom. An they were poor off. No work or nothin. So Tom told them one marnin, e said, "I'm going," he said, "for a job somewheres," he said, "if I can find—to make some money." Okay. The next marnin he takes his bundle an—lunch an off he start. So he travelled an travelled—through the fores—by an by he seen a *maudit* [damned, great] big lion. "Where you goin Tom?"—"Oh, she says, "that lion talks"—She says, "I don know if they all talks," she says, "I talk when I need, when I got need," she said. An she, "Where you going?"—"Well," she says, "me," he says, "I'm goin look for a job somewheres. Home," he said, "we're starvin," he says, "nothin to eat."—"Well," she said, this lion, "this forest," she said, "is alive with all kinds o wild beastses," she said, "an if they sees you, they're gonna eat you."—"Well," he says, "die here an die at home o starvation," he says, "it's the same thing."—"Well, okay," she says, "I'm gonna help you." She says, "Take a hair out o my tail, put it in your pocket and I'll see you to go. Now they'll be around you, those beastses, don't mind them, keep on goin, they wouldn touch you." Okay. Anyhow, all that time, he travelled for three days an three nights there, an at the end—o three nights—seen a little light in the woods. So goes into the camp—knocked at the door—an ole woman come to the door. She says, "Where you goin my poor Tom?" she says. "Well," he said, "granmother, I don know. I'm astray somewhere. I'm goin to find if I can find a job somewheres," he says, "we're starvin," he says, "at home."—"Well," she says, "you're gonna sleep with me tonight," she said, "now maybe you could sleep here tonight," she says, "an tomorrow you go further." Okay. So he was tired, n sleepy, hungry. So she got him his supper, then after supper he was there, he was fallin asleep. She says, "You sleepy, Tom?" He said, "Yes, granmother, sleepy."—"Well," she says, "you're gonna go to bed," she says. "It's not a nice room, but," she says, "but it's a nice bed," she says. Okay. So he, he got down, had to crawl on his hands an knees behind her, couldn see nothin at all. Dark as pitch. So she opened the room door, an she said, "Hold up now," she says, "what you do," she says, "don't you

169

rise out o your bed." Okay. He says, "Granmother, I'm too tired." Anyway, she shuts the door, when she shut the door, my God! The room come full o lights—an he look in the corner—beautiful lady! "Tom!" she says, "come on" she says, "come on, we'll have a good time tonight, me n you," she says. Well, my God! he was tired, *mais i l'a garâchée tout en grand*! [but he threw it (the blanket) over him!]

B.O.:   Ha ha ha ha! I guess!

—He trow the blankets over him an he took her! An he was jus gonna give her a kiss, *alle a rentré d'dans ielle, la vieille là* [she came in her, the old woman there].

B.O.:   Oh!

—"Ah ha! She told you," she said, "not to move from your bed, eh? Now," she said, "you're there, you're gonna stay there!" She turned him to a stone. Oh my! In a stone! Now all that time—that's what I hates, go over there—so anyhow, one marnin, Bill, "Now," he says, "Tom," he says, "maybe," he says, "Tom got a job," he says, "workin—me," he says, "I'm here," he says, "starvin. I'm goin too," he says, "tomorrow marnin." Okay. Nex marnin, takes his bundle an off he start. So he drove through the mountain, er through the fores—by n by—but he seen ahead of him a big er—lion. She says, "Bill," she says, "where you goin?"—"Oh, you talk!" She said, "Yes, I talk when I got need to," she said. An er, she said, "Where you goin?"—"Well me," he says, "I'm goin lookin for a job," he says, "if I can—I'm goin to look for to get—find a job. We were starvin at home," he says, "nothin to eat."—"Well," she says, "this forest," she said "is alive with all kinds of beastses, they gonna eat you!"—"I don care," he said. "Die here, die home o starvation it's the same thing. So I got to go anyway."—"Well," she said, "if you gonna go, well I'm gonna help you," she says. "Take a hair out o my tail, put it in your pocket an," she says, "keep on goin," she said—"they'll never harm you." Anyhow, he travelled three days an three nights too, an at the end o tree nights he came to that *cabane* [cabin, shack] too, there—camp. Knocked to the door—oh! the old woman come to the door. "Well, well, well," she says, "Bill," she says, "where you a goin?"—"Well, granmother," he says, "me," he says, "I'm goin to see if I can find a job. See, we're starvin," he says, "at home."—"Well," she said, "you'll stay here tonight, an tomorrow," she said, "you'll go further." He was glad. So—she got him his supper—he was starved—to eat. Then after, he sat down on the *banc* [bench] for to chat there. Ah! When she see he was fallin asleep, she said, "You're sleepy, Tom—Bill." He said, "Yes granmother, I'm tired," he said, "I'm all in."—"Well" she said, "go to bed," she said. So she takes him, puts him in the room there—was dark!—he had to crawl—his hands an knees behind her! "Now," she says, "Bill," she says, "you got a nice bed, the room's not very nice but the bed is nice. Now," she said, "if what you do, don't you rise out your bed!"—"No, no," he said, "granmother," he said, "I'm too sleepy an tired for that." Okay. She close the door behind her—the name o God! As soon she close the door, the lights in the room! S'cruel! An the lady in the corner—she was ten times prettier there!

B.O.:   Oh oh! [She claps her hands.]

—"Bill," she said, "come on!" she says, "have a good time, me an you tonight!" she says. He takes the blankets off then an fritch in the corner. [Laughter] An he got her there an took her round the neck for to give her a kiss *et la vieille rente*! [and the old woman comes in!] "Ah!" she says, "I tole you shouldn move from your bed, now," she says, "you're there, you're gonna remain there," she says. She turned him to a stone too. *Là* [There]. Anyway, keep on going just as well, I spose. So all that time, he—it was a long time an—Jack set out. He was only small, him—*tout ptit, tout ptit* [right small, right small]. Well, he told his mother an father, he says, "Now," he says, "Bill an Tom has gone," he said. "Maybe they're workin," he says, "havin a good time—me I'm starvin"—he said, "I'm goin tomorrow marnin." Ey said, "You

170

gonna all go an leave us alone—ole that we is."—"Well," he said, "I can't help that. Gotta go an look for something to eat," he says. Okay. Next marnin he takes his bundle an off he start. Goes in the fores an travel through the fores—by an by he look—he seen a big lion come toward him—he got scared. Him so small—right small he was. "Well," she says, "Jack," she says, "where you goin? A small little boy like you!"—"Well," he says, "granmother," he says—er—he said, "the lion talks in here?" She said, "Yes, I do. Of all talks, I talks—when I got need to," she said. "Where you goin?"—"Well," he said, "I'm goin," says, "where I can find a job," he said. "We're starvin," he said, "at, nothin to eat."—"Well," she said, "this place," she says, "this land, s'all kinds o beastses. They gonna find you, they gonna eat you!"—"I don't care—die here, die at home o starvation, it's the same thing," he said. "Well," she said, "if you're gonna go," she said, "I'm gonna help you along." She says, "Take a hair out o my tail, put it in your pocket," she says, "keep on goin," she says, "they'll never harm you. They'd be around you, but they wouldn hurt you." *C'tait ielle, la vache!* [It was her, the cow!] I should tell it just the same, no man ever know that though.

B.O.:   Ha ha! Makes no difference!

—So anyhow he travelled for tree days an tree nights too. So the last night, anyhow, he comes—seen the light there, he went an knocked at the door. "Oh my God!" she said, "Where you goin, poor little boy, where you going?"—"Well granmother," he said, "I'm goin to look for a job somewheres," he said. He says, "Home, we're starvin," he said, "my father an mother's ey's right old."—"Well," she says, "come on," she says, "the night, stay here, an go farther tomorrow." Okay. Comes in. She gives him his supper. Started chattin to him, by an by he was fallin asleep. She says, "You sleepy, Jack?" He said, "Yes, my granmother," he said, "sleepy an tired." Okay. She says, "You're goin a go to bed," she says. "It's a nice bed," she said, "but," she said, "the room's not very nice."—"It's nothin," he said, "I don care." So she goes ahead an him behind. Oh my God! Dark! Oh my God! He had to crawl behind her! Anyhow, she opens the door, nice bed. "Now," she says, "Jack, for what you do," she says, "don't you rise out o your bed!"—"No, no," he says, "granmother, I don care what I sees or what I hears, I don't get out—too tired! I'm all in," he said, "all in!" After she gone out the door, the door closed behind her, *mes amis de Dieu* [my friends by God], the lights in the room, s'cruel! An that pretty girl in the corner, she was ten times prettier again! "Come on Jack," she says, "come on!" she says—"have a time me an you tonight," she says, "pass away the night," she says. "If you wants a time," he says, "come find me! Me go find you, I'm not goin!" He cover his head.

B.O.:   Oh ho ho!

—So the next marnin, my gosh! get up—she was up her. "Well now," she says, "Jack," she says, "I'm gonna give you your breakfast an after," she says, "I'm gonna make a note out for you. You gotta go to the king's"—I don't know how many hundred miles from there the king was—I don remember that. An he was gonna be there for fair twelve o'clock. My gosh! He said, "I can't be there for twelve o'clock— bein so small."—"Nothin," she says, "I'll be there for twelve o'clock—jus." Okay. He eats his breakfast an she was makin a note—for the king now. "Now," she said, "you gotta go to the king," she says. "An you gotta get there at twelve o'clock— and—with the arms there, you know—eh?" Got arms there, you know—the—the—

G.T.:   On the clock?

—No no no no. Okay. My God!—Y'know, the soldiers n that—guardin—

G.T.:   Yes.

B.O.:   Oh yeah, yeah.

171

—Yeah—the guard the castle, eh? She said, "They're goin a rise their guns to shoot you but heist up your hand—they'll put down their guns." Okay. So—she gives him the note n—an right, twelve o'clock, he arrives to the king. So the mens is all there with their guns for to shoot him, eh? So he heists his hand—so they put down their guns. So—he went to the castle an he knocked to the door an he opened the door—e said, "I'm gonna see the king." So anyhow, the sarvent goes n tell the king—there was a little boy wanted him—a small boy. Right small, eh? He called him into his...er...er...what d'ye call it—set—sitting room—an he said, er—"Wha— what you come for?" he said. "Well," he said, "I got a note for you." So he guv him the note—an on that note—he had to show him all trough his barn. All trough his castle—everything he had. They had to show it to the little boy, now. It took tree days—to show him trough his house—an it took tree more days to show him trough his barn. But he was comin down to the castle—there was a small little barn there—a little, little grey mare inside. "Well," he says, "king," he says, "one thing you never showed me," he says, "you got to show me that too."—"Not at all," he says, that's no good, I'm not showin you that." He says, "I gotta see it!" He goes—he goes in the barn—the door was locked, an he was in there with the mare, eh? "Ah well," she says, that—she spoke, her—"Well," she says, "you're well fixed off now," she said. "The night," she said, "at eleven o'clock, the night," she says, "at eleven o'clock," she says, "the ole witch will be here. An if she finds you here, she's killin me an you too!"

B.O.:   Ah!

—He couldn get the door unlock. Okay. So anyhow, it was er...ten—ten to ten. "Now," she said, she says, "she's on er way. An she's comin an the nose is draggin the ground with vexation!"

B.O.:   Ha ha!

—"Now," she said—ha ha!—"I got a tooth loose in my mouth, take it out," she said, "an get in instead, you. There, she shouldn find you." Okay. By gosh! The mighty! By n by, here in she come. "Ah!" she says, "you got a boyfriend tonight!"— "Byfriend?" she says. "Well if you tink I got a boyfriend, well," she says, "go look for him!" She look—an look everywhere—she couldn find nothin. She guv her a trimmin—she had a whip—she's trim her down—till she drop, eh? The grey mare now. An then she took off. She had only strength enough to open her mouth for him to fall out, eh?

B.O.:   Oh!

—"Now," she said, "you sees that, eh? Now tomorrow night it's gonna be ten times worse. An if she finds you here she's gonna kill you." So anyhow he stayed all that day with her—"Now the night," she says, "she's gonna be here at twelve— eleven o'clock. Leven o'clock," she said, "in the night—an she's comin wicked," she said. Anyway, ten to eleven, "Now," she said, "she's comin. Now," she says, "there's a hole, there's a—a nail gone out of my shoe, eh, well now," she says, "get in place of the nail eh, dere she wouldn find you." She put a pint more in her, eh? The old witch. Okay. God! Eleven o'clock, *mes amis, arrive* [my friends, (she) comes]. She swings the door right open. She says, "You got a boyfriend here!" she says. "Well," she said, "if you think I got it, take a look out—look for him." She'd look every-where—she couldn find him! In her ears, in her mouth, everywheres. Couldn find him. Never look underneath of her shoe though. An then after she took poundin an poundin an poundin an she fall down. All in she was. So anyhow—she took off. So anyhow she heists up her body, he come out. Starts pullin her up. "Well," she says, "you see that—n the marnin she's goin a kill me."—"My sakes," he said, "no!" She said, "In the marnin she's gonna kill me for sure," she said. "An she'll be back," she says, "tomorrow night at twelve o'clock. Wicked jus like the devil." Okay. That day passed anyhow, ten to twelve, she says, "She's on her way. Ah!" she says, "she's not nice. Now," she said, "go in my head—there's only one place where I can hide you," she said—"you'll go in my manger—there's a small little bottle in there, eh? Well," she said, "get in that an I'll put you under my tongue. There...."

B.O.:   Haaa! ha ha!

—*C'est in conte!* [It's a story!] She says, "There, she wouldn find you, eh?" Okay. "Now," she said, "that's tonight I'm gonna die."—"Oh surely!" he said—"Yes!" she said, "After I'm dead, you'll split me open—take my heart an livers—and you'll burn it up, eh? An," she says, "put it in a white handkerchief, *les cendes* [the ashes], eh?" An she says, "You'll heave it over your left shoulder. Don look where it falls," she says. Okay. Sure enough. Ten to eleven, *mes amis* [my friends], he gets inside her tongue. In the bottle. She comes in—the witch—she says, "You got a boyfriend tonight!" She said, "If you tink I got a boyfriend, you look for him." She never looked for nobody but she took her—she tanned her, she was, well, alive—well she killed her—eh? She left the door open with the vexation. So he was all right—the door was open to go out, eh? She had jus the strength enough to open her mouth an the bottle fall out—an he start smoothin her up—she says, "Don't smooth me," she says, "I'm goin to die, I'm goin to die anyway." So she died. Splits her open—takes her livers an heart—he burns it—in ashes—an takes a handkerchief an he puts it in—an he goes out an he's ready to throw it over. She was enchanted—that was the king's daughter there!

B.O.:   Oh!

—Now I don know more n that—there's a... a lot more, my dear—I don't know—I don't remember.

B.O.:   You don't remember the rest of it?

—No... dat was a nice story, boy. Laugh! That was better yet! He got her at the last though! He had a hard time.

Commentary and Notes

Although this tale is incomplete, it is well told in terms of the criteria of excellence in Franco-Newfoundland tradition. Mrs. Kerfont faithfully adheres to the rules of repetition; the reader has only to compare her telling of the meetings with the lion and the old witch by the three brothers to recognize her fidelity. Her use of formulaic language is more rigorous in this tale than in any of her preceding narrations. Her dialogues are just as lively and succinct.

On the other hand, Mrs. Kerfont does not disguise her impatience with such repetition. At the conclusion of Tom's encounter with the old woman, she says: "...that's what I hates, go over there"—she does not like repetition. Just after Bill's transformation, she shows the same impatience: "Anyway, keep on goin just as well, I spose." And at the end of the tale, she makes no great effort to recall the remainder, which is a great pity.

Other characteristic features of the private or family tradition can be observed, especially the metanarrative exchanges between Mrs. Kerfont and Mrs. Ozon. Mrs. Kerfont betrays her French origins, too, by her use of French at particularly dramatic moments. Most of her experience of tales must have been acquired through the intermediary of French.

Mrs. Kerfont attributed the tale, or at least that part of it she told us, to Mrs. Olive Marche of Cape St. George.

Although *The Lion in the Forest* includes some very well known motifs, which bring to mind several international tale-types, identification according to *The Types of the Folktale* has not been possible. *Le Conte populaire français* is no more instructive. As far as motifs are concerned, included are P251.6.1, *Three brothers;* D1023.3, *Magic hair of lion's tail*; B211.2.2, *Speaking lion*; D517, *Transformation because of disobedience*; D231, *Transformation: man to stone*; C961.2, *Transformation to stone for breaking tabu*; D131, *Transformation: man to horse*; B211.1.3, *Speaking horse*; B133.1, *Horse warns hero of danger*; F1034, *Person concealed in another's body*; compare B529.1, *Animals (sow, bitch, mare) hide boy in their belly to protect him*; and H1242, *Youngest brother alone succeeds on quest*.

THE TWENTY-FOUR ROBBERS

Well, twenty-four robbers. It was a man an a woman—no!—a king an a queen. They had one daughter. An the king him, he was been gone sailin out—the sea—for six months. At the end of six months he was to return home, eh? So anyhow, the time he was gone—she was courtin her—a young prince. So anyhow, he was gone sailin—he had six months—at the end o the six months he came ashore. So he lost one of his men—so he was talk to his wife, he said, "I lost one o my men comin."— "Well," Jack said, "I'm a goin a go, me." Crazy Jack they called him. "You!" he said. "You're not comin, not you," he said. "We're king," he said, "to my kingdom yet. No, you're not comin. We'll get another one besides you."—"Oh!" he says, "king, take me with you—you, don't know what I can do."—"Okay," he says, "go in town, get a jar o rum, an some mutton, eh?" An he says, "Don be long gone," he said, "one o'clock we'll be sailin out." Okay. He takes off in town. On his way goin in he meet his friend who use to give him a drink here an a drink there, an he had him *jagué* [drunk]. So he goes in town—he finds his rum n dat—an his meat, an he was start to come home an he look, the, the—the boat was right out! He said, "She's gone!" he said, "I'm goin back," he said, "I'm goin a tap my rum," he said, "an we gonna have drinks," he said.

B.O.:   Ha ha ha!

—With his friend. He goes back, an they drinks the—the bottle, the gallon o rum. So anyhow, after, he comes home. That night, anyhow, that prince come down. An he ask the queen then an her daughter to go visit his castle—an he said, "Tomorrow night," he says, "I'll come down an get you," he said, "with the horses, with the horse n—the horse n—n a gig." They never asked Jack that. So anyhow, the nex day, stayed there till nine o'clock, at nine o'clock he went home. The nex day. The nex evenin, oh! They sees him comin. The queen an her daughter was riggin herself up to go out—never hasked Jack if he was goin or nothin, Jack said, "Where are youse goin?"—"Well," she said, "we're goin wi him."—"What about me's? I'm goin too," he said. "You never asked me to go visitin, I'm goin the same." He says, "Where my mistress goes, I goes." So he jogs behind him—jogs behind the—whaty-calls. They took off. Well, they drove until they got tired, tired, er—got hungry—so they called to a restaurant—an him—he never went while they was to eat, he use to go with the girls, eh? He use to know the girls so well. He eat with them, but he never paid, eh?

G.T.:   [changes the tape] Okay. I think that's okay. *Bon* [Good].

—An then when he came out the kitchen, to find them—they were gone. He just could make them—goin on the road, eh? The ways he was from them! He put his cap in his hand, an he was off—an he run an he run, run, run, an he got there into it—*il a floppé* là! [he flopped down there!]

B.O.:   Ha ha!

—When he reached them at all, he was all in! So anyway, they drove. When they go there, oh! there was a big castle! So they had tole the girl, the highway robber there, they had tole the girl from the town, eh? An she, an she knows, they knowed now the—they had gone there for to attend them, eh? An her, she was to like the queen an her daughter! Okay, went there, on way there, just her, now, eh, an him. So they had some soup for their supper. So anyhow they were at the table, now her

174

she makes a note an she told it to Jack, for Jack, told Jack, she said, "You're in a highway robber's camp, er castle, tonight," she said, "an there are twenty-four. An they brought youse to kill youse. But," she said, "if youse can get in a room where's a red door," she said, "there's lots of ammunition there an lots o guns." She says, "You could take your part, eh? But," she says, "don't you sleep clear the same room as your—as your mistress." Okay. They was at the table, so Jack hauled his plate, eh? It fell on his lap. *Il a gardé* [He looked]. There was him, then the queen, then her daughter, eh? He read it—he passed it to the queen. Ah! well her, she couldn eat. *Alle a attrapé eune venette!*

B.O.: Phew!

G.T.: What did she catch?

—a *venette*.

G.T.: What's that?

B.O.: fright.

—She was frightened, eh?

G.T.: Yeah—oh yes!

—An—ha ha! a *venette*! I didn't know that!

B.O.: We call that a *venette*, us!

G.T.: Yes.

—So she passed it to her girl, but she know she'd faint right there—she'd do that—she hadn't to pass it to her. So anyway....

B.O.: What was marked down on the note?

—Well, he had told you, eh? I told you, I said that already there.

B.O.: Oh.

—So he comes out, him. He says, "Nine o'clock," he says, "all hands to bed." Okay. "Now," he says, "Jack, you go sleep in that room."—"No. I'll sleep in the same room as my mistress. I'm use to," he says, "an since I'm there, I'll sleep in the same room as them."—"You're not ashamed?"—"No, I'm not ashamed—I don't sleep with her, I sleep in the same room." In bed. An happen it was a good room! Lots of ammunition there an guns an everything. "Now," he says, "we struck it lucky," he said. An then the womens started to cry an that, eh? He says, "Don't you cry! They'll want to find out then," he said, "we'll all be killed." He was crazy, but he was not crazy there! An then her daughter knowed that, eh? She done some bawlin, her! Anyway he load up twenty-five guns—so he made a kind of a place there, across the door, an he laid his twenty-four guns an—an he kept the other one. Anyhow, something to twelve. Oh! Dey hears the steps comin upstairs. Knocks at the door—"What do you want?" He says, "A little article," he said, "I forgot in de room the night," he says, Jack says, "it's mine. Go downstairs." By an by he hears them comin—he's countin them, too—twenty-four.

B.O.: Phew!

—Comes to the door. "You're gonna open us the door?"—"Well tell us how many of youse is there, I'll open the door, yes."—"We're twenty-four!"—"Okay," he said, "I'll open the door." *Il a halé dsus* [he let them have it], zing! ha ha! All the guns went off one time there! Then he gets up, he opens the door, an he take—he got the lady—the queen there—the odder gun, eh? An one had escape, eh? He was comin to another place there in the room—might be in the corner somewhere—she lined him up—she kill im—an then him before he move—he take the—second gun and bang! bang! Goes downstairs. The girl was there. He says, "That's all there is?"—"Yes. That's all the twenty-four of them. The worse one," she says, "the ole lady." Jack says, "Where is she?"—"She's in that room there."—"Don't worry," he

175

says, "I'll get her. Now," he said, "we're gonna make sure to get ready—we're gonna wish you goodbye! But," he says, "I'll be ready to fix her when she comes out the door." Anyhow, they range themselves, er... sham—waves her goodbye—then he goes behind the door. He goes behind the door. So, oh! the door opened! Ah! She says, "They gone?"—"Yes," she says, "they're right over there goin." She holds up her head—"They gone for sure"—when her head was clear of the door, he gives her one—down she comes!

B.O.:   What did he do?

—*Il a* [he]—he killed the ole woman. That's the mother there. She was the worse one, her. Ah well, anyhow....

B.O.:   *La vieille marabaisse!* [The old hag!]

—When the queen—was like that to Jack—no, no... so anyhow, Jack, he got a horse n carriage, for him an the queen an the daughter, an he got another one for the other girl. The girl went to her place. They kept on goin, them. So the queen, when she got home, she married Jack to her daughter. Well, the gladness, eh? An then she made a note—to the king, eh? All what happened, eh? An the day they got married, that's the day—the king sailed in.

B.O.:   Phew!

—Anyway, so she got a dory, an a man, y'know. An Jack, an his wife, on his knees, an her—they went to the boat, eh? When the king seen them comin—Crazy Jack—his daughter on Crazy Jack's knees—oh! my God, he almos come crazy! Told his man, he said, "Nab him, an put him in jail right away," he says, "don delay!" So wouldn—he was vexed, he was cross, walkin the deck, eh? She wouldn pass him the note—then, eh? Anyway, when she seen him, he was well, y'know, not so vexed—so she passed him the note. Drink! *Au nom de Dieu* [In the name of God] drink!

G.T.:   But I'm drinking from the bottle!

—*Eune pile* [A pile]! Look at mine, almost gone!

G.T.:   Ah!

—Ah... then he passed him the note. He read the note. "Well," he said, "surely to God it never happened?"—"Yes!" she said, "an," she said, "only for Jack," she says, "you wouldn find us here today," she says. "We'd been all killed."—"Well now," he told his men, "go an git Jack! Don't you hurt a hair on his head!" He said, "We're all gonna go ashore—an we're gonna marry them over an we're gonna have the wedding all over again!" An then—if they're not dead—they might be livin yet.

Commentary and Notes

Mrs. Kerfont grew more and more relaxed as our storytelling session progressed, and her dialogues became more and more lively. Thus it was that when I did not grasp the meaning of the expression "attraper eune venette," Mrs. Kerfont first, then Mrs. Ozon, both offered me an explanation. This apparent break in the narrative flow in no way seemed to disturb them. This kind of exchange is quite characteristic of the private or family tradition. There are other such exchanges in the course of this narration: exclamations from Mrs. Ozon, a teasing reprimand from Mrs. Kerfont addressed to me because I was not drinking my beer fast enough.

Note should be made of Mrs. Kerfont's use of a number of phrases in French, and the bilingual exchanges between the ladies themselves, and the ladies and myself. For the first time, Mrs. Kerfont uses the typical closing formula in Franco-Newfoundland tradition: "If they're not dead—they might be livin yet."

It has not been possible to provide a precise identification of this tale according to *The Types of the Folktale*. On the other hand, the archives of the Centre d'Etudes Franco-Terreneuviennes contain several versions of tales fitting in the section AT

950-969, *Robbers and Murderers*, notably in the series AT 956 which, in general fashion, deals with the execution of thieves. I propose for Mrs. Kerfont's tale the number AT 956E* (CEFT), *The Twenty-four Robbers*. Motifs in the tale include K1626, *Would-be killers killed*; Z71.8.6, *Formulistic number: twenty-four*; and L161, *Lowly hero marries princess*.

THE OLD WITCH AND THE BALL OF WOOL

...It start, it start by a woman an a... a man an a woman, a man and, well, a man an a woman, yes, eh? They had... a one daughter, eh? An... the ole woman died, eh? An he got married to another woman an she had tree daughters eh? An they use to give her misery there.

B.O.: Yes.

—That's how it start, eh?

G.T.: Well how does it go on from there?

—Well yes. They were jealous of the other—she was pretty, her eh? She was pretty, her. An she ad three an they were ugly as the devils. An now they use to put her—all—*cendes* eh? *A la place*, eh? [—ashes, eh? On the floor, eh?] [Looking fiercely at B.O.] *A sait tu sais!* [She knows you know!]

B.O.: Ah ha ha!

—In French it goes better, eh? It goes—it's a French story.

B.O.: Me I don't know that, my dear!

—*Ah, tu sais!* [Ah, you know it!]

B.O.: I heard it often but I don't know it! I was around ten, twelve years old when Olive told me that. I was sleeping over with poor Marie, I told the story about the ball of wool and I made her laugh! Ever since then I've never heard it.

—Yes, an the ole woman, she says, she tole her, she tole her, "Tomorrow," she says, "I'm gonna spin you a ball o wool," she says, "an you're gonna go down," she says, "in town," she says, "an get it all knitted to my likin," she says. "An if it's not to my likin," she says, "you know what you're gonna get!" Okay. "I'm gonna take a piece o you now, so as you knows." Anyway, she took off. When she got a ways down the yard, the ball o wool come out of her arms, eh? An it fell, an it started to roll, eh? An it fell in a hole, eh?... That's a thought!

B.O.: Ah ha ha ha!

—An den she run to get her ball o wool eh? She looked in the hole an saw a *vieille sorciaise là* [old witch there]. Ha ha ha! An ole witch there. She said, she said, "Gimme my ball o wool." An she says, "Come down, my little girl," she says, an she says, "we're gonna make your knittin for you," she said, "the way you want it," she said, "an you'll do our work for us." Good enough. She goes down. Then, er... she had to make the beds, wash the dishes, an cook dinner. She made the beds. So they were knittin there. They were three. So after the beds was made, she says, she asked, the old witch asked the little girl, she says, "How do you find my bed, little girl?" She said, "I wish to God I had one like that to sleep every night, I'd be able to sleep all the time," she said. An they use to put all kinds—there use to show her all kinds o things in the wood, all kinds o beasts n everything, eh?

B.O.: Yeah.

—But she wouldn have to say—so she washed the dishes. "How do you find my dishes my little girl?"—"I wish I had dishes like that at home," she says. "I'd be proud of it." Ah well, nice knittin she use to make, all beautiful knittin. An er... an then she cooked dinner. Now she... she made the soup herself eh? She knowed what she put in eh? But after the soup was cooked, well, *des garnouilles* [frogs] an all kinds o beasts to be seen eh?

B.O.:   Ahhh!

—An er... she says, "How do you like my soup, my little girl?"—"I wish I had soup like this at home," she said. "I'd be some proud." Well, they made lovely knittin—oh my God! An they use to like her! But it was seem to her—that it wasn't mean eh? Okay. "Now," she said, "my little girl," she said, "all your work is done. Your knittin is finished, the way you wanted it," she said. So they pack up her knittin eh? "Now," she says, "it's time for you to go home," she said, "Ah well," the oldest one, she said, "we know you're pretty," she said, "you'll be ten times prettier!" So the second oldest, "Yes," she said, "you're pretty, an you'll be ten times prettier, an when you talk," she said, "the roses come out o your cheeks."

B.O.:   Phew! Oh!

—An the youngest one, "Well," she said, "you know you're pretty, yes, you'll be ten times prettier again," she said—she said, "you'll roll money ahead of you," she said, "when you walks."

B.O.:   Phew!

—She took her knittin an off she starts. Oh!—an pretty, s'marder. Anyway, they looks out, the ole lady, she says, "Who's comin there?" she says. Be—she says, "That's our sister!"—"Don't be so crazy," she said, "so pretty as that!" She said, "Yes! Oh my!" An she says, "When she gets here, I'm gonna see that ole woman, I'm gonna get my knittin."—"Don't worry," she says—no, she had one daughter, her, that's all. There's a mix, a mix I had there. She had one, her, the ugliest devil. "Well," she says, "tomorrow," she says, "I'm gonna spin you a big ball o wool," she says, "an tomorrow," she says, "an you're gonna go." Okay. She spins a *maudit* [damn] big ball o wool for her. "Now," she says, "tomorrow mornin, you're goin—an get it done to my likin," she says. Okay. She was goin, the ball o wool in her arms—oh! when she got almost in the same place—the ball o wool fall out of her arms—phew!—*dans l'trou* [into the hole]. Then she went for her ball o wool—she said, "Gimme my ball o wool," she said. "Well my little girl," she said, "come down, she said, "an do some work for us, we'll do your knittin." Okay. She went down. So she had to make the beds, an cook dinner an wash the dishes. So anyhow she made the beds. "My little girl," she said, "how do you find my bed?"—"Well," she said, "I wouldn have it, I wouldn have a bed like that," she said, "because I wouldn leave my dog sleep in a bed like that," she says. They use to put all kinds o things on, eh? It seems to her, eh? They was mean, eh? There was a narry! Risin narry, you know—big holes in him. Okay. Then she washed the dishes. "How do you find my dishes, my little girl?"—"I wouldn have dishes like that home," she said, "I wouldn eat in them, anyway...."

B.O.:   Oh!

—"All full o holes." An then, then she made dinner—she made it theirselves, she didn know what they put in eh? After she was breasin the pot, y'know, searin the pot—she put three places on the table—she never puts hers though!

B.O.:   Hhhh!

—"My little girl," she said, "how do you find my soup?"—"Well, my, I wouldn eat soup like that!" she said. "No sir! I wouldn eat soup with all kinds o beasts in—no sir!" she said. Okay. There was a head on it like a Bison [a brand of beer]—

B.O.:   Huh!

—An er... after she was done, the dinner heat an that—knittin all great big holes—an narry an rise, oh! it was *fisire* [ugly]! Anyway. "Now, little girl," she says, "your knittin is ready." So, the oldest one, she said, "Now we know you're ugly—but," she says, "you'll be ten times uglier!"

B.O.:   Oh ho ho!

—"Ten times uglier!" she said. Okay. An the other one—she says, "Yes, you're ugly—she'll be ten times uglier," she said, "an when you talk, you'll say 'Prout-prout ma mère' ['Fart-fart my mother']!"

B.O.:   [Clapping her hands in glee] Ha ha ha!

—An er... dat's the way we heard it now—don't come tell me that! An er, so the youngest one, "Yes, we know she's ugly—but she'll be ten times uglier," she said, "an when she walks, she'll roll dung ahead of her!" I won't say 'pure'—dung, anyway. Ah! Anyhow, she gave her her knittin, an off she start. She hated her like pizen. Oh. She looked up, the old woman, she said, "It's some sight." She said, "That's my sister!"—"Shut your mouth, you," she says, "an go on in the room." She went in the room—an she said, er... "Where you come from, you?"—"Prout-prout ma mère, prout-prout ma mère!" [Fart-fart my mother, fart-fart my mother!]

B.O.:   Ha ha ha!

—She says, "Well you're pretty," she says, "pound on," she says, "pound on." She says, "Who made your knittin?"—"Prout-prout ma mère!" She couldn talk eh? That's the witch she made into her.

B.O.:   Oh my God!

—Now...

G.T.:   That's the end of the story?

—It's not the end of the story.

G.T.:   It's not?

—No.

G.T.:   No.

—No.

G.T.:   What happened then?

—Tiens maudit gârs [Look at the rascal], he winks!

B.O.:   Ah ha ha ha ha ha!

—I boit pas là! [He's not drinking there!]

G.T.:   Yes yes, I'm drinking.

—Ah, gardez, i boit pas, vous autes! [Ah, look, he's not drinking, you guys!] ... Look at me—I'm almos two bottles gone! J'vais m'jaguer! [I'm gonna get drunk!]

G.T.:   What is the end of the story?

—Anyway, well, the ole woman, she says, "Tomorrow night," she says, "there's a ball," she says, "at the king's tomorrow night. An," she says, "we're goin. An you," she said, "you're not goin, you're stayin home." They had her—always in the room, eh? Always in the room, old clothes on, all tored.

B.O.:   Jalouses! [Jealous!]

—An er... you know, when it's a long time you told stories, it's hard, you know.

B.O.:   Yeah.

—Oui. [Yes] So anyhow, the nex marnin, the nex night, "Now," she says, now before she left there, she put the, the, she took some ashes, she put all over the floor—an she told er, "An when I comes home tonight," she said, "if it's not cleaned up," she said, "like it is, like it was, well," she said, "take care o yourself—you're gettin it!" Oh, they rigged up, her, dressed up in the highest style, her girl—they took off to the ball. So anyhow, her, I'll tell you, she was there all alone, she started

179

to cry. An cry. By n by her godmother come in—she says, "What you got cryin, my poor little girl?"—"Well," she says, "look a here," she says, "look at the mess I'm in," she said. "My stepmother an her daughter," she says, "are gone to the ball, they're gone to the ball, an they put all that mess for me to clean," she says. "An I can't clean it," she says, "it's all ashes."—"Don worry about that," she said, "here's a stick," she says, "go down," she said, "to a rock down in the garden," she says, "an strike it," she says. "You're gonna go to the ball," she said, "an be home," she says, "for sharp twelve—sharp eleven o'clock. Be back for leven o'clock." All right. So anyhow, the girl takes the stick an she strucked on the rock, oh my God!—she got a suit colour o the sun! An a—what she had? A... a little waggon—by God!—*c'est pas des chouals, c'est pas des chouals* [it's not horses, it's not horses]. My gosh, *j'sais pas ça* [I don't know what it is]. Well, it put it for a horse anyhow, I forgets it. An er... I bet she wouldn do that for you—well, she cleaned up all the house, my son! Jus like a deck—like it was there, clean! When he got there, my God!—pretty she was—the crew, they was all lookin at her. They was all, "Who's that?" An the prince there, he was every dance was danced with her. He wouldn look at the other ones at all. The other one was *vilaine comme in diabe* [ugly as a devil]!

B.O.: Hee hee hee!

—Anyhow, they was havin a talk, she takes off. Nobody seen her goin, y'know. She took off like the reindeer. Anyhow, when she got home, it all went from her, eh? An she got herself back in her clothes, an—in the room. So by n by they come, them. "Well," they said, "we seed a pretty girl tonight—you'd see—she was dressed the colour of the sun!"—"No prettier than me," she said. Oh my God! They jumped on her, they almos kill her.

B.O.: Ah ha! Oh!

—An she says, "Tomorrow night, we're gonna see her again, I guess," she said, "we're goin again tomorrow night an you," she says, "you're gonna stay home."—"I don care," she said. So anyhow, the nex day passed, the night, she rigged herself all in white satin, all white vile dress, all everything she had, the ugly girl, eh? Do what you like, she was ugly. *A tait vilaine! Grand Bon Dieu, a tait vilaine* [She was ugly! Great Good God, she was ugly]! An—anyhow, fore dey left, they had to put the house full of—ashes again—an off they start. Ah! She was there cryin side the stove her. She caught her godmother come in again. "Ah!" she said, "what you got again tonight my little girl?" she say. "Well," she said, "look a here, what a mess! What a mess for me to clean!"—"Nothin for you to clean," she says. "You'll go," she says, "take that stick," she says, "an go back to the ball," she says. "An be home," she says, "at twelve o'clock. Fair at twelve though!" she said. No!—No, it's leven o'clock. I said—first time was eleven—twelve...

G.T.: Mmm.

—... D'you hear it before?

G.T.: No, that's what you said though.

—That's what I said?

G.T.: Yes... the first time was eleven o'clock.

B.O.: Yes, eleven o'clock the first time, yes.

—Yeah—but it's supposed to be ten. Three nights.

G.T.: On the first time was ten o'clock, the second time now is eleven o'clock.

—Now it's eleven o'clock, yeah.

G.T.: Right.

—"Now," she says, "be home, be back," she said, "for eleven o'clock." Okay. She goes down, struck on the rock, a dress the colour o the moon, now, an, an the waggon, an the horse, eh? Jumps in—gold slippers....

B.O.: Phew!

—Goes down there, the king seen her, oh my God!—They was sittin down too, there—they didn know her—she was too pretty, I spose—an he danced every dance with her.

B.O.: Phew!

—An her, she wasn dancin at all, the ugly one! Blank!

B.O.: *Trop vilaine* [Too ugly]!

—*Trop vilaine!... Gardez-la* [Too ugly!... Look at her]! After, anyhow, she looked at the time, just eleven o'clock—she takes off, my son, he nabbed her, but he missed her, eh? He said, "Me, tomorrow night, I'm not goin a miss you!" So anyhow, she goes home, she back evryting back again, an she goes behine the stove. By an by they comes in. "Well," she says, "if you'd know, but," she says, "the night she was pretty!" She says, "No prettier than me!"—"Oh!" she says, "mother, drop on to her an kill her, for God's sake!" They almos kill her, though, they almos kill her! "An tomorrow night," she says, "another one. Another ti—another ball again," she says, "tomorrow night an we're goin," she says. "An you're gonna stay to the house!"—"I don care!" she said. So the nex evenin comes—they done the same—they put all ashes on the floor—an they dressed up, an, "Be sure that you're gonna have it done!" But her godmother has it all done, clean, when she came there. An they took off. By n by she comes in again her, the godmother. She was cryin. "Now," she says, "go on," she says, "take that little stick," she says, "an go out the same place," she says, "an be home tonight at twelve o'clock. Sharp twelve o'clock you be home." Okay. She goes to the garden, she strikes on the rock, horse n carriage an—the horse n carriage the same colour as her there-colour o the stars tonight. She goes down, *mes amis de Dieu* [my good friends], seen the mother, her stepmother, an her sister there, sittin down. Nobody takes her for a dance—blank. An her, every dance she was on the floor—every dance she was on the floor. But he use to count the time, him, see eh? He knows the first time was ten o'clock, and—that night—fore that was eleven, eh? He said, "Tonight it's twelve o'clock for sure but," he says, "I'd better watch er." Anyhow er, twelve o'clock, he was there, outside the door. When she passed, he nabbed her, he cutch her by the—whatchercalls—by her slipper. Her golden slipper. But she never mind that, she took off the same. Well—not long she was home anyhow, she was behind the stove there in her same riggin—my gosh! she comes in, her mother an her sister. She said, "That girl was there again tonight." She said, "Now, the prince," she said, "got one of her slippers—an tomorrow he's goin round—who fits the slipper is goin to be his wife." Jeepers crams, she was cuttin a piece off her! She used to cut a piece off her feet her—pour *suiter* [to fit]....

B.O.: Yeah. To fit the slipper.

—Okay. She was in her room, her. So anyhow, "In the hour," they said, "the prince is comin!" She dressed up her, pretty. "Come in," he says, er..., "It suits you here, on your feet?" She try it. *Nom de Dieu* [In the name of God]! She couldn fit it! She use to—she use to cut it, y'know—her heel—it was too tight! Fits no one o the two! He said, "That's not belong to you," he said, "you got no other girls?"—"No!" she said, "I've only got a Cendrilloux there," she said. "You know, I'm ashamed to show her to you." *Mignonne* [Pretty]! She was there wid her, her, her *habit couleur de* [dress the colour of]—stars there. An one slipper on er feet, *mignonne* [pretty]. They open er door, he almos fall down! An them too—*j'dirons* [we'll say]—fall down, to see er! An e goes an e gets her the slippers—jus suit her feet. An she was dressed in the same, the same suit, eh? They almos died, they almos died, they almos died!

181

B.O.:   They were ugly them.

—*Oui oui* [Yes yes]. "You're gonna be my wife," he said. An they never had a chance to go see them gettin married, he was goin for all—but they fell in the river. They ad the chance to see her gettin married.

B.O.:   No!

—That's all I know, me.

Commentary and Notes

Mrs. Kerfont did not want to tell this story, although she did at first agree to summarise it. She claimed her friend knew the tale, but Mrs. Ozon could not or would not remember it. Mrs. Kerfont moreover made a mistake at the beginning of the story, attributing three stepsisters to *Cendrillouse*. We may suppose, too, that she would have preferred her friend to tell it, because "In French it goes better, eh? It goes—it's a French story." But after this preliminary discussion she nonetheless began to tell the tale.

Various kinds of metanarrative devices occur in this narration. After her first use of the French expression "*Prout-prout ma mère*," which produced an animated response in Mrs. Ozon, Mrs. Kerfont felt obliged to justify her use of the phrase—"... dat's the way we heard it now"—and to level at her a teasing reprimand: "don't come tell me that!" A slight reprimand is also implicit in her "*Gardez-la!*" which she addressed to me while indicating her friend, at the end of the episode of the second evening at the ball.

We have already noted the difficulty encountered by Mrs. Kerfont in starting her narration. She underlines the problem at the beginning of the second part of the story, when the stepmother announces the ball to be held at the king's castle: "... you know, when it's a long time you told stories, it's hard, you know." She also has a few small problems with the occasional detail: she cannot recall, for example, the name of the creature which was supposed to draw the carriage. She says it is a horse, but "... it's not horses, it's not horses. My gosh, I don't know what it is." She also makes a mistake of detail concerning the time *Cendrillouse* must return home.

I myself, not knowing the tale in the way Mrs. Kerfont was to tell it, caused a break in the narration. At the end of the first part of the tale, which I had recognized as a *Märchen*, I had not realized that in Franco-Newfoundland tradition this first part is often attached to a version of *Cinderella*. As I tried to cover my error, I winked at Mrs. Ozon, a wink which did not escape Mrs. Kerfont's eye and which led to her reprimanding me, because in Mrs. Kerfont's opinion, I was not drinking quickly enough. But she took up her narration immediately, an indication of the relaxed discipline of the private or family tradition.

In spite of these apparent breaks in the narration, the tale was told very well. Mrs. Kerfont had a captive audience.

After the tale's conclusion (without a closing formula), Mrs. Ozon added that it was "*le conte de Cendrillouse*" ["the story of Cinderella"] Mrs. Kerfont had just told. The latter had alluded to this title when calling the heroine a "*Cendrilloux*" although the name "*Cendrillouse*" does not appear in the tale itself. Amongst French New-foundlanders the names *Cendrilloux* or *Cendrillouse* are sometimes used to tease a person given to loafing about the house (like *Cendrilloux* in one of Emile Benoit's tales further on, who was always sitting behind the stove).

Both ladies attributed the tale to Mrs. Olive Marche, but neither was sure if she had told them "*les derniers temps qu'a conta les contes*" ["when she was telling stories on the last"] or "*les premiers temps*" ["on the first"], that is, at the beginning or at the end of her storytelling career. At the time I was living at Cape St. George, it was said that Mrs. Marche no longer told stories, despite her high reputation; as good luck would have it, one of my students was able to record her some years later, in a session in which she told several tales and sang a few songs.

Mrs. Kerfont's tale is well known in European tradition and indeed elsewhere. In reality we are dealing with the combination of two international tale-types, AT 480, *The Spinning Women by the Spring* (but titled *Les Fées* in Delarue and Tenèze's *Le Conte populaire français* II, 188-199) and AT 510, *Cinderella and Cap o' Rushes*. Motifs in the tale include S31, *Cruel stepmother*; L55, *Stepdaughter heroine*; L102, *Unpromising heroine*; H1226.4, *Pursuit of rolling ball of yarn leads to quest*; N810, *Supernatural helpers*; F92, *Pit entrance to lower world*; Q41, *Politeness rewarded*; D1860, *Magic beautification*; Q2, *Kind and unkind*; D1454.2.1, *Flowers fall from lips*; M431.2, *Curse: toads from mouth*; D1870, *Magic hideousness*; L131, *Hearth abode of unpromising hero (heroine)*; F311.1, *Fairy godmother*; D1473.1, *Magic wand furnishes clothes*; D1050.1, *Clothes produced by magic*; N711.6, *Prince sees heroine at ball and is enamored*; F821.1.5, *Dress of gold, silver, color of sun, moon and stars*; C761.3, *Tabu: staying too long at ball*; H36.1, *Slipper test*; K1911.3.3.1, *False bride's mutilated feet*; L162, *Lowly heroine marries prince (king)*.

In *Le Conte populaire français* Paul Delarue notes that French tradition frequently links AT 480 to AT 510 (which he subdivides into two variant forms only, 510A [*Cendrillon*] and 510B [*Peau d'Ane*], contrary to the tripartite division of *The Types of the Folktale*). Be that as it may, we have not collected sufficient Franco-Newfoundland versions to confirm or deny this link. The Centre d'Etudes Franco-Terreneuviennes possesses, in addition to Mrs. Kerfont's versions, one fragmentary version of AT 480, with no link to type 510, and two versions, from the same female narrator, which bring both types together but which differ widely from the tale analysis in *The Types of the Folktale*.

More generally, 35 versions of AT 480 are known in France, twenty or so from the French of North America; for AT 510A there are 36 versions from France, 28 from the French in North America. Many of these versions are of course linked. For a more detailed study of this series of tales, see *Le Conte populaire français* II, 278-280.

THE BLUEBIRD

One time there was a king an a queen. So was she pregnant. So anyhow—him—before she found her babies he went for a trip, eh? So after he was gone she found her babies, a boy an a girl. She had a sarvants er, staying with her see. A sarvin girl. So she tole her, she tole her, she said, "You take my baby," she said, "put er into a basket an go an drown them." Okay. The king wasn come yet, see. So after, after, de girl er, she took de babies, she put them into a basket—oh my God, they were cute! An she went down to the river. So she was sittin down dere, watchin dem, dey was sleepin. "Oh what a sin!" she said. "Dey're goin—an drown dat," she said. By n by she looked aroun, she seen a white bear. He said, "What you doin dere?" he said. "Well me," she said, "my mistress sen me," she says, "to drown de two kids," she said, "an I don like to drown them," she said. "Finds em a sin," she says, "dey're sleeping." She says, "Don't drown em," he says, "give em to me." So de white bear took de youngster—e took de basket in is mouth an er, takes off. An den she tole im, she tole er dat she ad drowned em, see. Okay. Anyway, dey—dat white bear reared em up. Dey were man a woman. "Now," e said, "you's man an woman now," e said, "I'm gonna build youse a little castle. For youse to go live in." So eh, e build dem a castle on, on de lower side de road. Now anyway—so de king came e didn know about is wife. She tole im she ad a dog an a bitch eh? She ad drowned dem, no more, no more said about it. Anyway, one marnin er, de, de king's servant went, took de, his cattle down de road eh? My God, e came aroun de castle. E says, "For all dat castle wasn't here before. What a pretty castle!" So e brought his cattle down de field an in de evenin e went an get em again. So de nex marnin when e brought dem down, well de sun was shinin eh, an de castle was *pretty*, oh! "Well," e says, "da's, da's, dat, da's, da's something in dat," e said. "I'm goin back." E told de king, he says, "King," e says, "is a castle over dere," e says, "dat wasn dere before." An e says, "Every marnin I goes down, i's, i's gettin prettier all de time."—"Ah," e says, "it's ony your eyes."—"Oh no," e said, "my eyes," e said. Well, nex marnin, de sarvant went out with his cattle again. My God, de sun was shinin so well, e said e couldn, e turned back. Tole de king, "Come down," e said. "You'll find out for yourself." So de king take is orse an carriage an e goes down. Shore enough! *Beautiful* castle, oh my gosh! "It wasn't ere before," e said. So anyway, de cou—de king goes down dere. She tole er brother, she said, "Look de king is comin ere." No, wait now, I'm ahead o my story again. Non, da's to de queen e was tellin dat, is to de queen. "Ah," she said, "you're crazy," she said, "is no, is no castle down dere." E says, "Come see for yourself." So she goes down dere, oh my God, it was pretty in dere—evrything was—dey ad evryting what you could mention, eh? In de castle. She tole er brother, she said, "The queen is comin ere." She comes in. My gosh, she ad, dey ad chairs, plush chairs to sit down on. She ad dinner order an everyting. Oh, she stayed dere a long time. Ah ah, "My God," she said, "you got a lovely castle!" she said. She said, "If you ad a blue bird an a golden cage," she said, "it'd be ten times prettier." An she said, "I's only you will get it." Okay. So anyhow, after she was gone, she tole it to er brother. She said, "De queen, she said our castle is beautiful. If we ad a blue bird in a golden cage, it'd be ten times prettier."—"Well," e said, "I'm goin tomorrow." So anyhow, de nex marnin de, de little boy rigged hisself an off e start. When e got down dere, *nom de dsous* [in the name of—]! Yes but e was, but e turned into a stone.

B.O.: Oh!

—E was a year today gone. No brother. So she goes an fine er ole bear. "Well," she said, "my brother is gone," she says, "a year an a day," she said. "Yes." An e says, er, she says, "E's gone to get er, de blue bird an de golden cage."—"My dear," e said, "i's not im is gonna get that—can get dat. I's ony you."—Blanche? [Pouring a beer, looking at Mrs. Ozon] "I's ony you," she says, "can get that. Now," she says, "go ome an get your big glass"—a big mirror she ad—"an come here," she says, "I'm gonna show you ow to do it." She goes ome, she gets er big lookin glass an she comes up now an e tells er. "Now," e says, "is a big, is a real big buildin an," she said, "a crack a de door is gonna be open an," she says, "when you gets—go to de door," she says, "you put de, de, de glass back to your face eh?"—"Yeah."—"An," she says, "you will have de bird. An," she said, "after," she said, "you'll go upstairs, you'll, you'll, you'll, you're gonna fine tree alf pint bottles a drop—de, er, water, eh?—an drop," e said, "on every spot you sees on de floor," eh? "You'll get your brother." Okay. She takes off. Shore enough. When she got down dere, oh, a moses big castle. De door was open. So she walks in wit de door, the back turned to er face eh? De glass, eh? De little bird comes to de door, she said, "I'm yours." She said, "I knows you're mine." So she goes upstairs an she fines a bottle, a tree alf pint bottle, water—an she dropped an dropped an dropped, oh my God, people in dere, dropped, de people. Dey was all enchanted, eh? An she ad one more drop left. No brother yet. So she said it was one by de step a de door she, she dropped it dere an it was im. "Well," she says, "it's almos time," she says, "fer you, for you to come ome," she said. "Long enough you're ere."—"Well," e said, "da's it." E goes ome. So anyway, after dey ad de castle—de bird an de golden cage—was prettier yet eh? So dat marnin dey, de whatycalls—de sarvan boy went out an put his cattle down, down de road again. Oh! Well, when e come back, e tole de king, "Well," e says, "king," e says, "if you ad seen de castle," e said, "i's on de lower side de road over dere," e said, "you'd be surprise." E said, "I got to go an see, see dat since you're complainin about it." Takes de orse an carriage an off e starts to go down dere. Now her she owns she knows er boy—er youngsters y'know. Sure. Oh, she tole er brother, she said, "De king is comin." Anyhow de king passed all before noon wit em. He eat an everyting wit em. An ah, anyhow before e left, e said, "Now you should come ome an ave supper with me."—"My brother goes," she said, "I'd go."—"Well," e said, "if you goes, I'll go." Okay. "Well," she said, "I'm not goin," she said "if I don't take my blue bird an my golden cage."—"Sure," e said, "take it wit you." So she takes it wit er. So when dey got to de king's, anyhow, she puts er bird above de door, eh? In de cage. An de king said, "Time," he says, "dey're gettin dinner," e said, "we'll go in my garden an see my flowers." Anyhow time de king was gone, dey rigged de table an dey put two places on de side, fer de girl an de boy, eh? An she put pisen in. She knowed it was er kids eh? Anyway, after dey come up. Dey went to de table. She was just takin a spoonful from er little brother's bowl. "Mistress an master," e said, "don't you eat what's on your plate," she said, "it's pisen."— "What!" e said. E never mind it, e took another spoon. E said, "Mistress an master," e said, "don't eat what's on your plate, it's pisen!"—"Pisen!" e said. De king said "What?" Well e takes his wife an e kills er dere. Den e know dat was is youngsters, eh?

B.O.: Ah yeah, yeah!

—So de king went put dem in de little dump, an if dey're not dead, dey're livin.

Commentary and Notes

Despite a lapse of memory by Mrs. Kerfont, this little story is well told; but the expression "I'm ahead o my story" is quite common in the private or family tradition. One should note the simple opening formula, common among French Newfoundlanders, and the somewhat abridged closing formula. Mrs. Kerfont could not recall from whom she had learned the story.

The tale appears to be a rather fragmentary version of the international tale-type AT 707, *The Three Golden Sons*, with the motifs T685, *Twins*; S301, *Children abandoned (exposed)*; B211.2.3, *Speaking bear*; B535, *Animal nurse*; S352, *Animal aids abandoned child(ren)*; H1331.1.1, *Quest for bird of truth*; D231, *Transformation: man to stone*; R158, *Sister rescues brother(s)*; D766.1, *Disenchantment by bathing (immersing) in water*; B131, *Bird of truth*; H151.1., *Attention drawn by magic objects: recognition follows*; B131.2, *Bird reveals treachery*; B521.1, *Animal warns against poison*; and Q261, *Treachery punished*.

This is the only version of the tale collected among French Newfoundlanders, although it is well known in France, with 35 versions noted in *Le Conte populaire français*, and in francophone North America, with 25 versions noted.

THE SILVER MOUNTAIN

One time dere was a man an a woman, dey ad tree daughters. An ah, *dame*, de two oldest ones signed deir name to de devil an dey was wit devils. But de youngest one her, she stayed home with her mudder an fadder. Anyhow, one ah, one evenin she wen—one Saturday evening she went down to de store. Er, one of her sisters was dere—an was ah, Mary was her name her. "Mary," she said, "what fer you don't come outside—come wit us?" she says. "We got lots o fun, lots o money. Dance every night"—"Oh well, me," she says, "I'm not goin me," she says, "my father an mother's ole," she says, "I'd like to stay wit dem." Uh, "If dey leave me go," she says, "I'll go." Okay. Anyhow she goes home in de evening, Saturday evening, she start workin, done all her work, in no time she's finish. So de ole woman, she says, "I spose Mary," she says, "you wants to go to de dance tonight?" She says, "Yes," she says, "if you leaves me go, I'll go."—"Well," she says, "ask your father." So she asked her fadder. "Well," he says, "you're a good girl," he says, "be home," he says, "at ten o'clock." So she could go. "De hour you want me," she says, "I'll come." An she tole er she says uh, she tole er, she tole er, she says, "An when you come down it'll be one—it'll be somebody waitin fer you." Okay. So she dressed up in her best clothes she had. When she wen outdoors, *dark* as de pitch! But dere was a man who, oh, a man dere, a young feller an a horse an carriage, waitin for er. She had to *feel* where to go, it was dat *dark*! So she gets aboard wit him an off he start. "Mary," he says, "what fer you don't sign your name to me?"—"No," she says, "I wouldn sign my name," she says. "I'll keep you company but," she says, "sign my name," she says, "I wouldn't." Anyhow, when dey got to de castle—my God! dey was dancin my son, belly to band. So uh, he tole her, he says, "At nine o'clock," he says, "the dance is gonna be finish an—Silver Mountain. Is you gonna come?"—"Well," she said, "you promise me come home—to bring me home de hour I wanted. Well," she said, "I'd go." He, she, he said, "Now," he says, "de dance is gonna be finish on Silver Mountain." So dey all took off.

B.O.:   Ohhh!

—Bad night! De seas bouting high an evryting. She was frightened but she wouldn tell him eh? "Is you frighten," he says, "Mary?" She said, "No, I'm not frighten." If she had said she was frighten, she was gone. So anyhow, when dey got on top of dat mountain, de ole devil put on his hat, come back de castle, lights evryting, oh! it was *pretty*. So anyhow, ten o'clock she says, "My hour's come." She says, "Take me home."—"Yes, sure," he says, "I'll take you home." So when she got to her place it was just ten o'clock. "Uh well," he says, "da's a good girl!" de ole man an de ole woman said. All right, all de week she work like a dog, all de week. Saturday evening she goes to de store, her sister was dere again. "Mary," she says, "What fer you don't come wit us? We got some fun us, y'know. Lots o money, lots a fun, dances."—"I don't care," she said, "if dey leaves me go," she said, "I'll go, if dey don't leave me go," she says, "I'm not goin." So anyhow, she goes home, she did all her day's work dere, nice work an evryting. "I spose Mary," she says, "you want to go to de dance again tonight?"—"Yes modder," she says, "if you leave me go."—"Well," she says, "ask your fadder." So she goes an ask her fadder. "Well," he says, "if you're a good girl! he says, "like you was last Saturday" he said, "right, well," he said, "you go tonight." He says, "You'll have an hour longer, leven o'clock tonight," he said. Oh! She was *glad*. So anyhow, she rigs herself an off she starts. She goes outdoors an he was dere again. *Dark* as pitch! She had to *feel* to get, y'know, to get where he'll be eh? So he gets aboard an off he starts. "Mary," he said, "sign your name to me eh?"—"No," she says, "I wouldn sign my name to you—I'll keep your company but," she says, "sign my name I wouldn't." He says, "Tonight," he says, "the dance is gonna be finish"—which time I said she had to go home?

G.T.:   Ten o'clock first.

—De first time?

G.T.:   Yeah.

—Uh yes. An ah, he says, "Gotta be finish," he says, "de dance gotta be finish, gotta go"—Ah me I gets puzzled, me—"De dance is gotta be finish, er, gotta be finished at nine o'clock, on Silver Mountain." He says, "You're gonna come with us?" She says, "*Sure*, if you comes home the hour I wanted," she says. He said "Yes." So anyhow, eleven, nine o'clock, de devil took off his hat off de ground. My God! evryting went black. An her now an him dey was in de carriage, horse n carriage an dey took off.

B.O.:   Ohhh!

—Bad night, oh my God! He says, "You frighten Mary?" he says. She says, "No." She wouldn have to say, you know. So anyhow, when dey got up dere, he put down his hat, de—castle come back an de *dancin*, my son, belly to band. Well now, leven o'clock was her time, to go home eh? "Now," he, she said, "my time is up to go home," she said, "I gotta go."—"Okay," he said. Takes her board an off they starts, an when she got home, it was just leven o'clock. "Well," he said, "da's what I calls a good girl now," he said. "Well," he says, "if you listens like dat again, nex, nex—"—"Is, ah, well," she says, "dere's only one more dance," she said, "nex

186

Saturday." She said, "If I goes nex Saturday," she said, "it'll be my last one." She said, "I'll stay home after with you," she says, "all time," she said. Okay.... Okay. All dat week she worked like a dog. Dat Saturday evening she went down to de store again. She was dere again. "Well, what fer you don't come wit us Mary?"— "*Non!*" She said, "I'm not goin."—"You're comin to de dance tonight?"—"Well," she said, "if dey leave me go," she said, "I'll go."—"But," she said, "it's de last one."—"Well," she says, "I'd, I'll go if dey leave me go." Okay. She goes home, she done all her evenin's work an evryting. "Well, I spose"—de ole woman, she says, "I spose, Mary, you'd like to go to de dance tonight?" She said, "Yes."—"Well," she said, "ask your fodder." She ask her fodder. "*Yes, sure,*" he said, "you'd go tonight, if you want. Twelve o'clock tonight." Longer see, eh? "Come home twelve o'clock tonight—" he says, "It'll be my last one anyway," she said, "I'm not goin no more." Okay. She goes upstairs, she rigs herself an goes outdoors, dark as pitch. Phew!

B.O.: Ha ha ha!

—Anyhow she got aboard. "Mary," he says, "come on," he says, "come on give me—sign me your name?"—"*Non!*" she says, "I wouldn sign my name. I'll keep your company," she says, "but sign my name," she said, "I wouldn." He says, "Gonna finish de time, de dance on ah, nine o'clock tonight again," he said, "on Silver Mountain?"—"Yes," she said, "if you promise me to come home—bring me de hour I wanted."—"Sure," he said. Okay. So anyhow at nine o'clock dey were down dere an anyhow dance till nine o'clock. Den de ole devil said, "Tonight, dance is gonna be finish on Silver Mountain." So dey all took off. When he got on top a de mountain he put on his hat, oh! de castle come full of lights an dey was startin dancin an evryting. So anyhow at nine o'clock, she got ah, thirsty for water, so she goes to, to de well eh? When she got down dere, dere was a little chapel eh? A little chapel. An to dat chapel was a road eh? So she had—she drink an after she—when she come up to de house, to de cha—to de whatyoucalls—to de time, de ole devil was dere wit a big book an a big pencil. "Now," he said, "Mary," he said, "now," he said, "you gotta sign your name."—"No," she said, "I'm not signin my name."—"You *got* to!" he said. She goes, she grabs de pencil from de, de devil, eh, an she made a big cross in de book.

B.O.: Ahh!

—Evryting went *en flammes* [up in flames]. An she was left alone! On de mountain! All night, alone!

B.O.: My God!

—She was in some friggin way now. The nex marnin, she, the nex marnin was come daylight anyhow, she was there on the Silver Mountain.

B.O.: My God!

—All fifty cents pieces all by gol—all by—like dat eh? She took a piece out. She was gonna take it wit er, eh? "No, I'm not gonna take it," she said, "it makes a hole there," she said. "I'm gonna put it back." So she tought about de little chapel she was in, eh? She goes dere. Shore enough, little chapel an a road to go eh? So anyhow, she took dat road. She travel an travel down dere, by n by she broke into a town. Ohh! My God! De people, de people, de people was cruel. So anyhow she seen a king an a queen an a young prince comin in—wit a harse n carriage eh. She was dere on side o de road her. Dey said, "You're gonna, you're gonna come wit us?"—"My God," she says, "no," she says, "I gotta go home," she says, "I'm gone since las night," she said. "My fodder an mudder is waitin fer me."—"Now, you're goin—comin wit us." So anyhow dey took her an dey put her wit de prince, behind. *Pense don* [Just think], a girl like her wit a prince. She almos fainted y'know! So de king he said, "How do you like Mary," he said, "dat you be my prince's wife?"— "King," she said, "don't make fun a me," she said. "I'm not makin fun a you," he

187

said. "Da's—you gonna be his wife. You unchanted us," he said. "We was all enchanted, us," he said, "you know. Da's you unchanted us," he says, "an you're gonna be"—an dat was de same feller was takin her home—dat was takin her to de time every night.

B.O.: *Non!*

—Take er, dey went to de king's dey ad dinner an dey got married her, eh? Den after, dey went to her place. So de ole woman, "Look over dere," she says, "comin." De king an queen an a young prince an a young—an his wife eh? A young lady. When she got in de house, she goes to her modder right away eh? She grabbed her holt [pause, while tape is turned]...

G.T.: That's right. So she comes to her mother.

—She says, she says, "I spose," she said, "you're tired waitin for me," she says, "gone since las night."—"What happened?" she said. "Well," she said, "da's it. I's ony now I can—I came," she said. "Well," de king said, he said, "she, she ah, was all enchant," she said, ah, de king tole her. "We was all enchanted. Da's her unchanted all de town," he said. "Now," he said, "she's my wi—my son'is wife." An e says, "You're gonna all come stay wit us," an dey're not livin—[she whistles]—gone king—

B.O.: Ha ha ha!

—Da's de last of it.

Commentary and Notes

The reader will appreciate the economy with which Mrs. Kerfont begins her story. After three sentences providing the context, we immediately enter the action with a direct and uncomplicated dialogue. Mrs. Kerfont will remain faithful to the first dialogue involving the heroine and her sister in the two subsequent ones. The same is true for the conversations between her and her mother, her and her father, her and the devil. Such repetition demonstrates that Mrs. Kerfont is perfectly capable of following the rules of the art—when it suits her.

It is rather difficult to evoke the atmosphere created by Mrs. Kerfont when Mary meets the devil and during the journey to the Silver Mountain. Without making great play with her voice, she nonetheless succeeds in provoking a shudder. The contrast between this encounter and the ball is all the more striking, with a single sentence: "My God! dey was dancin my son, belly to band" to conjure up the frantic activity of the ball.

Interaction between Mrs. Kerfont and her audience is now however limited to the "ehs?" and Mrs. Ozon's laughter. Mrs. Kerfont is obliged to ask us to remind her of the time Mary must return home, and admits that "...me I gets puzzled, me." Her version of the closing formula is even more abbreviated than usual, without however lessening the pleasure of the narration.

It has not been possible to identify this tale according to the international catalogues. It may be a rather abridged tale, or a few episodes from a much longer tale, but in this case Mrs. Kerfont would probably have said so.

Motifs in the tale include P252.2, *Three sisters*; Z71.1, *Formulistic number: three*; M211, *Man sells soul to devil*; D1067.1, *Magic hat*; D1131, *Magic castle*; D1131.1, *Castle produced by magic*; G303.16.3.4, *Devil made to disappear by making sign of the cross*; F768.2, *City of enchanted people*; D705, *Place disenchanted*; L162, *Lowly heroine marries prince (king)*.

THE GREEN DOG

It was a man an a woman, dey ad tree daughters so de ole woman died, left jus de man an tree daughters eh? So anyway one Sunday he was goin to mass. An when he got, in a place, was a great big garden eh? Garden o roses eh? What come out a dat, a green dog eh? He said, "You got a, go tell your oldest daughter, she's not here tomorrow, de, to, not here tomorrow to marry me, I'm gonna *heat* you."

B.O.: Oh oh!

—That's too bad.

B.O.: Oh ah!

—So he went to mass an he was late for dinner now. Dat was her now, dat was suppose to give him his dinner. An he was late. When he come in she was vex as the devil after her father. "What made you so late?" she said. "Well da's it," he said. "On my way comin," he said, "when I passed a big garden o roses," he said, "what come out of it, is a green dog an he tole me if he haven't got you to, be havin—"—my God me I can't pronounce it at all—"fer...er, he tole me fer you to go—fer you to marry him."—"Go an marry a dog?" she said, "You're foolish bye. You're sure to be eat by him. For sure I'm gonna marry a green dog." Well, he was real sorry. All de week he couldn eat no dinner...

B.O.: I don't know, me.

—So anyhow, passed a week, nex Sunday, he went again. Da's de second oldes was suppose to get his dinner. Went to mass, on his way comin when he got side a de garden again, what come out again, a green dog. He said, er, "If your oldes daughter don't want to marry me," he said, "you're gonna, I'm gonna *eat* you."— "Well," he says, "I'm gonna ask her, I donno." Anyway, e was late for his dinner again. An her, when she—when he come in de door she was wicked as a *lion*. She says, "Where you was today?" she says. "Well," he says, "he come," he says, "don't wants no dinner." An he looked—y'know he was down, he was gonna be eat, eh?

B.O.: I guess so.

—"Well," he said, "dat is de same trick as last Sunday," he said. "A green dog," he says, "come out an he told me if you weren't gonna marry him he's gonna eat me."—"Well," she says, "he can eat you if he wants! I's not me is gonna marry a green dog!"

B.O.: Ha ha ha!

—Well, he almos come *crazy*! Uh well, de nex time anyhow, it was de youngest one. Dat was her was suppose to get his dinner. Okay. So anyhow, de man when he, when he went to mass an on his way comin he come—he passed along dat garden again, out he comes. "You—if you haven't got de youngest one," he says, "tomorrow," he says, "to marry me," he says, "you're gonna be—I'm gonna eat you up," he said. Uh, he y'know he used to walk a step, back a step, a front step. He was all in wit de fright! Anyway, dat was her now dat was suppose to have his dinner. Anyway, a long time after, he come. "Ah!" she says, "Father," she says, "where you were you was late for your dinner?" she says. "Da's it," he said, "de green dog," he says, "come out today," he says, "he tole me if you don't marry him, well he was gonna eat me."—"Well, my son," she says, "I'm gonna marry de green dog, *sure, why not*?" Uh, well, he almos come crazy!

B.O.: I guess so.

—Okay. So anyhow, de nex Sunday when he went after mass, when de mass was over comin home, he met de green dog. He says, "What your daughter said?" He said, "She said yes, she'll marry you." He, "I'll be to your place in de afternoon." Anyway, afternoon, he comes, he comes an get her dere. She goes to do—she goes

189

wit him eh? When he gets to the garden, is a big hole, goes down underneat, a moses, a nice castle...

B.O.: Phew!

—Marder! "Now," he says, "what you want me to be," he says, "dog in de day or man in de day, or man in de day an dog in de night?"—"Oh," she says, "I radder for you to be dog in de day," she says, "man in de night."

B.O.: Ha ha ha!

—Okay. Now he was man in de night eh? Beautiful presents, marder! Now— wait now—yeah, but when de sisters come to hear dat now eh? Dat he was a beautiful prince in de night, dey got jealous of her eh? So one night dey went for a cruise eh, him—de two a dem eh? So he left his fur home eh? Time he was gone, time he was gone, de two sisters come eh? An dey, dey found his skin eh? Dis dog's skin eh? An burned it, eh? Yeah, but when dey burned it dey knowed dere, he knowed. He says, "Is somebody at my skin," he said, "le's go," he says. So when he got home, sure enough, it was gone. It was burned up eh? Trowed it in de stove. So, he says, "I gotta leave you," he says. "I can't stay wit you no longer." So her she grabbed him a holt an my God, screech—an screechin an evryting. "You can't...."— "No, no," he said, "I cant's stay wit you any longer," he said. "I gotta go," he said. An, ah, she scratched him in de face eh, and de blood's fallin on his shirt. "Look," she says, "you're goin but dat shirt, dat shirt dere, dat spot of blood," he said, "is nobody else is gonna take dat away," he said, "only my hands," she said. So she start... ohh! but I'll never tell you dat me, is too long, er...

B.O.: Ha ha ha!

G.T.: Go on, it's going fine. Nice.

—... Oh no.

B.O.: Come on.

... I can't.

G.T.: Why not?

B.O.: No pain to grow in his girl.

—*Ouais, mais tu sais bien, ej p... ej connais pas hein? Ej sais pas* [Yeah, but you knows, I c... I don't know eh? I don't know (it)].

G.T.: Well go on as much as you can.

—He said, "Before," he says, "you'll find me," he said, "you'll wear leather shoes [bang! on the table], steel shoes [bang!], iron shoes [bang!]." Da's before she'll find him eh? Dat was in clothes eh? An ah, anyway, she, he took off. An she took off too. When he used to go down in de valley, eh? She used to lose him outa sight eh? She was all tored up. She wored all—er, whatycalls, er leather shoes. She wored her steel shoes—she took it wit er though, she ad dem de same—an she wored iron shoes eh?—Now I'm able to tell it. Da's far as she went. Da's far I know she went. Is longer n dat dough. Olive knows dat, now.

G.T.: Yeah.

—*C'est eune maudite* [She's a devil] can say dat, my son.

B.O.: *T'as pas té chez Olive, t'as pas té chez Olive encore* [You haven't been to Olive, you haven't been to Olive yet]?

Commentary and Notes

When Mrs. Kerfont began this story, it was her sixth successive narration. One can readily understand her impatience therefore when she realizes how long her tale really is: "...ohh! but I'll never tell you dat me, is too long...". But this very impatience over the length of a tale, translated into an abrupt conclusion by Mrs. Kerfont, must be considered typical of the attitude of storytellers in the private or family tradition, even though this particular case is somewhat extreme.

The end of the tale, or at least the final sentences of the narration, provide us with its source, once again Mrs. Olive Marche. The sentence "*C'est eune maudite* can say dat, my son," must be construed as praise for Mrs. Marche, precisely because she is able to tell a very long tale in its entirety. Unfortunately, at the time I was living at Cape St. George, Mrs. Marche was not telling stories and I was not able to interview her.

The story fits under tale-type AT 425, *The Search for the Lost Husband*, the best known variant of which is probably *Beauty and the Beast* (AT 425C). Because the present version is incomplete, a more precise identification has not been proposed. The tale-type is indeed a complex one, with numerous variant forms. *Le Conte populaire français* identifies 118 French versions, and 63 for francophone North America. The tale's analysis in the French catalogue reflects its complexity, and I refer the reader to Vol. II, 72-109, for both an analysis and important study of the tale. The archive of the Centre d'Etudes Franco-Terreneuviennes has a second, more complete version of the tale.

The motifs appearing in the tale as Mrs. Kerfont tells it are: T111, *Marriage of mortal and supernatural being*; L54, *Compassionate youngest daughter*; L54.1, *Youngest daughter agrees to marry monster; later sisters are jealous*; D621.1, *Animal by day; man by night*; F721.5, *Subterranean castle*; C757.1, *Tabu: revealing secret of supernatural husband*; D721.3, *Disenchantment by destroying the skin (covering)*; H1385.4, *Quest for vanished husband*; and Q502.2, *Punishment: wandering till iron shoes are worn out*.

THE DOE

Uh well I guess the doe there now that's it, there's a man an a woman. They got married and they were young eh? And she got pregnant the woman, eh? And before she found her baby, eh, war was declared and her man had to go to the war, y'know. So now he had left a sarvant—he knew she had found a baby eh? He had left a sarvant to take care of her y'know. So he had told her, "*Whatever you do,*" he says, "don't harm her." It's because she had found her baby with him, eh? So anyway, he takes off to the war. There, he had left that feller there to take care of her and then, he'd tried to take, *you know, advantage* of her eh? He wanted her to obey him, y'know, because her man was gone eh? But she didn't want to y'know. There, so anyway he used to send letters eh, home. To his mother eh. To watch out for his wife while he's at the war. There anyway, what he does now—where they used to carry the *mail*, eh, well they couldn't carry the mail and come back the same day eh, they used to go halfway and sleep there, and the next day they used to take the mail to the battlefield. So anyway, that day, the *mailman*, he takes off and then, he has a chat with the feller who was looking after the woman eh? He has a chat with the feller when he was halfway there, we'll say eh. Or it was him carrying the mail, I don't know anyway. So what he had said was when the mail was coming, he should sleep over, he opened the mail to see if there were any letters for him—for her, eh. And if there were any letters for her well—"You'll read them." So anyway, she got a chance to send a letter to his mother and it said his wife had found a little boy eh. So anyway—when he got the news he was really proud. So anyway, he writes back, and he says to look out for her eh. So anyway him, that feller now he knew all that, the news he had sent, eh. So what he does, he writes a letter as if it had come from his mother, eh? And he, she says now on the letter that his wife had found a little dog eh?

A.K.: Heh heh!

—So he sends his answer back about the little dog or little cat to look after it like the eyes in his head eh? And now what happens now, but now you know this fellow eh, well he opens the mail bag and he reads the letter you know. So anyway, what he does, him, he writes another letter eh, and tells his mother to take that little dog—take her and her little dog and take them in the forest and kill them. If it was a little dog he didn't want it. When she receives the letter, the woman eh, she starts crying. And then he asks her what she was crying for. She tells him eh, she says, "I've had a letter from your husband," she says, "and he told me to send you into the woods as far as I could, send you and have you killed."

A.K.:   Oh ho!

—"Well," she says, "that's that." You've got to obey them, eh? So anyway, she asked two men. There the... man takes her in the woods to kill her, eh? So now, those men, those two men eh, well now, the, the last sickness, it was her who'd taken care of him now, saint Genevieve eh—it was saint Genevieve eh? So anyway, she takes those two men and they go off with her into the woods, her baby and her, both of them. And they had a dog with them, a big dog. So they'd gone a long way, anyway, they stop and then it was *deadlock*. So they had to kill her eh. Now he had said, eh, when they were going to kill her to pluck both eyes out of her head and bring them back to him for, for, for *proof* eh?

A.K.:   Little Golo.

G.T.:   Golo.

—Golo was his name, eh?

A.K.:   Oh yes, that was his name.

—That fellow—

A.K.:   Golo, Golo, yeah.

—When they were ready to kill the woman, they couldn't, they didn't have the heart. Her and her baby. So anyway, one of them says, "Well," he says, "me, I'm not killing her."—"But," he says, "she told us to bring back her eyes." He says, "If we don't bring them to him well he's going to kill us, eh?"—"Well," he says, "kill your dog." And he says, "we'll tear out the dog's eyes and wrap them up and take them with us, he'll think that's it eh." *All right.* But now she had to promise never to leave the woods. She had to stay in the woods—she had to stay there eh. She had nothing to eat, nothing to drink. Only her and her baby eh. *So okay.* They come back to the house and he says, "Did you do what I told you to do?" She said—they said, "Yeah." He says, "We've brought the two eyes." Well now, they had ah, the eyes packed up in a handkerchief, eh? Well he says, "Here, here are her eyes, the two eyes," he says—he didn't want to take them. He was sorry eh? So anyway, the war went on, and then, time goes by—it was a story. It went on for a little while, perhaps eh? So anyway, one fine day the, the, the... the war was over. Yeah. At that time eh. When she had—when she was in the woods with her baby, eh, well she killed some *buffalo*—some, some sheep and she made a dress with the sheepskin eh? And him, he was, the portrait, he was just his portrait eh? So anyway, the baby falls sick—one night there and she had no medicine for her baby, nothing to give him to eat, nothing at all. They were eating roots, eh? What could she do? So she would lose her baby eh? There anyway, she heard a scratching on the door right at midnight. In the forest now, all alone, the two of them eh? Her baby sick. She had made a cross with two sticks eh? And there she prays to the cross, eh, you can see her so well eh? He hears a sound at the door, she opens the door—a doe, a little doe, like a middling dog, we'll say eh. So he says, "My poor doe," she says, "if you only knew the trouble I'm in," she says, "my baby is sick," she says, "and there's nothing to drink, nothing to eat." She lies down. Her udder there well it's *right* big eh?

A.K.:   Ah, God dash!

192

—She had found her pups and her pups had died eh? So her udder was hurting her—she lies down for the baby to suck. So she takes her baby and he sucks on the doe, eh? After that, she came every day at the same time eh, she came every day for—the baby to suck on her—trying to calm her, you know. You can see the little doe—the dear little doe—lying down and the baby sucking eh?

A.K.: Ohh!

—So anyway, a long time after, I don't know how much time it took, anyway it took a long while. When she was in the woods—the war finished anyway, and so he comes home to see his wife and her—his baby eh? The baby was still alive. He asks his mother what she had done with his wife. She says, "Didn't you send for me to kill her?" He says, "What!" he says, "kill my wife?" he says. "I sent you a letter," he says, "and I told you to be really careful," he says, "with my wife and my baby."—"Well," she says, "that's it. You sent for me to get her killed and," she says, "now I had her killed."

A.K.: Ohh!

—There, he was crazy—gone crazy. He takes his horse and off—he takes. "Well now I'm not coming back until I find her. If she's dead or alive I've got to find her wherever she is, eh?" There so anyway, one day there's Genevieve eh, his mother and the little *God love*. Perhaps they were outside. They see a man coming. Because she had told him everything, eh? When they had taken her in the woods to kill her and everything, there were two men, they were to kill her. And so anyway they see this man coming. They were outside, they were—looking for roots to eat eh? He says, "Mother, look there who's coming now," he says, "to hurt us again. But," he says, "don't be afraid, I'm here, me," he says....

A.K.: Oh my God!

—He was nine, he was. "Don't be afraid," he says, "I'm here, me," and he grabs her and kisses his mother again, eh, and he waits for the man to come. And when he got there he threw himself on his knees in front of her and begged her pardon eh. Because he said he hadn't said that, him, it was only Golo there, it was only Golo....

A.K.: Yeah, Golo, yeah.

—who could have done that. So she says eh, the war was over and he'd come back, and he wouldn't—he wouldn't have died without finding her. There now when they're going eh, he takes her and takes her—home. But she hadn't lived very long without eating—they lived for maybe ten years on roots eh.

A.K.: Hmm.

—So him, he took him and chained him up like you would chain a dog up there. He chained him on a chain and you—"There," he said—lying on his side and he hauls on the chain to try and break it eh? And that's all I know.

A.K.: Little swine!

—It's only a piece eh.

G.T.: Hm.

A.K.: Da's de best kind dat.

G.T.: That's not finished?

—It's not finished—ah no! It's not the little quarter that, my dear. Not the little quarter. They had some misery. They had some....

Commentary and Notes

The reader will perhaps be struck by the somewhat dry narration Mrs. Ozon gives of her story; it is almost given as a summary, despite her use at various moments of lively dialogue, characteristic of her other narrations, and despite her comment that "it was a story"—the usual formula justifying the passage of time, or some unlikely event.

Mrs. Kerfont also knew the tale, since she brings to Mrs. Ozon's narration the addition of the name Golo, the villain of the story. Mrs. Kerfont's remark at the end of the tale is also significant: if she believes that "Da's de best kind dat," it is probably to let us know her preference in tales. It is not very long, lacks the repetition of *Märchen*, even though Mrs. Ozon insists that her version is far from complete.

As Hélène Bernier so well demonstrated in her book *La Fille aux mains coupées (conte-type 706)* (Quebec: Les Archives de Folklore 12, Presses de l'Université Laval, 1971), Mrs. Ozon's tale is a version, of literary origin, of AT 706, *The Maiden Without Hands*. As the characters' names suggest, moreover, we are dealing with a version of the legend of Saint Genevieve of Brabant which has since become traditional. Its literary history, as it appears in chapbooks, has been documented in the masterly work by Charles Nisard, *Histoire des Livres populaires ou de la Littérature de Colportage* (Paris: 2 vols., Maisonneuve & Larose, 1968; reimpression of the second edition, Paris: Dentu, 1864, vol. 2, 425-435). Bernier draws our attention to chapbooks which brought the story of Saint Genevieve to Canada in the nineteenth and early twentieth centuries. It is quite possible that Mrs. Ozon learned her version from an illustrated chapbook, although she claims to have heard it from her late husband, since she comments on two occasions, in her narration, how one can see so well the scenes she describes.

The story of Saint Genevieve is well rooted too in German language tradition. It is interesting to read Don Yoder's article "The Saint's Legend in the Pennsylvania German Folk-Culture" (*American Folk Legend: A Symposium*, ed. Wayland D. Hand, Berkeley: University of California Press, 1971, 157-183) which deals (164-171), with some apparent errors of detail, with the legend of Saint Genevieve in Europe and the United States.

Tale-type 706 is known in France in 47 versions, with some forty or so in North American French tradition. Mrs. Ozon's version is one of five collected from French Newfoundlanders, among whom can be found versions from both oral and literary tradition. Motifs in the tale include: K2110.1, *Calumniated wife*; K2117, *Calumniated wife: substituted letter (falsified message)*; S451, *Outcast wife at last united with husband and children*; S410, *Persecuted wife*; K2115, *Animal-birth slanders*; K512.2.0.2, *Eyes of animal substituted as proof for eyes of children*; S143, *Abandonment in forest*; K512.0.1, *Compassionate executioners*; S441, *Cast-off wife and child abandoned in forest*; B531.2, *Unusual milking animal*, and B535, *Animal nurse*.

THE LOST CHILDREN

Oh but the lost children, I only know a little piece in that.

A.K.: But yeah that don't matter, a little piece.

—Well it was a man and a woman, they had a little boy eh—his name was—I knew all their names eh? One was called—Pierre Col and the other was called— there were two Cols and now there was a little.... Now anyway they were two cousins, eh? So they were out playing one day and then he comes in to, to ask his mother for a slice of bread, a slice of bread that's a, a piece, a piece eh? She gives im a slap on his head and tells him to go away eh, she doesn't give him any bread. "Well," he says, "I'm going and I'm not coming back. You won't see me again," he says. Well, she thought he said that for *fun* eh? So they take off—*play* on the side of the street eh? Anyway, there's a man passing and he had three barrels on his cart eh—excuse me—and he takes the three little boys and puts each one in a barrel and takes them away, he steals them eh? He stole them. So—he mother and father were looking for him but they didn't find him, he was gone. So anyway, they were talking in the forest eh, the three of them. There, they walked and walked and walked. I

194

don't know how far it was before they found people, eh? So they came to an Indian cabin one evening eh, and it was only him brave, eh. He goes in. There was only a girl looking after it eh, and he asks her for something to eat, give him some bread or something. "I can't," she says, "my father and mother have gone and," she says, "if they find out they'll beat me."—"Oh but," he says, "we're not going to stay," he says, "we're gone travelling. We won't tell, nobody will know," he says. So there she gives him some bread and some tea and some milk and everything eh? And then they start travelling again and the little cousin, eh? There anyway, he was five years old when he left, there, him, from home eh. There anyway one time, after he'd finished travelling, we'll say eh—they had been travelling in the woods, him and his little brother—his little cousin, he falls sick him, eh. He was thirsty and he was hungry. And I don't know how many miles they had to trav—now he had to walk to fetch water for his little cousin, eh. He was sick for water eh. So anyway, you can see them, going along the two of them, they leave him there, eh. They take off, they walk together and nothing to put water in, only the barrel of his gun....

A.K.:   Oh gee whiz!

—So before they go to fetch their water and get back to him he was dead....

A.K.:   Oh dash!

—So they take him and bury him there and the two others split up, eh. So now, I don't know what happened to him, I don't remember. There anyway him, he walked long enough he tra—he fou—comes out into a village. So anyway, he goes looking for a job eh? Eh, he was old by now, he'd travelled a lot by that time. Well, he was five when he left home eh and by this time he was forty-five. It had been forty years he'd been travelling, eh.

A.K.:   Yeah.

—Yeah. And he was, he was to a house one day and they hired him eh. And every morning he would walk to work eh, he walked to work and on that—every morning when he went by there was a woman, she was sitting on the *balcony* eh. According to the story—and she watched him go by. So one morning—he told them there where he was staying that there was a woman who watched him go by every morning, he said, "I don't know why that is," he says, "I don't know who she is anyway." Well that morning anyway he was going by, eh, and the woman was outside and she asks him who he was because she wanted to know who he was, eh. She knew him and she couldn't say who he was. She couldn't say his name. She says she knows—we'll say....

A.K.:   She knowed him, eh?

—...that fellow eh. And he told her his name eh and it was his godmother.

A.K.:   Ahh!

—His beard had grown already eh, bearded, all beard eh. And she was his godmother her, eh? Every morning he went past his godmother's door and he didn't know her—I don't know anymore of it. I don't know any more, that's not the little quarter, the little quarter....

A.K.:   No.

G.T.:   Not the little quarter?

A.K.:   Yeah, she never tole it all anyway.

G.T.:   Do you know the rest of it?

A.K.:   She never tole it all anyway.

—I don't know the rest.

A.K.:   You tole longer n dat to me.

G.T.:   What came after?

—No no, that's, that's it, that's what I told you, well that's all I know eh.

A.K.: Da's a long—it's longer n dat. *De, i tait dans la grange là* [he was in the barn there].

—Not him.

A.K.: Who was it then? You knows.

—You're crazy you!

A.K.: Phew!

—Oh yeah. Yeah, uh yeah, yeah now....

A.K.: Ha ha ha!

—Now I remember, ah, ah! The first time he came to the village eh, he went to a house eh. There was only a man and a woman there eh, an old man and an old woman there eh. And he asks them to take him in as a boarder, but they didn't want to, eh. There anyway, he says, "The only place I can find is in my barn." So he goes and sets down in the barn, eh. And at midnight, he hears a noise and what it was was a man. He was coming to steal some hay eh, for his animals... [pause to change the tape; but Mrs. Ozon can add no more to her story.]

Commentary and Notes

Mrs. Ozon began her narration by warning us that she only knew part of the tale. She does indeed have to conclude her story well before its end, despite her friend's affirmation that on a preceding occasion she had told more of it; this provokes a minor exchange of teases. But in spite of Mrs. Kerfont's prompt, she is unable to remember more than an additional detail.

I have not been able to identify the tale according to *The Types of the Folktale*. Mrs. Ozon's allusion to the visual aspect of the story, "you can see them," suggests, as with the preceding tale, a printed source of the chapbook variety, and this has been confirmed by Luc Lacourcière. Professor Lacourcière is of the opinion that Mrs. Ozon's tale certainly derives from a booklet published in about 1888 by a certain Father Proulx, entitled *L'enfant perdu et retrouvé, Pierre Cholet* [Pierre Cholet, the child lost and found]. The hero of the tale, whose name closely resembles that in Mrs. Ozon's story, apparently told his adventures to the priest, who then put them into the form of a memoir. Professor Lacourcière also notes that the booklet was very popular around 1920. We do know that some older French Newfoundlanders received newspapers and other printed material from Quebec at that period.

THE THREE GOLD HAIRS

One time it was er, a man an a woman, dey had—you know dey were poor, dey were poor eh? Dey found a little baby, a little baby boy an evrybody was to see dat youngster, dey said—used... one day to come, he be, y'know, become a king eh? An evryone said that till it came to de king's ears, anyway. "I gotta go see," he said, "about dat baby," he said. Come one day anyhow, he come up dere. So he goes an he looks at de baby. Dat was shore. Y'know he looked like, y'know eh? An he tole de ole man de ole woman, he said, "Now," he said, "you got to make away wit your—dat, dat boy. Dat little boy o yours," he said. "An when dat boy is gone," he says, "come here." Pretty bad, deir own, own little boy dey had. But de king, so dat's what dey had to do. Anyway, after de king left, dey made a box—a box dat dey're shore it wouldn leak eh? Dey put him in an dey put down de river. So on de end of dat river dere was a man, he was all time fishin eh? An dey had no children. So dat day anyhow, he was dere fishin, he looked in de water was a box comin. He says "I wonder," he says, "what's in dat box?" He takes off fer to get it eh? He got dere, he opens it, he look in, de baby was *sleepin*. Cute. Well he never spared no time. He put it down in his dory an he took off for de shore. When he got to de house he tole his wife, he says, "Wife," he says, "I brought you sometin, what you're not expectin to

196

see," he said. An den he says, "Guess!"—"Well," she says, "I can't guess evryting." He says, "You wouldn guess it anyway." He says, "Come see." He showed her de little by. *Oh my God*! She almos come crazy wit de gladness. Er ad no young—no children eh? Okay. So anyhow, he was a big boy eh? So anyhow he got man, he had a mill eh? An evry day he was wit his father now—he used to call him his father eh? Wit his father, all, "Son." Anyway, de king come to hear about dat. Dat de youngster was alive eh? He was in some place eh? Anyway, he tole de queen, he says, "One day," he says, "I gotta go down dat way," he says. So anyhow to took off an he pass along where dat man was sawin. So he stop dere a long time talkin. An he tole de man, he says, "Ah, dat your son?" He said, "Yes!—*Not* my son," he says, "was a son," he says, "I found," he says, "on de water." He knowed it was den, was dat feller eh. "Look," he said, "look," he says, "before I left home I forgot to tell my wife," he said. He said, "Would you sen your little boy," he said, he said, "bring her a letter?"—"Sure," he said. So he made a letter an he said on de letter, when he get dere to kill him right away, no delay.

B.O.:   Oh oh!

—He wasn't a little boy, he was grown up eh? Anyway, he took off. So anyway he couldn get dere dat night. Ah, he pass in de woods eh, he got astray. He broke out to a camp in de woods so he knocked to de door an a woman opened de door. She said, "Where you're goin my little boy?" Tell er, tole him, "I'm astray," he said. He said, "De king," he said, "sen me," he says, "to bring a letter to de queen," he said. "And," he said, "I lost my road, I come here." He was all in, tired. "Uh well," she said, "you're not goin fudder tonight." She had twenty—*comment* [how many]?—She had twelve sons an dey were robbers, eh? Twelve o dem. So she gove the queen, de, de woman de letter to pick up see, so him, he went behind the stove an fell asleep. He never fell asleep you know. He heard all what was goin on. So de queen—de woman, her, she opened de letter, she looked at it eh? He was goin to his deat. Anyway, by n by her bys come. "Oh!" he says, "da's a *spy*!"—"No no," she said, "da's not a spy," she said, "da's a little by goin to his deat," she said. "Goin to his deat?"—"Yes," she said, "here's de letter." He give him de letter to read. "Well," he says, "we're robbers, we don't kill," he said. He said, "Da's, da's, da's, da's a shame," he says. He takes dat letter an heaves it in de stove an he makes anodder one. But he was a—write—his writnin-an he tole him de minute he gets home to marry his daughter! [laughter] He sign his daughter to him eh? Okay. So de nex marnin he got up, dey were gone before he got up. So he eat his breakfas an took off. Anyhow, he got to de king, passed de letter to de queen, "Well," she said, "I got to marry you," she said, "with my youngest daughter—i's de king's orders." Okay. She marry him. When dey come in de house, Mister Jack was dere. "Well," he says, "queen," he says, "did you read my letter?" She said, "Yes." He said, ah, "Da's not de way—"—"But," she said, "you tole me on your letter to marry him to de youngest daughter."—"Oh *non*!" he said. "Oh yes," she said. She said, "Here's de letter." She give him de letter. He's right seized, he can't say nothin else eh? He said, "I don't know what come over me dat day," he said. "Well, anyhow," she said, "we're gonna get him de same." I don't know, in dat place, anyhow, was a giant, eh, he had tree gold hair in his head. Anyhow, he tole Jack, he said, "Jack," he said, "tomorrow," he said, "you gotta go to dat giant," he said, "an you got to bring me," he said, "de tree gold hairs in his head,"—"I's a hard ting to do," he said. "Hard or not, you got to go, or your deat," he said. Okay. De nex marnin he took off, poor devil. So anyway, he travelled an travel until he came to, ah, it was—wait now—a ferryboat dere, used to cross de people eh? Ah, he puts Jack aboard—it's not Jack, I'll call him Jack anyway. So on his way goin across, dey tole him, he says, "It's twenty years I'm at dis job an I can't lose it."—Y'know, he can't, can't give it up eh? He said, "Could you tell me," he said, "what to do?"—"Not dis time but when I comes back," he

197

said, "I tell you." Okay. So anyhow, he took off. So anyhow, he g—he broke into anodder town. So as he—he went to a house an asked for something to eat. Dey brought him black bread. He says, "I don't want dat," he says, "white bread."—"Well," she says, "aroun here is all black bread, our wheat is no more good." He says, "You can't tell us," he says, "what is wrong?"—"No," he says, "I can't tell youse dis time. Maybe comin back I'll tell you." Anyway, he went into de odder town. He went to a house he asked for water. Dey brought him a glass o wine. He says, "I asked for water, I didn ask fer wine."—"Well, we got no wi—got no water," she said, "only wine," she said, "an we got to pay dear enough for it. Our well is all dried," he says, "you can't tell us what doos dat?" He says, "I can't tell you but when I come back I tell you." Okay. Anyhow, he took off. So anyhow dat night he broke out to de giant. He knocked to de door, de ole woman opened de door. "*My God!* Where you goin?" she said. "Well, me," he said, "I come here to get de tree gold hairs from de giant's head,"—"Who, who, he, da's a hard ting to do," she said. "If you be good," she said, "you'd do it fer me." "Well, all right," he says, "come on in." She gives him noting to eat. Now he tole her about de, de well dere—about de ferryboat. He said, "What doos dat?" She said, he said, "Dat ferryboat is twenty years now, he's on de job, he can't lose his job." He says, "I wonder what's de reason?"—"Ah," she says, "I don't know."—"Well," he says, "ask de giant, he might tell you." An he says, "In de odder town," he said, "dey're eatin black bread. An dey said dey can't get de white bread at all dere, black bread. Well ask him de reason de giant, what does dat now, dat deir wheat don come white no more eh? An in de odder town," he says, "dere's—deir wells is all dried, an dey can't get no water."—"Well," he says, "I'll hask him dat too." Okay. She had all aboard dere. "Now," she said, "I'll have to hide you in a place where he can't find you." Okay. So anyway, she hide him. An—ah, my God! by n by he arrived. *Pas beau* [Not pretty]! Ah, he comes in he start smellin, ah, he says, "Fresh meat in de house ole woman?"— "Sure," she said, "I got some for your supper," oh she gave him a big supper, My G—. After he was done supper, oh, "Ole woman," he said, "you know what you should do," he said, "look in my head,"—"Well," she said, "what happen? I's de firs time," she says, "you asked me dat."—"Yes," he said, "I'm tired," he said, "I wants you to look in my head." Okay. So he lays down, she lays down his head, an he fall asleep, dead to de worl. She had a gold hair eh? She comes across a gold hair, she pluck it out. Uhhh, he give a big kind a screech, almos struck her. He said, "What fer you're haulin my hair?"—"Well," she said, "somethin I got to ask you. Some ferryboat," she says, "over dere, is twenty years," she says, "dat man," she says, "he's, he's crossed de people across de lake an he can't get out of his job."—"Da's his fault," he says, "what fer he's so foolish?" He said, "De man now he's gonna cross across," he said, "well, before, before he gets ashore, well," he says, "ma—ask de odder man to row for him eh? To row. An," he said, "den after," he said, "when he gets ashore jump aboard—jump ashore him an push de boat. An," he said, "he's out of his job." Okay. But Jack heared, he use to hear all dat him. Fall asleep again. Her she was lookin, lookin. By n by she found anodder hair. She plucked it. Oh, *gee whiz*, he got *vex*. *"My God,"* she said, "ole man what's wrong wit you?" she said. "What fer you're pullin my hair?"—"Uh well," she said, "i's one ting I forgot to ask you. Uh," she says, "in a town dere," she says, "dey're always eatin black bread," she says. "Dey can't get no, no, no white wheat at all. All black."—"Da's, da's deir lazeness," he said. "If dey would get people, ploughs an horses," he said, "an er, an plough de lan," he said, "dey have white bread like *before*." All right, pass off like dat. He falls asleep again. By n—he was well asleep

anyhow, when she found de odder hair an, an she plucked it. *Oh my God!* He jump right up! Well he almos give her dat! He said, *"Garde!"* [Watch out!]—

B.O.:   Ha ha ha!

198

—"Oh, ole man," she says, "my God," she says, "you're *cross!*"—"Well," he said, "i's enough. You haulin—pullin my hair like dat."—"Well now," she said, "ole man, i's something I forgot to ask you. I's anodder town," she says, "dere," she says, "deir, deir—all deir wells are dry, all deir lakes, dey're dry. All dey drinks is wine."—"Da's deir lazeness," he said. He says, "In de bottom a de, de, is"—dey had a big well dere, y'know—used to support all de town eh? An in dat well e—was a, a, ah, comment ça? [What is it?]

B.O.:   *Garnouille?* [Frog?]

—Oh no, no no no—*in crapaud?* [a toad?]

G.T.:   *Crapaud?*

—*In crapaud.*

G.T.:   Eh? A toad.

—Yeah, I spose.

G.T.:   Toad, yeah, *un crapaud.*

B.O.:   Yeah.

—Yeah. Well da's it. Dat, dat now use to suck all de water. An de, de, de wheat dere I guess was de, de, a *souris blanche* [white mouse] fer to eat de, de, de... *machine là* [thing there].

G.T.:   Hm?

—*Des racines là* [The roots there].

B.O.:   Oh oh!

—De roots.

G.T.:   The roots?

—Yeah. Uh well now, he had it all een—knowed it all. He was some glad an he had de tree gold hair now. Anyhow when he got up de nex marnin, when dey got up, Jack was *gone.* Now she said, "Jack," she said, "you, you heared it all?" He said, "Yes, I heared it all." Okay. Anyhow he tanked her very much an put his hand—hair in his pocket an *futt! decolle* [whish! takes off]. Now anyhow when he got to er, to where de well dere—huh! when dey seen him comin my good gosh almighty dey start runnin to him. "I spose now," dey said, "you're gonna tell us."—"Yes, shore," he said, "I'll tell youse." He said, "De bottom o your well," he said, "is some *crapaud* [toad] an da's what sucks all de water from your well." He said, "If you could dig down enough an get, an get de *crapaud* an kill it, you get tousands o water." So anyhow, dey done it dere, he was dere, he stayed dere until dey done it. An shore enough. Dey found dat *crapaud* an kill it eh, *mes amis* [my friends]. De water, tousands. Well, de people was some glad, well, dey gove him *money* an gold an a horse an carriage. Took off. So anyhow dey got in de odder town where's black bread. Dey all come—when dey seen him comin—dey all come an meet him. "Now I spose," dey said, "you'll tell us wha—what happened to our wheat."—"Yes", he said, *c'est eune souris blanche,"* hein? [It's a white mouse eh?] I've got to French it. *"I's eune souris blanche,"* he said, "is eatin all the roots o yer, yer, yer ah...."

B.O.:   Wheat.

—"Wheat," right. Okay. Dey got horses an mans my son an ploughs an dey start ploughin. Ploughed. De foun it, de foun it an dey kill it. Then after, all right, dey was glad o dat. He gove Jack money an gole again dere, *oh my God!* he had tousands o money for himself. So he took off—until dey got to de, de lake. Now dat man was dere. "Now," he said, "you're gonna tell me—you're able to tell me de day what happened now I can't lose my job?"—"Shore," he says, "take me across first," he says, "I'll tell you first—I'll tell you after." Okay. So anyhow he takes him. Crossin de lake he tole him—an he got ashore now, he got out. "Now," he said, "de firs one now," he says, "is goin to come here to cross him across, well now," he said, "when you gets half ways across, eh, well give him your oars eh? An," he says, "make him pull de odder way, y'know, pull de odder half eh? An," he says, "when you gets almos ashore, jump out an push de boat, let him go. He's gonna be strayed him!" ...Ha ha! Okay. Anyhow he jumps on horse an carriage an now he starts for home. By n by de king looks out, he says, "Da's not Jack is comin dere?" He said, "Yes! Oh look a dat!" He went outdoors to meet him. "Well, well!" he said, "what you got all dat silver, gole?"—"My poor man," he said, "I knocked out de quarter of what I wanted to get...."

B.O.: Ha ha ha!

"—Dere's only more—tousands of it," he says. He said, "Rig yerself," he said, "an go." But de king, him, greedy—take de horse an carriage now he starts. When he got to de lake anyhow, he jumps aboard dat man dere. Hee hee hee! When he gets halfways across—an he said, gove de king de tree gole hair—not de giant give him all dat money, y'know, de gladness, he was goin back too him, to de giant, fer a load too, him. So anyhow when he got halfways de lake, de man says, ah, "You should," he says, "take de oars an give me a spell," he says, "me I'm all in. I'm all een."—"Shore," he said. So anyhow he took de oars an he start to row. When he got almos ashore, he jumps out dat man, he gives him a push. "Now!" he says, 'i's your turn," he said. "You, you row as long as I did," he said, "you'd know you, yer, yer job!"

B.O.: Ha ha ha!

—So c'est fini, c'est fini là [So that's the end, that's the end there]. Ha ha ha!

Commentary and Notes

The telling of this tale was proceeding nicely until problems of a linguistic nature arose. Mrs. Kerfont could not remember the English word for "crapaud" nor the English for "eune souris blanche." As she herself says, "I've got to French it." Such examples of macaronic language are common in Franco-Newfoundland tradition. Apart from a few minor problems of this kind, however, the tale was very well told, quite evenly, by Mrs. Kerfont at her best.

The story combines two international tale-types, AT 930, The Prophecy, and AT 461, Three Hairs from the Devil's Beard. Le Conte populaire français notes 18 versions of AT 461 and as many for French Canada. Although the two types are often combined internationally, only four such examples have been found in France. It should also be noted that nearly half the versions of AT 461 from France are localized in Brittany, which may explain its popularity among French Newfoundlanders; the Centre d'Etudes Franco-Terreneuviennes has five versions of the tale, told by three different narrators. Four of the five versions combine both types. Type AT 930 by itself, moreover, has not been found among French Newfoundlanders.

Motifs in the tale include the following: M312, Prophecy of future greatness for youth; M370, Vain attempts to escape fulfillment of prophecy; H1510, Tests of power to survive; M371, Exposure of infant to avoid fulfillment of prophecy; S331, Exposure of child in boat (floating chest); R131.4, Fisher rescues abandoned child; K978, Uriah letter; K511, Uriah letter changed; K1355, Altered letter of execution gives princess to hero; H1211, Quest assigned in order to get rid of hero; H1210.2, Quest assigned by king; H1273.2, Quest for three hairs from the devil's beard; H1292.8, Question (propounded on quest): when will a ferryman be released from his duties; H1292.1, Question (propounded on quest): why has the spring gone dry?; H1292.21* (CEFT), Question propounded on quest): why does the wheat not grow?; H1291, Questions asked on way to other world; H1292, Answers found in other world to questions propounded on way; G530.1, Help from ogre's wife (mistress); G532, Hero hidden and ogre deceived by his wife (daughter) when he says he smells human

200

blood; H1243, *Riches the reward of questions solved on quests;* P413.1.1, *Ferryman puts oars into king's hand and he must remain ferryman.*

Mrs. Kerfont learned the tale from Mrs. Hélène Renouf, her late husband's mother-in-law from his first marriage. Mrs. Renouf was a Pieroway from St. George's.

THE KING OF THE FISHES

B.O.: *L'âroi des poissons* [The king of the fishes].

A.K.: I knowed one all right, but I fergets it, *non.*

G.T.: About the man who didn't have any children an he went fishin and ah, I don't know it eh? An he fished up the king o the fish?

A.K.: Right.

G.T.: Is that it?

A.K.: Yes.

G.T.: Go on then.

A.K.: Uh well, I don't know eh?

G.T.: Well you recognize it when I say it, that beginning part.

A.K.: I's de start of it, yes.

G.T.: An the fish says, "Throw me back in an fish on the other side," or something an he does that three times.

A.K.: Yeah.

G.T.: And um, the third time he takes a fish in and the fish says to cut him up.

A.K.: Yeah. Ah, give de guts—wait now, wait now—de meat to his wife, de   bones to his dog—to his bitch dere—an de guts, ah, wait now....

B.O.: *Mette dans son jardin* [Put in his garden].

A.K.: *Ouais.* So his wife'll have tree twins eh, tree boys, his dog have tree chops—pups an have tree roses in de garden eh.

G.T.: Well tell de story then.

A.K.: Oh, i's a nice story, I donno dat *mignon.*

G.T.: Start from the beginning, maybe it'll come back to you.

A.K.: Da's, da's de beginnin.

G.T.: No, well, right, y'know, I said the first bit but you start right from the very beginning, cos I mean, I don't know the way to say it you see, I just heard a little bit....

A.K.: But me my dear, da's all, da's all I can remember is dat dere. My God! I donno de name o de house dere.

G.T.: Eh?

B.O.: Eh heh!

G.T.: An he goes—the boys go off one at a time and ah....

A.K.: Who here tells dat story?

B.O.: It's Bill an Tom and Jack eh? Yeah.

G.T.: Yeah. No, I read about it once. Um, and they met an old witch or somethin.

A.K.: They got married eh?

G.T.: I don't know.

A.K.:   Is one got married, I know. De first one got married eh?

G.T.:   I never heard dat.

B.O.:   Yeah.

A.K.:   An when he went to say his prayer in de night eh....

B.O.:   He used to sleep with one leg out of the bed. Used to sleep....

A.K.:   Oh well, when he, when he said his prayers, I donno what kind a house, de, de—my God, de name o de house now. I fergets de name o de house now. Anyway, he tole his wife, he says, "What's dat house over dere?"— "Well," she said, "What goes dere never returns."

G.T.:   Start from the beginning and try to tell me as much of it as you can and maybe Blanche can remember odd bits and pieces.

A.K.:   Oh my gosh, *j'sais pas* [I don't know]. You said the first, you.

G.T.:   Well no, I didn't, I just said the first words but you—I would like you to say it in your words, the way you say it.

A.K.:   My God, Blanche?

B.O.:   Well there was a man and a woman they had—they were married eh? And him he was a fisherman and he used to go fishing eh. And one day he caught this cod eh, and so he told his wife he'd caught a cod, a pretty fish, eh. And she says, "Tomorrow," she says, "if you catch another one you'll bring it to me, to eat." You see, that's how it goes eh?

A.K.:   Yeah yeah, da's de way it was tole here, here.

B.O.:   And the next day, he went an caught a fish, that cod, eh, and he took it and cooked it and she ate it, she, she—she ate the meat, she gave the bone to her dog and the guts she planted in her garden eh.

A.K.:   *Ouais, ouais d'méme* [Yeah, yeah, like that].

B.O.:   Oh yeah. And ah... his wife found three little boys eh—

A.K.:   Yeah.

B.O.:   And so that was Tom an Bill an Jack.

A.K.:   Yeah.

B.O.:   That was their names y'know. The first one to go away was Bill. Bill went away and he got married and so anyway when he said his prayers in the night going to bed eh....

A.K.:   Pick that up!

B.O.:   Eh?

A.K.:   *Pick that up* eh!

B.O.:   No difference. When he went to go to bed he said his prayers there anyway he saw this house eh, and he asked her see what—what kind of house it was and she said to him, she said, "*Don't*," she said "*bother* about that house," she says, "everything that goes there—that goes there doesn't come back." And so anyway, he went to bed, his belly in the air in the bed and he had—one leg out of the bed eh? So anyway, when his wife had gone to sleep he took off and he didn't come back anyway. So anyway, the next day Bill takes off, Bill—Tom.

A.K.:   He goes in the garden firs.

B.O.:   No no. Yes, and when they left there now I forgot eh, when they left—well yes, exactly, that's how it is I think—there anyway Tom left after eh.

G.T.: What about ah....

B.O.: He had to go look for his brother who had gone eh.

G.T.: Blanche, what about the, the three things that the, the, ones they gave the dog and ah, the one she planted in the garden? What happened to that?

A.K.: He went with the dog. Bill, ah—*Tom a té avec son chien* [Tom went with his dog] eh—now when, when he was enchanted dere eh....

B.O.: Well yes, well now....

A.K.: Well, one o de roses was down eh?

B.O.: Yeah.

A.K.: De nex marnin, so Bill went to de garden eh?

B.O.: She's telling the story look. Tell it you.

A.K.: No no, you tell it.

G.T.: Tell it, Blanche.

B.O.: I don't know it.

A.K.: No no, you talks good you.

B.O.: And there anyway, in the evening he's walking and when he comes to that house eh, well his wife asks him where he's come from. "Oh," he says, "I've been around," he says. So anyway in the night they get dressed for bed, she says, "Now you're going to come to bed," and there when you know, he starts trying to see what that house was. She says, "I told you last night," she said, "what that house is," she says. "Everything that goes there never comes back." So anyway it happened that his brother had been there eh. So anyway, he goes to bed again just like his brother he lies down with one leg out of the bed eh. So she says to him, she says, "Why is it you sleep with one leg out of the bed?" She says, "Last night you slept with one leg out of the bed and," she says, "tonight you're sleeping again with one leg out of the bed." He says, "That's all right," he says, "that's how I sleep." So anyway when his wife was asleep he goes to the house again eh. *Dame*, I can't tell you what happened to them anyway. Anyway he pass....

A.K.: Dey was turned, dey was turned to a stone.

B.O.: To a stone.

A.K.: Yeah.

B.O.: And there anyway, the next morning they go in the garden there was another flower lost again—fallen down eh. That was the second. So there Jack gets dressed and he takes off. He says, "I've got to find my two brothers," he says. "And," he says, "if I can't find my two brothers," he says, "well," he says, "the roses will come back to life."

A.K.: Yeah.

B.O.: That's what he said, eh?

A.K.: Yeah.

B.O.: When he comes to that house anyway, ah, well now he goes in an anyway his wife there. They go to bed in the night.

A.K.: *Oh non*, but you said, "Where you come from?" she said.

B.O.: She asks him, "Where you come from?" she says. She says, "That's two nights in a row you take off and you don't come back." She says, "Where do you go?"—"Ah," he says, "I go looking around," he says, "visiting."

So anyway that, that night when they're going to bed, he gets down on his knees again to say his prayers. So anyway, eh, he asks her what that house is. She says, "The third night tonight you ask me the same thing," she says, "I'm telling you," she says, "not to *bodder* with that house because," she says, "everything that goes there never comes back." So he goes to bed with one leg out of the bed eh. She says, "Why is that," she says, "can't you sleep in the bed?"—"Well," he says, "that's the way I sleep."

A.K.: Poor way!

B.O.: "Third night tonight," she says....

A.K.: Ah ha ha ha!

B.O.: "you're sleeping with one leg out of the bed." So he says, "That's okay," he says, "go to sleep." When she was asleep, he *goes back* again eh. So he doesn't come back. But now me I don't know there, there. I don't know it eh.

A.K.: He came back him.

B.O.: But anyway the next morning when his father got up he went to the garden....

A.K.: No no, wait now. It was an ole witch in dere y'know. Er....

B.O.: I don't know.

A.K.: Well yes now, when—de two of dem when dey went wit deir dogs eh? So anyhow when ah, when ah.... When she come she said, "Oh my God, I'm frighten your dog," she said, "tie your dog!"—"My dog is not cross," he said. He said to hisself, "Da's what it is, da's what it is dere. An she said—he said, "My dog is not cross," an den ah, now, ah, wait now, *c'est là c'est pire* [that's where it's hard].... Ah, someting about his brudders anyway, he said... ah. He said, "If you don't," he said, "tell me where's my brudder," he said, "I'm gonna—my dog," he said, "is gonna eat you alive."—"Oh my God!" she says, "No!" she says. She says, she says, ah, "Well," she says, "dey're dere, dey're dere, dey're in a stone eh? Deir dog an deir two selves. Well here," she says, "bottle o w—bottle o water," she says, "drop it on everyone you sees dere," she said. [pause to change the tape]

G.T.: An she gives him a bottle of, ah....

—Water, an he drops it in evry pla—y'know, in evry stone eh?

G.T.: Yeah.

—So anyhow his two brudders come to, an de two dogs eh. An when dey come, my son, dey took her. Dey tored her up in pieces. Den after now dey was unchanted eh? So anyhow dey goes down to de house eh—his wife an ah.... Yeah, but when dey got in dere de tree brudders, de tree—dey looks alike an she didn know who was her husband, which now.... is her husband eh? An eh, well so den anyhow it was Tom eh, "Well now," he said, "I'm your husband," he said. "An," she says, "where you was all de time?"—"Well," he says, "da's de way," he says, "we went in dat house," he said, "it was enchanted. A good chance for my brudder John, ah, Jack," he says. "Da's him cha—unchanted us." Well now, da's far as I heard it eh?

G.T.: Hm. But ah, did Blanche leave any of it out? I mean she didn't ah....

A.K.: She never mentioned de dogs.

G.T.: No. Oh, ah, yeah, that's right.

A.K.: An de dogs now goes wit dem eh?

204

G.T.:	Yeah. Did they have horses as well?
A.K.:	Yes, now I tinks about it, de harses too bye.
G.T.:	Yeah.
A.K.:	Wait now. When, well was de meat fer de hor—de woman, de bones fer de dog, de guts fer de....
G.T.:	Garden?
A.K.:	... de garden an de skin fer de horses eh?
G.T.:	Yeah.
A.K.:	De mare eh?
G.T.:	Yeah.
A.K.:	Something like dat anyway.
G.T.:	Hm. And the horse had three....
A.K.:	Tree foals an dey had each one eh?
G.T.:	Hm, right.
A.K.:	Da's how it goes... i's hard y'know i's a long time I never tell dose stories. *Des chouals ouais, chaque in choual* [Horses yeah, each one a horse].
B.O.:	*Chaque in choual* [Each one a horse].
A.K.:	*Chaque in chien* [Each one a dog].
B.O.:	These days people don't tell stories anymore....

Commentary and notes

This tale is extremely interesting, not for its narrative content which is very fragmentary, but because it illustrated perfectly the cooperation which is so typical of the two ladies' storytelling. Neither could remember the story well, but together they were able to reconstitute its main elements as they knew them. In any event, it is the only story collected which so well illustrates the macaronic aspect of Franco-Newfoundland tradition. With much coaxing at the beginning, Mrs. Ozon begins the story, in French, to be replaced, half-way through the tale, by Mrs. Kerfont, speaking in English. The reader will also notice the numerous details that each lady brings to the other's narration at moments of memory lapses.

The story is a very fragmentary version of the international tale-type AT 303, *The Twins or Blood-Brothers. Le Conte populaire français* notes some 70 French versions of the tale, and seven for French tradition in North America. This last figure is of course out of date; in his 1961 revision of *The Types of the Folktale*, Stith Thompson noted 15 Franco-American versions. Apart from Mrs. Ozon and Mrs. Kerfont's version, six others have been recorded from French Newfoundlanders, and the tale seems to be one of the most popular in this tradition. Neither lady could provide the source of their versions, which they must have heard on several occasions.

Motifs from tale-type AT 303 in this version include: P251.6.1, *Three brothers*; T511.5.1, *Conception from eating fish*; T589.7.1, *Simultaneous birth of (domestic) animal and child*; F577.2, *Brothers identical in appearance*; E761, *Life token*; E761.3, *Life token: Flower fades*; G263, *Witch injures, enchants or transforms*; D231, *Transformation: man to stone*; K1311.1, *Husband's twin brother mistaken by woman for her husband*; and D700, *Person disenchanted.*

THE BIG GREY DOG

One time dere was a man an woman dey had tree sons, Jack an Bill an Tom. Well Ja—Tom said, he says, "I gotta go tomorrow," he says, "to see if I can fine work somewheres." He said, "Three big boys to de house," he says, "an nobody movin." Okay. De nex marnin anyhow, he takes off. He was travellin, travellin, walkin trough de country. He looks up before him, a big grey dog, he start to growl an he start to growl an he start chasin him. Ha ha ha! You should see de legs go home you! He got in de house, he fell in de door, he almos died wit de fright. Dey couldn get noting out of him. Dey said, "What in de name o God you got?"—"Well," he said, "I don't know." He said, "I's a big grey dog," he says, "up dere," he says, "almos frighten me to deat." Bill said, "You should be ashamed o yourself," he said, "frighten of a dog."—"You never seen de dog," he said. Okay. He says, "I'm goin tomorrow marnin," he says, "I gonna fine him." De nex marnin anyway, Bill, he takes his bundle an off he start. Ah, he was goin wit his head down, y'know, not tinkin about notin. When he looks up de mister dog was dere, right in de front of im. He start to growl an chase im, he start to run, he run, he fall in de door he almos kill hisself. "Ahhh!" he said, "da's de way eh?"—"*Ben* [Well]," he said, "I wasn frighten of a dog." He said, "I's not a dog," he said, "it's the devil."—"Well," he said, "I don't know what it is."—"Well," Jack says, "sometin," he says, "be frighten of a dog. Well, me, I'm goin tomorrow marnin," he says, "an I bet you I'm not gonna come back."—"*You!*" he said, "You'll be like us." Okay. De nex marnin Jack takes his bundle an off he start. Ah, he was goin now, "I'm goin up to de country." He looks up he seen him sittin down on his starn—an he start growlin eh? "You can growl if you wants," Jack says to hisself, "I'm goin—I'm goin—I'm facin you." He faced him, he sit down. He start sayin—you know he start to growl after Jack an he start to run after Jack eh, but Jack never mine him, he kept on goin. He comes facin Jack,"Well," he says, "is de firs man I never frighten from dis country," he said. "Takes a dog," he says, "to frighten me." Okay. He said, "We're gonna be buddies togedder." He says, "Where you *goin*?"—"Well," he says, "folly me," he says. De dog tole him, he said, "Folly me, come wit me," he said. Okay. So anyhow dey start takin off. When dey got in de... aroun twelve o'clock in de night. He says, "you know dat house dere," he says. "Go," he said, "knock to de door," an he says, "if he don't want fer you to come in," he says, "me, me an you," he said, "I'm gonna show him my teet," he said. "Dey're gonna bring me een." Okay. When dey got dere, de ole woman come an answer de door. When she seen de dog, she got frighten, eh? "My gosh!" he said, "can I sleep here tonight?"—"My gosh," she says, "no," she says, "my hus—my boys is gone."—"Well," he says. "I wants to sleep an if you ref—my dog is dere." He showed his teet. "Come on een," she says, frighten to death. She gives him his supper an he was to feed de dog well too eh. He was to feed de dog an all. Den he says, "Ask her fer, fer a room."—"Well," she says, "I got no rooms," she said, "All de rooms is dere is my bys owns." I don't know how many boys she had. Ah, tree bys. She said, "Dey got each a room, ah."—"Well," he says, "I wants a room," he said. "If you don't my dog—if you don't give me a room to sleep een," he said, "my dog is dere. He showed his teet to her again. "Oh!" she says, "go on," she says. Went upstairs. Now de dog tole Jack, "Go on to bed," he said, "sleep happy you," he said. "Me I'm gonna watch." Okay. Roun twelve o'clock, *mes amis*, he heard de racket comin. Her bys. Comes een. So she gove em deir supper. He said, ah, "Who's in my room?"—"Well," she said, "a little boy," she said, "an a dog."—"Well, I'm gonna go see about dat me," he said. So he goes upstairs de dog him he goes on de edge where's de whole upstairs eh, an he says—an he lays down dere, *mes amis de Dieu*, he was goin a see, when he got de las step above he made a growl an de giant he never went downstairs, he *fell* downstairs. He almos *killed* hisself!

B.O.:   Ha ha ha!

—"My God," he says, "modder," he says, "tomorrow marnin," he says, "wake us up early," he says, "to be gone fer when dey gets up." Okay. So anyhow, before daylight she wakes dem up an dey're gone. So Jack never heard notin at all, him.

206

Blank! So his dog wake him up. He says, "Get up master," he said. He said, "I's time to get up to go." He gets up, goes downstairs, "My God," he says, "take care you don't down—don't break down de stairs," he said. He tole his dog. "Oh no," he said. Anyhow, when he got downstairs, now before he went downstairs, he tole, he tole his—"Jack," he said, "you're gonna ask em fer her fartune. She got a fartune. An you—she's gonna say she got none. She got some. She got one, a fartune," she said. "An tell her to give it to you." Okay. So anyhow dey had deir breakfast dere an he haves a smoke. Now. "Now," he says, "before I leaves here," he said, "I wants a fartune. Dere's a fartune here," he said, "an I wants it."—"My poor man," she says, "I got no fartune here."—"Yes," he said, "an if you don't gimme it," he said, "my dog is dere." So anyhow, she went an she got it. I donno de name o de—I donno what's de name o de, de whatyoucalls de name of it....

G.T.:   The fortune?

—Was a fartune eh, but I donno what dey had it een eh, i's something I know, I fergets what it is anyway.

G.T.:   The fortune was in something?

—Inside, yeah.

G.T.:   Like a big chest?

—Yes. So anyhow she gives him—she gives him dat an off dey start. So anyhow, now, "Look," he said, "dere, dere, dere comin down," he said, "her sons dere," he said, "wit each a bag o money. Now," he says, "you'll keep behind me, me I'll go face dem," he said. Dey was comin down, dey was sayin, "I wonder if de boy an de dog is *gone*—I wonder dey're gone. I hope dey're gone fore we gets down dere." When he looks up *mes amis de Dieu*, de dog was dere. He start to growl, dey start, dey left evryting—each a bag of money dey had—dey left evryting an off dey starts trough de woods evrywheres. So anyhow, he tole Jack, he says, "Take dem bags," he says, "an tie dem togedder. An put dem across my back. I'll carry it me," he said. So Jack went ahead an him, he was behine. So when Jack look aroun, he says, "Where's de bag o money?"—"Well," he said, "I sent it down," excuse me, he said, "I sent it down to yer fodder," he said, "I know he's in bad need of it."—"Oh well, okay." So anyhow dey was goin aroun till dey got to a town. Now he tole Jack, he said, "You go to de store," he says, "you'll get, ah, two prince suit." Da's from de head now to de feet eh, whole suit an prince. Okay. Anyway, Jack go to de store, took two prince suits so when he comes back, so, ah, he give him one in his mout to de dog eh? Well de dog tole him, he says, "I'm gonna go," e says, "take a visit aroun," e says. "Wait for me here. An," he says, "don't you move."—"Oh no," he said. So e goes in de woods, he turns back to a prince dere. Jack had a prince. So anyhow, he never know dat see. So he put on his suit, a beautiful prince. So anyhow he comes down an Jack was dere sittin down on side de road. He said, "What yer waitin fer," he said, "boy?"—"Well, me," he said, "I'm waitin fer my dog."-"Waitin fer yer dog?" he said. He said, "Yes, he's gone an take a turn in de woods somewhere," he said. He said, "You'd know—if you'd see yer dog, you'd know yer dog eh?"—"Sure," he said, "I'd know my dog."—"Well," he said, "I'm yer dog." He said, "You're not my dog," he said, "you're a prince."—"Well," he said, "you ah, you unchanted me," he said. "I was enchanted to a prince, er a dog." Uh well, he was some glad. "Now," he tole Jack, he said, "down home," he says, "is two weddings tonight," he said. "My sister got married as yer—" —an ah, wait now, yeah, his sister got married—an ah, wit one of his brodder, an ah, my God, I can't place it togedder now. Tom got married to de king's daughter eh, an de king's son got married wit Jack's sister, see? Now dat was said on de first dat was said on de last. Okay. "Now," he said, 'i's one right here," he said. "We'll go to dat one an if it don't suit us," he said, "we'll go somewhere else." So anyhow, de first time dey goes dere, oh, was all some small, little people eh. Right small. He tole Jack, he says, "You like here you?" he said. "No, I don't like it. Too small," he said. "Too small people."—"Well, we'll go to de odder one." Da's to, da's to his fodder's de king. So anyhow, dey went in to de king, dey stayed to de door. So de king he start lookin. So he goes een to see his wife, he tole, he tole de queen, he says, "I's two princes come dere, two prince," he said. "I'm sure," he said, "our one—one of dem is our prince."—"Well," she said, "I'm goin an see, me," she said, 'if i's him," he says—she says—"I'll know him." Okay. She goes an she looks. She said, "Yes, da's our prince." Oh my God! Was no, no delay. Dey had to go een, eh? So anyway—no, Jack.... I's hard, my son. I's hard.

G.T.:   Think a moment.

—I'm ahead o my story. Tom got married de king's daughter all right but—ah, Jack's sister wasn married at all. She was home, still home eh? So ah, anyway, ah, he went in de parlor anyhow where dey was chattin dere. So he said, he ask Jack, "You," he said, "Jack, you'll get married my sister," he said, "an I'll get married wit yours," he said, "have de tree weddings togedder." He said, "Sure," he said. So he asked his fodder. "Shore," he said. So anyhow Jack got married wit de king's daughter an his prince got married wit Jack's sister so, dey're not dead dey're livin yet. I's ony a small little shart one eh?

Commentary and notes

This short tale has some moments of humour, notably in the confrontations with the dog at the beginning, and the confrontation of the old woman's son with the dog. Mrs. Kerfont had to be seen at these moments of tension, her eyes bright with mischief. The reader will note how she stops in full narrative flight to ask for a word from one of her audience, and how she covers up a moment of confusion towards the end of the tale, when she tells us, "I'm ahead o my story"—a common enough sentence in the private or family tradition, less so in the public tale tradition of French Newfoundlanders. Mrs. Kerfont attributed the tale to a sister of her mother, "poor aunt Christine." She could not say when she had heard it told.

Despite some similarities with tale-type AT 545, *The Cat as Helper*, it has not been possible to identify the tale with any precision. Its motifs include: P251.6.1, *Three brothers*; D141, *Transformation: man to dog*; D754, *Disenchantment by serving transformed person*; D777, *Disenchantment by covering with cloth*; H1242, *Youngest brother alone succeeds on quest*; and L161, *Lowly hero marries princess*.

FEARLESS RICHARD

Well Fearless Richard now, it was a man and a woman, they had a son eh. His name was Richard and he had never been frightened. He'd never seen anything that could frighten him eh. So he used to say so to his mother every day he said, "I'd really like something which would—" —which could frighten him eh. And he'd never been frightened and he couldn't, he couldn't believe that he could be frightened. So anyway, she was saying to her husband that evening, she said, "Tonight you're going to frighten Richard." He says, "Yeah. How?"—"Well," he says, "tonight I'm going to pretend—I won't fetch water for the night eh. Well," he says, "when it's dark I'm going to roll you up in a white sheet," and she said, "that you'll go an lie down in on the path. And," she says, "when the night is really dark well then," she says, "I'm going to tell him I haven't got any water and," she says, "I'll send him for water, eh?" She says, "Lie across the path." Anyway when night comes now ah, "Well," she says, "Richard," she says, "I haven't got any water for the night." She says, "You're going to have to go fetch some." Now there the old man had gone eh. He says, "Yeah." She says, "You're not afraid to go?"—"Afraid!" he says, "I've never yet seen anything to frighten me." She says, "Don't know, could see something."—

208

"Well," he says, "if I see something, I'll know what to do—I'll know what to do with it."

A.K.: Ha ha ha!

—Anyway, he takes the two pails and goes to the brook—it's a long ways to go to the brook eh? When he known—when he, when he had—he got to the brook, he dipped his water pails and he starts to come back, eh. When he's come some distance he was halfway, he sees this thing on the path, white as snow lying on the path. He comes up to him, he says, "What are you doing here, you?" He says, "Let me pass."

A.K.: Ah ha ha ha!

—It wasn't moving, it was rolling eh? "Well," he said, "I'll tell you twice, the third time if you don't get out of my way I'll get you out of it, me." Okay. There, he says it for the second time—that's when he was rolling about, eh? He was rolling about like he should eh. "Well," he says, "that's the last time. Go away!" He doesn't listen to him, he pulls himself up. Puts his two pails down and he takes him and he gives him a damn good licking. He almost kills him. So he takes him and throws him alongside the path and picks up his two pails and takes off for home. And now anyway, he got home and she said to him, "Well," he said, she said, "Richard," she says, "you didn't see anything?"—"I saw something on the path there," he said. He says, "He didn't want to let me pass but I passed." Ha ha ha! "I guarantee you," he says, "with what I gave him," he says, "he's not, he's not going to get up from that tomorrow." She says, "What!" She says, "You didn't beat up your father?"—"It wasn't my father who was foolish enough to go and put himself on the path?" he says.

A.K.: Eh heh heh heh!

—"I'm tired of telling my father," he says, "to stop trying to frighten me. So," he says, "it's not him the man to frighten me." He says, "I gave him a good trimming and I threw him on the side of the path. Well that," he says, "now if he was foolish enough to, to go there well," he says, "that's that."—"Well," she said, "you gave your father a beating perhaps you've half killed him so," she says, "we can't keep you. You've got to go." Yeah. He goes away. He doesn't wait at all, he takes off. See. Anyway he walks and he walks and he walks, *God knows* how many days and nights eh? So anyway, he's in the forest anyway, he comes to a big house. There anyway, he goes in. It was night eh. And he goes in there, there was a stove, there was everything he needed, except something to eat, eh? And he had something to eat on him eh. So anyway, he lights the stove and he starts making pancakes eh? So anyway he hears, "Look out above Richard, look out above," he says. "Fall down if you like," he says, "but don't fall in my stove."

A.K.: Hee hee hee!

—There a leg falls down. Oh, he takes the leg and he stands it up. Well, the start of a man anyway. So anyway, a little while after, they said, he said, "Look out above." Okay. He says, "Look out above but," he says, "don't fall in my stove. Pay attention!" There the other leg falls down eh. Well he's all in pieces we'll say eh.

A.K.: Yeah yeah.

—To cut up the little body, we'll say. There, the, the body fell down, he takes the body—he stands the two legs up—he takes the body and stands it on—he puts them, puts it on the two legs. Yeah. There, the shape of a man eh. Soon an arm falls down. There he takes the arm and sticks it. There, there, a while after, the other arm falls down, he puts it there. "Ah!" he says, "I'm listening to the head. When the head falls," he says—"I'll have company." Not afraid. So still anyway. Soon he says there, *"Ah well,"* he says, *"come on."* A man's head falls down. Well he takes the head right quick and sticks it on. "Ah well," he said. "I'll have company now." Yeah. So

209

anyway, "Ah well," he says, "Jack," he says—not Jack but "Richard," he says, "you'll, we'll have a *game* of cards."—"Okay," he says. "Can you play cards?"— Yeah, I play cards, me." So they start. Anyway, they play cards. Ah, a while after he sees it, the ugly beast, the devil eh. He drops a card. He says, "Look, you've dropped a card. Pick it up."—"Oh," he says, "pick it up yourself." No, the, the devil says, eh, he says, "You've dropped a card."—"No, it wasn't me," he says, "it was you." He says, "Pick up your card." And so he picks it up. So anyway, he does that about three times eh. The third time he does it anyway, he says, "Look! You dropped a card there." Jack says to him, "It wasn't me." Not Jack but *but* Richard tells him, "It wasn't me, it was you." And he says, "Pick up your card."—"I'm not picking it up, you've got to pick it up. It's you who dropped it," he says, "you're going to pick it up." So the devil leans under the table to pick his card up and there, he hooks him by his body and makes the sign of the cross on his head eh. He'd got him. What could he do? And he said, now the devil was dead. "And before, before," he says, "you leave here," he says, "you've got to sign on this here on condition you never have anything more to do here. With the blood from your little finger there," he says, "you've got to cut the tip of your finger and sign a paper that you're never going to trouble me again." The devil had to cut the tip of his finger and he signs a paper.

A.K.:   Ha ha ha! He gave him a fright!

—So there anyway, they hear talk of Fearless Richard who had never been frightened. So the king has a big *party* eh, and so he invites Richard to go to his party. He'd never been frightened. So he says, "If there's a way to frighten him, I'm going to frighten him." He says, "If I can't frighten him, he can't be frightened." So he gets all his servants to make a *puttin*, a big puttin and put a rooster in the puttin eh.

A.K.:   Yeah.

—So when everybody was there anyway—they all sat down so they could all have their lunch eh. So they had to cut open the puttin, and when they'd cut the puttin, Richard fainted. He couldn't talk.

A.K.:   No?

—Hmm. The rooster came out from inside eh and that frightened him.

A.K.   It never took him much this time eh?

—No. Finished. That's all I know in it me, anyway. Don't know if that's all of it.

Commentary and notes

Richard's meeting with his father, and especially his conversation with the devil while preparing his meal, were related so seriously by Mrs. Ozon that Mrs. Kerfont and I had smiles on our faces throughout the narration. The end of the story, which hardly lived up to expectations, only increased our amusement.

The tale is a version of AT 326, *The Youth Who Wanted to Learn What Fear Is*. It is widespread in Europe, with some fifty versions recorded in France and over sixty from French sources in North America. Mrs. Ozon's version, on the other hand, is the sole example collected from French Newfoundlanders.

The tale's motifs are: H1376.2, *Quest: learning what fear is*; H1400, *Fear Test*; H1401.3* (CEFT), *Fear test: father disguises himself as ghost to frighten fearless son*; H1411.1, *Fear test: staying in haunted house where corpse drops piecemeal down chimney*; H1421, *Fear test: playing cards with devil in church*; G303.16.3, *Devil's power avoided by the cross*; and H1441.2* (CEFT), *Fearless hero frightened by appearance of rooster when pie is cut*.

THE WOMAN WHO HAD A FOAL

Ah, one time was a man an a woman dey had no children eh, but she was pregnant
eh? So one day he—her husban tole er, "Le's go fer a walk up in de, up in de fiel."
Den dey went fer a walk in de field, it was tree nice little, ah, what you call it? Ah,
des poulains là, comment? [Ah, foals there, what?]

G.T.:   Foals?

—*Foals*. Tree nice little foals in de.... She says, "I wish to God," she says, "I had
one like dat." Pass off like dat. Yes but, when she had her baby, i's a foal she had.
So de ole man died dere eh?

B.O.:   It's worse than Mister, Mister Limpet!

G.T.:   What? Worse than what?

B.O.:   Mr. Limpet eh?

G.T.:   Who's Mr. Limpet?

B.O.:   No, it's, it's a, it's a, a story on the TV eh?

G.T.:   Ah yes.

B.O.:   That feller, he had, he wanted, he liked codfish enough eh?

G.T.:   Yes.

B.O.:   That he wished enough to be—too much you know to be a codfish he   turne
into a codfish. [Laughter] That's what I ca—what I called Robert
          after that there, Mr. Limpet!

—An—ah, an so anyhow she foun a foal. So she had a sarvin boy, an he was to
go in, marnin an de evenin fer to feed de foal. So anyway dat marnin, when de
sarvant went up an ah, to feed de foal, he spoke, "You see," he said, "you tell modder
if she haven't got de king's daughter, de oldest daughter to sleep wit me tonight.
Well," she says, "I's gonna kill her." Oh, de poor little boy run out to de house *cryin*,
breakin his heart. She said, "What you got cryin?"—"Well," he said, "de foal tole
me—" —"De foal!" she said. "Yes, he tole me if you haven't got de king's oldes
daughter sleep wit him tonight, he's gonna kill you." My God! she almos come *crazy*!
"Go de, de king—to de king's daughter."—"Well," she says—he says, "I's no harm
fer you to go an see." So anyway, he gets up, she gets ready now an off she starts
now, fer de king. So anyhow when she got dere, opens de door, de king—"Well,"
de king said, "Sometin happen? What's wrong?" he said, "de firs time you come
here," er, y'know. She said, "Yes." But she was, she was scared to ask him eh. He
says, "Something brought you here," he said. "You never come here for noting."—
"Yes," she says, "king, I come fer someting but," she says, "I don't tink," she
said,"I'm goin to succeed of it."—"Well," he says, "hard to tell."—"Well," she says,
"I came see if you could leave your oldest daughter come sleep wit me tonight," she
said, "I'm all alone, to keep me company." [Pause to change tape] *Il est maudit, moi
ej te dis* [He's a devil, me I'm telling you].

B.O.:   Heh heh heh!

G.T.:   She was afraid?

—So anyway, she said ah, "Yes, sure," he says, "she can go." An her she was
so—she was only too glad to go. She usen't to go nowhere. Anyhow she got dere,
well de little boy was glad to see de girl come too, y'know eh? Anyway, so anyway
after dark, she tole de girl, she said, "You should go to de well," she said, "get me,"
she says, "a little saucepan o water fer our night?"—"Shore," she said. So anyway
she takes her little saucepan, she goes to de well, she dips her water an before she
got to de house she met a young prince. He said ah, "Do you know," she said, "what
dat woman wants you fer tonight?" She said—he said, "No." She says, "She wants

you to go sleep wit her, her foal in de barn tonight."—"Me," she says, "wit a foal! No no," she said, "I don't like dem enough," she says, "fer dat." So anyway, sappeared away again an ah, she goes over to de house. So anyhow, when de time comes anyway y'know, fer her to go to de barn anyway. "Ah," she says, "I got someting to ask you," she said, "an I hates to ask you." She says [Mrs. Kerfont whispers] "You wouldn go," she says, "sleep wit my foal tonight in de barn?"—"I spose," she said. She wouldn refuse her, see. So anyhow de little boy took her an brought her to de barn an when de foal seen her comin in de barn he start to kick an kick an kick an kick, he almos tore down de barn, an he close de door an he left her dere an took off fer de house. So when he went down to de house, he tole his mistress, he says, "My God," he says, "I'm sure she's gonna be killed de morrow marnin." He says, "De horse is wile in de barn." So anyhow she, she never sleep all night her. So de nex marnin early him he gets up, he goes to de barn, *my gosh*! he only finds her in pieces in de drain.

B.O.: Oh oh!

—She was in pieces in de drain. "Tell modder," he said, "if she haven't got," she said, "de secon oldes to sleep wit me tonight, I'm gonna kill her." He was *toute à faite* [altogether] vex. He had take her an put her in—he buried her in de, de dump was dere. So he goes to de house blue marder, cryin. Tole his mistress, "My gosh!" she said. "De night, an he said fer you to go an get de secon oldest. An if you don't go, he said he'll give you!" Oh my God! Ah well she was half crazy. "Well," he said. "Try it," he said. "I's no harm to try." Anyway, she rig herself an off she start. Honest. She hate to go een eh? When she got dere she hate to go een. So anyway, she knock to de door. Sarvant opened de door. She said, "I want to see de king." So she went een. Well de king said, "Someting, me gosh, someting goin wrong," he said, "fer you to be here so," you know, "*often*," he said. She was down eh. "I knows dere's someting wrong wit you." he said. "Well," he—she said. "I don't tink I'm gonna succeed dis time."—"Well," he said, "if I can I'll do." Anyway. "Well," she said, "I come to see you fer your second oldest daughter, to, to stay wit me," she said, "yer—de older one," she said, "is lonesome eh, an she would like to have her sister wit her?"—"*Sure*," he said, "he can go." Anyway—an she was glad. Dey took off. Anyway, she got dere to er house, she said, "Where's ah my sister?" She said, "She's upstairs." Anyways, dey was dere chattin y'know. An anyway, when de time come to go to de well, she tole her. She says, "You're gonna go an get me a saucepan o water?"—"*Sure*," she said. "You're not frightened?"—"No," she said, "I'm not frighten." She goes to de well, she dip her d-saucepan o water, den she comes back to de house. When she got halfways she met a young prince again. He said, "Do you know what dat woman wants you to do tonight?" She said, "No."—"To sleep wit her foal in de barn."—"Well," she said, "I'm gone, sleep wit a foal in de barn," she said, "me I don't like foals an I don't like horses eiter." So he sappeared away now, she went to de house. So when de time had come to go an ask her to go to de barn her—ah, she was down. Anyway, "I's no harm," she said. She said, "You'd do one ting fer me?"—"Well," she said, "if I can do it, I'll do it fer you."—"You wouldn go," she said, "sleep wit my foal in de barn de night?" She says, "I spose." She was glad. Anyway, de little boy took her up. De little foal, he was dancin, dancin, dancin in de barn. So he put her een, an e locked de door an he took off. Ohh! what a racket dey had in dere. He goes to de house he tole her. He says, "Anodder one," he says, "is gonna be dead again tomorrow marnin," he said, "fer sure," he said. "De horse is goin wile in de barn." Ah well, he was half crazy. So anyway, dat night pass, de nex marnin he goes early to de barn. Face n face wit her chowder. *Oh*! my G—an he was vex! Ohh! "She haven't got de youngest one to sleep wit me tonight," he said, "I'm gonna kill her," he says, "I'm gonna kill her!" Well de little boy, he was half crazy. He had to take her now an had buried her, de same place. He goes to de house, he said, "He said like dat, if you haven't got de youngest one to sleep wit him tonight he's goin to kill you."—"My gosh!" she said, "wha—what is gonna be," she said, "what de king is goin to say to me so often as dat!"—"Well," he says, "he's—is no harm to try," he says. "Try it," he says. "She might come. He might leave her come." Anyway she goes. Anyway she got dere. She tole an—she knock to de door, de sarvant open de door. She said, "I want to see de king." So she—he took her inside. "Ah," de king said, "my God you comes often," he said. "Someting happen," he said. "*Well*, well," she said, "yer—de two—yer two girls want de youngest one to go wit dem tonight," she says, "to sleep wit dem tonight."—"Well," she said, "she can go fer tonight, but," she said, "she can't stay very long, just fer tonight," she said. "Well," she said—[the telephone rings]

G.T.: Hello? Yes. *C'est pour vous. Venez* [It's for you. Come on].

A.K.: Hallo?

G.T.: She was gonna go down....

B.O.: What is it, the, the power?

A.K.: Ina.

B.O.: What's Ina want?

A.K.: Her girl, Wal—

B.O.: Which one?

A.K.: Wally's...

B.O.: Again! Ah, ah!

A.K.: Where was I?

G.T.: She—the youngest girl was gonna go down an spend the night.

—Yeah. So he said, "I's only her I got in de house to tend de barns," he said. "I's her tends de barns fer me." Okay. Anyway, when she got to de house, she said, "Where's my sister?"—"Oh," she said, "dey're upstairs. Stay here wit me, you," she says. Was chattin an evryting. Now it come de time to go to, to de well, she tole her, she said, "You're gonna go an get a saucepan o water fer our night?"—"*Shore*," she said. "Yer not frighten?"—"No," she said. Anyway she goes to de barn—to de well an she, dips her water. When she was halfways goin to de house she met wit de prince again. He said, "You don't know what dat girl, dat woman wants you to do tonight?"—"No," she said. "She wants you to sleep wit her foal."—"Well me, I likes foals so much," she says, "I'll like it."

B.O.: Ha ha ha!

—"Oh," she says, "my trade," she says, "keepin de barn," she said, "fer de foals an dat, y'know, I'll like it." All right so he sappeared away an he—so now she was to hate to ask her eh? Ohh! she—it killed two eh? So anyway, oh, was time to come, anyhow fer to go to de barn, she ask her, she says, she said, "I got someting to ask you," she said, "but," she said, "I don't know, if I'm gonna succeed or not." She said, "You wouldn go—you wouldn go sleep wit my foal in de barn tonight?"—"*Sure*, why? I like de foals," she said, "like myself." Oh! Well she was glad de woman. So anyway, de little boy took her an went to de barn, never heard a soun or nothing. He opens de barn, she goes een, she goes to de foal, she smooth him down an she was pretty. An dey had a room oh, on de barn eh, an t'was all nice, big bed an evryting. Okay. So, she, she was dere wit him a long time den after when de time come to go to bed, she went. Oh! she got in de bed a nice bed an eh, gosh, by an by she look is a young prince comin een marder!

B.O.: [she whistles] Woh! what a night! Ha ha ha ha!

—He jumped in dere wit her too y'know!

213

B.O.: Ha ha! I guess!

—So anyhow, de little boy he goes to de house, he said—ah, ah—"De foal never done noting," he said, "never bawled, never kicked or noting," he said. "She— seemed he like her eh?" De nex marnin he gets up, *my God*! it wasn't a barn was, was a castle, a *beautiful* castle, *beautiful* castle. He goes to an—to his missus' room door he says, "Come up," he said. "Get up." He says, "Come see what is dere dis marnin." She gets up in a run her, she goes to de window an she look. *Beautiful* castle.

B.O.: My God!

—"Well," she said...

B.O.: Ha hah hah!

—Well anyway dey got married, de two o dem an de ole woman stayed wit dem. Dey're not dead an dey're livin yet.

Commentary and notes

This tale demonstrates, through the subtle allusions made by both ladies, that the *Märchen* always was, and remains, an adult genre. The narration also illustrates the ease with which, in the private or family tradition, one may interrupt the storyteller. At the very beginning of the tale Mrs. Ozon inserts her aside, perfectly appropriately moreover, on a character in a children's television programme. Mrs.Kerfont, far from disapproving, gives her approbation by laughing. The Robert in question, whom Mrs. Ozon had nicknamed *Mr. Limpet*, is a nephew of her's who used to tease her a lot. The telephone call did not seem to interfere overly with the narration; one word was enough to put Mrs. Kerfont back on the right track.

The tale seems to be an episode taken from the beginning of the international tale-type AT 425 *The Search for the Lost Husband* (see Mrs. Kerfont's *The Green Dog*, above), but for want of a greater development of the tale, it is not possible to furnish a precise identification. If it is indeed a very abridged version of this tale-type, one should not be surprised; for it is a well-liked tale in Brittany, where some twenty versions have been recorded. The tale seems to be little known in Quebec, however.

Motifs in the tale include: C758.1, *Monster born because of hasty (inconsiderate) wish of parents*; D131, *Transformation: man to horse*; D621.1, *Animal by day; man by night*; P252.2, *Three sisters*; L50, *Victorious youngest daughter*; and D735.1, *Disenchantment of animal by being kissed by woman*.

DE BUMBLE BEE

Well one time it was—a man an a woman, dey had a, a boy an a girl so de ole man died an left just de girl an de boy an de woman. So her, de girl, her she was goin aroun a young prince eh, a long time. So anyhow, her modder one day she says—ah, she says, "Me an your brudder," she says "we're gonna go in town," she says, "fer a cruise."—"Sure." So she—dey took off an dey never return. She wait for dem, wait for dem, never return back. An her, she was to go wit dis young prince now. So one night, before he left, he said, "Should come," he says, "over tomorrow," he said, "to visit my castle."—"Ah well," she says, "tomorrow, I can't promise you fer tomorrow. Well," she said, "ask for tomorrow," she says, "I'll go. Tomorrow," she says, "I got work to do eh? But I'll do my work tomorrow an after tomorrow I'll have noting to do, I'll go tomorrow—after tomorrow."—"Well okay," he said, "I won't have to wait fer you tomorrow."—"No," she said, "don't wait fer me tomorrow." Okay. So anyhow he stayed dere till nine o'clock. Nine o'clock he went home, no more dan dat. So de nex marnin she gets up. She does her work. She said, "I tole him I wasn't goin today but," she says, "I goin to see." She rigs herself up, an off she start. When she got dere, de doors were open. Nobody dere. She goes upstairs. She opens a room door, *my God*! de clothes, de clothes in dere, clothes. She seen her

214

modder, she seen her brodder's clothes. She shut de door an she goes to de window again to see if dere was anybody comin. No, nobody comin. She opens de odder one, *oh my God*! de bodies, de bodies in de room, *cruel*. Some was jus dead eh, det was crawlin. Oh my God, she got frighten to deat. She goes to de window, was nobody comin. Anyway, was anodder room she had to go. She went in anodder room, i was a, a, an axe, choppin block an a tub, half full o blood. She goes to de window, he was *comin*. He was comin wit a girl by de hair. Now she was in a fix. She goes downstairs an it was—under de stairs was a hole eh? She was—shove herself in dere, only fer dat—she couldn hide herself clear o dat. By n by he comes een, de poor girl screechin de top of her voice. *Pense don* [Just think]. Well, he took her—he was takin her upstairs. See, she caught holt of de step eh, wit her han, he took a knife, he cut off her han an de han fall in her *lap* her, underneat de stairs. An when she heard de bang o de axe eh, she took off, fer home. Ohh! She almos kill herself, she goes to de king. An she tole de king to have—make a time eh. An now she tole de king her story dere. How it happen eh? An now she tole de king, she said, "After lunch," she said, "make everyone tell a story here. Dream or stories or someting like dat," eh. "An leave me fer de las one," she said, "I'll tell my story." Okay. She goes back home. She leaves de hand to her—to de king see, she goes home. She bashed up her hair—her head. Not dat night, de nex night. Not dat night now.

G.T.: Hm.

—De nex night now was supposed to be a time to de king. Ah, by n by she looked, she—he was comin. *Peur, phew* [Afraid, phew]! So anyhow he comes een. He said, "I wait fer you today," he said. "Oh my gosh," she said, "I almos died dere," she said, "a headache," she says, "cruel," she says, "I almos died." And—ah, anyhow he stayed dere till nine o'clock. "Now," he says, "tomorrow yer gonna come."—"Me, my gosh," she says, "tomorrow night," she says, "de king got a time tomorrow night," she says, "come fine me," she says, "we'll go to de king's. To de time."—"Sure," he said. Anyway, goes home. After he was gone, she, she, she lock de doors an de windows, she was scared eh? She knowed it was him eh. Anyway de nex evenin, oh, she look, she seen him comin. T'was, t'was daylight yet eh. She goes down wit him to de king. Anyway, he had—ah, Mounties an dat to de house too eh.

G.T.: What did they have?

—De Mounties eh. Dey had Mounties dere too see eh. Anyway, so anyway nine o'clock so dey had lunch. So after lunch, now de king said, he said ah, "After everyting is, is fixed up, fixed up back," he said, "all hands got to tell a story or a yarn or a dream or someting like dat, y'know eh?" Okay. Anyway, dey all tole deir story an den it come to him. He was to help de poor, he was to give dem money an everyting. Oh, it was nice, it was Mary was her name, her. "Now," he says, "Mary," de king says. "Well me," she says, "king, I got noting to say. Ony a dream. But," she says, "a dream's noting a dream."—"No," he says, 'i's noting a dream, i's not—anyway," he said, "you gotta tell it de same." Okay. "Well," she says, "I dream," he said, "my fodder—my brodder an my modder went in town," he says, "dey never return. An ah," an he—she said, ah, "I dream," she said, "I went to a castle one day. I got een dere," she said, "I went upstairs, I open a room door, ohh!" she says, "it seemed to me, de clothes was in dere oh my I tought I had seen my modder an my fodder's clothes—my brodder's clothes in dere too," she said. "I tought now," she said, "king, i's ony a dream." Oh! my God he was gettin frighten him. "King, can I go outdoors?"—"No," he said, "no one's allowed before de story's tole." Anyway, she said, "I open de—it seem to me I open de odder room door," she said, "Oh! I seen de bodies," she says, "dey was crawlin fer one de odder," she says. "Crawlin over one odder. My God," she said, "what a fright I was een. Maybe," she says, "i's ony a dream." The king says, "I know,"—"An den," she says, "I shut dat door an I went to de window," she said, "dere was nobody comin. I open de odder room door," she said. "Oh my gosh!" she said, "was a tub dere half full o blood, an axe," she said, "an a choppin block. Well," she said, "what a fright I was into myself," she said. "I went to de window," she said, "I seen a man comin. I went downstairs," she said, "an I hide behind de stairs, an he was comin wit a girl by de hair,"—"King, can I go out please?"—"No," he said,"you can't go out, not before de story is tole. Nobody moved fer your story or nobody else's story, you shouldn move either," he said. Okay. An ah, she said, ah, "Den I got under de stairs. He come wit dat girl she was screechin well to me it was pitiful to see her screechin. An," she said, "on her way upstairs—"

B.O.:   Oh my God, have I got a sore stomach.

—Sore?

B.O.:   Tired eh.

—Oh yeah. "She caught holt o de step wit de—de step eh, it seemed to me he cut off her hand."

B.O.:   Oh!

—Yeah, now she had her hand—she had de hand in her breast eh, in her.... "An ah," she says, "it seemed to me de hand fall in my lap," she says. "*My God* what a fright, I seem to myself," she said. "An ah," she said, "when I heared," she says, "when I tought," she says, "I heard de noise of de axe," she said, "I run fer home."—"An," he said, ah, "wid de han?" She said, "Yes." An she says, ah, "You don't know if you got de han in yer—onto you dere?" An she put her hand in her breast, she said, "Here's de hand," she said, "my cousin Hélène's hand," she said. "An—ah," she says, "da's de guy kill her." She says, "If I had knowed you was here tellin news to de king, you'd never tell it, you'll never—"

B.O.:   Ha hah hah!

—"You'll never tell news to de king if I had knowed dat," she said—he said. De king says, "It's too late fer you now." So anyway, de—she said, "I'll go show you," she said. So he made him give him de keys—give her de keys eh. So anyhow, her ahead an de Mounties now, an de, an de, an de—wit him, wit him eh. He goes to de first castle. Oh *jay whiz crumbs!* She opens one door she said, "Look a dere," she said. "Da's my modder's clothes an my brodder's clothes"—an den she opens de odder one, "Look a de bodies,"—Oh my God! dey was *crawlin* in pieces. An she open de odder one. "Look," she said. Tub half full o blood, an axe, choppin block. [She whistles] Remind o poor Alfie.

B.O.:   Hah hah hah!

—Or Josie. Den, dey, dey tooked him—dey took him, dey tied him down an dey put kerosene all over de place an dey set fire een, dey burn him all an den dey an *dame*, dey're livin yet.

Commentary and notes

This tale, the last to be recorded from the two women's repertoires, is certainly the most dramatic of all. Mrs. Kerfont was able to create a tension which she sustained throughout the narration. Mrs. Ozon's interjection, when she complained about her stomach ache, in no way interfered with the tale's progression, any more than mine did when I wanted to verify that I had indeed heard the work "Mounties," officers of the Royal Canadian Mounted Police.

The tale is a version of the international type AT 955, *The Robber Bridegroom*. It does not seem to have been collected frequently in France or French Canada, with only eight and seven versions for each respectively noted in *The Types of the Folktale*. Given that the tale does not include magical elements, and that collectors have generally tended to favour *Märchen* at the expense of other types of tale, these figures perhaps give a poor reflection of its real popularity. Two other variants of the tale have been recorded from French Newfoundlanders, and the general theme of the heroine (or hero) opposed to robber-murderers is quite common.

Motifs in the tale are: K1916, *Robber bridegroom*; H57.2.3* (CEFT), *Severed hand as sign of crime*; H11, *Recognition through storytelling*; Q211, *Murder punished*; Q414, *Punishment: burning alive.*

XII

The Public Tradition:
Folktales of Emile Benoit
Commentary and Notes

THE GUESSER

Oui ben in coup y avait eune bonne fois—[Yes well once there was a good time—]

G.T.: It's in English now.

—Oh yes. One upon a time [laughter] there was a fella he was not too kind. [Laughter] He was lazy and he was—and he was saucy and he was everything, I think. He was a good-for-nothing—to tell the truth. So he was walkin an he played tricks an all kinds of stuff like dat, you know? An he used to hurt people an eh, he was no good, no good! No good! So anyhow, good enough, anyow [laughter]. Good enough, [laughter] well eh you got to laugh—when a fella talks English like me, you shouldn laugh! An e was walkin along de road n by n by he broke up to a farm. An e seen dat bunch a crows flyin off in de air an down an up an down an up an down. "Yes but what de heck is goin on over dere? I gotta see what, what's goin on." So e goes. When e got close, here's the crows all gone! Sshht! All gone away. It was a horse had died—ole horse. A big son of a—an de crows—an de crows now dey were—havin deir dinner on to im. An dey had de whole, dey had de skin all—chopped—all in, all in de hole y'know—for to get to de meat see. So—[he coughs]—excuse me. Okay. Good enough. Là. "Now," e said, "if only I had one a dose crows, dat'd be a nice pastime for me den." Y'know? Nothin to do. "If I had one a dose crows—I hope I could catch one." An e made up his mind—e s—it comed in his mind, e said, "If I get inside dat horse now, an stay dere, an by n by," e said, "for sure," e said, "dey're gonna come back." So good enough. So e settle inside a de harse. Oh e was dere about an hour. An by n by e eard, "Craa, craa, craa, craa, craa, craa!" I s'en veniont [They were coming]. "It's comin, dey're comin!" But dey wouldn, dey go for to pitch on de harse but dey hauls back again—but dey kept on goin for about, maybe ten or fifteen minute. An by gee, by n by, one took a chance. Jumped on, bien—niam, niam— [well—yum, yum—] [laughter]. Get a few bite out of it anyway. So e hauled back. So he comes back again. An when e seen there was no, no sign, no move or nothing, well den by geez, well den when e sees, dey see, de rest seed—dat e, e was havin a good feed—en nothin to, to trouble im, so dey all jumped. Oh oh oh geez aha ha ha! an dey was in wid deir paw an hm an hm an a haul an haul an push. Good enough. By n by dey didn't to slip is paws, is, between de ribs y'know. E, e caught de paw, caught im by de paw. Hold on—wid is hand, wid is hand. All right. Jeepers crumbs dey could de, de, de—de crow start to screech an everything. And—all de rest took off. So e put, e, e got out a bit an e put his hand over de, de, de rib a de harse, so e, so e got de, got de crow on de other side.... So den he pulled hisself out. So e had de crow. So he took de crow by de two paws, but de two paws an e old under is arms. He was walkin—an goin—walk, walk, walk, walk, long, long ways, i dit [he says]. First thing, e broke, e broke up to a house. So e goes dere, e knocks to de door an—de lady come an open de door—is that talkin loud enough dere eh? [He points to the tape-recorder]

G.T.: Hm.

—Yeah? De lady come open de door, "Oh," she said, "hallo." E said, "Hello, Ma'am." "Madame," e said. Yeah. She said, "You look tired."—"Yes," e said, "I'm a bit tired, yeah I'm tired."—"You hungry?"—"Yes," e said, "euh—I'm gettin hungry."—"Come in, come in," she said, "my husband soon be here." So all right, she said, "sit down." Cos she was lookin at, she didn't like to ask him, y'know, what, she, what he had under his arm dere, but she was lookin at it—she was tinkin, "Now is dat a crow or whatever it is?" Euh, she wasn't sure. So euh—by n by de husband comes in, well she said, euh, this was, euh, is name was Stanley, eh. [Laughter] So all right. She said euh, "Dat's Stanley—dat's my husband." Euh, they shake hand and euh, hah hah, in a present, in a present way. "Well," e said euh to de, "e's, e, e's hungry, so I told him to wait until you come." So, she had the supper ready you know, so she gives her husband a supper here an, an him there his supper. Dey were

220

havin supper an she, she—e said euh, "What you got dere den?"—"Oh," e said, "dat's euh—my guesser."—"Oh, oh, a guesser?" e said. "Yeah." A right. E had is supper an—euh, but e went good, had a big chat. Talk about dat, de, de, de fellow, de you know, they learned den how to, how to do it y'know? De fellow had de crow, eh, de other guy, e thought now dat was a kinda big, big shot, or something, y'know? They are m—talkin. Good enough. Ten o'clock. Go to bed. Gone to bed. All right. Dey was dere bout euh, half an hour I spose—e heard somebody [Emile taps four times on the table] a-knockin to de door dere. De feller had de crow dere y'see? Now, de euh, lady euh de woman in de house—heard him too. But euh, her husband didn, didn't get up because e was tired, y'know? So she got up. And she knowed who it was. So he done down stairs an he started—listenin y'know. Puts is ears to de—listenin. And euh—so he got to de door and euh, to bring a bottle a wine, y'know? He said, "I brought de bottle, a bottle a wine," e said. So he said, "You take de bottle a wine," e said, "and hide it," e said, "put it in de cupboard—for tomorrow night," e said, "well—I don't wanna work night shift," next night y'know. [Emile whispers] *"So we'll have a drink a wine y'know."* An he—[laughter]—and Stanley was lis, was listenin, listenin to all dat him you see. He was listenin, listenin dere. So all right! Good enough. Next morning he got up, his breakfast ready—and, euh, Stanley got up too. So dey had breakfast together. So euh, "Well, it's too, it's too bad," he said, euh, "I haven't got a drink of wine to give." E says euh, "It's a nice while since we had w, wine in de house," he said. "Oh," he said, "it's okay." And den pulls on de crow an de crow "Craa!" He said euh, "What e sayin dere?"—"Ah, not too much, no matter what dat, dat, e's, e's tellin me something but euh, it's not too much of it."—"Ah, no, but what he's tell you, what e said there?" Hey, he wanted de, he wanted de, "I'm, I don't, I don, I'm not," he said, "you said like that you never had no wine and euh, since a long, long time, but he's tellin me," he said "there's a bottle up there"—hah!—"in the cupboard." Hah! "Yes! No, dat, that's not true." So e, with that, he jumps right up and he, he goes an he looks in the cupboard [Emile gets up and mimes looking in a cupboard] and here it was, the bottle a wine. So all right. Got out the bottle a wine.

G.T.: Hm.

"Boy," e said, "look, dat must be hid dere for years and years and years!" E said, "I don't think but euh..."—"but look at dat," e said. He says, "You should sell me that, you!"—"Oh no!" he said, "I can't sell you that." He says, "Why?"—"Because," he said, "euh, da's jus nice there," e said, *"vieux* [old] guesser," e said. "Gee!" e said, "like to have that!" Well, ma, co, he coaxed him a while and—he said, "I'll give you five hundred dollars for dat!" No, he said, "I'll give you euh, a hundred," and he started, a hundred, two hundred, three hundred and, euh, e, "No, no, I didn want dat." An when e come five hundred, well euh, "Yeah, okay," he made his mind. So, so, he went to de bank an e got a loan of five hundred dollars and—now e told him about de, de, e said, "You're gonna buy dis from me," e said, "but," e said, "I'm gonna tell you about it." He said, "You haven't, you gotta get a cage," he said, "and euh, and euh—y'know, put de crow in because he, he'll fly away," e said, "you because e gotta be kept in de cage."—"Oh yes," she said, "I'll get dat de same time." So good enough. So e went an e euh, bought de cage, got de loan, a five hundred dollars an euh, got de cage—he brought it home, an put de crow in. Hung it on de wall. *Là!* Now he is goin. "Now I'm gonna tell you," e says first, eh. Now is wife was dere. "I'm gonna tell you something first before I goes, y'know."—"Yes," he said, euh, "Don't leave nobody piss in his eyes—[laughter]—because if dey, anybody pisses in his eyes, he'll never guess no more." [Laughter] So—it's all right. "Oh, don't you worry about dat. Dere's nobody's gonna piss in his eyes. Don't worry." So good enough. That's fine. So e put it n e's gone to work him. And him he's gone. He's gone travellin again. Bummin is way an dis an dat. So that night e had to work all night, that, euh, er husband had to work all night. So euh, da's de night now your euh, er boyfriend was comin to see her. So he come in about ten o'clock. So good enough. Come in dere right brazen y'know. E, "H-sh-sh-t-t-t, look out, look out!" E said, "Why is dat?"—"My husband bought a, bought a guesser this morning." [Laughter]—"Yeah? A guesser. But dat don't mean nothing, be guessin."—"No, no but e, he, he, he-e-e tells y'know," heh! "if anything goes on or something like that, if he's happen to see me n you there e'll euh, tell but euh, I hear, I heard my, I heard im tellin my husband, dat it's right easy to, to fix im." [Laughter] She said, "Guess what it is?"—"Well," e said, "like dat euh, for not nobody, to let nobody piss in his eyes because *les, les* [the, the], de, de, is guesses is all gone, is all finish, *fini, fini* [finished, finished]!"—"But," e said, "da's, da's nothing, it's not hard work piss in his eyes." Pshee! So good enough. He goes, him. And he was there now, t'was listenin, it was listenin. But de crow now when e seen dat coming he used to do dis—do dat! [Emile covers his eyes with his hands] But by n by it starts to fall, starts to fall an then he was finish. But he never got de crow, hah! Ha ha! *Là.* "Now I'll tell you what we're goin to do."

G.T.:   Eh?

        —true dough.

Commentary and notes

Emile narrated this humorous tale to a class of students in a course on the traditional culture of French Newfoundlanders. Ever delighted to have an audience, he gave himself wholeheartedly to his narration. He told this tale in English, for the benefit of the few folklore students in the course whose knowledge of French was not good. The fact that he did not know all the students explains his reticence to speak a little more frankly at the end of the tale.

On the other hand, he is skilled at putting his audience at ease, and this is why he made fun of his English at the tale's beginning, by parodying the English opening formula and exhorting his listeners not to mock his speech. Much of the laughter Emile brought forth from his relatively young audience came from his onomatopaeas on the one hand, evident even on the printed page, and on the other hand from the grimaces often accompanying the onomatopaeas. His "niam, niam"—suggesting crows pecking at the dead horse, are far more than simple noises. Emile went without his dentures for many years, which seems to have added to the elasticity of his face; while saying his "niam, niam," he put one in mind of a gluttonous banquet, as he rolled his eyes and twisted his lips.

Emile is a past-master of the allusion. When the woman's lover gives her the bottle of wine, saying "So we'll have a drink a wine y'know," Emile utters the words in a way suggestive of far more than an innocently shared glass of wine. On the other hand, he knows how to use blunt speech to good effect. When he warned the husband that the only way in which the crow could be deprived of its talent was by pissing in its eyes, he looked straight at his audience, a gleam in his eyes and a smile on his lips, before saying the phrase "piss in his eyes"—vulgar, but absurd too. It was a combination that prompted uncontrolled laughter.

The ending of the jest cannot be rendered by words alone. Imitating the contortions of the poor woman squatting over the cage, trying to free herself from the clutches of the crow, Emile created a moment of supreme mimed farce. In sum, it was a wholly unrehearsed performance of comic genius.

While this jest fits under no precise tale-type, it is related to the general type AT 1535, *The Rich and the Poor Peasant*, and especially to section III which involves the sale of a pseudo-magical object to the husband of an adulterous woman. On the other hand, the deception leading to this sale is enshrined in the tale-type AT 1358C, *Trickster Discovers Adultery: Food Goes to Husband Instead of Paramour*. Not identified, however, is the tale element which, from the point of vies of this narration is just as important—the attempts made to relieve the crow of its gift—and which, from the performance aspect is even more important, since it encompasses a highly comical ending.

Motifs in the jest include: K1571, *Trickster discovers Adultery: food goes to husband instead of paramour*; K137, *Alleged speaking animal sold*; K114, *Pseudo-magic oracular object sold*; and based on this last motif, the new number K114.2.1* (CEFT), *Alleged oracular bird sold* is proposed.

THE SEVEN-HEADED MONSTER

Once upon a time—there was a woman an a man—they had a son. And euh, his name was Jack heh heh! It's like they say, it's all the time Jack, Jack. You don't say John you say Jack. Well, ah they had raised their children, they had a little farm, a couple of cows *an so on*, some sheep—enough to, to live off. And, the boy worked, he worked, he worked all the time—but in those times—well—you had to be twenty-one before you—before you were on your own. When you were twenty-one, ah well *dame*, you were on your own. Well, that's good. Anyway, here's his—his birthday comes round—twenty-one. Hah! Oh, it's not a small business there, he's a man there now, d'you see, oh ho! I guarantee you! He wasn't slow either. There! Yeah, and the ole man and the ole woman they were startin to get old, they were in their, their fifties, something like that, and euh—only boy they had—and I guarantee you, when he said—to his father, to his mother, but he says, "Papa and Mama," he says, "you know I think," he says, "I'm goin," he says euh, "to take off," he says. "I'm goin to see a little bit—of the universe." Because where they lived, there was nothing at all—there was a, a little shack perhaps every, every two, three miles something like that, there was not too many people in those times—not like n-not like now. "Ah!" he says, "Papa," he says, euh, he says, "I'm goin, I think I'm goin to go now, see," he says, "a little bit of the universe," he says, "that'll teach me a bit," he says, he says, "you taught me a little bit of school," he says, "but not much." And he says, "I could go," he says, "and maybe," he says, "I could do good for myself." And he said, "If I don't do good well," he says, "there," he says, "I could pay you back—make you happier than you are."—"Ah," he says, "my child," he says, "we're not so miserable as that yet, we've got something to eat." Ah yeah, so that's good... he's talkin. Well there, the next marnin he takes off anyway—he takes a little, a little, euh, couple of small—whatyecalls, small cakes you calls them, made with molasses, and euh—so he takes off. And there he walks and walks and walks and walks—soon here's the night come.... So there he makes a kind of a small shack with branches and he—hauls under that—and he lies down and goes to sleep. The next marnin he gets up—and he eats a couple of molasses *buns* and and then he's gone again, and walks and walks and walks and walks. And euh... that's good. Soon it's night again—pah! There he has a rest again. And he walked like that for three days. The next day—the same thing happened, and he walks and walks. And all of a sudden—kind of as night was falling—he sees—"Hey! Well look over there! Look at the houses!" he says. "Ah! well look at that," he says, and he looks, "There," he says, "what's that they've got flying in the air?" he says. All the, the, the, the poles he could see, the posts and things like that, there were, there were pieces of cloth on them they calls it, or pieces of guinea cotton, stuff like that d'you see, he didn't know they were flags y'know, but it was, it was all *black*. Anyhow that's good, so there he has a wash for the night there, in his little shack made of branches and euh, the next marnin—not—well yes, the next marnin there he takes off for there. And anyway off he goes. And there—everybody dressed in black—the women, the men, flags all black—he says, "What's the matter," he says, "is the whole world," he says, "like that? Is it like that," he says, "a misery, if

223

I had known that I wouldn't have left home. I'd have stayed, there's more, there's more fun at home than there is here, heh! Gee, it's sad!"

G.T.: Hm.

So there he started to walk around through the people, he was say to say, "How are you, how are you,"—they didn't answer. They all had their heads down and—black shawls on their head—"Gee! what the *diggen*—is going on here?" He says, "Well what's the matter?' Anyway he walks by the people, here, there, there's not a big crowd of people but euh, more than he had ever seen in his life. So anyway he, he says, speaks to one of them, a man who was there but he was an old man—he says, "Well what's the matter," he says, "what, is everybody," he says, "in the universe," he says, "like that?"—"Ah!" he says, "my poor boy," he says. "We're all ·sad today." He says, "Yes," he says, "I can see that," he says, "you're sad," he says, "are you like that all the time?"—"Ah! no, no," he says, "we're not like that all the time." He says euh, "Every year," he says, "it happens like that here." He says, "Yes? Well," he says, "so tell me," he says, "what's the matter, so what is the matter, what is it? That happens! That has happened to you, what is it?"—"Ah! yes," he says, he says to him, "yes." He says, "There's a seven-headed beast," he says—"it comes every year, to take one of our girls. And," he says, "this year," he says, "it's the worst year of all. It's coming this year to take," he says, "the, the, the king's daughter."— "Well, well," he says, "the king's daughter." He says, "She's gonna be eaten tomorrow," he says, "tomorrow at eleven o'clock."—"Yeah?" he says—"eaten by what?"—"Well," he says, "by the seven-headed beast. *By geez* it's an ugly beast! Oh! You ought to see it!" And he says, "We can't kill it or nothing at all, I can't do anything with it?"—"Naaa! It's too strong, it's, they can't do nothin with it, they shoot cannons at it—they can't, it doesn't do nothin at all."—"But, but it can't be possible," he says. So there he says, "It, it, it, it doesn't surprise me," he says, "you're, euh, all in mourning here," he says. "Eh! Yeah," he says, "I'm goin to see your king." Takes off. Knocks on the door [Emile raps the table]. The mistress comes, opens the door—Mister Jack was there—a fine fellow there, too, a handsome man, handsome, I guarantee you. Well, he says, "The king," he says, "is home?" She says, "Yes," she says, "but he doesn't want to be disturbed."—"Oh-oh," he says, euh, "I have to see the king," he says. "Ah," she says, "no, you can't, he doesn't want to see you."—"But tell him I want to see him. It's important." Ah! She takes off. She tells him, and there was the king, his head between his legs huh! He was really sad. She says to him, "In the, there's a young man who wants to see you," she says. "Ay!" he says, "I'm not going to see him," he says, "I'm not goin to see nobody."—"Well," she says, "I'm goin to see you, absolutely. It's *important*." Euh... there he gets up and—he comes— has a look—a right small man. "And what's that?" he says. And the girl now she, she, she—saw him—but, the handsomest man she had ever seen in, set her eyes, her eyes on. Oooh! She fell in love with him. My God, my God, she felt so sad, she was goin to be eaten the next day but, the sadness she had in her heart! She fainted, she went, she looked at him, she heaved a big sigh—"But, but, but, but, but, but, but I could eat him!"—to herself she said that y'know—there the king says, euh, he says, "What's your name?" He says euh, "My name is John," he says—"Jack."—"Oh-ahhr!" he says, "Jack," he says, "We've heard talk," he says, "of names like that," he says. He says euh, "What do you want?" he says. "Ah," he says, "my dear euh, king," he says, "I heard," he says, "your daughter is gonna be eat tomorrow."— "Yes," he says, "it's really sad,"—and he starts crying. "Oh!" he says, "don't cry. Don't cry. I've come to help you."—"My poor boy," he says, "my poor boy! Go back home!"—"Ha ha ha!" he says, "listen to that now, listen," he says. "Ha ha ha! Go back home, and not before my work is finished!" The king, he starts, he, his two eyes hauled right up, he says, "What's that? A little man like that," he says, "what can *that* do? They fire great, great big cannons at it *an so on*, and they can't—blank—it

224

didn't mind it at all—blank! Neh!" That's good. He says, "Come in! Come in! Come into my parlour." Ah. Jack goes in. And he sits down. He says euh, "What have you got to do now?" He says euh, "Is it, is it far from here," he says, "for where there's the, the, the found, the, the—the foundry euh! To smelt the, the—
G.T.:   The foundry.

—The foundry, the foundry, yeah. Ah. "Well," he says, "it's a couple a miles." He says, "What d'you want to do?"—"Because," he says euh, "I'd like to have a sword made."—"Yes?" he says. "Why?" he says. "Well," he says, euh, euh, "I want it," he says—"to defend myself—because," he says, euh, "me an the seven-headed beast," he says, "we're gonna have a battle tomorrow."—"Oh! Poor boy, now don't talk like that!"—"But," he says, *never mind*," he says, "now," he says, "I've got a knife made—a sword—"—"Well," he says, "yes," he says, "I could get a sword made for you because," he says, "they've got all sorts of steel there and everything," he says, "we've got the best quality in the world."—"Well," he says, "that's what I want." He says, "You're going," he says euh, "to send," he says, "one of your—of your men," he says, "to the found—to the foundry—and euh, get a knife made. I want a knife," he says, "six feet long—and the *blade*," he says, "the, the edge," he says, "six inches wide—and three qua—three quarter inch thick."—"But," he says, "what are you going to do with that?"—"*Never mind!*" he says—"That's my business." And he says, "I want that knife." And he says, "Made with the best steel—in the world." Well, that's it, there he calls his—his soldiers and euh, he tells him there, he says, "You're going to go to the foundry," he says, "and take one of my horses there," he says, "and euh, off you go," he says, "and euh, get that knife made," he says, "like, like Jack wants there." He looked at Jack there now, and the knife, just think, you. Anyway that's that. He takes off and mixes in and then they make the knife. But it took two men to carry it! Well! Yeah. Oh! a little while, the next marnin—nine o'clock in the marnin—there! They come with the knife. It took two men to carry it into the house. Ah, euh, like that, well, Jack takes the knife by its handle—he starts sw—swinging, swinging it in the air and *soon*—the king fell over backwards, he falls down on his backside—he says, "What sort of a man is that?"—The sword heavier than him! "Well," he says, "it's not too bad—it's not too bad." That's good. There. There now they're waiting for eleven o'clock, well that's it, there's the girl, he took her, they took the girl by the arm and take her to the—down by the sea. There! that's good. At eleven o'clock—Jack—gets there. He stands alongside the girl—with his knife in his hand. Soon they saw a big swell rising in the sea—it went right up in the air! And it was coming near there, oh! Now *that* was frightening! Everybody, the women an all that they had all hidden their, their eyes and all that with the black shawls they had, all hidden their eyes, they got down on their knees, they didn't want to look or nothing, they, they knew that the, the seven-headed beast was going and they were going, it was going to devour the *two* of—the girl and the, the boy. Ah! They were upset! Ah good God, good God. Anyway, that's good. Th-e-e-re, another big swell comes, it rises up in the air again and it's coming there, and then all of a sudden there they could see the heads, the seven heads, it was rising up there and it was kind of in a slope there. I told them there, t'was, I marked it on the paper how the seven-headed beast was made d'you see, it was kind of in the *jib* there y'know.
G.T.:   Hm.

—How it was made there now, how it was, it had seven heads in it, and—but it's hard for me to mar, mark on the tape there. Well anyway it had the—seven heads. All at once she comes on shore. When she got on shore she pushed the water, and the water came half, half, up to their wais, up to their waists, the boy and the girl there. "Oh! Well!" she says, "Hah! Well," she says, "today oh, I'm gonna have a good meal. Two! Hah! That's," she says, "that's gonna, that's gonna be eaten!"—

225

"Well," he says euh, "we're gonna see about that," he says—Jack he says—"we're gonna see about that," he says. "Who's gonna be eaten first." Anyway that's good. There, here comes the beast to arrgnrr! to, to hook them. Yes but him he jumps and he tang-leeng! he takes the small head first, he takes the small head—vling! Gee! The head drops off! On his sword! There she hauls back again. Only six heads left there. Hauls back. And there I'm, there now, ar-r-r! there she gets mad, the, the, the foam comin out of her eyes. There she comes again and like—she's comin again like a spinning-wheel, the other head—the second, second—small—smallest head there. He was taking them goin up d'you see, to weaken her eh? *A right.* Oh, look, two heads on his sword. And the blood—ah! the blood! The blood, the blood, was pissing out, pissing out—the girl was full of blood, he was full of blood, it was euh, it was nothing but blood. Anyway that's good. There she hauls back again and comes up again and he does the same thing again—plingco! he—sticks the other head on— only four more left now. There. He, he hauls back again oh! this time, me, this time, oh! only the end of her tail was, was right in the water. The way she was twisting in the air to have a real good shot this time, ah! hoh hoh hoh! Yes but, vling! again—another head again, that's four gone. Yes but she was startin to get weak. She jumps back again but *dame*—she's—only half her body she, she, she raised up. Ahh, startin to get weak—there! She comes again, ho ho ho! she gets up on the shore the same again, oh that's it, the same, come on, he says, "That's it, eat, eat!" He gives it to her *bang!* again—well—he did that—until the last head was—and when the biggest head—when she left her place it was the size, and everybody watching!—the size of her head—there—that she—but it was a *big* head, oh! Anyway that's good. *By de geezus, so den* two whacks on the side there, and he gives it to her. And he only cut it in half. Yeah. That was a big whack, ole man. Oooho! Oh! You should have seen it. Pshee! An he took it again, he took er again on the other side, e gave her one like that, on, on the right then he turned er over on the other side on the left an flack! he cuts it, he cuts off the head. There. Well there, well if you had seen that—if you had seen that. The people—the black shawls were gone it was, was gone right out of their hands—and then they jumped on Jack and hug him and her now she wanted to kiss Jack too but she couldn't there was, there were three of them around her there—and that's how it went. And—oh! he had like a *hard time.* Him it was worse than the seven-headed beast—and he had a *hard time* with the seven-headed beast, but with the people, oh! It's not *fit,* it's not *fit,* he was shouting, oh! And he says there the king he says to "Leave him alone, leave him alone!" Anyway they left him alone. There. In the house now, there's a lad my man, how he was received! And there Gerald! Well my good God! Well it was, laugh, ah, he couldn't walk at all! They carried him to, to the castle, he was carried to the food and everything, he, he, ah! the candles were shining and everything, oh! it was, it's, it was too nice, too nice. There. After it was all finish, but he says, "To see you such a small man," he says, "and to see you," he says, "with so much power." He says, "I give you," he says, "half my kingdom," he says, "and my daughter in marriage. And you're not gonna get married tomorrow," he says—he says, "straightaway. I'm going to marry you straightaway." Well, that's good. There—they send for the minister, and they get married, and when they had their wedding party—but me now I couldn't play the fiddle much in those days! But the time of their party they were about, in the, on a *spree*—they had *homebrew* made out of spruce, heh! *Holy gee!* They got me to co—"Come in!" But I was well received *dough, bye*—I played for—a, a part of their dance—and all—but I was well received. Yeah.

Commentary and notes

It is a measure of Emile Benoit's talent that he can take what is normally no more than an episode from a *Märchen* and make a complete narrative out of it, full of drama and artistic verve. As may readily be seen, this is due in part to his gift for creating lively conversations in which he puts himself heart and soul into the roles of the speakers. The hero, Jack, speaks frankly to his parents as he notes the little instruction they have given him, while his parents remain proud of their estate. Further on, Emile evokes the king's chagrin faced with his daughter's sacrifice, and her falling in love at the first sight of Jack. Emile by no means has the monopoly on creating dialogue among Franco-Newfoundland storytellers, but he is certainly one of its better practitioners.

To the reader's eyes, Emile's characters' monologues may sometimes seem confused, but in fact, this apparent confusion represents the storyteller's very acute perception. At moments of high tension, a speaker cannot always utter his words as fast as he might like, and Emile has grasped this fact. His conversations in tales represent a conscious effort on his part to capture the spontaneity of his scenes.

On the performance plane—specifically, Emile's body language—it should be realized that the onomatopaeas which he uses so enthusiastically are accompanied on the one hand by facial gestures, and on the other hand, should the need arise, by vigorous physical gesticulations. One has to visualize Jack's combat with the seven-headed monster, in which Emile stands up, swirls and twists like a man fighting for his life.

The aside made by Emile as he tries to explain how he had drawn his vision of the monster on a piece of paper, refers to a sketch he made for some reporters from Radio-Canada who had visited him for filming purposes, some years ago.

The reader will notice how Emile is able to draw his audience into the very heart of what he is describing. He does this not only with his "D'you see"s and "you know"s but also by speaking directly to an individual, by the person's name, for example, as when he brings me into the party which followed the monster's death. Emile creates links between the past of the tale and the present of the narration, by the use he makes of the closing formula. By having himself invited to the hero and heroine's wedding party, he asks the listener to look at him in his more usual role—that of the local fiddler. This link adds a new dimension to the *Märchen*: its characters now enter the real world, and do not remain isolated in their magical realm.

The Seven-Headed Monster (or *Beast*, as Emile most frequently calls it) as narrated here, is a version of the international folktale type AT 300, *The Dragon-Slayer*, although Emile's tale is composed in fact of episodes II, III and IV only according to the break-down in *The Types of the Folktale*. It is therefore a very abridged version of a tale which has apparently been recorded in some thirty examples only in France, although it is one of the most widely collected folktales in European tradition. Of the French versions, approximately one third were recorded in Brittany. A half-dozen versions have been collected from French Newfoundlanders, though not from the same number of narrators. But the tale seems to be widely known, for numerous informants have mentioned the tale by name, even if they were unable to tell it.

The international motifs in this version include: L100, *Unpromising hero*; S262, *Periodic sacrifices to a monster*; B11.10, *Sacrifice of human being to dragon*; D1081, *Magic Sword*; B11.2.3.1, *Seven-headed dragon*; B11.11, *Fight with dragon*; R111.1.3, *Rescue of princess (maiden) from dragon*; T68.1, *Princess offered as prize to rescuer*; and Q112, *Half of kingdom as reward*.

Emile was not sure to whom he should attribute his version of the tale, but mentioned the names of two storytellers of an earlier generation, Jack Tourout and Narcisse Chaisson, who lived at Mainland.

JOHN-OF-THE-WOODS (WOODEN LEG)

G.T.: Do you know a story euh, where there's—a cat—who talks?

E.B.: A—a cat who talks.

G.T.: Yes.

E.B.: Yes. Yes, I've heard that story already.

G.T.: Yes?

E.B.: But gee, I don't know if I can tell it the right way but I think....

G.T.: Do you want to try?

E.B.: I can try, for sure.

G.T.: What, what is it called?

E.B.: Euh, it's called, "John" and he was called euh— "John-of-the-Woods" or something like that.

G.T.: Yeah?

—Euh, he, he, well he lived with his father an mother until he was an age to, to, to look out for himself, you know, it was in—those days euh, it was twenty-one years old before you could move from the house. Younger than that it was, you weren't the *boss*, you weren't the chief—you had to listen and obey every, euh, word your parents said to you. But gee, when you got to be twenty-one, oh oh! gee, chee! you could go where you like but *dame*, you couldn't play the fool of the, in the house, the, the, the, the, in your father's castle we'd say. He had his orders and it had to go like—li—like he, like he wanted. Well there was this man, his name was John, John—that—something, I don't remember no more—maybe you heard that, John, John-of-the-Woods or something like that.

G.T.: Yes, John-of-the-Woods.

—It's something like that, John-of-the-Woods. Anyway euh, all his, his life, that he had lived, with his father an his mother—he had a cat—and euh—he thought a lot of his cat. It was the only company he had to speak the plain truth. Euh—he loved his father an his mother, but his cat, ahh! Well that! His cat! He loved his cat. Well, it went on, it went on. Well anyway euh, when he reached the age of twenty-one, he said to his father an mother he says "I thin—Dad," he says, "and Mom—I think me," he says, "I'm goin-to—to take off from here, me." He says, "Around," he says, "here,"—euh there wasn't much to see, but euh—"I'm gonna go see—hear, I've seen a couple of, of, of neighbours," he says, "around, they told me there are some beautiful places to see. It's just like another world. And me I listened to that and I've got that on my mind, it's three or four years now they've been talking to me about that, you've heard that, we've met those neighbours—and I've got it on my mind, and that's why I want to go an see—what it's like, what it's like—in the universe."—"*What*! Well," he says, "my boy," he says, "you've got your age, well, *dame*," he says, "you can do what you want." Good, that's good. Well then he, he, his mother takes off, she cooks some little cakes, little biscuits and all kinds a things like that, biscuits and everything. Well he says euh, there were no m, no, no automobiles an all that—in those days—there was nothin like that—you had to walk, walk, walk, walk or you had a horse. Well, that's good. You w—can go on a horse—but *dame* clear of that, you had to walk. Well that's that. He takes off there—heads off with his—his little package of, of, of *bun* and little cakes and *so on* and all that—and euh, he takes off. And he was euh, pretty upset—that—he'd gone maybe a quarter of a mile—"Look at that!" he says, "My cat! I've forgotten my cat!" There! Turns around. Ah ha! He gets to his house—"Oh!" she says, "You're back?"—"Yes," he says, "for sure I'm back, I've come for my cat," he says—"my cat! Oh my dear cat!" Ah ha! And the lad, when the cat saw him, "M-miaow!" Heh!

228

He cried out eh? "Ah!" he says, "time," he says, "my little puss," he says, "come with me. I can't go," he says euh, "without you with me." Ah well that's good there, they're gone. And they walk, walk all that day, and they walk part of the night and there they're really tired—well there he gets some brush an all kinds a things like that, little branches and he makes a little bed—for the night. And euh, that's good. Ow! They lie down—him an his cat, ah! he takes his cat in his arms and hugs him. With his cat it was like his life was saved. He had the universe in his arms. Well! That's pretty good. There. That's that. Soon, it's daylight—"Ah!" he says, "my little pussycat,"—hah! He says, "We're goin to go—travellin again." Oh here they are leaving. That's good. There, they're gone. Walk an walk an walk an walk all day long again. An there was nothin to see, no buildings, there was nothing, *nothing*! It was all b, b, b, bogs and little clumps of spruce an here an there and mountains and, and valleys and everything and—little streams to cross and they walk and they walk and they walk. And they ate little cakes from time to time, they didn't have a big appetite but even if they had a good appetite I think he didn't want to eat too much, he wanted to save his food he didn't know when he would—euh, when he would—have seen something—that he'd, that he'd stop to eat or something like that. Well that's good, they walk all day long again—until after nightfall—and then well, *dame*, then, then it's the night. Hm well, they have a rest again. And he takes his cat in his arms again and hugs him! And that, and he says, "My little pussycat, my little pussycat! And without you," he says, "I'd be so lonesome." Euh, that's good. The next day—gone again—at the break of day they get up and they're gone again. They walk! Walk, walk, walk! Walk, walk, walk. All of a sudden—the cat—he says, "My master!" Ehh? He says euh—he says if they go real quick he says, "to come in, in, into a village—here there."—"What!" he says—"Well," he says, "I didn't think cats could talk."—"Well," he says, "cats don't talk but me, your cat here, he talks!"—"But why didn't you talk to me before?" he says. "Oh no!" he says, "I wouldn't have wanted to talk before," he says, "because you weren't in, in, in need of me talking. I kept myself to myself all the time," he says. "But," he says, "now where I'm speaking to you there,"—he says, "you're going to come pretty soon," he says, "near a, near a village there—it won't take the whole day," he says, "walking an all that," he says, "before we get there. But *dame*," he says, "you're gonna have to listen to me," he says. "Whatever I tell you," he says, "is gonna be right." Well there, I guarantee you John-of-the-Woods there, he, he, he, it's, it, it, it was his shoulder, it's the, his skin there climbed up his back to his ears, his, it pushed his ears up!

G.T.: Hm.

—The way he was surprised enough—and to see a cat talking he'd never hea, heard that before. And never seen it—and that's, well, he was delighted! "But, but, but, but! And it talks, a cat that talks!" he says, "Well, well, well, well! It's wonderful!" he says, "Something like that." Well that's good. There—the cat, he don't say no more there. An there they walk, they walk, they walk. Well there all at once—the cat says—"Well—the village isn't far there." There he says, "Now—my dear master," he says, "we're gonna have to—make a little shack here for ourselves—with brush," he says, "and little euh—little roots an all that," he says, "we're gonna make a lodging for ourselves," he says, "now, here. We've got to make a lodging," he says. "It's not like yesterday night or the night before that, or the night before that—now we've got to make a lodging. And we'll settle right here. Me an you," he says, "my dear master. Because," he says, "I've always loved you, me." The cat said to, to John-of-the-Woods there. "I've always loved you, me. But I never wanted to say nothing. But," he says, "I'm going to do my best for you, me." Ah! That's good, there, they build their, their shack—with roots and brush and, and, and, peat and all kinds a things like that but they didn't make it, not too bad—tight, all that. It's not, it's not euh, it wasn't too cold. Well—that's good. There—it's going good there—soon the *buns* there are starting to get low—there's almost nothing left to eat. Well he says, "My, my dear cat," he says euh, "I'm going to tell you something, me," he says—"our cabin's built now—and us, us, our food," he says, "it's, it's starting to get pretty low. And there's not much," he says, "around here there's any way of getting." Well the cat says, "Hah! you think that you. Heh! Me," he says, "I, I know me there's, there's, there's rabbit, there's birds, there's food, there's food! There's food here around here."—"Oh you think so you?" he says, "nah!" he says, "there's nothing here."—"Ah yes!" the cat says, "Ah yes! Ah yes there's food here, around here." Bah, he doesn't know, him. But he says, "I'm gonna tell you—I'm gonna tell you a little something," he says—the cat says to, to John-of-the-Woods—"I'm gonna tell you a little something," he says. He says, "What is it, what are you going to tell me?"—"Me," he says, "I'm gonna tell you me—listen—tomorrow euh, you're gonna, you're, early in the morning that, early—at—before daybreak you've got to be up"—the, the cat said to John-of-the-Woods—"Ah, it's before daybreak you've got to be up—and you've got to be there for day*break*." And he says, "You're going euh, you're gonna go," he says, "like, ahh, maybe a mile from here there—back," he says, "in the forest," he says. "And you're gonna take a, a, a bag with you," he says, "a, a bag," he says. He says, "What for?"—"Well," he says, "you, you've got to take a bag with you," he says. He says, "What kind of a bag?"—"Well," he says, "the, the, the sacks," he says, "that, that farmers," he says, "they're there, you don't have to go very far, there are farmers, there are kings, there are all kinds here," he says, "all kinds! All kinds around here."—"But," he says, "how do you know that, you?"—"*Well*, I know," he says. "I'm a cat," he says, "I'm, I'm, I'm presented like a cat but I'm not just a cat," he says, "I'm something," he says, "which is more valorous than a cat, and you don't know it. But," he says, "you're in good hands." Heh! Well! And then he says, "My dear cat," he says, "that's it," he says, "you, like you'll tell me, like you'll, like you're going to tell me, well, I'll do it." Ha ha! "Well," he says, "that's that," he says. He was glad, the cat said, "Miaow!" Hah! Well that's that. That's good. There! He says, "You're gonna euh go further back over there," he says, "it's not too far to walk," he says—"you'll find a big barn there," he says, "you'll find some, some sacks," he says, "they've thrown out," he says, "big sacks, bags all full o holes," he says, "sideways," he says, "they're all knitted up," he says, "and all—*slack*," he says. And he says, "You're gonna pick up one like that," he says. "And then tomorrow marnin," he says, "you're gonna go," he says, "in the woods and you're gonna catch some rabbits," he says. "You put that," he says, "stretched out just like a snare," he says—he showed, showed John-of-the-Woods what, what to do, d'you see.

G.T.:   Yes.

—Then he takes off there, but he, he, he wasn't *smart*, you see, if he had been smart he would have caught some but he wasn't smart! Slow! It took him two days to, to, to, to turn around. Oh he was! Lazy and all and ta, ta, he was really slow! But *dame* it was, lazy or not, that's, it had to be done. But early next morning there he is, gone. With his sack. And there he does like the cat told him to do—and then he starts driving the rabbits now there, and—the rabbits started jumpin here an there—soon, look! Two of them in the sack! But—before he got to the sack, the two rabbits are out of it. There! Phew, *cheepers!* Smart, no! Nah, the rabbits out of it and there they were, gone, and he, he, he comes back to the house—to the cabin and, and, "Where are the rabbits? No rabbits?" he says. "There are no, no rabbits," he says, "there were two in the sack."—"But if you had been smarter," he says, "you'd have caught some," he says, "you're pretty euh, pretty slow," he says, "you know it," he says, "when are you going to learn to be a bit smarter?" he says. He says, "I don't want you to watch cats," he says, "cats are smart, eh? But you," he says, "you're pretty far from being a cat. Hah! You're not smart!" He says, "You're not, you don't know what to do you!" He says, "Me, I'm going tomorrow morning, hah!" He says, "Are you going tomorrow marnin, you?"—"Yes!" he says, "I'm going tomorrow morning, but now *dame*," he says, "I'm gonna tell you something me. I don't want to go and get my paws wet me. Because there—there are sort of bogs there, going around there, going around there! Hey! I want me—little boots me. And there are some," he says, "there's a store there,"—and he knew everything eh? That cat he *knew* everything my old buddy. He was a witch, y'know. He was a *witch*, a *witch* they calls eh, a *sorciaise*. But him he didn't know, he didn't know, he thought he was a cat like the other cats—but.... He says, "You're gonna get me a pair of boots, you. Me I can't go. Because they wouldn't sell me a pair of boots," he says, "not, not to a cat. But you now there, you," he says, "you can get the boots there, you." And he says, "What size will that be?"—"Well," he says, "it'll be *number* one—a small size," he says. Ah, it's about four inches long, *I suppose*, three and a half to four inches. Number one, that's a small number, small number. "Take care," he says, "don't ask for a big number," he says, "because I, I won't be able to put them on my paws—"—"You won't be able to stay in them,"—"Neh! Too—they'll be—too big for me." Oh, that's good, there he is the next morning, there he is gone to get the, the, for—to look for the boots. Seems he went to three, two or three stores. The third store, by geez he found—number one. Ahh! Small number! Oh! it was about three inches long. Three inches, small boots, ah, they were about four, eight inches high there, heh, pretty little boots! All flowers, oh they were pretty! That's good, he gets to, ah, a face on him, the cat looks, "Well," he says, "I couldn't have done better myself!" Hah hah! *Dame*! "Na-a-r-aow! R-a-aow!" He says! Hee hee! He shouts out like a, he shouts out there! Good! That's good. There, there he says now, "I'm goin me, tomorrow morning there I'm goin after rabbits me. And I'm not strong," he says, "because—I haven't eaten, I haven't eaten, I'm weak too, me. I don't know how long we're gonna be able to be hungry like that," he says—"but—I want something to eat. Well," he says, "tomorrow morning I'm going me." Hm. Off he goes—the next morning at the break—first light of day there, the, the cat's gone there. He puts on his boots an he's gone. My great good God. He wasn't gone too long—well he left—he left at half past five—it was in the autumn there—well it was, it was just at daybreak—in October or something like that there, y'know—

G.T.:   Hm.

—Well, rabbit time, you know how it is—and there he is, gone. And euh, he says euh, he says, "Don't forget the sack there." John-of-the-Woods said to the rabbit—"Oh! Well yes, here, you,—if you hadn't, hadn't reminded me," he says, "I'd have forgotten that. Of course," he says, "the sack, sure, give it here." Well then John-of-the-Woods gives him the sack and there he's gone, he takes off there. He takes off. He was walking on his hind legs heh! He was standing up. Like a man. That's good. There he was, gone—he wasn't gone any time at all—look! He heard, he, he, around, he was gone about an hour an a half or something like that—and he heard a noise something tapping its feet—outside. He says, "And what's that?" he says, "is it a lynk, or, or, what is it?" He was afraid. Well he finds the door opening—his cat! "But," he says, "you're not back already!" He says, "You gave me, you gave me a scare!" he says—"Hoh! You almost curdled my blood!" He thought, he said it was a lynk or something like that. "Oh oh shoo, sheece." And he says, "Have you got something to eat?" he says. "Yeah," he says. There he, he, he shuts the doors and he empties the sack—three rabbits! Three rabbits! "Oh well," he says, "my dear cat, now come in now! Oh well I'm gonna cook that, me."—"Oh ho!" he says, "You better believe you're gonna cook you because me," he says, "me, I'm tired, me. It took me, heh heh! it took me a good little while before, I caught those rabbits there euh, I did better, I did better than you, you, you went yesterday," he said, "you came, you came back with euh, the sack all empty. But me," he says, "I, huh! I worked for that, me. Hah hah! Look out!" he says, "heh heh! Hi ha ha!" And he says, "Waow, waow, waow!" sometimes he says, "Waow waow!" y'see, he did that and, yeah, but the cat—he talks now but me, I can't do like him now— y'know, it's so long that, like, it's like I can't remember now how it, you know, how it was. But it's something like that anyhow. Well that's good. There! That's that, tears the skin off it and fry it euh, fry it right dry—no butter, no grease—nothin at all—fry it right dry. Well—now fried that in the soup—so it wouldn't burn d'you see, he had to—he put a little bit of water in it and he heated them, him, he *steamed* them they call it, heating them there.

G.T.:   Hm.

—And after when it was cooked right there—then they start eating. There's the cat and euh, John-of-the-Woods there, and they eat, "Ahhhooah!" *Dame* it was good! Ohh! Well him there, John-of-the-Woods, he lies down him—and he falls asleep. He was pretty happy with his belly, his stomach full—pretty happy enough it, it seemed like he had died and had gone to heaven. Ah! But the cat—him—he had eaten well too, but *dame* he was thinking all the time, he had something in his mind. Thinking. And he knew there was, there were three giants there, in, in, in, in the village there—there was three giants. And his, his, John-of-the-Woods, his master there, well, he loved his master—he had alw, he had always loved his master—he was a good person d'you see, he had never hit his cat or nothing at all like that—he was good to him. And ah, he says, "It's, I've got to do something good—for John-of-the-Woods, I've got to do something good for him, some time," d'you see, "and there's, there's three giants there," he says. An he was calculating now what he was going to do—but he didn't tell John-of-the-Woods, he didn't say, no, but he was calculating that now, and he knew there was a, a king there, where he lived, an he had a beautiful daughter. "Well if," he says, "if only I could," he says, "succeed with that and," he says euh, "he could," euh, John-of-the-Woods now, "could marry the king's daughter there now," he says, "a beautiful girl like that," he says, "and if I could euh, destroy the three giants me" he says, "if I could find a plan—a way—and, and he, and could give, give him that for a, for a surprise, something like that now—how proud he would be!" he says. "it, it, it'll put joy into his heart again. Well, he's been so good to me in, in all my life. He's been so good." Anyway John-of-the-Woods was snoring him it was, and the cat him he, he was calculating—what he was going to do. Anyhow he says nothing to John-of-the-Woods, he don't say nothing. Anyway that night went by [Emile coughs]—excuse me. That night went by, ate well an all that—sleep. Well the cat was sleeping him he had his, his paw under his ear there, like that, and he was thinking, and he was thinking what he was going to do. Well he had to calculate his idea just right, so he could do what he had in his mind. And if he had made, euh, a, a *mistake*, or a, a, a, a fault ah *da, dame* well he was done for. Well he knew that. Like that well, he had it all—figured out. Well he says nothing to John-of-the-Woods. He keeps his secret to himself, his secret, that. He says nothing. The next morning they get up—and euh, that's good. "Well," he says, "me," he says—when it was about ten o'clock, or half past ten, something like that—because he had it all figured out there in, in his mind what he wanted to go an do and everything—this n that—ah there's, "Well," he says—he says to John-of-the-Woods he says, "My master," he says—"you're gonna stay," he says, "in the house," he says, "you're gonna"—not in the house but in, in the cabin because it was a cabin—it wasn't a house, made with roots and, and moss y'know, turf and, it was a little hiding-place they had. "You're gonna stay here," he says, "and me," he says, "I'm gonna—take a little trip," he says, "I'm gonna *sneak* around, I'm gonna take a little trip around. Ah, I'm a cat," he says, "nobody's gonna pay no attention to me— they're gonna think I'm, a cat after rats, or mice or something like that." And he says euh, euh, euh, "I'm gonna go see my little boy, myself, an when I come back well if I've got anything, well I'll tell you. And like that nobody'll know nothin." Hoy! That's that. There, off he goes. And, "Miaow," it's, "miaow," there and euh, and if he met people an so on he'd go an rub his head, on their legs, and then, "Miaow," and then they'd say, "Oh dear little pussycat, dear little pussycat! Pretty little cat! Isn't he friendly!" And it went like that and it went like that. Well—he goes off to the giants, one of the giants there, there, there was a giant, three giants were there, three brothers—and they had each a farm. And each—a castle! *And* they were castles! It wasn't their, their little cabin they'd made with roots and, and peat—and—and moss! Heh heh! I guarantee you that. Heh heh! I guarantee you it shined that castle there! Eh! He goes off there and he, the, the, the, the, the oldest, the oldest of the brothers. And there, there, he was eating there the, doing his—he's eating his dinner. They weren't married or nothing, there, there was no woman, there was no woman giants d'you see, it was all giants, big men of, seven and eight hundred pounds—and women ah well, the women who were there were only women of—a hundred an fifty pounds, a hundred an seventy-five pounds, but they wouldn't have married men like that because they were-they were like mountains! Heh! They couldn't have girls or nothing, they had to live by themselves with—with them-selves, ah yes, with themselves and I mean to say, and what I mean—it wasn't easy for them to have a woman—they couldn't. Neh! Impossible! Like that they stayed, they, they're *bachelors* we'll say, it's like that, that's how I'll pronounce it, *bachelors*. They, they were cooking their food—and they ate. And that's that. Well here's the cat comes in and euh—he goes, "Miaow, miaow," and he goes rub his head on the giant's leg—and the giant is eating and he gave little pieces of meat to the cat and the cat ate that, and he rubbed his head some more on the giant's leg, and the giant stroked his head and the charming little cat, that's that. The charming little cat! And they were eating and it was great company for the giant—that now the giant liked that. Oh ha ha ha ha! He liked that. That's good. Ah he says, after he had finished eating well he says, "My little pussycat, my little pussycat," he says there, "my little cat no, my little pussycat," he says. And he says, "I'm gonna have a little nap. Me," he says, "I work hard—and I eat—and after I've eaten I've got to have an hour, an hour, an hour's rest—an hour of rest. Before I go back to work." And the cat he was there "Waow, waow," he, "waow, waow," he was stroking his head.

G.T.:   Yes.

—An then there's the giant who lies down on the floor face up and the cat was there rubbing his head on his face and then, "Little pussycat," and, "little pussycat," and, "little pussycat."—"Hnn-r-r-r!" and soon there's the giant—"Hn-r-r-r-r! kn-r-r-r! hn-r-r-r!" There's the giant—gone! He was gone—asleep. There the...[pause to change the tape]... cat, "R-a-a-a-ow!" He hooks him by the throat and drives his teeth right through his, his throat—*he cuts his throat right to the back*! [spoken with a ferocious voice] "Ahr-r-r-r!" He couldn't get his breath—he was—dead there. There he had—where he was lying was right where he—where he had his cellar. The cat hooks his paws on the, on the cellar door he, and the, the thing, a door he had there which closed down, down in the floor—he hauls that—and there he starts—he forced him—the cat wasn't big but he was strong—because he was, he, he was a, a *witch*, was a witch. He was strong. And he hauls, and he hauls, and he hauls, and he shoves him in the cellar. And he jumps on him with his, kick, kicking him and he *pushes* the giant into the cellar. And he *shuts* the door.... "Well," he says—the cat gets back to the house—to John-of-the-Woods' place, his master's, "Well," he says, "my cat," he says, "what have you seen today?"—"Ah! not too much," he says, "not much," he says, "lots of people," he says euh, "I saw the giants an all that," he says euh, "they gave me something to eat," he says. "I was at a giant's there, he ga, gave me some meat—to eat—well," he says, "they are good, fine people." That's good, that's fine. There. Next marnin—"Well," he says, "John-of-the-Woods," he says, "we've got some rabbit left," he says—he says, "so we ate one yesterday. And we ate another one today and another one tomorrow," he says, "that'll do, it's food, that's food," he says. "Well you'd better believe it," he says, "if it wasn't for you," he says, "my little cat," he says—"hah! I'd be dead me now me—I could have had something to eat. But I can't get anything to eat, me—I'd be dead, me." Hah! "Ah well *dame*," he says, "that's that. You, you fed me," he said, "all the time I was with you," he says, "your, your father and your mother, they, you—gave me food, you fed me, gave me food—but I didn't ferget that, me." Hm. "Ah! That was good that. Now it's my turn." Ah well that's good, well, well there the next day you come again euh, "Well," he says, euh, "John-of-the-Woods," he says, "my master," he says, euh, he says euh, "I'm gonna go for a little walk again. You, I want, don't you mind that," eh—"I'm coming back—don't you be afraid," he says, "I won't leave you, me."—"Ah," he says, "nah," he says, "me," he says, "me," he says, "I don't know, I'm not used to people me," he says, euh, "and I'm shy an all that," he says, "I've never seen a girl in my life clear of my mother," he says, "my mother," he says, "I know, my father—but I've never seen—other girls—I never had no sister, I never had nothin at all—I'm only an only child me."—"Ah but," the cat says, "well yes, oh yes," he says, "but *dame*," he says, "you're used to that," he says, "that don't make no difference—maybe a day will come," he says, "it, it'll come to your turn for that," he says. "Oh I don't know!" he says, "my cat," he says, "I don't know."—"Ah well," he says, "I'm gonna go for a little walk again," he says, there, he's gone again. Aiee, there the cat's gone to the other giant's, the, the, the, the second of the brothers there now, the other, the other, the second oldest we'll say who's alive there. Off he goes there and then he, he, noon time, and the giant was there eating and he had fried meat and he, he, and he was eating! And the cat comes in there—and "Maow-waa-waa," and he rubs his head, on the, on the giant's thigh—and then the giant says, "Little pussycat, little pussycat," and he cuts off a piece of meat and he gives it to the little pussycat, and little pussycat eats it. He didn't know that little pussycat could talk him but he thought it was a, a cat like the other there—and he gives him some food, food, and after he had finished eating, well did they eat, it wasn't little, little *bills* y'know—he said fifteen gallons of, of food there, well, they took—a calf, a two hundred pound calf there—that's what they'd cook up for their meal them. Oh now us now I know y'see euh—a pound is enough—but them, with them it's two hundred pounds and, and two hundred and fifty pounds for a meal—that's, those are big meals—a couple of small pieces—well you can't give too much because that's, that's a big appetite, big men, eight to nine hundred pound—there were some—a thousand pound there! Ho ho ho! They were big men, old man! Well that's that, but the cat was there rubbing, and he was saying, "Little pussycat, little pussycat!" Ah well that's good. "Well," he says, "my little pussycat," he says euh, "we eat," he says—"and after we've eaten, I—we have a rest." Ah and the, the, there the giant lies down—on the floor, his face in the air and the little pussycat was there and he's rubbing his face—on the, on the giant's face—he had a big beard—he—his beard was six inches long! Ah! it was, it was like hair! It was, there were no scissors in those times he, to *trim* it y'see.

G.T.:   Hm.

—It grew, t'was just like hair it was. Only his two eyes you could see, y'know. Oh! it was, oh it was, it was like, not worse than animals, worse than animals—with animals their hair doesn't grow long—but, them, them there, oh! That's good! There! There all of a sudden the giant's gone. "Hn-r-r-r! hr-r-r-r! hn-r-r-r!" And he was sleeping, he was sleeping and when the little pussycat saw he was sleeping so well, "A-a-a-gr-aow, raow!" He hooks him by the throat—he *drives* his teeth through—his throat—cuts his throat—cuts it—*clean off*! Cruh! The poor giant—he was gone him—he can't, he's gone—he's *finished*! No way to catch his breath, he breathes—at the bottom of his throat—eeeh! but he, he couldn't push it ba, back—it was, no, he was gone, the veins were cut right up, the veins to the heart, all cut! It was—in no time at all the blood was *pissing* out. My God it was, oh! it was terrible, terrible, terrible! There! He didn't live long—like five minutes and the giant was gone. There he—he miaowed, three giants—the same cellar—they were lying, it was right next to the cellar, the, the door they had to put their vegetables in y'see eh?

G.T.: Hm.

—Anyway the cat hooks his paws on—but there was no misery d'you see, he was, *dame*, a witch, d'you see, that weighed a lot there—a cat by himself, he couldn't do it—but with the, the witch there euh—a witch—a witch. There! Hooks the door and opens the door and there my man, there! he set to, he hauls on it, and he hauls, hauls, hauls! And all at once the latch there, *flick*! And he's gone. Stretches out in the, in the, in the, in the cellar. Then he shuts the door there—and then he takes off to John-of-the-Woods again. "Yeah! What sort of a day did you have today, pussycat?"—"Ah!" he says euh, "my dear master," he says euh, "all right, all right. All nice people they gave me something to eat and all that and—ah! it gave me a lot of pleasure. And," he says, "it's not too long ago you," he says, "you're going, a time, you were shameful," he said, "but you're gonna have to come with me too."—"Well," he says, "when you want," he says, "when you want," he says, "when you think I can go—I'll go." Now they still had another rabbit left. "Well," he says, "we've, we've got another—*puddin* there," he says—"another meal." And he says, "After, after that, well then," he says, "we'll be able to go—hunting again," he says, "I'll catch some more."—"Oh, we don't need that," he says, "for sure," he says, "for sure."—"Oh," he says, "not me," he says, John-of-the-Woods he says, "not me, me, my stomach's full," he says, "it's good food, good food! Ho! I'm not complaining, me," he says, "it's not, I'm fed better than when I was home! Yeah! I wasn't fed so well as that at home," he says. Oh ho! "Well, that's that," he says. Well, that's good, but *dame*. The next day—it's the last rabbit—ah ha! Well *dame* there were three giants and there's the last giant, too eh. But John-of-the-Woods didn't know nothing about that him—he didn't know! Neh! All he thought about was the rabbits—and he was thinking after—that rabbit was gone, we're gonna have another one again—that's all he was thinking about, eh?

G.T.: Yes.

—What are we gonna do, we're gonna, gonna, y'know eh? Ah? Well everybody's like that, we're gonna, let's say—well, what we're gonna do tomorrow, what are we gonna do? Well that's that, that's that. It's, it's, the—people in those days are like people now—they're the same. There, that's good. There! That's that. The next day—there! about eleven o'clock—"Well," he says, "John-of-the-Woods," he says, "my master," he says, "I'm going off on a little journey. Again," he says, "to stroll around, have a look, you see, and after, when I'm sure—they don't know I can talk, me," he says, "they don't know that. I talks to nobody, me," he says. "And they think I'm a cat eh, like you, you thought too there. But uh, heh heh! we'll, we'll *trick* them there." All right. He says euh, "I'm gonna go again." Ah well, all of a sudden it's half past ten goin on eleven o'clock, the cat's gone again. Ahh! Jack cooks the rabbit him, the rabbit he had and—he euh, he says euh, "you're gonna cook the rabbit today," he says, "but," he says, "don't save any for me," he says, "because me," he says, "he'll give me something to eat over there, me." He says, "Fill up your stomach right good you. To put a little bit of fat on you," he says, "you're thin, you! *Jeepers crumbs!*" he, and, "You're like that!" And he says, "Fatten yourself up properly," he tells him, "eat!" And he says, "Don't take too much for me," he says, "because me," he says, he, "when I go off like that there, they give me bits of meat an all that an I eat and I fill my stomach, and you," he says, "you're suffering for

235

me. Me," he says, "I'm starting to get smart, me, I'm starting to think, you've got to live too, you." And Jack he was falling down y'know! Such a handsome cat he had, eh? You know? Ah! That's good. There. That's that, there's the cat gone again. Ah well, he goes off now to the other giant—and it's the same thing, the same thing that happened with the two others. It's what happened with the two, the first two—happened to this one too. He rubbed his, his head on his leg and the, the giant fed, fed him and so on, and—he hooks him by the—the throat to make the story a bit shorter and he does the same thing—and there that's that. There. Now, the cat, him, he was eh, he was a witch eh? He was a witch or a person who had been turned into, into a cat by a witch—and y'see, it's, it's—

G.T.: Enchanted people there.

—Yeah, yeah, yeah! Enchanted, enchanted, yeah, enchanted, yes. Had been turned to a cat eh? That's why now d'you see eh? Well that's good. There. There the cat—he could write a bit him—well he made some, some, some, some *poster*, some things, some posters there eh? And euh he says euh, "The property,"—she marks it on the, the poster—the little piece of paper he had and he says, "This property here," he says, "belongs to John-of-the-Woods," an he sticks that on the post there—and then he goes off to the other one—and he says, "This property belongs to John-of-the-Woods." And he goes to the other one and he does the same thing again—like that he had three there—three castles—and three farms belonging to John-of-the-Woods—and John-of-the-Woods didn't know nothing about it. There. That's good. He goes home. "Ah," he says, "what did you see today euh, my little pussycat?"—"Ahhh!" he says, "not much," he says. "But," he says—"I saw the king's daughter there—ahh!" he says, "that's a beautiful girl! She's a beautiful creature!" He says, "Yes?"—"Ah yes," he says, "but," he says, "it won't be me who'll get her. Ahh!" he says, "p—attention!" he says—ha ha ha! He says, "Do you know," he says, "there are not many, many, I've seen loads of, of young fellows like you there," he says, "but do you know there aren't any so good looking as you? I didn't see one. Some had big ears, big noses all twisted—mouths all twisted," he says, "eyes all—sideways—but her there—but her," he says, "she's beautiful, her two eyes right straight, her cheeks right red, beautiful red lips," he says—"and built so well," he says, "built so well. And I'm sure," he says, "if you would because you, you'd see yourself, I'm pretty sure, you'd be well dressed," he says, "I'm sure," he says, "she'll fall in love with you! Right away!" Well, that's good. Well, "Ah no, not me, ah no, ah no, my little pussycat—no," he says, "not me. No no. Me I'm not a handsome fellow, I'm not a handsome fellow, me."—"Listen to me I tell you—you *are* a handsome fellow—I didn't know it before—but now—I know, me—*now* I know."—"You know? Well—I believe you, I believe you," he says, "because," he says, "you've done enough, e, done enough now," he says, "for me," he says, "I believe what you'll say."—"Now," he says, "I'm gonna tell you, me—I'm gonna tell you something—Wooden-Leg I'm gonna tell you,"—that's the cat talking—"I'm gonna tell you something me,"—he says—"you're gonna go," he says, euh— "there's a store there—" euh, he, he said the name of the store, now me I can't remember its name, the name—but he said it—and then he said, "A *suit* of clothes there," he says," and," he says, "there's, they're, there's all sorts of colours—well," he says, "you," he says—"I'm gonna tell you the colour you've got to get—you've got to get."—"But," he says, "how can I go an get a suit of clothes, I've got no money."—"That don't make no difference, that," he says, "don't make no difference," he says, "listen to me what, what I'm tellin you there, me," he says, "that's me talking to you—your cat," he says. He says euh, "Look," eh, "you're gonna go," he says, "into that store and you're gonna get a suit," he says, "in, euh, black serge," he says, "it's euh," and he says, "it, it shines—and then," he says, "you're gonna get a white shirt," he says, "they've got some there," he says—"and the, the, the *neckties* there," he says, "with, bow-ties they call them—they're made," he says, "like euh, a fan there," he says, euh, y'know, "and they call that bow-ties. And it's there," he says, "it's, it's marked," he says, "the pictures are there and everything, it, you, you can see when you go in, you look and you'll see yourself there, you'll see yourself there—now," he says, "that's what you've got to take, you." He says, "What for?" She says to him, "Look," he says—"if you only knew," he says, "what, if, if you had seen," he says, "what I saw, me," he says—"What did you see?"—"Well," he says, "I went to the king's me—"—"You went to the king's you?"—"Oh yes!" he says, "I went there, went around, I didn't go inside," he says, "but I went around—and then I saw the king's daughter," he says, "she was picking, she was outside, she was picking flowers, she was, she was making bouquets there. But," he says, "she's a beautiful girl! Ahh! Like I told you just then," he says, "red, cheeks right red, lips right red, long blond hair, and—blue eyes and she's so pretty!" he says. "But me," he says, "well it's like I told you! I told you you're the best looking fellow! That I've seen, me! They're all twisted noses and best mouths and cross-eyes—and that's why," he says, "I—I told you—You! You! You! You! You'll have her! You'll have her! It's guaranteed! There!" he says, "go on—like I told you—you want some money—I've got money here." There. He gives him some money. He says, "That'll cost you—heleven—heleven dollars—for the, for the costume." Now I guess it costs about, about five hundred, five hundred dollars—but it cost heleven dollars—in those times. Heleven dollars. She gives, the, the cat gives heleven dollars, I don't know, he had stolen it from the giant or what, but he, he had eleven dollars—there he had, he gave to, to John-of-the-Woods. There's John-of-the-Woods gone. But he was *trembling* like that there. He, he, he, don't know but he was in another world he, he, he couldn't believe it eh? He couldn't believe it. Well, that's good. There. [Emile coughs and chokes] Excuse me. When he goes in the store—he sees the pictures all that there—there—and he sees his suit there. And he sees the white shirt and the, the, the bow-tie on it. Well there, the, the, the, the clerks come to him, he says, "What can we do for you?" He says, "I want the, that suit there—and euh, the shirt, and the, and the, the, the bow-tie, the, the, what do you call it—there—the, the ecktie—the goat—the goat ecktie?

G.T.: Hm.

—The goat ecktie—the *bow-tie*. He says, euh, "I want that there. And how much does it cost?"—"Eleven dollars." Ah, ah. The cat, the cat knew—euh, he, he, but he's a witch—he knew, he hadn't been there but he knew, y'see. Anyway that's good. Buys the, the, the—suit, and then, I took the sh, the shoes too eh? Oh he'd told him that, forgot to say it there. The shoes and the, the hat and everything. And he buys it. And it cost—euh, thirteen dollars for, for the, the, the shoes and everything. There. He gets back—there. He, there, he, the, the cat he'd, he was boiling water the time he was gone. And he, he, he'd set up, he'd made it with galvanized iron, a, a, a thing, a *bathtub* there—the, he made it with galvanized iron—and he heaves the water into it and he says, and they he heaves the, the, the, Wooden-Leg into it and he washes him. And I guarantee you he scrubbed him, my son. But he didn't—scratch him with his claws oh! But *dame* he drew his claws back there and scrubbed him with his paws y'know. And there are, in the bush, there were all kinds of things he could hook—but he scratched him a couple of times when he was encouraged enough to, because he loved his master eh? You know some times, you know, heh heh! Gee! Well that's good. Well then he, he was kind of mad—he didn't know what the cat—but he, he, y'know, he trusted him, he listened to him because he trusted him—even if he would be hung the next day—euh, *still* he trusted him. Well that's good. There. There. Well he'd dressed him, my son, there he dresses him. Oh! Holy Catoos! That was—handsome, my son! Handsome man. Oh! There he says, "Now go to the king's!"—"Me?" he says, "to the king's?"—"Oh ho ho! Yes!" he says.

"You're gonna go to the king's," he says—and he says, "You're gonna—knock on the door—and you're gonna—I—lift your hat when they come open the door—and euh—and it's her," she said, "who's gonna come open the door."—"Well,"—"But," he says, "don't be shy. Don't be shy! Tell her, 'Hello Miss—and when she sees you—she's gonna fall in love with you, she's gonna say, 'Come in! Come! Come in!'" Well that's good. There. He takes off. Ah ha! But *dame* his two knees were knocking together like that there [Emile taps the fingers of each hand together in quick time]—shyness—and he didn't know you see? He was—he was born in the woods—never seen people before—who would be brave like that! Oh ho ho! He, he, but he, he listened to his cat—he *goes*. So there he knocks to the door. Oh my good God! When she opened the door—she looked at him—she takes off, leaves the door open she takes off, hooks him around his neck, she hugs him—and hauls him into the house. Well him, he didn't, almost like a, he had a—heart—attack, atta, attack. Ah! It came close! My good God—for a girl to go an do something like that—for the first time in his life! She didn't say, "Come in," or nothing like that, she hauls him! Hauls him inside! The first good looking man she had ever seen in her life. Well, that's that. Then he comes in! And the king said, so goes to her father she says, "My father," she says, "this is, the charming man," she says, "I've got here. Oh! That's nice!" And he says, "What's going on then? What's going on then?" But she says, "Come see!" And I saw the king, the old king him but he was, well his nose, and he had two, two—*kinks* in his nose him—and his mouth all twisted as well! But his daughter, her—was, was—a beautiful person. Ah ha! She was, she was the, the, the—the the, oh, "*A top choice of the world,*" as they say eh? Well that's good. He comes there—and the—the man y'see—so charming, all that now it's the cat did all that y'see eh? Ah? The witch ah? He gave him all—the right manners—so the girl would—ah?

G.T.:   Hm.

—And he was—a witch eh? There aren't any now but in those times, there were lots of, of witch—they knew, they could—swear—they knew everything, they knew everything. Well that's good. Well, well he goes in there. And then there's a, there's a, there's a big supper there, all, all, all kinds—of things there to eat—and he was received like a—gentleman. Well, that's that, he couldn't go back home that night, no, no, no, he had to stay, had to stay. Well that's good. M—well he stays. Pass the evening—and they played cards—and-it went by, it went by and the next morning well he says, "I've got to go back home." Well, the king he says euh, "Listen," he says, "my dear young man," he says, "Come again. Come again."—"Well," he says, "thank you very much—I'll come back—for sure." Anyway he takes off home him there. And he gets there he says, "How did you get on?" the cat says, "How did you get on euh, John-of-the-Woods?"—"Well, well," he says, "It was extrominary. But," he says, "it was good, I had a fine evening."—"I said you would," he says, "I told you so!" And he says, "I was, I wasn't asked to come back again." He says, "What, did he tell you you have to come back?"—"No—but he, he told me co, come again."—"Well well," he says, "that's what that means—it's for you to go back again. Huh! That's, that's what that means—if he had said 'Come and see us some time,' but he said 'come again'! Well, that means—come again tonight! Hoh!"— "Well I'm h-h-hungry y'know," and then he *gives it, my son,* they ate—and he had, he had been out rabbiting him, he'd caught some rabbit, the cat y'know—and he'd cooked up a *feed*—oh—and it, it, t-t-t!—better than the giants could do ah ha! And they eat! They eat! Good. There. Euh.... That's good. Yeah, well, the cat was satisfied and the young fellow too, him, well, he was starting to come—he was thinking he was in the meat—and he was thinking—there was something in it—and he was happy his little heart was coming back in, in, in, in *shape*—oh, it was a—good life and he was thinking, the beautiful girl, the beautiful girl, the beautiful—ah well,

well, well he didn't sleep at all that night—he didn't, he didn't sleep, he didn't sleep, nah! t'all he didn't sleep. Nah! That's good. There the night passed. There the next day, there's the cat starts again he had th, the clay hard there, the *basin* he had made there it was soft, it had gotten hard, oh! gee it was almost eaten like, like rocks. There. There he shoves the, the, the, Wooden-Leg into it and puts in the water and the cat he, from, from, from the lake, and he tips that on his back and he rubs, rubs, rubs—and washes him right good. There were no *perfumes* or nothing like that y'see—in those times—there was nothing like that y'know—only flowers eh—they rubbed themselves with flowers, there, nice smelling flowers eh? There that's, that's enough there. It worked—oh! they had a way, they had a way, they had a way of doing things. Ah! That's good. There. Again—dressed again there. The same change of clothes—and there he's gone again, same hat and all. There he's gone again. Ah that's good he gets there, knocks to the door—oh, opens the door, "Eh, eh! You, come in, come in, come in, come in, come in, come in, come in, come in! But why didn't you come quicker, but why didn't you come quicker?" But it was, t'was only the evening before and euh, it's only the night now d'you see? Oh, the girls like for you to come see them at noon, at noon or in the, in the day. He, but, got to go, she's not sick she missed him, oh! oh! Oh, seven and eight o'clock or nine to ten o'clock or something like that—missed him—oh! And it, and ah but d—there it starts warming up my man, it's starting to warm up! Ho ho ho! Whacko! Yeah, well, that's good. There the king he found he was a charming man—and he could see his daughter—was pretty pleasant—and euh, pretty proud to meet that young man and then him, ah well, he's, he's a young man—it, it, it pleased him pretty much too—he, he didn't know what to say, he, he was gonna, he was, he was gonna speak and he stopped, he stops, stopped. And all at once it came out—"Well," he says, "my dear man," he says—but his daughter she was around—around twenty-three years old, d'you see.... It was about time in those times to get married d'you see? Ah—and he knew that y'see? He says euh, "Euh, my, my dear John-of-the-Woods," he says euh, "that's your name,"—he says, "Yes, euh, my name, yes, John-of-the-Woods, Yes."—"Well," he says euh, "would you like," he says, "euh, to marry my daughter," he says. "Oh yes," he says, "that would give me great pleasure if I had the chance," he says, "if you would give me the, the, cause," he says, "to, to act," he says, "so I could, you could give me your daughter—if, if she's in love with me." Oh she says, "Yes! I'm in love with you!"—"And me too," he says, "I'm in love with you." And he says, "We're not lucky enough to be able—for us to be able to be put together," he says. "Well," he says euh the king says to him, "I give you my consent, my consent," he says, "get married!" He says euh, "I'll get the minister—and you'll be married. Whenever you want." Well that's that there, he takes off to get his cat there. Heh heh! He gets back about two o'clock in the morning—*now*—the cat was sleeping. In the hay. Sleeping, he says, "Waow! waow!" Well... John-of-the-Woods gets there, opens the door, he says, "Hay! Haow—waow-waow," the cat he says, "you woke me up," he says. "Ah well," he says, "what kind of a night did you have?" Well there now John-of-the-Woods tells his story, tells his story to his cat—"But," he says, "that's that, d'you see? That's the story," he says—the cat says to, to John-of-the-Woods. "The wedding," he says, "it's right close eh?"—"Well," he says, "that's right."—"Ah well," he says. Now the, the king thought him he was—he wasn't a rich man—he thought he had nothing y'know, John-of-the-Woods he thought, he didn't think—but *dame*—for his, for his daughter—he's her love, she had fallen in love with him and she, she was such a beautiful creature—in her person—that—he took pity on his daughter, d'you see, there, he, that made him—-love his daughter—ten times better—than he had loved her before. Because she had found her choice. Heh? Well that's good. There. Anyway, the next morning, my friend, he was up again and eating rabbit again and heh heh? and he heaves him in

239

the tub again and another wash again—and that's that, he's gone. Gone. Gets there...
[pause to change the tape]
G.T.:   No.

—Yeah. Well, that's good. There that's, he, he goes in and goes to where the girl was—goes in an this an that. There—euh, they were chatting for a little bit and then they started talking about marriage and this an that and euh—straight off to get the minister—he wants to get them married right away. Yeah, that's good. Oh the minister's there—the minister comes. Well now the cat him, he, the cat came there too. When those times came, it was close, well the cat comes there too—but he was around y'know, "Miaow, miaow, miaow"—but they didn't mind the cat because he was a cat. But they didn't stroke him or nothing like that—he was a pretty little cat. That's good. There. Ayyy. There the minister marries them. Well, after they were married—there. He says euh—they had had their dinner—and then he says to his master, Wooden-Leg he says, "Now," he says euh, "tell the king," he says, "to—get," he says, "two horses an a carriage. And euh, tell him like that that you want—two horses and a carriage—and then we're going—I—that you want to go and see," he says, "your, what, what you've—belongs to you." Ah—he says, "What?" he says, "I've got nothing belonging to me."—"I told you, say that." He says, "All you've got, all you've got to say is that—and," he says, "shut your mouth." Well, that's good, that's good. Yeah, he tells the king he says, "Now," he says—"I want you to get two—two horses," he says, "and euh, a carriage—and," he says, "I want," he says, "you to go to, with me," he says—"me and my wife—and you and your, and your, your lady." He had a wife too the king euh—but she was quiet, her she never said nothing—she was right y'know euh quiet, she was quiet. That's that. Good. There he says,"Do what I told you now." And he says, "You're gonna go," he says, "to the three giants there," he says. "Bu—there where they, they live over there on their farms. And euh, say nothing," he says. And he says, "I can't go there," he says, "me, all the, the giants."—"I told you! Go! Get in the carriage and come on! And don't say nothing! Now listen to me," he says. Well that's good there he tells the king and all that—and he gets in the carriage, the horses and all that—and off they go! And then they go to the giants'. When he gets there the first *gate*, the, the, the propiety, the propriety—propr-ity—hah! no way to say it!—belongs to Wooden-Leg. The king looks at that. He says, "What's this!" he says, "What's this?" he says. "John-of-the-Woo—Wooden-Leg's property?" He says, "Is that you?"—"Oh yes," he says, "that's me." D'you see there—goes through the farm—the other gate again then—"Wooden-Leg's—property"—big castles, it, it was shining eh? Wah! But, but, but, the king his ears were rising up, it's, it's, he had a hat on his head and his ears, they were growing, ha ha ha! up in the air—and all at once there's his hat off his head! He was pretty surprised! Off they go again, further—and it was John's—Wooden-Leg's property again! "Well," he says, "that can't be, that." Oh yes there, the cat gave the, the keys to, to Wooden-Leg and there, "Wooden-Leg," he says, "open the castles," and they went inside but—but it was smelling a bit—because the giants were starting to, starting to, heh heh heh! they were starting to rot! But that made no difference, because he was a farmer d'you see eh, had been for a long time! Eh hee hee! He just passed his nose over it like that. And when I got there, that's just where they were—but *dame*—between me and Wooden-Leg and the cat—we buried the giants—and euh, we got clear of the, the, heh heh! the, the smell and if they're living with the young couple—they're living!

Commentary and notes

This tale, perhaps the longest of all those I have recorded, is a narrative *tour de force*. Starting from the simplest of themes—the hero, helped by his cat, wins the hand of a princess—Emile has created a zesty and dynamic tale which serves to evoke, to whomever cares to appreciate the fact, the days of the first French people living on the Port-au-Port Peninsula. The landscape, the isolation, the food (numerous old settlers have spoken to me of the old days when they had little more than rabbit to eat during the long, hard winters), the practical philosophy of the cat, all these elements combine to reflect a past when life was not easy. Emile evokes it with much humour.

A question comes immediately to the mind of one interested in the art of the public storyteller: how does he manage, with a minimum of narrative motifs, to create such a long story? In the chapter dealing with his art, Emile had spoken, without going into details, of ways of lengthening a story. The tale of John-of-the-Woods well illustrates his procedure. Firstly, physical movement is relatively brief in the tale, but the surrounding dialogues are very long. The conversations between John, to a degree playing the part of a child, and the cat, playing the sometimes patient, sometimes irascible father, are filled with counsel and advice; they are always lively, with the cat aroused by the rather negative attitude of John, and his protests.

Emile lengthens his narration with asides. One thinks, for example, of his account of the giants' habits, or of the cat's monologue after the first dinner in the shack, in which the cat in fact anticipates the tale's ending. The tale of course does not lack action. The cat's confrontation with the giants is more than lively, both in words and in Emile's body movement and vocal play.

But these matters, which have to do with technical analysis, cannot be properly appreciated without the tale's terminal context. Reproduced below is the conversation following the conclusion of the narrative:

G.T.: Ha ha! Ho! That's a great story, Emile. That's a great story. You told it really well. Who told you that one? Do you remember?

E.B.: You did.

G.T.: Eh?

E.B.: You!

G.T.: Me?!

E.B.: Yeah!

G.T.: I told you?!

E.B.: Yeah yeah! What you're going [two or three indistinct words]

G.T.: I told you that?

E.B.: Yeah! Last year—not this year—last year—but not so long as that eh?

G.T.: But you, you'd heard it before?

E.B.: No, never.

G.T.: You'd never heard that told?

E.B.: No, you told it last year.

G.T.: That can't be true!

E.B.: It's God's truth.

G.T.: And you'd never heard it before? No?

E.B.: It was you told me that.

It is quite remarkable that a man who had heard no more than the broad outline of a tale over a year before can take such a sketch and make such a well developed narrative out of it. I had myself forgotten I had told it to him, as the conversation above indicates. In fact, numerous storytellers, male and female alike, have told me that a single hearing of a tale was enough for them to know it; but this is the proof of it. The version Emile had learned from me was no more than the skeleton of one I had myself heard told by Mrs. Elizabeth Barter, a gifted storyteller from Mainland; I had related it to him following a recording session when, at his request, I told him a story.

The tale itself is a version of the international tale-type AT 545, *The Cat as Helper*. It does not seem to be widely distributed in France; *Le Conte populaire français* notes only some fifteen versions for France and its dependencies and eight only for French tradition in North America. I refer the reader interested in the original version of this variant to the article by Geraldine Barter entitled "'Sabot-Bottes et P'tite Galoche': A Franco-Newfoundland Version of AT 545, *The Cat as Helper*," *Culture & Tradition* I (1976), 5-17.

Motifs in the tale include N411.1.1, *Cat as sole inheritance*; B211.1.8, *Speaking cat*; B422, *Helpful cat*; B581, *Animal brings wealth to man*; B582.1.1, *Animal wins wife for his master* (Puss in Boots); L161, *Lowly hero marries princess*; and compare F771.4.1, *Castle inhabited by ogres*.

CENDRILLOUX

Well Cendrilloux—the story of Cendrilloux, he had a, a, a mother—she had a child. And euh, she raised her child euh, she had had a husband but she was married but she wasn't married long and she lost her husband. In the, the first war. Her husband was, was in the war and he was, he was killed. She stayed with her child. And she raised him up until he was twenty-one years old—but he'd never gone out of the house. He was all the time sitting behind the stove. And she called him Cendrilloux. His name was John. But she didn't call him John, she calls him Cendrilloux. And everybody—ca—called him Cendrilloux. It's a, a *nickname* y'know eh?

G.T.: Hm-hm.

—And—that's good, went by, went by, went by, went by—until he was twenty-one years old. Well there she says—well it's different eh?

G.T.: Hm.

—Cendrilloux eh?

G.T.: Hm-hm.

—Her she was a girl and him he was, he was a boy. Well there—she says, "My dear child," she says—"if you are going," she says, "to be like that there, for the rest of your days—if you live to be fifty, or sixty or seventy, seventy-five, eighty years old," she says, "maybe even a *hundred*—and your, your name is gonna stay," she says, "Cendrilloux. Because," she says, "you're all the time behind the stove! Everything, you haven't come out from behind it in your life yet," she says. "Since I've known you, since you've been in the world," she says, "you've been, that's where I've seen you—where I've seen you all the time," she says. "Behind the stove. My Cendrilloux." She calls him Cendrilloux. And everybody calls him Cendrilloux. Well there that's good. There. She's twenty-one years old, he's twenty-one years old. Well, "Now," she says, "my dear young, my dear young man," she says, "get up, get up!" she says. "My—nah!" he says, she says, "Now get up!" But, but euh [whispers; the snivelling fool] —he tried to pick himself up—he couldn't—he couldn't—he was all the time sitting down eh? Was, was, he had the, the cramps eh? Well there she hooks him there. She, he tried and he couldn't. Well, she knew there, d'you see, he had the will—but he couldn't. There she hooks him and hauls him up there. And there, there she, she, she makes him walk, oh oh! And he was, he, he was walking like an old man I guess a hundred, hundred—hundred years old, a hundred and ten, a hundred and fifteen years old, something like that. And she hauls him up and she walks him, he walks, he walks, he walks and ooh! but in a couple of days—chee! He, he's starting to get some strength. And he starts walking by himself. There. "Now," she says—"there, d'you see now," she says, "that's it," she says, "d'you see, you've had, you've had, you've had the, the, the excise, the exercise," she says, "d'you see that?" she says—"You're starting to walk," and him he was starting to get proud, he was starting to get proud eh? Heh heh! He was starting—it was like another, another world eh? All the time sitting down, all the time sitting down eh? And all at once his mother gets him to walk—his—but it wasn't, it wasn't something—heh heh! new for him that! Ha ha! Oohh! There! *By gosh*, he started to learn how to get up—and he started to move his arms and—and it was moving there. And, and he was walking there. Oh and they'd passed a week like that there—passed a week. "There now," she says, "d'you see? Me," she says, "I'm starting to get old, me," she says,—"your mother—there—she's starting to get old, her, me, I'm sixty-eight now there," she says. He says, "Yes." But him he was only—thirty-five. There. Nah—I've made a mistake—twenty-one years old I mean.

G.T.:   Hm.

—She was sixty-eight and him he, he was—twenty-one. She had got behind— euh, Cendrilloux. Ah—there. "Now," she says,"the, the king there," she says, "there—euh, the farmer up over there—not the king, the farmer,"—she says, "he's got a beautiful daughter there. Oh oh oh! Well," she says, "euh me," she says, "I find her a pretty—a charming person," she says—"she's friendly, she's always got a smile on her face," she says, "and she works—she works like a dog. And," she says, "if you could only," she says—"you, you're a handsome fellow, you," she says—"you're a handsome fellow. And if you could change a little bit and move a little bit," she says, "and you could go there," she says—"and cast an eye from time to time. Oh, cast an eye from time to, not, you don't have to, not too, you're too quick—you take your time," she says-"take your time! Only you've got to listen to that," she says, "it, it's not polite that. That's wild, that. But you take your time— and," she says, "you cast an eye at her from time to time—and then after a little while," she says, "it works there," she says, "and it gets going. And soon," she says, "it comes to something!" Hah hah! "But you mustn't be too brazen! Look out!" And I mean ah, he didn't know too much and then—it was only in those times that his mother started her, all the time his ears were getting, "Cendrilloux, Cendrilloux, Cendrilloux." But it was starting to change there. Anyway—that's good. There. Ah, it was like that for that week and another week, and another week—and he was walking, and he was moving, and he was starting to come around, and it was going good—there! She says, "You're in pretty good shape now there, you." There. She says, "You're gonna go to the, the farmer's," she says—"you don't forget—euh, cast an eye from time to time!"—"Well, cast an eye from time to time! Oh well that's that." That's good. There. So the time came there and it was the time—it was the Saturday night. Syoo! "There, like I told you," she says—"you're gonna go there with some respect," she says, "Good evening euh, Sir, good evening Ma'am, good evening, Miss—look out!" she says—"do it right! And then, when the old man and the old woman—euh, aren't looking," she says, "cast an eye! At the girl."—"Yes mother," she says, "Well,"—"Well that," he says, "isn't hard to do." Good. Ah, that's good. Ah, that's good. Well that's it there—he, then he gets dressed, she, she, she washes him right and euh—she dresses him up in those times there weren't many fine clothes but *dame* huh! you dressed up y'know, it was all clothes made on the loom, they used to make a loom eh?

G.T.:   Yes yes.

—With wool and looms—and they used to make pants and, and, and—shirts and—Well that's that. She dressed him up right anyhow. The, the best way she could. But he was a good looking man. Pah! I guarantee you. He wasn't skinny like me heh!

G.T.:   Hm!

—Well that—he's gone. There. Like that around eight o'clock in the evening. Oh it was dark. There. In his mind now he says, "Mother told me—to cast an eye—well—and cast an eye," he says, "euh the farmer, him, he's got cows, he's got sheep—and that there"—there he goes and he hooks a fork there were three arm forks—three arms were in it heh! Well he takes a fork and puts it in his pocket. He's gone. Ah! That's good. When he got to the, to the farmer's barn—and—he, he goes into the barn. He looks for the sheep—and sheep their eyes are so bright ah, it's like flashlights their eyes eh. He goes up—and he gets his fork to, he hooks the sheep and sticks his fork into an eye, he pulls it out! He hooks another and sticks the fork in and he pulls it out! Ha ha! He pulls out five or six—five or six there. [laughter] "Well," he says, "that should do, five or six eyes," he says, "that's enough that—for tonight." Heh heh!

G.T.:   Heh heh heh!

—Well that's good. Well there he is, gone. Well my old man when he, he, after there—he knocks to the door—and the girl went to open the door—ooh! She had never seen him and he, he, he didn't live too far from there. But she had never seen him, she had never been there y'see.

G.T.:   Hm.

—The charming young, young man! Oh oh oh oh oh the handsome man! Stiew! Aowaowaow! Hee! Ha ha! Cacko! She says, "Come in, come in, come in! Dada! and euh, Mama!"—"What?"—"Look, the young man," she says, "look! Some—oh, good evening, come in, come in! Dear friend, come in!" But they didn't know he was the, the, the, she had fixed him up d'you see she had dressed him there—he, he passed for a Cendrilloux all the time y'know—

G.T.:   Hm.

—That was his name he had never been—stood up—she—in his life eh? Y'know, he was, he was abandoned, they didn't know that—when they saw him—they thought he was somebody coming from, from, from foreign countries or something like that eh?

G.T.:   Yes yes.

—Ah. Anyway that's good. *By de gee*, the girl, my God she, oh, oh, oh, oh! She, she, she loved him, she loved him, she loved him. The handsome man, the handsome man, and—so much spirit, so much spirit, so—so well brought up eh? She says, "Sit down." Well there he sits down—and then the old man and the old woman they were there talking, they were chatting, about this, about that, and the girl she was there—she, she was showing herself there, she was a little bit smart, she was smart and y'see—oh, waow! Heh! She, she was, she was, pretty intelligent, I guarantee you. There that's good. There. Soon there's the old man and the old woman, they turn their backs eh, he grabs an eye in his pocket and he throws it at her, pock! He smacks it in the side of her mouth [Emile is contorted with laughter]—the girl's face! She looks at him he says, "Pssshh!" She points to her father and mother she says, "Pop and Mom, and you do something like that!" she says. Oh! "Pss! They're not going to like that!" Do you see, she meant to say, y'know....

G.T.:   Hm.

—That it was a sign—and then there he turned around and they start talking again and then all at once they turn their backs again [bang!] he fires, throws another

244

one again hah! Another eye again! Yeah! Oh she gets—ss—she meant to say—
"Don't do that! Don't do that!" But she wasn't saying it but she was making signs
with her hand y'see? There's her father and mother turn around again but they start
talking again and everything was going just fine oh oh! it was serious business—
there. Soon there, they turn around again and there he throws another eye again—
her—he hits her in the eye—this time. [laughter] Right—oh jeez, he aims just right!
Rrraow! There she goes and says in his ear—she says [Emile whispers], "Don't do
that, don't do that no more!" she says, "because perhaps Pop and Mom won't like
something like that," she says. Ah that's good, there, oh, he didn't do it no more.
But he still had three more eyes in his, in his pocket! Hah hah! But he didn't do it
no more, he didn't do it no more. Ah, that's good. There he goes home. "Good
evening—oh, the king says, euh the farmer says, "Come back again, come again!"—
"Oh," she says [in a simpering girl's voice], "come back again"—the girl eh, the
king's daughter said, "Oh come again!"—"Well yes, oh yes," he, he says, "I'll come
back," he says [in a weirdly deep and garbled voice], "oh yes." Well that's good.
There. That's good, takes off. There he gets back to his, he gets home—his mother
she, she was sitting in her rocking-chair, she was there she, she was knitting, her.
She was knitting. Ah hun! Rayum! "Hoho!" she says, "you're back!" She says to
him, "How was it?"—"Oh," he says, "not bad Mom, not bad." She said, "Did you
cast eyes like I told you to?"—"Oh I cast three eyes," he says. And she says, "Did
she play anything?"—"Oh, she, she told me like that euh, she said, 'Don't do that
no more,' she says, 'in case,' she says, 'Pop and Mom see, see you!'"—"Ah! I told
you, me! I told you! Better than sitting behind the stove all the time," she says, "heh
heh heh! Now tomorrow—tomorrow," she says, "now there—I'm gonna tell you
me. Tomorrow I'm going to get the girl me—and," she says, "you're gonna cook
dinner." Now—they had a—a little dog called "Three Sorts."

G.T.:   "Three Sorts."

—"Three Sorts." The little dog, a little *cracky dog* they call it, eh?

G.T.:   Yes yes.

—Her name was "Three Sorts"—and they had a, a—a goose—which, which
was sitting—well, be—he's behind the door, they had made a cage for it.

G.T.:   Yes yes, yes yes.

—And there was a dozen eggs—and they had their goose—was—sitting on
them. There. That's good. Ah! Anyway, the next day comes, "Well now," she says,
she says, "you're gonna cook dinner—ah well," she says, "you're gonna cook three
sorts,"—she meant to say meat, turnips—and potatoes! She says, "You're gonna
cook three sorts—and me, I'm gonna go get the girl—and then I'm gonna—bring—
bring her here—and it's like that," she says, "everything's gonna get done—start,"
she says, "and then—the deal's gonna be made. It's a long time I've been waiting
for that, me!" she says—"now," she says, "there's joy in my heart now, I'm happy,"
she says, "to see what you've done. I never thought," she says, "you were so
smart—as you are. To see you—I used to call you Cendrilloux all the time—yes but
I'm really sorry. If I had known," she says, "never! I would have called you
something like that. A mother should pay attention," she says, "to what she says to
her child." He don't say nothing, him. But—that's good, good, ten o'clock comes
around, she says, "I'm, I'm going to get the girl now, well," she says, "I'm gonna
chat for a little while and," she says, "you—*tree, tree*."—"*Tree* what?"—"And euh,
that, that, that won't be too bad," she says, "that won't be too bad." All right. Now
him he, he, three sorts, and there the dog was called "Three Sorts"—but her she
meant to say euh, some meat, some, some potatoes, and some turnips. Three sorts,
y'know. Hm.

G.T.:   But that's a funny name for a dog.

—Eh?

G.T.:   That's a funny name for a dog.

—Yeah! Yeah, yeah, but three sorts, that's not the dog.

G.T.:   Yes yes!

—Anyway heh! that's good. There. There when she's, when she'd gone—he, he didn't ask for more because he was—his way was—say quick—and after she was gone he started to think—he—"What's he saying that, that, what did she *mean* by that," he says, "three sorts!" he says. "What sort of affair I've got to cook, three sorts?" Y'know if he had thought quicker there—he would have asked what it was—what sort of three, three sorts I've got to cook? But he says d'you see ki, kind of puzzled there, had kind of—of, of—contradicted there—but she was gone now—and he was there—but, "It isn't, it wouldn't be the little dog there? It wouldn't be the little dog? Three Sorts. For the turn," he says, "that's it. *I bet you a darn* that's what she meant! The little dog! Ah no!" he says, "not that! But," he says, "I don't know what it is! Three Sorts," he says, "I call, I call it, the little dog," he says, "Three Sorts. Well," he says, "you've got to think," he says, "it's that. But," he says, "that's that, I'm not gonna take the chance anyhow," he says, "that's that, she said Three Sorts but that's that. That's that." There he gets a pot of water my man and he boils it there.

G.T.:   Ha ha!

—And he hooks the dog by the, by the back of its neck when the pot was boiling just right, and he heaves the dog in but my God in life eh the dog eh [laughter], t'was, "Wah wah wah wah wah wah wah wah wah wah wah!" And then, then, the goddarn goose sitting behind the door—Holy gee when she heard that and she knew what she, what he had done—she knew, her—she could talk—but she knew there that he had heave the little dog—into, into the boiling water there and then, well, she started carrying on, "Quack! quack! quack! quack! quack! quack! quack! quack!" Well he says, "Watch out, you!" he says—"if you don't shut your mouth—well you," he says, "you're goin in with Three Sorts!" [laughter] And there he said that, it—she gets madder yet! She quack quack, quack, qu-a-a-a-ck, qu-a-a-ck! Quack, quack, quack! *Oh jeepers cripes!* He, she was *crazy*, my man! She was spitting fire! Cendrilloux, he grabs by the neck he tears her—out of her cage, where she was in the cage eh—and he takes her and he *heaves* her into the—into the tub with Three Sorts—and he pushes her right—over the side and he bangs the lid down—all at once there and—nothing to hear. There's the goose gone. And four sorts. Well after his anger had passed—[laughing]—"Oh my great good God," he says, "what have I been and done? But," he says, "got to think I'm crazy a'right. Oh I'm gone out of my head," he says, "I'm gone! That's not what Mom, Mom told me to do! Three Sorts! I bet you it's sorts of of of, of, of of vegetable or something like that, meat or something like that. There perhaps potatoes or perhaps turnips—or perhaps cabbages," he says. He—d'you see? He says, "Pay attention," he says, "after all." He says, "Look," he says, "and my mother," she says, "had fourteen eggs there," he said, "being hatched," he says—"to have some, some geese," he says, he says, "for, for euh, food. Well," he says, "she's not gonna be pleased! My God, what am I gonna do? Look it's not," he says, "it's, it's no good," he says. "It's crazy," he says, "for the trouble. Oh well *dame*," he says, "now," he says, "I know I'm crazy—now," he says, "I *know*! Cendrilloux! It wasn't wrong," he says, "to call me Cendrilloux. And not only that she should have called me as well—as well—should have called me 'Stupid,'" she says, "the, the, the n—all sorts of things like that." There. "Look at the eggs," he says—"it's not as bad yet as Three Sorts," he says, "and the goose," he says. "No, look at the eggs," he says, "over there," he says, he says, "what is Mom

246

gonna say?" Ah well there he was there, my old buddy, he got right wild, my old buddy—Holy cat! Well there he said, "Now my man," he says, "that's that, well I've got no choice. I've got no more choice. I'm gonna have to sit on the eggs myself," he says, "to hatch those eggs. Because," he says, "if I don't hatch those eggs—I'm ruined! [laughter] We'll have nothing to eat! [Emile laughs while speaking, swallowing his words] Nothing to eat!" He says ch—the, if, if, ah if you could hear him there, my man, and there, he sits down on the eggs! He sticks his backside on the eggs. And then soon here—she's coming [in a little old lady's voice]—"You paid good attention to my child, a charming man, my charming boy that you are there—" and then he says, "So kind," and he could hear...his mother, his mother and the girl coming to eat three sorts! Heh heh! Mom! [pause to reverse tape] "Here, your boy he's so kind, dinner tonight"—"Oh yes, that's so, I know he's a charming boy." [high-pitched old woman's voice] Well, well it went good. Well there they get there and they open the door eh. When they open the door eh, "Qua qua, qua, qua, qua, qua qua qua qua!" Well he was there—him she looks the girl comes in too she was looking over there he was there—all naked on the ha ha ha ha! All naked on the eggs! All naked on the eggs ah, "Wah, wah, wah wah," he was saying, he was saying! [laughter]

Commentary and notes

This narration was the last of a fairly long session, during the course of which Emile and I had done justice to a bottle of rum. I had first asked him if he knew a tale whose heroine was named "Cendrillouse", hence the explanation shortly after the tale's beginning ("Her she was a girl and him he was, he was a boy"). If I mention a bottle, it is because this kind of humorous tale is much more entertaining when storyteller and audience have become unconstrained. What would normally seem quite ordinary then seems extremely amusing.

At the tale's end, we were both bent in two with laughter, and for at least a quarter of an hour after the formal conclusion of the story Emile went on making us laugh as he repeated the squawks made by Cendrilloux sitting on his eggs, and replayed the tale's ultimate scene. In fact, we had a fit of uncontrollable laughter, due as much to the onomatopoeias scattered throughout the story and Emile's facial contortions, as the humour inherent in the narrative situation.

The tale combines two international tale-types, At 1685, *The Foolish Bridegroom*, and AT 1218, *Numskull Sits on Eggs to Finish the Hatching*, the motifs of which include J2462.2, *Casting sheep's eyes at the bride*; J2462.1, *The dog Parsley in the soup*; and J1902.1, *Numskull sits on eggs to finish the hatching*. Fool tales are extremely widespread in French tradition (see Mme A. Cadet & Gerald Thomas, *Contes de Jean-le-Sot, Société d'Etudes Folkloriques du Centre-Ouest*, special number, 1972, 2-62) although *The Types of the Folktale* recognizes only seven versions of AT 1685 from France, six from Canada and three from Louisiana. Only a single version of AT 1218 has been recorded for France, none for the French in North America. On the other hand, statistics established in 1964 by Luc Lacourcière for his *Catalogue raisonné du conte populaire français en Amérique du Nord* included two versions of AT 1218 and ten of AT 1685. We may assume that M. Lacourcière's *Catalogue raisonné* will include many more when it eventually appears.

Curiously, while the Archives of the Centre d'Etudes Franco-Terreneuviennes include several versions of fool tales, the types represented in Emile Benoit's version are the only ones so far recorded. Emile learned the tale from his late father.

THE TALE OF THE BLACK MOUNTAIN

The Tale of the Black Mountain. Hm. Well I guess. It's a story which is a bit long too there it's, it's—after a bit I'll tell it. I think I can remember a bit of it. Well, once, once upon a good time — like it's always upon a good time in the old times it, it happened

I guess in the—four and five centuries ago. There was a man—his name was—euh—Johnny—in English it's Jack. Well that's how I heard it, that's the name—because—Johnny was a man who had never been beaten. He, he was a smart man, he was sharp and—he had all kinds of, of, of, of good ideas and all that. He, he always won. In all the stories that, that we've, that have been, have been resisted, have been told. Well, that man, that man there—he was a man I guess who had been born euh, to his euh—way, to his work—but his gift was—a card-player. And he played poker. And he *played* poker. He played for years and years—and everyone who played with him—he beat. He beat them. And they came from all parts of the world—parts you, cha, cha, channel, channels [challenge] they calls it—and they came—*and* he beat them, he beat them. Well, he came to be pretty rich—he built castles—euh, his father and his mother and he built a castle for himself—and he had lots of land, land and he started to, to build ho, hotels—and all that. Ah! He became—a millionaire, millionaire. Well, everyone gave up playing with him—because they were all ruined—he'd made them all poor, everybody poor. They were all ruined, they had played all their, their money, all their wealth, he had wealth everywhere, all over the universe. That he had won. Well—once upon a good time he says, "Look at that!" he says, "that," he says—"look at that. I'm the champion," he says, "of the whole universe—at playing poker. Now," he says, "the only man I haven't played with," he says, "is the devil. And," he says, "I wouldn't mind playing with him. Pah! Because if I would beat him—anyway." Oha! That's good, it was like that for—well perhaps for a couple of days—all of a sudden, here's a stranger comes in. Wah! Ha ho! A handsome man—a fine black hat on his head and, a fine black suit and the fine, a fine white shirt and a bowt—a, a, a bow—machine, what do they call it, the bowties there—the cat's ecktie we used to call it before. That's good. There. Hey! "How are things?" he says the first thing he asks the, the devil, but he didn't know it was the devil—he didn't know it was the, the demon—he says euh—"Can you play poker, you?" Asks the devil—"Can you play poker?"—"Ah! not much—a little bit," he says, "a little bit. Not much. "He says euh, "I'm a poker player, me," he says—"and there's no one who can beat me."-"No?" he says, "No one can beat you."—"No," he says, "no one can beat me," he says, "they've come from every part of the world—to try," he says, "to beat me but they haven't been able to beat me. Like that," he says, "I'm the champion—at poker in the universe."—"Hah? Well," he says, "that," he says, "that's really nice, that's, that's, that's good that." Yeah. Well—he says euh, "Do you want to have a game with me, do you want to try a game?"—"Oh," he says, "we won't play for a lot of money," he says, euh, "me," he says, euh, "I'm not, euh, euh, I'm not rich. I'm a, a poor man."—"Oh well," he says, "we're not going to bet too much," he says, "because...." Ah well that's that. That's good. There. Take the cards and there they start there. They play. Well he puts, he, he, he, he, the, the, the champion he puts ten dollars on the table—he didn't want to go too high because the, the, the, that man who was there him he, he had just played with euh, with Johnny just for them—to pass the time—he didn't want, he didn't want to be too hard on him. Well that's good. There. There, the demon put ten dollars down too—and they, show their cards, look see! Johnny—wins. Ah! Twenty dollars. Hauls it in.

G.T.: Hm.

—Yes but—he was so used—to betting you see—eh—he kind of went out of his head. Anyway—by gosh he hauled twenty—twenty dollars in, there, another one again, another hand there. And then euh, "Ah," he says, "look! We're gonna put fifty—fifty dollars." Oh euh, the devil don't want, "Well, me," he says, "I haven't got much money," he says "but euh..." he says—"Well I can—I can, I can put fifty dollars too." There he takes fifty dollars and he throws it in the, to meet J, John—meet the, John's bet, yeah, all at once there John euh, hauls in again. Yeah, that's

248

that—there that makes a hundred dollars there. That makes a hundred and twenty dollars—the two hauls. Ah, and he thinks to himself—"Bu—yeah, it's no use me playing with that, me," he says, "because I'm gonna haul, haul everything, take all the money he's got in his pocket." That's good. There. Ah! The third—round of cards—the third—there! "Hey!" he says—"Euh—a hundred dollars." The devil puts—two hundred dollars! "Oh gee!" John found that—really funny. Ho! He didn't have much money on the first and there all of a sudden, hey, he puts a hundred dollars down—and the demon puts—two hundred dollars! Ho, when he saw that—well there he puts—euh two hundred dollars with what—the hundred he had put before. Well there the devil puts—two hundred more dollars—and then it starts going up, going up, all of a sudden there the devil puts—a thousand dollars! Well the other fellow there, there, he, the, the, John, he puts—fifteen thousand dollars! And then it starts going, and up it goes, and up it goes, and up it goes! And look! he, the, the, he, that man had no money—and look at the money he's got! Ha! Well it's foolishness going up I guess like a hundred thousand dollars there. There! That's that. There, lay their cards down—ah! the devil hauls in. By gosh! He was starting to, to think there. Oh! But he says, "It was dealt like that." Well there, my old buddy, he, he, John, it's John's turn to deal the cards. So he deals them. Well he—there. He gave out the cards to the demon and himself and that's that. There him there, he doubles there. Heh heh hundred thousand dollars, two hundred thousand dollars— "For sure there he, he, he's not going—he's not going to attack me because he hasn't got the means." There the devil tips up his money—he redoubles! John there, John doubles. Oh, lucky sign. Spreads his cards—look! He had a, the, the, a straight there right up eh! Well! John loses again—and so it went, so it went, so it went and there his money all at once it's gone, look! No more money left! The devil had it all! Anyway that's good. But he says, "I can't play no more—I've got no more money."— "Oh but," he says, "you've got lots of wealth."—"Oh yes," he says, "but," he says, "I can't play for that."—"Ah *dame*!" he says, "that's it," he says—"it's, it's—chee! That's it," he says, "that's, that's the game!"

G.T.:   Yes.

—And it was like that that he always was, him euh, John there, he played, played, played until there was nothing left, nothing at all! He, he, put his face on the ro—on, on the rock. Ah ah, the, the demon does, did the same thing as him there. Well, oh *dame* he had a place here, he had a, a village he had here, he had, he had that and there plays and the devil was winning and he was winning, and he was winning, and when it came to the end of the story—he's got everything—pl—euh, played for, for what he had—and everything he had left after—he even played for the, the, the, the castle he had built for his father and his mother—he played for that and he lost it—and he had euh, everything he had left after—was his father and his mother. "Well," he says, "I've got nothing left at all. I've got nothing else."—"Well," he says, "you have got something else." He says, "What's that?"—"Your father and your mother."—"Well, well yes," he says, "but I, I'm not going to play my father and my mother."—"Oh well," he says, "that's, that's the game. That's that. Ah, that's that, play for your father and your mother." Well he's got his father and his mother too. There. "But," he says, "I've got nothing at all left to play with. And I've got no—I've got nothing else. You've put me on, on my face," he says, "on, on, on the rock. I've got nothing else, I can't play no more, can't play no more."—"Oh yes!" he says—"Now," he says, "I can play for, for yourself—for you."—"Play for me?" he says. "Oh yes," he says, "that's, that's, that's the game," he says. "Well! Ah *dame*, that's that." There, play the cards again and—it—the devil's got him. There! "Well," he says, "you're the champion now," he says-"I've never been beaten. But," he says, "you've got me, you've beaten me." He says, "You've got to think," he says, "that you're not a man, not an ordinary man."—"No!" he says—he says, "I'm the demon,"

249

he says. He says, "I might have known! You were something like that."—"Well," he says, "it's your own fault," he says, "if you had, you hadn't named me—I wouldn't have come and I wouldn't have come to get you, you, here. But," he says, "you said that—it was only the devil you hadn't played with and—you were afraid to play with me—and this and that." He says, "That's why I came. To make you see—that was your, with your champion and this and that—that you were pretty far from being a champion. Now," he says there, "I'm gonna tell you something—I want you," he says, "at the Black Mountain—in a year and a day from now. Now—a year and a day from now! I want you at the Black Mountain." And he says, "Where is that?"—"Ah *dame!*" he says, "it's up to you to find where it is." He says, "I'm not going to tell you where it is—it's up to you, that. And if he can't come there—to the Black Mountain, you can't get there in a year and a day—I'll be here to get you. And my little boy," he says, "it, it's not gonna be too pretty for you." Well there euh, John oh ho, he came—on—with all his pleasure and all his, his fine manners and everything he had—euh, euh, he came all, all—sad. That's good. There the devil disappeared—and him he was there—sitting on a rock—gn—chewing on his nails. There. [Emile coughs] Excuse me. Arrh! There! Anyway, he stayed at home that night—not at home, because he didn't have a home no more, he had nothing. The next morning—at the break of day—he left. And he started walking—and walks and walks and walks! And when he had left the place where there was not a lot of people, there were a few, a few, there was a—a family here, a, a family over there and this and that, t'was, t'was in little groups they gathered together y'know—and perhaps you had to walk about—a hundred thousand miles to find another, another little place like that again, if there was any more, more, more inhabitants, you see—perhaps well five or six families and something like that—living in small—ca, ca, brush cabins they call them—something like that. And some others made with, with, with bits of wood, logs, log cabins there. Anyway that's good. Well he walks, he walks, and he walks and he walks and he walks, and nothing to eat but *dame*, he wasn't clumsy and he, he, he would throw a, a, a few stones and he would kill small birds and soon and—he'd cook that and—ah, he held on, kept going.

G.T.:   Hm.

—Well he walked—for two to three months—through the forest—and all at once—night was starting to come on, he caught sight of—a small light—ahh! it's kind of red, the light. Anyway he heads for it, he says, "What is that now?" he says, "what is, what is it? What is that?" he says, "I see there?" Anyway he comes up, comes up, comes up—when he got there it was a little shack—and it was all covered with moss and, there were, there was, oh there was trees growing on the r, on the, the roof, ah! I guess it was—a thousand years old! And there was a door there—it was made with roots—so he goes there, looks around—"Well," he says, "that's really funny," he says. Well he, he goes and knocks to the door. Hah! He heard something—someone move, someone moving inside. All of a sudden here's the door opening—ah my good Lord, you should have seen that! Oh well well well well wah well well! An old woman, she was an old witch—and old woman—oh I guess she was like—fifteen hundred years old or, or eighteen hundred years old, something like that—oh was old, old, her, her, her teeth there hanging down black, hanging down over her lips there—he and the, the big hairs—the, the, the, eh, big white hairs coming out of her nose, and the warts on her nose the, the warts on her, her, on her chins and all that oh! oh! Ah, he, he's pretty shaken—he couldn't talk—he, he was—shaken—he's, oh! It was, it was, he'd never seen anything so ugly in his life. And she says, "Oh don't be afraid [in a little old woman's voice]! Come on in!" she says, "my little boy, come in!" [Emile stretches out the last few words] Well, there, him—he, he goes in but his, his, his two knees were knocking together! He—so afraid! "I'm not going to hurt you, I'm not going to hurt you!" [Old woman's

250

voice] And, "So where are you going, what's happened?" And it's all kinds of things like that—"What has happened and—" Well there he tells her his story, well there. "Ahhh! yes, my dear child, that's how it is, when you're young you don't know what you're doing. And you shouldn't have done something like that," and *dame* he shouldn't have but *dame* he did! And that's that! And now it's too late! And she says now, he tells her about the Black Mountain, he had to be there in a year and a day—and then, and he didn't know what it was, and this an that. And he knew that more or less. "Well," she says, "I've—got a sister"—she says, "I guess she's still alive—but she's older than me." Well he thought to himself now—"Well if she is older than them—than you, and she, and, and she is no more beautiful than you are—my God, my God! What have I got to do? I hope to tell you my blood doesn't turn," he says, "for the fright—because," he says, "I've had enough with this one here"—was thinking to himself that, he had that in his mind there. Anyway, that's good, they were chatting all night—m—oh he was comfortable, ah, she was good to him, she was good to him, she gave him something to eat, she, she, she was pre, she was a witch d'you see? And she could have whatever she, whatever she wanted. There she would have said like that well, "I want—euh—a loaf of bread there on the table"—there, the bun would have come there, d'you see? Whatever she wants she, she, she got it. Y'know. She had so much power y'know. And him now, he, he, she asked for some tea, and she asked for some milk and it came there and him, all scared him! He was scared. Anyway, that's good. "Well," she says, "to tell you— where the Black Mountain is, I, I don't know. But," she says, "my sister," she says, "she lives like—like a hundred—hundred miles from here," she says. "Well," she says, "perhaps," she says, "she'll know." Well that's that, well—well, that, he was gonna go see her anyhow. Well there that's good.

G.T.: Yes.

—The next morning comes, and there then she gives him something to eat, some biscuits and everything and then—whatever he wanted she, she had it, because she, she wished for it and it came—it fell there on the table. And she takes a sack—oh, he had a great big sack—and he had a misery to carry it—so he whacks it on his back and then he takes off. And there he walks, he walks, he walks, he walks—through the woods more or less here and there—and he walks. Night and day. He didn't go fast. Because the, the, the road is so bad—he couldn't go quick. And to do those hundred miles there, it took him pretty close to a month. And he had something to eat all the time it's like a, euh, euh, when he, when he would eat a, a, a cake, there was another cake came there d'you see, it's, it's her power, the, the witch's there now there. She had so much power d'you see and she liked the boy because he was so—nice like that you see. He wasn't a bad person only, d'you see—he, he, he hadn't done things right. That's good. Walks and walks and walks and walks. Well, it took him a month for sure before he got there. Anyway it was the same he got there about night, nightfall there—he looks ahead, chee! sees a little, little light. So there he, he makes for it, "Well," he says, "got to think it's her sister—oh well," he says, "got to think," he says, "because—oh for sure," he says, "I've walked a hundred miles now, oh for sure, oh, it's guaranteed, that. So it must be her." But when he got there my, my old buddy, the cabin, the shack was even—even older—than the one he'd seen first. Now the first one there, it was the youngest was there, the youngest of the sisters you see—and—they were three sisters there in all. Well she didn't tell him there, her, she said she had a sister. She remembered—because—so old d'you see, I guess she was like—eighteen hundred years old, nineteen hundred years old, something like that, y'know your, your memory y'see, it, it goes y'know. Anyway that's good. Ah. He gets there. So he knocks and then he thinks to himself—"Now d'you see I've got to, I, euh, I'd better

251

get myself right now," he says, "and it's—and I'd better not be, be too afraid." Ah. My dear friend!

G.T.: Hm.

—He knocks to the door, she opened the door. Ah oh oh oh! When he looked at her—and still he had made up his mind the right way now not to—d'you see! Not to have a, an attick, an attack, a heart attack. But he fell down! He fell down. Yeah. He fell down, backwards. When he saw that. Oh she was ugly! Ah! Oh, big teeth down to her chin there and *black*! And she had white spots and, and black spots, on her there—and all twisted up there—and wa-warts coming out of her nose there, all pointed! Well, my friend—her she was ugly! Oh she was ugly! And her, her, her, her eyebrows there—was all curled there like, all like hair—and her, her eyelashes—was all curled up like, like, like trout hooks there. And her two eyes was flashing! It was flashing! It was like candles! Oh she was ugly, ugly, ugly! Well she, she said, John jumps out, she hooks him and he, he had fainted, he had fainted. And so she—rubbed him with water, I don't know what it was anyhow—they didn't tell me—but euh, he, he came to. But she was good to him, even better than the, the first one. Even better! Well after a little while well he came—but—she wasn't pretty to look at, but, *dame*, she was so good! So good, it's more, ah, oh, oh! Well he didn't sleep on the, on, on brush that night, she took him in her arms and she—rocked him all night long. Like he had been a little baby. Ah he's happy, happy! Anyway that's good. There. He tells her his story and everything, "Well," she says, "my dear—not much I can do for you," she says, "my dear child." Well *dame*—he was upset, upset, upset. "Ah! don't know what you're gonna do—but *dame*," she says, "I've got a sister—I've got a sister who lives—like—oh it'll take like—six months, six to seven or eight months—to get there."—"What!" he says, "grandmother," he says—"six, seven or eight months to get there?"—"Oh yes," she says—"Her, she's the oldest of my sisters," she says, "and she's old, she's old, oh she's—twenty-five hundred years old," she says, "she is. Oh," she says, "well it's hundreds of years, thousands of years I haven't seen her," she says. "it's a good two thousand years for sure," she says, "I haven't seen her. But," she says, "she must still be alive." Well—well goldarn that wasn't a little ways—six or seven months to walk—before he manages to get there. Ah! And he was counting the days now there, y'know, he was counting them there. Well he had to be there in a year and a day—well now if he had no more luck—than he had now with the first two sisters—well *dame* he'd had it! He'd had it. So John goes to find her, there, there, there was no, no danger, he found her. Anyway that's good. "Well, well, now," she says, "there," she says to, wish for food and this an that, whatever he wanted to eat and everything—there. She says, "Now," she says—"you've got enough food there," she says, "for, for your *journey*," she says. "It might take you a good six months, seven months—maybe even eight months—but," she says, "you've got enough food." *Dame*, well that's that. He's gone. He didn't kiss her but almost—because she was so kind. I can't kiss you. It was all warts, and hairs and, and great big long teeth and all that there, oh-ha! Was ugly! Oh, it, it turned your stomach! Anyway, he takes off. He walks, he walks, he walks, he walks, and walks and walks. He'd lie down at night and then first light be up and walk—and he walked, too—for eight months. And there's still nothing to see, nothing! And he walks and still walking—almost another month again or a couple of weeks or something like that, I can't remember exactly but—euh, it took more than eight months. Well, all at once it's the same thing again—it's coming around nightfall, look, saw a little light again—"Ah well," he says, "got to think this is where it is." There. Off he goes. Well now he had had two frights but the second fright was a lot worse than the first one. "But," he says, "this one here," he says, "I ca—I'm gonna—perhaps I'm gonna die from this one. If she's, if she's not more beautiful," he says, "than, than her sisters—than her two sisters,"—that's good.

252

G.T.:   Hm.

—Off he goes. He takes a chance. And then he knocks to the door and he jumps back there around like ten yards back there—and he looks, she's opening the door. Ah! When she opened the door—and he looked at her—her front, her teeth came down—below her chin eh? And her there—the two, the two front teeth, that's all she had left. And she, they were sticking into her knees—she, she, she, it was like, but she would hold her head up and her two teeth, y'know stopped at her knees. "Well wha' doin' here?" [Emile speaks in a high but guttural falsetto, swallowing his words] Well him there, he was oh, well there, he, he passed clean out. And the big warts, the, hairs there, and her, her hair there, it was just like ah, ah, ah, ah four inch nails there, thick, thick hair y'know, and they were, like ah, like, like rope there oh! Now that was ugly, my old buddy—great big warts there and there was moss growing on top of all that. Oh! She wasn't fit to look at, but he passed out, he passed out, he didn't—but she brought him to, because she was, she was a witch eh, witch eh? She could do anything. There. The only thing, they didn't know where the Black Mountain was. Well that's good, there he tells his story, he goes in, but she was good to him. He goes in and she gives him something to eat—whatever he wanted to eat—she wished for it, try an see what it was—cakes and, and, was, was all kinds of bi, of birds euh, b-baked, anything—she wanted, whatever she wanted, she got it. A good chance, because she would, she couldn't have lived alone her, there was no farm around nothing at all, he would have, she would have *died*. Died right there! But—she had so much power y'know. There. That's good. But he tells his story and all that and what had happened, he had had loads of money and everything and then he had lost it all and this and that... [pause to change tape]. He says, "Well, look it was the devil," and he says—he would have beaten him an this an that. Yes, but he says—that man came and there he tells—he tells the whole story, d'you see. "Well," she says, "my dear child, that's the way it is," she says—"you can't know." She says, "That fellow," she says, "you've got to look out for him," she says—"you should never," she says, "mention his name too often—because," he says, "all the words you—when you speak his name," he says, "he comes closer all the time and that's not good! No, we should leave him alone," she says. "And now," he says, "I've got to go to the Black Mountain," and this and that euh, told the whole story—"Well," she says, "me," she says, "I don't know where the Black Mountain is, I don't know, me," she says. "But I've got some, I've got some eagles," she says. "Every day they go off looking for food, they fly everywhere euh, all over the universe. And," he says, "they come back," she says euh,—"well," she says, "they tell me the news, whatever they see and this an that an so on. And," she says, "that's my hobby." Ah, that's good, soon, mor, morning came an this an that well the eagles had gone, she says, "They're going, they're going to come back later on," she says.

G.T.:   Yes.

—Well-they spent the whole day together—they, they, they chatted there the two of them together—and it came into a habit, well she was so kind, d'you see? She was ugly but—so kind that—he loved her—he loved her. There anyway the afternoon about three o'clock in the afternoon euh, here the eagles starting to get back. And it's "Qua-qua-qua!" and, "Qua-qua-qua!" And they flew down and this an that and then she'd call them, she says, "Any of you," she says, "knows where the Black Mountain is?"—"No! No! No! No! No! No!" There was about fifteen of them I guess—"No! No! No! No!" It was all noes, they didn't know. Well him, he was two or three times falling over on his, on his side. Oh well he was discouraged. Well he knew he was—he's done for, he was, he was finished. He was finished. Her there she, she was in the back and—so he called her 'grandmother,' too, him. But he says, "Grandmother," he says, "I'm, I'm done for." She says, "Soon oh," she says, "I don't think they're all here yet," she says. Y'know there was an old one—an old

253

one—old eagle—an eagle there the—she says, "He's—he's not back yet," she says, "there's one missing." Oh she looked up in, in the sky, she was looking, "Oh!" she says, "he's coming," he was over two thousand years old. Oh he was old, he didn't fly too quick, he, he was taking his time, the young ones they, they, they were there before their time. "Oh!" she says, "He's coming, I can see him over there." She says, "Could be he knows, him." Ah all at once he gets there, "Raow, raow, raow, raow, raow." Sets down where she was. She says, "Euh, you know you where the Black Mountain is?"—"Yes," he says, "yes, that's where I've come from." He says euh—to his mistress. Oh, well, there John him there, ho ho! Well he, proud d'you see? Hah! Well that's good—after being so sad all the time, well that made him feel good, that. He knew where the Black Mountain was. "Yes," he says, "ah," he says, "that's where I've come from," he says. "Oh well," she says, "my dear child," she says, "you've got it made," she says. "Ah *dame* yeah! Yeah." Well she says, "Tomorrow morning now"—there's—"Well," he says, "tomorrow morning," he says, "that's gonna be just," he says, "a year and a day—yes, just a year and a day tomorrow morning," he says. "Yeah. And I've got to be there tomorrow. A year and a day is what he told me."—"Well right, you don't have to be afraid," she says,"that—you're gonna be all right." She says, "I'm gonna—"—she asked her, her eagle she says euh, euh, "Are you going to, to take him there?"—"Oh yes," he says, "oh yes." She says, "Do you think you'll be strong enough to do it?"—"Oh yes, yes, yes, yeah." Well that's good. There. The next morning they left at—daybreak. Now she gives him a bottle of medicine. She says, "I'm gonna give you this little bottle of medicine here. And you're gonna get up on his back—and," she says, "when he asks you—when he's hungry he's gonna ask you for—a bite to eat—you're gonna"—she says "I've got a, you've got a knife here, you're gonna take that knife with you—and," she says, "you're gonna cut a piece out of your body," she says, "and you're gonna give it to him. Because if you don't feed him," she says, "he won't be able—to, to, to haul you to take you there." Anyway that's good. "Well," she says, "after you've cut off the piece—you take the, the medicine," she says, "and you rub some on the piece—what you cut—and," she says, "it'll come just as good as before." Oh, there, "That's good, grandmother," he says, "well that's good." Well that's that the, the, the time comes and there he, he gets up on the, the, on the eagle and then—the bottle of medicine and the knife and that's that. And from time to time the, when they were up in the air the eagle asks him, "Qua-qua! I'm hungry." So there he cuts a piece off himself—it hurt, too—but *dame* heh! that's that. Cuts! And then he gives it to him. "Myammyam," and he swallowed it and then he took his medicine and then it's, it's, it's like—like he hadn't touched his body at all. Well that's good. There. They fly and they fly and they fly and they fly. And ah, at nightfall—they got there.

G.T.:   Yes.

—It took him twelve hours—to fly there—and a bird goes, it goes fast d'you see? Hm. We'll say thirty, thirty-five miles an hour or something like that—it goes fast. Faster than walking. Anyway, that's good. He gets there, there the eagle comes down he comes down he comes down and he *lands*. And then—John—gets off the eagle—then he says, "Now," he says, "you're gonna go," he says, "and knock to the door. And then," he says euh, "that's where the devil is," he says, "that's where he lives." Ah! That's good. Well they get to saying goodbye to each other and all that and then the eagle's gone again—home. And then euh, John goes to the euh, devil's door, the devil's castle, knocks, the devil comes, opens the door. "Ahhh! Ah well," he says—"you made it. Well," he says, "you're lucky, I was just thinking about you," he says. "Your time is up today and," he says, "here you are. Well," he says, "that's not bad. That's not bad. Well," he says, "come in. Come in." When he came in, the devil's wife was there—and he had three daughters, well, and, and there was one.... He looked at her and she looked at him too and then oh! she laughed, she smiled,

"The handsome man, the handsome man," she thought—and him too—"Oh oh oh oh," the most beautiful girl he had ever—laid his eyes on. That's good. There wasn't a big, big fuss there—oh and everything. That's good. They stayed chatting until ten o'clock and then it's time to go to bed because he says, "Tomorrow," he says, "we—John has got his work to do." There. John—that, him he thought he didn't sleep all night long because he, he was thinking about what kind of work it was going to be. Okay. Good. Next morning comes—six o'clock—up. For breakfast. And he—ate. "There," he says, "come with me." But all the time he was watching the girl in secret and when the devil turned his back and the old woman—and he looked at her and made little winks d'you see? And her too—oh! She loved him! Oh but, but, but, but! And she was so beautiful. Anyway—that's good, he says, "Come with me now," he says, "I'm gonna take you to your work." That's good—he came out euh, the devil goes ahead and him behind, and he goes to a building and he opens up the building—and there are some machines, some, some *millsh, millshed* you calls that? There. And euh—he, he, he goes in and he, he takes an axe—an axe made out of paper. John him he was looking at that and, "What's he gonna do with that?" Anyway he takes the axe and he puts it on his back and the, the, the handle bent in two and the, the, the axe's blade was in—in his back. Rubbing on his—his back. And he takes him to, there's some—there was an acre of, of wood—there. Gets there. And still John didn't know what was going on. "There," he says, "J, John," he says—"There," he says, "your work for today, my friend." He says, "What? Sort of work?"—"There," he says,"you've got to cut down all the wood that's there," he says—"and you've got to, to get it it all, all stacked," he says, "in piles"—and he says, "that's got to be done," he says, "by six o'clock tonight." And he says, "If you can't do it—my poor child," he says—"you're—you're in for a sad—a sad time when I come for you." There he says, "Here! There's the axe," he says euh, "you've got to cut that. Cut—that wood there."—"But," he says, "how can I do that with that, me?"—"Hoh! That's up to you," he says—"there's the axe." That's good. No way he can say much. Here! There. He takes the axe, the devil takes off—and he takes the axe and he, he, he, he lets her go—against the tree. Jeepers cr—the axe blade—the piece of paper the handle broke, the axe fell off—there. There he sits down—and he cries, he cries, he cries, he cries, he's pretty sad—and ah! "Well," he says, "I've had it. It's just as well I make up my mind now," he says, "and—get ready," he says, "for—to go down to hell," he says, "for eternity. Well," he says, "it's just as well I make up my mind." There's no resources. No, there's no resources. No. Ah, that's that. So there he stops crying. He, he, he consoles himself and that's that, finished—say no more. He makes up his mind.

G.T.:   Hm.

—Soon, noon comes—he was sitting down, like that—and all at once he heard a racket there, he looks—the young girl! The girl he had fallen in love with—coming with his dinner! "Well look at that now," he says, "what a pity," he says, "if only I could do that now," he says, "and look!" And oh, oh, oh, oh, oh—"I'd be so happy for the rest of my days—with a woman like that," he says, "a beauty like that," he says—all sorts of b—ideas passing through his head. So she gets there—and she says, euh, "What's the matter then, what's going on?"—"Well," he says, "your father," he says, "gave me some, a paper axe," he says, "and he told me to, I've got to cut all that," he says, "and pile it—have it stacked by six o'clock."—"Well," she says, "I've brought you your dinner there."—"No!" he says, "I don't want any dinner, I don't want to eat. Because," he says, "for the time," he says, "that I'm here now," he says, "it's gonna be a long time like that," he says euh, "I've given up."—"Go on with you!" she says, "you're not so foolish," she says, "eat, eat!" she says, "eat your dinner! You won't be sad like that." Ah. She says, "Where's your axe?" She says, "The, the," he says, "the axe is there, with the broken handle there."

255

A'right—she grabs the axe her— and flick! flick! flick! flick! like that—she makes a couple, a couple of little *signs*, the trees started to fall down, the branches were flying in the air in the sky, and the—logs starting to pile up and everything, in like, like five minutes—you've got the whole f—the, the, the acre was all, all cut down, all stacked up! "Ooh!" Ah he gave a big sigh. Well well well! Well there he lo, his, the girl there, she loved him—oh a hundred times worse, oh, he was in, in a sad shape my old buddy—with the love he had for her. Well, well, well, well, well, well! There, that's good. There. Well he's happy, so she says, "Tonight you're gonna take the, the axe," she says, "and you're gonna give it to Dad," she says—"he's gonna ask you if you've done your work and," she says, "say 'yes'."

G.T.:   Yes.

—That's good, there he stays there till six o'clock in the evening and—he, he takes off. Gets there he says, "But," he says, "have you done your work?"—"Yes," he says,"I've done my work. But," he says, "if I had had a good axe now—but a paper axe," he says—"that, that made me work hard."—"Well," he says, "that's a job of work."—"Oh yes yes yes."—"Oh well, that's that," he says, "that's fine, that's good," he says. He says, "Another one tomorrow," he says. He was thinking now, "What sort of other one? What sort of other one?" Anyway that's good. That night he goes but he—doesn't sleep at all because he was pretty eh, upset and all that. Just think. It was hard—and he was thinking about the girl—and, y'know, he had all that in his head—oh! They were mixed up like a, a minister—it, it, it was hard. The next morning—there. Eats his breakfast, up at, at six o'clock, breakfast, and that's that. They take off, he says, "Come on! I'm gonna give him his work for today again," he says. The devil goes off again to his dairy there—and he opens the door and he, he, he goes, he comes out with, with a basket. A basket made out of straw there. And he thinks to himself he says, "What's he gonna do with that," he says, "what, there was, wa—what's he got to do?" He says, "Follow me." He takes him—to a lake. Oh, the lake was about euh, hm, well it was a big lake—like a mile around I guess—you know, all around, y'know? *Diameter* they calls it. It was a big lake—there he says euh, "Here"—he gives him the basket—he says, "You've got to dry up that lake," he says, "get it dried up for euh, six o'clock tonight." Well—not much he could say—the devil's gone. Takes the basket anyhow and then when he takes the basket and dips it in the lake—but before he'd put his foot on the side the, the basket was dry! The water had all run through the, the, the—the straws—the sides there. "Bee bee! me I can't," he tried five or six times to dr—where—he throws the basket down and there he is all upset again. There he is upset again. Ah! An it's almost noon, at noon he didn't hear anything, nothing, then, look! Oh! The same one again! Coming with his dinner again. Huh! "Well," he says, "that's not bad." Well he's kind of consoled by what she had done yesterday—he says,"What are we gonna do today—but she'll never be able to do anything with, not with that basket in the water. No way!" Gets there, she says, euh, she says, euh, "Hey, what's the matter? Well," she says, "that it," she says. He says euh, "Your father gave me a basket," he says,"to dry up that lake—but," he says, "I tried it but," he says, "before I got the basket—euh, hauled ashore, there's nothing left in it," he says—"It all falls, all falls in the, in the, in the—back in the lake again!" She says,"Look, don't get upset, euh, eat your dinner." And she says, "I hope you like your dinner."—"Oh yes," he says, "I guess," he says, "yesterday," he says, "you brought a fine dinner. It, it, I really enjoyed it. And I know," he says, "this one here smells good, ah it's good too." She says, "Don't get upset about nothing, so tuck into your food there." And then he sets to it and he eats and it's good. Yeah he's eating now. Her she takes the basket and she, she—just one basket full—flick!—like that—the lake dry! "Well," he says, "that's not bad! Oh look at that now! Done so quick," he says. There. That's good. Ah, she picks up the dishes and that and she goes back home. The she says—euh,

before she left she says euh, "Listen," she says, "John," she says—"You've still got another—another job to do. And it's not too—too easy. It, it's gonna be the hardest job of all! But," she says, "if you can do it, well you're clear away with your life." There—she's gone. Six o'clock—he comes back—to the devil's with the basket and—"Well," he says,"did you do your job?"-"Eh yes," he says, "I managed," he says, "I worked hard but I managed there. The lake is dry."—"Ah that's very good." He says, "Tomorrow you've got another one again," he says—but the devil said there—"you've got another one again—another job again. Tomorrow's the last one," he says, "if you can do that one—you're clear—you're free." Ah that's very good—there. Off he goes to bed—and then six o'clock the next morning—up again.
G.T.: Hm.

—Breakfast—"There," he says, "come with me." But—he doesn't go to his store or nothing at all. He takes him—to a, a pole—that was a hundred feet high. A glass pole. he says, "D'you see that pole?"—"Well," he says, "yes. Of course," he says— "it's a glass pole."—"Oh yes," he says. He says, "There's a blackbird's egg—up there on top of the pole." And he says, "I want," he says, "for you to bring me—that egg at six o'clock tomorrow night—tonight," he says. He didn't say nothing because euh, the girl and this an that, she, he, he, but he didn't know what sort of plan she, he didn't know nothing about that. Anyway that's good. There. There she knew— that her father was a smart man. She says, "For sure," she says, "he's gonna send one of my sisters," but her two sisters, they, they, they couldn't do that them. Ah, they they were like their mother eh, they, they, they couldn't wish them for nothing at all like that there they couldn't do that—it's only her had her father's secret eh? But her father didn't know either—he thought it was only him but her she was euh, as good as him. Anyway that's good. Hey. He takes him there—he says, "Come with me," well then he says euh, "That's that"—like I just said. And then euh when it came to eleven o'clock—"There," he says, "who is going to take John his, his, his dinner there." Well her so quick—she says, "Me, I'm not, me, I'm not going! I don't want to go, me, take him his dinner this time [little girl's voice]. Let my sister go!"—"Well," he says, "look here," he says, "because you spoke so good—so rude," he says, "so *sharp*"—well he says, "you're gonna take his, his food to him"—Because that's why she had—why—because if she hadn't said, said that he would have sent—the others, her other sisters eh? "Ah ha!" he says, "well since you spoke so, so light, so cruel—you're gonna go take him his food." And her, she did what she wanted, d'you see? So like that she puts on her coat and then—there she takes his food—and off she goes. And when she goes out there she hauls the door, bang! not—she wasn't pleased y'know. There. Well on her way, her, she goes by the store and she takes a, a, a, a boiler there, a, it held about—like ten to fifteen gallons y'know. Takes it with her. And his food. She got there, he was sitting by the pole, by the pole. And he tried, he tried, he tried, he tried and euh—he falls down again—and it was slippery—he couldn't he couldn't—he couldn't he couldn't—it was impossible. The ice—glass there, it, it, he tried to climb up but he couldn't—he'd slide down. Anyway very good. She gets there. With his food. There. She says, "Eat!" She says, "Have you got, have you got the egg?"—"No," he says, "it's impossible, I tried," he says, his, his trousers were all—his trousers were all in, the, the, the, side of his trousers, the inside of his trousers were all worn out. It would rub on the glass when he was trying to climb up, he couldn't do it. She says, "Eat." Well that's good, he's eating, he's eating. And her she takes off and she breaks off some little boughs and—small bits of wood—all kinds of things—and she makes a fire. And—after the fire was made—he says, "What are you going to do with that?"—"Well," she says—"that's it," she says—"what I'm going to do with that," she says, "eat your dinner." And she put the, the, the pot—the boiler on it—and she made her fire. And she pours some water into it—and then it's boiling, boiling.

G.T.:   Hm.

—While he was eating there, it was boiling, oh it's going—and he thinks to himself, "But what are you going to do with that? What's she going to do with that?" Ah, it was boiling, she says, "Have you finished eating now?"—"Yes," he says, "and," he says, "it was good food, too. But," he says, "what are you going to do with that there?"—"Well," she says, "now—I'm gonna tell you something," she says. "Euh, this here it's gonna be hard for you to do," she says. He says, "What is it?" Well she says, "You've got to take me—and put me in that boiler—into that boiler," she says, "and euh, boil me until the flesh falls off my bones." And she says, "You're gonna take my bones—and you're gonna stick them," she says, "on this glass pole there—and you're gonna make a, a ladder," she say. "And you're gonna climb up—and you're gonna take the egg," she says, "and put it in your mouth," she says—and then she says, "as you come back down pick up my bones and when you get down—put them in the pot." And she says, "I'll come back to myself again."— "Ah," he says, "that's hard to do, after all the kindness you've done me. And me," he says, "I love you so much," he says. "I'm in love with you," he says. "Well," she says, "in love or not," she says, "it's, you're gonna have to do it," she says. Ah, that's that, he takes her and flicks her, he shoves her in the, in the boiler and then, my man—boil! Boil, boil, boil, boil, boil. Soon all the flesh has fallen off her bones—so then he picks up all her bones—and then he sticks them against the, the glass pole and then he—climbs up. And he gets up to the top, he had just enough bones to—make—the—the ladder to grab the egg. Anyway he grabs the egg and puts it in his, in his mouth—and then he climbs down. And there he picks up the bones as he comes down, picks up, picks up, picks up the bones as he comes down. And when he got down—he throws the, the, the bones into the boiler like she had said—and it all jumped up—just like—as if she hadn't been bothered, heh! Yes, she looks at herself, ah! she says, "You didn't pick up all the bones!"—"Oh yes!"—"Oh no," she says, "look," she says, "my little toe," she says—"it's gone, my little toe isn't there. But now—ah well," she says, "that don't make no difference," she says. Well, that's good. Ah! That's that.

G.T.:   Yes.

—There. Gets to the—she goes off home and in the evening at six o'clock—he gets there and hands over the egg—to the devil—"Here," he says—"Well," he says, "my dear friend—well," he says to him, "you've done your *duty*—ah! like that," he says, "you're clear. There now," he says, "look. Because now—you, you're smart, you were a good poker player,"—and he says, "if I hadn't been—I didn't have the power," he says, "I would never have beaten you either—but I had the power. And like that," he says, "well, I beat you—and then I told you to come," he says, "in a year and a day, and you came—and then euh you've had lots of things to do. Well," he says, "now," he says—"I'm gonna give you one of my daughters in marriage— because you've done your work properly." Well.... "Well," he says, he says, "would you mind having one of my girls?"—"No!" he says, "I love, I'd love to have one of your girls. Hm. I'd like to get married." Well that's that. There. Well he says now—oh they'd had a, a good, good conversation the two of them and soon and this and that—"Here tomorrow morning," he says, "now," he says, "I'm gonna put a—a— handkerchief on you," he says, "over your eyes—and you're gonna put my three girls," he says, "side by side"—and then he says, "you're gonna," he says, "you—I'm going to give you the auth—the authority to touch their feet. And then the one you're gonna, that you'd like to have—well you, you'll say, 'this one'. If it's the oldest or the youngest or the second one or whatever it is, that's it," he says. "That's the one you'll have. But," he says, "I'm not going to let you choose with your eyes." That's good. But there! Well that's that—but he thought, he thought eh about the little toe—"Well," he says, "that's not bad!" he says. "Now look if I didn't do the right thing—forget that toe there." Hah! Thinks to himself, says to himself. He don't say nothing. Anyway the next morning six o'clock they're up—and they—a good breakfast—and euh, there. Then he puts a handkerchief over your eyes—and then he puts his three girls—side by side—and then him—he feels there—their, their, their, their feet, their toes there. Soon he gets to—to, to the one who only had nine toes. She says to him, "This one," he says, "is the one I want." Ah well *dame* that's that. This one. The, the devil didn't notice that she didn't have a toe d'you see. He didn't notice that. Y'know he was starting to get old—because he couldn't see too well, heh heh! Anyway that's good. Ah! Well—he married them there. That's that—he marries them, straight away. Well they were man and woman—married. There. It was like that euh, for a couple of days—maybe a week or something like that—oh I can't remember how—how long it was but—well now between euh, him and his wife—they were chatting d'you see, they were talking—and he was saying what—where he came from—a beautiful place to live it was and everything. And now her where she was, well it had, there was nothing to see and nothing at all—it was only her father and her mother and her two sisters—she had never seen nothing else, y'know, he was, he was the first man she had seen and euh, they, they was all the time chatting. He says euh, "I wonder," he says, "if there was a way for us to have the chance," he says, "for us to get away from here," he says. "For us to, to go where I want, where I was living, me, before, before I came here," he says. "Well," she says, he says "Oh yes," he says, "if I had the chance, but *dame*," he says, "it's, it's not easy to find chances."—"Well," she says, "I don't know," she says, "I don't know. If you know the way you euh, euh, I could euh, arrange something." She says, "Me, I can do a lot."—"Oh," he says, I know that. Because if it wasn't for you," he says, "I wouldn't be here—I wouldn't have you for my wife now." Well, that's good. [Pause to change tape]

G.T.:   Good, go on.

—There that's good. There. It happened that—they had made some, some plans together and there it was important for them, for them, to run away. But *dame*, they had to leave—in the night. Around midnight or one o'clock or something like that—so that her father and mother wouldn't notice. Well they made their, their plot together, they had really worked it out. There. That's good. There. She says, "Now I'm gonna make—it's tonight we're gonna leave."—"Yes," he says, "if there's any way at all."—"Yes," she says, "it's tonight we're gonna go—we're gonna go—at one o'clock—tomorrow morning." And she says, "I'm gonna make three cakes—which talk like me—and we're gonna take pop's horse—his white horse—because he, he goes like the wind." But he said to him, "If we take euh, his, his other horses—the red horses or the black horse"—she says, "and he notices—he won't be long getting on our tail. But if we take his horse—well—that's...." There that's good. There. Well they get dressed there. And they go to bed and then—the old man and the old woman go to bed and euh, when midnight came—there—she says, "Me, I'm gonna make-the cakes, the three cakes—and you," she says, "you're gonna put the saddle—on the white horse." And she says, "Don't make too much, too much noise—and then bring the horse here to the door and me, I'm gonna make the three talking cakes—and I'm gonna put them on the stair—and euh, like that when I've done that and I'm gonna come out, I'll be ready to get—in the saddle with you." And she says, "We're gonna move." There, that's good. She took care of everything. There it's the cakes, him takes off to get, get the, the white horse. The white horse. Hey! When she got there, at the door—she was ready. The cakes were made, they were placed on the stair and she gets upon the, on the horse and that's that, they're gone there—and they, they move. And they move! Hah hah hah! It's a—flash! There. Soon about two o'clock—in the morning, the old woman started to, to tap him in the back, she says, "Old man!"—"What do you want?" The old man said, his wife, "What it's telling me," she says, "what it's telling me about," she says—"is our daughter is gone. And John too."—"Ah, what's the matter with you, you're a foolish old woman!" he says, "Sleep! You know they haven't gone," he says, "they're too happy here."—"No!" she says, "they've gone somewhere. They've gone."—"Ah go to sleep!" Well she sta—picking after him again—well she says to him euh, there he says euh, he called her by her name, euh I don't know if it was Cecilia or euh, Genevieve or what kind of name she had—but she, he shouts out, she says, "Are you asleep there?"—She says euh, eh, "No," she says, "I'm not sleeping."—"There, do you see? Crazy fool! She's there! And what are you—go to sleep!" he says, "Leave, leave me alone me I'm tired, me—I want to go to sleep, me." Anyway it went like that but her she couldn't sleep—it wasn't m—what he was saying there. Soon at three o'clock—three o'clock in the morning—she started poking him with her elbows—she says, "Old man, old man! Old man!" There. "What's the matter again you crazy old fool!" he says. She says, "I'm sure," she says, "that they've gone, I'm *sure* they've gone!"— "But you *know*, you told me that just now but," he says, "I spoke to them, and I spoke to her and she—they were there! She's there, she answered me, it's her!"—"No no!" she says—"And there's something going on there." Well there he says, he shouts out, "Jane!" he says, "Are you asleep there?"—"Ah!" she says, "Well," she says, "I was sleeping," she says, "but you woke me up!"—"Will you go to sleep! Crazy old woman! Look!" he says—"If you, you have, you could have, you can't sleep—you're gonna cat, you're gonna catch my hand in your mouth," he says. "Ohhh! You don't have to be mean," she says, "because," she says, "I know something's going on," but he says, "I know he told, she said to me, spoke—haven't you got—are you deaf?"—"Oh no I heard it."—"So go to sleep! You crazy old woman, go to sleep!" And then hnrrr! There he's sleeping, sleeping, sleeping but her, she not sleeping, not her—but him, he is sleeping—falls asleep—tired y'know, tired.

G.T.:   Hm.

—Soon at four o'clock in the morning there she starts prodding him again. "Ah well," he says, "you," he says, "I should have done something with you—because I told you she's there and you keep going on that's she's not here—that she's gone! And me talking to her all the time, twice already! And why can't you leave me alone so I can sleep! Tomorrow," he says, "I, I won't be able to do nothing!" But she says, "She's gone, she's gone." Well he calls out, calls out again—"Ginny! Are you asleep?"—"Well," she said, "I was sleeping," she says, "but you woke me up."— "Well do you see? Go to sleep! Go to bed and sleep! Because if you're gonna, give up, I'm gonna—settle that," he says, "for, for the first time in my life I'm gonna hit you. Go to sleep! Crazy old woman, go to sleep!" Well like that, that's alright. Anyway it went on again—until five o'clock—yes, but them, they were moving along there, they were going there. Five o'clock in the morning—the old woman again she prods him again. There he turns around and hooks her by the throat— "Look!" he says, "I've got a good mind to strangle you," he says, "my damned old witch!" he says, "what if I strangled you now!" he says. "And do you think you'll let me sleep?" he says to her. "But I'm telling you she's gone, me!"—"Ah, ah, ah—look!" he says. "Ginny! Are you asleep?" [Emile projects his voice, calling to the distance] No answer. "Ginny, are you asleep?"—"There do you see? D'you see? D'you see? D'you see? D'you see!" she says. "Well no but he, she's asleep."—"There I'm telling you they've gone." Well the old man he jumps, jumps up! He hauls on his pants he only put, only put one leg—one leg on, he, hah hah! it, he, he was in such a hurry he, ho! he was dragging the other leg! In his underclothes on one side and his pants on the other side! And then he gets a move on—and he goes to their bedroom—gone!

G.T.:   Hm.

260

—"Well!" he says, "if only I had listened to you!"—"If only you had listened!"—"Ah gee that was well, well, well, well, well said! Now are we going to catch them? It's all right! If they haven't taken my horse. But if they've taken my horse," he says—"I'm gonna have some misery! They're gonna give me some misery. Well, well, well, well, damn fool—that I was—and why didn't I listen to you?"—"Well I told you! I told you!"—"Yes, you did indeed"—No my man, he takes off to the barn and—on his way he loses his, he loses his pants! He was in his longjohns—he hauls back on his horse and then there he is, off he goes—and off he goes. He had so much power d'you see, the horse, it, it, it could go too. It was a red horse, white horse, black horse, it's no different—he, he had power to put, put, put *good* in it there. Well that's good. There. There he's going! And he moves, and he goes. And, and then John and, and the, her, the, the, his wife—they were going too. And lumps of earth were flying the mud, little stones were flying in the air it was, w, w, w, oh t'was just like a real—*demon starm*. There—and the devil—moving too him. He's coming there! Ho! On his way! That's good. There. He's going, he's going, he's going, he's going, oh but it was broad daylight—it was around ten o'clock—but the poor horse there he, was white but he was twice as white because he was all—the sweat, it, it was, it was all the foam—coming from, from, from his sides and all—hair—and everything. And she says, "Stop!" she says, "stop now," she says, "and I'm gonna put my ear to the ground," she says, "see if I can hear Pop coming. And if I don't hear him coming," she says, "we've got a small chance," she says. She says, "How far is it still?"—"But," he says, "it's still—as far as I know," he says, "about—like a hundred miles for sure."—"Well," she says, "we're gonna have some misery to do it because Pop's coming fast." She says, "Pop is by himself on the back—on his horse and us we're two of us on his horse. I know his horse is, is much faster than the—but he, it's a big load to carry. But," she says, "Let—let's go," she says, "come on," and she says, "Give it to him. Give it to him!" And him, my man, he let you have it he had a, pieces of rope there, the, reins—and he gives it to him on the belly, and—he, the horse going like the wind. Him, she moves, he moves, and you give it, and you give it, yes but she can hear the ground trembling the devil was coming behind there. And they're going, and they're going, and they're going, and they're going, and they're going. Well it was, to finish the story a little bit, a little bit quicker—it was quick enough, quick enough and euh, and close enough— that when—when they got to like we'll say—like a hundred yards from the Holy Land—she looks behind she says, "Pop's back there," she says, "he's coming," she says, "I can see him coming," she says—"he, he's, he's gonna, he's gonna catch us," she says, "give," she says, "give it to him! Give it to him!" Oh well there, my old buddy, he gives it to him on the horse's belly, oh oh! It, the horse was, was *flying* like the devil. And the devil was closing on them—her father was approaching— [Emile coughs]—ah this damned cough I've got. Anyway he was getting closer, getting closer, getting closer, quick enough that, that, they, they thought—they think he's gonna—he—he would have caught them. But—I guess it's the power she had too her—they, they made it because—when they had, when the, the white horse put its two front legs in the Holy Land—the devil was there. It was—ah but I guarantee you! And when he got there the, the, he turned his horse around like that but he hooked the tail, the white horse's tail—and that's all he got, tore off the tail from the white horse's body! And he couldn't, he couldn't go—couldn't—put his foot in the Holy Land he was obliged to turn around—and he [Emile, in his excitement, swallows two or three words]—ehh! and he guarant—oo, er he, er, a, ah—he, he, he couldn't speak he was stuttering! For the anger he felt. And *dame* he was obliged to go back home and—me I was there—it was, and it was one, one of my uncles, the one who had come—when they had got there, well, he says, "She's a beautiful woman though, boy. Beautiful woman." I was there when they got there with their, their, with the white horse—but a pretty little horse it was too. Yeah. Yeah and they

261

had the devil of a wedding, ho, holy gee! Yeah we had some fun! Lots of home-brew there—hah hah! Yeah! It was all right.

Commentary and notes

This tale, a narration of some seventy minutes, was even longer than *John-of-the-Woods*. Emile himself felt obliged, towards the end, to "finish the story a little bit, a little bit quicker", although our session was to continue for another fifty minutes. But it is only when one is nowadays face to face with storytellers like Emile that one can begin to appreciate what the talent (and the endurance) of old-time storytellers must have been. One begins too to appreciate the pace of life, so different from our own, of former generations: they loved spending long hours with a gifted storyteller.

The Tale of the Black Mountain, as we shall shortly see, is one of the most complex of *Märchen*. Even in Newfoundland versions of the tale have been collected which include many more motifs than this one (for example, with the addition of the fugitives' transformations into obstacles to the pursuing devil, and the final episode in which the hero temporarily forgets his wife until reminded of her by the story of the old and the new keys); but no other version takes up more time, and the duration of a tale was important in the public storytelling tradition.

A single example from Emile's story will suffice to demonstrate how he lengthens his narrations. The first motif in the tale involves the card game pitting the devil against John, in the course of which the latter loses his wealth as well as his soul. In itself, it is a motif which can be quickly and simply presented. Emile makes of it an epic encounter, equal to any classic cinematographic drama. The game begins with a highly confident hero facing a seemingly mediocre opponent, one moreover who loses the first few hands. But the hero's reputation, based on uninterrupted successes, can only lead, as in Greek tragedy, to a total and demoralizing defeat. Emile leads us through to the hero's inevitable downfall. It is an incredibly dramatic and finely sustained introductory episode.

Good storytellers know how to manipulate their audience's emotions, and Emile is no exception to this rule. After such a dramatic opening, he then leads us, in the first part of the hero's journey, through a bleak but calm countryside, to plunge us into unrestrained laughter with his description of the first sister. He brings her to life with visual details but also with vocal effects, as when he marvelously imitates the old woman's words. To this he adds grimaces which only compound the comic aspect of the situation. Not only does Emile maintain this pace until the hero's arrival at the devil's domain, but he also manages to increase the comic effect with his successive meetings with the other two sisters.

It is however important to remind ourselves here of Emile's attitude towards the devil; for him, the demon is a reality. It is therefore significant that we are dealing in this story with a devil and not with a giant; and that the third sister advises John not to name the devil by name too often. These are Emile's own words when he speaks about his personal philosophy. The *Märchen* is here filling a didactic role.

From time to time, Emile humorously evokes the behaviour of his characters in a way which demonstrates how fine an observer of human psychology he is. One thinks in particular of the series of confrontations between the devil and his wife, at the time of John and his wife's flight. Despite her husband's threats, she proves to be correct; but even after hearing the devil's self-castigation of his behaviour, she cannot resist underlining her triumph with her two well placed, "I told you's".

In concluding this commentary, I must once again draw the reader's attention to Emile's closing formula. He brings the audience back to everyday reality with his participation in the festive triumphal return of the hero and his wife.

The Black Mountain is a version of the international tale-type AT 313, *The Girl as Helper in the Hero's Flight*; it is one of the most widely known tales in French tradition. *Le Conte populaire français* gives some ninety versions for France and another twenty or so for French Caribbean islands; seventy-nine versions of the tale from French tradition in North America are noted in *The Types of the Folktale*. The tale is found in Europe, western and eastern Asia, in Africa and, of course, in America. As Paul Delarue said so well in his commentary (*Le Conte populaire français* I, 234): "This tale is the lengthiest of the Indo-European repertoire, one of the best composed and best loved; and in no other does one find so many elements brought together from the distant past: bird-girls, metamorphoses, enchantments, speaking objects and animals, and very diverse magical doings of an occasionally disconcerting oddness. But these motifs, the considerable antiquity of which leaves no doubt, are clearly anterior to the creative operation which picked them out from so many others or set them apart from already existing combinations to make of them a coherent and logical construction, a veritable work of art which has endured the test of time." Emile Benoit's version and his performance of it most certainly add a new dimension to these comments. His is one of the best of the dozen or so collected from French Newfoundlanders. He learned it from the late Julien Chaisson, who had told it to him in his youth, and claims not to have told it himself more than half a dozen times (at least until recently).

The chief motifs in the tale include the following: N4, *Devil as gambler;* S221.2, *Youth sells himself to an ogre in settlement of a gambling debt;* G461, *Youth promised to ogre visits ogre's home;* Z72.1, *A year and a day;* C12, *Devil invoked: appears unexpectedly;* H1235, *Succession of helpers on quest;* N825.3, *Old woman helper;* G201, *Three witch sisters;* G202, *Beneficent witches;* G236, *Witch lives in forest;* G214.1, *Witch with long teeth;* D810, *Gift of a magic object;* D812.6, *Magic object received from witch or wizard;* D1472.1.22, *Magic bag (sack) supplies food;* B455.3, *Helpful eagle;* B322.1, *Hero feeds own flesh to helpful animal;* D1503.13, *Magic potion heals wounds;* G465, *Ogre sets impossible tasks;* H1010, *Impossible tasks;* H1095, *Task: felling a forest in one night;* H1095.2, *Task: stacking wood from felled forest in one day;* H1116.2.1* (CEFT), *Task: felling a forest with a paper ax;* H1143.2* (CEFT), *Task: emptying a lake in one day with a straw basket;* H1114, *Task: climbing glass mountain;* H1114.1.1* (CEFT), *Task: securing an egg from top of glass tower;* H335.0.1, *Bride helps suitor perform his tasks;* G530.2, *Help from ogre's daughter (or son);* F848.3, *Ladder of bones;* E64.2, *Resuscitation by magic cauldron;* E15.1, *Resuscitation by boiling;* E33, *Resuscitation with missing member;* H57.0.1, *Recognition of resuscitated person by missing member;* compare B652.1, *Marriage to swan maiden* (not explicit in this version, although the hero does marry the devil's daughter); G550, *Rescue from ogre;* and D1611.8, *Magic cakes answer for fugitive.*

(UNTITLED STORY I)

Well, once upon a time there was a man and a woman—and they had a child. A girl. They had a small farm—couple of cows—and they euh, every time they used to make, they used to make butter—they would send a piece of butter to the priest. She used to send her daughter with a—saucerful of butter. Well that was fine—good, he made good butter and everything—but this one time—it was in the month of August—hot weather—and euh, that Saturday ah well she says euh, she takes the saucerful of butter and she says to her daughter, she says, "Take that," she says, "to the priest," she says. To the priest. Ah! But the butter was soft ah! Anyway that's good, she takes off with the m—the pat of butter and she goes to the priest's—she says, "Here, Father," she says, "mom's sent you a saucerful of butter again," she says. "Ah! Well, well, well," he says, "is your butter soft," he says, "today?"—"Ah yes, Father," she says—"it's as soft as shit!" Oh! Well, there he didn't say much—but he found it pretty—insolent. Ah! Three or four days later he, he had to go on—on missions because in those times, d'you see, they had to walk—from place to place, perhaps five or six miles and then they had euh a mission and this and that—confess people and—so on. And euh, well on his way—he—it was always there, he passes

263

by the old, by the old woman's—and the old man's place. But the old man wasn't there, was only the old woman. Anyway when, euh, he gets to the door, he knocks to the door, she opens the door, "Aye--gran," she spoke funny y'know, *"Come in Father, come in, come in! Come in!* "—*"Oh, you know* euh, euh, I haven't got the time to come in," he says euh, "I'm going," he says euh, "on a mission there." Oh well, so they mention the place where it was, all that—well that's that, oh well *dame*—euh, "Thank you very much," he says, "for the butter you send me every Saturday."— "Oh that's nothing, that's nothing!. Well *dame* it's a great pleasure!" But he says, "Yes but," he says, "you sent me a piece," he says, "last Saturday," he says, "a saucerful of butter," he says and euh, euh, "I said to your daughter the butter was soft."—"Ah yes yes Father," she says, "it was soft," she says—"it's hot weather." "Yes yes but," he says, "she told me that, I said that the butter was soft and she said to me that the butter was—'yes Father,' she says, 'like, like shit'. Soft as shit!"—"She didn't say that to you! Father?"—"Well yes," he says—and he says, "It would be a'right for you," he says, "to, to correct her," he says there, "because it, those aren't fine words to speak! Things like that."—"No danger Father! She's not here. She's gone out somewhere. But when she gets back—I'm gonna learn her Father, Father, Father, I won't fail—I'm gonna beat the shit out of her!" Well, by the gee, there, him he, looks, takes off, well it was all shit, he takes off. He doesn't go too far—there was—her husband he was put, putting a, a roof on a, on a cellar. "Hey! Good evening!" he says, "Good—good, good day," he says, "Father." Euh, "Good day," he says euh, George I think it was, George was his name—he says euh, "Where are you going there?"—"Well," he says, "I'm going on a mission there." He says, "Could I speak with you for a minute?"—"Of course," he says, "why not," it, George comes down from the barn—he says, "What's the matter, Father?"—"Well," he says euh, "I have, I have to tell you, euh, y-y-you've failed," he says, "a little bit with—with your daughter—so that—"—"My daughter?" he says, "What's the matter then, what's the matter then?"—"Euh, yes," he says euh, "I passed by your, your wife there just now," he says euh, "but she had sent a piece."—but he tells the story, what had happened—and he says, "I get there to, to your wife," he says euh, "she, she, she—the, I told, told her about it she said she's gonna beat the shit out of her and stuff like that," he says, "it's—"—" Oh ha ha ha ha! Ha ha ha! Father—heh heh! You don't find that funny. Because—I know, me—I know all that, me. "—"And what is it, what is it?"—"Well—look Father—I'm gonna tell you something. Me," he says, "I'm a person—who—I don't want no foolishness and there are some every day-- that the Good Lord brings—I,'ve, I've got my story to tell—and I tell them how to do this and that—and how—to be converted amongst the people and everything. But Father it's no use talking, there are people like that," he says. "Those people—no way you can get anything into their head—they're crazy as my ass." Ha ha ha!

Commentary and notes

This brief story, told with considerable seriousness, in order to underline by contrast the family's vulgar language, was to lead, as we shall see, to another "priest story" and a few short jokes and legends which brought the session to a close. One should take note that the insolent daughter's mother first speaks to the priest in English. It is a very common feature among French Newfoundlanders, when telling a "priest story" in French, to have a person addressing the priest speak in English, for practically their whole experience has been with anglophone priests, to whom one not only owed respect (hence, by its absence, the story's humour), but also the English language. The priest has always been an authority figure in the eyes of French Newfoundlanders as indeed in the eyes of others; the genre is quite common in the province as a whole. Emile learned his version from a septuagenarian neighbour, Mr. Joe Bozec.

The tale has not been identified, although it has its place in *The Types of the Folktale* in the section covering jokes about priests and religious orders (AT 1725-1874). It may well be that the story has been collected, but omitted from classification because of the somewhat coarse language. On the other hand, it can be classified under the general motif X434, *The parson put out of countenance*.

[UNTITLED STORY II]

There was a mother like that too there, euh, and euh, he used to catch a rabbit, he was, he was like twelve years old eh—so not too big—just a little finger [of rum in his glass]—he was like twelve years old—and every Saturday he, he used to catch rabbits like a son-of-a-gun—there was lots of rabbits. Anyway euh, she says now, she says euh, "Go take a rabbit to the priest—and every Saturday—take a rabbit to the priest." Well he used to go, he, he took a rabbit to the priest. Yes but it was like that for five or six months—used to take a rabbit to the priest, every Saturday, every Saturday. That's good. He says, "I'm starting to get tired of all that, me," he says, "me, it costs me money, me," he says, "to buy sn, sn, snares and all that, w, wire to make snares and all that—and the priest has never given me nothing, me." But he doesn't say so to his mother—he's thinking that in his mind now, y'know. He's *fed up. He, he didn't want to go—always taking rabbits—he didn't want to go.* "Oh," she says, "you've got to go—hoh! Dame!" she says. "Our priest," she says, "he's got to eat too." And she says, "You're gonna go—take him his rabbit, like you always do." Well that's that—he had to obey there, that's the, her orders it's this, it's that. There he takes the rabbit and off he goes—both his eyebrows hauled down over his cheeks. Oh oh! He wasn't pleased! That's good. He gets to the priest's—doesn't tap, knock the door or nothing, he opens the door—and he throws the rabbit in the, in the kitchen. And he shuts the door and he takes off. The priest there—he was sitting at his table—his desk, he looked at the rabbit there—but the—he didn't know who had come in and thrown in the rabbit, where—gee he was surprised—anyway he gets up and he goes and—he opens the door and he looks—the little boy who came every—"Eh hay!" he says, "What's the matter, what's the matter today?" he says—"What's the matter? Come here, come see, come see my little boy, come see, come see, come here, come!" Little boy turns around he, he says, "What's the matter Father?"—"Oh," he says, "Did you, you, but it was you brought that rabbit there?"—"Oh," he says, "it was me, yes yes, it was me."—"But," he says, "it's not like that you bring a rabbit to the priest! Oh ho ha hee!"—he laughs, "heh heh!—Oh no, it's not like that," he says, "well come in my little boy, come-come-come-come-come-come-come-come!" So the little boy comes in—"Look," he says—"you're a handsome little fellow, you," he says—"I like you—but," he says, "d'you see, you haven't, you haven't been raised up right—and your father and your mother, well you, you haven't got a father, you," he says, "your father is dead—but if your mother would have," he says, "you would have been raised properly there, the way," he says, "you should have been—well you wouldn't have done that there," he says, "you didn't do right there." And he hunches his shoulders and he doesn't say nothing—he just lifts his, his—he wanted to say he didn't know. He says, "Look," he says, "just between me and you," he says—he says, "I'm gonna take my cassock—and I'm gonna—you," he says, "you're going to be the priest. I'm going to put my cassock on you and you're going to sit in my chair—and me," he says, "I'm going to be the little boy—and I'm going to take the rabbit—and," he says, "like you're going to see me do—well there," he says, "you'll do the same as me and it'll be right."—"Ah yes, Father," he says, "it's—I'd like to learn that." A'right. So the priest takes his cassock off and hangs it on the little boy but *dame* it was—too big for him—but *dame* it didn't make no difference—he was the priest there. So the priest goes out with the rabbit—and then the priest knocks [Emile raps the table] on the door. Well the little boy said euh, "Come in!" The priest opens the door. The priest

265

comes in holding the rabbit in his hand, he says, "Here," he says, "Father—I've brought you a rabbit for your dinner tomorrow." The little boy says—"Ah thank you very much, my little boy, that's very kind of you." The little fellow, there was a little jar with some, some, some, some quarters in it euh, he lifts up the, the cover and he takes a quarter out he says, "Here," he says, "my little boy, twenty-five cents," he says, "for your rabbit!" Ah ha ha ha!

Commentary and notes

In a very short narrative, Emile succeeds in very rapidly characterizing the two antagonists. He evokes the boy's frustration and the priest's impatience faced with the former's seeming rudeness. This he does above all by means of conversation, in monologue or dialogue form. As ever, one must visualize the elastic-faced Emile, and in particular the priest's little pout as he preaches to the lad.

The Types of the Folktale has a whole series of anecdotes numbered from 1832A* to 1832K* which oppose a priest and a clever boy, the only versions of which are from Quebec. The sub-type AT 1832E*, *Good Manners*, is precisely Emile's tale, although he could not remember his source. Emile's version is the second collected from French Newfoundlanders. Perhaps because this series of anecdotes seemed restricted to French-Canadian tradition, Stith Thompson did not give them precise numbers in his *Motif-Index of Folk-Literature*; this tale must therefore be classified under the general number X434, *The parson put out of countenance*.

[TWO STORIES ABOUT MOSEY MURRIN]

G.T.:   ...Tell me some, some stories about Mosey, Mosey Burns there. You've heard the old stories they tell about him.

—Ah! Yes. Mosey Born—euh, Mosey Burn—he was in Stephenville but he was everywhere—but he was in Stephenville in those days—and they were making moonshine in the, the, the—Moonshine Valley they used to call it—they called it, they gave it that name because they used to make moonshine there. Anyway, the police were trying, trying to catch them but they couldn't. Anyway, they had asked, they had met Mosey, he asks, asked Mose, "Mose," he says euh, Mose knew him but *dame*—and euh, he says, "Can you tell me who makes the moonshine in the—*Who makes the moonshine*," he says, "*in Moonshine Valley?*"—"Oh yes, sure."— "*Who?*"—"Hoh hoh!—*Me I'm not gonna tell you,* I'm not gonna tell you," he says. "Why not? Why not? If I give you some money," he says, "will you tell?"—"Ho yes!" he says. He says euh, "How much would you want?"—"Give me five dollars I'll tell you," he says. "Five dollars and I'll tell you who makes the, the moonshine," he says, "in the, the, Moonshine Valley."—A'right the, the *ranger* gives him five dollars. There! "Who is it?" He says, "It's God." Ah ha ha!

G.T.:   Ha ha!

—It's true as well.

G.T.:   Yes yes.

—Moonshine—the moon—was shining.

G.T.:   Did he tell him after euh, "If you give me five more dollars I'll tell you who makes the, the, the sun shine?'

—Mm! Mm.

G.T.:   Eh?

—They didn't give it to him though.

G.T.:   No—ha ha ha!

—Huh! They didn't give it to him.

G.T.:   Have you heard any others there?

—There was another one he euh, there was a man who euh, he had a horse—euh in those days, well they had euh, euh, nail bags there.

G.T.:   Yes.

—They weighed fifty pounds euh, it was fifty pounds of nails. And they used to put oats in it there and they used to put a little piece of line — over the horse's head and they'd put a gallon of oats in it and the horse would eat in the bag and like that he didn't lose any.

G.T.:   Hm.

—Anyway euh, Mose Burns is going past—he was just putting, he was putting the, the, the horse's head in the bag. He says to this fellow, he says, "My poor man," he says, "it's, it's, it's no good what you're doing there." He says, "What?"—"It's no good," he says, "you'll never put the horse in the bag!" Heh heh! Heh heh heh!

Commentary and notes

Moses Murrin (1908?-1980), born in Spaniard's Bay (Conception Bay), was an eccentric character who spent the greatest part of his life on the west coast of Newfoundland, first at Lark Harbour, then at Corner Brook and, for almost twenty-five years, in Stephenville. He was a man whom one spoke of as a "wise-fool", earning his livelihood by begging and through intermittent peddling. He was recognized as a master of retort and repartee. The two anecdotes told by Émile form part of a whole series current on the West Coast.

Emile, who began his narration in French, felt obliged to resort to English in order to convey the pun of the first anecdote. Although most French Newfoundlanders are bilingual, and therefore understand the puns which so frequently occur in "Mosey" stories, they often switch from French to English in order to give the crux of the anecdote in its language of origin.

The Centre d'Etudes Franco-Terreneuviennes has an abundant documentation on Mosey Murrin (Murn, Burn, Burns), and it is as much a part of the French folklore of the region as it is of the English. I intend to devote a study to him in the near future.

"WE THREE"

—Ah yes for the three young fellows who had learned to speak.

G.T.:   What's that story called?

—Well, I don't know the name of the story—but it's—the way I heard it well—it's—one time there was three-three young fellers—and euh they had decided to go—look for work. But now *dame*—they spoke French—not a word of English—for them—really, t'was really difficult for them. If they had been to a place and there was work and the people spoke English and them they couldn't speak a word of English well they had been really disappointed. Anyway that's good. By gosh there was one person there anyway who spoke English and French—and they had decided to go and find this—this person—to try and learn a few words in English. Well—eh well they go, well—they had started to discuss—well they were going to look for work. Well the—the feller who could speak English—he tells them, well, he says, "Why," he says—euh—"don't one of you learn," he says euh, "'*We three*'— and then the other eh well—'*Lookin for a job*'—and the oth, the other well, '*Lookin'*, euh,—'*Quicker de better*'. If they ask you, '*What you lookin for?*'—well, '*We three*'— "well, he says, "'*Lookin for a job*' and '*How—what time you want to go to work?*'—Well, '*Quicker de better*'." Well *dame* they got that—well they practiced that in—in themselves y'know. "*We tree, we tree*" and euh, "*We're lookin for a job*" well, "*Quicker de better*." Well that's that. Well, all at once they got that in their head, stuffed in their head and—they take off there. Well it took a few days before they got there. Anyway on their journey—they had found—a—a dead man—on the side of the path. "Look! Look there! It's a dead man"—There, he says, "That's bad, that." Come up to the man, hey, a knife in his, stuck in his back. "Well," he says, "look," he says, "someone," he says, "killed that man." Ah! They look, one of them looks up—the one who had learned euh, "We three"—he looks—a policeman by him. He says, *"Oo killed that man?"* He says, *" We three."*—*"Why did you kill im?"*—The other one replies—*"Lookin for a job."*—*"But you're gonna be ung—hung."* Huh! The other feller says to him euh, *"Quicker de better"*! Hah!

Commentary and notes

This story has a certain piquancy on the Port-au-Port Peninsula, not because it describes an event which actually took place, but because linguistic problems provoked by bilingualism, and more especially those raised in the pre-bilingual period, affected the French more than the English. There are still people who make fun of the accent of French Newfoundlanders when they speak English (and even those who do not speak French are very conscious of their French accent), but the French have their revenge with a series of anecdotes, some quite vulgar, in which a Frenchman who speaks English badly is pitted against an anglophone figure of authority such as the priest.

This tale is a version of the international type AT 1697, "*We Three; For Money.*" The tale seems quite well known in France (21 versions), but surprisingly less well known in North America where, for French tradition, only three Quebec and three Louisiana French versions have been recorded. Given that both Quebec and Louisiana French are surrounded by anglophones, one might have expected a wider distribution of the tale. Its motif is C495.2.2, "*We three*"—"*For gold*"—"*That is right*"; *phrases of a foreign language.*

The reader will appreciate how much more effective this story is when told in French to a bilingual audience; italicized phrases in the translation were in English in the original narration. Emile attributes the tale to his late father, who told it to him in his youth.

The preceding tales by Emile Benoit represent the sum of his tape-recorded repertoire at the time of the original French edition of this work; since then, some half-dozen or so hitherto unrecorded tales have been collected and will eventually be published. It would, however, be a pity not to offer the reader a sampling of his personal experience narratives, his memorates, and a few of the introductions with which he prefaces fiddle tunes of his own composition; this, after all, is how his narrative abilities have been made known to a wider public. While he cannot permit himself the luxury of narrating a *Märchen* in a festival or a bar, because to do so would take far too much time, he can and does link his tunes with personal experience stories.

Following the series of recordings made with him in November 1980, he told the following story to his audience. He had told it the preceding evening, too, to one of his daughters, Shannon, and a friend of hers, with considerable effect, and was requested to repeat it for recording.

THE HORSE THAT SAW A GHOST

G.T.: Tell us, tell us, tell us about that again Emile.

—Well—yeah. I lived here—I never said I lived here last night—but—it—as the story goes. I live here—that was on a—now to remember de day it was, if it was Monday or Tuesday or Wednesday or whatever it was—but I went up to euh—I was single—I wasn married or nothing—that was in my—seven years euh you know—single. So—I had a nice horse—at dat time—I had paid—two hundred and fifty dollars for the horse—it was a tall horse—shin horse—e was, is mother was a racer—an e could ave been a racer too—if e ad been—y'know teach to it. But at that time two undred and fifty dollars—you wouldn get a harse no less that eight—seven or eight hundred—

G.T.:   Hm.

—A harse like that now. You know?

S.K.: Why?

—So euh, good enough. I left here an I went up—to my brother Ben—I got dere—Three Rock Cove—I stayed here, I ad supper dere—so I said now I said, "I'm gonna go up," I said—"to my—to my sister"—Yvonne—my brother Ben's sister too—she lived about a mile from dere—"So I'm gonna go up," I said euh, I said, "I'll be back for around nine o'clock. I'll be back." So all right—that's good enough. So I takes the harse an euh—puts him in the s—they ad a Santa Claus sleigh you know, dem euh, y'know—shart sleigh y'know—eh?

G.T.:   Hm.

—Oh a nice sleigh—Santa Claus sleigh dey calls, you sees dem on the, on the picture eh? An er, I'm gone. An when I got dere I ad to—open de gate an go trough de field an I had about—two hundred yards I suppose to go before I get—she used to live up top of the hill—*descend dans le* [comes down in the]—they calls euh, Roun Head. So a'right—went there to my sister—tied the horse up behind the house—the wind was nar-wes—tied de house behind, the harse behind the house an I give im—one of the hay—eat away. So I goes in to my sister's. An euh, we start chattin, chattin, chat, chat, an dere was a couple a girls there—girls around my age— women—y'know—as usual—y'know, kind of a—so on—tinkin an er, figurin—an everything like that. Not much show wid dat but euh, still, y'know—lookin for worse to—y'know—but—not too much, thanks [I pour him a drink]—So nine o'clock—oh! I said eh! Nine o'clock—I'm goin. An moonlight! A nice night! Oh! Just like dey show on the television—it shines! Heh! You could see—I'm sure—euh at twenty-five steps you could see a—little bird—pitch on a limb—it was dat clear. That snow eh? Oh! Beautiful! So a'right. Well, I said, I told Ben, I said I was gonna be back for nine o'clock so—I'm not gonna be there for nine o'clock but euh, I'm goin, anyhow. An so I got aboard the sleigh—an I'm gone. Turn de harse around— an set—aboard the sleigh. Now dem time I used to smoke euh Beaver Tobacco—

G.T.:   Hm.

—A knife an—plug tobacco y'know.

G.T.:   Yeah.

—Plug eh. Goddam. Den I get euh, de brown paper there an—y'know. See. Chew on dat—then we stick it—an then light it. Brown paper—tobacco. I should make one tomorrow show you ow we use to make it.

S.K.:   I've made them before.

—You make them too? *Oh ben dame c'est ça* [Oh well *dame* that's that].

S.K.:   Ha ha ha ha ha!

—You know how it is. So a'right—started going through the field—when I got to the gate—got out, opened the gate—the horse out—to the gate again—then I sets down—an I start—cut some tobacco now. It's nice, so calm—y'know.

G.T.:   Hm.

—Not a draught of wind, or nothing, right—cosy—not cold—right nice! An I was makin my cigarette—an den I—pretty—de harse stop. I look at de harse—I said, "Go on!" So I'm, y'know, give a look for a match to—by an by I said, "Go on!" Start backing up. You know, you get—euh—funny eh?

G.T.:   Hm-hm.

269

—You get something funny in your brain, dis n dat. I said, "Go on!" An when I said dat he'd *back* up again. That's the first time y'know dat, dat had happened to me.

G.T.:   Yes.

—Back up again. So I starts to lookin around there, looking long the fence an euh, lookin everywhere. I—lookin at is head he was dere—lookin like dat. But when I say nothing e, e don't move, e's dere. An e's lookin.... Start lookin too, me, at dat—funny, I never seen anything like dat. But I said, "There's nothing dere!" I said, "Goddarn fool is, dere's notting dere!" I said, "Go on! Go on," I said. Back up again. *Ben tchiens*—oh it come to my mind, look between de, de two horse's ear—an you'll see what e sees. So a'right, I got up on the shaft, got over the dashboard an [Emile gets up and moves away from the table] got over an I'm lookin up over the ear—but couldn see nothing there [he sits down]. So I set down again—he was dere my son, "Hneuh! hneuh!" like that eh. Well, I said, "There's nothing there—"—So that's the word I said. I took, I took—I had a whip—eh—took the reins—"You goddarn son of a bitch!" That's the word I said. An I give im that. Oly jeepers! [Emile blows a kiss]

S.K.:   Ha ha ha ha ha!

—Flack! An wid dat my son look, e stood up like this—[he imitates a rearing horse]—an that was—in a second eh—in a m—that *lightning*—phooit! Jus like that—an e took off—an de sl, an de sleigh didn upset. It was a good chance it was shart—ony for that mind e would a broke the shaft or whatever—but dat, dat's, they turned like the, like a spintop.

G.T.:   Hm.

—An I lost the reins—I hook on to dat board—when I went fo, for to, y'know, tip over I hook on, I hook on the dashboard like that—an—before I got, y'know, e—to sit down for to hook the reins—e was dere at the gate *là*. He was there—e was back there already.

G.T.:   Hm.

—Cos it wasn't too far, you know. My jeepers cripes, y'know, dat—*là*. When I got to myself I got the reins an everything—e was quite, quite, quite. But my son—e was about dat high from the ground, he was like [two or three indistinguishable words] I was goin to say about de harse, about de devil—nah. I got out of the sleigh. So I took him by the halter. I says, "Come on," I said, "we can't go out there, they got no barn up there—*pas d'grange en-haut là*"—*j'y parle* [no barn up there"—I talk to him]—in French y'know.

G.T.:   Hm-hm.

—"Come on! Come on!"—"Euh-euhrah-a-chrnn! Achrrr!" Like e was talkin to me—pounds ees, ees, ees foot in de—well den I tooks de rein, I goes in the back of him an, I tell wid de rein eh? An de e *back up*, e *back*—well—I had to quit. Because e would ave break, e would ave fall on the shaft, break my shaft. So I had to quit. So. I turn him around. I would to turn him around this way—but turn him around *this way*. Oh *ouais*—turn him around this way.

G.T.:   Hm-hm.

—Funny you know.

G.T.:   Yeah.

—Open the gate—den—went to my sister's again. So I—she said, "Oh you're back! What happened?" I said, "My horse didn want to pass." So I said, "I come fer a—you for to come with me." My sister was pious and euh, Fintan, e's dead now Fintan, my brother-in-law, him—I said, "Come on with me." An then they told me about the, the mailman had come there an euh, e was goin back home—an e was stuck—e ad to go back an sleep with euh—my brother's euh, fadder-in-law.

G.T.:   Hm.

—That's where he had to pass in—dat night—with his mail—couldn get his horse to go—the harse had turn around same way, same story as I said with mine. I said, "Come on with me, come on!" No sir. So e put his cows out—e ad two cows—put out the—two cow out the barn—an put my harse in the barn. Two men, they wouldn come with me. Ah! Pen—

G.T.:   What was there, Emile?

—Eh?

G.T.:   What was there?

—Whatever was there—it wasn't pretty. No *mon ami*. Oh I don't know what was there—but—I guarantee you—I was proud that I didn see what was there. It wasn't pretty, what my harse seen there.

G.T.:   Hm.

—So all right. I wasn frighten you know—ah—I'm pretty bold y'know, in my time.

G.T.:   Hm.

—Even dat skeleton an all that there, but I got a fright—but euh, it's a true story that—that's true that.

G.T.:   Oui oui.

—You know—fergit. So all right. Nex marnin I left—was about four or five o'clock, well—it was before daylight—an de *same kind of weather*. You could hear a person say—Hello! E could be a *mile* away an I'm sure you would hear the echo.

G.T.:   Yeah.

—*Not* a drap o wind de same ting like—last night we'll say eh?

G.T.:   Hm.

—An—it was when the harse, when the sleigh eh, e use to crack eh? The sleigh eh?

G.T.:   Hm.

—M-m-hn-hn—make noise on the, on the, on the snow eh?

G.T.:   Hm-hm.

—Frost, see. It was in March, that. So—right—well now I said—to meself—"I'm goin a know if it's dere." So put the r—put the reins behind the dashboard, I let them go—I never said, "Go on", I never said *nutting*! But I watch is *ears*—I watch im. I watch em now.

G.T.:   Yes.

—See—if she was gonna pay any attention—on de way, you see? Go—the harse, goin, goin, the head like this—walkin—[Emile imitates a plodding horse] when they got there in the same place—e didn even look. I don't know if she look like this—but the head didn move.

G.T.:   Hm.

—[plodding steps again] *Là*. Funny that?

G.T.:   Yeah.

—Why did e, didn—if it was a people's piece of paper or if it was—a some—or if it was a rat or *what*? It's funny you get—

G.T.:   Don't be afraid! [Emile pinches S.K. in the ribs]

—It's funny dat e, e didn look see if the rat was there—no that's true dough!

271

G.T.:   *Tu l'as affrayée—tu l'as peurée* [You frightened her—you scared her].

S.K.: That's not funny, Gerald.

—No, no, that's what I find funny—it's funny dat—dat e didn look for dat again, see, see if it was there.

G.T.:   Hm-hm.

—*Ah tu sais ça* [Ah you know that]. Ah! I got my mind too, me, I don't worry now.

G.T.:   Hm-hm.

—I'm smart in my way see. Ho ho! What they say about the harse eh?

G.T.:   Hm.

—If he sees something dere—now—an take im out an bring him back, e go—when he come back he's gonna look see if it's there—suppose e takes it away—he's gonna turn *his* head see if he see—eh?

G.T.:   Yeah.

—You see a little glimp of his euh—of his mokin.

G.T.:   Hm.

—But see—no mokin at all. Well I say I wouldn like to see—what e seen. I wouldn like to see it.

G.T.:   Hm.

—It would frighten the shit out of me all right. Whatever it was—I don't know what it was—I don't know—but whatever e seen—to frighten, frighten him like that—that wasn't pretty. It wasn a good thing. It wasn God for sure he seen. No...

Commentary and notes

This narrative, in the form of a personal experience story, clearly demonstrates the difference between a tale and a legend. Only too often in collections of legends one sees the account presented as a sustained narrative. The legendary narrative, however, when related in a natural context, has nothing to do with the *Märchen*. Emile looked for my every reaction to the happenings he was relating, hence my so frequent 'hms' and 'yeahs'. This then was a story told with considerable natural-ness—not without a certain dramatic manner of course, but it is in the nature of the storyteller to dramatize even the most ordinary narratives. One might point to the asides on tobacco or the atmosphere in his sister's home as narrative-length-ening devices; but in this kind of story they derive rather from a desire for accuracy of detail and thus, of authenticity.

During the telling of the event we were joined by Stephanie Kelly, a friend, the S.K. of the text. The previous evening Emile had told his "ghost story" to his daughter and her friend; Stephanie Kelly had witnessed the fright he gave them. She was a good listener for Emile, who managed to frighten her in the course of his narrative; both took the events of the story very seriously, not that that prevented Emile from teasing the girls. The inherent seriousness of the topic did not divert the narrator from his natural proclivities. He is well aware of the potential of ghost stories, whether his audience believes him or not. He has his own personal convic-tion, as is evidenced by his comment on the point at the conclusion of the narrative.

The memorate itself can be classified under the motif E421.1.2, *Ghost visible to horses alone.*

To conclude this sampling of Emile Benoit's narrative art, here are two exam-ples of the stories he uses as introductions to his fiddle compositions. Depending on the audience, he will naturally vary the story's length; in a noisy bar, he will tend to shorten it, doing likewise for an impatient fieldworker. Faced with an admiring audience, however, he is quite able to make such a story last twenty minutes. The following version, which he tells equally well in French or English, is one of average length. I have heard it told on many occasions, always with the same enthusiasm, the same verve and the same sincerity. It is "The Skeleton."

THE SKELETON

—Now. Yeah—well—dere's one time I was seventeen years old—I was chasin de girls—like every young feller I spose—but I had a girl friend—an I use to go see her every Saturday night—not every night but every Saturday—so I had four miles to walk—so is a long ways. So very good, euh, went on an went on, an went on for a couple a years an euh, it happened that one night, special night—dat I was comin home—euh, I had to pass the graveyard every time I used to come down—but that special night—when I passed the graveyard—I look on, on my right side—here's a skeleton—standin dere—at my side. So I turns around—an I—looked at him like dat—an I wasn frightened—not a bit in the world—I said, "What do you wants?" E didn answer. So I said, "If you're under the protection of God," I said—"tell me what you wants," I said, "an I'll do it for you." So e don answer. So I said, "If you're under the protection of the devil," I said, "go on, in the name o God." So e disappeared—e'd *gone*. So it went on like dat—for to make the story shorter—I had to—to go over a mile—about a mile an a quarter or something like, maybe not dat, I don know—but anyhow, it's a long ways. And euh, e done dat—all the ways—I, I used to walk about twenty-five or tirty yards an here he was—so I talk to him—same thing as I said there—until I got down the shore here—right here in—dis—dis is the place—where I'm talkin now—so when I got down below to the shore there—mister Man! I looked like dat on the side, an here he was—about twenty-five feet high—I figured—he could be tirty—I don't know—but I figured about twenty-five feet—in the air, an e was about fifteen feet wide an de arms on dat an de, de bones—I could see the *bones* eh—Ah! my good heaven! I fell down—back firs—an I fell on a piece of wood with—a big piece o wood—on the bank dere now. So I fell on that—an I lost—conscioun—lost my senses—so a'right. By n by I don know how long I was dere, ten minutes, fifteen minutes, twenty minutes—I *don't* know—but I come to—an when I come to—de water was pourin off a me—*pourin* off—same like I took a bucket of water an throw it on me—I was *soakin*, soakin, soakin wet. So I looked around n nothing to see—*nothing*, nothing in the world, nothing, gone, disappeared, I couldn talk to him dat time—da's all—he frightened me. So okay. So I tried to get up—fall down—I use to get up—fall down—the leg—couldn get no use of my leg—went off, dey were gone, see, couldn—but after—you know, a while, well I got to, I got up on my leg anyhow—but I was goin up same like I was drunk y'know—goin this way an that way, zig-zag-gin—so I managed to come up to de house—God, I climb up dat hill up dere. An when I put my foot on the platform—for to open the door—I looks at the corner here he was dere again—like I seen him before you know—standin—standin dere—lookin at me dere, right to the corner by the farm. So I went in. So er, when I got in, that I was inside the door—my father jumped up an Mam an then Mam was cryin an er *c'est la petite affaire* [it's (not) a small matter]—oh they say, "What's wrong? What's wrong? What's wrong?" Now I didn want to say nothing because the ole man didn want to believe in ghostses, e didn *believe* in dat him. No. Well if I were to tell im well now, er, get mad, see. So er, I didn want to say notting. So I went to bed. But I never slept that night—ha! An I was two years after—dat I couldn go out in de night—I couldn g—in the night I couldn go outdoors! Right? Always to have somebody with me, my sisters or my brothers. But er, the way it went—but two years—two years an a half before I, I, I was—I got bold again. So dat passes. But now I composed a reel—an I said—ha! for to remember my—my fright—I'm gonna call it—"The Skeleton Reel." An da's the way it goes. [Emile plays his tune]

Commentary and notes

Emile had told this story for the American folklorist Kenneth S. Goldstein, who had accompanied me, in July 1978, to do some fieldwork among French Newfoundlanders. The story of the "Skeleton Reel" is one of the favourites of the many audiences for whom Emile has played, and with good cause. He presents his case, as one can see, without in any way protesting too loudly about the truthfulness of the happening. He does not force his experience upon the listener, but convinces by the simplicity and sincerity of his account.

There are several motifs incorporated in The Skeleton: E422.1.11.4, *Revenant as skeleton*; E261.4, *Ghost pursues man*; E265, *Meeting ghost causes misfortune*; E273, *Churchyard ghosts*; E293, *Ghosts frighten people (deliberately)*; compare also E265.1.1, *Blow received from a spirit at night; that side paralyzed*; and E443.5, *Ghost laid by adjuring it to leave "in the name of God"*, (even if, as in the case of Emile's skeleton, success was only temporary). See Ch. IV for another version of this story.

The last narrative is more amusing. Emile tells how, for the first time in his life, he composed a tune while dreaming:

EMILE'S DREAM

G.T.:   Emile, can you tell, can you tell the story there about, about Emile's Dream there now?

—Yes yes, I can tell it to you. Euh, it was last Spring—well we'll say in 1977. Euh—seventy-seven I mean to say—seventy seven? Yeah, seventy-seven. Well—I'd gone to bed that morning, it was in March, and that evening—and then euh, about three o'clock in the—after midnight—I dreamed—I dreamed a—a reel—and euh, it woke me up. I jumped up—from in my bed and then I run for the violin—I didn't have time to put my clothes on or nothing, I take off and—euh, I hook my violin and there I play it and play and play—and I played for over an hour there. And because it was the first one I had dreamed—in my life—I've dreamed I've been in dances and I've heard tunes and music and everything—but I never dreamed of, of, of composing a reel in my dream. Anyhow, that's good. I played the reel—and then when I had finished, well I say in case I forget it I'm gonna phone my sister—and I'm gonna ask her to tape it—the, the reel. Well, that's good. I phone her, and she gets up. Like they say it was *"Emergency"*—that's good. She says, "What's the matter?—*What is* wrong?" in, in English—she thought it was a, an English fellow talking. "Well," I say, "I've composed an eight and I'd like," I tell her, "for you euh, you to tell your boy to get up and to tape it for me." Well so all right—she tells her boy, he gets up and there he gets his machine and so I play and he tapes—that's good. There—I go back to bed. And so I wake up at seven o'clock in the morning. And I get up, light my stove and I pick up my violin—and I try—and I try to remember it—and I was trying—no! It's gone. It's gone. That's fine, so I phone—and I say euh, "Tell your boy," I tell her, "that he can put the tape on and he can give me a couple of notes." That's good. There. She tells him. So he gets up and then euh, he, he, put the receiver over it and I listen. *Two* notes and I say, "That's good, I' got it." There I hang up the, the telephone and I take my violin and I play it. Well, I say that's not bad—it's a dream, well, I say, I'm gonna call it—I'm gonna call it "a dream", I'm gonna call it "Emile's Dream". Like that, I say, it would be something, I say, to think about, you know, to have something in your mind to say, well Emile, he dreamed a reel—so, a, a reel. That's that. And it goes like this here. [He plays it]

Commentary and notes

This story by no means exhausts Emile's repertoire on the composition of his many tunes, a selection which are recorded on his first album, *Emile's Dream*. His second album, *Ça vient du Tchoeur/It come from the Heart*, combines a good selection of his compositions with the accompanying narratives, some in French, others in English, with a booklet containing texts and tunes.

It might have been fitting to attribute to this story the motif E722.2.5, *Saved soul leaps from body on hearing heavenly music*, but it would not be strictly accurate.

XIII

Original French Transcriptions

This chapter provides the texts as they appeared in the French edition of this work. It includes, in order, long quotations from chapters V and VI (indicated in the present study by an asterisk), the texts of tales told by Mrs. Blanche Ozon, and those told in French by Emile Benoit.

The purpose of providing the French texts is to allow the reader, should he or she desire, to compare them to my translations. Most readers of this edition will probably not be fluent in French, however, so these texts will at least allow them to *see* what Newfoundland French is like. They may then better comprehend the difficulties, not only of writing down an approximation of a hitherto purely oral form of French, but also the difficulties of rendering such French into a reasonable English equivalent, bearing in mind that the many forms of regional Newfoundland English also differ markedly at times from standard English.

The original French edition included tales and quotations in English. As a courtesy to French readers, French translations were offered. While all texts in the main body of this edition are in English, providing the original French serves as an equitable balance for a work which serves a potentially bilingual readership.

References preceding the extracts or tales are to the page on which each begins.

(p. 91)

J'tais pas gros. Et euh, i, le docteur a dit à mon père, i dit, "Pour sauver çte petit gamin-là," i dit, i dit, "tu vas ête obligé," i dit, "de tonde de la laine, de la laine de d'sus d'un mouton,"—et ça c'est dans mars—"et pis pas laver la laine—la quitter—comme alle est—et pis paquer ton enfant dedans," i dit, "pour dix-huit jours." Ienque ça sus moi. Et euh i dit, "Tu pourras pt-ête le sauver." Toujours i m'avont paqué dans la laine pis i m'ont tenu en'd'sous le poéle—un de les gros poéles, les *Waterloo* là. Et i m'ont ieu là pour dix-huit jours, tchinde le feu—pour tchinde la même chaleur vous savez pis euh—j'ai—j'ai ressuscité.

(p. 91)

G.T.:   Quoi faire que tu as quitté l'école après le grade trois là?

E.B.:   Bien, le temps tait dur à vive—et pis euh, moi j'tais le, le pus vieux de la famille.

G.T.:   Hm.

E.B.:   Pis mon père bien i portait l'*mail*—pis ça y prenait euh—trois et quate jours dans l'hiver pour—pour faire son *mail*, parce faulait qu'il alle de, à Clam Ban' Cove, jusqu'en bas au boute d'la Barre.

G.T.: Oui.

E.B.: A Long Point qu'il appelont. (Une vingtaine de kilomètres)

G.T.: Oui oui.

E.B.: Pis ça prenait trois-quate jours dans l'hiver parce qu'i y a des piles de neige, des piles de neige pis ç'ta, à choual et pis tu pouvais pas faire ça dans eune jornée—ç'ta impossibe.

G.T.: Fallait descende là pour pelleter, euh, pellayer—

E.B.: I faulait couper du bois.

G.T.: Oui.

E.B.: I faulait faire attention aux—animaux—

G.T.: Oui.

E.B.: Que j'avions. Comme ça j'pouvais pas aller à l'école—tout en grand arait péri.

G.T.: Oui oui.

E.B.: Comme ça que j'ai pas ieu d'école.

(p. 92)

G.T.: La, la première chose que t'avais fait ç'tait d'aller à la pêche avec ton père?

E.B.: Ouais.

G.T.: Tu avais tchel âge—douze ans?

E.B.: Euh... non—j'avais euh, j'avais neuf ans d'çte temps-là.

G.T.: Neuf ans.

E.B.: Quand j'ai té l'premier coup.

G.T.: Ç'tait euh...

E.B.: Ah—j'assayais à s'prende la morue à la faux mais j'ai pas pu. Mais—pis lui n'en prenait—pis j'sais pas quoi-ç-qu'i faisait ça que fait ça. Mais euh—oh, il a pris joliment de morue pis moi j'ai pas pu n'en prende ieune. Bien, ça, ç'tait bien. "Ben," i dit, "fait pas d'diffarence," i dit, "ça m'ersembe,"—i m'dit ça asteure là—j'ai pas oublié—i dit, "Ça fait pas d'diffarence," i dit "pt-ête bien," i dit, "le Bon Dieu," i dit, "va pt-ête bien te donner ieune comme ça," i dit, "c'est malaisé d'dire." T'sais? Toujours—i nageait—moi aussi j'nageais mais eune ptite paire d'avirons, j'mettais pas d'force mais dame assez j, j—toujours—i dit euh, i prend eune morue pis i l'jette par-dessus bord pis eune, eune morue ça, ça flotte et moi j'tais, j'nageais de—darrière et pis lui i nageait—devant hein? Pis j'avais l'dos viré à lui. I dit, "Garde-la, garde-la, garde-la sus—"—J'ergarde, garde la morue a flotte! *Holy Jaze* là je saute—j'saute à la mer moi!

G.T.: Heh!

E.B.: J'as trapé la morue!

G.T.: Heh!

E.B.: I m'a crocheté t'sais! Heh! I m'a crocheté par le bas des tchulottes pis m'a halé d'dans encore. Pis j'avais la morue! Ooh! J'tais tout trempe! Ac la tét ç'tait en-d'sous de l'eau et tout. Mais j'avais la morue.

G.T.: Ouais.

E.B.: "Là, y ois-tu? J't'ai dit," i dit. "Le Bon Dieu t'ara donné eune morue." Pis, ç'tait pas eune ptite fierté que j'avais Gerald, j'ai jamais oublié ça garde.

278

E.B.: Ça—euh, non. j'ai té, j'ai travaillé dans les bois—j'étais in, in coup—quand j'étais veuve—j'ai té pour cinq mois. J'étais *cookie*—dans l'bois.

G.T.: Ailloù, ça?

E.B.: A *Camp* Tchinze—i appellent ça—en bas d'Black Duck.

G.T.: Ah oui.

E.B.: Black Duck Siding.

G.T.: Oui.

E.B.: Ouais. J'étais là cinq mois parti. Et pis j'avais mes soeurs ici qui restaient avé, avec mes enfants, pis faisaient attention, comme ça.

G.T.: Étais-tu bien payé?

E.B.: Oh ben, j'ai euh, travaillé cinq mois—et j'ai venu à la maison avec six cents pièces.

G.T.: Six cents pièces.

E.B.: Ouais, pour cinq mois.

G.T.: Ç'tait pas pire pour ç'temps-là.

E.B.: Oh oui mais dame j'ai pas sorti à nulle part ni arien, j'ai...

G.T.: Non, non.

E.B.: J'ai gardé mon argent.

G.T.: Le samedi au souère, quoi-ç-que vous faisiez le samedi au souère?

E.B.: Ça jouait du violon pis là i faisiont des concerts, des, des, des *concert* là.

G.T.: Ouais.

E.B.: J'avions dans l'bout d'la *bunkhouse* et pis j'mettions des, des, des couvartes—en avant.

G.T.: Ouais.

E.B.: Pis là pou—m'en on—on s'arrangeait avec in, in cordage et pis—j'halions sus le cordage pour—fârmer les couvartes, j'halais sur l'cordage pou ouvrir les couvartes—quand qu'les—oh j'avais du *fun*.

G.T.: Tu avais toujours ton violon avec toi.

E.B.: Oh ouais ouais ouais. On faisait des, des, des, des ptits ramates [des bagaelles] à nous autes t'sais mais ç'tait des beaux concerts t'sais.

G.T.: Ouais.

E.B.: Pas d'danger! D'quoi nous faisions nous autes mêmes t'sais...

G.T.: Est-ce que le monde contiont des contes dans ces concerts-là?

E.B.: Uh non, non, oh non, non non. On est venu finir tout—passe...

G.T.: Des chansons pis des...

E.B.: Ouais, ouais—pis parler comme d'autes et euh, vous savez *performer comme d'aute monde.*

G.T.: Oui oui.

E.B.: Et so on... Oh! on avait du plaisir! Le monde en parle encore, les vieux t'sais.

G.T.: Ouais.

E.B.:   Ouais. J'avais du *fun*. Oh ieux avaient du *fun*, ieux—mais moi c'est mon plaisir moi asteure.

G.T.:   Oui oui.

E.B.:   Ça m'faisait du bien moi.

(p. 94)

G.T.:   Quand c'est que tu as commencé à euh, disons, quoi, travailler ac les bêtes là, arranger les bétes?

E.B.:   Oh bien c'était—dans l'temps d'mon père.

G.T.:   C'est ton père qui t'avait appris ça?

E.B.:   Ben i a—pas tout—pas tout—non, pas tout. Euh—i fais—i arrangeait les bétes, i les marquait et *so on*.

G.T.:   Oui.

E.B.:   Moi ben quand j'ai, je m'as marié, je m'ai mis à—à faire cela, la même *job* aussi.

G.T.:   Hm.

E.B.:   J'allais pas l'trouver—j'le faisais moi-méme.

G.T.:   Oui.

E.B.:   Et puis tout d'in coup i y avait in, ma grand-mère alle avait eune, eune vache—euh, alle allait aouère in veau—pis la vache tait malade et son côte est tout sor—sorti ois-tu?

G.T.:   Hm.

E.B.:   Et pis y avait mon onque Lecoure, Job Lecoure—i tait in, il avait in—live de docteur—mais dame j'pouvais pas ouère le live moi—parce que faulait tère—i faulait ête marié pou ça ois-tu. On pouva pas ouère ça d'ces temps-là.

G.T.:   Non.

E.B.:   Non—toute caché entor-z-eux. Bien çte vache-là a pouvait pas aouère son veau parce que tout son côte tait sorti—pis la vieille a mis à—*smoother*—et pis a voulait aouère le veau. Bien euh—le vieux Tacannou lui, c'est—i croyait qu'i tait d'quoi aussi—mais il a pas venu m'donner la main—et je... Bien c'est pour ça qu'a voulait—pis ça donnait que ç'tait eune taure.

G.T.:   Ouais.

E.B.:   Ouais. I y avait eune grosse *job* là. Mais ça c'est mes, mes gros, ma grosse entorprise.

G.T.:   Et...

E.B.:   Pis après ça.

G.T.:   Tchel âge t'avais quand tu as fait ça?

E.B.:   J'avais vingt-deux ans.

G.T.:   Vingt-deux ans... Et après ça tu as fait toutes sortes d'affaires avec les bêtes.

E.B.:   Après ça—fait toutes sortes d'affaires.

(p. 95)

G.T.:   Tchelle sorte de maladies i avions le monde le pus souvent, que tu pourrais djérir?

280

E.B.: Bien y avait euh, y avait eune tapée d'monde poitrinaire et toutes sortes d'affaires comme ça... et euh—

G.T.: Quoi-ç-que tu ieux donnais?

E.B.: Ben—i vouliont pas l'prende moi j'ai, j'tais poitrinaire aussi pis je m'ai djéri.

G.T.: Oui.

E.B.: Et mon père et ma mère m'a pas dit d'el faire mais euh j'savais que j'tais poitrinaire ben j'ai attrapé eune euh, eune purisie—et pis euh, ej savais qu'ej tais poitrinaire.

G.T.: Oui.

E.B.: Bien là—j'ai té dans la fôssière à la côte là pis je—ej pêchions dans le temps là et pis j, j'sauvions tous les foies d'morue.

G.T.: Oui.

E.B.: Pis j'mettions ça dans des, dans des barils j'appelons—

G.T.: Hm.

E.B.: Des fossieres, tcheque chose comme ca--et pis j'quittions ca a fonde le soleil pis la on prenait, c', on tirait l'huile la aus de d'sus pis dame on avait—vingt-cinq sous le, le le gallon.

G.T.: Oui.

E.B.: Dans çtés temps-là. Euh c'est, ç'tait beaucoup.

G.T.: Hm.

E.B.: Ben—c'est bien. A çte—çt hiver-là ça m'a c—le coup j'ai été attaqué de poitrinaire—ç'tait dans mars—dans ma jeunesse—m'en as dix, dix, dix-sept ans j'avais çte temps-là—oh euh, joliment de, de, de seize et dix-sept et dix-huit ans qui m'arrivait là—

G.T.: Hm.

E.B.: J'ai fait en masse pis y en a en masse qui m'a arrivé et toute en grand, ça, ç'a té euh, in *blockade* t'appelles là euh... C'est bien. Là. J'dis j'sus poitrinaire. Et j'm'en vas à la côte—euh—pis, j'ergarde dans l'baril pis ç'ta—Gerald—c'est nouère, nouère, pareil—comme de l'encre.

G.T.: Hm.

E.B.: Là—pis les mouches dessus là! Ç'tait—plein d'mouches. Ça c'est vrai—ça qu'ej dis là là, c'est pas d'menteries dedans.

G.T.: Non.

E.B.: C'est vrai, c'est toute la varité là qu'ej dis là.

G.T.: Hm hm.

E.B.: J'ai regardé ça. *Lovely*! Heh! Mourir! Ha ha! Comme i disont ah? *Live or die.*

G.T.: Right.

E.B.: Ej prends ma bouteille—j'avais eune bouteille comme ça ici j'avais *my son*—

G.T.: Oui.

E.B.: Trois-quarts—eune bouteille de *t'ree half-pint* qu'i l'appelont.

G.T.: Hm.

281

E.B.:	Pis j'pousse les mouches de côté pis j'la pousse dedans—pis justement pour prende le lhuile là. Pis ç'tait comme du *coaltar* hein.
G.T.:	Oui oui.
E.B.:	Pis ça vidait, ça vidait, ça vient s'emplisait, s'emplisait et tout d'in coup tchiens! La bouteille pleine. Là j'm'en viens à la maison pis je la mis sous l'châssis—droite comme ça. Et l'endemain matin—je m'ai levé—la bouteille ici—tait—tout ça là ici en d'sous là—la motché d'la bouteille—a tait tout blanc pareil comme in—ç'tait pas blanc—ç'tait mangnière de jaune et d'quoi d'même hein?
G.T.:	Hm.
E.B.:	Et tout l'reste là—eç tait de, de l'enque nouère. Du charbon, heh! Là! Ej prends eune ptite tchuillerée comme ça ici—pis j'le vide—pis je l'avale.
G.T.:	Le nouère ou—le, le clair?
E.B.:	Le nouère!
G.T.:	T'as—t'as—
E.B.:	J'l'ai pas brâssé ni arien du tout, je l'ai quitté—
G.T.:	Non!
E.B.:	Comme ça, j'ai pris le nouère.
G.T.:	Hm.
E.B.:	Bien mon ami—j'ai tout brûlé ma bouche en-d'dans—et c'est pareil comme j'arais pris eune bouchée de l'acide. Aïe, toute la jornée ça venait *back* vous savez, c'est euh, l'odeur hein.
G.T.:	Hm.
E.B.:	Ah mon cher homme ah ç'ta—i faut in, i faut in estomac pou prende d'quoi d'même—euh... y a parsonne d'aute qui pou, qui pourrait l'attaquer—non non. Assayez-vous à la, non non, i pouviont pas. Et j'ai fait ça pour neu matinées—sept matinées—et la septième matinée—j'tais en train d'déjeuner—et pis ej tais comme ça ici—m'assis à la tabe—pis j'ai fait ça comme ça ici [se pince la peau du poignet]—ça—ç'etait—ç'tait *huileux*, lhuileux, il ava, le, le dos de ma main là—hein?
G.T.:	Oui oui.
E.B.:	Pis là—in *spell*—dis, on arait dit in cordon de—la droche eh, de la, de la, l'odeur là.
G.T.:	Oui.
E.B.:	Là j'lève ma chemise comme ça—pis j'ramâsse in ptit euh, morceau de, de bois qu'i y avait sus la place—pis j'fais ça comme ça—et quand qu j'arrivais là—y avait la grosseur de ça—en travers d'ma main ici là.
G.T.:	Oui.
E.B.:	La droche eh? C'est comme la couleur de l'enque qu'i tait—en-dessous là de l'huile là.
G.T.:	Oui oui.
E.B.:	Comprends-tu ça asteure?
G.T.:	Oui oui.
E.B.:	Oui.
G.T.:	Oui.

E.B.: Là. J'ai pris ça pour neu jours—neu matinées—si ma mère sera en vie—
alle est pas en vie, alle est partie—mais si a sera en vie—a pourrait t'dire—
a pourrait t'dire. Pis j'portais des, des hardes de d'sous de laine—

G.T.: Hm.

E.B.: Parce le docteur euh, avait ieu dit à mon père—de me mette sous la
laine—euh, pas mette de coton sus moi—jamais! Je n'en ai jamais usé d'la
laine pour le reste de mes jours.

G.T.: Hm.

E.B.: [...] Toujours c'est bien. La neuvième jornée—ouais—pis parsonne m'a dit
parsonne dans l'monde—m'a dit de faire ça—la neuvième jornée, j'dis à
ma mère—j'dis— "Ajord'hui—ej m'en vas asteure," je dis, "prende des
purges." J'm'en prende in patchet de—de—*salts* eh, les, les, des *Epsom
Salts* qu'il appelont.

G.T.: Ouais.

E.B.: C'est pour les bétes, c'est pas pour du monde—mais i aviont ça par ptits
patchets, j'crois qu'ç'tait eune once.

G.T.: Oui oui.

E.B.: Par patchet—eune once. Bien—ej prends deux, deux... Bien, c'est bien. Là
j'prends ma, ma purge—asteure vlà comment, comment j'ai fait.

G.T.: Hm.

E.B.: J'prends mon patchet de *salt*, ej prends deux *pill*, des, des *Dr. Chase
Kidney Liver Pills* qu'i l'appeliont de çte temps-là. Ç'tait en ptits barils là.

G.T.: Oui.

E.B.: Ej prends deux—pis je l'ai quitté là pour—comme cinq heures—pis là
j'prends le patchet d'*salt*—pis j'le cale par-dessus ac in verre d'eau. Là.
L'endemain matin—non, pas l'endemain matin, c'est, ç'tait pas trop
longtemps—mais mon ami—euh, Gerald—ça fait peur quoi a sorti
d'dans moi—ça fait peur. Et si j'arais pas fait ça—j'aras mouri—ça
m'arait tué.

G.T.: Quoi-ç-qui avait sorti?

E.B.: D'la droche et de la, toute, toute, toutes sortes d'affaires moi, ej peux pas
t'dire—j'peux pas—y avait pas d'sang don. Mais le resse—oh! C'est
effroyabe!

G.T.: Hm.

E.B.: Là. Là j'dis asteure là à ma mère—a va bouillir de l'eau—pis j'avions les
grosses bâilles là t'sais, ça tchenait euh comme treize à tchinze gallons,
quatorze gallons, tcheque chose comme ça t'sais des grosses bâilles.

G.T.: Oui oui.

E.B.: J'avions pour les, les, pour nous laver d'dans eh?

G.T.: Oui oui.

E.B.: C'tait en galavanaille là. Toujours c'est bien. Bouillit l'eau—pis a met in
ptit peu d'moutarde dedans, d'la moutarde heh—d'la moutarde sec.

G.T.: Hm.

E.B.: Eune ptite tchuillerée de moutarde sec... Et là j'me saque dedans—pis
j'tire mes hardes—pis j'me fous dedans—ben, avec du savon—de huile de
morue asteure—j'avions pas d'savon, de, de, de, de t'*ilet* soap, les, les, les

toilette là, neh! Non—s—avions ça avec du, d'la cende et pis de, de, de—du huile à morue puis on bouillait ça ensembe avec eune canne de, de, de, gellac—*Gillett lye* qu't'appeles là.

G.T.: Hm.

E.B.: Y avait in lion d'sus hein—hm. Pis ça ça tchuisait la, la—pis on s'lavait avec ça. Ho! Hah hah! Pis les filles qui tiont—faut aller les ouère heh heh heh! C'est bien—là. Là! Ma maman a garde mes hardes, a dit, "Mon cher enfant," a dit—a dit, "vas-tu brû, brûler ça!" A dit, "Ça," a dit, "jamais, jamais," a dit, "j'vas—j'tirons l'odeur d'là-d'dans." Pis a faulait qu'a brochait d'çtés temps-là, brocher les hardes de d'sous de laine hein.

G.T.: Hm.

E.B.: Ç'tait dur, t'sais eh, là! Ben c'est ça. Quoi faire eh? Ben a brûle les hardes—par ptits morceaux—parce ça l'ara foutu tout le, le, complet d'dans—bien la maison arait pris en feu.

G.T.: Oui.

E.B.: C'est bien. Là. Gerald—me lave comme i faut—ça m'a pris deux bâilles d'eau—après que j'tais lavé—y avait bien in doigt comme ça—par dessus—ç'tait encore le *stuff* que j't'ai montré là—hah?

G.T.: La droche.

E.B.: Oui. La droche là—hein—sus l'eau, qui flottait sus l'eau eh? Ç'ta ça encore.

G.T.: Qui est sorti d'ton corps.

E.B.: Sorti d'mon corps—la chance du Bon Dieu—sorti—sorti d'mon corps—pis j'pouvais laver le resse après qu'la purge eh?

G.T.: Hm.

E.B.: T'sais eh? Ç'tait tout là hein? pis parsonne m'a dit hein? Quoi faire hein?

G.T.: Hm. Ça t'avait djéri.

E.B.: Hein?

G.T.: Ça t'avait djéri.

E.B.: Mais oui—pis—j'tais *a'right* après.

G.T.: Oui.

E.B.: Ouais.

G.T.: Pas croyabe eh.

E.B.: Ouais, c'est dur à crouère—mais c'est vrai.

(p. 99)

G.T.: Et tu as ieu du monde mourir qui tiont poitrinaire.

E.B.: Ouais—ma femme tait poitrinaire pis j'y ai dit—"Fais que j'ai fait," pis j'y dis, "tu vas—

G.T.: A voulait pas—

E.B.: J'y ai donné eune tchuillerée alle a pris-t-in ptit peu, *holy Moses*! Ça a mis à pleurer alle m'a dit, "J'vas mourir," a dit, "parce j'peux pas la prende." Là.

G.T.: Hm.

E.B.: Là j'dis, "Oui, moi aussi," j'dis.

G.T.: Tchel âge qu'alle avait quand qu'alle a mouri?

284

E.B.: Alle avait euh—aussi bien dire trente ans, vingt, vingt-neuf ans, voyez,   vingt-neuf aller sus trente ans.

G.T.: Hm.

E.B.: Bien alle a mouri. Pis si a m'ara couté—pis n'en prende—

G.T.: Hm.

E.B.: Pis aouère le *pluck* là—mais alle a pas ieu d'*pluck* mais c'est ça.

   (p. 100)

E.B.: I y avait mon frère là, il ava arrivé ici in coup avec la, la mâchouère câssée de deux places.

G.T.: Oui.

E.B.: Le nez fendu, la bouche fendue—

G.T.: Joachim là?

E.B.: Joachim.

G.T.: Oui.

E.B.: Pis ergarde l'ouvrage j'ai fait d'sus là eh.

G.T.: C'est toi qui as fait tout ça?

E.B.: C'est moi qu'a fait ça.

G.T.: Comment qu'tu as fait?

E.B.: Ma, j'ai mis sa, sa mâchouère ensembe—

G.T.: Oui.

E.B.: L'ai bandé et toute eh?

G.T.: Il a pas pu manger pendant in boute.

E.B.: Oh non—i—i avait qu'in-in bouillon don, j'faisais du bouillon.

G.T.: Hm.

E.B.: Ouais, oh ouais.

G.T.: Comment qu'il a ieu fait ça? Comment qu'il a fait ça?

E.B.: Il a fait ça, il a tapé dans, dans eune planche, pis l'chval l'a *kické* a—

G.T.: Oh mon Dieu! Oui.

E.B.: Commencer ici.

G.T.: Oui.

E.B.: Le nez coupé là. J'ai gardé comme i faut euh, eune bonne *job*.

   (p. 100)

E.B.: Asteure mon oncle Jean il avait eune, eune cartouche—qui a câssé dans la main, i-z-y a défoncé la main—i tait en train t'sais eh, pis i corchait la capsule parce qu'alle avait—raté j'allons dire eh.

G.T.: Hm hm.

E.B.: Pis quand qu'i la hale ça l'a fait partir—mais dame i y avait pas d'plomb dedans.

G.T.: Hm.

E.B.: Mais elle a defoncé pis ç'a toute déchiré sa main, son pouce ici est tombé en bas là—

G.T.:	Hm.
E.B.:	Toute la peau elle est partie de d'sus et toute. J'ai été le charcher en bas à la Barre—
G.T.:	Hm.
E.B.:	Avec mon chval—pis j'l'ai amené ici. Pis je l'ai, j'avais des, des, des, des *salt* et pis j'avais du sel—j'ai tout mis ça dans de l'eau bouillante—pis je l'ai fait s—*soaker* sa main là-d'dans.
G.T.:	Oui.
E.B.:	La sueur frette y coulait sus la fidjure.
G.T.:	Oui.
E.B.:	Ah! mon ami ç'tait pas joli. I y avait deux, deux soeurs, Bernadette et pis Marie, elle est en vie ielle—Bernadette est morte—et i l'avont regardé pis il ont evanoui ieusses.
G.T.:	Hm.
E.B.:	Pouviont pas le *fécer* [angl. to face].
G.T.:	Et tu l'as cousu après.
E.B.:	J'y ai pas coudu, non.
G.T.:	Non?
E.B.:	Non non. J'ai toute—lavé comme i faut—
G.T.:	Oui.
E.B.:	Pis j'ai remis son pouce ensemble—pis j'ai tenu à laver ça, je l'ai t—j'ai regardé par-d'sus lui pour onze jours—mais dame j'pouvais pas arien faire—pis la pêche s'en venait et pis toute en grand—
G.T.:	Oui.
E.B.:	Pis faulait qu'ej gagne ma vie aussi moi.
G.T.:	Oui oui, oui oui.
E.B.:	Pis j'l'ai amené à l'hôpital. Et pis euh—j'allais avec lui, le docteur a regardé sa main pis il a demandé comment longtemps que ç'tait fait. Ben y avait onze jours. Çte journée-là—j'l'ai amené au Crossing. Le, le vieux là disait plusse qu'in coup. "Tu m'as sauvé la vie toi," i dit. Ha! Il aurait oublié jamais ça, i dit.
G.T.:	Oui oui.
E.B.:	Qu'av—m'avez sauvé—y avait sauvé la vie.
G.T.:	Hm.
E.B.:	Pis le docteur a gardé sa main. Ben i dit, i dit, "C'est-i toi qu'a fait l'ouvrage?" Et j'y dis, "Oui, c'est moi." Mais i dit, "Y a pas d'docteur ou arien," i dit, "qui peut faire mieux que t'as fait."
G.T.:	Eh ben! Ça c'est in beau compliment, eh?
E.B.:	Il a dit ça t'sais, ouais. I dit, "Ça c'est d'la bonne ouvrage," i dit.
G.T.:	Ouais.
E.B.:	I dit, "I y a pas d'câgrane dedans, *no gangarene in it, nothin.*"
G.T.:	Hm hm.
E.B.:	"*It's natural.*" Ben là i l'ont gardé à l'hôpital pis i n'avont coupé des morceaux de sa fesse pis il avont—
G.T.:	Oui.

E.B.: Empli sa main ois-tu.

G.T.: Oui.

E.B.: Ben moi j'pouvais pas faire ça.

G.T.: Non non.

E.B.: Mais euh—je l'ai—je l'ai sauvé.

G.T.: My God!

E.B.: Ah!?

G.T.: Oui oui.

E.B.: Selon pour moi et il arait mouri là. Cancrène arait pris dedans pis il ara mouri.

(p. 102)

E.B.: J'avais ma soeur—euh, j'tais à m'greyer çte souerée-là—

G.T.: Tu as, tu as fait naîte in enfant.

E.B.: Oh ouais.

G.T.: C'était pour qui ça? Tchel enfant que tu as fait naîte? C'était—

E.B.: Oh—oui, oui, c'est ma soeur.

G.T.: Ta soeur.

E.B.: Ma soeur—je l'ai pas ené—j'ai pas ené l'enfant—mais euh, je l'ai mis sus la route.

G.T.: Oui. Oui.

E.B.: A pouvait pas aouère son enfant, a tait deux jours et deux nuits dans l', l'agonie là, à souffrir.

G.T.: Oui oui.

E.B.: Eh? Pis j'ai té, alle a, alle a demandé pour moi parce que—j'sus son pârrain—

G.T.: Hm.

E.B.: Avec ça—pis son frère.

G.T.: Mais t'arais pu— [...]

E.B.: Toujours j'ai été, euh, pis là j'y ai dit, j'y dis, "Si tu restes là—i vont coucher plus tard," j'dis, "mais—tu vas ête partie."

G.T.: Oui oui.

E.B.: Mais j'y dis, "Tu vas ête bigée d'dégager de d'là,"—j'dis, "si tu veux aouère ton enfant."

G.T.: Hm.

E.B.: "Non," a dit, "j'peux pas."—"Ben," ej dis, "si a peut pas—si a peut m'acouter j'm'en vas. J'm'en vas *back*, m'en vas *back*."

G.T.: Oui.

E.B.: J'y dis, "Tu vas pas aller loin." Mais a dit, "Quoi-ç-qu'i faut qu'ej faise?" Mais j'y dis, "Faut qu'tu t'lèves au de d'là." Là j'prends la couvarte pis j'la pâsse sus la place. Là. J'dis, "Viens-t'en."—"Non non, j'peux pas." Ben j'dis, "Viens-t-en!" J'dis, "Peux pas ou qu'tu peux—c'est ça!" Et là j'dis, "Le Bon Dieu a souffri pou nous autes aussi—pis i l'a pris—" Bien j'dis, "Faites-lui i dit pis prends-là aussi. Vlà c'est toute."

G.T.: Hm.

287

E.B.:	Maman asteure a entendu ça, les cris, "Hôa-ta-coin-coin-coin-coin-coin-coin!"—mais la vlà a s'couche, la couche. Pis là j'me mets—a tait couchée la fidjure en l'air, la fille là sus la place—sous la couvarte. Pis là Gerald, a va aussi vrai comme i y a Bon Dieu—j'ai commencé à peser sus son estomac là eh—
G.T.:	Oui.
E.B.:	Pis j'le fais—pis j'ai attendu—quointe! Alle a parti en bas—il a parti, a parti, eh—
G.T.:	Oui oui.
E.B.:	Pis là j'la quitte. Pou l'ouvrage—j'ai pas té *busynose* arien du tout moi.
G.T.:	Non non.
E.B.:	M'en vas en bas pis—devant l'mirouère. Pis quand j'tais devant le mirouère pour arranger mon *neck-tie*, faut j'm'en allais moi—à courser ah ah! Tais veuve, eh, tais veuve.
G.T.:	Oui oui.
E.B.:	"Oueh!" Elle! Déjà!
G.T.:	Ouais.
E.B.:	Pis j'y dis ça i faut croire—euh déjà, l'temps d'venir en bas—
G.T.:	Oui.
E.B.:	Pis arranger mon *neck-tie*—après trois ou quate minutes là—
G.T.:	Quoi-ç-tu l'avais fait ç'tait, t'avais retourné le bébé.
E.B.:	Ouais ouais ouais, là, i tait, i tait d'travers.

(p. 103)

E.B.:	Ben. Si j'arais ieu l'instruction Gerald, j'arais té euh—in docteur.
G.T.:	Ou, oh oui.
E.B.:	J'arais été—*surgery* ou—
G.T.:	C'est ç'que tu arais—
E.B.:	J'arais été den, in dentiste, ou j'arais été quoi.
G.T.:	C'est que tu arais voulu faire.
E.B.:	Oh oui, c'est ça d'mon tchoeur ça.
G.T.:	Oui oui, oui oui oui, oui. Pour djérir l'monde.
E.B.:	T'aras pu s'couper en deux, ça c'est pas d'diffarence pour moi ça. Ça j'arais, j't'arais coudu ensembe.
G.T.:	T'arais—t'arais voulu ête ça—in docteur.
E.B.:	Oh oui! J'arais voulu ête ça!
G.T.:	Oui oui.
E.B.:	Oh j'arais voulu ête ça. Oui oui oui. J'arais voulu, ç'tait mon tchoeur ça.
G.T.:	Oui oui oui, oui oui oui.
E.B.:	Ça m'a, ça m'faisait grand plaisir.

(p. 104)

E.B.:	Ben Gerald, j'm'en vas, ej m'en te dire eune ptite histouère par là—de mon intention de ma vie—euh, j'ai joué en masse pour arien—et toute mon intention tait bien, l'Église eh, l'Église—dans ma—ma qualité de la religion qu'ej sus dedans. Euh—mon Église. Bien, j'allais jouer—bien

288

fatigué—pis là jouer et jouer et jouer, jouer et joue. Bien ça fa arien—ben j'l'ai fait pour mon Église. Mais jouer ac les autes là il aviont des—des amoureux, des, des filles et *so on*, ej parlons ici et là pis moi j'pouvais pas aouère de, faulait qu'ej joue moi, et joue et joue et joue pis là faulait qu'ej marche après six et sept milles—dans la vâse et toute—ben j'disais, "Ben c'est pour l'Église."

G.T.: Hm.

E.B.: Pis tout d'in coup—i y a ieu trois ou quate-z-églises qui taient euh pour ieusses bâtir pis ç'tait déchiré encore—et tout d'in coup tchiens, y en a eune église qui s'bâtit—que j'ai travaillé tant pour—Gerald—et tout d'in coup vlà qu'in homme qui s'en vient pis i dit, "T'as eune *job* sus l'église? Viens-t-en travailler."

G.T.: Hm.

E.B.: Pis i tiont là comme ça des vers pour in ouvrage là—moi j'ai pas té charcher pour l'ouvrage—il ont venu m'trouver.

G.T.: Hm.

E.B.: L'église, va-t-en, travaille chez l'église. Et j'ai travaillé, j'ai été.

G.T.: Hm.

E.B.: Pis après ça mon *luck* a changé après ça—nah!

    (p. 107)

G.T.: Et si je me trompe pas Émile, un des grands plaisirs, dans ta vie, c'est de faire rire le monde.

E.B.: Ah oui, ouais, ah oui, c'est vrai ça—c'est vrai ça.

G.T.: T'as tout l'temps té d'même.

E.B.: J'ai—faire rire le monde et pis assayer d'mette le monde hereux. C'est euh, c'est ma vie ça.

G.T.: Ouais. Et tu feras n'importe quoi pour l'faire.

E.B.: Ouais, ouais, ouais, je—me garâcherais à la mer si j'pouvais vous faire assez, vous faire rire.

    (p. 107)

E.B.: Pis tout-ç-t'attendais ç'tait chez l'diable. Tu sais qu'ej pense à ça moi—*souvent*, Gerald. J'ai tendu dire moi, c'est dans mon temps t'sais—

G.T.: Hm.

E.B.: Plusse que tu nommes le nom du diable, pus proche qu'i vient.

G.T.: Hm.

E.B.: Asteure tu prends toutes les, les, les apôtes qu'i y a asteure. Mais c'est pas souvent qu'i vont dire—le diabe. I vont pt-ête bien dire les, *the Evil* eh, *Evil Spirit* eh?

G.T.: Hm.

E.B.: Mais c'est pas souvent—mais d'çtés temps-là—mais bon sang d'la vie tu peux pas prende vent mais *tu allais* chez l'diabe! Mais le diabe va t'aouère! Le diabe tait là et, le diabe te course—pis i ouoyont toutes sortes d'affaires, toutes sortes de, de, de—euh—sais-tu j'pense à moi-même des fois ois-tu, euh, euh, j', j'ai pas d'instruction—

G.T.: Hm-hm.

289

E.B.: Mais l'instruction compte pas—quoi-ç-qui vient dans la tête là. Eh?

G.T.: C'est juste ça, oui.

E.B.: I tait, i tait assez nommé—qu'i-z-y disent—quasiment les prende en charge.

G.T.: Ouais.

E.B.: Ouais! Mais asteure i quittont trantchille. Y a plus arien asteure.

G.T.: Ouais.

E.B.: T'entends plus parsonne dire mais j'ai vu ci hier au soir, j'ai vu ça hier au soir. T'entends plus arien. Eh?

G.T.: Oui.

E.B.: I l'ont quitté trantchille. Tu sais—j'dis ça à Rita des fois aussi là—ej devrions pas euh—nommer le nom de, de çt homme-là.

G.T.: Ouais.

E.B.: J'devrions pas y nommer son nom du tout.

G.T.: Oui oui.

E.B.: Non, j'devrons quitter trantchille. Là.

G.T.: Oui oui.

E.B.: C'est mon *idée* asteure là.

G.T.: Oui oui, j'comprends.

E.B.: Tu sais ça qu'ej veux dire eh. Devrons quitter trantchille. Comme ça bien i nous quittera trantchille aussi—i nous gardera clair.

(p. 113)

G.T.: Ç'tait euh, tchel moment de l'année où i—commenciont à—aller veiller?

E.B.: Oh—quand ça arrivait dans l'alentour de, d'octobe, de novembe, ça commençait de... ouais.

G.T.: Et pis ça allait jusqu'à, jusqu'à quand, jusqu'à avril?

E.B.: Oh ça allait jusque dans avril, oui, ouais. Asteure la Carême oh dame, y avait pas arien comme ça ois-tu, ç-tait abandonné toute en grand pour la Carême.

G.T.: Oui.

E.B.: Ça dansait pas, ça, ça—y avait arien, arien qui bougeait.

G.T.: Oui oui.

E.B.: Mais dame quand ça venait, le—jour de Pâques, ah ben dame là, là—*gee*! Là c'est des coups d'fusil, big-et-di-bang! C'est pareil comme des noces.

G.T.: Oui oui.

E.B.: Oh, ça, ça c'est du plaisir. I vont tirer in coup d'fusil ici, pis n'attendait in coup d'fusil là-bas et in aute coup d'fusil là-bas et euh—ç'tait pareil comme eune djerre mon ami. Heh!

G.T.: Heh! Ouais.

E.B.: Tout l'monde avait eune barrique de vin ou d'quoi d'même ou eune barrique de bière de fait pis ça faisait...

G.T.: Ç'tait la plus grosse fête dans ç'temps-là qu'asteure.

E.B.: Oh oui—asteure ben il allont aux *clubs* et *so on*—mais çte temps-là ben on restait tout à la maison—no allait chez les oisins, chez, ici et là vous savez, et pis...

G.T.: Et quand qu'i, disons qu'il ara ieu une veillée, ici à souère, à tchelle heure le monde arait ieu venu—pour commencer ça?

E.B.: Oh—ç'tait—ç'tait avant la nuit ici.

G.T.: Oui.

E.B.: Ouais. Ç'arrivait à l'entour de six heures, de cinq heures, de—ça boivait pis ça dansait pis—mais asteure—ça prend dix ou onze heures en nuit avant qu'le monde commence à bouger.

G.T.: Oui oui.

E.B.: Mais asteure dans mon temps moi ç'tait toute—pis ça allait jusqu'au jour le matin.

G.T.: Oui. Et le monde, il arait ieu fait des *games* de cartes ou...

E.B.: Oh oui oui. Ouais, ouais. Faut qu'tu vas bouère comme ça à faire, faire la, la noce de même, i jouiont aux cartes—oh oui.

(p. 114)

G.T.: Quand tu tais gamin—y avait-i beaucoup de veillées?

E.B.: Oh oui, oui—ben—eune fois par semaine—et des fois deux fois par semaine. Des veillées—oh oui.

G.T.: Dans l'hiver.

E.B.: Dans l'hiver, ouais.

G.T.: Oui.

E.B.: Et des fois des ouoyageurs—i venaient de la Grand'Terre, y en avait du Cap et ça ouoyageait l'idée d'venir bien ça passait à la maison pis euh, là, le, le bonhomme i laimait les contes. Pis là i l—euh, i faisait conter des contes. Bien asteure moi j'tais gamin—j'acoutais—pis j'les ramâssais. Mais i y en avait—n'en savais joliment des contes, eune tapée d'contes— mais j'en ai noublié eune tapée vous savez—parce que...

G.T.: Le monde contait...

E.B.: Pas, pas, pas, d'—continué la, la, la pratique, continué la pratique—mais ça, ça...

G.T.: Quand qu'i euh, quand qu'i y avait une veillée, y arait ieu combien du monde euh—dans la maison?

E.B.: Oh—la famille.

G.T.: La famille.

E.B.: La famille, oh oui.

G.T.: Et...

E.B.: C'est bien rare qu'i y avait des, d'autes qui venaient vous savez parce qu'i taient tout occupés ici et là et i pâssiont des veillées vous savez—n'en— de place en place—i n'en ont pt-ête bien té asteure chez euh, j'allons dire chez, chez mon onque ou d'quoi d'même. Ben il ont tenu aller là—ont té bien eune vingtaine ou eune trentaine de zeux—pis quasiment tous les souères i tiont là.

G.T.: Oui.

291

E.B.: Pis après in boute là i changiont d'place, là il alliont dans in—aute maison pis là—ça, ça jouait d'la musique et...

(p. 115)

G.T.: Tu m'as dit là que t'avais oublié joliment de contes.

E.B.: Ah oui, j'ai oublié eune tapée.

G.T.: J'sais c'est parce qu'i y a pus la pratique de ça—mais t'as—tu t'as souvenu de—de certains contes. Quoi faire que tu t'as souvenu de, disons, de la Montagne Nouère ou euh, ou les, la Bête à Sept Tétes, ces contes-là, plutôt que d'autres contes? Quâ faire que tu as gardé ces contes-là dans ta téte?

E.B.: Parce que je les ai contés un peu plus souvent que les autes, vous savez.

G.T.: Oui, oui, mais—quand, quand est-ce que tu les contes? Quand c'est que tu les contes?

E.B.: Ben, quand qu'ej vas comme ça vous savez—d'in—ou clair—d'la compagnie qui vient pis i m'demandont de conter in conte—des fois les ouoyageurs—comme vous et *so on*.

G.T.: Oui oui, oui oui. Mais avant là, quand qu'i y avait pas beaucoup d'monde comme moi qui veniont...

E.B.: Oh ben oui, bien ouais.

G.T.: De St. John's ou n'importe ailloù mais—quand qu'i y avait ienque des Français.

E.B.: Oh bien, on, on avait, on boivait la goutte pis euh, tout d'in coup bien iun "Mets là, donnez-nous là, allons, in ptit conte, allez!" "Ben là, pis c'est ça, ben." "Donne-nous la Bête à Sept Tétes, donne-nous-le, enouoie-nous-le..."

G.T.: I demandiont les contes—par leus noms.

E.B.: Oh ouais ouais, ouais ouais, oh! ouais, ouais. Ouais.

(p. 116)

G.T.: Pis euh, alors à ç'moment-là i, i y avait des, des gens qui, qui tiont connus pour ête de bons conteurs?

E.B.: Oh oui, oh oui, oui oui.

G.T.: Dis-moi les noms de...

E.B.: Ben i y avait iun qui s'appelait euh—Jack Tourout.

G.T.: Oui.

E.B.: Pis y avait in aute qui s'appelait euh, euh... Narcisse Chaisson—ça c'est in beau conteur de contes aussi—et pis euh et son frère euh, Julien, Julien, Jules qu'i l'appeliont, Julien Chaisson—i tait in bon conteur de contes aussi. Oui euh, français pis anglais. Oh c'est, c'est eune belle compagnie— i compreniaient pas la motché d'quoi-ç-qu'i disait vous savez mais dame ç, ç'allait—pis ça sonnait, pis c'est ça.

G.T.: Tchi-ç-qui, tchi-ç-qui comprenait pas la moitié?

E.B.: Euh, ben, c'est euh...

G.T.: Le monde?

E.B.: Le monde, ouais, nous autes, moi et mon frère j'avions té chez euh, euh comment-ç-qu'i vous l'appelle euh, l'appelle—Julien, Julien Chaisson. Il

292

avait eune, eune cruche de, de—de bière de fait—et pis euh, i nous a
donné chaque in coup—mais lui c'est déjà sus l'tchoeur—*spree*. Bien j'y
avons demandé pour chanter eune chanson—euh, i s'mit. Là, i chante.
Ah! i tait là pis i sautait d'bord en bord dans la, sus la place, bien j'avons
manqué d'mourir moi et mon frère, mon frère Joachim, bien, bien, bien,
bien—ç'tait pas trop dur à comprendre, dans son tchoeur, son amour et
pis, c'est ça—mais le reste c'est pas, y avait pas de, pas moyen
d'comprendre arien du tout—mais dame—ç'allait!

G.T.: Euh...

E.B.: Pis là ej demandons, i dit ça i voulait des chansons anglaises? Ouais! J'sais
des chansons anglaises! J'te pense! i dit. Pis là i chantait là aussi—pis c'est
"toute mon amour", "*my heart and my love*" an "*broke my heart*" pis le reste
c'est [Émile chante des paroles déformées, délibérément]—"*broke my
heart*"—d'quoi d'même, t'sais! Des ramages—des, des—mais c'est du
fun don!

G.T.: Oui oui.

E.B.: Oh ça, ça faisait rire, t'sais, eune plaisir t'sais! Ça faisait du *fun*.

   (p. 117)

E.B.: Tchiens! Goutte! I boiviont du, du, de, i boiviont du, de la bière et des
choses comme ça i, i...

G.T.: Chantiont-i les, "La Marseillaise" là?

E.B.: Oh oui, oui.

G.T.: "Allons enfants de la patrie".

E.B.: Oui.

G.T.: Sais-tu chanter ça?

E.B.: Le, le vieux Scardin là. lui i chantait ça lui.

G.T.: Oui.

E.B.: Ouais, ouais. Mais les autes, i pouvaient pas, ç'tait pas des chanteurs.

G.T.: Non.

E.B.: Le, le vieux Lecore là, là. Job Lecore i savait pas chanter neh!

G.T.: Non.

E.B.: I y avait, i chantait ieune en anglais—"*She be down,*" i dit, "*she,*" i y avait
pas de "*a*" d'dans du tout lui, c'est toute "*she*". Pis le vieux Tacannou
ç'tait toute "i"—"i", "i".

G.T.: Ha ha ha!

E.B.: Si ç'tait eune fille, tait "i".

G.T.: Ha ha ha!

E.B.: Pis le vieux Lecore, "*she*"—ç'tait toute "*she*"! "*She be dere, she be, she be
come*" euh, oh ouais. I chantait là euh, "*She be down the numbornal* [?], *she
be down the numbornal,*" pis là i, i, i disait tcheques paroles avec ça là pis
i dansiont ois-tu.

G.T.: Oui oui!

E.B.: Toi essuie pas! Les gros—heh heh! Avions du *fun* don!

G.T.: Ouais.

E.B.: Ej veillais ça moi—mais, tu sais j'ai *enjoyé* ça moi?

G.T.:   Ouais ouais, ouais ouais.

E.B.:   Pis d'çtés temps-là i y avait arien à vouère—mais—ej laimais ça.

(p. 118)

G.T.:   Dis-moi si euh j'ai raison, quand je, si je crois que—quand on contait des contes, le monde autour, i disiont pas arien.

E.B.:   Oh non!

G.T.:   I coutiont.

E.B.:   I éc—i riiont dame, si ç'tait euh... oui.

G.T.:   Oui oui.

E.B.:   Ouais.

G.T.:   Mais—y avait-i des conteurs si, vous aviez moqué de lui peut-être...

E.B.:   Oh oui.

G.T.:   Ils araient ieu té fâchés—ou—s'i contait son conte et pis euh—

E.B.:   Oh non, non non, i faisiont pas d'quoi d'même non.

G.T.:   Non parce qu'il arait été fâché.

E.B.:   Oh oui oui, oh oui oui. Non non. Tout—tchequ'un s'i faisait quoi-ç-qu'i voulait faire, on s'moquait pas d'lui. Non.

(p. 118)

G.T.:   Tchel âge, tchel âge avais-tu quand t'as commencé à conter des contes?

E.B.:   Oh, à l'entour de—dans les dix-sept ans.

G.T.:   Devant le monde. Dix-sept ans.

E.B.:   Dix-sept ans, j'ai commencé, oui.

G.T.:   Et euh—t'avais été quoi, tout petit quand qu't'avais entendu les contes.

E.B.:   Oh, ouais, une douzaine d'années, de quoi d'même, eune tchinzaine d'années, *so on.* C'est durant ma jeunesse.

G.T.:   Oui.

E.B.:   J'avais le violon eune tapée dans l'idée vous savez.

G.T.:   Oui.

E.B.:   C'est ça ç'qui—mais ç'ava pour ça...

G.T.:   Plus que les contes.

E.B.:   J'arais, m'aras ieu toutes ces contes-là, mais dame—ois-tu?

G.T.:   Oui oui.

E.B.:   Mais mon intérêt était plus dans le, dans ma musique, que les contes.

G.T.:   Ouais, ouais. Ouais.

E.B.:   Ouais. N'on, on avait, avait du plaisir.

G.T.:   Oui.

E.B.:   Oh ç'tait, ça pâssait du beau temps. Ça m'ersembe... que j'avions plus de beaux temps dans çte temps-là qu'on a asteure.

G.T.:   Oui oui.

E.B.:   Oui—y avait plus de, ça paraît—plus, plus de joie.

(p. 119)

294

G.T.:   Et si je me trompe pas Émile, un des grands plaisirs dans ta vie, c'est de faire rire le monde.

E.B.:   Oh oui, ouais, ah oui, c'est vrai ça—c'est vrai ça.

G.T.:   T'as tout l'temps té d'même.

E.B.:   J'ai—faire rire le monde et pis assayer d'mette le monde hereux. C'est euh, c'est ma vie ça.

G.T.:   Ouais. Et tu feras n'importe quoi pour l'faire.

E.B.:   Ouais, ouais, ouais, je—me garâcherais à la mer si j'pouvais vous faire assez, vous faire rire.

G.T.:   Heh heh!

E.B.:   Ouais, ouais.

G.T.:   Ouais, ouais.

E.B.:   Pis j'sais pas, j'sais pas m'—nager.

(p. 119)

G.T.:   Et tchel âge avais-tu quand qu'il avont commencé à te demander des contes comme ça?

E.B.:   Oh j'avais à l'entour de dix-sept ans—seize ans.

G.T.:   I saviont déjà que tu savais conter des contes.

E.B.:   Oh ouais ouais ouais.

G.T.:   Oui oui.

E.B.:   Et euh j'actais pis je les faisais rire! Lo! Oh! Ouais.

(p. 120)

G.T.:   Toi, quand tu contes une histoire ou un conte, toi tu es tout l'temps—deboute...

E.B.:   Ah oui, ah oui.

G.T.:   Et pis euh...

E.B.:   Oui.

G.T.:   Alors i disont que ça c'était comme les vieux Français. Alors—c'est vrai ça?

E.B.:   Oh oui c'est vrai, oh oui.

G.T.:   Quand qu'tu tais gamin, est-ce qu'i contiont comme ça—comme les vieux Français d'avant?

E.B.:   Oh oui y en avait, oui—tu, tu prends comme euh le, le, le Julien Chaisson—je vous as dit là.

G.T.:   Oui.

E.B.:   Lui là il était, i faisait du gibas comme ça lui aussi. Mais euh, j'sais pas—mais ç'tait risibe là.

G.T.:   Oui.

(p. 120)

E.B.:   Il avait, i contait là le coup qu'il avait conté le coup—le conte de la Montagne Nouère. Mais i dit—quand qu'ça a venu sus pour finir là—quand qu'le, quand qu'le diabe avait marié la, sa fille pis et pis çte—son garçon. Fait qu'ça a venu au boute et qu'—le, le, i faulait qu'il arriviont asteure sus la Terre Sainte tu sais et euh, i dit, i dit, ça, ça ici, sa fille i dit

295

a descendu i dit de d'sus le choual et pis elle a mis son, son oreille à la terre—pis a dit—"Pâpa s'en vient." Pis il aviont pus qu'cent varges à faire i dit pour aller à la Terre Sainte, heh! Toujours i dit, c'est bien. Là alle embarque, a dit, "Pâpa s'en vient," a dit, "pis il est proche." Bien i dit, "Mon bon Dieu de Dieu," lui asteure, "là," i dit, "là," i dit, "ça ç'tait mouche, là," i dit, "ça va là-bas, j'te garantis là qu'ça va ça," i dit, "le vente," i dit, "qui est pas pus haut," i dit, "quate pouces de la terre, pis ça va là asteure, cent varges, hm! hm!" Bien, c'est bien, c'est bien, ça va pis ça va pis ça va, pis ça va, pis ça va, pis ça va. Et après in boute a dit euh, "Pâpa approche, pâpa approche." Ben alors i s'en prit à donner in coup d'fouette qu'i dit en-d'sous le vente du choual—ah le choual i dit, "Là. Bien," i dit, "là! ça asteure! *Asteure* ça va! *Asteure* ça va! Là— asteure," i dit, "armasse ton avouène," i dit, "armasse ton avouène!"— de quoi de même—t'sais. Toujours—alle avait pus qu'quate varges— "Ben," a dit, "Pâpa est darrière là-bas je le ois," a dit, "pus qu'quate varges à faire," a dit, "pour, pour sauter sus la Terre Sainte. Pus qu'quate varges—ah! Mon bien Dieu de Dieu là, toh! aaah, téorh! ça va, là asteure, ah! Asteure là," i dit, "ça là, ça c'est, c'est, ah! Astchuse les sotties," lui i dit. Hah! Ça ça marche. *Asteure* ça marche—quate varges—ben c'est ça qui faisait rire ois-tu là. Oui. C'est pas in ptit boute assez qu'i tait avec ses quate varges là avant qu'il arrive là tout d'in coup vlà le diable qu'arrive pis i le croche le choual pis justement i sautait dans la Terre Sainte—pis i y restait la tcheue dans la main i dit. Ben c'est ça qui, qui faisait rire là.

G.T.: Oui.

E.B.: Penses-tu Sainte-Barbe pis pendant cinq minutes pour dire ça asteure.

(p. 121)

G.T.: Bien—quand qu'tu—t'avais commencé à conter les contes toi—tu voulais les conter comme lui par exemple?

E.B.: Oh ben, un peu comme lui mais dame, j'les contais pas comme lui pareil.

G.T.: Non non.

E.B.: Parce qu'i mettait trop d'sus lui—vous savez.

G.T.: Mais tu cherchais...

E.B.: Oui oui.

G.T.: A y mette la vie dedans.

E.B.: Ouais ouais, oh oui, à mette la vie dedans. Oh oui, bien sûr.

G.T.: Penses-tu enfin, y avait-i pas beaucoup de conteurs comme ça?

E.B.: Non—i y en avait pas beaucoup.

G.T.: Du monde qui...

E.B.: Asteure i y avait Jack Tourout, i contait des—des histoires aussi, des contes—les vieux contes d'avant—mais dame i actait pas avec le, avec le conte, quand i les contait. Euh, Narcisse Chaisson pareil—i contait les contes aussi mais euh... comme ça.

(p. 121)

G.T.: Mais—j'comprends que tu aimes mieux la musique que les contes—mais tu t'souviens quand même de, de, des contes—euh, quoi-ç-que c'est dans les contes que, que tu estimais?

296

E.B.: Aaah... bien—les contes que j'estimais, ben ça c'est joliment du diabe dedans, le, le, les, *y'know*... et pis quand tu contes les contes et pis ces, les affaires comme ça, ben—ça, ça, ça frissonne ois-tu, ça, pis tu actes là.

G.T.: Oui oui.

E.B.: Ouais, ça, ça, ça, ça touche, ois-tu.

G.T.: Ouais.

E.B.: Oh ouais. Clair de ça—le, le—le conte sera, sera pas tchurieux.

    (p.122)

E.B.: Mais euh moi, la façon que j'ai, que je les contais, mais dame, ça faisait rire le monde t'sais, faulait qu'ej parle comme la vieille sorciaise et pis— faulait qu'ej parle comme l'aute, t'sais, t'sais, changer la voix *an so on*.

G.T.: Oui.

E.B.: Pis—asteure dans mon temps je—i y avait pas d'télévision, i y avait pas d'radio, i y avait arien comme ça, mais faulait faire du *fun* ois-tu—m'en jouer du violon in boute et pis euh, après ça faulait conter des contes. Bien alors j'avais, des, des, des, des fois j'mettais de la laine filée—sus la tête pou faire les chouveux longs, pis j'me faisais des dents avec du papier, des, des dents nouères, des longs dents—pis ej me collais ça dans la djeule pis euh, là j'faisais comme la vieille sorciaise et pis euh menaçais le monde, pis ça, ça, ça riait là, ça faisait du *fun* t'sais.

    (p. 122)

E.B.: J'avais in coup j'avais, i y avait in préte, euh—i avait venu ici—pis i béguait—vous savez—i faisait toujours "brouou"—et pis ben moi j'ai té à sa maison—ben i me disiont, "Fais don le préte là." Ben là je me mis pis je parlais comme le préte. Pis, pis, j'prêchais comme qu'i prêchait ois-tu, prêchait au monde *an so on*. Ben ça les faisait rire hein. Tout d'in coup là je me mis là, in chou. J'arrache le tchoeur du chou pis je me fourre le chou sus la téte pis j'ai les fientes en haut, pis là j'ai commencé à acter comme le préte là. Bien i ont manqué d'mourir, c'est pas utile ça, ça, my—j'ons ieu du *fun*, j'ons ieu du *fun*—du plaisir, grand plaisir. Ouais.

    (p. 122)

G.T.: Dis-moi—les contes là—on m'avait, on m'a dit que souvent ç'tait bien long à conter—eh, des fois trois ou quatre heures. C'est-i vrai ça?

E.B.: Oh oui, oui. Oh oui.

G.T.: Un conte qui durait trois ou quatre heures?

E.B.: Oui. Pas quatre heures mais euh—deux ou trois heures pour sûr.

G.T.: Oui.

E.B.: *Oh my!* Ouais. Mais dame ois-tu, tu peux longer les contes ois-tu là—tu peux les longer hein.

G.T.: Oui oui.

E.B.: Oh oui.

G.T.: Comment tu fais pour ça?

E.B.: Ben tu mets des ptits morceaux d'dans et *so on* pis tu—les alentours, ici et ça là, oh oui.

G.T.: Oui.

E.B.: Oh oui, pas d'danger—pis c'est meilleur aussi t'sais.

G.T.: Oh oui oui, oui oui.

E.B.: Pis des ptits morceaux avec pour pass—pour parsouter. Oh ouais.

G.T.: Oui.

E.B.: Oh oui oui. Ça colle mieux t'sais.

G.T.: Pis quand tu fais, tu fais des magies là sus la place, j'pense que ça, ça longit aussi hein?

E.B.: Oh oui, bien sûr, oh oui.

(p. 125)

E.B.: Là—i enouoyont quri le minisse, et pis i s'mariont, et pis quand qu'il aviont les noces—mais moi j'pouvais pas jouer beaucoup jouer du violon de ces temps-là! Mais le temps de leus noces i tiont entor, dans le, dans l'*spree*—il aviont du *home-brew* fait avec du prusse, heh! *Holy gee!* I m'a fait ve—"Rente là!" Mais j'tais bien reçu *though, bye*—j'ai joué pou— eune, eune partie d'leu danse—et toute—mais j'tais bein reçu. Ouais. (Conclusion de *La Bête à Sept Têtes*).

(p. 125)

E.B.: Et dame il a té obigé de s'en aller *back* chez lui pis—moi j'tais là—c'est, pis c'est ienne, ienne d'mes onques, çui-là qu'avait venu—quand qu'il avont arrivé là ben i dit, "C'est eune belle femme *though, bye*. Belle femme." J'tais là quand qu'il avont arrivé ac leu, leu, avec le cheval blanc—mais in beau ptit cheval aussi. Ouais. Ouais pis i avont ieu eune noce de diabe, *ho, holy gee!* Ouais y a ieu du *fun!* Du *home-brew* en masse là—hah hah! Ouais! C'est *all right*. (Conclusion du *Conte de la Montagne Nouère*).

(p. 125)

E.B.: Et quand j'ai arrivé là, quand j'étais là, ça a donné justement comme ça— mais dame—entor moi pis Jambe-de-Bois pis l'chat—j'avons enterré les géants—pis euh, j'avons clarci d'la, la, heh heh! la, l'odeur pis s'i vivont ac les deux mariés—i vivont! (Conclusion de *Jean-des-Bois* ou *Jambe-de-Bois*)

(p. 127)

E.B.: Il a tombé à, à la renvarse. Quand qu'i oit ça. Oh ça ç'tait vilain! Ah! Oh, les grands dents ça descend en-bas d'son menton là pis nouères! I y avait des plaques blanches pis des, des plaques nouères, dessus là—pis places corbues là—pis des gu—des verrures qui sortaient d'son nez là tout pointues! Ben mon ami—ça ç'tait vilain! Oh ça ç'tait vilain! Pis les, les, les, les zusses là—ça *corlait*? [Eng. to curl] là c'est comme des, tout des choueux—pis les, les poils des yeux là—c'est toute *corlé* comme des, des, des crocs à truite là. Pis les deux yeux ça flambait! Ça flambait! Ç'tait comme des chandelles! Oh ç'tait vilain, vilain, vilain!

(p. 128)

E.B.: Pis, ma, i dit, "C'est, faut qu'ej fais du bien—à Jean-du-Bois, faut que j'y fais du bien tcheque temps," ois-tu, "pis y a, i y a trois géants là," i dit. Pis i cartchulait asteure quoi-ç-qu'il allait faire—mais i disait pas à Jean-du-Bois, i disait pas, non, mais i carculait ça là asteure, pis i savait qu'avait in, in roi là, ioù i restait, pis il avait eune belle fille. "Ben si," i dit, "si par quand," i dit, "j'pourrais réussir là pis," i dit euh, "qu'il ara," euh, Jean-du-Bois asteure, "arait pu marier asteure la fille de l'aroi là," i dit, "eune belle fille comme ça," i dit, "pis qu'ej pourrais euh, détruire les

298

trois géants moi," i dit, "si j'pourrais trouver in plan—eune façon—pis, pis i, pis faut y, y donner ça pour in, pour eune surprise, de quoi d'même là—comme i sera-ti fier!" i dit. "Ça, ça, ça i y donne encore de la joie dans l'tchoeur. Bien i a té si bon à moi dans, dans toute ma vie. Il a té si bon."

(p. 128)

E.B.:   Bientôt à trois heures—trois heures du matin—alle a commencé à l'proguer ac ses coudes—a dit, "Vieux, vieux! Vieux!" Là. "Quoi-ç-qu'a encore ça sacrée vieille folle!" i dit. A dit, "J'sus sûre," a dit, "qu'i sont partis, j'sus *sûre* qu'i sont partis!"—"Mais tu sais bien, tu m'disais ça tantôt mais," i dit, "j'ieuse ai parlé, pis j'y ai parlé pis a—i-z-étiont là! Alle est là, a m'a repondu, c'est ielle!"—"Non non!" a dit—"Pis y a d'quoi là-d'dans." Ben là i dit, il a enouoyé, "Jane!" i dit, "Dors-tu là?"—"Ah!" a dit, "Bien," a dit, "j'dormais," a dit, "mais vous m'avez reveillé!"- "Dors-tu! Sacrée vieille folle! Garde!" i dit—"Si tu, t'as, t'arais, tu peux dormir—tu vas att, tu vas m'attraper ma main dans la djeule," i dit. "Ohh! T'as pas besoin d'ête méchant," a dit, "parce que," a dit, "j'sais y a d'quoi," mais i dit, "J'sais bien i t'a, a m'a dit, parlé—t'as pas de—es-tu sourd?"—"Oh non j'ai entendu ça."—"Et euh, dors! Sacrée vieille folle, dors!" Pis là hnrrr! Là ça dort, ça dort...."

(p. 130)

E.B.:   Et, le garçon a travaillé, i travaillait, i travaillait tout l'temps—mais çtes temps-là—bien—faulait qu't'avais vingt-et-une ans avant qu'tu—que tu tais toi-même. Quand qu'tu avais vingt-et-une ans, ah ben dame, tu tais à toi-même. Bien c'est bien. Toujours, vlà son—sa naissance qu'arrive— vingt-et-une ans. Hah! Oh c'est pas eune ptite affaire là, c'est in homme là asteure, ois-tu, oh ho! je le garantis!"

Tales Told By Blanche Ozon

(p. 150)

LE CONTE DE JEAN ET JEANETTE

Ç'ta in homme et eune femme, i viviont tout seuls, eh, tous les deux. Et alle éta pas tout là, ielle, vous savez, comprenez eh? Ça fa *anyway*, i faisiont in jardin pis i aviont des bétes eh? Des vaches pis il aviont des cochons. Ça fa *anyway*, lui travaillait et asteure ielle soignait ça. Ça fa que quand ç'a vnu dans l'temps d'l'automne *anyway*, il aviont eune vache à tuer eh? Ça fait, il avont tué la vache. Pis i dit, "J'avons in grand jardin de choux," eh? Ça fa, i dit, "J'mettrons in morceau à chaque chou"—ça fa, i y ava pas expliqué, vous savez, comment-ç-qu'il alliont mette in morceau à chaque chou. Si a comprenait, alle a pas compris qu'il alliont tchuire in morceau d'—viande, pis in morceau d'chou eh, in chou. Ça fa *anyway*, i dit, "J'allons mette in morceau à chaque chou," *anyway*, c'est d'méme qu'i conte eh? Et là lui s'en va travailler. Ça fa *anyway*, ielle éta pas tout là, eh? Quand qu'il éta parti, a prend la viande, a la coupe—et a va dans l'jardin pis a mis in morceau à chaque chou, eh? [Elle rit] Ça fa *anyway*, ça va de méme. Mais apras in boute asteure a trouvait ça drôle qu'a tchuisa pas d'viande, t'sais? Asteure son nom ta Jeanette, pis lui son nom ta Jean—ta Jean et Jeanette eh? Mais lui ç'ta Jean l'Sotte, j'dirons. Ça fa *anyway*, i dit, "Quoi-ç-qui est la cause que tu tchuis pas d'viande, j'avons d'la viande en masse."—"Oui," a dit, "mais," a dit, "m'as-tu pas dit de mette in morceau à chaque chou?" [Elle rit] I dit, "Tu vas pas vnir me dire que t'as mis in morceau à chaque chou?" A dit, "Oui!"—"Mais, i dit, "c'est pas d'méme que je t'avas dit, j't'avas dit de tchuire in morceau d'viande et in chou," eh? A dit, "J'ai mis in morceau d'viande à chaque chou!" Il ont pardu la viande *anyway*!...Ça fa *anyway*, il aviont don in cochon à tuer, eh, quand que ç'a vnu dans les temps d'Noël, là, bien, i tue son cochon. Pas asteure i y dit, "Asteure," i dit, "ça c'est pour Noël," i dit, "in morceau pour Noël, et in morceau pour le Jour de l'An." Ouais. S'en va—travailler. *So anyway*, la veille d'Noël, pas la veille mais in coupelle de jours avant Noël, il arrive in homme là. Ça fait, i dit, "Bonjour Madame!" A dit, "Bonjour Monsieur," m'a dit, "j'vous connais pas." I dit, "Vous m'connaissez pas?"—"Non," a dit, "j'vous connais pas." "Mais," i dit, "moi, j'sus Noël."—"Oh," a dit, "j'pense que vous êtes vnu pou vote morceau d'cochon." [Elle rit] I dit, "Ouais, j'ai vnu pou mon morceau d'cochon." Teuh! A y donne son morceau d'cochon pis i s'en va avec. Quand que son homme vient le souère, eh, "Bien," a dit, "Jean," a dit, "j'ai ieu in *visitor*." I dit, "Oui?" A dit, "Oui," Alle a dit "Oui, j'ai vu vieux Noël aujourd'hui." I dit, "Vieux Noël? J'ons pas encore rendu à Noël!" Bien, a dit, "Il a vnu pou son morceau de cochon," eh! [Elle rit] I dit, "T'y as pas donné in morceau d'cochon?" A y dit, "J'y ai donné sa pârt," eh, "t'as dit que c'est pour Noël et le Jour de l'An, bien, j'y ai donné sa pârt," eh? I dit, "Asteure i reste in aute morceau." Pis i dit, "Asteure, souais de pas l'donner—ça," i dit, "c'est pour le Jour de l'An," eh? Ouais! Tant mieux. *Anyway*—i s'en va encore travailler. Jean s'en va travailler. Oh! quand que ç'a vnu pour le Jour de l'An, *anyway*, là, le méme homme arrive eh? I dit, "Bonjour Jeanette." A dit, "Bonjour, Monsieur," a dit, a dit, "j'vous connais pas."—"Non?" i dit. "Mais," i dit, "moi, j'sus le Jour de l'An," eh? "Oh!" a dit, "j'pense que vous êtes vnu pou vote cochon," eh? [Elle rit] I dit, "Oui, j'sus vnu pou mon morceau d'cochon." I dit, "Moi, j'sus le Jour de l'An." A y donne le morceau d'cochon pis i s'en va. S'en va avec. *Anyway*, quand que Jean arrive eh? "Bien," a dit, "Jean," a dit, "j'ai ieu in aute *visitor*." I dit, "Oui? Tchi-ç-qu'il est?" A dit, "Le Jour de l'An." A dit, "J'y ai donné sa pârt de cochon, pis il est parti avec." [Elle rit] Là i s'enrage! "Bien," i dit, "t'as donné toute la viande aux choux, pis t'as toute en grand donné l'cochon à l'méme homme. Pis asteure," i dit, "nous vlà sans viande!" eh? "Bien," i dit, "j'm'en vas." Pis i dit, "Quand j'arai trouvé aussi fou comme toi, m'en vas ervnir!" [Elle rit] *Okay*. Vlà parti. I marche, i marche, couple de jours *anyway*, i erconte deux hommes, avec eune vache. Pis i tiont en astinement asteure, eh? Y ava eune bâtisse pis y ava du foin qui poussa dsus, eh? Pis i *wonderiont* comment-ç-qu'il ariont pu faire pour aller en haut asteure pou que la vache mange le foin. Pis y en a iun qui dit, "T'es fou, eh, moi," i dit, "j'sais!" i dit. "Quoi-ç-que vous avez à vous astiner?"—"Bien," iun dit, y en a iun qui dit, "asteure," i dit, "y a du foin là," pis i dit, "j'voudarions l'aouère pour la vache," pis i dit, "asteure j'porrons pas saouère comment faire pour l'aouère!"—"Mais," i dit, "montez en haut, pis coupez-lé pis t'en vas donner à la vache."—"Non," i dit, "c'est pas d'méme j'allons faire." I dit, "J'allons couper la téte de dsus la vache pis," i dit, "mette la téte en haut!" [Elle rit]—"Bien," i dit, "j'ai trouvé aussi fou comme Jeanette." Ça fa il orvire de bord, pis s'en va chez ieusses. Fa *anyway*, il arrive chez ieusses, "T'es ervnu?" I dit, "Oui, j'ai ervnu trouver," i dit, "j'ai trouvé aussi fou comme toi! J'sus arvnu *back*." Pis i dit, "J'reste pas." I dit, "J'm'en vas." A dit, "Moi aussi, m'en vas." [Elle rit] Fa *anyway*, i s'greye. Pis i sort la porte, pis a dit, "M'en vas aussi."—"Bien," i dit, "farme la porte!" A prend la porte et a l'emporte avec ielle! C'est in conte eh?... *Anyway*, i marchont, pis i marchont, i marchont *anyway*. Il entendait du train, il entendait du monde, eh, ça fa don i monte dans in âbe. Tous les deux. Quoi-ç-que ç'ta, ç'ta quate voleurs. I vienniont de voler de l'argent, eh? Pis i arrivont au pied de l'âbe ailloù-ç-qu'il étiont, en haut là, ieusses. A monte la porte avec ielle, eh? I mettont leu porte, i faisont—eune a-a-affaire, i mettont la porte don hein? Tchuire d'la soupe. *Anyway, okay*. Vlà don les voleurs à compter leu-z-argent. Ça faisa don, eh. "C'est ma pârt," i dit, "'-ç-qu'est la mienne moi?" Bien i *maillndiont* [angl. to mind] pas, i comptiont eh? Là a dit, "Jean, *my God*," i dit, "j'ai envie d'pisser!"— "Bien," i dit, "pisse de branche en branche, pou pas qu'les voleurs t'entendent," eh? S'assit. A pisse dans l'potte, [elle rit] potte des voleurs. Oh, y en a iun qui dit, "Écoute don," i dit, "écoute, écoute!" i dit—i dit, "Le Bon Dieu qui nous envoie du vinaigue!" I brâssa l'potte pis i disa ça, "Le Bon Dieu nous envoie du vinaigue!" [Elle rit] *Okay*. Là i prenont encore à compter—"Ma pârt, la mienne, la tchienne," pis l'aute i n'ava pas, eh? Non, y a pas d'pârt pou lui. Là les vlà pris en qurelle. "*Oh my God!*" a dit, "Jean, j'envie d'chier!"

A.K.: (qui vient de rentrer): Oh my God!

—Pis i dit, "Tu chies de branche en branche pou pas qu'les voleurs t'entendent!" A s'braque, pis a chie [elle rit] dans l'potte!

A.K.: Ha ha!

—Ha! "Oh!" i dit, "garde! Le Bon Dieu," i dit, "nous envoie d'la moutarde!" I s'prend à brâsser dans l'potte, brâsser la marde comme d'la soupe, vlà *anyway*... vlà don, et les vlà pris en qurelle encore compter leu-z-argent—mais pouviont pas compter la pârt de quate—pouviont ienque compter la pârt de trois—mais lui, vlà le pauve diabe, pas d'argent—il éta aussi voleur comme ieusses—i voula sa pârt!

A.K.:   Oui! J'sais!

—Oh, in boute apras, i s'avont mis en qurelle, *by geewhiz Chris'*, ç'ta chaud! "Oh bien," a dit, "Jean, j'peux pus *stanner* [angl. to stand]," a dit, "j'ai la porte sus l'dos, pis j'peux pus la tchinde!" I dit, "T'as pas monté la porte?!"

A.K.:   Ha ha ha!

—A dit, "Tu m'as dit de porter la porte."—"Non," i dit, "j't'avas dit d'la fârmer!"—"Bien," a dit, "je l'ai!" [Elle rit]—"Bien," i dit, "largue-lé de branche en branche pou pas qu'les voleurs t'entendent!"

A y *goddam* in coup d'pied à la porte! [Elle rit]

A.K.:   Ha ha ha!

—Vlà les voleurs pris à crier la peur, le diabe qui s'en vnait! Mais lui là, qui a pas ieu sa pârt, reste là, eh?

A.K.:   Ah!

—Il avaient tout quitté l'argent, pis il ont frangi, il ont peur, eh?

A.K.:   Yes!

—Anyway, i descendont, Jean et Jeanette d'en haut. Ça fa *anyway* i croyont qu'c'est l'diabe qui s'en vnait, tout ç'temps-là, ç'ta la porte. Ça fa *anyway*, i dit, "Quoi-ç-que tu fais là, toi?"—"Bien," i dit, "moi, j'mange d'la soupe," pis i dit, "ma soupe est chaude."—"Mais," i dit, "t'es pas fin," i dit, "gratte ta langue!" I gratte sa langue, oui, la soupe c'est pas chaude, eh? I dit, "Avec quoi j'vais gratter ça, moi?"

—"Donne-moi in couteau! [rires] Donne-moi in couteau, j'vas gratter ta langue, moi!" I prend in grand couteau pis il allonge sa langue et, plus qu'i grattait, plus qu'il allongeait sa langue, quand qu'alle éta longue assez, i la coupe!

A.K.:   Oh my gosh!

—Pis le vlà pris à crier pis s'pointer, étiont campés à eune distance hein? Les autes hein? Vlà qu'i commence à crier, "Lire-la, lire-la, lire-la," i pouva pas parler, eh? Il avont dit, "Je nous allons lire-la," i s'en allont, pis c'est ça! [Rires] C'est fini! [Rires]

(p. 164)

LE CONTE DU JARDINIER

Ça ç'tait in homme et eune femme, il aviont ç'ptit-là hein. Il aviont, il étiont loin d'l'église pis y avait ienque ieusses d'habitants hein? Pis i pouviont pas trouver d'parrain et d'marraine pour leu ptit, hein. Ça fa eune jornée, a prend son bébi a l'paque *anyway*, la femme, pis là a dit, a dit, "I faut qu'ej trouve eune marraine et in parrain pou mon bébi aujourd'hui parce qu'il est temps qu'i seye baptisé." Ça fa a dit, "Le promier qu'ej vas trouver, ej vas l'prende parrain et marraine." Ça fa a prend son bébi pis a s'en va pis là *anyway* a marche in boute pis là a renconte eune femme, hein? A y dmande est-ce qu'alle aime son bébi. A dit, "Ej m'en vas l'faire baptiser mais j'ai pas d'marraine." A dit, "Viendrez-vous marraine pou mon bébi?" A dit, "Oui." A dit, "Allez-vous en église," a dit, "ej srai là aussi." Ça fa a dit, "J'ai pas d'parrain," hein, "mais," a dit, "le promier qu'ej vas trouver va aller parrain pour mon bébi." Ça fa *anyway* a marche in boute pis là a renconte çt homme-là hein. "Ailloù-ç-que vous allez avec vote bébi?"—"Bien," a dit, "ej vas l'faire baptiser," a dit, "j'ai trouvé eune marraine mais j'en as pas d'parrain." A dit, "viendrez-vous

303

parrain?" I dit, "Oui, tout d's uite." I dit, "Allez-vous-en," i dit, "j'allons ête là bientôt. Ej srai là bientôt," i dit. Là a va don dans l'église, hein. Et là l'préte i vient pis là quand qu'alle arrive i sont là toutes les deusses. Ça fa qu'alle a baptisé son bébi et a s'en vient chez ieusses. I dit, "As-ti ieu in parrain pis marraine?" A dit, "Oui." Ça fa a sava pas tchi-ç-qu'i tiont hein. Ça fa le bébi a grandi *anyway* jusqu'à temps qu'i vient en âge d'aller à l'école. Ben eune jornée *anyway*, i s'en allait à l'école et i pâssait au rain in ptit risseau et toutes les fois qu'i pâssait l'ptit risseau-là i s'amusait dans l'risseau hein. *Anyway* ç'jornée-là i s'mat à s'amuser dans l'risseau pis là quand i s'lève pou s'en aller, hein, bien çte femme-là s'présente devant lui, hein. Ça fa i dit, "Allo," pis a dit, "Allo," a dit, "tu m'connais pas j'pense." I dit, a dit, "J'sus ta marraine." Ça fa *anyway*, a dit, "Mets ta téte dans l'risseau," a dit, "jusqu'au niveau d'tes choueux," hein. A dit, "Fa attention d'pas aller pus loin." A dit, "Au niveau d'tes choueux, trempe-les dans l'eau," hein. *Anyway*, fa comme sa marraine y a dit, hein, sa téte dans l'risseau. Et là apras qu'i s'ara ieu enlevé i ava don les choueux en or, hein. Ça fa *anyway* a y prend in béret pis a y met sus la téte au niveau d'ses choueux hein. Pis lá a dit, "Asteure,"—a y dit, hein?—"Ortire pas çte calotte-là d'd'sus ta téte avant qu'ej te dis," hein. Ça fa *anyway* à toutes les souères le ptit vnait à la maison, i vouliont ortirer sa calotte pis i voulait pas hein? Ça fa ça, c'est long aussi, hein? Là *anyway*, i grandit pis là quand qu'i tait clair d'l'école i dit, "M'en vas charcher pou d'l'ouvrage," hein. Son père et sa mère tiont pauves tu sais. Ça fa *anyway*, i marche, *anyway*, i marche et i marche pou des jours et des nuits, hein. Là *anyway*, i arrive à in château, in château d'l'âroi. A la porte. I s'en va lui ouvrir la porte. A dit, "Quoi-ç-que tu veux?" I dit, "Ej veux ouère l'âroi, ej veux l'parler." A dit au roi, pis là *anyway* l'âroi y dit d'rentrer, hein. Qu'in ptit garçon qu'i voulait, hein. I dit, "Dis-y qu'i rente." Là i rente pis i s'en va au âroi pis i dit asteure, "Quoi-ç-que tu veux?"—"Ben," i dit, "moi, ej charche eune *job*." I dit, "Mon père et ma mère sont pauves pis," i dit, "y a ienque moi pis," i dit, "ej voudras aouère d'l'ouvrage pour les *helper out*."—"Bien," i dit, "j'ai pas d'l'ouvrage à t'donner ienque," i dit, "in *helper* pour mon jardinier." I dit, "J'as in jardinier pis," i dit, "il est tout seul ça fait," i dit, "tu peux—j'vas t'garder pou y donner d'la main." Ça fa *anyway* le lendemain matin—couché en l'souère—l'endemain matin il a ieu s'levé pour aller prende sa *job*, t'sais. I s'en va au jardin. Sa marraine arrive. A dit, "Asteure fais comme ej vas t'dire." A dit, "Moi, j'sus ta marraine." A dit, "Fas comme ej vas t'dire," a dit. A dit, "Tu sras *okay*," a dit. A dit, "Plante pas tes fleurs la racine en bâs. Plante tes fleurs la racine en haut."—"Mais," i dit, "ça va pas pousser." A dit, "Oui, ça va pousser." Là *anyway* i fait comme sa marraine y a dit. I plante ses fleurs, i plantait ses fleurs les racines en haut, hein? Pis là asteure l'aute jardinier i y dit, i dit, "Quâ faire qu'tu fais ça?"—"Bien," i dit, "c'est d'méme qu'ej plante mes fleurs, moi," i dit, "ac la racine en haut."—"Mais," i dit, "t'es fou! Tes fleurs allont pas pousser," i dit, "t'as la racine en haut."—"Uh bien," i dit, "c'est ça. C'est d'méme faut qu'ça va." Le lendmain matin quand i s'lève, pis i s'en va dans son jardin, les fleurs tout en fleur, hein?

A.K.: Oh my God!

—Pis l'aute ses fleurs tiont *dull* t'sais. Ça fait, i n'en fa ça pour longtemps. Là, vlà l'aute tait jaloux, lui. *Anyway*, i conte des menteries au âroi pis là l'âroi l'appelle pis i dit, i dit, "Ej peux pas t'garder." I dit, "Ej peux pas l'faire," i dit. I dit, "L'aute jardinier est supposé d'ête le *boss*." I dit, "Asteure tu fais in meilleur jardin qu'lui, ça fait," i dit, "i est pas content." Ç'à cause du bribe, ça. Ça fa i dit, "Ej vas t'mette à sor—soigner les chouals." Ça fa *anyway*, "Content?"—"Oh ouais," i dit, i aviont, i avait trois chouals hein. Et *anyway* la première matinée qu'i tait pour s—sarvir ses chouals sa marraine vient là hein. Et i y en ava in vieux, in vieux choual. Il avait la misère à s'bouger, hein? A y dit, "Asteure, *feedes* çui-là meilleur qu'les autes. Ça fa" a dit, "tu vas faire du cas d'çui-là." *Okay*. A dit, "Moi, j'sus ta marraine." Ça fa don dans arien d'temps les chouals s'avont rabicoté. Le vieux choual il a vnu aussi jeune comme in, in choual de trois ans, hein. I *feedait* bien tu sais. Temps en temps a vnait ouère. Ça fa *anyway*—euh, l'âroi don i ava trois filles. Ça fa *anyway* i s'mettont jaloux. Là, le, le, l'aute jardinier l'en voulait pas hein. Ça fa i dit au roi, i dit, "Faisez-moi faire eune ptite cabane dehors et pis j'irai rester là, dans ma cabane, tout seul." Ça fa i dit, "Ej sras chez nous, fais comme ej voudrais." *Okay*, fait eune cabane pis là i s'en va. Rester dans, dans la ptite cabane. Ça fa *anyway* les trois filles du roi là asteure, hein, i tiont en haut dans leu chambe là ieusses. *Anyway* la première soirée—là i tait, i tait manière d'*in-love* avec ieune de ieusses là t'sais. I tiont pas allouées d'aller à sa cabane. La première soirée eune fois qu'la nuit tait bien fârmée, i tire sa calotte pis i fait in tour à l'entour d'la cabane, in tour d'dans. I voyiont ça. La pus vieille a dit, "Y a d'quoi là-d'dans," a dit, "ej m'en vas ouère." Ben ouais, tape à la porte. I ouve la porte. I dit, "Ouais? Où-ç-que tu vas?"—"Moi," a dit, "ej viens ici." I dit, "Va-t-en. Ej t'ai pas besoin ici. Ton père m'a amné là-dsus," i dit, "i va encore me challer et i va m'enoueyer."—"Non," a dit, "j'avons vu d'quoi," a dit. A dit, "C'est comme eune clarté." A dit, "Ça fa in tour à l'entour d'ta cabane et pis ça a rentré."—"C'est pas vrai, ça," i dit. "Décolle, décolle chez vous. T'as pas besoin ici." A s'en va *anyway*. La soirée là pâsse et l'endmain au souère don la fille, le deux, hein, la *second one*, a dit, "Moi, à souère, ej m'en vas," a dit, "ej m'en vas ouère tchi-ç-que c'est ça, veiller." *So*, i fait deux tours à l'entour d'la cabane et pis piouque! rente d'dans encore. Ouais, va en-d'dans. Pis alle arrive là, tape à la porte. I dit, "Où-ç'tu vas?" A dit, "J'ai vu d'quoi d'joli tantôt," a dit. A dit, "Ça semblait comme eune clerté," a dit, "a fait deux tours en, entour d'ta cabane pis," a dit, "il est rentré."—"Pas vrai, ça," i dit. "Ej sais ç'que tu fais. Tu veux vnir ici, vous voulez vnir ici, ta soeur pareille a vnu hier à souère," i dit. "Vous voulez vnir ici m'faire parde ma *job* encore." I dit, "Décolle! Veux pas d'toi ici." A s'en va. Fa *anyway*, sans moyen, hein. "Ah!", a dit, "Y a pas moyen d'faire arien avec," a dit, "ej sais pas." A dit, "Ej vas pus." Bien la pus jeune a dit, "Demain au souère moi ej vas aller. *I bet* you," a dit, "ej vas saouère moi. M'en vas saouère quoi va en-d'dans là." L'endmain au souère don, à la nuit, i tiont en haut, hein. Tire sa calotte, i fait bien nouère...

A.K.: Tire tes doigts d'ta djeule! Tire tes doigts d'ta djeule!

—Oh toi, t'es folle!

A.K.: Ha ha ha!

—Là *anyway*, la troisième soirée, là c'est la pus jeune hein. Fa trois tours à l'entour d'la cabane pis piouque! dans la cabane encore. A dit, "Ej m'en vas." A y dmande pour saouère la varité. Ça fa, ouais, tape à la porte. Ouve la porte. "Où-ç-que tu vas?" A dit, "J'sus vnue."—"Bien," i dit, "rente."—"Bien," a dit, "j'avions vu d'quoi d'joli." A dit, "A souère, i faut qu'ej saille la varité." A dit, "Y a d'quoi ici." I dit, "Quoi-ç-que tu crois qu'y a ici?"—"Bien," a dit, "ej sais pas." A dit, "Ça fa trois tours à l'entour d'ta cabane pis ça a rentré pis," a dit, "c'est ici d'dans."—"Ah!" i dit, "moi j'as rien vu." Là *anyway* i s'faisont l'amour...

A.K.: Uh dame, c'est bon ça!

—Ouais, faisont l'amour. Là *anymore* quand qu'i tait longtemps assis, i l'enoueye. I dit, "Va-t-en. Si ton père sait ça," i dit, "i va m'faire parde ma *job* encore." Là *anyway*, a s'en va chez ieusses. Là ses soeurs y dmandont. "Ah!" a dit, "Y a pas moyen d'faire arien avec."—"Mais," i avont dit, "quoi-ç-qu'est la cause qu't'as rentré et j'as pas pu rentrer nous autes?"—"Uh dame," a dit, "ej sais pas, j'peux pas vous l'dire." Ça fa à tous les souères quand ses soeurs taient endormies ielle allait, hein, le trouver et—ouais. Ça fa *anyway*, jusqu'à temps qu'i l'a dmandé en mariage hein? Ça fa *anyway* a dit, "Ouais. Mais," a dit, "mes parents va iête à contre ça," a dit, "toi t'es in jardinier." Là *anyway* i dit, "L'âroi m'a mis dsus." Pis i dit à sa fille, "Tu maries pas çte jardinier-là, pas toi! Eune fille comme toi," i dit, "marier in

305

jardinier! Quoi ça va ressembler," i dit, "déshonorer ma famille, c'est tout." I la fout dhors. Là a y a dit, là a dit, "Pourtant, ej m'en, ej l'enbandonne pas." A dit, "Ej mets l'feu."—"Bien," i dit, "va-t-en! Descends pus!" I la fout dhors *anyway*. Ça fa *anyway* don quand ça vient pou l', l'mariage, i voula pas l'entende parler. Non. Non, c'est pas d'méme. La, la première s'marie, la plus vieille, s'marie avec in prince. Il ont pas té dmandé aux noces—ieusses. Et la deuxième s'a marié. Non. C'est pas d'méme. Quand la promière s'a marié là, hein, ben i tiont mariés là, ieusses, i sont mariés là *anyway*.

A.K.: Tchi?

—I sont mariés, l'prince, l'prince pis l'jardinier. J'me trompe. Là *anyway* la plus vieille s'a marié, pis i tiont pas dmandé aux noces, hein. Ça fait i dit à sa femme i dit, "J'allons aller aux noces à souère." A dit, "T'es fou, toi." A dit, "J'ons pas dmandé." A dit, "J'avons té *manager* le château d'mon père," a dit, "c'est pas pour aouère le méme droit," i dit, "ouais, j'allons aller." *Anyway*, i rente dans sa chambe, sa marraine ta là, hein. Pis a y donne trois noix—vous savez quoi-ç-que c'est eune noix, hein?

G.T.: Hm.

—Noisette. A dit, "Asteure là-d'dans," a dit, "y a chacun in habit. Pis," a dit, "y a trois soirées d'noces, ça fa," a dit, "vous allez aux trois noces, aux trois soirées." Et a dit, "Vous allez aouère in changement d'habits à chaque noix," hein. Ça fa *anyway* quand ça a vnu pour s'greyer, i dit, "C'est temps qu'tu t'greyes," hein. "Mais," a dit, "ej vas pas aux noces pas moi," a dit, "j'ai pas d'robe."—"Ben," i dit, "tchiens, câsse çte noix-là," i dit, "ton *suit* est là-d'dans." Là a câsse son noix hein. A l'a mis, a l'ava vu, la couleur du soleil hein?

A.K.: Oh God!

—Dans l'noix, hein? Pis lui câsse la sienne pis ç'ta pareil hein? Chacun in habit la méme couleur. Ça fa, sa marraine y a dit, a dit, "Quand vous srez pârés, y ara in choual pis eune carrosse pou vous prende là-bâs." Ça fa i s'greyont pis s'en allont. Quand qu'il arrivont là, bien, l'âroi, parsonne les connaissait, hein?—"Garde!"

A.K.: Oh!

—Faisa des contes d'méme. Vous faisiez ça d'abord. Là *anyway* ça s'pâsse. La deuxième soirée don quand ç'a vnu i câssont la deuxième noix. Bien là, tait don in habit d'couleur—qu'la lune. Ça fait i s'en allont mais parsonne les connaissait hein. Ça fa don quand la noce tait fini don i s'en avont té, hein. Et vlà in ptit peu pus tard la troisième soirée, i câsse don la troisième noix i n'avait don l'habit couleur d'étoiles. Ça fa don la troisième soirée faula don—qu'i contiont chacun eune histouère.

A.K.: Oh ouais?

—Ça fa *anyway*—là toutes les autes contiont des histouères c'est ienque les deux dârniers qu'avont resté, hein. Ces deux-là hein. Ça fa don i s'mat à conter hein. Quand qu'il avait parti d'chez ieusses et, i dit qu'il avait té chez l'âroi pis il ava séjour i dit. "C'est ici j'ai travaillé—vous erappelez-vous," i dit, "du ptit jardinier," i dit, "qui planta ses fleurs la racine en haut?"—"C'est pas toi!" i dit. I dit, "Ouais, c'est moi." — "Bien," i dit, "vous m'avez *banishé* du château," i dit, "pis," i dit, "asteure j'sus aussi bon comme toi. J'ai marié vote fille pou—content—contentement, mais," i dit, "j'sus aussi bon comme vous quand méme." Pis ç'a fini là.

(p. 168)

CINQ SOUS L'POIL

Ej sais qu'i voulait enoueyer son garçon vende sa vache—ç'ta Jack, hein?

G.T.: Oui.

A.K.: Cinq sous l'poil.

G.T.:   —Ouais.

G.T.:   Hein?

  —A y dmande cinq sous l'poil.

G.T.:   Ouais.

  —Pou sa vache, hein?

G.T.:   Ouais.

  —Il erconte in homme, i dit, "Où-ç-que tu vas avec ta vache?"—"M'en vas la vende," i dit. "Comment qu'tu dmandes pou ta vache?"—"Bien," i dit, "Ej la vends cinq sous l'poil."

A.K.:   Ha ha ha!

  —C'est in conte! "Bien," i dit, "tu dmandes pas in ptit coup pou ta vache."—"Uh bien," i dit, "ceux qui m'donnent pas cinq sous l'poil a pas ma vache." *Anyway*, qu—qu'i va marcher, eh. I rencontre in aute. *Anyway* i dit, "Où-ç-que tu vas avec ta vache, Jack?"—"Ouais," i dit, "ej m'en vas avec ma vache. Ej m'en vas la vende." I dit, "Combien qu'tu dmandes pou ta vache?"—"Cinq sous l'poil."—"Uh," i dit, "tu dmandes trop cher pou ta vache. Tu la vendras pas."—"Bien," i dit, "i faut qu'ej dmande le *worth* [angl. la valeur] d'ma vache." I dit, "Si tu m'donnes pas cinq sous l'poil," i dit, "ej la vendras pas." Tchiens! *Anyway*, i trouve le troisième pis i dmande pareil, hein? Ça fa i dmande où-ç-qu'i va avec sa vache pis i dit, "Ej m'en vas vendé ma vache." I dit, "Comment-ç-qu'tu dmandes pou ta vache?" I dit, "Ej dmande cinq sous l'poil." I dit, "Bien," i dit, "tu la vendras pas."—"Ben," i dit, "quitte-lé, tu la veux pas, quitte-lé. Dmandez in aute prix d'ma vache," i dit, "aspère." *Anyway* i marche. Il arrive à l'église. Il amârre sa vache dhors pis i rente. Là *anyway*, i voit l'estâtue d'la Saint Viarge. I s'en va, y a dit, "Tu veux acheter ma vache, toi?" Pas d'raponse. Ç'ta eune stâtue, hein. I dit, "Ej te dmande si tu veux acheter ma vache." Pis i dit, "Raponds! Si tu raponds pas," i dit, "tu vas aouère des rgrets."

A.K.:   Ha ha ha!

  —Uh, là, *anyway*, rapond pas. Ouais. "Bien," i dit, "ej te dmande pour le troisième coup. Dis," i dit, "si tu m'donnes pas d'raponse," i dit, "tu vas m'raponde bien don, tu vas aouère des rgrets." I y dmande si alle ara acheté sa vache—encore pour le troisième coup. Pas d'raponse. I prend in bâton pis i la colle ça. I la câsse. Mais c'est là qu'alle a l'trésor, hein!

A.K.:   Ohhh!

  —Pis là i s'met à ramasser, i disait, "Y en a assez, y en a assez, y en a assez!" I dit, "Pas trop, pas trop!"

A.K.:   Ha ha ha!

  —Pis ç'ta tchurieux, hein? Ça continuait à couler eh?

A.K.:   Ben ouais.

  —Il a pris eune saquée d'argent pis quitte la vache là pis s'en va avec la saquée d'argent chez ieusses, hein? Il avait ieu assez, cinq sous l'poil!

A.K.:   Uh ouais!

  (p. 191)

LA BICHE

Uh bien j'pense que la biche là asteure c'est ça, y a in homme et eune femme. I s'aviont marié et pis i tiont jènes eh? Et alle a vnu enceinte la femme, hein? Et avant qu'alle a trouvé son bébé, hein, la djerre s'a declaré et pis son homme tait bugé d'aller à la djerre, t'sais. Ça fa là il avait quitté in sarvant—i savait qu'alle avait trouvé in bébé hein? Il avait quitté in sarvant pou la soigner t'sais. Ça fa i y avait dit, "*Whatever you do*," i dit, "fais-y pas mal." C'est comme alle avait trouvé in bébé par lui, hein?

Ça fa *anyway*, i s'en va à la djerre. Là, il avait quitté çte gars-là pour la soigner et pis là, il ava assayé d'aouère *you know, advantage* d'ielle hein? I voula qu'alle obéit à lui, t'sais, parce que son homme tait parti hein? Mais alle a pas voulu t'sais. Là, ça fa *anyway* il enoueyait des lettes, hein, chez ieusses. Sa mère à lui, hein. De faire attention à sa femme tant qu'il est à la djerre. Là *anyway*, i fait asteure—où-ç-qu'il alliont porter le *mail*, hein, ben i pouviont pas aller porter le *mail* pis s'en vnir *back* la méme jornée hein, i alliont eune motché l'chmin pis i couchiont là, pis l'endmain i alliont porter l'*mail* sus l'champ d'bataille. Ça fa *anyway*, çte jornée-là, le *mailman*, s'en va *anyway* pis alors, i fait la langue avec çte gârs-là qui soignait la femme hein? I fait la langue avec çte gârs qu'était eune motché l'chmin là, ej dirons hein. Ou c'est lui qui portait l'*mail*, ej sais pas *anyway*. I avait dit d'méme que quand qu'el *mail* alla vnir, foulait qu'i pâsse à coucher, ç'a ouvri le *mail* pis faire attention qu'y avait des lettes pour lui—pour ielle, hein. Pis s'i avait des lettes pour ielle bien, "Tu les liras." Ça fa *anyway*, alle a trouvé l'occasion d'enoueyer eune lette à sa mère pis i dit sa femme avait trouvé in ptit garçon hein. Ça fa *anyway*—quand qu'il a rçu les nouvelles i tait bien fier. Ça fa *anyway*, lui, i savait tout ça là asteure çte gârs-là, nouvelles qu'il enoueyait, hein. Ça fait quoi-ç-qu'i fait, i fait eune lette comme si ç'ara vnu d'sa mère à lui, hein? Pis i, a y dit d'méme sus la lette que sa femme avait trouvé in ptit chien hein?

A.K.: Heh heh!

—Ça fa i renoueye la raponse de ç'ptit chien ou ptit chat d'y faire attention comme les yeux d'sa téte hein? Et asteure qui pâsse asteure, tu sais mais asteure çte gârs-là hein, bien i rouve le sac de *mail* pis i lit la lette tu sais. Ça fa *anyway*, quoi-ç-qu'i fait lui, i fait eune aute lette hein, pis i dit à sa mère de prende çte ptit chien-là—la prende ielle pis son ptit chien-là hein et les emmener dans l'bois pis les tuer. Si c'est in ptit chien i n'en voula pas. Quand qu'a reçoit la lettre la femme, hein, a s'met à pleurer. Pis là i y dmande quoi-ç-qu'alle ava à pleurer. A y dit hein, a dit, "J'ai ieu eune lette de ton homme," a dit, "pis i m'dit pou t'enoueyer dans l'bois aussi loin comme qu'ej pourrais t'enoueyer pis de t'faire tuer."

A.K.: Oh ho!

—"Bien," a dit, "c'est ça. I faut les obéir hein?" Fa *anyway*, alle a dmandé deux hommes. Là le... homme la prend dans l'bois pou la tuer, hein? Ça fa asteure, ces hommes-là, ces deux hommes-là, ces deux hommes-là hein, bien là, le, la dârniere maladie, ç'tait ielle qui l'avait soigné asteure, sainte Geneviève hein—sainte Geneviève ça hein? Ça fa *anyway*, a prend don ces deux hommes-là pis i s'en allont avec ielle dans l'bois, son bébé pis ielle, tous les deux. Pis il aviont in chien avec ieusses, in gros chien. Ça fa qu'il avont té loin assez *anyway*, i s'arrétont pis là eç tait *deadlock*. I faula don la tuer hein. Pis asteure il ava dit, hein, quand qu'il alliont la tuer d'y arracher les deux yeux d'la téte pis y apporter pour, pour, pour *proof* hein?

A.K.: Ptit Golo.

G.T.: Golo.

—C'est Golo qu'était son nom, hein

A.K.: Oh ouais, ça tait son nom.

—Çte gârs-là—

A.K.: Golo, Golo, ouais.

—Quand qu'il arrivont pour tuer la femme, i pouviont pas, il aviont pas l'tchoeur. Ielle pis son bébé. Ça fa *anyway*, i y a iun qui dit, "Ben," i dit, "moi, ej la tue pas."—"Mais," i dit, "a nous a dit d'apporter les deux yeux." I dit, "Si j'y portons pas ben i va nous tuer, hein?"—"Bien," i dit, "tue ton chien." Pis i dit, "J'allons arracher les yeux du chien pis j'allons les paquer j'allons les emmener, i va croire qu'c'est ça hein." *All right*. Dame, faula qu'a promette de jamais en sortir du bois.

Faula qu'a reste dans l'bois—faula rester là hein. Alle ava arien à manger, arien à boire. Ienque ielle et son bébé hein. *So okay.* I s'en venont à la maison et i dit, "Avez-vous fait ça ej vous ai dit d'faire?" A dit—i ont dit, "Ouais." I dit, "J'avons emmené les deux yeux." Ben asteure, il aviont ah, les yeux d'paqués dans in mouchoir de poche hein? Ben i dit, "Tchiens, vlà les deux yeux, les deux yeux," i dit—i a pas voulu les prende. Il avait d'l'argret hein? Ça fa *anyway*, la djerre allait *on*, et pis là, ça pâsse—ç'ta in conte. Ça pt-éte in ptit bout hein? Ça fa *anyway*, eune bonne jornée la, la la...djerre a fini. Ouais. A çte coup-là hein. Quand qu'c'est qu'alle a ieu—qu'alle a té dans l'bois avec son bébé, hein, bien alle a tué des *buffalo*—des, des moutons pis alle a fait eune robe avec la peau d'mouton hein? Ça ç'tait, portrait, ç'tait juste son portrait hein? Ça fa *anyway*, l'bébé tombe malade—eune soirée pis là don alle avait pas d'médecine pou son bébé, pas arien à y donner à manger, n'arien du tout. I mangiont des racines, hein? Quoi faire? Don alle ara pardu son bébé hein? Là *anyway*, i l'a entendu gratter à la porte dans l'tchoeur d'minuit du soir. Dans la forêt d'méme, tout seuls, tous les deux hein? Son bébé malade. Alle a eune croix de fait avec deux bois hein? Pis là qu'a prie à la croix, hein, tu la vois si bien hein? Il entend don à la porte, a rouve la porte—eune biche, ptit biche, comme in moyen chien, ej dirons eh. Ça fa i dit, "Ma pauve biche," a dit, "si tu sarais don la misère qu'ej sus d'dans," a dit, "mon bébé est malade," a dit, "pis y a arien à boire, arien à manger. A s'couche. Son ermelle là bien c'est *right* gros hein?
A.K.: Ah, God dash!
—Alle avait trouvé des ptits chiens pis ses ptits chiens avont corvé hein? Bien don son ermelle faisait mal—a s'couche pou qu'le bébé téte dsus. Ça fa don prend le bébé pis a téte sus la biche, hein? Après ça, à tous les jours a venait à çte moment-là hein, tous les jours a venait pour qu'a—le bébé téte sus ielle—assaie d'la soulager, tu sais. Tu vois la ptite biche—la chère ptite béte—couchée pis l'bébé téte hein?
A.K.: Ohh!
—Ça fa *anyway*, in grand boute aprés, ej sais pas combien qu'ça a pris d'temps, *anyway* ça a pris pas in ptit coup. Quand alle était dans l'bois—la djerre finit *anyway*, pis là don lui qui s'en vient chez ieusses pour ouère sa femme et pis sa—son bébé hein? Le ptit ta encore en vie. I dmande à sa mère quoi-ç-qu'alle avait fait avec sa femme. A dit, "M'as-tu pas enoueyé d'la tuer?" I dit, "Quoi!" i dit, "faire tuer ma femme?" i dit. "Ej t'avais enoueyé eune lette," i dit, "pis ej t'avais dit de faire bien attention," i dit, "à ma femme pis mon bébé."—"Bien," a dit, "c'est ça. Tu m'enoueyais d'la faire tuer pis," a dit, "asteure ej l'ai fait tuer."
A.K.: Ohh!
—Là, l'vlà fou—parti fou. I prend son choual pis i s'p—lance. "Bien asteure ej viens pas avant qu'ej la trouve. Qu'a seye mort ou en vie il faut ej la trouve n'importe ioù-ç-qu'alle est, hein?" La ça fait *anyway*, eune jornée don Geneviève eh, sa mère chez l'ptit *God love*. Ç'ta pt-éte d'en-dhors. I voyont in homme vnir. Parce a y ava toute conté, hein? Quand qu'il aviont l'emmenée dans l'bois pour la faire tuer et toute en grand, i y avait deux hommes, y avait pour la faire tuer. Pis ça fait *anyway* i voyont çt homme-là vnir. I tiont dhors, i bat—charchiont des racines manger hein? I dit, "Maman gare là qui s'en vient encore," i dit, "pour nous faire du mal. Mais," i dit, "aies pas peur, j'sus ici moi," i dit...
A.K.: Oh my God!
—I tait neuf ans qu'i avait. "N'aies pas peur," i dit, "j'sus ici moi," pis i l'attrape et l'embrasse encore sa mère, hein, pis i aspère l'homme à vnir. Et quand que c'est qu'il arrivait là i s'a jté à gnoux à ielle pis i s'dmandait pardon hein. Parce qu'i dit qu'il avait pas dit ça, lui, c'est ienque Golo là, c'est ienque Golo...
A.K.: Ouais, Golo, ouais.

—Qu'a pu l'faire. Ça fait a dit eh, la djerre a fini pis i ta ervnu pis il ara pas ieu—il ara pas mouri sans la trouver. Là asteure quand qu'i s'en allont hein, i la prend pis i l'emmène—chez ieusses. Mais alle a pas vi autchun temps quand qu'alle a pris la nourriture de—i demeuriont pt-éte bien eune dizaine d'années sus les racines hein.

A.K.:   Hmm.

—Ça fa lui, i l'a pris pis i l'a chaîné comme tu aras chaîné in chien là. I l'a chaîné à chain pis tu l'—"Vlà," i dit—couché sus l'côté pis i hale sus la chaîne pour assayer d'la câsser hein? Pis c'est toute qu'ej sais.

A.K.:   Ptit maudit!

—C'est ienque in morceau hein.

G.T.:   Hm.

A.K.:   Da's de best kind dat.

G.T.:   That's not finished?

—C'est pas fini—ah non! C'est pas l'ptit quart ça, mon cher. C'est pas l'ptit quart. I n'a pâssé d'la misère. I n'a pâssé..

(p. 194)

LES ENFANTS PARDUS

Oh mais les enfants pardus, ça ej sais ienqu'in ptit morceau de d'dans.

A.K.:   Mais ouais ça fait arien, in ptit morceau.

—Bien ça ç'ta in homme et eune femme, il aviont in ptit garçon hein—i s'appelait—ej savais toutes leus noms hein? Y en a iun qui s'appelait—Pierre Col et pis l'aute s'appelait—y avait deux Col pis asteure y avait in ptit... Asteure *anyway* ça ç'tait deux ptits cousins, hein? Ça fa i tiont à carnasser dhors eune jornée pis là i rente pour, à dmander à sa mère pour eune tranche de pain, eune tranche de pain c'est eune, eune taille, eune taille hein? A y fout in plein claque sus la téte pis a y dit d's'en aller hein, a y donne pas d'pain. "Bien," i dit, "ej m'en vas pis ej erviens pus. Tu m'eroiras plus," i dit. Bien, a croyait qu'i disait ça pour *fun* hein? Ça fa i s'en allont—*play* sus l'bord d'la rue hein? *Anyway*, y a in homme qui pâsse pis i ava trois barils sus sa chariot hein—tchusez-moi—là i prend les trois ptits garçons pis i les met don dans chaque des barils pis i les emporte, i les vole hein? I les a volés. Ça fait, il y a—sa mère et son père charchaient pour lui pis i ont pas trouvé, i tait parti. Ça fait *anyway*, i marchiont dans la forêt hein, tous les trois. Là il ont marché, il ont marché, il ont marché. Ej sais pas combien tait avant qu'il avont trouvé des habitants, hein? Ça fait, il avont arrivé à eune cabane savage eune soirée hein, pis ç'tait ienque lui qui tait hardi, hein. I rente. Y avait ienque eune fille qui soignait hein, pis i dmande pour y donner à manger, y donner du pain pis y donner d'quoi d'méme. "J'sus pas capabe," a dit, "mon père et ma mère sont partis pis," a dit, "s'i venont à déclarer ça i vont m'batte."—"Oh mais," i dit, "ej vons pas rester," i dit, "ej vons m'ballader. Ej vons pas l'dire, parsonne va saouère," i dit. Là a y donne du pain et du thé et du lette et toute en grand hein? Pis là i s'prenont à *traveller* encore et l'ptit cousin, hein? Là *anyway*, y avait cinq ans quand qu'il a parti, là, lui, d'chez ieusses hein. Là *anyway* in coup, après qu'il était fini d'*traveller*, ej dirons là—i aviont *travellé* dans l'bois, lui pis son ptit frère—son ptit cousin, i tombe malade là lui, hein. Il avait soif, pis il avait faim. Pis ej sais pas combien d'milles foulait qu'i *trav*—asteure foulait qu'i marche pour aouère du l'eau pour son ptit cousin, hein. Il avait la pépie hein. Ça fait *anyway*, tu les vois, i s'en allont tous les deux, i l'quittont là, hein. I s'en allont, i marchont ensemble pis arien pour mette l'eau d'dans, ienque la canon d'son fisil...

A.K.:   Oh gee whiz!

310

—Ça fa avant qu'il avont té arendu pour aouère d'l'eau et ervnu *back* à lui i ta mort...

A.K.: Oh dash!

—Ça fa i l'prenont pis i l'enterront là pis les deux autes se prenont, hein. Ça fa asteure, ej sais pas quoi-ç-que c'est qu'a devnu lui, ej me souviens pas. Là *anyway* lui, il a marché assez qu'il a *tra*—il a cha—sort dans in village. Ça fa *anyway*, i va charcher pour eune job hein? Eh, i ta vieux çte temps-là, il ava *travellé* toute en grand çte temps-là. Ben, i avait cinq ans quand qu'il a parti d'chez ieusses hein et là çte temps-là i avait quarante-cinq. Ça fa quarante ans qu'i y ava qu'i *travellait*, hein.

A.K.: Ouais.

—Ouais. Et i a, i a té eune maison eune jornée pis i l'avont engagé, hein. Et à tous les matins i s'emmenait à l'ouvrage à pied hein, i marchait à l'ouvrage pis à çte—toutes les matins quand qu'i pâssait y avait eune femme, a tait assis sus l'*balcony* hein. Selon l'conte—pis a l'veillait pâsser. Ça fa eune matinée—là i leu y dit ailloù-c-qu'i restait qu'y avait eune femme qui l'veillait pâsser à tous les matins, i dit, "Ej sais pas quoi-ç-qu'est la cause de ça," i dit, "ej sais pas tchi qu'alle est *anyway*." Bien çte matinée-là *anyway* i pâssait, hein, pis la femme tait dhors et a y dmande tchi qu'il était parce a voulait saouère tchi-ç-qu'i tait, hein. A l'connaissait et pis a pouvait pas dire tchi-ç-qu'i tait. A pouvait pas dire son nom. A dit qu'a sait—ej dirons...

A.K.: She knowed him, eh?

—...çte gârs-là hein. Pis i y a dit son nom hein pis ça ç'tait sa marraine.

A.K.: Ahh!

—La barbe tait poussée là déjà lui hein, barbeux, toute en grand barbeux hein.

Pis ça ç'ta sa marraine ça, hein? I pâssa à toutes les matins à la porte à sa marraine pis i la connaissa pas—ej sais pus, ça. Ej sais pus ça, c'est pas l'ptit quart, l'petit quart....

A.K.: Non.

G.T.: C'est pas l'ptit quart?

A.K.: Yeah, she never tole it all *anyway*.

G.T.: Do you know the rest of it?

A.K.: She never tole it all *anyway*.

—Ej sais pas le restant.

A.K.: You tole longer n dat to me.

G.T.: What came after?

—Non non, c'est, c'est, ça, c'est ça là qu'ej t'as conté bien c'est ienque ça qu'ej sais hein.

A.K.: Da's a long—it's longer n dat. De, i tait dans la grange là.

—Pas lui.

A.K.: Tchi qu'c'est don? Tu sais bien.

—T'es folle toi!

A.K.: Phew!

—Oh ouais. Ouais, uh ouais, ouais asteure...

A.K.: Ha ha ha!

—Asteure ej me rappelle, ah ah! Le promier coup qu'il a sorti au village hein, bien il a té dans eune maison hein. Y avait ienque in homme pis eune femme, in vieux pis eune vieille qui tiont là hein. Pis i leu demande pour le *lodger* pis i voulont pas, hein. Là *anyway*, i dit, "La seule place qu'ej peux trouver c'est dans ma grange." I va pis i s'met dans la grange, hein. Et à minuit l'souère, il entend du train pis quoi-ç-que ç'tait, ç'tait in homme. I s'en vena don voler du foin hein, pou ses bétes... [pause pour changer de bande; mais Mme Ozon n'a plus rien à ajouter au conte.]

(p. 201)

L'AROI DES POISSONS

B.O.: L'âroi des poissons.

A.K.: I knowed one all right, but I fergets it, non.

G.T.: About the man who didn't have any children an he went fishin and ah, I don't know it eh? Ah he fished up the king o the fish?

A.K.: Right.

G.T.: Is that it?

A.K.: Yes.

G.T.: Go on then.

A.K.: Uh well, I don't know eh?

G.T.: Well you recognize it when I say it, that beginning part.

A.K.: I's de start of it, yes.

G.T.: An the fish says, "Throw me back in an fish on the other side," or something an he does that three times.

A.K.: Yeah.

G.T.: And um, the third time he takes a fish in and the fish says to cut him up.

A.K.: Yeah. Ah, give de guts—wait now, wait now—de meat to his wife, de bones to his dog—to his bitch dere—an de guts, ah, wait now...

B.O.: Mette dans son jardin.

A.K.: Ouais. So his wife'll have tree twins eh, tree boys, his dog have tree chops—pups an have tree roses in de garden eh.

G.T.: Well tell de story then.

A.K.: Oh i's a nice story, I donno dat *mignon*.

G.T.: Start from the beginning, maybe it'll come back to you.

A.K.: Da's, da's de beginnin.

G.T.: No, well, right, y'know, I said the first bit but you start right from the very beginning, cos I mean, I don't know the way to say it you see, I just heard a little bit...

A.K.: But me my dear, da's all, da's all I can remember is dat dere. My God! I donno de name o de house dere.

G.T.: Eh?

B.O.: Eh heh!

G.T.: An he goes—the boys go off one at a time and ah...

A.K.: Who here tells dat story?

B.O.: C'est Bill et Tom et Jack hein? Ouais.

G.T.: Yeah. No, I read about it once. Um, and they met an old witch or somethin.

A.K.:   They got married eh?

G.T.:   I don't know.

A.K.:   Is one got married, I know. De first one got married eh?

G.T.:   I never heard dat.

B.O.:   Ouais.

A.K.:   An when he went to say his prayer in de night eh...

B.O.:   I s'couchait avec eune jambe au bord du lit. Couchait...

A.K.:   Oh well, when he, when he said his prayers, I donno what kind a house, de, de—my God, de name o de house now. I fergets de name o de house now. Anyway, he tole his wife, he says, "What's dat house over dere?"— "Well," she said, "What goes dere never returns."

G.T.:   Start from the beginning and try to tell me as much of it as you can and maybe Blanche can remember odd bits and pieces.

A.K.:   Oh my gosh, *j'sais pas*. You said the first, you.

G.T.:   Well no, I didn't, I just said the first words but you—I would like you to say it in your words, the way you say it.

A.K.:   My God, Blanche?

B.O.:   Bien y avait in homme et eune femme il aviont—i tiont mariés hein? Pis lui ç'tait in pêcheur pis il allait pêcheur hein. Pis eune jornée là il a pêché, çte morue-là hein, pis là il a dit à sa femme qu'il ava pris eune morue, in joli poisson, hein. Pis a dit, "Demain," a dit, "si tu n'en prends in aute tu vas me l'emmner, manger." Vois-tu c'est d'méme hein?

A.K.:   *Ouais ouais*, da's de way it was tole here, here.

B.O.:   Et l'endemain, il a té pis il a trapé eune morue, çte morue-là hein, pis i l'a emmené pis i l'a fait tchuire pis a l'a mangé, alle a, a—alle a mangé la viande, alle a donné les os à son chien et les tripes a les a plantés dans son jardin hein.

A.K.:   Ouais, ouais d'méme.

B.O.:   Oh ouais. Et ah... sa femme don alle a trouvé trois ptits garçons hein—

A.K.:   Ouais.

B.O.:   Pis ç'ta don Tom et Bill et Jack.

A.K.:   Ouais.

B.O.:   Ç'tait leus noms t'sais. Le promier qui s'en était, ç'tait Bill. Bill a té pis i s'a marié et ça fa *anyway* quand qu'il a dit ses prières le soir pour aller s' oucher hein...

A.K.:   Ramasse ça!

B.O.:   Hein?

A.K.:   *Ramasse ça* hein?

B.O.:   Pas d'diffarence. Quand qu'il a té pour s'coucher i dit ses prières pis là *anyway* il a vu çte maison-là hein, pis i y a dmandé ouère quoi-ç-que— tchelle sorte de maison qu'ç'tait pis a y a dit, a dit, "*Don't*," a dit, "*bother* pas pour çte maison-là qu'," a dit, "tout-ç-qui va par là—qui va là vient pas." Et là *anyway*, i s'a couché, le ventre en l'air dans l'lit pis il ava— eune jambe en bas du lit hein? Ça fa *anyway*, quand sa femme était endormie il a parti pis il a pas ârvnu *anyway*. Fa *anyway* l'endemain Bill pârt, Bill—Tom.

313

A.K.: He goes in the garden firs.

B.O.: Non non. Oui, pis quand qu'il ont parti là asteure j'ai oublié hein, quand qu'il ont parti—bien ouais, justement, c'est d'méme qu'ej pense—là *anyway* Tom a parti après hein.

G.T.: What about ah...

B.O.: I foulait qu'il alle charcher son frère qui tait parti hein.

G.T.: Blanche, what about the, the three things that the, the, ones they gave the dog and ah, the one she planted in the garden? What happened to that?

A.K.: He went with the dog. Bill, ah—Tom a té avec son chien hein—now when, when he was enchanted dere eh...

B.O.: Bien ouais, ben asteure...

A.K.: Well, one o de roses was down eh?

B.O.: Ouais.

A.K.: De nex marnin, so Bill went to de garden eh?

B.O.: A conte ouère. Conte-lé toi.

A.K.: Non non, conte-lé toi.

G.T.: Conte, Blanche.

B.O.: Ej le sais pas.

A.K.: No no, you talks good you.

B.O.: Et là *anyway*, le souère i marche pis quand qu'il arrive à çte maison-là hein, ben sa femme y dmande ioù qu'i dvenait. "Oh," i dit, "j'ai té à l'entour," i dit. Ça fa *anyway* le soir là i s'greyont pour aller s'coucher, a dit, "Asteure tu vas vnir t'coucher," et là quand, tu sais, i s'met d'à ouère quoi-ç-que c'est que ç'tait çte maison-là. A dit, "Ej t'ai dit hier à souère," a dit, "quoi-ç-que ç'tait çte maison-là," a dit. "Tout-ç-qui va ârvient pas." Ça fa *anyway*, i s'couche encore pareil comme son frère, i s'couche eune jambe en bâs du lit, hein. Ça fa a y dit, a dit, "Quoi-ç-qu'est la cause que tu t'couches avec eune jambe en bâs du lit?" A dit, "Hier à souère t'as couché avec eune jambe en bâs du lit pis," a dit, "à souère tu t'couches encore avec eune jambe en bâs du lit." I dit, "C'est *all right*," i dit, "c'est d'méme que je m'couche." Ça fa *anyway* quand sa femme tait endormie i s'en va encore à la maison hein. Dame, ej peux pas vous dire quoi-ç-qu'a devenu d'ieusses *anyway*. *Anyway*, il a pas...

A.K.: Dey was turned, dey was turned to a stone.

B.O.: To a stone.

A.K.: Yeah.

B.O.: Et là *anyway*, le lendemain matin il allont au jardin y ava encore eune fleur de part—de tombée hein. Ç'tait la deuxième. Pis là Jack i s'greye pis i s'en va. I dit, "I faut qu'ej trouve mes deux frères," i dit. "Et," i dit, "si ej peux pas trouver mes deux frères," i dit, "eh bien," i dit, "les rosiers allont vnir back en vie."

A.K.: Ouais.

B.O.: C'est ça i a dit, hein?

A.K.: Ouais.

B.O.: Quand qu'il arrive à çte maison-là *anyway*, ah, bien asteure i rente pis là *anyway* sa femme. I allont s'coucher le souère.

A.K.: Oh non, but you said, "Where you come from?" she said.

B.O.: A y a dmandé, "Ioù-ç-que tu d'viens?" a dit. A dit, "Vlà deux soirées de rang qu'tu t'en vas pis t'ârviens pas." A dit, "Ioù-ç-tu vas?"—"Ah," i dit, "ej vas ouère à l'entour," i dit, "visiter." Ça fa *anyway* le, le soir quand qu'il allont s'coucher, i s'met encore d'à gnoux pour dire ses prières. Ça fa *anyway*, hein, i y dmande quoi-ç-que tait que ç'tait çte maison-là. A dit, "La troisième soirée à souère," a dit, "tu m'dmandes la méme chose," a dit, "ej te dis," a dit, "de pas *bodderer* dans çte maison-là parce que," a dit, "tout-ç-qui va ârvient pas." Ça fa s'couche avec eune jambe en bâs du lit hein. A dit, "Quoi-ç-qu'est la cause de ça," a dit, "t'es pas capable de t'coucher dans l'lit?"—"Bien," i dit, "c'est d'méme qu'ej couche."

A.K.: Poor way!

B.O.: "Troisième soirée à souère," a dit...

A.K.: Ah ha ha!

B.O.: "Tu t'couches avec eune jambe en bâs du lit." Ça fa i dit, "C'est *okay*," i dit, "dors." Quand alle a té endormie, i *ârtourne* encore don hein. Ça fait il a pas ârvnu. Mais asteure moi ej sais pas là, là. Ej sais pas ça hein.

A.K.: Il a ârvnu lui.

B.O.: Mais *anyway* le lendemain matin don quand son père s'a lvé il a té à l'jardin...

A.K.: No no, wait now. It was an ole witch in dere y'know. Er...

B.O.: Ej sais pas.

[The rest of the tale is told by A.K., in English]

(p. 208)

RICHARD-SANS-PEUR

Bien Richard-sans-Peur asteure, ça, ç'tait in homme et eune femme, il aviont in garçon hein. Son nom tait Richard pis il avait jamais té peuré. Il ava jamais vu d'quoi qui pouvait l'appeurer hein. Ça fait i disait ça à sa mère à tous les jours i dit, "Ej voudras bien aouère d'quoi qui l'ava—,"—qui pouvait l'appeurer hein. Pis il ava jamais té peuré pis i pouvra pas, i pouvra pas croire qu'i pouvait éte appeuré. Ça fa *anyway*, a disait à son homme le souère, a dit, "A souère tu vas appeurer Richard." I dit, "Ouais. Comment?"—"Ben," i dit, "à souère ej vas faire mine qu'—ej vas pas chailler d'l'eau pour la nuit hein. Ben," i dit, "aprés la nuit j'vas t'rouler dans in drap blanc," et y a dit, "qu'tu vas aller t'coucher dans l'chemin. Pis," a dit, "quand qu'la nuit va éte fârmée bien noire là ben," a dit, "ej vas y dire qu'ej as pas d'eau pis," a dit, "ej vas l'enoueyer quri d'l'eau, hein." A dit, "Couchez à travers le chemin." *Anyway* quand le soir vient asteure ah, "Ben," a dit, "Richard," a dit, "j'as pas d'eau pour la nuit." A dit, "Tu vas ête bugé d'aller n'en quri." Là l'vieux tait parti là hein. I dit, "Ouais." A dit, "T'as pas peur d'aller?"—"Peur!" i dit, "j'ai jamais vu d'quoi-ç-qui m'a appeuré encore." A dit, "Sais pas, pourras ouère de quoi."—"Bien," i dit, "si j'vois d'quoi, ej m'en saouère quoi faire—saouère quoi faire avec."

A.K.: Ha ha ha!

—*Anyway*, prend les deux siaux pis i s'en va au risseau—c'est eune grande distance aller au risseau hein? Quand qu'i sait—qu'i, qu'il a—qu'i va au risseau, i pêchait les siaux d'eau pis i pârt à s'en vnir, hein. Quand qu'il arrive eune distance i tait à motché l'chmin, i voit çt affaire-là dans l'chmin, blanc comme la neige qui s'trouvait dans l'chmin. Il arrive à lui, i dit, "Quoi-ç-tu fais ici toi?" I dit, "Quitte-moi pâsser."

A.K.: Ah ha ha ha!

315

—Ça bougeait pas, ça s'roulait hein? "Ben," i dit, "ej vas t'dire deux fois, la troisième coup si t'ertires pas de d'dans mon chmin ej vas t'ertirer moi." *Okay*. Là, i dit pour la deuxième coup—c'est là qu'i s'roulait, hein? I s'roulait comme i faut hein. "Ben," i dit, "c'est l'dârnier coup. Va-t-en!" I l'coute pas, i s'tire dsus. Met ses deux siaux en bâs et i l'prend pis i l'donne eune maudite râclée. I manque d'le tuer. Ça fait i l'prend pis i l'jette à côté du chmin pis i prend ses deux siaux pis i s'en va chez ieusses. Pis asteure *anyway*, i arrivait chez ieusses pis a y dit, "Bien," i dit, a dit, "Richard," a dit, "t'as pas arien vu?"—"J'ai vu eune affaire qu'y avait dans l'chmin là," i dit. I dit, "I voula pas m'quitter pâsser mais j'ai pâssé." Ha ha ha! "Ej te garantis," i dit, "avec ça qu'ej y as donné," i dit, "i va, i va pas s'en lever dmain." A dit, "Quoi!" A dit, "T'as pas batti ton père?"—"C'est pas mon père qui tait fou assez aller s'mette dans l'chmin?" i dit.

A.K.: Eh heh heh heh!

—Et j'sus fatigué d'dire à mon père," i dit, "d'arrêter d'm'en peur. Ça fait," i dit, "c'est pas lui qu'est l'homme à peurer." I dit, "Ej l'ai donné eune belle râclée pis j'l'ai jté à côté du chemin. Ça ben," i dit, "asteure si i tait fou assez d', a'aller là bien," i dit, "c'est ça."—"Ben," a dit, "t'as foutu eune douille à ton père tu l'as pt-ête tué eune motché ça fait," a dit, "ej pouvons pas t'garder. Tu vas t'en aller." Ouais. S'en va. Spère pas plus, i décolle. Voyez. *Anyway* i marche et i marche et i marche, *God knows* combien d'jours et nuits hein? Ça fa *anyway*, c'est dans la forêt *anyway*, il arrive une grande maison. Là *anyway*, i rente. Ç'tait la nuit hein. Pis i rente là i y avait in poéle, y avait tout-ç-qu'i foulait, ienque d'quoi à manger, hein? Pis il ava d'quoi à manger sus lui hein. Ça fa *anyway*, il allume le poéle pis i s'prend à faire des crêpes hein? Ça fa *anyway* i entend, "Gare de dsus Richard, gare de dsus," i dit. "Tombe si tu veux," i dit, "mais tombe pas dans ma poéle."

A.K.: Hee hee hee!

—Là eune jambe tombe. Oh, i prend la jambe pis i la pique deboute. Ben, l'commencement d'in homme *anyway*. Ça fa *anyway*, in ptit boute aprés, i s'ont dit, i dit, "Gare de dsus." *Okay*. I dit, "Gare de dsus mais," i dit, "tombe pas dans ma poéle. Fa attention!" Là l'aute jambe tombe hein. Ben il est toute en grand par morceaux ej dirons hein.

A.K.: Ouais ouais.

—Pour couper l'ptit corps, ej dirons. Là, la, le corps a tombé, i prend le corps—i pique les deux jambes deboute—i prend l'corps pis i l'pique sus—i les met, met sus les deux jambes. Ouais. Là, la forme d'in homme hein. Bientôt, i tombe in bras. Là i prend l'bras pis i l'colle. Là, là, in boute aprés, i tombe l'aute bras, i l'met là. "Ah!" i dit, "j'écoute la téte. Quand i va tomber la téte," i dit,—"j'arai d'la compagnie." Pas peur. Là toujours *anyway*. Bientôt là i dit, "*Ah well*," i dit, "*come on*." Tombe la téte d'in homme. Ben i prend la téte bien vite pis i l'pique dsus. "Ah bien," i dit. "J'arai d'la compagnie asteure." Ouais. Ça fa *anyway*, "Ah bien," i dit, "Jack," i dit—pas Jack mais "Richard," i dit, "tu vas, j'allons jouer eune *game* de cartes."—"*Okay*," i dit. "Peux-tu jouer aux cartes?"—"Ouais, joue aux cartes moi." Prend don. *Anyway*, jouont aux cartes. Ah, in boute aprés i voit ça, la vilaine béte, le diabe hein. I largue eune carte. I dit, "Gare, t'as largué eune carte. Ramasse-lé."—"Oh," i dit, "ramasse-lé toi." Non, le, l'diabe i dit, hein, i dit, "T'as largué eune carte."—"Non, c'est pas moi," i dit, "c'est toi." I dit, "Ramasse ta carte." Là pis i la ramasse. Ça fa *anyway*, i fa ça vers trois fois hein. Vlà l'troisième coup qu'i fait *anyway*, i dit, "Gare! T'as largué eune carte là." Jack y dit, "C'est pas moi." Pas Jack mais *but* Richard y dit, "C'est pas moi, c'est toi." Pis i dit, "Ramasse ta carte."—"Ej la ramasse pas, ç'à toi à la ramasser. C'est toi qui l'as larguée," i dit, "tu vas la ramasser." Ça fa le diabe se baisse en dsous la tabe pour ramasser sa carte pis là, i l'croche par le corps pis i l'fait la signe de croix sus la téte hein. I l'avait. Quoi faire? Pis i dit, asteure le diabe ta mort. "Pis avant, avant," i dit, "qu'tu pars d'ici pis," i dit, "faut qu'tu m'signes ça qu'y a ici en dsus condition que jamais qu't'as affaire ici. Avec le sang d'ton ptit doigt là," i dit, "i faut qu'tu coupes le bout d'ton doigt pis tu m'signes in papier comme quoi tu vas jamais m'troubler." Le diabe il a bugé d'couper l'bout d'son doigt pis i signe in papier.

A.K.:   Ha ha ha! I l'a fait peur!

—Là vlà *anyway*, il attendont don parler d'Richard-sans-Peur qu'il ava jamais té appeuré. Ça fa qu'l'âroi fait in grand *party* hein, pis il invite don Richard pour aller à son *party*. Il ava jamais té appeuré. Ça fa i dit, "Si y a in moyen de l'appeurer, ej vas l'appeurer." I dit, "Si ej l'appeure pas, il est appeurabe." Ça fa i fait ses sarvants pis ses sarvantes qu'i faire eune *puttin*, *gros* puttin pis mette in coq dans la *puttin* hein.

A.K.:   Ouais.

—Ça fa quand qu'tout l'monde a té là *anyway*—i s'mettont là pour tout aouère chaque leu *lunch* hein. Faula don couper la *puttin*, et quand qu'il avont coupé la *puttin*, Richard a vanoui. Parla pas.

A.K.:   Non?

—Hmm. Le coq a sorti de d'dans hein pis ça l'a peuré.

A.K.:   It never took him much this time eh?

—Non. Fini. Ça qu'ej sais d'dans moi *anyway*. Sais pas si c'est toute.

Tales Told By Emile Benoit

(p. 223)

LA BÊTE À SEPT TÊTES

Un coup par eune bonne fois—y avait eune femme et une homme—il aviont in enfant. Et euh, son nom était Jack heh heh! C'est comme on dit, c'est tout l'temps Jack, Jack. On dira pas Jean on dit Jack. Bien, ah il aviont levé leu-z-enfants, il aviont eune ptite farme, eune coupelle de bétes à cornes *an so on*, tcheques moutons—assez pou, pou vive dessus. Et, le garçon a travaillé, i travaillait, i travaillait tout l'temps— mais çtés temps-là—bien—faulait qu't'avais vingt-et-une ans avant qu'tu—que tu tais toi-même. Quand qu'tu avais vingt-et-une ans, ah ben dame, tu tais à toi-même. Bien, c'est bien. Toujours, vlà son—sa naissance qu'arrive—vingt-et-une ans. Hah! Oh, c'est pas eune ptite affaire là, c'est in homme là asteure, ois-tu, oh ho! je le garantis! I tait pas moisi non plus. Là! Ouais, pis le vieux pis la vieille ça commençait à vieillzir, i sont dans leu, leu cinquante ans, d'quoi d'même, et euh—seul garçon qu'il aviont—ej j'te garantis, quand qu'il a dit—à son père, à sa mère, mais i dit, "Pâpa et maman," i dit, "vous savez qu'ej crois," i dit, "qu'ej m'en vas," i dit euh, "me lancer," i dit. "M'en vas aller ouère in ptit peu—l'univers." Parce ioù-ç-qu'i restiont, y avait arien du tout—y avait pt-ête bien, un ptit *shack* à toutes les, à toutes les deux, trois milles d'quoi d'même, y avait pas grand monde d'ces temps-là—pas comme qu'ass—pas comme asteure. "Ah!" i dit, "Pâpa," i dit, euh, i dit, "j'vas m'en aller, j'crois qu'ej m'en vas m'en aller asteure, ouère," i dit, "in ptit peu de l'univers," i dit, "ça va m'instruire in peu," i dit, i dit, "vous m'avez appris in ptit peu d'école," i dit, "mais pas beaucoup." Pis i dit, "J'pourrais aller," i dit, "et pis pt-ête bien," i dit, "faire bien pou moi-même." Pis i dit, "Si j'fais pas bien ben dame," i dit, "là," i dit, "j'pourras vous recompenser—vous mette plus hereux que vous êtes."—"Ah," i dit, "mon enfant," i dit, "j'sons pas encore si miserabe que ça, j'ons d'quoi à manger." Ah ouais, c'est bon là... i parle. Ben là, le lendemain toujours i s'pousse—i s'prend in, in ptit euh, coupelle de ptits—des, des machines, des ptits gâteaux que tu appelles, faits à la melasse, et pis euh—là i s'pousse. Pis là i marche et marche et marche et marche—bientôt vlà la nuit qu'arrive... Fa là i s'fait eune manière de ptite cabane de brousse et pis i s'—hale en-d'sous d'ça—pis i s'couche pis i dort. L'endemain matin i s'erlève—et i mange eune coupelle de *buns* à la melasse pis là i s'pousse encore, et marche et marche et marche et marche. Et euh...c'est bon. Bientôt la nuit arrive encore—pah! Là i s'erpose encore. Pis il a marché comme ça pour trois jours. L'endemain—ç'a arrivé pareil, pis ça marche et marche. Et tout d'in coup—manière dans la brume d'la nuit—i s'aparçoit—"Hey! garde don là-bas! Garde les maisons!" i dit. "Ah! garde don ça," i dit, pis i ergarde,

"Là," i dit, "quoi-ç-qu'il avont là à voler en l'air?" i dit. Toutes les, les, les, les poteaux qu'i voyait, les parches et quoi d'même, i y avait des, des morceaux d'linge dessus il appelle ça, ou des morceaux d'*guinea*, d'quoi d'même ois-tu, i savait pas que c'est des pavillons t'sais, mais c'est, c'est tout *nouère*. Toujours c'est bien, là i s'lave là pour la nuit là, dans sa ptite cabane de brousse pis euh, l'endemain matin—pas—ben oui, l'endemain matin là i s'pousse là. Toujours pis i s'en va. Et vlà—tout l'monde habillé en nouère—les femmes, les hommes, les pavillons nouères—i dit, "Quoi-ç-qu'i y a," i dit, "c'est comme ça," i dit, "qu'le *world* est? C'est-i comme ça," i dit, "c'est in misère, si j'arais su j'aras pas bougé d'chez nous. J'arais resté, y a pus, y a pus d'plaisir chez nous qu'ici, heh! *Gee*, c'est trisse!" Pis là il a commencé à marcher parmi l'monde pis, i disait, "Comment ça va, comment ça va,"—i repondiont pas. C'est toutes la téte en bas pis—des châles nouères sus la téte—"*Gee*! quoi-ç-que le—*diggen* qui marche ici?" I dit, "Quoi-ç-qu'i y a don?" Toujours i passe entor du monde, ici, celle-là, i y a pas grand monde mais euh, plus qu'il avait jamais vi d'sa vie. Toujours i, i dit, parle à iun, in homme qu'i y avait là mais y avait in vieux—i dit, "Quoi-ç-qu'i y a don," i dit, "quoi-ç-que, c'est-i comme ça," i dit, "tout l'monde est," i dit, "dans l'univers?"—"Ah!" i dit, "mon pauvre enfant," i dit. "J'sons toute trisse aujourd'hui." I dit, "Oui," i dit, "j'ois ça," i dit, "vous êtes trisse," i dit, "c'est-i comme ça vous êtes tout l'temps?"—"Ah! non, non," i dit, "c'est pas comme ça j'sons tout l'temps." I dit euh, "A toutes les ans," i dit, "ça ç'arrive ça ici." I dit, "Oui? Bien," i dit, "dis-moi don," i dit, "quoi-ç-qu'i y a, quoi-ç-qu'i y a don, quoi-ç-qu'i y a? Ça arrive! Ça vous ara arrivé, quoi d'même—"Ah! oui," i dit, i y dit, "oui." I dit, "Y a eune béte à sept tétes," i dit—"qui vient à toutes les ans, ramasser ieune de nos filles. Et pis," i dit, "çt année," i dit, "c'est la pire année de tout en grand. A s'en vient çt année pour ramasser," i dit, "la, la, la fille du roi."—"Penses-tu," i dit, "la fille du roi." I dit, "A va-ti ête mangée demain," i dit, "demain à onze heures."—"Ouais?" i dit—"mangée par quoi?"—"Ben," i dit, "par la bète à sept tétes. *By geez* c'est eune vilaine béte! Oh! Tu devrais la ouère!" Pis i dit, "J'pourras pas la tuer ni arien du tout, j'porras pas arien faire avec?"—"Naah! C'est trop fort, c'est, i pouvont pas arien faire, i tiront dsus des coups d'canon—i pouvont pas, ça y fait arien du tout."— "Mais, mais c'est pas possibe," i dit. Là i dit, "Ça, ça, ça, ça m'étonne pas," i dit, "vous êtes, euh, toutes en deuil ici," i dit. "Hein! Ouais," i dit, "m'en vas aller ouère vote roi." S'en va. Frappe à la porte [Émile frappe sur la table].

La maîtresse s'en vient, rouve la porte—Monsieur Jack tait là—in joli homme là, aussi, in bel homme, beau, j'te garantis. Bien, i dit, "L'aroi," i dit, "est à la maison?" A dit, "Oui," a dit, "mais i veut pas être derangé."—"Oh-oh," i dit, euh, "j'ai à ouère l'aroi," i dit. "Ah," a dit, "non, tu peux pas, i veut pas t'ouère."—"Mais dis-y qu'ej veux l'ouère. C'est important." Ah! A s'en va. A y dit, pis vlà l'aroi avait là, la téte là entor les deux jambes huh! I tait bien trisse. A y dit, "Dans la, y a in jène homme qui veut t'ouère," a dit. "Aiy!" i dit, "j'vas pas l'ouère" i dit, "vas pas ouère parsonne."—"Ben," a dit, "j'vas t'ouère, absolument. C'est *important*." Euh...là i s'lève pis—i s'en vient—pis i ergarde—in tout ptit homme. "Et quoi c'est qu'ça?" i dit. Pis la fille asteure a l', a, a—l'a vu—mais, l'pus bel homme qu'alle avait jamais vu de, mis ses yeux, yeux dsus. Oooh! Alle a tombé en amour avec. Mon Dieu, mon Dieu, le chagrin qu'alle avait, alle allait ête mangée l'endemain mais, le chagrin qu'alle avait dans l'tchoeur! A s'a pâmé, ç'a parti, a l'a regardé, alle a pris in grand soupir—"Mais, mais, mais, mais, mais, mais, mais c'est-i-mangeabe!"—dans ielle-même a dit t'sais—là l'aroi i dit euh i dit "Quoi-ç-qu'est ton nom?" I dit euh, "Mon nom est Jean" i dit—"Jack."—"Oh-ahhr!" i dit "Jack" i dit, "j'ons tendu parler" i dit "mon cher euh, aroi," i dit, "j'as tendu" i dit "qu'ta fille va ête mangée demain."— "Oui" i dit, "c'est bien malheureux"—pis i s'mit à pleurer. "Oh!" i dit, "pleure pas. Pleure pas. J'sus venu ici pour t'aider."—"Mon pauvre enfant" i dit, "mon pauvre enfant! Va-t-en chez vous!"—"Ha ha ha!" i dit, "acoute don là, acoute" i dit. "Ha ha ha! M'en aller chez nous, et pas avant qu'mon ouvrage va ête fini!" Là l'aroi i commence, i, les deux yeux à haler en haut, i dit "Quoi c'est qu'ça? I tirent lui en-dessus à coups des, gros coups d'canon *an so on*, pis i pouviont pas—plette—a *maillndait* pas ça du tout—plette! Neh!" C'est bon. I dit "Rente! Rente! Rente dans mon salon." Ah. Jack rente. Pis i s'assit. I dit euh, "Quoi t'as asteure à faire?" I dit euh, "Y-a-ti, c'est-i-loin ici d'ici" i dit "pour ioù-ç-qu'est la, la, la fondière la, la—la *foundry* euh! Pour fonde la, les —

G.T.:   La fonderie.

La fondrie, la fondrie, ouais. Ah "Ben" i dit, "c'est eune coupelle de milles." I dit "Pourquoi faire?"—"Parce qu'" i dit euh, "j'voudrais aouère eune epée de fait."—"Oui?" i dit. "Pourquoi?" i dit. "Ben" i dit, euh, euh, "j'veux ça" i dit—"pou me defende—parce qu'" i dit, euh, "moi pi la béte à sept tétes" i dit "j'allons aouère eune bataille demain."—"Oh! Pauvre enfant, parle pas don comme ça!"—"Mais" i dit *"never mind"* i dit "asteure" i dit "j'ai in couteau de fait—eune epée—"—"Ben" i dit "oui" i dit, "j'pourras t'en faire eune epée parce qu'" i dit "il avont toutes sortes de, de, d'acier là et toute en grand" i dit, "nous avons la meilleure qualité du monde."—"Ben" i dit, "c'est ça ç'qu'ej veux." I dit "Tu vas" i dit euh, "enouoyer" i dit, "iun d'tes—de tes hommes" i dit, "à la fondière—à la fondrie—et pis euh, faire faire in couteau. J'veux in couteau" i dit "de six pieds d'long—et la *blade*" i dit, "le, le taillant" i dit, "six pouces de large—et pis trois cour—trois quarts de pouce d'épais."—"Mais" i dit "quoi-ç-tu vas faire avec ça?"—*"Never mind!"* i dit—"Ça c'est mes affaires." Et i dit "J'veux ç'couteau-là." Et i dit "Fait avec la meilleure acier—du monde." Bien, c'est ça, là il appelle ses—ses gendarmes pis euh, i y dit là, i dit "Tu vas aller à la fondrie" i dit "pis prends iun des chevals là" i dit "pis euh, va-t-en" i dit "pis euh, faire faire le couteau là" i dit, "que, que Jack veut là." Il a ergardé Jack là asteure, le couteau là, penses-tu toi. Toujours c'est ça. S'en va pis mêle en-d'dans pis là i faisont le couteau. Mais ça prenait deux hommes pour le porter! Bien! Ouais. Oh! bientôt, l'endemain matin—à neuf heures du matin—là! Il arrivont avec le couteau. Ç'a pris deux hommes pour le porter dans la maison. Ah, euh, comme ça, ben, Jack prend l'couteau par la manche—i commence à sc—à secouer, à secouer ça en l'air et *so on*—l'aroi il a tombé en arrière, i tombe en bas sus ses fesses—i dit "Quoi sorte d'homme que c'est ça?"—Le couteau plus lourd que lui! "Ben" i dit, "c'est pas trop pire—c'est pas trop pire." C'est bien. Là. Là i spèront asteure pour onze heures, ben c'est ça, vlà la fille, i l'a, il avont pris la fille par le bras pis i l'amenont au pl—auprès de la mer. Là! C'est bien. A onze heures—Jack—arrive là. I s'pique deboute au ras la fille—avec son couteau dans la main. Bientôt il ont vu eune grosse houle qui se lève à la mer—ça s'a levé en l'*air*! Pis ça s'en venait là, oh! Ça ça faisait peur! Toute le monde, les femmes et toute ça il avont tous caché leu, leu-z-yeux et tout ça avec leu châle nouère qu'il aviont, tout caché leu-z-yeux, i s'ont mis à genoux, i vouliont pas regarder ni arien, i, saviont que la, la béte à sept tétes allait pis i alliont, alle allait devorer les *deux*—la fille et le, le garçon. Ah! I tiont depités! Ah bon Dieu, bon Dieu. Toujours c'est bien. Là-à-à, ç'a pris encore eune aute houle encore ça monte en l'air là et pis ça s'en vient là, pis là tout d'in coup là i voyiont les têtes, les sept tétes, a montait là pis ç'tait manière d'fait en biais là. J'eux ai dit là, tait, ç'ta, j'les ai marqué sus l'papier comment-ç-que la béte à sept tétes tait fait ois-tu, ç'tait manière dans le *jib* là t'sais.

G.T.:   Hm.

—Comment-ç-qu'a tait fait asteure là, comment a tait, alle avait sept tétes n'en, pis d'—mais c'est dur pour moi mar, marquer sus *tape* là. Bien *anyway* alle avait le—sept tétes. Tout d'in coup alle arrive à terre. Quand alle arrive à terre alle a poussé l'eau, pis l'eau a venu à, la motché d', jusqu'à la cein, jusqu'à la ceinture, le garçon pis la fille là. "Oh! Ben!" a dit, "Hah! Bien" a dit, "aujourd'hui oh, j'vas aouère in beau repas. Deux! Hah! Ça" a dit, "ça va, ça ça va ête mangé!"—"Ben" i dit euh, "j'allons" i dit euh "ouère ça" i dit—Jack i dit—"j'allons ouère ça" i dit. "Tchi-ç-qui va ête mangé l'premier." Toujours c'est bien. Là, vlà la béte s'en vient pour arrgnrr! pour, pou les crocheter. Oui mais lui i saute, pis i tang-liing! i prend la ptite téte le premier, i prend la ptite téte—vling! Gee! La téte qui tombe! Sus l'sâbe! Là ça hale en arrière encore. Y a pus qu'six tétes de resse là. Hale en arrière. Pis là m'en, là asteure, ar-r-r! là a s'enrage, l', l', l'etchume ça sortait des yeux. Là a s'en vient encore pis là com—a s'en vient encore m'en ête l'arouet, l'aute téte—la deuxième, deuxième—pus—ptite téte là. I prenait ça à monter ois-tu, pou l'affaiblir t'sais euh? A right. Oh tchiens, deux tétes sus l'sâbe. Pis le sang—ah! le sang! Le sang, le sang, ça pissait, ça pissait—la fille tait plein d'sang, i tait plein d'sang, ç'tait euh, ç'tait ienqu'in sang. Toujours c'est bien. Là a s'en hale en arrière encore pis a s'en vient encore pis i fait encore la même affaire—plingco! i—colle l'aute téte de dsus—c'est ienque pus quate de resse là. Là. I s'en, ça hale encore oh! ç'coup-là,moi, là ç'coup, oh! euh, ienque le bout d'la tcheue qui tait, tait tout fait sous l'eau. La façon qu'ça s'tord en l'air pour faire in beau coup ç'coup-ici ah! hoh hoh hoh! Oui mais, vling! encore—y a encore eune aute téte, vlà quate de parti. Oui mais a commençait à devenir faibe. A saute en arrière encore oui mais dame—alle a—ienque la motché du corps qu'a, qu'a, qu'a, a relevé. Ahh, ça commence à faiblir—là! A s'en vient encore, ho ho ho! alle a levé sus l'bord pareil, oh c'est ça, pareil, viens-t-y, i dit "C'est ça, mange, mange!" I t'enouoie bang! encore—bien—il a fait ça—jusqu'à temps qu'la darnière téte a té—et quand qu'la grosse téte—c'est d'sa place qu'a quitté ç'tait la grosseur, pis tout l'monde gardait!—la grosseur d'la téte—là—qu'alle a—mais ça ç'tait eune grosse téte, oh! Toujours c'est bien. By de geezus, so y a den deux coups sus l'côté là, pis i l'enouoie ça. Pis i l'a ienque coupé en motché. Ouais. Ça c'est in gros coup mon vieux. Ooooho! Oh! T'arais dû ouère ça. Pchi! Pis i l'a pris encore, i l'a pris encore sus l'aute bord i l'a enouoyé in coup comme ça, à, à droite pis i l'a renversé sus l'aute bord à gauche et flac! i la coupe, i l'a coupé la téte. Là. Bien là, ben si t'arais vu ça—si t'arais vu ça. Le monde—les châles nouères étiont partis ç'tait, ç'a parti d'la main toute en grand—pis là i sautiont sus Jack pis l'embrassont et pis ielle asteure a voulait embrasser Jack aussi pis a pouvait pas i y en, i n'en avait trois là autour de ielle—et pis c'est comme ça qu'ça allait. Pis—oh! il a comme des hard-time. Lui c'est pire qu'la béte à sept tétes—pis il a pas ieu in hard-time ac la béte à sept tétes, mais ac le monde, oïe! C'est pas fitte, i criait, oh! Pis i dit là l'aroi i dit de "Quittez-le trantchille, quittez-le trantchille!" Toujours i l'ont quitté trantchille. Là. Dans la maison asteure, là ça c'est in gârs mon homme, qui ta reçu! Pis là Gerald! Mon bon sang d'la vie! Bien ç'tait, ri, ah, i tait parti, i marchait pas du tout! I l'avont porté à, au château, i l'ont porté pour à manger et toute en grand, i, i, all les chandelles ça lumait et toute, oh! ç'tait, c'est, ç'tait trop beau. Là. Après c'est tout fini, mais i dit, "Te ouère in si ptit homme" i dit "et à te ouère" i dit "avec tant de pouvouère." I dit "J'te donne" i dit "la motché d'mon royaume" i dit "pis ma fille en mariage. Pis tu vas pas s'marier à demain" i dit—i dit "tout d'suite. M'en vas t'marier toute d'suite." Bien, c'est bien. Là—i enouoyont quri le minisse, et pis i s'mariont, et pis quand qu'il aviont les noces—mais moi j'pouvais pas jouer beaucoup jouer du violon de ces temps-là! Mais, le temps de leus noces i tiont entor, dans le, dans l'spree—il aviont du home brew fait avec du prusse, heh! Holy gee! I m'a fait ve—"Rente là!" Mais j'tais bien reçu dough, bye—j'ai joué pou—in, eune partie d'leu danse—et toute—mais j'tais bien reçu. Ouais.

322

(p. 228)

JEAN-DU-BOIS (JAMBE-DE-BOIS)

G.T.: Connais-tu un conte euh, ioù-ç-qu'i y a—in chat—qui parle?

E.B.: In—in chat qui parle.

G.T.: Oui.

E.B.: Oui, Oui, j'ai entendu çt histoire-là déjà.

G.T.: Oui?

E.B.: Dame j'sais pas si j'peux la conter comme i faut mais dame ej crois que—

G.T.: Veux-tu essayer?

E.B.: J'peux assayer, bien sûr.

G.T.: Comment que, comment que ça s'appelle?

E.B.: Euh, s'appelle, "Jean" et i s'appelait euh—"Jean du Bois" ou tcheque chose comme ça.

G.T.: Oui?

—Euh, i, i, ben i vivait ac son père et sa mère jusqu'à temps qu'il a ieu l'âge de, de, de quitter à lui-même, vous savez, ç'tait dans—les temps-là euh, ç'tait vingt-et-une ans avant que vous pouviez bouger d'la maison. En-dsous d'ça c'est, tu tais pas *boss*, tu tais pas chef—faulait qu't'acoutes et obéir à toutes euh, les paroles que tes parents te disaient. Mais dame, quand qu't'arrivais à vingt-et-une ans, oh oh! dame, tch! tu pouvais aller ioù-ç-que tu veux mais dame, tu pouvais pas faire le fou de la, dans la maison, le, le, le, le, dans l'château d'ton père qu'ej allons dire. I avait ses ordes pis faulait qu'ça va comme—c—comme i, comme i voulait. Bien il avait çt homme-là, i s'appelait Jean, Jean—que—tcheque chose, me'n rappelle pus du—t'aras pt-être pas entendu ça Jean, Jean-du-Bois ou tcheque chose comme ça.

G.T.: Oui, Jean-du-Bois.

—C'est tcheque chose comme ça, Jean-du-Bois. Toujours euh. toute sa, sa vie, qu'il a vi, avec son père et sa mère—il avait in chat—et pis euh—il en croyait eune tapée d'son chat. C'est de la seule compagnie qu'il avait pour dire la franche varité. Euh—i laimait son père et sa mère, mais son chat, ahh! Ben ça! Son chat! I laimait son chat. Ben ç'allait, ç'allait. Bien toujours euh, quand qu'il a arrivé à l'âge de vingt-et-une ans, i dit à son père et sa mère i dit "Ej crois bien—pâpa" i dit, "et maman—j'crois bien moi" i dit "j'm'en vas—té—j'm'en vas m'pousser hors d'ici moi." I dit "A l'entour" i dit, "ici"—euh i y avait pas grand'chose à ouère, mais euh—"j'm'en vas aller ouère—attends, j'ai vu eune coupelle de, de, de oisins" i dit "à l'entour, i m'avont dit qu'i y a des belles places à vouère. C'est pareil comme d'in aute monde. Pis moi j'acoutais ça pis j'ai ça dans l'idée, y avait trois ou quatre ans d'ça asteure qu'i m'parlont dsus, vous avez entendu ça, j'ons rencontré çtés oisins-là—pis j'ai ça dans l'idée, pis c'est pour ça qu'ej voudrais aller ouère—quoi ça parait, comment qu'ça parait—dans l'univers."—"*What*! Ben" i dit "mon enfant" i dit, "t'as ton âge ah bien dame" i dit "tu peux faire quoi-ç-tu veux." Bien, c'est bien. Ben alors i s, i s, sa mère va, a tchuit des ptits gâteaux, des ptits bistchuits et toutes sortes d'affaires comme ça des, des galettes et toutes. Bien i dit euh, i y avait pas de m, de, du, automobile et toute ça—d'çtés temps-là—y avait arien comme ça—faulait qu'tu marches, marches, marches, marches ou t'avais in cheval ben c'est bon. Tu m—peux aller à choual—mais dame clair de ça, faulait qu'tu marches. Bien c'est ça. I s'en va là—s'pousse avec son—son ptit paquage de, de, de, *bun* et pis des ptits gâteaux et *so on* et toute ça—et euh i s'pousse. Et i tait assez euh, boulevarsé—qué—il a pt-être té comme pt-être bien in quart de mille—"Gare tchiens!" i dit, "mon chat! J'oublié mon chat!" Là! Orvire de bord. Ah ha! Il arrive à la maison—"Oh!" a dit "t'as revenu?"—"Oui" i dit "bien sûr j'as revenu, j'ai vnu quri mon chat" i dit—"mon chat! Oh mon cher chat!" Ah ha! Pis le gârs quand que le chat i l'a vu "M-miaou!" Heh! I crie eh? "Ah!" i dit "le temps" i dit "mon ptit poussinne" i dit, "viens-t-en avec moi. Ej peux pas m'en aller" i dit euh, "sans que t'es ac moi." Ah bien c'est bon ben là, i sont partis. Pis là ça marche, marche toute ce jornée-là, pis ça marche eune part d'la nuit pis là c'est bien fatigué—ben là i s'arrange des brousses et toutes sortes d'affaires comme ça des ptits bois pis i s'fait eune ptite couchette—pour la nuit. Pis euh c'est bien. Aïe! S'erposent—lui pis son chat, ah! i prend son chat dans ses bras pis l'souque. Avec son chat c'est pareil qu'la vie tait sauvée. Il avait l'univers dans les bras. Ben! C'est bien bon. Là. C'est ça. Bientôt vlà l'jour qui s'fait—"Ah!" i dit, "mon ptit *pussycat*"—hah! I dit "j'allons aller—en ouoyage encore." Oh les oici en partant. C'est bon. Là vlà i sont partis. Marche et marche et marche et marche toute la jornée là encore. Pis y avait arien à vouère, y avait pas d'bâtisses, y avait arien, *arien*! Ç'tait toutes des, des, des, des borbiers et pis des ptites prussières et ci et ça et des montagnes et des, et des vallons et toute en grand et—des ptits risseaux à traverser pis ça marche, pis ça marche, pis ça marche. Pis ça mangeait des ptits gâteaux d'temps en temps, ç'avait pas grand appétit pis quand même qu'il arait ieu l'appétit j'crois bien qu'i voulait pas manger trop, i voulait menager sa nourriture i savait pas quand c'est qu'il arait—euh, qu'il arait—vu d'quoi—qu'i, qu'i s'arrêtait pour manger ou tcheque chose comme ça. Bien c'est bien, ça marche toute la jornée là encore—jusqu'après la nuit—et pis là bien dame là c'est, c'est la nuit s'en vient. Hm ben, ça s'erpose encore. Pis i prend son chat dans ses bras encore pis ça souque! pis ça, et pis i dit "Mon ptit poussinne, mon ptit poussinne! Et sans là pour toi" i dit "je m'ennuierais." Euh, ça va. L'endemain—encore partis—à la câssée du jour ça s'lève pis là c'est parti encore. Ça marche! Marche, marche, marche! Marche, marche, marche. Tout d'in coup—le chat—i dit "Mon maîte!"

Ehh? I dit euh—i dit qu'i allont bien vite i dit "arriver dans, dans, dans in village—ici là."—"Quoi!" i dit—"Ben" i dit "j'croyais pas que les chats parlaient."— "Ben" i dit, "les chats parlent pas mais moi ton chat là, i parle!"—"Mais que faire tu m'as pas parlé avant ça?" i dit "Oh non!" i dit, "j'aras pas voulu t'parler avant ça" i dit "parce que tu tais pas dans la, la, ne, la nécessité pour parler. Je tchenais tout l'temps moi-même moi" i dit. "Mais" i dit "asteure ioù j'te parle là"—i dit "tu vas bien vite arriver" i dit "proche d'in, proche d'in village là—ça va pas prende la jornée" i dit "à marcher et tout ça" i dit "pour avant qu'ej arrivons là. Mais dame" i dit "tu vas ête obugé de m'acouter" i dit. "Quoi-ç-qu'ej vas vous dire" i dit "ça va ête juste." Bien là, j'te garantis Jean-du-Bois là, i, i, i, c'est, c'est, ça, ça, ç'avait té son épaule, c'est l', sa peau là montait en haut en arrière sus ses oreilles, ses, ça poussait ses oreilles en l'air! La façon qu'il a té assez surpris pis—et c'est pis oir in chat parler qu'il avait jamais en, entendu ça encore. Et jamais vu ça—et c'est, ben, i tait dans l'transport! "Mais, mais, mais, mais! Et que ça parle in chat qui parle!" i dit, "Bien, bien, bien, bien! C'est formidabe!" i dit, "d'quoi d'même." Bien c'est bon. Là—le chat i dit pus arien là. Pis là i marchont, i marchont, i marchont. Ben là tout d'in coup—le chat dit—"Bien—le village n'est pas loin là." Là i dit "Asteure—mon cher maître" i dit "j'allons ête obigé d'nous faire—eune ptite cabane ici là—avec des brousses" i dit "et des ptits euh—des ptites racines et toute ça" i dit "j'allons nous faire in logement" i dit "asteure, ici là. Faut nous faisons in logement" i dit. "C'est pas comme hier au soir pis avant hier au soir pis la soirée d'avant ça—asteure faut qu'ej nous faisons in logement. Pis j'allons—establir ici là. Moi et toi" i dit "mon cher maîte. Parce qu'" i dit "j't'ai toujours laimé, moi." Le chat dit à, à Jean-du-Bois là. "Je t'ai toujours laimé, moi. Mais j'ai jamais voulu arien dire. Mais" i dit, "m'en vas faire mon mieux pour toi, moi." Ah! C'est bien, là, i s'bâtissont leu, leu cabane—avec des racines pis des brousses et pis des, des, des, de la t, de la tourbe et toutes sortes d'affaires comme ça mais i l'ont fait pas, pas trop pire—étanche, tout ça. C'est pas,

324

c'est pas euh, ç'tait pas trop froid. Bien—c'est bon. Là—ça marche là—bientôt les *buns* là ç'a commencé à venir pas mal rare—i y a quasiment pus arien à manger. Ben i dit "Mon, mon cher chat" i dit euh, "j'm'en vas t'dire eune chose, moi" i dit—"la cabane est bâtie asteure—pis de d', nous, note nourriture" i dit, "c'est ça commence à venir pas mal rare. Pis y a pas grand'chose" i dit "à l'entour ici qu'i y a moyen d'aouère." Ben le chat dit "Hah! tu crois ça toi. Heh! Moi" i dit "ej, ej sais moi qu'i y a, y a, y a du lapin, y a d'la volage, y a d'quoi, y a d'quoi! Y a d'quoi ici à l'entour ici."—"Oh crois-tu toi?" i dit, "nah!" i dit, "i y a arien ici."—"Ah oui!" Le chat dit "Ah oui! Ah oui qu'i y a d'quoi ici à l'entour." Mah, i sait pas lui.

Mais i dit "M'en vas t'dire—j'm'en dire eune ptite chose" i dit—le chat dit à, à Jean-du-Bois—"m'en dire eune ptite chose" i dit "Quoi-ç-que c'est, quoi-ç-tu vas m'dire?"—"Moi" i dit "j'm'en vas t'dire moi—acoute—demain euh, tu vas te, te, de, de bon matin ça, du—bonne heure—a—avant jour faut qu'tu seyes deboute"—le, le chat a dit à Jean-du-Bois—"Ah, c'est avant jour faut qu'tu seyes deboute—pis faut qu'tu seyes là pour la *câssée* de jour." Pis i dit "Tu vas euh, tu vas aller" i dit "comme, ahh, pt-ête bien in mille d'ici lâ—en arrière" i dit "de la forêt" i dit. "Pis tu vas prende in, in, in sac avec toi" i dit, "in, in sac" i dit. I dit "Pouquoi faire?"—"Ben" i dit, "tu, faut qu'tu prends in sac ac toi" i dit. I dit "Tchelle sorte de sac?"—"Bien" i dit, "des, des, des sacs" i dit "que les, les farmiers" i dit, "i y en a là, t'as pas besoin d'aller bien loin, y a des farmiers, y a des rois, y a toutes sortes ici" i dit "toutes sortes! I y a des géants, y a toutes sortes, toutes sortes! Toutes sortes à l'entour ici."—"Mais" i dit "comment qu'tu sais ça toi!"—"*Bien*, j'le sais" i dit. "Ej sus in chat" i dit "j'sus, j'sus, j'sus présenté comme in chat mais j'sus pas ienqu'in chat" i dit "ej sus d'quoi" i dit "qui est pus valeureux qu'in chat, pis tu l'sais pas. Mais" i dit "t'es dans les bonnes mains." Heh! Ben! Pis là i dit "Mon cher chat" i dit, "c'est ça" i dit "tu, comme tu m'dirais, comme tu m'am, comme tu vas m'dire, bien, j'vas l'faire." Ha ha! "Bien" i dit, "c'est ça" i dit. I tait content, le chat disait "Miaou!" Hah! Bien c'est ça. C'est bien. Là! I dit "Tu vas euh aller pus en arrière là-bas" i dit "c'est pas bien loin à marcher" i dit—"tu vas trouver eune grosse grange là" i dit, "tu vas trouver des, des, sacs" i dit "qu'il avont jté dehors" i dit "des gros sacs, des, des, des bottes qui taient tout pleins d'trous" i dit "en travers" i dit, "c'est toujours broché" i dit "et tout—*slack*" i dit. Et pis i dit "Tu vas ramasser iun comme ça" i dit. "Pis là demain matin" i dit "tu vas aller" i dit "dans l'bois et pis tu vas aller attraper des lapins" i dit. "Tu vas mette ça" i dit "à tende pareil comme in collet" i dit—i y a montré à, à Jean-du-Bois comment, comment faire, vois-tu. Pis là i s'en va, mais i, i, i tait pas *smart*, ois-tu, s'il arait té *smart* i n'arait attrapé mais i tait pas *smart*! Longir! Ça prenait deux jours pou, pou, pou, pou s'orvirer d'bord. Oh i tait! Lâche et toute et ta, ta, ça c'est bien tard! Mais dame c'est lâche ou pas, ça c'est, faulait qu'ça s'faise. Mais au ptit jour l'endemain matin là le vlà parti. Avec son sac. Pis là i fait comme le chat y a dit d'faire—et pis là i commence à draillver [angl. to drive] les lapins asteure là, pis—les lapins commençaient à sauter ici et là—bientôt tchiens! Y en a deux qui s'en va dans l'sac! Mais—avant qu'il arrivait au sac, les deux lapins sortis de d'dans. Là! Phiou, *cheepers*! *Smart*, non! Nah, les lapins sortis de d'dans pis les vlà pa, partis pis là i, i, i s'en vient à la maison—à la cabane pis, pis, "Ioù-ç-qu'est les lapins? Y a pas d'lapins?" i dit. "I y a pas d', pas d'lapins" i dit, "y a deux qu'étaient dans l'sac"—"

Mais si t'aras té pus *smart*" i dit "vous aras attrapé" i dit, "tu sais assez euh, assez lâche" i dit "tu sais ça" i dit, "quand vas-tu t'apprende à iête *smart* in ptit peu" i dit. I dit "J'veux pas qu'tu zing [veilles, regardes] les chats" i dit "c'est *smart* les chats eh? Mais toi" i dit "t'es bien loin d'être in chat. Hah! T'es pas *smart*!" i dit "T'es pas, tu sais pas comment faire toi!" I dit "J'vais moi demain matin, hah!" I dit "Vas-tu aller demain matin, toi?"—"Oui!" i dit, "j'm'en vas demain matin, mais dame asteure" i dit, "m'en vas t'dire eune chose moi. J'veux pas aller mouiller mes pattes moi. Parce c'est—c'est des manières de borbiers là, aller à l'entour là, aller à l'entour

325

là! Hé! j'veux m—des ptites bottes moi. Et pis y en a" i dit, "y a eune boutique là"—pis i savait tout eh? Le chat i *savait tout* mon vieux. C'est eune sorciaise, t'sais. Ç'tait *witch*, in *witch* qu'il appelont eh, eune sorciaise. Mais lui i savait pas, i savait pas, i croyait ç'tait in chat comme les autes chats—mais...I dit "Tu vas aller m'quri eune paire de bottes, toi. Moi j'peux pas aller. Parce qu'i m'vendront pas d'bottes" i dit, "pas, pas à in chat. Mais toi asteure là toi" i dit "tu peux y aouère les bottes toi." Et i dit "Quel nombe ça va prende?"—"Ben" i dit "ça va prendre *number* iun—in ptit nombre" i dit. Ah, c'est à l'entour de quate pouces de long, *I suppose*, trois pouces et demie à quate pouces. Nombre iun, c'est in ptit nombe, ptit nombe. "Attention" i dit, "dmandes pas in gros nombe" i dit "parce ça j'vas pas pououère les mette sus mes djin—"—"Tu vas pas pououère rester avec"—"Neh! to—ça va ête—trop grand pour moi." Oh, c'est bien, oh le vlà l'endemain matin le vlà parti quri les, les pour—garder pour les bottes. Paraît qu'il a été dans trois, deux ou trois boutiques. La troisième boutique, *by geez* il a trouvé—nombre iun. Ahh! Ptit nombe! Oh! ç'tait à l'entour de trois pouces de long. Trois pouces, des ptites bottes, ah, il aviont à l'entour de quate, huit pouces de haut là, heh, des belles ptites bottes! Tout fleuries oh ç'tait joli! Ça c'est bien, il arrive à, ah, ac d'la djeule, le chat regarde "Bien" i dit, "j'aras pas pu faire mieux moi-même!" Hah hah! Dame! "Na-a-r-aou! R-a-aou!" I dit! Hi-hi! I crie comme in, i crie là! Ben! C'est bien. Là, là i dit asteure "J'm'en vas moi, demain matin là ej m'en vas quri des lapins moi. Pis j'sus pas fort" i dit "parce que—j'ai pas mangé, j'ai pas mangé, j'sus faibe aussi, moi. Ej sais pas comment longtemps j'vons pouoir ête à faim comme ça" i dit—"mais—j'veux d'quoi à manger. Ben" i dit "demain matin j'm'en vas moi." Hm. Ça va—l'endemain matin à la câ—ptite câssée du jour là le, le chat a parti là. I mit ses bottes pis il est parti. Mon ami du bon sang de la vie. I tait pas trop longtemps parti—ben il a quitté—il a quitté à cinq heures et dmie—ça ç'tait dans l'automne ça—ben ça ç'tait, ç'tait justement la câssée du jour—dans l'octobe ou d'quoi d'même là, t'sais—

G.T.:   Hm.

—Ben l'temps des lapins, tu sais comment c'est—et pis le vlà parti. Puis euh, i dit euh, i dit "Oublie pas l'sac là." Jean-du-Bois a dit au lapin—"Oh! Ben oui, tiens, t'es d'selon—selon que tu m'as, tu, tu m'arais pas rafraîchi" i dit "j'aras oublié ça. Bien sûr" i dit, "le sac, bien oui, pâsse." Ben là Jean-du-Bois i pâsse le sac pis là i s'parti, i s'pousse là. I s'pousse. I marchait sus les pattes d'arrière heh! I tait droite deboute. Pareil comme in homme. C'est bien. Le vlà parti—i tait pas parti autchun temps—tchiens! Il a tendu, i, i, n, à l'en, i tait parti comme eune heure et dmie ou d'quoi d'même—pis il a tendu du carillon, de quoi s'tapait les pieds—dehors. I dit "Et quoi c'est qu'ça?" i dit, "c'est-i in loup-çarvier ou, ou quoi-ç-que c'est?" Il a ieu peur. Ben i la trouve la porte qui rouve—son chat! "Mais" i dit "t'es pas venu déjà!" I dit "Tu m'as, tu m'as foutu eune frousse!" i dit—"Hoh! Tu m'as manqué d'tourner le sang!" I croyait, i dit qu'ç'tait in, in, in loup-çarvier ou d'quoi d'même. "Oh oh chu, chisse." Pis i dit "As-tu d'quoi à manger?" i dit. "Ouais" i dit. Là i, i, i s'fârme le porte pis i vide le sac—trois lapins! Trois lapins! "Oh bien" i dit "mon cher chat, viens dame asteure! Ben j'm'en tchuire moi là."—"Oh ho!" i dit "j'te pense tu vas tchuire toi parce qu'moi" i dit "moi, j'sus fatigué moi. Ça m'a, heh heh! ça m'a pris in bon ptit boute avant, j'ai pu attraper ces lapins-là euh, j'ai fait mieux, j'ai fait mieux qu'toi, toi y a toi, t'as pâssé hier" i dit, "t'as, t'as venu avec euh, le sac tout vide. Mais moi" i dit "je ch, huh! j'ai travaillé pour ça moi. Hah! Hah! Attention!" i dit "heh heh! Hi ha ha!" Pis i dit "Ouaou, ouaou, ouaou!" des fois i dit "ouaou ouaou!" ois-tu, i faisait ça et pis, ouais, mais le chat—i parle asteure ça t'sais ej peux pas faire comme lui asteure—t'sais, c'est si longtemps qu'ça comme, c'est pareil qu'ej peux pas me rappeler asteure là comment qu'i, tu sais, comment que ç'tait. Mais c'est tcheque chose comme ça *anyhow*. Ben c'est bien. Là! C'est ça, arrache la peau de dsus pis ça fricasse euh, fricasse tout sec—pas d'beurre, pas d'graisse—

326

arien du tout—fricasse tout sec. Ben—pis faisait fricasser ça dans la soupe—pou pas qu'ça brûle ois-tu, faulait qu'i—i y mettait in ptit peu d'eau d'dans pis i les, i chauffait ça, lui, i *steamait* qu'i l'appelont euh chauffait là.

G.T.:   Hm.

—Pis après quand c'tait bien tchuit là—là i s'mettont à manger. Vlà le chat et pis l', Jean-du-Bois là, et ça mange, "Ahhhoua!" Dame ça ç'tait bon. Ohh! Ben lui le, Jean-du-Bois i, i s'couche lui—pis i tombe endormi. I tait assez heureux avec le vente, l'estomac plein—assez hereux qu'i, i paraît qu'il avait mouri pis i tait parti au paradis. Ah! Mais le chat—lui—il a bien mangé aussi, mais dame i pensait tout l'temps, il avait d'quoi dans l'idée. Pensait. Pis i savait i y avait, i y avait trois géants là, dans, dans dans, dans le village là—i y avait trois géants. Pis son, son, Jean-du-Bois, son maître là, bien, i laimait son maître, il a touj, toujours laimé son maître—ç'tait eune bonne parsonne ois-tu, il a jamais tapé son chat ni arien du tout comme ça—i tait bon à lui. Pis ma, i dit, "C'est, faut qu'ej fais du bien—à Jean-du-Bois, faut que j'y fais du bien tcheque temps", ois-tu, "pis y a, i y a trois géants là" i dit. Pis i cartchulait asteure quoi-ç-qu'il allait faire—mais i disait pas à Jean-du-Bois, i disait pas, non, mais i carculait ça là asteure, pis i savait qu'avait in, in roi là, ioù i restait, pis il avait eune belle fille. "Ben si" i dit "si par quand" i dit "j'pourrais reussir là pis" i dit euh, "qu'il ara" euh, Jean-du-Bois asteure, "arait pu marier asteure la fille de l'aroi là" i dit "eune belle fille comme ça" i dit, "pis qu'ej pourrais euh, détruire les trois géants moi" i dit, "si j'pourrais trouver in plan—eune façon—pis, pis i, pis faut y, y donner ça pour in, pour eune surprise, de quoi d'même là—comme i sera-ti fier!" i dit, "Ça, ça, ça i y donne encore de la joie dans l'tchoeur. Bien i a té si bon à moi dans, dans toute ma vie. Il a té si bon." Toujours Jean-du-Bois i ronflait lui ç'a té, pis le chat i, i carculait lui—quoi-ç-qu'il allait faire. Toujours i dit arien à Jean-du-Bois, i dit pas arien. Toujours ç'a pâssé çte soirée-là [Émile tousse]—estchuse-moi. Ç'a pâssé çte soirée-là, bien mangé et tout ça—dormont. Bien le chat dormait lui il avait sa, sa patte en-dsous son oreille là, comme ça, pis i pensait, pis i pensait quoi-ç-qu'il allait faire. Ben faulait qu'i cartchule son affaire comme i faut, pour pouoir faire quoi-ç-qu'il avait dans l'idée. Pis s'il arait fait, euh, in, in *mistake*, ou de, de, de, eune faute ah da, dame là i, i tait baisé. Ben i savait ça. Comme ça bien, il avait toute en grand—cartchulé. Bien i dit arien à Jean-du-Bois. I tchient tout son secret, sa secret ça. I dit arien. L'endemain matin i s'levont—et pis euh, c'est bien. "Ben" i dit "moi" i dit—quand qu'ça arrivait à l'entour de dix heures, ou dix heures et dmie et d'quoi d'même—parce qu'il avait toute cartchulé là dans, dans son idée quoi-ç-qu'i voulait aller faire et tout—ci et ça—ah y a, "Ben" i dit—i dit à Jean-du-Bois i dit "Mon maître" i dit—"tu vas rester" i dit "à la maison" i dit, "tu vas"—pas à la maison mais à, à la cabane parce ç'tait eune cabane—ç'tait pas eune maison, c'est fait de racines et de, d'la mousse t'sais, des plouses et c'est eune ptite cachette qu'il aviont. "Tu vas rester ici" i dit "pis moi" i dit "j'm'en vas—faire in ptit ouoyage" i dit, "m'en vas *sneaker* à l'entour, m'en vas faire in ptit ouoyage à l'entour. Ah, j'sus in chat" i dit, "parsonne va faire attention à moi—i vont crouère j'sus, in chat pour des rats, des souris ou d'quoi d'même." Pis i dit euh, euh, euh, "J'm'en vas ouère mon ptit gamin moi-même, pis quand j'vas vnir ben si j'as d'quoi, ben j'vas t'dire. Et comme ça parsonne sara arien.

Hoï! C'est ça. Là i s'en va. Pis "miaou" c'est "miaou" là pis euh, pis s'il a rencontré du monde et d'quoi d'même il allait pis i s'frottait la téte, leus jambes, pis là "Miaou" pis là pis i disiont "Oh cher ptit poussinne, cher ptit poussinne! Le joli ptit chat! Il est-i ami!" Et pis ça allait comme ça pis ça allait comme ça. Bien—i s'en va chez les giants, iun des giants là, i, i y avait in giant, trois giants il y avait là, trois frères—pis il aviont chaque eune farme. Pis chaque—in château! Pis ç'tait des châteaux! Ç'tait pas leu, leu ptite cabane qu'il aviont fait avec des racines et pis de, pis d'la tourbe—pis—pis d'la mousse! Heh heh! J'te garantis ça. Heh! heh! j'te garantis ça *chaillnait* [angl. to shine] le château là! Hein! Il s'en va là pis i, la, la, la, le, le pus vieux, le pus vieux des frères. Pis là, là, i tait en train d'manger là le, faire son—i mange son dîner. I tiont pas mariés ni arien, i, i avait pas d'femmes, y avait pas d'femmes giants ois-tu, c'est toutes des giants, des gros hommes de, sept et huit cents lives—pis des femmes ah bien, les femmes qu'i y avait là c'est ienque des femmes de—cent cinquante lives, cent-soixante-tchinze lives, mais il aront pas marié des hommes comme ça parce ç'tait—ç'tait comme des montagnes! Heh! I pourriont pas aouère des filles ni arien, i tiont obigés d'vive par ieux avec—comme-z-eux-mêmes, ah oui, avec ieux et j'veux dire, pis ça qu'ej veux dire—c'est pas aisé pou ieusses aouère eune femme—i pourriont pas. Neh! Impossible! Comme ça i restiont, i, i sont des *bachelor* j'allons dire, c'est comme ça, vlà comment qu'ej vas l'prononcer, des *bachelor*. I, i tchuisiont à manger—et pis i mangiont. Pis c'est ça. Ben vlà le chat qui rente et pis euh—i fait "Miaou, miaou", pis i s'en va pis i s'frotte la tête sus la jambe du giant—et pis le giant i mange et pis i donnait des ptits morceaux de viande au chat pis le chat mangeait ça, pis i s'frottait la téte encore sus la jambe du giant, pis le giant pâssait la main sus la téte et pis le charmant ptit chat, c'est ça. Le charmant ptit chat! Et pis ça mangeait et pis ç'tait eune grosse compagnie pour le géant—ça là le giant laimait ça. Oh ha ha ha ha! I laimait ça. Ça c'est bon. Ah i dit, après qu'i tait fini d'manger ben i dit "Mon ptit poussinne, mon ptit poussinne" i dit là, "mon ptit chat non, mon ptit poussinne" i dit. Et i dit "J'm'en vas prende in ptit repos. Moi" i dit "j'travaille dur—pis j'mange—pis après j'mange faut j'ai eune heure, eune heure, eune heure d'erpos—eune heure d'erpos. Avant qu'ej vas à l'ouvrage encore." Pis le chat i tait là "Ouaou, ouaou" i, "ouaou, ouaou" i frottait la téte. Et pis vlà le géant qui s'couche sus la place la fidjure en l'air pis le chat tait là qui s'frottait sa téte sus sa fidjure et pis "Ptit poussinne" et "ptit poussinne" et "ptit poussinne."—"Hnn-r-r-r!" pis bientôt vlà le géant—"Hn-r-r-r! kn-r-r-r! hn-r-r-r!" Vlà le géant—parti! I tait parti—endormi. Là le... [pause pour retourner la bobine]... chat "R-a-a-ou!"

I croche à la gorge pis i draillve ses dents droite à travers de son, sa gorge—*i coupe la gorge droite en arrière!* [voix féroce] "Ahr-r-r!" Il a pas pu prende son vent—i ta—mouri là. Là il avait—ioù-ç-qu'i tait couché c'est droit ioù-ç-qu'i—ailloù-ç-qu'il avait sa cave. Le chat croche ses pattes sus la, sus la porte d'la cave, pis les, machine, eune porte qu'il avait là qui fârmait par-dessus, de dsus la place—i hale ça—pis là i s'mit—il l'a forcé—le chat était pas gros mais i tait fort—parce qu'i tait, ce, ç'tait in, in *witch*, ç'tait *witch*. I tait fort. Pis i hale, pis i hale, pis i hale, pis i y fout dans la cave. Pis i saute dessus ac les, à, à coups d'pied pis i *pousse* le géant dans la cave. Pis i *fârme* le porte... "Bien" i dit—le chat arrive à la maison—chez Jean-du-Bois, son maîte, "Ben" i dit, "mon chat" i dit, "quoi-ç-t'as vu aujourd'hui?"—"Ah! pas grand'chose" i dit. "Pas grand'chose" i dit, "en masse du monde" i dit euh, "j'ai vu les géants et tout ça" i dit euh, "i m'avont donné à manger" i dit. "J'étais chez in géant là, i m'a do, donné d'la, manger d'la viande, toute ça" i dit "i m'a, i m'a donné des morceaux d'viande—manger—ben" i dit "i sont bons, du beau monde." C'est bon, c'est bien. Là. Sus l'endemain—"Ben" i dit "Jean-du-Bois" i dit, "j'ons aouère du lapin de reste" i dit—i dit "don j'ons mangé iun hier. Pis j'ons mangé encore in aute aujourd'hui pis in aute demain" i dit, "ça va faire, c'est d'la nourriture, ça fait d'la nourriture" i dit. "Ben j'te pense" i dit "sinon pour toi" i dit "mon ptit chat" i dit—"hah! J'serais mort moi asteure moi—j'arais pu aouère d'quoi à manger. Mais j'peux pas aouère d'quoi à manger, moi—j'serais mort, moi." Hah! "Ah ben dame" i dit, "c'est ça. Toi tu m'as nourri" i dit "tout l'temps qu'ej tais ac toi" i dit, "ton, ton père pis ta mère, i, tu—m'donnais à manger, tu me faisais manger, m'donne à manger—mais j'ai pas oublié ça moi." Hm. "Ah! Ç'tait bon ça. Asteure c'est mon tour." Ah ben c'est bien, ben, ben vlà l'endemain tu en viens encore euh "Ben" i dit euh, "Jean-du-Bois" i dit, "mon maîte" i dit, euh, i dit euh, "ej m'en vas faire in ptit tour encore. Tu, j'veux, pas qu'tu maillnes [angl. to mind] pas ça" eh—"j'vas revenir—tu vas pas aouère la peur" i dit, "j'vas pas t'quitter moi."—"Ah" i dit, "nah" i dit "moi" i dit, "moi" i dit "ej sais pas, j'ai pas l'habitude parmi le monde moi" i dit, euh, "pis j'ai honte et toute ça" i dit "j'ai jamais vu eune fille d'ma vie clair de ma mère" i dit, "ma mère" i dit "ej sais, mon père—mais j'ai jamais vu d'—d'autes filles—j'ai pas ieu d'soeur, j'ai pas ieu arien du tout—j'sus ienqu'in seul enfant moi."—"Ah mais" le chat dit "mais oui, ben oui" i dit "mais dame" i dit "t'as l'habitude à ça" i dit "ça fait pas d'diffarence—pt-ête bien in jour viendra" i dit, "ça, ça viendra à ton tour à ça" i dit. "Oh j'sais pas!" i dit "mon chat" i dit, "j'sais pas."—"Ah bien" i dit "m'en vas aller faire in ptit tour encore" i dit, là, le vlà parti encore. Aïe, là le chat a parti chez l'aute giant, le, le, le, le deuxième des frères là asteure, l'aute, l'aute, l'aute pus vieux j'allons dire, qui est en vie là. S'en va là et pis i, il, temps d'midi, pis le géant tait là en train d'manger pis il avait la viande fricassée pis i, i, pis ça mangeait! Pis le chat qui rente là—pis "Maou-oua-oua" pis i s'frotte la téte, sus la, sus la tchuisse du géant—et pis le giant dit, "Ptit poussinne, ptit poussinne" pis il y coupe in morceau d'viande pis i y donne au ptit poussinne, pis ptit poussinne mange. I savait pas qu'ptit poussinne parlait lui mais i croyait que ç'tait in, in chat comme les autes là—pis i donne à manger, à manger, et pis après qu'il avait fini d'manger, ben ça mangeait, ç'tait pas des ptites, des, des, des ptites *bill* t'sais—i disait tchinze gallons de, de nourriture là, ben, i preniont là—in veau, in veau d'deux cents lives là—c'est ça qu'i fricassiont ieusses pour leu manger ieusses. Oh nous autes là je le sais ois-tu euh—eune live c'est assez ça—mais ieusses c'est deux cents lives et, et deux cents cinquante lives pou in repas—c'est, c'est des gros rpas—eune coupelle de ptits morceaux—ben tu peux pas donner trop parce ça c'est grand appétit, des gros hommes de huit à neuf cents lives—i y en avait qu'y a—là eune mille lives! Hoh hoh hoh! Ç'tait des gros hommes mon vieux! Bien c'est ça, mais le chat qui tait là i frottait, pis i disait "Ptit poussinne, ptit poussinne!" Ah bien c'est bien. "Bien" i dit "mon ptit poussinne" i dit euh, "on mange" i dit—"pis après qu'on a fini d'manger, mo—on s'erpose." Ah pis le, le, là ça le giant se couche—sus la place, la fidjure en l'air pis le ptit poussinne tait là pis i s'frotte la fidjure—sus la, sus la fidjure du giant—il avait eune grosse barbe—i la—sa barbe était six pouces de long! Ah! ç'tait, ç'tait, ç'tait comme des choueux! C'est, y avait pas d'ciseaux d'çtes temps-là i, pour *trimmer* [angl. to trim] ois-tu.

G.T.: Hm.

—Ça poussait, ç'tait comme des choueux que ç'tait. Ienque les deux yeux qu'tu oyais t'sais. Oh! ç'tait, oh ç'tait, ç'tait comme des, pas pire que des bêtes, pire que des bêtes—des bêtes le poil pousse pas long—mais des, ieusses là, oh! C'est bien! Là! Là tout d'in coup le giant a parti. "Hn-r-r-r! hr-r-r-r! hn-r-r-r!" Et ça dormait, ça dormait pis quand le ptit poussinne a vu qu'i dormait si bien, "A-a-a-gr-aou, raou!" I y croche la gorge—i *draillve* ses dents à travers—la gorge—y coupe la gorge—coupe—*clean off*! Creuh! Le pauvre giant—i tait parti lui—i peut pas, i, il est parti—il est *fini*! Pas moyen de prende haleine i prend haleine—en bas d'sa gorge—eeeh! mais i, i pouvait pas la, la, la pousser *back*—ç'tait, non, i tait parti, les veines taient coupées toute en grand, les veines du tchoeur, c'est toute coupé! C'était—il a pas ieu autchun temps le sang ça *pissait*. Mon Dieu ç'tait, oh! ç'tait froyabe, froyabe, froyabe! Là! Il a pas vi longtemps—comme cinq minutes pis le géant tait parti. Là il a binn—il a miaulé, trois giants—eune même cave—i s'y couchiont ç'tait droite au ras la cave, la, la porte qu'il aviont pour mette les ledjumes dedans ois-tu euh?

G.T.: Hm.

—Toujours le chat croche les pattes dessus—mais ç'a pas d'misère ois-tu, c'est, mais dame c'est *witch*, ois-tu, ça pesa joliment là—in chat lui-même, i pourra pas le faire—mais ac la, la *witch* là euh—eune sorciaise—eune sorciaise. Là! Croche la porte pis rouve la porte pis là mon homme, là! i s'prend, i hale dessus, pis i hale, hale, hale! Et tout d'in coup l'latchille là, *flick*! Pis il a parti. I longe dans la, dans la, dans la, dans la cave. Pis là i fârme la porte—pis là i s'en va pis Jean-du-Bois encore. "Ouais! Tchelle sorte de jornée qu'tu as aujord'hui, poussinne?"—"Ah!" i dit euh, "mon cher maîte" i dit euh, "*all right, all right*. Toute du beau monde i m'avont donné d'quoi à manger et tout ça et des—ah! ça m'a fait grand plaisir. Pis" i dit "y a pas bien longtemps d'ici toi" i dit "tu vas, in boute, tu étais honteux" i dit "mais tu vas ête obigé d'venir avec moi aussi."—"Bien" i dit, "quand qu'tu voudras" i dit, "quand tu voudras" i dit, "quand tu saras qu'ej peux aller—j'irai." Asteure il aviont encore in aute lapin de resse. "Ben" i dit "j'ons encore in aute—*puddin* là" i dit—"in aute erpas." Pis i dit "Après, après ça, ben là" i dit "j'allons pououère aller—*hunter* encore" i dit, "m'en vas attraper d'autes."—"Oh, j'avons pas besoin d'ça" i dit, "pas d'danger" i dit, "pas d'danger."—"Oh" i dit "pas moi" i dit, Jean-du-Bois i dit "pas moi, moi, mon estomac est plein" i dit "c'est d'la bonne nourriture, bonne nourriture! Ho ho! j'm'en plains pas moi" i dit, "c'est pas, j'sus mieux nourri qu'ej tais chez nous! Ouais! J'sus pas si bien nourri que ça chez nous" i dit. Oh ho! "Ben, c'est ça" i dit. Ben c'est bon, mais dame. L'endemain—c'est l'darnier lapin—ah ha! Ben dame y avait trois géants pis c'est l'darnier giant aussi eh. Mais Jean-du-Bois savait arien d'ça lui—i savait pas! Neh! Tout-ç-qu'i pensait, c'est les lapins—pis i pensait après—çte lapin-là tait parti, j'vons encore aouère in aute—c'est tout-ç-qu'i pensait, eh?

G.T.:   Oui.

—Quoi-ç-qu'ej allons faire, j'allons, ça va, t'sais hein? Ah? Ben tout l'monde est comme ça, j'allons, disons—ben, quoi j'allons faire demain, quoi j'allons faire? Ben c'est ça, c'est ça. C'est, c'est l—le monde de ç'temps-là est pareil à l'monde asteure—c'est pareil. Là c'est bien. Là! C'est ça. L'endemain—là! à l'entour de onze heures—"Ben" i dit "Jean-du-Bois" i dit "mon maîte" i dit "ej m'en faire in ptit ch—in ptit ouoyage encore moi" i dit. "M'en faire in ptit ouoyage. Encore" i dit "pour bistronner à l'entour, ouère, ois-tu, pis après quand qu'ej vas ête sûr—i savont pas qu'ej parle moi" i dit, "i savont pas ça. J'parle pas à parsonne moi" i dit. "Pis i croyont qu'ej sus in chat eh, comme tu croyais toi aussi là. Mais euh, heh heh! j'vons les, j'vons les *tricker* là." *All right.* I dit euh, "M'en vas aller encore." Ah bien, tout d'in coup vlà dix heures et dmie à onze heures, le chat a parti encore. Ahh! Jack tchuit le lapin lui, son lapin qu'il avait pis—i euh, i dit euh, avant, ej me trompe là, avant qu'il a parti—i dit "Jack" i dit euh, "tu vas tchuire le lapin aujourd'hui" i dit "mais" i dit "sauve-la pas pour moi" i dit "parce moi" i dit "i m'donnera à manger là-bas moi." I dit "Emplis-toi l'estomac comme i faut toi. Pour t'engraisser in ptit peu" i dit, "t'es maigue toi! *Jeepers crumbs!*" i, pis "T'es d'même!" Pis i dit "Engraisse-toi comme i faut" i y dit, "mange!" Pis i dit "Prends pas trop d', pour moi" i dit "parce moi" i dit, i, "quand qu'ej vas comme ça là, i m'donnent d'les morceaux d'viande et toute ça pis j'mange pis j'm'emplis l'estomac, pis toi" i dit "tu t'fais souffrir pour moi. Moi" i dit, "j'commence à ête *smart* moi, j'commence à penser, faut qu'tu vis aussi toi." Pis Jack ça tombait t'sais! C'est in si beau chat qu'il avait eh? Tu sais? Ah! C'est bien. Là. C'est ça, vlà le chat parti encore. Ah ben, i s'en va asteure à l'aute giant—et c'est la même affaire, le même chose qu'avait arrivé avec les deux autes. C'est quoi-ç-qui arrivait ac les deux, les deux premiers—arrivait à çui-là aussi. I frottait la, la téte sus la jambe pis le, le giant le, le nourrissait et pis ça, pis—i le croche par la j—la gorge pou faire l'histoire pus court pi i fait la même affaire—pis là c'est ça. Là. Asteure, le chat lui, ç'tait eh, ç'tait in sorciaise eh?

Ç'tait eune sorciaise ou eune parsonne qu'avait té tourné en, en chat par eune sorciaise—et ois-tu, c'est, c'est—

G.T.:   Du monde enchanté là.

—Ouais, ouais, ouais! Enchanté, enchanté, ouais, enchanté, oui. Avait té tourné en chat eh? C'est pour ça asteure ois-tu eh? Ben c'est bien. Là. Là le chat—i pouvait écrire in peu lui—ben i faisait des, des, des, des *poster* [des affiches], des machines, des *posters* là eh? Pis euh i dit euh "Le bien"—a y marque sus la, la *poster*—le ptit morceau d'papier qu'il avait pis i dit "Le bien ici là" i dit, "c'est à Jean-du-Bois" et pis i colle ça sus l'poteau là—pis là i s'en va à l'aute—pis i dit "Le bien icitte appartient à Jean-du-Bois." Et pis i s'en va à l'aute pis i fait encore pareil—comme ça i avait trois là—trois châteaux—et trois farmes qu'appartenaient à Jean-du-Bois—pis Jean-du-Bois savait arien d'ça. Là. C'est bien. I s'en va chez lui. "Ah" i dit, "quoi-ç-t'as vu aujourd'hui euh, mon ptit poussinne?"—"Ahhh!" i dit, "pas grand'chose" i dit. "Mais" i dit—"j'ai vu la fille à l'aroi là—ahh!" i dit, "ça c'est eune belle fille! Ça c'est eune belle créature!" I dit "Oui?"—"Ah oui" i dit "mais" i dit "c'est pas moi qui vas l'aouère. Ahh!" i dit "p—attention!" i dit—ha ha ha! I dit "Sais-tu" i dit "qu'y a pas grand, grand, j'en ai vu en masse des, des jeunes hommes comme toi là" i dit, "mais sais-tu qu'i y en a pas d'si beau qu'toi? J'en ai pas vu iun. Y en avait des grosses oreilles, des gros nez tout tordus—des djeules tout tordues" i dit, "les yeux tout—travers—mais ielle là—mais ça" i dit "c'est l'beauté, les deux yeux sont tout droites, les joues est tout rouges, les belles babines rouges" i dit—"et si bien bâtie" i dit, "si bien bâtie. Pis j'sus sûr" i dit "que si t'arais à cause tu m', tu t'oyais, j'te crois bien, tu seras bien habillé" i dit "j'sus sûr" i dit, "a tombera en amour avec toi! Tout droite!" Bien c'est bien. Ben, "Ah non, pas moi, ah non, ah non, mon ptit poussinne—non" i dit, "pas moi. Non non. Moi j'sus pas in bel homme, moi j'sus pas in bel homme."—"Orvenez-moi j'te dis que—que t'es in bel homme—je l'savais pas avant—mais asteure—je l'sais moi—as*teure* je le sais."—"Tu l'sais? Ben—j'y crois, ej crois" i dit "parce qu'" i dit "t'as assa, a, assez fait asteure" i dit "pour moi" i dit "qu'ej te crois quoi-ç-tu diras."—"Asteure" i dit "m'en vas t'dire moi—m'en dire eune chose—Jambe-de Bois m'en vas t'dire"—c'est l'chat qui parle—"m'en dire eune chose moi"—i dit—"tu vas aller" i dit euh—"y a eune boutique là—" euh, il, il a dit l'nom d'la boutique, asteure moi j'm'en rappelle pas le nom, le nom—mais i l'a dit—et pis il a dit "In *suit* de hardes là" i dit "pis" i dit "c'est des, i y en a, i y en a de toutes sortes de couleurs—ben" i dit "toi" i dit—"ej m'en vas t'dire la couleur que tu faut qu'tu prends—que tu prends."—"Mais" i dit "comment j'peux aller quri in *suit* de hardes j'ai pas d'argent."—"Ça fait pas d'diffarence ça" i dit "ça fait pas d'diffarence" i dit, "acoute-moi quoi-ç, quoi-ç-qu'ej te parle là moi" i dit, "c'est moi qui t'parle—ton chat" i dit. I dit euh, "Garde", eh, "tu vas aller" i dit "dans çte boutique-là et pis tu vas prende in *suit*" i dit "de, euh, sarge nouère" i dit, "c'est euh", et i dit "ça, ça brille—et pis" i dit "tu vas prende eune chmise blanche" i dit, "i y en a là" i dit—"pis y a les, les, les *necktie* là" i dit "qu'a, les *bow-tie* qu'il appelont—c'est fait" i dit "comme euh, en sifflette là" i dit euh, t'sais "et i appelont ça des *bow-ties*.

Et c'est là" i dit, "c'est, c'est marqué" i dit "les portraits sont là et toute en grand, ça, tu, tu peux ouère quand tu rentres, tu gardes pis tu t'ois là, tu t'ois là—asteure" i dit "c'est ça faut qu'tu prends toi." I dit "Pourquoi faire?" A y dit "Garde" i dit—"si tu sarais" i dit, "quoi-ç, si, si tu t'arais vu" i dit "quoi-ç-que j'ai vu moi" i dit—"Quoi-ç-que t'as vu?"—"Bien" i dit, "j'étais chez l'aroi moi—"—"T'as té chez l'aroi toi?"—"Oh oui!" i dit, "j'ai té là à l'entour j'ai pas rentré dans la maison" i dit—"mais j'tais à l'entour—et pis j'ai vu la fille du roi" i dit, "a câssait, a tait d'hors a câssait des fleurs, a les, a faisait des boquets là. Mais" i dit "ça, c'est beau! Ahh! Comme je t'ai dit tantôt" i dit, "les rouges, les joues tout rouges, les babines tout rouges, les grands choueux jaunes, et les—z-yeux bleus et c'est si beau!" i dit. "Mais moi" i dit, "ben ec est comme ej t'ai dit! Ej t'ai dit que t'es l'pus beau! Que j'ai vu moi! C'est tout des nez tordus et les djeules tout travers, des yeux croches—et pis c'est pour ça" i dit "que—ej t'ai dit—toi! Toi! Toi! Toi! Tu l'aras! Tu l'aras! C'est garanti! Là!"

i dit, "vas-t-en—comme je t'ai dit—tu veux de l'argent—j'ai de l'argent ici." Là. I y donne l'argent. I dit "Ça t'coûte—honze—honze dollars—pour le, pour le costume." Asteure j'pense ça coûte dans les, dans les cinq cents, cinq cents dollars—et honze dollars ça coûtait—çtés temps-là. Honze dollars. A donne, le, le chat donne honze dollars, j'sais pas i l'avait volé du giant ou quoi, mais i, il avait honze dollars—là il avait, i donne à, à Jean-du-Bois. Vlà Jean-du-Bois parti. Mais i *tremblait* comme ça là. I, i, i, sais pas mais i tait dans in aute monde i, i, i s'croyait pas lui-même eh? S'croyait pas lui-même. Ben c'est bien. Là. [Émile tousse, s'étouffe] Estchusez-moi. Quand qu'i rente dans la boutique—i oit les portraits tout ça là—là—pis i oit son *suit* là. Pis i oit la chemise blanche et la, la, la *bow-tie* là-dessus. Ben là, les, les, les, les commis s'en vient à lui, i dit "Quoi-ç-qu'ej pourrons faire pour toi?" I dit "Ej veux le, le *suit* là là—et euh, la chemise, et la, et la, la, le *bow-tie*, le, le comment t'appelles ça—là—la, l'*ecktie* de—le bouc—l'*ecktie* de bouc?

G.T.: Hm.

—L'*ecktie* de bouc—le *bow-tie*. I dit euh, "J'veux ça là. Et comment ça coûte?"— "In honze dollars." Ah, ah. Le chat, le chat savait—euh, i, i mais, c'est sorcier—i savait, il avait pas té là mais i savait ois-tu. Toujours c'est bon. Achète la, la, la—*suit*, pis là, j'ai pris les sou, les souliers aussi hein? Oh i y avait dit ça, oublié d'dire ça là. Les souliers et la, le chapeau et toute. Pis il achète ça. Pis ça a coûté—euh, treize dollars pou, pou le, le, les souliers et toute. Là. Ça arrive—là. I, là, i, le, le chat il avait, i bouillait de l'eau le temps qu'i tait parti. Pis i, il avait arrangé, il avait fait ça avec d'la fer grâsse, in, in, in machine, in *bathtub* là—les, il a fait ça avec d'la fer grâsse—et pis là i fout de l'eau d'dans et i dit, et pis i fout le, le, le, Jambe-de-Bois d'dans pis là i l'lave. Et j'te garantis qu'i l'a frotté mon vieux. Pas don de—grafigné avec ses ongues oh! Mais dame i halait ses ongues en arrière pis là i frottait ac ses pattes t'sais. Pis c'est des, dans la brousse, y avait toutes sortes d'affaires i pouvait crocheter—mais i le grapigne eune coupelle de fois quand i tait assez encouragé pour le, parce qu'i laimait son maîte eh? Tu sais des fois, tu sais, heh heh! *Gee!* Ben c'est bien. Là, ben, c'est bon. Ben là i, i tait la manière d—ma—d'affolé lui—Jean-du-Bois i tait manière de fou—i sait pas quoi-ç-que le chat—mais i, i, t'sais, i s'fiait dans lui, i l'acoutait parce qu'i s'fiait dans lui—quand même qu'il arait été pendu l'ende-main—euh, *still* i s'fiait dans lui. Ben c'est bon. Là. Là. Ben i l'avait greyé mon homme là i l'habille. Oh! *Holy* catouse! Ça ç'tait j—beau mon vieux! Bel homme. Oh! Là i dit "Va-t-en chez l'aroi asteure!"—"Moi?" i dit "chez l'aroi?"—"Oh ho ho! Oui!" i dit. "Tu vas aller chez l'aroi" i dit—pis i dit "Tu vas—frapper à la porte—et pis tu vas—s—*saluter* quand qu'i vont venir rouvrir la porte—et euh—pis c'est ielle" alle a dit "qui va venir rouvrir la porte."—"Ben"—"Mais" i dit "aies pas honte. N'aies pas honte! Dis-y 'Salut mademoiselle'—pis quand qu'a va t'ouère—a va tomber en amour avec toi, a va dire 'Rente! Approchez! Rente!'" Bien c'est bien. Là. I s'en va. Ah ha! Mais dame les deux genoux ça tapait ensemble comme ça là [Émile tape les doigts de chaque main ensemble]—la honte—pis i savait pas ois-tu? I tait—i tait éné dans les bois—jamais vu du monde avant—tchi-ç-qui ara du courage comme ça? Oh ho ho! I, i, mais il a, l'a acouté son chat—i *va*. Là i frappe à la porte. Oh mon bon sang de la vie! Quand qu'alle a rouvri la porte—alle l'a rgardé—a s'en va, quitte la porte rouvrie a s'en va, a l'croche tout l'tour du cou, a l'embrasse—pis a l'hale en d'dans la maison. Ben lui, il a pas, manière quasiment in, il a in—coeur—attaque, atta, attaqué. Ah! Ç'a venu proche! Bon sang d'la vie—pour eune fille aller faire d'quoi d'même—pou le premier coup d'sa vie! Alle a pas dit "Rente" ni arien comme ça, a l'hale! A l'hale dedans! Hale! Le premier bel homme qu'alle avait jamais vu d'sa vie. Bien, c'est ça. Là i rente! Pis l'aroi a dit, a s'en va à son père a dit "Mon père" a dit "c'est, le charmant homme" a dit "que j'ai ici. Oh! C'est agréable!" Pis i dit "Quoi-ç-qu'i y a don? Quoi-ç-qu'i y a don?" Mais a dit "Venez ouère!" Pis j'ai vu l'aroi, le vieux roi lui mais pis ç'tait, ben le nez pis il avait deux, deux—*kink* dans

l'nez lui—pis la djeule toute tordue aussi! Mais sa fille, ielle—tait, tait—tait eune
belle parsonne. Ah ha! A tait, a tait la, la, la—la la, oh "*A top choice of the world*" qu'i
disont eh? Ben c'est bien. I vient là—pis le—l'homme ois-tu—si charmant, tout ça
mais c'est l'chat qui faisait ça ois-tu eh? Ah? Le sorciaise ah? Il y donnait toutes les
façons d'faire—pour que la fille—ah?

G.T.:   Hm.

—Pis c'est—in sorciaise eh? Asteure i y en a pas mais ces temps-là, i y avait
eune tapée des, des sorcis—i saviont, i pouviont—jure—i saviont tout, i saviont tout.
Ben c'est bien. Ben, ben ça rente là. Pis là c'est in, c'est in, c'est in grand souper là,
de, de, de toutes sortes—d'affaires là à manger—pis i tait reçu comme in—monsieur.
Ben, c'est ça, i pouvait pas aller chez lui çte soirée-là, non, non, non, faulait qu'i reste,
pis i reste. Bien c'est bien. M—bien i reste. Pâsser la souerée—pis i avont joué aux
cartes—et—ça pâssait, ça pâssait et l'endemain matin ben i dit "Faut qu'ej m'en vas
chez nous." Ben, l'aroi i dit euh, "Acoute" i dit "mon cher jène homme" i dit, "orviens
encore. Orviens encore."—"Ben" i dit "marci beaucoup—j'erviens encore, bien sûr."
Toujours i s'en va chez lui là. Et il arrive là i dit "Comment qu't'as réussi?" le chat
dit "Comment qu't'as réussi euh, Jean-du-Bois?"—"Bien, bien" i dit "c'est extromi-
naire. Mais" i dit "ça c'est bien, j'ai pâssé eune belle souerée."—"J'ai dit ça" i dit "ej
t'ai dit!" Pis i dit "J'm'as, j'me demandais pus à venir." I dit "Que, t'a-t-i dit qu't'as
à revenir?"—"Non—mais i, i m'a dit or, orviens encore."—"Ben, ben" i dit "ça veut
dire ça—c'est pour ortourner encore. Huh! Ça, ça veut dire ça—s'il ara dit 'Viens
nous ouère tcheque temps', mais i dit 'erviens encore'! Ben, ça veut dire ça—viens
à souère encore! Hoh!"—"Ben j'ai f-f-faim t'sais" pis là i *donne my son*, i ont
mangé—pis il avait, il avait té aux lapins lui il avait attrapé du lapin, le chat
t'sais—pis il avait fait in *feed*—oh—pis ça, ça, t-t-t!—meilleur que les géants pouvaient faire ah ha! Pis ça mange! Ça mange! Bon. Là. Euh... C'est bien. Ouais, ben,
le chat tait satisfait et pis l'jène homme lui, bien, i commençait à venir—qu'i pensait
qu'i tait dans l'viande—pis i pensait que—i y avait d'quoi dedans—pis i tait heureux
son ptit tchœur orvenait en, en, en, en *shape*—oh, c'est eune—bonne vie pis i pensait,
la belle fille, la belle fille, la belle—ah ben, bin, ben il a pas pu dormir d'la nuit—il
a pas, il a pas dormi, il a pas dormi, nah! *t'all* a pas dormi. Nah! C'est bien. Là ç'a
pâssé la nuit. Là l'endemain, vlà l'chat prend encore il avait la, la champeux durcie
là, la *basin* qu'il avait fait là ç'tait grâsse là, ç'avait durci, oh! gee c'est quasiment
mangé comme des, comme des câilloux. Là. Là i fout le, la, la Jambe-du-Bois d'dans
pis i mit le l'eau pis le chat i, du, du, du lac, pis i chavire ça sus l'dos pis i frotte,
frotte, frotte—pis i l'lave comme i faut. Y avait pas des *perfumes* ni arien comme ça
ois-tu—çtés temps-là—i y avait arien comme ça t'sais—ienque des fleurs hein—i
s'frottiont ac des fleurs, là, des fleurs d'odeur euh? Là ça c'est, c'est assez là. Ça
marchait—oh! il aviont eune façon, il aviont eune façon, il aviont eune façon d'faire.
Ah! C'est bon. Là. Encore—greye encore là. La même change de hardes—pis le vlà
parti encore, même chapeau et tout ça. L'vlà parti encore. Ah c'est bien i arrive là,
frappe à la porte—oh, rouve la porte "Eh, eh! T'as, rente, rente, rente, rente, rente,
rente, rente, rente! Mais quâ faire t'as pas venu plus vite, mais quâ faire t'as pas venu
plus vite?"

Mais c'est, c'est justement la soirée d'avant pis euh, pis c'est justement la nuit
ois-tu? Oh on laime aller les ouère les filles à midi, à midi ou dans la, dans la jornée.
I, mais, faut les va, c'est pas malade a l'avait manqué, oh! oh! Oh, sept et huit heures
ou neuf à dix heures ou d'quoi d'même—manqué—oh! Pis ça, pis ah mais d—là ça
commence à chauffer, mon vieux, ça commence à chauffer! Ho ho ho! *Wacko!* Ouais,
ben, c'est bien. Là l'aroi i s'trouvait ç'tait in assez charmant homme—pis i ouoyait
sa fille—tait assez plaisant—et euh, assez fière d'encontrer çte jène homme-là pis lui,
ah bien, c'est i, c'est l'jeune homme—le, ça le, le, le plaisait assez bien—qu'i, i savait
pas quoi dire, i, i allait, i tait, i tait pour parler pis il arrêtait, il arrête, arrêtait. Et tout

d'in coup ç'a sorti—"Ben" i dit "mon cher homme" i dit—mais sa fille a tait à l'entour de—à l'entour de vingt-trois ans, ois-tu... C'est quasiment temps d'çtés temps-là d'se marier ois-tu? Ah—pis i savait ça ois-tu? I dit euh, "Euh, mon, mon cher Jean-du-Bois" i dit euh, "c'est ton nom"—i dit "Oui, euh, mon, nom, oui, Jean-du-Bois, oui."—"Ben" i dit euh, "aimerais-tu" i dit "euh, marier ma fille" i dit. "Oh oui" i dit "ça m'fera in grand plaisir si j'arais la chance" i dit, "si vous m'donnerez la, la causation" i dit "de, d'agir" i dit "que j'pourrais vous pourriez m'donner vote fille—si, si alle est en amour avec moi." Oh a dit "Oui! j'sus en amour avec toi!"—"Et moi aussi" i dit "j'sus en amour avec toi." Et i dit "J'sons pas chanceux assez de pouvouère me—de te pououère ête mis ensemble" i dit. "Ben" i dit euh l'aroi y dit, "je vous donne mon consentement, mon consentement" i dit, "mariez-vous!" I dit euh, "J'arai le minisse—et vous srez mariés. Quand qu'vous voudrez." Là c'est ça là, i s'en va quri son chat là. Heh heh! Il arrive là entor d'deux heures du matin—now—le chat dormait. Dans l'foin. Dormait, i dit "Ouaou! ouaou!" Ben... Jean-du-Bois arrive, rouve la porte, i dit "Hé! Haou—ouaou-ouaou" le chat i dit, "tu m'as reveillé" i dit. "Ah ben" i dit "tchelle sorte de souerée qu't'as pâssé?" Ben là asteure Jean-du-Bois conte, conte au chat—"Mais" i dit "c'est ça là, ois-tu? Vlà les contes" i dit—le chat dit à, à Jean-du-Bois. "Les noces" i dit "c'est tout proche eh?"—"Bien" i dit, "c'est ça."—"Ah bien" i dit. Asteure le, l'aroi croyait lui qu'ç'tait—que ç'tait pas in homme riche—i croyait il avait arien t'sais le, Jean-du-Bois i croyait, i croyait pas—mais dame—pour sa, pour sa fille—c'est son amour, alle avait tombé en amour avec lui pis a, ç'tait eune si belle créature—de parsonne—que—il a pris pitié à sa fille, ois-tu, là, il a, ça y a fait—laimer sa fille—dix fois mieux—qu'i l'avait laimée avant. Parce qu'alle avait trouvé son choix. Heh? Ben c'est bien. Là. Toujours, l'endemain matin mon ami i tait encore deboute pis i mange du lapin encore pis heh heh! pis i fout dans la bâille encore pis eune aute laverie encore—pis c'est ça, il a parti. Allé. Arrive là... [pause pour changer de bande]

G.T.: Non.

—Ouais. Bien, c'est bien. Là ça c'est, i, i rente et va ioù qu'la fille tait—rente et ci et cela. Là—euh, ça jasait in ptit peu pis là ça a commencé à ête à parler de mariage et ci et cela et euh—va à la fois aouère le minisse—déjà i veut les marier. Ouais, c'est bien. Oh y en a le minisse—le minisse s'en vient. Ben asteure le chat lui, le, le chat a venu aussi là. Quand ç'a venu çtés temps-là là, ça ç'tait proche, ben le chat vient aussi là—mais i tait à l'entour t'sais, "Miaou, miaou, miaou"—mais i maillndiont pas le chat parce ç'tait in chat. Mais i tait pas frotté ni arien comme ça—ç'tait in beau ptit chat. C'est bien. Là. Aïe. Là le ministe les marie. Bien, après qu'i sont mariés—là. I dit euh—il avont ieu leu, leu dîner—pis là i dit à son maîte, Jambe-du-Bois i dit "Asteure" i dit euh, "dis au roi" i dit "de—aouère" i dit "deux chouals et pis eune voiture. Et pis euh, dis-y comme ça que tu veux—deux chvals et eune voiture—et pis j'allons—ej—qu'tu veux aller ouère" i dit "ton, quoi-ç-que, quoi-ç-que t'as—t'appartient." Ah—i dit "Quoi?" i dit, "J'as arien qui m'appartchient."—"Ej t'ai dit, dis ça." I dit "Tout-ç-t'as, t'es tout-ç-t'as à dire—pis" i dit "fârme ta gueule." Ben, c'est bien, c'est bien. Ouais, i dit au roi i dit "Asteure" i dit—"ej veux que vous avez deux—deux chvaux" i dit "et pis euh, eune voiture—pis" i dit "j'veux" i dit euh "vous allez venir a, avec moi" i dit—"moi et ma femme—et vous et vote, et votre, votre dame." Il avait eune femme l'aroi aussi euh—mais ielle était trantchille a disait jamais rien d'quoi—a tait bien t'sais, euh trantchille, a tait trantchille. C'est ça. Ben. Là i dit "Fais quoi-ç-qu'ej t'ai dit asteure." Pis i dit "Tu vas aller" i dit "là à les trois géants là" i dit. "Ma—là ioù-ç-qu'i, i vivont là-bas dans leus farmes. Et pis euh, dis arien" i dit. Pis i dit "J'peux pas aller là" i dit "moi, toutes les, les géants."—"Ej t'ai dit! Va! Embarque à bord d'la voiture pis viens! Et pis dis arien! Asteure acoute-moi" i dit. Ben c'est bien là i dit au roi et toute ça—pis i embarque dans la voiture, les chevaux et toute ça—les vlà partis! Pis s'en va là chez les géants. Quand qu'il arrive là la première *gate*, la, la, la propriétié, la proprieu—proprit-itié—hah! pas moyen d'le dire!—est à Jambe-du-Bois. L'aroi garde ça! I dit "Quoi don?" i dit, "Quoi don?" i dit. "La propriété à Jean-du-Bo—à Jambe-de-Bois?" I dit "C'est toi ça?"—"Oh oui" i dit "c'est moi." Ois-tu là—pâsse à travers la farme—encore l'aute *gate* encore—"La propriété à—Jambe-du-Bois"—des grands châteaux, ça, ça mirait eh? Ouah! Mais, mais, mais, l'aroi ses oreilles ça montait, c'est, d'la, il ava in chapeau sus la téte pis les oreilles, ça poussait, ha ha ha! en l'air—et tout d'in coup vlà le chapeau par-dessus d'la téte! I tait assez surpris! Les vlà partis encore, pus loin—pis ç'tait encore la propriété à Jean—à Jambe-de.Bois encore! "Ben" i dit "ça peut pas s'faire ça." Oh oui là, le chat a donné les, les clés à, à Jambe-du-Bois pis là "Jambe-du-Bois" i dit "rouvrez les châteaux" pis il y rentiont là-d'dans mais—mais ça puait in peu—parce les géants commenciont à, commenciont à, heh heh heh! i commenciont à pourrir! Mais ça fait pas d'diffarence, parce ç'tait in *fârmer* ois-tu eh, depis longtemps! Eh hé hé! Ça pâssait l'nez dessus comme ça. Et quand j'ai arrivé là, quand j'étais là, ça a donné justement comme ça—mais dame—entor moi pis Jambe-de-Bois pis l'chat—j'avons enterré les géants—pis euh, j'avons clarci d'la, la, heh heh! la, l'odeur pis s'i vivont ac les deux mariés—i vivont!

    (p. 241)

G.T.:   Ha ha! Ho! Ça c'est in beau conte, Émile. Ça c'est in beau conte. Tu as bien conté. Tchi-ç-qui t'avait conté ça? Tu t'souviens?

E.B.:   C'est toi.

G.T.:   Eh?

E.B.:   Toi!

G.T.:   Moi?!

E.B.:   Ouais!

G.T.:   Moi j't'ai conté ça?

E.B.:   Ouais ouais! Quoi tu vas [deux ou trois mots indistincts]

G.T.:   Ej t'ai conté ça?

E.B.:   Ouais! L'année pâssée—pas çt année—l'année pâssée—mais pas si long qu'ça eh?

G.T.:   Mais tu, t'as entendu ça déjà?

E.B.:   Non, jamais.

G.T.:   T'avais jamais entendu conter ça?

E.B.:   Non, tu n'en contais ça l'année pâssée.

G.T.:   C'est pas vrai!

E.B.:   Varité du Bon Dieu.

G.T.:   Et tu avais jamais tendu ça? Non?

E.B.:   C'est toi qui me l'a conté.

(p. 242)

CENDRILLOUX

Ben le Cendrilloux—l'histoire de Cendrilloux, il avait eune, eune, une mère—alle avait in enfant. et pis euh, alle a levé son enfant euh, alle avait ieu in homme mais alle a té mariée mais alle était pas longtemps mariée qu'alle a pardu son homme. Dans les, la première djerre. Son homme tait, était dans la djerre pis il a, il a été tué. Alle a resté avec son enfant. Pis a l'a élevé en, en, jusqu'à temps qu'il avait vingt-et-une ans—mais il avait jamais sorti d'la maison. I tait tout l'temps assis darrière le poêle. Pis a l'appelait Cendrilloux. Son nom était Jean. Mais a l'appelait pas Jean, a l'appelle Cendrilloux. Pis tout l'monde—le—l'appelait Cendrilloux. C'est in, in *nickname* t'sais eh?

G.T.:   Hm-hm.

—Pis—c'est bien, ç'allait, ç'allait, ç'allait, ç'allait—jusqu'à temps qu'il a té vingt-et-une ans. Ben là a dit—ben c'est diffarent eh?

G.T.:   Hm.

—Cendrilloux hein?

G.T.:   Hm-hm.

—Ielle tait eune fille et lui ç'tait, ç'tait in garçon. Ben là—a dit "Mon cher enfant" a dit—"si tu vas" a dit "ête comme ça là, tout le reste d'tes jours—si tu vis cinquante ans, soixante ans, soixante-dix ans, soixante-tchinze ans, quatre-vingt ans" a dit "pt-ête bien *cent* ans—pis ton, ton nom va rester" a dit "Cendrilloux. Parce" a dit "t'es tout l'temps darrière le poêle! Tout-ç-qui, t'as pas sorti dehors d'ta vie encore" a dit. "Depis qu'ej te connais, depis que t'as té dans l'monde" a dit, "t'as té, c'est là qu'ej t'ai—qu'ej t'ai vu tout l'temps" a dit. "Darrière le poêle. Mon Cendrilloux." A l'appelle Cendrilloux. Pis tout l'monde l'appelle Cendrilloux. Ben là c'est bon. Là. Alle a vingt-et-une-ans, il a vingt-et-une ans. Ben "Asteure" a dit "mon cher jeune, mon cher jeune homme" a dit, "lève-toi!" a dit. "*My*—nah!" i dit, a dit "Lève-toi dboute!" Mais, mais euh [voix basse; le sot qui pleurniche]—il assayait d'se lever deboute—i pouvait pas—i pouvait pas—i tait tout l'temps assis eh? Tait, tait, il avait les, les crampes eh? Ben là a l'croche là. A, il assayait pis i pouvait pas ben a savait là ois-tu, il avait la volonté—mais i pouvait pas. Là a l'croche pis a hale dessus là. Pis là, là a, a l'fait marcher, oh oh! Pis i tait, i, i marchait comme in vieux j'pense de cent, cent—cent ans, cent, cent-dix ans, cent-tchinze ans, d'quoi d'même. Pis a hale dessus pis a l'marche, i marche, i marche, i marche pis ouh! mais dans eune coupelle de jours—tchi! I, i commence à prende d'la force. Pis i commence à marcher tout seul. Là. "Asteure" a dit—"là, ois-tu asteure?" a dit, "c'est cela" a dit, "ois-tu, t'as, t'as, t'as le, le, l'accis, l'axcisse [l'exercice]" a dit "ça ois-tu?" a dit—"Tu commences à marcher" pis i commençait à ête fier lui, i commençait à ête fier eh? Hé hé! I commençait—c'est pareil comme in, in aute monde eh? Tout l'temps assis, tout l'temps assis eh? Et tout d'in coup sa mère l'a fait marcher—son—mais ç'tait pas, ç'tait pas d'quoi—heh heh! d'nouveau pour lui ça! Ha ha! Oohh! Là! *By gosh*, il a commencé à apprende à lever—pis il a commencé à bouger les bras pis—pis ça bougeait là. Pis, pis i marchait là. Oh pis ça avait pâssé eune semaine comme ça là—pâssé eune semaine. "Là asteure" a dit, "ois-tu? Moi" a dit "j'commence à vieillsir moi" a dit—"ta mère—là—ça commence à vieillsir ça, moi j'sus soixante-huit ans asteure là" a dit. I dit "Oui." Mais lui il avait ienque—trente-cinq ans. Là. Nah—je me trompe—vingt-et-une ans j'veux dire.

G.T.:   Hm.

—Alle avait soixante-huit ans et lui i, lui avait—vingt-et-une ans. Alle avait debougé darrière de—le Cendrilloux. Ah—là. "Asteure" a dit "le, l'aroi là" a dit "là—euh, le farmier en-haut là-bas—pas l'aroi, le farmier"—a dit "i n'a eune belle

336

fille là. Oh oh oh! Bien" a dit "euh moi" a dit "ej trouve c'est assez—eune charmante parsonne" a dit—"c'est ami, ç'a toujours in sourire sus la fidjure" a dit "pis ça travaille—ça travaille comme eune béte. Pis" a dit "si tu pourrais don" a dit—"toi t'es in bel homme toi" a dit—"t'es in bel homme. Pis si tu pourrais convartir in ptit peu pis bouger in ptit peu" a dit, "pis tu pourrais aller là" a dit—"pis jter in oeil d'temps en temps. Oh, jter in oeil d'temps en, pas, t'as pas, pas trop t'es trop vite—tu prends ton temps" a dit—"prends ton temps! Faut qu'tu coutes ça seulement" a dit, "ça, ça c'est pas poli ça. C'est sauvage ça. Mais tu prends ton temps—pis" a dit "tu y jettes in oeil d'temps en temps—pis là après in ptit boute" a dit, "ça travaille là" a dit, "pis ça bouge. Pis bientôt" a dit "ça arrive à d'quoi!" Hah hah! "Mais faut pas ête trop fronté! Attention!" Pis j'veux dire ah, i savait pas grand'chose pis là—c'est ienque çtés temps-là qu'sa mère a commencé ielle, tout l'temps qu'il attendait à ses oreilles "Cendrilloux, Cendrilloux, Cendrilloux." Mais ça commençait à changer là. Toujours—c'est bien. Là. Ah, ç'a té comme ça pou çte semaine-là pis eune aute semaine, pis eune aute semaine—pis ça marchait, pis ça bougeait, pis ça commençait à s'convartir, pis ça allait—là! A dit "T'es pas mal in beau *shape* asteure là toi." Là. A dit. "Tu vas aller chez le, le farmier" a dit—"tu oublies pas—euh, jette in oeil d'temps en temps!"—"Ben, jette in oeil d'temps en temps? Oh pis c'est ça." C'est bien. Là. Vlà le temps arrivait là et ça ç'tait le temps—ç'tait le samedi au souère. Siou! "Là, comme ej t'ai dit" a dit—"tu vas aller là d'la respecte" a dit, "Bonsouère euh, Monsieur, bonsouère Madame, bonsouère Mademoiselle—attention!" a dit— "fais ça comme i faut! Pis là, quand qu'le vieux pis la vieille—euh, n'ergardent pas" a dit, "jette in oeil! A la fille."—"Oui maman." A dit "Bien."—"Bien ça" i dit "c'est pas dur à faire." Ben. Ah, c'est bien. Ah, c'est bon. Ben là c'est ça—i, là i s'greye, a, a, a l'lave comme i faut pis euh—a l'arrange de çtes temps-là ç'tait pas beaucoup des belles hardes mais dame, huh! s'arrangeait t'sais, c'est toutes des hardes d'étoffe du métier, i faisiont in metchier hein?

G.T.:   Oui oui.

—Avec d'la laine et des léleurs [?]—pis i faisiont des, des, des tchulottes et des—chemises et des...Ben c'est ça. A l'a greyé comme i faut *anyhow*. La, la meilleure façon qu'a pouvait. Mais c'tait in bel homme. Pah! J'te garantis. I tait pas in maigue comme moi heh!

G.T.:   Hm!

—Bien ça—il est parti. Là. Comme ça à l'entour de huit heures du souère. Oh, i faisait nuit. Là. Dans son idée asteure i dit "Maman m'a dit—à jter in oeil—bien—et jter in oeil" i dit "euh le farmier lui, il a des cornes, il a des moutons—pis ça là"—là i va pis i croche eune forchette et y avait des forchettes à trois bro—trois bras tait dans ça heh! Bien i prend eune forchette met dans sa poche. Il a parti. Ah! C'est bien. Quand qu'il a arrivé à la, à la grange du farmier—pis—i, i rente dans la grange. I garde pour les moutons—pis les moutons ça a les yeux si clairs ah, c'est comme des *flashlight* les yeux eh. I s'pousse—pis i pique la forchette pour, i les croche les moutons pis i la pique la forchette dans in oeil, i l'arrache! I croche in aute pis i pique la forchette pis i l'arrache! Ha ha! I n'arrache cinq ou six—cinq ou six là. [rires] Ben" i dit "ça c'est quoi faire, cinq ou six yeux" i dit "c'est assez ça—pour à souère." Heh heh!

G.T.:   Heh heh heh!

—Ben c'est bien. Ben le vlà parti. Ben mon vieux quand qu'i, i, après là—i frappe à la porte—et pis la fille a té rouvrir la porte—ooh! A l'avait jamais vu pis i, i, i restait pas trop loin de d'là. Mais a l'avait jamais vu, alle avait jamais té là ois-tu.

G.T.:   Hm.

—Le charmant jène, jeune homme! Oh oh oh oh oh le bel homme! Stiou! Aououaou! Hi! Ha ha! Caco! A Dit "Rente, rente, rente! Papa! et euh, maman!"—

"Quoi?"—"Argardez, le jeune homme" a dit, "gardez! Des—oh, bonsoir, rentrez, rentrez! Cher ami, rentrez!" Mais i saviont pas que ç'tait le, le, le, a l'avait arrangé ois-tu a l'avait greyé là—i, i pâssait pour in Cendrilloux tout l'temps t'sais—

G.T.: Hm.

—Ç'tait son nom il avait jamais té—piqué dboute—a—d'sa vie eh? T'sais, c'est, i tait abandonné, i saviont pas ça—quand qu'il ont vu ça—il croyiont que ç'tait d'quoi qui venait dans les, dans les, dans les autes pays ou d'quoi d'même hein?

G.T.: Qui oui.

—Ah. Toujours c'est bien. *By de gee*, la fille, mon Dieu a, oh, oh, oh, oh! A, a, a l'aimait, a l'aimait, a l'aimait. le bel homme, le bel homme, pis—tant d'esprit, tant d'esprit, tant—si bien élevé eh? A dit "Assoueyez-vous." Ben là i s'assit—et pis le vieux pis la vieille i tiont là qui parliont, i jâsiont, d'ci, d'cela, pis la fille a tait là que—a, a s'faisait ouère là, a tait in ptit peu *smart*, a tait *smart* et ois-tu—oh, ouaou! Heh! C', c'était, pas mal intelligent, j'te garantis. Là c'est bien. Là. Bientôt vlà le vieux pis la vieille, i viront l'dos eh, i rafle in oeil dans la poche pis il y enouoie ça paque! I claque ça dans l'côté d'sa djeule [Emile se tord de rire]—fidjure d'la fille! A l'ergarde i dit "Pssch!" A pointe à son père à mère a dit "Papa et maman, toi faire d'quoi d'même!" a dit. Oh! "Pss! I vont pas laimer ça!" Ois-tu, a voulait dire, t'sais...

G.T.: Hm.

—Que c'est signe—et pis là il a orviré d'bord pis i commencent à parler encore pis là tout d'in coup i s'orviront l'dos encore [clac!] i tire, enouoie encore in aute hah! In aute oeil encore! Ouais! Oh a s'en va—ss—a voulait dire—"Fais pas ça! Fais pas ça!" Mais a disait pas mais a faisait signe ac sa main ois-tu? Vlà son père et sa mère virent de bord encore mais i commençont à parler encore pis toute allait bien oh oh! ç'tait pas des ptites affaires—là. Bientôt là, i orviront d'bord encore pis là qu'i *saque* in autre oeil encore—I—i la tape dans l'oeil—ç'coup-là, [rires] *Right*—*oh gees* i vient juste! Roh! Là a s'en va pis a dit à son oreille—a dit [Emile parle à voix basse] "Fais pas ça, fais pus ça!" a dit "parce pt-ête bien papa et maman laimera pas d'quoi d'même" a dit. Ah c'est bien, là, oh, il a fait pus. Mais il avait encore trois autes yeux dans la, dans la poche! Hah hah! Mais i l'a fait pus, i l'a fait pus. Ah, c'est bien. Là i s'en va chez lui. "Bonsoir"—oh, l'aroi dit, euh le farmier dit "Erviens encore, viens encore!"—"Oh" a dit [voix de jeune fille sotte] "erviens encore"—la fille eh, la fille du roi a dit "Oh viens encore!"—"Ben oui oh, oui" il, i dit "m'en viens *back*" i dit [d'une curieuse voix profonde et brouillée] "oh oui." Ben c'est bon. Là. C'est bien, s'en va. Là il arrive à sa, il arrive chez—sa mère a, a tait assis dans la chaise à barcer, a tait là a, a brochait ielle. A brochait. Ah hum! Réumme! "hoho!" a dit "t'es venu!" A y dit "Comment qu'ç'a été?"—"Oh" i dit "pas pire maman, pas pire. A dit "As-tu jté des yeux comment qu'ej t'ai dit?"—"Oh j'ai jté trois yeux" i dit. Pis a dit "Ç'a-t-i joué d'quoi?"—"Oh, a, a m'a dit comme ça a dit euh, a dit 'Fais pus ça' a dit 'en tout cas' a dit 'papa et maman te, te oueraient!'"—"Ah! J't'ai dit, moi! Ej t'ai dit! Meilleur qu'à ête assis darrière le poêle tout l'temps" a dit "heh heh heh! Asteure demain—demain" a dit "asteure là—m'en vas t'dire moi. Demain j'm'en vas quri la fille moi—pis" a dit "tu vas tchuire à dîner." Asteure—il aviont in—in ptit chien qui s'appelait "Trois Sortes."

G.T.: Trois Sortes".

—"Trois Sortes." Le ptit chien, in ptit *cracky dog* qu'il appelont eh?

G.T.: Oui oui.

—Elle s'appelait "Trois Sortes"—et pis il aviont in, in—in zoie—qui, qui couvait—ben, d—il est derrière la porte, il aviont ieu fait eune cage.

G.T.: Oui oui, oui oui.

—Pis i y avait eune douzaine d'oeufs—pis i aviont leu zoie—à—à couver dsus. Là. C'est bien. Ah! Toujours l'endemain arrive, "Bien asteure" a dit, a dit "tu vas tchuire à diner—ah ben" a dit "tu vas tchuire trois sortes"—a voulait dire c'est d'la viande, des choux-raves—pis des patates! A dit "Tu vas tchuire trois sortes—et pis moi j'vas aller quri la fille—et pis j'm'en vas—l'—l'amener ici—pis c'est comme ça" a dit "tout va s'faire—commencer" a dit "et pis—l'affaire vas ête faite. I y a longtemps que j'aspère pour ça moi!" a dit—"Asteure" a dit "j'sus dans mon joie asteure mon tchoeur est heureux" a dit "à ouère quoi-ç-que t'as fait. Ej croyais jamais" a dit "que tu tais si *smart*—que t'as. A t'ouère—je t'appelais tout l'temps Cendrilloux—oui mais j'ai bien d'ergrets. Si j'arais su" a dit "jamais! qu'ej t'arais appelé d'quoi d'même. Eune mère devra faire attention" a dit "quoi-ç-qu'i t'a dit à son enfant." I dit pas arien lui. Mah—c'est bien, bon ça arrive à dix heures, a dit "M'en, m'en vas aller quri la fille asteure bien" a dit "ej m'en vas jâser in boute pis" a dit "toi—*tree, tree*."—"*Tree* quoi ça?"—"Pis euh, ça, ça, ça, sra pas trop pire" a dit "ça sra pas trop pire." *All right*. Asteure lui i, i, trois sortes, pis là le chien s'appelait "Trois Sortes"—mais ielle a voulait dire euh, d'la viande, des, des patates, pis des choux-raves. Les trois sortes t'sais. Hm.

G.T.:   Mais c'est in tchurieux nom pour in chien.

—Eh?

G.T.:   C'est in tchurieux nom pour in chien.

—Ouais! Ouais, ouais, mais trois sortes, c'est pas l'chien.

G.T.:   Oui oui!

—Toujours heh, c'est bien. Là. Là quand que c'est, quand qu'alle est partie—i, il a pas dmandé pus long parce qu'i ta—sa manière tait—dis vite—pis après qu'a tait partie il a commencé à penser—i—"Quoi-ç-qu'i dit que, que, quoi-ç-qu'alle a *meané* avec ça" i dit, "trois sortes!" i dit. "Tchelle sorte d'affaire faut qu'ej tchuise, trois sortes?" T'sais s'il ara pensé plus vite là—il ara demandé quoi-ç-que ç'tait—tchelle sorte de trois, trois sortes faut qu'ej tchuis? Mais i dit ois-tu ma, mangnière de *puzzlé* là, avait mangnière de—de, de—*contredicté* là—mais a tait partie asteure—pis i tait là—mais "C'est, ç'sera pas l'ptit chien là? Ce sera pas l'ptit chien? Trois Sortes. Pour l'tour" i dit "c'est ça. *I bet you a darn* c'est ça qu'a voulait dire! Le ptit chien! Ah non!" i dit "pas ça! Mais" i dit "j'sais pas quoi-ç-que c'est! Trois Sortes" i dit "j'appelle, je l'appelle le ptit chien" i dit "Trois Sortes. Ben" i dit "faut croire" i dit "c'est ça. Mais" i dit "c'est ça, j'vas pas prendre la chance *anyhow*" i dit "c'est ça, alle a dit Trois Sortes mais c'est ça. C'est ça." Là i prend la potte d'eau mon homme pis i la bouille là.

G.T.:   Ha ha!

—Pis i le croche le chien par la, par la darrière du cou quand la potte bouillait comme i faut, pis i fout le chien dedans mais mon Dieu d'la vie eh le chien eh [rires], c'est "Ouah ouah ouah ouah ouah ouah ouah ouah ouah ouah ouah!" Pis là, là, le *goddarn* zoie qui fait darrière la porte—*Holy gee* quand alle a tendu ça pis a savait quoi-ç-qu'a, quoi-ç-qu'il avait fait—a savait ielle—a pouvait parler—mais a savait que là il a foutu le ptit chien—dans, dans l'eau bouillant pis là ben alle a commencé à disputer, "Coâque! coâque! coâque! coâque! coâque! coâque! coâque! coâque!" Ben i dit "Garde-toi!" i dit—"si tu taises pas la gueule—ben toi" i dit "tu vas ac Trois Sortes!" [rires] Pis là il a dit ça d'quoi—a enrage de plusse! A coâque coâque coâque, coâ-â-â-que, coâ-â-que! Coâque, coâque, coâque! *Oh jeepers cripes*! i, a s'*enrageait* mon homme! A crachait l'feu! Cendrilloux i la croche par le cou i l'arrache—sort de la cage, d'ioû-ç-qu'a tait dans la cage eh—pis i la prend pis i la *fout* dans l—dans la bâille avec Trois Sortes—pis i la pousse droite—par-dessus l'bord pis i cale les couverts en bas—tout d'in coup là pis—arien à tende. Vlà l'zoie parti. Pis quate sortes. Ben après qu'la colère tait pâssée—[rires]—"Oh mon grand Bon Dieu" i dit "quoi j'ai té faire? Mais" i dit "faut crouère qu'ej sus fou *a'right* . Oh j'sus parti d'la téte" i dit, "j'sus parti! C'est pas ça qu'maman, maman m'a dit d'faire! Trois Sortes!

339

I bet you c'est sortes de de de, de, de de lédjume ou d'quoi d'même, d'la viande ou d'quoi d'même. Là pt-ête bien des patates ou pt-ête bien des choux-r—ou pt-ête bien des choux" i dit. I—ois-tu? I dit "Faire attention" i dit, "après tout." i dit "à couver" i dit—"pour aouère des, des zoies" i dit, i dit "pou, pour euh, la nourriture. Ben" i dit "a va pas ête contente! Mon Dieu, quoi j'vas n'en faire? Garde c'est pas" i dit "c'est, c'est pas utile" i dit. "Ça c'est fou" i dit "pour la peine. Oh ben dame" i dit "asteure" i dit "j'sais j'sus fou—asteure" i dit "j'le sais! Le Cendrilloux! C'est pas mal" i dit "de m'appeler Cendrilloux. Pis pas ienque ça alle ara dû m'appeler aussu—aussi—ara dû m'appeler 'fou'" a dit, "le, le, le n—toutes sortes d'affaires comme ça." Là. "Orgarde les oeufs" i dit—"c'est pas encore si pire des Trois Sortes" i dit "pis l'zoie" i dit. "Non, garde les oeufs" i dit "là-bas" i dit, i dit "quoi-ç-que maman a va dire?" Ah bien là i tait là mon vieux il a venu farouche mon vieux—*Holy cat!* Ben là il a dit "Asteure mon homme" i dit "c'est ça, ben j'ai pas d'*choice*. J'ai pus d'*choice*. M'en vas être obligé de m'assire sus les oeufs" i dit "pour couver ces oeufs-là. Parce qu'" i dit "si j'couve pas ces oeufs-là—je sras ruiné! [rires] J'arons pas arien à manger! [Emile parle en riant, d'une voix avalée] Pas arien à manger!" i dit ch—les, si, si ah si tu l'entends là mon homme pis là, i s'assit sus les oeufs! I s'colle le darrière sus les oeufs. Pis là bientôt vlà—a s'en vient [petite voix de mémère]— "T'as fait bien attention à mon enfant, in charmant homme, mon charmant enfant qu'tu es là—" et pis i dit "Si gentil" pis il attendait... sa mère, sa mère pis la fille s'en venaient pour manger trois sortes! Heh heh! Maman! [pause pour retourner la bande] "Tiens votre enfant il est si gentil, déjeuner à souère"—"Oh oui, c'est ça, je le sais qu'c'est in charmant enfant." [petite voix de vieille] Bien, bien ça marché bien. Bien là alle arrivont pis i rouvront la porte eh. Quand i rouvront la porte eh, "Couâ, couâ, couâ, couâ, couâ, couâ, couâ, couâ, couâ!" Ben i tait là—lui a rgarde la fille rente aussi a rgardait là-bas i tait là—tout nu sus les ha ha ha ha! Tout nu sus les oeufs! Tout nu sus les oeufs ah, "Ouâ,ouâ, ouâ, ouâ" i faisait, i faisait! [rires]

(p. 247)

LE CONTE DE LA MONTAGNE NOUÈRE

Le Conte de la Montagne nouère. Hm. Bien j'pense. C'est in conte qui est in peu long aussi là c'est, c'est—après in boute vas l'conter. J'pense j'peux me rappeler in peu. Bien, in coup, in coup par eune bonne fois—comme c'est toujours par eune bonne fois les temps pâssés ça ça arrivait j'pense dans les—quate et cinq siècles de ça. Y avait eune homme — i s'appelait — euh — Johnny —en anglais c'est Jack. Ben c'est comme ça j'l'as entendu, c'est l'nom—parce que—Johnny c'est eune homme qui avait jamais té gagné. I, ç'tait in homme qui tait *smart*, i tait déluré et—il avait toutes sortes de, de, de, de bonnes idées et tout ça. Il a, il a toujours gagné. Dans toutes les histouères que, que j'avons, qu'a té, qu'a té résisté, qu'a té conté. Bien, ç'homme, çt homme-là—c'était eune homme ej pense qu'avait été éné euh, à son euh—façon, de son ouvrage—mais son *gift* était—in joueur de cartes. Pis i jouait *poker*. Pis ça *jouait poker*. Il a jouè pour des années et des années—pis tous-ç-qui jouaient avec lui—i gagnait. I les gagnait. Pis ça venait d'toutes les parts du monde—parts vous, des, des, des *channel*, des *channels* [challenge, un défi] qu'il appelont, les—et pis i veniont—*pis* i les gagnait, i les gagnait. Ben, il a venu assez riche—il a bâti des châteaux—euh, son père et sa mère pis ç'a bâti in château pour lui-même—pis il avait de la terre en masse de la terre pis il a commencé à, à bâtir des, des hôtels—et toute ça. Ah! Il a devenu—millionaire, millionaire. Bien, toute le monde a abandonné jouer avec lui—parce qu'i tiont toutes enruinés—i les avait toutes pauves, toute du monde pauve. I tiont toutes enruinés, i aviont tout joué leu, leu l'argent, toutes leus biens, il avait du bien partout, dans toute la grandeur de l'univers. Qu'il avait gagné. Ben—par eune bonne fois i dit "Tchiens!" i dit "ça" i dit—"vois ça. Ej sus le champion" i dit "de tout l'univers—à jouer le *poker*. Asteure" i dit "le seul homme que j'ai pas joué avec" i dit, "c'est le diabe. Pis" i dit "j'*maillnderais* pas le

340

jouer avec lui. Pah! Parce si je le gagnerais—*anyway*." Oha! C'est bon, c'était comme ça pour—pt-ête bien eune coupelle de jours—tout d'in coup, vlà in étranger qu'arrive. Oua! Ha ho! In bel homme—in beau chapeau nouère sus la téte pis des, in beau *suit* nouère et la belle, eune belle chemise blanche pis in *bowt*—eune, eune, in *bow*—machine, comment-ç-qu'il appelont ça, les *bowtie* là—les *ecktie* de chat qu'ej appelions ça auparavant. C'est bien. Là. Haïe! "Comment c'est?" i dit la première affaire i dmande au, au diabe, mais i savait pas que ç'tait le diabe—i savait pas que ç'tait le, le démon—i dit euh—"Peux-tu jouer l'*poker* toi?" Dmande au diabe—"Peux-tu jouer l'*poker*?"—"Ah! pas beaucoup—in ptit peu" i dit, "in ptit peu. Pas beaucoup." I dit euh, "J'sus in joueur de *poker* moi" i dit—"et i y a parsonne qui peut m'gagner."—"Non?" i dit "Parsonne peut t'gagner."—

G.T.: Hm.

—"Non" i dit "parsonne peut m'gagner" i dit, "il avont venu d'toutes les parts du monde—assayer" i dit "d'me gagner mais i ont pas pu m'gagner. Comme ça" i dit "j'sus le champion—à jouer le *poker* de l'univers."—"Hah? Ben" i dit "ça" i dit "c'est bien beau, c'est ça, ça c'est bien ça." Ouais. Ben—i dit euh, "Veux-tu jouer in *game* avec moi, voulez-vous assayer in *game*?"—"Oh" i dit "j'allons pas jouer pour grand argent" i dit, euh, "moi" i dit euh, "j'sus pas, euh, euh, j'sus pas riche. J'sus in, in pauve."—"Oh ben" i dit, "j'allons pas" i dit euh, "*better* [parier] trop" i dit "parce que..." Ah ben c'est ça. C'est bien. Là. Prendont les cartes pis là ça commence là. I jouent. Ben i mit, i, i, i, le, le, le champion i mit dix dollars sus la tabe—i voulait pas aller trop haut parce que le, le, le, çt homme-là qui tait là lui i, il avait justement joué avec euh, avec Johnny justement pour ieux—pâsser l'temps—i voulait pas, i voulait pas ête trop dur sus lui. Ben c'est bon. Là. Là, le demon mit dix pièces aussi—pis i, ouvront la main d'cartes, tchiens! Johnny—gagne. Ah! Vingt pièces. Hale ça d'dans. Oui mais—i tait si à l'habitude—à *better* ois-tu—hein—il a mangnière de partir hors d'sa téte. Toujours—*by gosh* il a halé vingt—vingt dollars dedans, là, encore eune aute, eune aute main là. Et pis euh, "Ah" i dit "tchiens! On va mette cinquante—cinquante dollars." Oh euh, le diabe veut pas, "Ben moi" i dit "j'ai pas grand argent" i dit "mais euh..." i dit—"Ben ej peux—ej peux, ej peux mette cinquante dollars aussi." Là i prend cinquante dollars pis i jette dans la, à la rencontre de, à J, à Jean—rencontre la, du *bet* à Jean, ouais, tout d'in coup là Jean euh, hale dedans encore. Ouais, c'est ça—là ça fait cent pièces ça. Ça fait cent vingt pièces—les deux hales. Ah, pis i pense à lui-même—"Ma—ouais, c'est pas utile qu'ej joue avec ça moi" i dit "parce que j'm'en vas t, tout haler, arracher tout l'argent qu'il a dans la poche." C'est bien. Là. Ah! La troisième—tour de cartes—la troisième—là! "Tchiens!" i dit—"Euh—cent dollars." Le diabe mit—deux cents dollars! "*Oh gee!*" Jean trouvait ça—bien tchurieux. Ho! Il avait pas grand argent en premier pis là tout d'in coup tchiens, i mit cent dollars—pis le démon mit—deux cents dollars! Ho, quand qu'il a vu ça—ben là lui i n'en mit—euh deux cents dollars avec quoi-ç-que—le cent qu'il avait mis. Ben là le diabe mit—deux autes cent dollars—pis là ça commence à monter, à monter, tout d'in coup là le diabe qui mit—mille dollars! Ben l'aute là, là, i, le, le, Jean, i mit—tchinze mille dollars! Et pis ça ça va, pis ça monte, pis ça monte, pis ça monte! Pis tchiens! i, les, les, i, çt homme-là avait pas d'argent—pis garde là l'argent qu'il a! Ha! Ben c'est eune bêtise à monter j'pense comme cent mille dollars là. Là! C'est ça. Là, ouvent les cartes—ah! Le diabe hale dedans. I savait pas que ç'tait le diabe—i savait pas lui. I hale dedans.

G.T.: Oui.

—*By gosh!* I commençait à, à penser là. Oh! Mais i dit "Ça donnait comme ça." Ben là mon vieux il a, i, Jean, c'est l'tour à Jean d'*dealer* les cartes. Là il les *deale*. Ben i—là. I s'enoisait les cartes au, au démon pis lui pis c'est ça. Là lui là, i double là. Héhé, cent mille dollars, deux cent mille dollars—"Pour sûr là i, i, i va pas—i va pas m'enplatcher [attaquer] parce qu'il a pas les moyens." Là le diabe renvarse l'argent—i erdoube! Jean là, doube Jean. Oh, signe de *luck*. Ouvent les cartes—garde! Il avait in, les, les *straight* là tout droit hein! Ben! Jean pard encore—pis ç'a té, pis ç'a té, pis ç'a té pis là l'argent a va d'in coup tchiens! Plus d'argent de resse! Le diabe avait tout! Toujours c'est bien. Mais i dit "J'peux pus jouer—j'ai pus d'argent."—"Oh mais" i dit "t'as en masse du bien."—"Oh oui" i dit "mais" i dit, "ej peux pas jouer pour ça."—"Ah dame!" i dit "c'est ça" i dit—"c'est, c'est—tchi! C'est ça" i dit, "c'est, c'est l'*game*!" Pis c'est comme ça qu'il a toujours lui euh, Jean là, i jouait, jouait, jouait jusqu'à temps qu'i n'en avait pus, pus arien du tout! I, i, i, mettait la face sus le câill—sus, sus la roche. Ah ah, le, le démon fait, faisait pareil comme lui là. Ben, oh dame il avait eune place ici, il avait in, in village il avait ici, i avait, il avait ça pis là joue pis l'diabe gagnait pis i gangnait, pis i gangnait, pis quand qu'ça a venu au boute du conte—il a tout-ç—j—euh, joué pour, pour ç'qu'il avait—pis tout-ç-qu'il avait de resse après—il a *even* joué pour le, le, le château qu'il avait bâti a son père et sa mère—il a joué pour ça il a pardu ça—pis il avait euh, tout-ç-qu'il avait de resse après—c'est son père et sa mère. "Ben" i dit "j'ai pus arien d'resse. J'ai pus arien."—"Ben" i dit "t'as d'quoi d'resse." I dit "Quoi-ç-que c'est?"—"Ton père et ta mère."—"Ben—ben oui" i dit "mais ej, j'vas pas jouer mon père et ma mère."—"Oh ben" i dit "c'est, c'est l'*game*. C'est ça. Ah, c'est ça. Ah, c'est ça, joue pour ton père et ta mère." Ben il a son père et sa mère aussi. Là. "Mais" i dit "j'ai pus arien à jouer. Pis j'ai pus—j'ai pus arien. Tu m'as mis sus la, la face" i dit, "à, à, sus la roche. J'ai pus arien, j'peux pus, pus jouer."—"Oh oui!" i dit—"Asteure" i dit "j'peux jouer pou, pou toi-même—pour toi."—"Jouer pour moi?" i dit. "Oh oui" i dit, "c'est, c'est, c'est la *game*" i dit. "Bien! Ah dame, c'est ça." Là, joue les cartes encore pis—ça—le diable l'a. Là! "Ben" i dit, "c'est toi qu'est le champion" i dit—"j'ai jamais été gangné. Mais" i dit "tu m'as, tu m'as gagné." I dit "Faut crouère" i dit "que t'es pas eune homme, eune homme euh, ordinaire."—"Non!" i dit—i dit "j'sus le démon" i dit. I dit "J'me doutais! Tu tais d'quoi d'même."—"Ben" i dit, "c'est d'ta faute" i dit, "si t'as, m'arais pas nommé—ej arais pas venu pi j'arais pas venu te, te, ici.

G.T.:   Hm.

—Mais" i dit "t'as dit que—c'est ienque le diabe qu't'avais pas joué avec pis—t'avais peur de jouer avec moi—pis ci et cela." I dit "C'est pour ça qu'j'ai venu. Te faire ouère—que tait ton, avec ton champion et ci et ça—que tu tais bien loin d'ête in champion. Asteure" i dit là, "ej m'en vas t'dire eune chose—ej te veux" i dit "à la Montagne nouère—dans in an et in jour d'ici. *Now*—in an et in jour d'ici! Ej te veux à la Montagne nouère." Pis i dit "Ioù-ç-que c'est, ça?"—"Ah dame!" i dit, "C'est *up* à toi" i dit "à charcher ioù-ç-que c'est." I dit 'vas pas t'dire ioù-ç-que c'est—c'est *up* à toi ça. Pis s'i peut pas venir là—à la Montagne nouère, tu peux pas ête là in an et in jour—ej serai icitte pou te quri. Et mon ptit garçon" i dit "ça, ça va pas ête trop beau pour toi." Ben là euh, Jean oh ho, il a venu—sus—avec tout son plaisir et toutes ses, ses faraudries et toute-ç-qu'il avait—euh, euh, il a venu bien, bien—en chagrin. C'est bien. Là le diabe a disparu—pis lui était là—assis sus eune roche—à g—à ronger ses ongues. Là. [Émile tousse] Là—estchusez-moi. Arrh! Là! Toujours il a resté çte soirée-là chez lui—pas chez lui parce qu'i avait pus d'chez lui, il avait arien. L'endemain matin—à la câssée du jour—il a quitté. Pis i s'a mis à marcher—et marche et marche et marche! Et quand qu'il a quitté la place ioù-ç-qu'i y avait pas grand monde, i y avait des, des, ç'avait eune—eune famille ici, eune, eune famille là-bas et ci et cela, c'est, c'est par ptits groupes i ramassiont t'sais—et pt-ête bien faulait qu'tu marches à peu près—cent mille milles pour trouver eune aute, eune aute ptite place comme ça encore, s'i y avait encore des, des, des habitants, ois-tu—pt-ête bien des cinq à six familles et d'quoi d'même—qui vivaient dans les ptits—d, d, des cabanes en brousse qu'il appelont là—d'quoi d'même. Pis d'autes faits avec des, des, des morceaux d'bois, des billots, des *log-cabin* là. Toujours c'est bon. Ben ça marche, ça marche, pis ça marche pis ça marche pis ça marche, pis par arien à manger mais dame, i tait pas maladroite pis i, i, i garâchait des, des, des roches et pis i tuait les ptits gibiers et *so on et pis*—i tchuisait ça pis—*a, i s'y tenu, tenu aller. Ben il a marché*—*pour deux à trois mois*—*à travers d'la forêt*—*et tout d'in coup*—*ça commençait à venir la nuit, il aparçoit*—*eune ptite lumière*—*ahh! c'est manière de rouge, la lumière. Toujours i s'pousse pour là, i dit "Quoi-ç-que don?" i dit "qu'est, quoi c'est qu'ça? Quoi-ç-que c'est ça" i dit "je vois là-bas?" Toujours il approche, approche, approche*—*quand qu'il a arrivé là ç'tait eune ptite shack*—et ç'tait toute plein d'mousse et des, y avait des, des, oh i y avait des âbes qui poussaient sus le, c, sus la, la couvarture, ah! ç'avait j'pense—mille ans! Pis i y avait eune porte là—eç tait fait avec des racines—là i va là, rgarde à l'entour—"Bien" i dit, "ça c'est bien tchurieux" i dit. Ben i, i va pis i frappe à la porte.

G.T.:   Oui.

—Hah! I a tendu d'quoi—tchequ'un bou, tchequ'un bougeait d'dans. Tout d'in coup vlà la porte qui s'rouve—ah mon grand seigneur de, t'as vu ça! Oh bon bin bin bin bo ben ben! Vlà eune vieille, ç'tait une vieille sorciaise—eune vieille—oh j'pense qu'alle avait comme—tchinze cents ou, ou dix-huit cents ans, d'quoi d'même—oh tait vieille, vieille, les, les, les dents ça pendait dans l'nouère, ça pendait par-dsus les babines là—i pis les, les gros pouels—le, le, le, eh, des gros pouels blancs qui sortaient de son nez, pis les verrures sus l'nez les, les verrures sus la, les, sus les mentons et tout ça oh! oh! Ah, i, il est assez saisi—i pouvait pas parler—i, i tait—saisi—il est oh! C'est, c'est, i avait jamais vu d'quoi si vilain d'sa vie. Pis a dit, "Oh n'aies pas peur! N'aies pas peur [voix de petite vieille]! Allez rente!" a dit, "mon ptit garçon, rente!" [Émile allonge ces derniers mots] Bien là lui—i, i rente mais ses, ses, ses deux genoux ça tapait ensemble! I—si peur! "Ej vas pas t'faire mal, ej vas pas t'faire mal!" [voix de vieille] Pis "Ioù-ç-que tu vas don, quoi-ç-qui a arrivé?" Pis c'est toutes sortes d'affaires comme ça—"Quoi-ç-qui a arrivé et pis—" Ben là i y conte l'histouère, bien là. "Ahhh! oui mon cher enfant, c'est comme ça qu'c'est, quand qu'on est jeune on sait pas quoi-ç-qu'on fait. Pis t'arais pas dû faire d'quoi d'même" et dame ç'ara pas dû mais dame i l'avait fait! Pis c'est ça! Pis c'est trop tard asteure! Pis a dit asteure, i y a conté pour la Montagne nouère faulait qu'i seye là dans in an et in jour—et pis, pis i savait pas ce que ç'tait, pis ci et ça. Pis i savait là à peu près. "Bien" a dit "j'ai—eune soeur"—a dit "j'pense qu'elle est encore en vie—mais elle est pus vieille que moi." Ben i pensait à lui-même asteure—"Ben si alle est pus vieille que ieu—que vous, pis a, pis, pis alle est pas pus belle que vous êtes—Mon Dieu, mon Dieu! Que j'en dois faire? Ej souhaite te dire que mon sang tourne pas" i dit "par la peur—parce qu'" i dit "j'en ai ieu assez d'cette-là-ici"—pensait à lui-même ça, il avait ça dans l'idée là. Toujours, c'est bien, ça jâsait tout la nuit—m—oh i tait confortabe, ah, alle était bonne à lui, a tait bonne à lui, a y donnait à manger, a, a, alle a té as, a tait eune sorciase ois-tu? Pis a pouvait aouère quoi-ç-que a, quoi-ç-qu'a voulait. Là alle arait dit comme ça ben "J'veux—euh—eune *bun* de pain là sus la tabe"—là la *bun* de pain arait venu là ois-tu? Quoi-ç-qu'a voulait a, a, a l'avait. T'sais. Alle avait tant d'pouvouère t'sais. Pis lui asteure, i, i , a demandait pour du thé, pis a demandait pour du lait pis ça venait là pis lui toute effarouché lui! I tait effarouché. Toujours, c'est bien. "Bien" a dit "pour te dire—ailloù-ç-qu'est la Montagne nouère, je, je ne sais pas. Mais" a dit "ma soeur" a dit "a reste comme—comme cent—cent milles d'ici" a dit. "Ben" a dit "pt-ête bien" a dit "a l'sara." Bien c'est ça, ben—ben, ça, il allait la ouère *anyhow*. Ben là c'est bon. L'endemain matin arrive, et puis là a y donne d'quoi à manger, des galettes et toute en grand et pis—tout-ç-qu'i voulait a, a l'avait, parce que a, a souhaitait pour pis ça venait—ça tombait là sus la tabe.

G.T.:   Hm.

—Pis a prend eune saquée—oh, il avait eune grosse saquée—pis il a ieu d'la misère à la porter—là i fout ça sus l'dos pis là i s'pousse. Pis là i marche, i marche, i marche, i marche—en travers du bois à peu près ici et là—pis ça marche. Nuit et jour. Ç'allait pas vite. Parce que la, la, la route est si mauvaise—qu'i pouvait pas aller vite. Et pour faire çtés cent milles là, ça y a pris pas loin d'in mois. Et pis il avait tout l'temps d'quoi à manger c'est pareil comme in, euh, euh, quand qu'ti, quand qu'i mangeait in, in, in gâteau, i y avait in aute gâteau qui venait là ois-tu, c'est, c'est, c'est son pouvouère de la, la sorciaise là asteure là. Alle avait tant d'pouvouère ois-tu pis a laimait le garçon parce qu'i tait si—gentil comme ça ois-tu. Ç'tait pas eune mauvaise parsonne ienque, ois-tu—i, i, i s'avait mal entorpris. C'est bon. Marche et marche, et marche et marche. Ben, ça y a pris in mois pour sûr avant qu'il a arrivé là. Toujours ç'tait pareil qu'il arrivait là à l'entour de la câ, d'la câssée d'la nuit là—il garde en avant, tchi! oit eune ptite, ptite clarté. Pis là i s, i s'pousse là "Bien" i dit "faut crouère c'est sa soeur—oh bien" i dit "faut crouère" i dit "parce que—oh pour sûr" i dit "j'ai cent milles à marché asteure, oh pour sûr, oh, c'est garanti, ça. Pis ça doit ête ielle." Mais quand qu'il a arrivé là ma mon vieux, la cabane, la *shack* ta encore—encore pus vieux—que ceux-là qu'il avait vu là en premier. Asteure la première là, c'est la pus jeune qu'a là, la pus jeune des soeurs ois-tu—pis—i tiont trois soeurs là en tout. Ben i y a pas dit ielle là, a y a dit alle avait eune soeur. A se rappelait—parce—si vieux ois-tu, j'pense qu'alle avait comme d'—dix-huit cents ans, dix-neuf cents ans, d'quoi d'même, t'sais la, la mémoire ois-tu, c'est, ça s'en va t'sais. Toujours c'est bon. Ah. Il arrive. Là i frappe et là i s'pensait à lui-même—"Asteure ois-tu faut qu'ej m'en, m, euh, faut qu'ej me mis comme i faut" i dit "pis que c'est—pis j'faus pas qu'ej, ej aie trop peur." Ah. Mon cher ami! I frappe à la porte, alle a rouvri la porte. Ah oh oh oh! Quand qu'i l'a regardée—pourtant il avait fait son idée comme i faut asteure pour pas—ois-tu? Pour pas attraper eune, eune attique, eune attaque, in attaquement d'tchoeur. Mais il a tombé don! Il a tombé. Ouais Il a tombé à, à la renverse. Quand qu'i oit ça. Oh ça ç'tait vilain! Ah! Oh, les grands dents ça descend en-bas d'son menton là pis *nouères*! I y avait des plaques blanches pis des, des plaques nouères, dessus là—pis places corbues là—pis des gu—des verrures qui sortaient d'son nez là tout pointues! Ben mon ami—ça ç'tait vilain! Oh ça ç'tait vilain! Pis les, les, les, les zusses là—ça *corlait* [angl. to curl] là c'est comme des tout des choueux—pis les, les poils des yeux là—c'est toute *corlé* comme des, des, des crocs à truite là. Pis les deux yeux ça flambait! Ça flambait! Ç'tait comme des chandelles! Oh ç'tait vilain, vilain, vilain! Ben a, a dit, Jean saute dehors, a l'croche pis i, i tait vanoui, il a vanoui. Et pis a l'a—frotté avec de l'eau, j'sais pas quoi-ç-que c'est *anyhow*—i m'avont pas dit—mais euh, i, il a revenu *back*. Mais a tait bonne à lui, encore meilleure que la, la première.

G.T.: Hm.

—Encore meilleure! Ben après in ptit boute ben là il a venu—mais—a tait pas jolie à regarder, mais, dame, a tait si bonne! Si bonne, c'est pus, ah, oh, oh! Ben il a pas couché sus la, sus, sus les brousses ç'soir-là, a l'a pris dans ses bras pis a l'a—bârcé tout la nuit. Comme ç'arait té in ptit bébi. Ah il est heureux, heureux! Toujours c'est bien. Là. I conte l'histouère et toute en grand, "Ben" a dit "mon cher—pas grand'chose qu'ej peux faire pour toi" a dit "mon cher enfant." Bien dame—i tait deconforté, deconforté, deconforté. "Ah! sais pas quoi tu vas faire—mais dame" a dit "j'ai eune soeur—j'ai eune soeur qui resse—comme—oh ça prenra comme—six mois, six à sept ou huit mois—pour aller là."—"Quoi!" i dit "grand-mère" i dit—"six, sept ou huit mois pour aller là?"—"Oh oui" a dit—"Celle-là c'est la pus vieille de mes soeurs" a dit "et alle est vieille, alle est vieille, oh alle a—vingt-cinq cents ans" a dit "qu'alle a. Oh" a dit "bien i y a des cents ans, des mille ans je l'ai pas vue" a dit. "Y a bien deux mille ans pour sûr" a dit "ej l'ai pas vue. Mais" a dit "a doit ête en vie encore." Bien—bien bon sang d'la vie ç'tait pas in ptit boute—six ou sept mois à marcher—avant qu'i réussit à y arriver. Ah! Pis i comptait les jours asteure là, t'sais, i les comptait là. Ben faulait qu'i seye là pour in an et in jour—ben asteure s'il avait pas plusse de chance—qu'il avait asteure ac les deux

344

premiers soeurs—ben dame i tait foutu! I tait foutu. Ça fait qu'Jean va la trouver, i, i, i y avait pas, y a pus d'danger, i l'a trouvée. Toujours c'est bon. "Ben bien asteure" a dit "là" a dit de, souhaite pour la nourriture et ci et cela, quoi-ç-qu'i laimait manger et toute pis—là. A dit "Asteure" a dit—"t'as assez d'nourriture là" a dit "pour, pour ton *journey*" a dit. "Ça va pt-ête bien prende six mois, sept mois—pt-ête bien huit mois—mais" a dit "t'as assez d'nourriture." Dame, bien c'est ça. Il est parti. I l'a pas embrassée mais quasiment—parce qu'a tait si bonne. Ej peux pas t'embrasser. Ç'tait toutes des verrures, pis du poil et pis des, des, des, les grands dents longues et tout ça là, oha! ç'tait vilain! Oh, ça, ça tournait l'tchoeur! Toujours i s'en va. I marche, i marche, i marche, i marche, i marche, et marche et marche. I s'couchait la nuit et puis là au ptit jour deboute pis i marche—ben il a marché—pour huit mois. Et i y a pas encore arien à ouère, arien! Pis ça marche pis à marcher encore—quasiment in aute mois encore ou eune coupelle de smaines ou tcheque chose comme ça, m'en rappelle pas comme i faut mais—euh, ça a pris plus que huit mois. Bien, tout d'in coup c'est encore pareil—ça a arrivé à la brune d'la nuit, tchiens ç'a vu-t-encore eune ptite clarté—"Ah bien" i dit "ben faut crouère que c'est là qu'c'est." Là. Le vlà parti. Ben asteure il avait attrapé deux peurs mais la deuxième peur tait beaucoup pire qu'la première. "Mais" i dit "cette-là-ici" i dit "j'p—j'vas aou—j'vas pt-ête bien mourir d'cette-là-ici. Si c'est qu', si t-i y a pas pus belle" i dit "que, que ses soeurs—que ses deux soeurs"—c'est bien.

G.T.: Oui.

—I s'en va. I prend eune chance. Pis là i frappe à la porte pis là i saute en arrière là à l'entour comme dix varges en arrière là—pis il argarde ça a rouve la porte. Ah! Quand qu'alle a rouvri la porte—pis i l'a regardé—les premières, les dents ça descendait en-bas d'—le menton euh? Et ielle là—les deux, les deux dents de dvant, ç'tait tout-ç-qu'alle avait de resse. Pis alle a, a piquait ça sus ses genoux—a, a, a, c'est pareil mais a tchenait sa tête en haut pis les deux dents, t'sais arrêtaient sus ses genoux. "Ben quâ aller qué cotte?" [Émile parle très haut, d'une voix gutturale, avalant ses paroles] Bien là lui là, il était oh ben là, il, i vanouit tout nette. Pis les grosses verrures, les, pouels là, pis les, ses choueux là, eç tait pareil comme des, des, des, des, des, des clous d'quate pouces là, des gros, gros choueux t'sais, pis ç'tait les, pareil comme des, des, des, des, du cordage là oh! Ça ç'tait vilain mon vieux—des grosses verrures là pis i y avait d'la mousse qui poussait dsus tout ça là. Oh! Ç'tait pas *fitte* à rgarder, mais il a vanoui, il a vanoui, il a pas —mais a l'a fait revenir, parce que c'est, c'est eune sorciaise eh, des *witch* eh? Ça pouvait faire n'importe quoi. Là. La seule affaire i saviont pas ioù-ç-qu'était la Montagne nouère. Ben c'est bien, là i conte son histouère, i rente, mais a tait bonne à lui! I rente pis a y donne à manger—ça qu'i voulait manger—a souhaitait pour assayer ouère ça c'est—des gâteaux c'est des, des, ç'tait toutes sortes des oise, des zoiseaux euh, *b-béqués* [angl. to bake], toute—ça qu'a voulait, ça qu'a voulait, a l'avait. Eune chance, parce qu'alle ara, alle ara pas vi à part ielle i y avait pas d'farme pis à l'entour d'arien du tout, il ara, alle arait *mouri*. Mouri plein! Mais—alle avait tant d'pouvouère t'sais. Là—c'est bon. Mais i conte l'histouère et toute et quoi-ç-qui a arrivé, il ava en masse de l'argent et toute et pis il avait toute pardu pis ci et ça... [pause pour retourner la bande]... I dit "Tchiens c'est la vilaine bête" pis i dit—i l'arait gagné ci et ça. Oui mais i dit—çt homme-là arrivait pis là i conte—i conte tout l'histouère ois-tu. "Bien" a dit "mon cher enfant, c'est comme ça" a dit—"peux pas saouère." A dit "Çte gars-là" a dit "faut qu'tu y fais attention" a dit—"faut jamais" a dit "qu'tu l'nommes trop souvent—parce" i dit "i y a toutes les paroles que tu n—quand que tu parles d'son nom" i dit "là il approche tout l'temps et pis c'est pas bon! Non j'el devrons quitter trantchille" a dit "Pis asteure" i dit "faut qu'ej vas à la Montagne nouère" et ci et ça euh, contait toute l'histouère—"Bien" a dit "moi" a dit "j'sais pas ioù-ç-qu'est la Montagne nouère, moi j'le sais pas" a dit. "Mais j'ai des, j'ai des aigues" a dit. "A

345

tous les jours i sont partis pour de quoi à manger, i volont partout euh, toute la grandeur de l'univers. Pis" i dit "i ervenont *back*" a dit euh,—"bien" a dit "i m'contont les nouvelles, quoi-ç-qu'i ouoyont et ci et ça et *so on*. Pis" a dit "c'est mon pâsse-temps." Ah, c'est bien, bientôt, le, la matinée arrivait et ci et ça bien les aigues tiont partis, a dit "I vont, i vont arriver pus tard" a dit.

G.T.: Oui.

—Bien—ça a pâssé là toute la jornée—i, i, il avont jâsé là tous les deux ensembe—pis il a venu qu'il aviont l'habitude, ben a tait si bonne, ois-tu? Ç'tait vilain mais—si bonne que—i la laimait—i la laimait. Là toujours c'est l'après-midi à l'entour de trois heures de l'après-midi euh, vlà les aigues qui commencent à arriver. Et c'est, c'est "Coin-coin-coin!" et "Coin-coin-coin!" Pis ça s'posait pis ci et ça pis là a les appelait, a dit "Y en a tcheques d'vous autes" a dit "qui sait ioù-ç-qu'est la Montagne nouère?"—"Non! Non! Non! Non! Non! Non!" N'en avait eune tchinzaine ej pense—"Non! Non! Non! Non!" C'est tout des non, i saviont pas. Ben lui, i tait deux ou trois à tomber en bas, à ses, à ses côtes. Oh ben i tait découragé. Ben i savait qu'i tait—il est baisé, i tait, i tait foutu. I tait foutu. Ielle là a, c'est en arrière pis—fa qu'i l'appelait "grand-mère" aussi lui. Mais i dit "Grand-mère" i dit "c'est, c'est foutu." A dit "Bientôt oh" a dit "crois pas que c'est tout ici encore" a dit. T'sais i y en avait in vieux—in vieux—vieux-n-aigue—in aigue là les—a dit "C'est—il est pas ici encore" a dit, "i y en a iun qui manque." Oh alle a rgardé dans, dans l'ciel a rgardait, "Oh!" a dit "i s'en vient", il avait pâssé deux mille ans. Oh i tait vieux, i volait pas vite, i, i prenait son temps, les jeunes ieusses i, i, i tiont là avant leu temps. "Oh!" A dit "I s'en vient, j'le vois-là-bas." A dit "Pt-ête bien lui i sait." Ah tout d'in coup il arrive, "Raou, raou, raou, raou, raou." S'pose en bas ioù a tait. A dit "Euh, tu t'sais-ti toi ioù-ç-qu'est la Montagne nouère?"—"Oui" i dit, "oui, c'est là que je deviens." I dit euh—à sa maîtresse. Oh bien là Jean lui là, ho ho! Ben i, fier ois-tu? Hah! Ben ça c'est des bonnes—après si trisse tout l'temps, ben ça l'a rejoui cela. I savait ioù-ç-qu'i tait la Montagne nouère. "Oui" i dit, "ah" i dit "c'est là qu'ej deviens" i dit. "Oh bien" a dit "mon cher enfant" a dit "tu l'as d'fait" a dit. "Ah dame ouais! Ouais." Ben a dit "Demain matin asteure"—y a—"Bien" i dit "demain matin" i dit "ça va ête juste" i dit "in an et in jour—oui, juste in an et in jour demain matin" i dit. "Ouais. Pis faut qu'ej seye là demain. In an et in jour qu'i m'a dit."—"Ben entendu, t'as pas besoin d'aouère peur" a dit "qu—tu vas ête *a'right*." A dit "J'vas y—"—alle a demandé à son, son aigue a dit euh, euh, "Vas-tu l'a, l'amener là"—"Oh oui" i dit, "oh oui." A dit "Crois-tu qu'tu sras capabe assez?"— "Oh oui, oui, oui, ouais." Ben c'est bon. Là. L'endemain matin il avont quitté à la—câssée du jour. Asteure a y donne eune bouteille de medecine. A dit "J'm'en vas t'donner çte ptite bouteille de medecine là. Et pis tu vas embarquer sus son dos—pis" a dit "i va t'amener là. A la Montagne nouère. Pis" a dit "quand qu'i va t'demander—quand qu'il ara faim i va t'demander pour—eune bouchée à man-ger—tu vas"—a dit "j'ai in, t'as in couteau ici, tu vas prende ç'couteau-là avec toi—pis" a dit "tu vas couper in morceau dans ta chair" a dit "pis tu vas y donner. Parce si tu l'nourris pas" a dit "i va pas pououère—te, te, t'haler pour t'amener là.

G.T.: Hm.

—A la Montagne nouère. Pis" a dit "quand qu'i va t'demander—quand qu'il ara faim i va t'demander pour—eune bouchée à manger—tu vas"—a dit "j'ai in, t'as in couteau ici, tu vas prende ç'couteau-là avec toi—pis" a dit "tu vas couper in morceau dans ta chair" a dit "pis tu vas y donner. Parce si tu l'nourris pas" a dit "i va pas pououère—te, te, t'haler pour t'amener là." Toujours c'est bien. "Bien" a dit "après qu't'as coupé l'morceau—tu prends le, la medecine" a dit "pis tu l'frottes sus l'morce—ce que t'as coupé—pis" a dit "ça va venir pareil encore." Oh, là, "C'est bien grand-mère" i dit, "ben, c'est bon." Ben c'est ça le, le, le jour qu'arrive pis là i, il embarque sus la, la, sus l'aigue et pis—la bouteille de médecine pis l'couteau pis

346

c'est ça. Pis d'temps en temps le, le, quand qu'il ont rentré en l'air l'aigue y dmande "Coâ-coâ! J'ai faim." Là i s'coupe in morceau—ça faisait mal—mais dame heh! c'est ça. Coupe! Pis là i y donne. "Miamiam" pis il a avalé ça pis là i prendait son medecine pis là c'est, c'est, c'est pareil—comme il arait pas ieu touché sa chair du tout. Bien c'est bon. Là. Ça vole et ça vole et ça vole et ça vole. Et euh, à la brune d'la nuit—il ont arrivé. Ça y a pris douze heures—pour voler là—pis in gibier ça va, ça va vite ois-tu? Hm. J'dirons les trente, trente-cinq milles à l'heure ou d'quoi d'même—ça va vite. Pus vite que marcher. Toujours c'est bien. Il arrive là, là l'aigue descend i descend i descend pis i s'*pose*. Pis là—Jean—s'debarque sus l'aigue—là i dit "Asteure" i dit "tu vas aller" i dit "pis frapper à la porte. Et pis" i dit euh, "c'est là-ç-qu'est l'diabe" i dit "c'est là-ç-qu'i reste." Ah! C'est bon. Ben i s'en vont s'souhaiter au-vouère et tout ça pis là l'aigue ç'a parti encore—chez lui. Et pis euh. Jean va à la porte du, du diabe, le château du diabe, frappe, le diabe s'en vient, rouve la porte. "Ahh! Ah bien" i dit "tu l'as fait. Ben" i dit "tu es chanceux, j'pensais justement à toi" i dit. "Ton temps est à boute aujourd'hui pis" i dit "t'arrives. Ben" i dit, "c'est pas pire. C'est pas pire. Ben" i dit "rente. Rente." Quand qu'il a rentré, la femme du diabe tait là—pis il avait trois filles, bien, pis, pis i y en avait ieune. I l'a regardé pis a l'a rgardé aussi et pis oh! a s'a fait rire, sourire, "Le bel homme, le bel homme" qu'alle a pensé—et pis lui aussi—"Oh oh oh oh" la pus belle fille qu'il avait jamais—mis ses yeux dsus. C'est bien. Ça a pas fait grand, grand chamaille là—oh et tout. C'est bon. N'on restait à jâser jusqu'à dix heures et pis là i faut aller s'coucher parce qu'i dit "Demain" i dit "on—Jean a son ouvrage à faire." Là. Jean—ça, lui i pensait il a pas dormi d'la nuit parce qu'i, i pensait à tchelle sorte de *work* ça va iête. Allez. Bon. L'endemain-t-arrive—six heures—deboute. Pour déjeuner. Et ça—déjeune. "Là" i dit, "viens avec moi." Mais tout l'temps i gardait la fille en cachette pis quand qu'le diabe virait l'dos et la vieille—pis i gardait pis i faisait des ptits coins d'oeil ois-tu? Pis ielle aussi—oh! A l'aimait! Oh mais, mais, mias, mais! Pis a tait si belle.

G.T.: Oui.

—Toujours—c'est bon, i dit "Viens ac moi asteure" i dit "j'm'en t'amener à ton ouvrage." C'est bien—i sortait euh, l'diabe s'en va à l'avant pis lui s'en va par derrière, pis i s'en va à eune bâtisse pis i rouve la bâtisse—pis y a des machines, des, des *millsh*, les *millshed* t'appelles là? Là. Et euh—i, i s'en, i rente dedans pis i, i prend eune hache—eune hache en papier. Jean lui i gardait ça pis "Quoi-ç-qu'i va faire avec ça?" Toujours i prend la hache pis i l'mit sus son dos pis le, le, le, le manche a pleyé pis le, le, le taillant d'la hache était dans—dans l'dos. Frottait sus son d—son dos. Pis i l'mène à, i y a d—i y avait in arpent de, de bois—là. Arrive là. Pis encore Jean savait pas quoi-ç-qu'i y avait. "Là" i dit "J, Jean" i dit—"là" i dit "ton ouvrage pour aujourd'hui mon ami." I dit "Quoi? Sorte d'ouvrage?"—"Là" i dit "faut qu'tu coupes tout çte bois-là qu'est là" i dit—"et faut qu'tu le, tout, tout l'apiloter" i dit—"par piles"—pis i dit "faut qu'ça seye sorti" i dit "pour six heures à souère." Pis i dit "Si tu peux pas faire ça—mon pauvre enfant" i dit—"t'es—tu as in triste—eune trisse temps quand j't'arviens pour toi." Là i dit "Tchiens! Vlà la hache" i dit euh. "faut qu'tu bûches ça. Bûche—ce bois-là."—"Mais" i dit "comment l'faire ac ça moi?"—"Hoh! C'est *up* à toi" i dit—"vlà la hache." C'est bien. Pas moyen d'dire grand'chose. Tchiens! Là. I prend la hache, le diabe s'en va—pis i prend la hache pis i, i, i, il enouyait ça—sus l'âbe. *Jeepers cr*—le taillant d'la hache—le morceau d'*paper* la manche a câssé, la hache a tombé—là. Là i s'assit—et i pleure, i pleure, i pleure, i pleure, il a du chagrin—et ah! "Ben" i dit "je suis foutu. C'est aussi bien qu'ej fais mon idée asteure" i dit "puis—me mette" i dit "au f—aller en fond de l'enfer" i dit "pour l'éternité. Ben" i dit "c'est aussi bien qu'ej fais mon idée." I y a pas d'ressources. Non i y a pas d'ressources. Non. Ah, c'est ça. Là i pleure plus là. Il a, i, i s'raconsole et pis c'est ça, c'est fini—parle pus. I fait son idée. Bientôt, midi

347

arrive—i tait assis comme ça—et tout d'in coup il a tendu du carillon là, i ergarde—la jeune fille! La fille qu'il a tombé en amour avec—qui s'en venait avec son dîner! "Bien ergarde don ça" i dit "c'est-i bien dommage" i dit "si j'pourrais faire ça asteure là" i dit "pis garde!" Pis, oh, oh, oh, oh, oh—"J'serais-ti heureux pour le reste de mes jours—avec eune femme comme ça" i dit, "eune beauté comme ça" i dit—toutes sortes de b—des idées y pâssaient dans la téte.

G.T.:   Hm.

—*So* alle arrive là—pis a dit, euh, "Quoi-ç-qu'a don, quoi-ç-qu'i y a?"—"Ben" i dit "ton père" i dit "m'a donné des, eune hache en papier" i dit "pis i m'a dit de, faut qu'ej coupe tout ça" i dit "pis piler ça—ouère ça d'pilé par six heures."—"Ben" a dit "j't'as apporté ton dîner là."—"Non!" i dit "j'veux pas d'diner, j'veux pas manger. Parce qu'" i dit "pour le temps" i dit "que j'sus ici asteure" i dit "ça va ête longtemps comme ça" i dit euh, "j'ai abandonné."—"Va-t-en!" a dit "t'es pas si fou" a dit "mange, mange!" a dit, "mange ton dîner! T'as pas d'chagrin comme ça." Ah. A dit "Ioù-ç-qu'est ta hache?" A dit "La, la" i dit "la hache est là, le manche câssé là." *A'right*—a prend la hache ielle—pis flic! flic! flic! flic! comme ça—a fait des, des ptits *sign*, les âbes a commencé à tomber, les branches ça volait en l'air dans l'ciel, et pis les—bois commençaient à s'piler et tout ça, dans comme, comme cinq minutes—t'as tout la f—la, la, l'arpent tait toute, toute bûché, toute pilé! "Ooh!" Ah il a pris in grand soupir. Bien, bien, bien! Ben là i l'a, sa, la fille là, a l'laimait—oh, cent fois pire, oh, i tait dans, dans eune triste position mon vieux—avec l'amour qu'il avait pour ielle. Bien, bien, bien, bien, bien, bien! Vlà, c'est bon. Là. Ben il est content, *so* a dit "A souère tu vas apporter la, la hache" a dit "pis tu vas donner ça à papa" a dit—"i va t'demander si t'as fait l'ouvrage pis" a dit "dis 'oui'." C'est bien, là i s'reste là jusqu'à six heures du souère pis—i, i s'en va. Arrive là i dit "Mais" i dit "as-tu fait ton ouvrage?"—"Oui" i dit, "j'ai fait mon ouvrage. Mais" i dit "j'arais ieu eune bonne hache encore—mais eune hache de papier" i dit—"ça, ça m'a fait travailler dur."—"Ben" i dit "ça fait in ouvrage."—"Oh oui oui oui."—"Oh ben, c'est ça" i dit "c'est bien, c'est bon" i dit. I dit "Encore in aute demain" i dit. I pensait asteure "Tchelle sorte d'aute? Tchelle sorte d'aute?" Toujours c'est bon. Çte soirée-là i va mais i—dort pas d'la nuit parce qu'i tait assez eh, chagriné et tout ça. Pense. Ç'tait dur—pis i pensait à la fille—pis, t'sais, il avait tout ça dans la téte—oh! I tiont boulangé comme in, in minisse—ça, ça, ç'tait dur. L'endemain matin—là. Mange le déjeuner, deboute à, à six heures, déjeune, pis c'est ça. Vlà partis, i dit "Viens-t-en! M'en vas y donner son ouvrage pour aujord'hui encore" i dit. Le diabe va encore à sa laiterie là—et i rouve la porte pis i, i, i va, i sort avé, avec in panier. In panier fait avec d'la paille là. Pis i pense à lui même i dit "Quoi-ç-qu'i va faire avec ça" i dit, "quoi, i y avait, av—quoi-ç-qu'il a à faire?" I dit "Suis-moi." I l'amène—à in lac. Oh, le lac avait comme euh, hm, ben ç'tait in grand lac—comme in mille de tour j'pense—vous savez, tout l'tour, t'sais? *Diameter* qu'il l'appelont. Ç'tait in grand lac—là i dit euh, "Tchiens"—i y pâsse le panier—i dit "I faut qu'tu chesses ç'lac-là" i dit, "vous l'avez sec pour euh, six heures à souère." Ben—pas beaucoup qu'i pouvait dire—le diabe a parti. Prend l'panier *anyhow* pis là quand qu'i prend l'panier pis i, l'pêche dans le lac—mais avant qu'il avait mis la patte de côté le, le panier tait sec! L'eau avait tout pâssé à travers des, des, des—des pailles—les côtés là.

G.T.:   Hm.

—"Bi! bi! moi j'peux pas" il a assayé cinq ou six fois de t—aillou—i jette le panier en bas pis le vlà encore depité. Le vlà encore depité. Ah! Ah c'est presque midi, à midi il a tendu arien, arien, là, garde! Oh! encore la même! S'en vient ave son dîner encore. Huh! "Ben" i dit "ça c'est pas mal." Ben il est manière d'consolé par ça qu'alle avait fait hier—i dit "Quoi-ç-qu'ej allons faire aujord'hui—mais a va jamais pouvoir faire de quoi avec, pas ac le pangnier de l'eau. Pas moyen!" Arrive là, a dit euh a dit euh, "Allez, quoi-ç-que t'as? Ben" a dit "c'est ça" a dit. I dit euh

"Ton père m'a donné in pangnier" i dit "pour chesser çte lac-là—mais" i dit "j'l'as assayé mais" i dit "avant qu'ej ai l'panier—euh, halé d'côté, i y a pus arien d'dans" i dit—"ça tombe, tout dans le, dans le, dans le, dans le—dans l'lac encore!" A dit "Garde, chagrines-toi pas, euh, mange ton dîner." Pis a dit "J'souhaite tu laimes ton dîner." "Oh oui" i dit "j'te pense" i dit "hier" i dit "t'avais in beau dîner. Ça m'a, ça m'a fait grand plaisir. Pis j'sais" i dit "ça sent bon ça ici, ah ça c'est bon." A dit "Te chagrines pas d'arien, *so* mange comme i faut là." Pis là i s-t-y mit pis i mange pis ç'tait bon. Ouais ça mange. Ielle prend l'panier pis a, a—justement in panier plein—flic!—comme ça—le lac sec! "Bien" i dit "ça c'est pas mal! Oh, garde don! Si vite fait" i dit. Là. C'est bien. Ah, a prend les plats et cela pis a s'en va chez ielle. Là a dit—euh, avant qu'alle a quitté a dit euh, "Acoute" a dit "Jean" a dit—"t'as encore eune aute—in aute *job* à faire. Pis c'est pas trop—trop aisé. Ça ça va ête la pus dure *job* de toute en grand! Mais" a dit "si tu peux l'faire, ben ta vie t'est claire." Là—alle a parti. Six heures—i s'en vient—chez le diabe avec le panier pis—"Ben" i dit, "as-tu fait la *job*?"—"Eh oui" i dit "j'ai ressi" i dit "j'ai travaillé dur mais là j'ai russi. Le lac est sec."—"Ah c'est bien bon." I dit "Demain t'as encore in aute" i dit—ma l'diabe a dit là—"t'as encore eune aute—eune aute *job*. Demain c'est la darnière" i dit, "si tu peux faire cette-là—t'es clair—t'es *free*." Ah c'est bien bon—là. Ahh! Ça va aller s'coucher—et pis six heures l'endemain matin—deboute encore. Ça déjeune—"Là" i dit "viens avec moi." Mais—i pâsse pas au magasin ni arien du tout. I l'amène—à in, in poteau—qui avait cent pieds de haut. In poteau en vite. I dit "Ois-tu ç'poteau-là?"—"Bien" i dit "oui. Bien sûr" i dit—"c'est in poteau en vite."—"Oh oui" i dit. I dit "I y a in oeuf de marle—dans l'boute du poteau en haut là." Pis i dit "J'veux" i dit "que tu m'apportes—çt oeuf-là à six heures demain souère—à souère" i dit. Il a pas arien dit parce euh, la fille et ci et cela, a, i, i, mais i savait pas tchelle sorte de plan a, i savait arien d'ça. Toujours c'est bon. Là. Là ielle savait—que son père ç'tait in gars *smart*. A dit "Por sûr" a dit "i va enouoyer ienne de mes soeurs" mais ses deux soeurs, i, i, i pouviont pas faire ça ieusses.

G.T.:   Oui.

—Ah, i, i tiont comme leu mère eh, i, i, i pouviont pas ieusses souhaiter arien du tout comme ça là i pouviont pas faire ça—c'est ienque ielle qu'avait le, le, le, le secret d'son père eh? Mais son père savait pas non plus—i croyait ç'tait ienque lui mais ielle a tait euh, aussi bon comme lui. Toujours c'est bien. Allez. I l'emmène là—i dit "Viens avec moi" ben là i dit euh, "C'est ça"—comme j'ai dit de suite. Et pis euh quand ç'a arrivé à honze heures—"Là" i dit "tchi va aller apporter à manger à, à Jean là." Ben ielle si vite—a dit "Moi j'vas, moi j'vas pas! Moi j'veux pas aller, apporter à manger çte coup-ci [petite voix de jeune fille]. Que mes soeurs va!"— "Ben" i dit "garde" i dit "parce qu't'as parlé si bon—si bâssi" i dit, "si *sharp*"—ben i dit "tu vas aller y porter son ma, son manger"—Parce que c'est pour ça qu'alle avait ça—pour que—parce si alle ara pis dit dit ça il ara enouoyé—les autes, ses autes soeurs hein? "Ah ha!" i dit "ben pis parce t'as parlé si, si volant, si cruel—tu vas aller y porter son manger." Pis ielle a fait ça qu'a voulait ois-tu? Comme ça a va a s'couve pis là gu—là a prend à manger—pis a s'en va. Pis quand qu'a sort là a prend la porte, *bang*! pas m—a tait pas contente t'sais. Là. Bien en s'en allant ielle a pâsse au magasin pis a prend in, in, in, in boulouère là, eune, ça tenait à l'entour de—comme dix à tchinze gallons t'sais. Prend ça ac ielle. Pis son manger. Alle a arrivé la, i tait assis au poteau, au poteau. Pis il a assayé, il a assayé, il a assayé, il a assayé pis euh—i tombe encore—pis ça glissait—i pouvait pas, i pouvait pas—i pouvait pas, i pouvait pas—c'est impossibe. La glace—vite là, ça, ça, i assayait d'monter mais i pouvait pas—ça glissait en bas. Toujours bien bon. Alle arrive. Ac son manger. Là. A dit "Mange!" A dit "As-tu, as-tu l'oeuf?"—"Non" i dit "c'est impossibe, j'ais assayé" i dit, il av, il avait pus d'tchu—toutes ses tchulottes en, le, le, le, le bord d'ses tchulottes, le bord d'en-d'dans c'est toute usé. A frottait sus la

349

vite quand i assayait d'monter en haut, i pouvait pas. A dit "Mange." Ben c'est bon,
i mange, i mange. Pis ielle a s'en va pis a câsse des ptites brousses et—des ptits
morceaux d'bois—toutes sortes d'affaires—pis a fait in feu. Pis—après qu'le feu était
fait—i dit "Quoi-ç-tu vas faire avec ça?"—"Ben" a dit—"c'est ça" a dit—"quoi j'vas
faire avec ça" a dit, "mange ton dîner." Pis alle a mis le, le, la potte—la boulouère
dessus—et pis alle a fait le feu. Pis a fout de l'eau d'dans—et pis là ça bouille, ça
bouille. Tandis qu'i mangeait là, ça bouillait, oh là c'est—pis i pense à lui-même,
"Mais quoi-ç-tu vas faire ac ça? Quoi-ç-qu'a va faire avec ça?" Ah, ça bouillait, a dit
"As-tu fini d'manger asteure?"—"Oui" i dit "et" i dit "ç'tait bon à manger aussi.
Mais" i dit "quoi-ç-tu vas faire avec ça là?"—"Ben" a dit "asteure—j'm'en vas t'dire
eune chose" a dit. "Euh, ça ici ça va ête dur pour toi à faire" a dit. I dit "Quoi-ç-que
c'est?" Ben a dit "Faut qu'tu m'prende—et me mette dans çte *boiler*-là—dans çte
bouillère-là" a dit "et euh, me bouillir à jusqu'à temps que la chair tombe sus mes
os."

G.T.:   Hm.

—Pis a dit "Tu vas prende mes os—pis tu vas les coller" a dit "sus çte poteau
en vite là—pis tu vas faire in, eune échelle" a dit. "Pis tu vas monter en haut—pis
tu vas prende l'oeuf" a dit "pis mets-lé dans ta bouche" a dit—et pis a dit "à mesure
qu'tu redescends ramasse mes os et pis quand qu'tu vas arriver en bas—mets-les
dans l'potte." Pis a dit "J'm'en vas revenir—à moi-même encore."—"Ah" i dit "ça
c'est dur à faire, après tout l'bien qu'tu m'as fait. Pis moi" i dit "j'te laime tant" i dit.
"Ej sus en amour avec toi" i dit. "Ben" a dit "en amour ou pas" a dit "c'est, tu vas
ête obigé d'faire ça" a dit. Ah, c'est ça, i la prend pis i la flic! i la fout dans le, dans
la boulouère pis là mon homme—bouille! Bouille, bouille, bouille, bouille, bouille.
Bientôt toute la chair a tombé sus les os—ben là i ramasse tous les os—pis là i s'colle
ça sus la, la poteau en vite pis là i—monte. Pis i va en haut, i y avait juste assez d'z-os
pour—faire—l'e—l'echelle pour attraper l'oeuf. Toujours il attrape l'oeuf i l'mit
dans sa, dans sa bouche—pis là i descend. Pis là i ramasse les os à mesure i ramasse,
i ramasse, i ramasse les os à mesure. Et quand qu'il a arrivé en bas—i f—fout le, le,
les os dans la boulouère comme ielle avait dit—et toute a sauté deboute—pareil
comme—s'alle a pas té derangé heh! Oui, a s'argarde, ah! a dit "T'as pas ramassé
tous les os!"—"Oh oui!"—"Oh non" a dit, "garde" a dit "ma ptite orteil" a dit—"alle
est partie, ma ptite orteil est pas là. Mais asteure—ah ben" a dit "ça fait pas
d'diffarence" a dit. Bien, c'est bon. Ah! C'est ça. Là. Arrive à l'—a s'en va chez ielle
et pis au souère à six heures—il arrive pis i pâsse l'oeuf—au diabe—"Tchiens" i
dit—"Ben" i dit "mon cher ami—ben" i y dit, "t'as fait ton *duty*—ah! comme ça" i
dit "t'es clair. Là asteure" i dit "garde. Parce ast—tu, t'es *smart*, t'as té in beau joueur
de *poker*"—et i dit "si j'arais pas té—j'arais pas ieu le pouvouère" i dit, "j't'arais
jamais gagné non plus—mais j'avais le pouvouère. Pis comme ça" i dit "ben, je t'ai
gagné—et pis j't'ai dit d'venir" i dit "dans in an et in jour, pis t'as venu—et pis euh
toute en grand t'es derangé. Ben" i dit "asteure" i dit—"ej m'en vas t'donner ieune
de mes filles en mariage—parce t'as fait ton ouvrage comme i faut." Ben... "Ben" i
dit, i dit, "*maillnderais-tu* aouère ieune de mes filles?"—"Non!" i dit, "j'laime,
j'laimerais aouère ieune de tes filles. Hm. J'laimerais ête marié." Bien c'est ça. Là.
Ben i dit asteure—oh il avont ieu eune, eune bonne, bonne convarsation entor-z-
eusses *so on* et ci et ça—"Ici à demain matin" i dit "asteure" i dit "j'm'en vas t'mette
in—in—mouchouère" i dit "sus les yeux—pis tu vas mette mes trois filles" i dit
"côte-à-côte"—pis là i dit "tu vas" i dit "tu—j'vas t'donner l'aut—l'autorité de
toucher leurs pieds. Et pis cette-là que tu vas, que tu laimerais d'aouère—ben tu, tu
diras 'cette-là'. C'est la pus vieille ou la pus jeune ou la deuxième ou quoi-ç-que
c'est, c'est ça" i dit. "Cette-là que t'aras. Mais" i dit "j'vas pas t'donner ton choix ac
tes yeux." C'est bien. Mais là! Bien c'est ça—mais il a pensé, il a pensé eh à la ptite
orteil—"Bien" i dit "ça c'est pas mal!" i dit "Garde ça si j'ai pas bien fait—oublier

350

cette orteil-là." Hah! Pense à lui-même, dit à lui-même. I dit pas arien. Toujours l'endemain matin six heures les vlà deboute—pis ça va—in bon déjeuner—pis euh, là. Là i met in mouchoir sus tes yeux—et pis i pique ses trois filles d'—côte-à-côte—pis là lui—i tâte là—les, les, les, les pieds, les orteils là. Bientôt il a arrivé—à, à cette-là qu'avait ienque neuf-z-orteils. A y dit "Cette-là" i dit "que j'veux." Ah ben dame ç'est ça. Cette-là. Le, le diabe a pas fait attention qu'alle avait pas d'orteil ois-tu. Il a pas fait attention à ça. T'sais i commençait à vieillsir—parce qu'i oyait pas clair, heh heh! Toujours c'est bien. Ah! Ben—i les marie là. C'est ça—i les marie, toute d'suite. Ben i tiont homme et femme—mariés. Là. Ça a té comme ça euh, pour eune coupelle de jours—pt-ête eune semaine ou tcheque chose comme ça—oh j'me rappelle pas comment—comment temps qu'ç'tait mais—bien asteure entor euh, lui et sa femme—i jâsiont ois-tu, i parliont—pis i disait comment—ioù-ç-qu'i dvenait—eune belle place à vive et toute en grand. Pis asteure ielle ioù-ç-qu'a tait, bien ç'avait, i y avait pas arien à vouère ni arien du tout—ç'tait ienque son père et sa mère pis ses deux soeurs—alle avait jamais vu arien d'aute t'sais, c'est, c'est l'premier homme qu'a oyait pis euh, t'sais, c'est en masse i jâsiont entor-z-eux. I dit euh, "I wonder" i dit "si j'arais pas moyen d'aouère eune chance" i dit "d'nous degager d'ici" i dit. "Pour nous en, en aller ioù-ç-qu'ej veux, qu'ej vivais moi, avant, avant qu'ej ai venu ici" i dit. "Bien" a dit, i dit "Oh oui" i dit "si j'arais la chance, mais dame" i dit "c'est, c'est pas aisé d'aouère des chances."—"Ben" a dit "j'sais pas" a dit, "j'sais pas. Si tu sais la route toi euh, euh, j'pourras euh, arranger tcheque chose." A dit "Moi j'peux faire joliment."—"Oh" i dit "j'sais ça. Parce selon pour toi" i dit, "j'serais pas ici—j't'arais pas pour ma femme asteure" Ben, c'est bien. [pause pour changer de ruban]

G.T.:   Bon, vas-y.

—Là c'est bien. Là. Ç'a venu que—i s'avont fait les, les plans ensembe pis là ça met sus l'importance de se, de se, se faufiler. Mais dame, faulait qu'i quittiont—dans la nuit. A l'entour de minuit ou eune heure ou d'quoi d'même—pour pas qu'le père et la mère s'ava aparçu. Ben i s'faisiont leu, leu complot ensemble, il avont bien arrangé ça. Là. C'est bien. Là. A dit "Asteure là j'm'en vas faire—c'est à souère j'allons quitter."—"Oui" i dit, "s'i y a moyen du tout."—"Oui" a dit "c'est à souère j'allons quitter—j'allons quitter—à eune heure—demain matin." Pis a dit "J'm'en faire trois gâteaux—qui parlent comme moi—et pis j'allons prende le cheval à pâpa—son cheval blanc—parce ça, ça va comme la vision." Mais i y a dit "Si j'prenons euh, les, les autes chvals—les chvals rouges ou l'chval nouère"—a dit "pis i s'aparçoit—i va pas ête longtemps à mette sus nos pattes. Mais en prenant son chval—bien—c'est à y..." Là c'est bon. Là. Bien ça s'greye là. Pis i allont s'coucher et pis—le vieux et la vieille s'en va s'coucher et euh, quand qu'ç'a arrivé à minuit—là—a dit "Moi, m'en vas faire—les gâteaux, les trois gâteaux—et pis toi" a dit "tu vas aller mette la selle—sus le chval blanc." Pis a dit "Fais pas trop, trop de bruit—et pis amène le chval ici à la porte pis moi j'm'en faire les trois gâteaux qui parlent—pis j'vas mette ça dans l'escalier—et euh, comme ça quand j'aras cela et j'm'en vas sortir, ej srai pârée à embarquer—sus la selle avec toi." Pis a dit "J'allons nous pousser." Là, c'est bon. Alle a tout arrangé. Là c'est les gâteaux, lui s'en va qu, quri le, le chvau blanc. Le chval blanc. Allez! Quand qu'alle y a arrivé, à la porte—a tait pârée. Les gâteaux tiont faits, i tiont placés dans l'escalier pis alle embarque sus le, sus le cheval et pis c'est ça, i sont partis là—pis i, ça marche. Pis ça va! Hah hah hah! C'est in—sifflet! Là. Bientôt, à l'entour de deux heures—du matin, la vieille a commencé à l', l', à le taper dans l'dos, a dit "Vieux!"—"Quoi-ç-tu veux?" Le vieux a dit, sa femme "Quoi qu'i m'dit" a dit "de quoi qu'i m'dit" a dit—"que note fille est partie. Et pis Jean."—"Ah, quoi qu't'as, t'es eune vieille folle!" i dit "Dors! Tu sais bien qu'i sont pas partis" i dit, "i sont trop hereux ici."—"Non!" a dit "i sont partis à tcheque part. I sont partis."—"Ah dors!" Bien a comm—à pigouiller après lui encore—ben

351

a y dit euh, là i dit euh, i l'appelait par son nom, euh j'sais pas si ç'tait Cecilia ou euh, Genevieve ou tchelle sorte de nom qu'a y—mais a, i crie, a dit "Dors-tu là?"—A dit euh, eh, "Non" a dit "j'dors pas."—"Là ois-tu? Sacrée folle! Alle est là! Et quoi-ç-que tu—dors!" i dit. "Quitte, quitte-moi trantchille moi j'sus fatigué moi—j'veux dormir, moi." Toujours ça a té comme ça mais ielle a pouvait pas dormir—c'est pas m—de quoi qu'i disait là. Bientôt à trois heures—trois heures du matin—alle a commencé à l'proguer ac ses coudes—a dit "Vieux, vieux! Vieux!" Là. "Quoi-ç-qu'a encore ça sacrée vieille folle!" i dit. A dit "J'sus sûre" a dit "qu'i sont partis, j'sus sûre qu'i sont partis!"—"Mais tu sais bien, tu m'disais ça tantôt mais" i dit "j'ieuse ai parlé, pis j'y ai parlé pis a—i-s-étiont là! Alle est là, a m'a repondu, c'est ielle!"—"Non non!" a dit—"Pis i y a d'quoi là-d'dans."

G.T.:   Hm.

—Ben là i dit, il a enouoyé, "Jane!" i dit, "Dors-tu là?"—"Ah!" a dit "Bien" a dit "j'dormais" a dit "mais vous m'avez reveillé!"—"Dors-tu! Sacrée vieille folle! Garde!" i dit—"Si tu, t'as, t'arais, tu peux pas dormir—tu vas att, tu vas m'attraper ma main dans la djeule" i dit. "Ohh! T'as pas besoin d'ête méchant" a dit, "parce que" a dit "j'sais y a d'quoi" mais i dit "J'sais bien i t'a, a m'a dit, parlé—t'as pas de—es-tu sourd?"—"Oh non j'ai entendu ça."—"Et euh, dors! Sacrée vieille folle, dors!" Pis là hnrrr! Là ça dort, ça dort, ça dort mais ielle dort pas, pas ielle—mais lui i dort—tombe endormi—fatigué t'sais, fatigué. Bientôt à quatre heures du matin là a commence à le proguer encore. "Ah bien" i dit "toi" i dit, "ej m'en ai dû faire d'quoi avec toi—parce qu'ej t'ai dit qu'alle est là pis tu m'progaches qu'alle est pas ici—qu'alle est partie! Pis moi qui y parle tout l'temps deux fois déjà! Et quoi faire tu m'quittes pas trantchille qu'ej peux dormir? Demain" i dit "ej, j'vas pas pouoir arien faire!" Mais a dit "Alle est partie, alle est partie." Ben i crie, crie encore—"Ginny! Dors-tu?"—"Ben" a dit "j'dormais" a dit "mais vous m'avez raveillé."—"Ben vois-tu? Dors! Couche-toi et pis dors! Parce si tu vas, artires, j'm'en—satrer ça" i dit "pour, pour le premier coup de ma vie te, te frapper. Dors! Sacrée vieille folle, dors!" Bien comme ça, ça va. Toujours ça allait encore—jusqu'à cinq heures—oui mais ieusses i s'dehaliont là, ça allait là. Cinq heures du matin—la vieille encore a l'progue encore. Là i s'vire de bord pis i la croche à la gorge—"Garde!" i dit "j'ai bonne envie de t'trangler" i dit "ma saprée vieille witch!" i dit, "comment si j'te tranglais là!" i dit. "Et crois-tu qu'tu m'quitteras dormir?" i y a dit. "Mais j'te dis qu'elle est partie, moi!"—"Ah, ah, ah—garde!" i dit. "Ginny! Dors-tu?" [Émile projette une voix éloignée] Pas d'reponse. "Ginny, dors-tu?"—"Là vois-tu? Ois-tu? Ois-tu? Ois-tu? Ois-tu!" a dit. "Ben non mais i, a dort."—"Là j'te dis qu'i sont partis." Ben le vieux i saute, saute deboute! I s'fourre ses tchulottes i a ienque mis, mis ienque eune jambe—eune jambe dessus, il a hah hah! ça a fait, i tait assez pressé il, ho! il draguait l'aute jambe! En hardes de dsous sus in bord pis en tchulottes sus l'aute bord! Pis là i s'pousse—pis i va dans la chambe—partis! "Ben!" i dit "si j't'arais écouté!"—"Si t'arais don acouté!"—"Ah gee ç'tait bien, bien, bien, bien, bien dit! Asteure j'vons-ti les attraper? C'est all right! S'il ont pas pris mon cheval. Mais s'il ont pris mon cheval" i dit—"ej vas aoir d'la misère! I vont m'donner d'la misère. Bien, bien, bien, bien, sapré fou—qu'ej tais—et quâ faire qu'ej t'ai pas couté?"—"Ben j't'ai dit! Ej t'ai dit!"—"Vous m'avez bien."—Non mon homme, i s'en va à la grange pis—en s'en allant i pard ses, i pard ses tchulottes! I tait dans in long-john—i hale back sus son cheval pis là le vlà, i s'pousse—pis là i s'pousse. Il avait tant de pouvouère ois-tu le cheval ça, ça, ça allait aussi là.

G.T.:Hm.

352

—Ça tait in cheval rouge, cheval blanc, cheval nouère, c'est pas d'diffarence—i, il avait du pouvouère pour le mette du, du, du *good* là. Ça c'est bien. Là. Là ça va! Pis ça pousse, pis ça va. Pis, et pis Jean pis, pis la, celle, la, la, sa femme—ça s'pousse aussi. Et les boules de terre ça volait la vase, les ptits câilloux ça volait en l'air tait, t, t, oh tait pareil comme in vrai—*demon starm*. Là—pis le diabe—pousse aussi lui. I s'en vient là! Hoh! Ça marche! C'est bien. Là. Ça va, ça va, ça va, ça va, oh mais i tait grand jour—c'est à l'entour d'dix heures—mais le pauvre cheval là i, tait blanc mais i tait deux fois pus blanc parce qu'i tait en—la sueur, ça, c'est, c'est, l'etchume—qui sortait des, des, des côtes et tout—pouel—et toute. Pis a dit "Arrête!" a dit "arrête don" a dit "pis j'm'en vas mette mon oreille à la terre" a dit "ouère si j'entends pâpa s'en venir. Pis si j'l'entends pas s'en venir" a dit "j'avons eune ptite chance" a dit. A dit "Comment loin qu'i y a encore?"—"Mais" i dit "i y a encore—comme je crois" i dit "à l'entour de—comme cent milles pour sûr."—"Ben" a dit "j'allons ouère de la misère à l'faire parce pâpa s'en vient vite." A dit "Pâpa est tout seul sus l'dos—sus l'cheval pis nous autres j'sons à deux sus son cheval. J'sais qu'son cheval est, est beaucoup plus vite que le—mais, i, c'est in gros charge à porter. Mais" a dit "pot—partons" a dit, "viens-t-en" pis a dit "fouille ça. Fouille ça!" Pis lui mon homme i t'a enouoyé ça il avait in, des boutes des cordeaux là, les, cordes—pis i t'a enouoyé ça sus le vente, pis—i, le cheval n'en l'avait des vents. Lui a pousse, i pousse, que t'astiques, que t'astiques, oui mais alle entend la terre ça tremblait le diabe s'en venait en arrière là. Pis ça va, pis ça va, pis ça va, pis ça va, pis ça va. Bien ç'a té, pour finir l'histouère in ptit peu, in ptit peu vite—ç'a té assez, assez vite pis euh, pis assez proche—que quand que—quand qu'il ont arrivé comme j'allons dire—comme cent varges de la Terre Sainte—alle ergarde en arrière a dit "Pâpa est là-bas" a dit "i s'en vient" a dit "j'le ois s'en venir" a dit—"i, il est, i va-ti, i va nous attraper" a dit, "fa" a dit, "fouille ça! Fouille ça!" Oh ben là mon vieux i t'enouoie ça sus l'vente du cheval, oh oh! Ça, le cheval n'en, n'en *volait* ac le démon. Et pis le diabe approchait dsus—son père approchait—[Émile tousse]—ah cette malheureuse toux que j'ai là. Toujours il approchait, approchait, approchait, assez vite qu'ec, qu'ec, i, i s'croyont—i croyont que la, qu'il l'ar—il—i les arait ieu attrapé. Mais—ej pense que c'est son pouvouère qu'alle avait aussi ielle—il, i l'ont fait parce—quand qu'i avont, quand que le, le cheval blanc a mis ses deux pattes de dvant sus la Terre Sainte—le diabe tait là. C'était—ah mais ça j'te garantis! Et quand qu'il a arrivé là le, le, il a viré son cheval de bord comme ça mais il a crocheté la tcheue du, du cheval blanc—et pis c'est tout-ç-qu'il a ieu, arraché la tcheue du corps du cheval blanc! Pis i pouvait pas, i pouvait pas aller—pouvait pas—mette son pied sus la Terre Sainte il a té bigé d'ervirer d'bord—pis il [Émile, dans son excitation, avale deux ou trois mots]—ehh! qu'i garant—oo, er, i, er, a, ah—i, i, i pouvait pas parler i beguait! Pour la colère qu'i tait d'dans. Et dame il a té obigé de s'en aller back chez lui pis—moi j'tais là—c'est, pis c'est ienne, ienne d'mes onques, çui-là qu'avait venu—quand qu'il avont arrivé là ben i dit "C'est eune belle femme *dough, boy*. Belle femme." J'tais là quand qu'il avont arrivé ac leu, leu, avec le cheval blanc—mais in beau ptit cheval aussi. Ouais. Ouais pis i avont ieu eune noce de diabe, *ho, holy gee!* Ouais y a ieu du *fun!* Du *home-brew* en masse là—hah hah! Ouais! C'est *all right*.

(p. 263)

[HISTOIRE SANS TITRE I]

Bien, in coup par eune bonne fois i y avait eune homme et eune femme—pis il avont in enfant. Eune fille. Il avont eune ptite farme—coupelle de vaches—et puis euh, à tous les fois qu'i faisont, i faisiont du beurre—il enouoyiont in morceau de beurre au prête. Alle aouoyait sa fille avec in—soucoupée d'beurre. Ben ça allait bien—du bon, i faisait du bon beurre et toute—mais çte coup-là—c'était dans le mois d'août—les temps chauds—et pis euh, le samedi là ah ben a dit euh, a prend la soucoupée

353

d'beurre pis a dit à sa fille a dit "Apporte ça" a dit "au tchuré" a dit. Auprête. Ah!
Mais le beurre tait mou, ah! Toujours c'est bien, a s'en va ac le m—l'atchet d'beurre
pis a pâsse au prête—a dit "Tenez mon père" a dit "maman vous a enouoyé eune
soucoupée d'beurre encore" a dit. "Ah! Bien, bien, bien" i dit "vote beurre est-i mou"
i dit "aujord'hui?"—"Ah oui mon père" a dit—"c'est mou comme d'la marde!" Oh!
Ben là il a pas dit grand'chose—mais il a trouvé ça pas mal—insolent. Ah! Trois ou
quate jours après i, faulait qu'il alle faire des—des missions parce d'ces temps-là
ois-tu, faulait qu'i marchiont par—place en place, pt-ête bien cinq ou six milles pis
là i faisiont euh eune mission et là et ci et ça—confesser l'monde et—*so on*. Et euh,
bien en s'en allant—i—ç'tait toujours là, i pâsse chez la, chez la vieille—pis l'vieux.
Mais le vieux tait pas là c'est ienque la vieille. Toujours quand que, euh, il arrive à
la porte, i frappe à la porte, a rouve la porte "Aii—gran" a parlait tchurieux t'sais,
"*Come in Father, come in, come in!* Rente!"—"*Oh, you know* euh, euh, j'ai pas l'temps
de rentrer" i dit euh, "j'm'en vas" i dit euh "faire eune mission là." Oh ben là i disent
la place qu'alle était, tout ça—ben c'est ça oh ben dame—euh, "Ej vous ramarcie
beaucoup" i dit "pour le beurre vous m'enouoyez tous les samedis.—"Oh pas
d'quoi, y a pas d'quoi! Ben dame ça fait grand plaisir!" Mais i dit "Oui mais" i dit
"vous m'avez enouoyé in morceau" i dit "samedi pâssé" i dit "pis eune soucoupée
d'beurre" i dit pis euh, euh, "j'ai dit à vote fille le beurre tait mou."—"Ah oui, oui,
mon père" a dit, "c'était mou" a dit—"ç'in temps chaud."—"Oui oui mais" i dit "a
m'a dit que, j'ai dit qu'le beurre tait mou pis a m'a dit que le beurre tait — 'oui
mon père' a dit, 'comme, comme d'la marde'. Mou comme la marde!"—"A vous a
pas dit d'quoi d'même! Mon père?"—"Mais oui" i dit—pis i dit "Ça srait *a'right*
pour vous" i dit "la, la *correcter*" i dit là "parce qu'i, c'est pas des belles affaires
à dire! D'quoi d'même."—"Y a pas d'danger mon père! Alle est pas ici. Alle est
partie dehors à tcheque part. Mais quand qu'a va venir—ej m'en vas l'apprende
mon père, mon père, mon père, j'vas pas la manquer—m'en vas la batte en
marde!" Bon sang de la vie, là, i, i, garde, i s'pousse, ben ç'tait toute d'la marde,
i s'pousse. I s'en va pas trop loin—i y avait—son homme i tait en train de, d'mette
du, eune couvarte sus eune, sus eune cave. "*Hey!* Bonsouère!" i dit, "Bonj—bon,
bonjour" i dit "monsieur le tchuré." Euh, "Bonjour" i dit euh, George j'crois que
c'est George qui est son nom—i dit euh, "Ioù-ç-que vous allez là?"—"Ben" i dit
"j'm'en vas sus eune mission là." I dit "J'pourrais-ti t'parler pour eune minute?"—"Bien sûr" i dit "pourquoi pas" ça le, George sort dessus la grange—i dit
"Quoi-ç-qu'i y a don mon père?"—"Ben" i dit euh, "j'ai, j'veux te dire, euh, t, t,
t'as failli" i dit "in ptit peu de—pour ta fille—ça que—"—"Ma fille?" i dit
"Quoi-ç-qu'i y a don, quoi-ç-qu'i y a don?"—"Euh, oui" i dit euh, "j'ai té pâsser
chez ta, ta femme ici betôt de suite là" i dit euh, "mais alle a enouoyé in
morceau"—mais i conte l'histouère, quoi-ç-qu'i y avait arrivé—pis i dit "J'arrive
là à, à ta femme" i dit euh, "a, a, alle—le, j'y ai dit ça alle a dit a va la batte en
marde et d'quoi d'même" i dit, "c'est—"—"Oh ha ha ha ha! Ha ha ha! Mon
père—heh heh! Vous trouvez pas ça tchurieux. Parce que—je sais moi—je sais
toute ça moi."—"Et quoi-ç-que c'est, quoi-ç-que c'est?"—"Bien—regardez mon
père—m'en vas vous dire eune chose. Moi" i dit "j'sus eune parsonne—que—ej
veux pas d'folies—i y a toutes les jours—que le Bon Dieu amène—j'ai, j'ai mon
histouère à conter—ej y dis comment faire et ci et cela—et comment—se convartir parmi le monde et toute en grande. Mais mon père c'est pas utile de parler, i
y a du monde comme ça" i dit. "Çte monde-là—pas moyen d'y armette ni arien
dans leu tête—c'est fou comme mon tchul." Ha ha ha!

(p. 265)

[HISTOIRE SANS TITRE II]

Il avait eune mère comme ça aussi là, euh, pis euh, il attrapait du lapin, il avait, i tait comme douze ans eh—pas beaucoup don—justement in ptit doigt—il avait comme douze ans—pis à tous les samedis i, i prendait du lapin comme in *son-of-a-gun*—y a en masse du lapin. Toujours euh, a dit asteure a dit euh, "Va-t-en porter in lapin au prête—pis à toutes les samedis—vas porter in lapin au prête." Ben il allait, i, i portait in lapin au préte. Oui mais c'était comme ça pour cinq ou six mois—portait in lapin au préte, à toutes les samedis, à toutes les samedis. C'est bien. I dit "J'commence à ête fatigué de tout ça moi" i dit, "moi ça m'coûte de l'argent moi" i dit "pour acheter des, des, des collets et tout ça, du, du *wire* pour faire des collets et tout ça—pis jamais le préte m'a donné arien à moi." I dit pas à sa mère don—i pense ça dans son idée t'sais. I est *fed up*. I, i voulait pas aller—porter toujours le lapin—i voulait pas aller. "Oh" a dit "tu vas ête obigé d'aller—hoh! Dame!" a dit. "Note préte" a dit "faut qu'i mange aussi lui." Pis a dit "Tu vas aller—porter son lapin, comme tu fais tout l'temps." Ben c'est ça—i tait obigé d'obéir la, c'est le, les ordes c'est ci, c'est ça. Là i prend le lapin pis i s'en va—les deux zusses dehalaient en bas sus ses joues. Oh oh! I tait pas content! C'est bien. Il arrive là chez l'préte—i tape, frappe pas la porte ni arien, i rouve la porte—pis i jette le lapin dans le, dans le *kitchen*. Pis i fârme la porte pis i s'en va. Le préte là—i tait assis à sa tabe—son bureau, il ergardait le lapin est là—mais le—i savait pas tchi-ç-qui avait rêntré pis jeté ç'lapin-là, ailloù—*gee* i tait surpris—toujours i s'lève pis i s'en va pis—i rouve la porte pis i garde—le ptit garçon qui venait à tous les—"Eh hé!" i dit, "Quoi-ç-qu'i y a, Quoi-ç-qu'i y a aujord'hui?" i dit—"Quoi-ç- qu'i y a? Viens-ti, deviens oir, viens oir mon ptit garçon, viens oir, viens oir, viens ici, viens!" Ptit garçon ervire d'bord i, i dit "Quoi-ç-qu'i y a mon père?"—"Oh" i dit, "t'as, tu, mais c'est toi qu'a porté l'lapin là?"—"Oh" i dit "c'est moi, oui oui, c'est moi."—"Mais" i dit "c'est pas comme ça faut porter in lapin au préte! Oh ho ha hi!"—i rit, "heh heh!—Oh non, c'est pas comme ça" i dit, "ben rente mon ptit garçon, rente-rente-rente-rente-rente-rente-rente-rente!" Vlà le ptit garçon rente—"Garde" i dit—"t'es in beau ptit garçon toi" i dit—"ej te laime—mais" i dit "ois-tu, t'as pas bien, t'as pas té bien élevé—pis ton père et ta mère, ben tu, t'as pas d'père toi" i dit "ton père est mort—mais si ta mère ara" i dit, "t'aras té elevé comme i faut là, comme la façon" i dit "que ça devrait ête—ben t'aras pas fait ça là" i dit, "t'as pas bien fait là." Et pis i s'lève les épaules en l'air pis i repond pas—justement i s'lève les, les—en voulant dire i savait pas. I dit "Garde" i dit "justement entor mois et toi" i dit—i dit "J'm'en vas prende ma soutane—pis j'm'en—toi" i dit "tu vas ête le préte. Ej m'en mette la soutane sus toi pis tu vas t'assire ici dans ma chaise—pis moi" i dit "j'vas ête le ptit garçon—pis j'vas prende le lapin—pis" i dit "comme tu vas m'ouère faire—ben là" i dit "tu pourras faire pareil comme moi pis ça sra jusse."—"Ah ouais mon père" i dit "c'est—j'laimerais apprende ça." *A'right.* Là le préte tire sa soutane de sus lui pis i l'croche sus le ptit garçon mais dame ç'tait—trop grand pour lui—mais dame ça fait pas d'diffarance—i tait l'préte là. Là le préte sort dehors ac le lapin—pis là le préte frappe [Émile frappe sur la table] à la porte. Ben le ptit garçon a dit euh, "Rente!" Le préte rouve la porte. Le préte s'en va avec le lapin dans la main, i dit "Tchiens" i dit "mon père—je vous as porté in lapin pour votre dîner demain." Le ptit garçon dit—"Ah marci beaucoup mon ptit garçon, c'est bien gentil d'toi." Le ptit, il avait eune ptit cage avec des, des, des, des vingt-cinq cennes dedans euh, i lève le, le couvert pis i prend in vingt-cinq cennes i dit "Tchiens" i dit "mon ptit garçon, vingt-cinq sous" i dit "pour ton lapin!" Ah ha ha ha!

(p. 266)

[DEUX HISTOIRES DE MOSEY MURRIN]

G.T.:   ... Dis-moi des, des histoires à Mosey, Mosey Burns là. T'as tendu les vieilles histoires qu'i racontent sus lui.

—Ah! Oui. Mosey Born—euh, Mosey Burn—i tait à Stephenville mais i tait partout—mais i tait à Stephenville çtes temps-là—pis i faisont du *moonshine* dans le, le, le—Moonshine Valley qu'i l'appeliont—i l'ont appelé, i avont donné ç'nom-là parce qu'i y faisiont le *moonshine* là. Toujours la police assayiont, assayait d'les attraper mais i pouvait pas. Toujours il avont demandé, i avont ercontré Mose, i demande, demandait à Mose, "Mose" i dit euh, Mose savait lui mais dame—et euh, i dit "Peut-tu m'dire tchi-ç-qui fait le *moonshine*—*Who makes the moonshine*" i dit *"in Moonshine Valley?"*—*"Oh yes, sure."*—*"Who?"*—"Hoh hoh!—*Me I'm not gonna tell you*, j'vas pas t'dire" i dit. "Quoi faire? Pourquoi faire? J'te donne d'l'argent" i dit, "diras-tu?"—"Ho oui!" i dit. I dit euh, "Comment tu le voudrais?"— "Donne-moi cinq pièces j'te dirai" i dit. "Cinq dollars ej te dirai tchi-ç-qui fait le, le *moonshine*" i dit "dans le, le, *Moonshine Valley*."—*A'right* le, le *ranger* y donne cinq pièces. Là! "Tchi-ç-que c'est?" I dit "Le Bon Dieu." Ah hah ha!

G.T.:   Ha ha!

—C'est bien vrai.

G.T.:   Oui oui.

—*Moonshine*—la lune—*shaillnait* [angl. to shine].

G.T.:   Y a t-i dit après euh, "Si tu me donnes encore cinq pièces je te dirai qui fait le, le, le *sunshine*?"

—Mm! Mm.

G.T.:   Eh?

—I y ont pas donné don.

G.T.:   Non—ha ha ha!

—Huh! I y ont pas donné.

G.T.:   As-tu tendu d'autes là?

—I y avait eune aute i euh, i y avait in gars qui euh, i avait in cheval—euh çtes temps-là ben il aviont des, des sacs à clous là.

G.T.:   Oui.

—Ça pèse cinquante lives euh, ç'tait cinquante lives de clous. Pis i mettiont de l'avoine là d'dans pis i mettiont in ptit morceau d'lingne—par-dsus la tête du cheval pis i mettiont in gallon d'avoine dedans pis le cheval mangeait dans l'sac pis comme ça i n'en pardait pas.

G.T.:   Hm.

—Toujours euh, Mose Burns pâsse—i lui mettait justement i mettait le, le, la tête du cheval dans l'sac. I dit à çte gars-là i dit "Mon pauve gars" i dit, "c'est, c'est, c'est inutile quoi-ç-tu fais là." I dit "Quoi?"—"C'est inutile" i dit "tu mettras jamais le cheval dans l'sac!" Heh heh! Heh heh heh!

(p. 267)

"WE THREE" ("NOUS TROIS")

— Ah oui pou les trois gars qui avaient appris à parler.

G.T.:   Comment qu'ça s'appelle çte histoire-là?

— Ben j'sais pas l'nom de l'histouère—mais c'est—la façon qu'ej l'ai entendue ben—c'est—in coup i y avait trois—trois jeunes gars—et euh i s'aviont décidé

356

d'aller—charcher de l'ouvrage. Mais dame asteure—i parliont français—pas in mot anglais—ça ieux—joliment, de, de, joliment d'difficulté pou-z-eux. S'il ariont té à eune place qu'il ariont de l'ouvrage pis le monde parlait anglais pis ieusses pouvaient pas parler in mot anglais ben ça il avont té bien désappointés. Toujours c'est bien, *by gosh* y en avait iun toujours qui parlait anglais et français—et i s'avont décidé à aller trouver çte—çte parsonne-là—pour assayer à apprende tcheques mots à parler anglais. Bien—eh bien il allont bien—il avont commencé à discuter—bien il alliont pou charcher de l'ouvrage. Ben le—le gars qui pouvait parler anglais—i ieux dit, bien i dit "Quâ faire" i dit—euh—"que iun d'vous autes apprend pas" i dit euh, "'*We three*'—et pis l'aute eh ben—'*Lookin for a job*'—pis l'au, l'aute ben '*Lookin*, euh,—'*Quicker de better*'. S'i vous demandont '*What you lookin for?*'—ben '*We three*' — ben i dit '*Lookin for a job*' pis '*How—what time you want to go to work?*'—*Well, 'Quicker de better'.*" Ben dame il aviont ça—ben ça a pratiqué ça dans—dans eux-mêmes t'sais. '*We tree, we tree*' pis euh '*We're lookin for a job*' ben, '*Quicker de better.*' Ben c'est ça. Ben tout d'in coup il aviont ça dans la téte, fourré dans la téte pis—i s'poussont là. Ben ça a pris tcheques jours avant qu'il avont arrivé là. Toujours dans leu ouoyage—il avont rencontré—in—eune mort—sus in côté du chemin. "Tchiens! Garde là! Il y a in homme mort"—Là i dit "Ça ça va mal." Vient au l'homme, tchiens in couteau dans l', *draillvé* dans l'dos. "Bien" i dit "garde" i dit "tchequ'un" i dit "qui a tué çt homme-là." Ah! I gardont i y en a iun qui garde en l'air—çui-là qu'avait appris euh, '*We three*'—i garde—in *policeman* au ras lui. I dit "*Oo killed that man?*" I dit "*We three.*"—"*Why did you kill im?*"—L'aute rapond— "*Lookin for a job*"—"*But you're gonna be ung—hung.*" Huh! L'aute y dit euh, "*Quicker de better*"! Hah!

(p. 274)

LE RÊVE D'ÉMILE

G.T.: Émile, can you tell, peux-tu conter l'histoire là du, du rêve d'Émile là asteure?

—Oui oui, j'peux vous conter. Euh, ç'tait le printemps pâssé—ben j'allons dire en dix-neuf-cent-soixante-sept. Euh—soixante-dix-sept j'veux dire—*seventy-seven*? Ouais, soixante-dix-sept. Bien—j'ai té me coucher çte matinée-là, ç'tait dans mars, bien çte soirée-là—et pis euh, à l'entour de trois heures de la—après minuit—j'ai rêvé—j'ai rêvé in—in *reel*—et euh, ça m'a raveillé. J'ai sauté dboute—de dans mon lit et pis je cours pour le violon—j'ai pas eu l'temps de mette mes hardes dessus ni arien, j'm'en vas pis—euh, j'croche le violon pis vlà qu'ej le joue et joue et joue—pis j'ai joué pour une heure de temps là. Pis parce que ç'tait le promier j'avais rêvé— dans ma vie—j'ai rêvé j'ai té dans des danses et j'as tendu des, des musiques et toute en grand—mais j'ai jamais rêvé à, à, à composer in *reel* dans mon rêve. Toujours, c'est bien. J'ai joué l'*reel*—pis là quand que j'ai ieu fini, ben j'dis à tout cas je l'oublie je m'en vas *phoner* ma soeur—et j'm'en vas y dmander pour l'*taper*—le, le *reel*. Bien, c'est bien. J'la *phone*, bien a s'lève. Comme i disont ç'tait '*Emergency*'—c'est bon. A dit "Quoi-ç-qu'y a?—*What is wrong?*" en, en anglais—a croyait ç'tait in, in Anglais qui parlait. "Bien" j'dis, "j'ai composé in huit pis j'voudrais" j'y dis "qu'tu euh, tu diras à ton garçon d'se lever pis de le *taper* pour moi." Ben comme de fait—a dit à son garçon, i s'lève pis là i prend son mecanique pis là je la joue pis i *tape*—c'est bien. Là—je m'artourne m'coucher. Et pis je me raveille à sept heures du matin. Et j'me lève, j'allume mon poêle et pis j'prends mon violon—et pis j'assaie—et pis j'assaie à me rappeler—pis j'assayais—non! Il est parti. Il est parti. C'est bien, là qu'ej *phone*—et j'dis euh, "Dis à ton garçon" y dis "qu'i pourra mette le *tape* dessus pis i pourra m'donner eune coupelle de notes." C'est bien. Là. A y dit. Là i s'lève et pis euh, i, i, a mis la *receiver* dessus pis j'l'attends. *Deux* notes et j'dis "C'est bon, je l'ai."

Là, j'pends le, le téléphone et pis j'prends le violon pis je le joue. Ben j'dis ça c'est pas mal—c'est in réve ben j'dis j'vas l'appeler—m'en vas appeler "in rêve" ej vas l'appeler "Le Rêve à Émile." Comme ça ej dis ça srait d'quoi ej dis pour penser, vous savez, pour aouère de quoi dans l'idée à dire, ben Émile, il a révé in *reel*—*so*, in, in *reel*. C'est ça. Pis ça va comme ça ici. [Il l'interprète]

XIV

Tale Types and Motifs

Tale-type numbers are from Antti Aarne and Stith Thompson's *The Types of the Folktale*; motifs are from Thompson's *Motif-Index of Folk-Literature*. Page references are to the beginning of tales in which given types and motifs occur. Page numbers in parentheses indicate a problematic identification. An asterisked number followed by (CEFT) indicates a proposed new number.

359

MOTIFS

B. Animals

C. Tabu

D. Magic

365

XV

Bibiliography

Aarne, Antti & Stith Thompson, *The Types of the Folktale*. FF Communications No. 184, revised edition. Helsinki: Academia Scientiarum Fennica, 1961.

Arnaudin, Félix, *Contes populaires de la Grande-Lande (Première série)*. Bordeaux: Groupement des Amis de Félix Arnaudin, 1966.

Arsenault, Georges, "La Marlèche (Conte-type 56B)". *Culture & Tradition* I (1976), 19-31.

Aucoin, Gérald E., *L'oiseau de la vérité et autres contes des pêcheurs acadiens de l'île du Cap-Breton*. Montréal: Les Quinze, 1980.

Babcock-Abrahams, Barbara, "The Story in the Story: Metanarration in Folk Narrative". *Studia Fennica* 20 (Helsinki, 1976), *Folk Narrative Research*, 177-184.

Ball, John, "Style in the Folktale". *Folk-Lore* LXV (1954), 170-172.

Barbeau, Marius, Gustave Lanctôt *et al.*, "Contes populaires canadiens". *Journal of American Folklore* XXIX (1916), 1-151; XXX (1917), 1-157; XXXII (1919), 90-167; XXXIV (1923), 205-272; XXXIX (1926), 371-449; XLIV (1931), 225-294; LIII (1940), 89-191.

Barbeau, Marius, Georges Mercure, Jules Tremblay et J.-E.-A. Cloutier, "Anecdotes populaires du Canada". *Journal of American Folklore* XXXIII (1920), 173-297.

Barbour, Robert Wayne. "The Community of Mainland, 1884-1921: A Factual Report". Unpublished MS., C.E.F.T., Memorial University of Newfoundland, 1975.

Barter, Geraldine, "'Sabot-Bottes et P'tite Galoche': A Franco-Newfoundland Version of AT 545, *The Cat as Helper*". *Culture & Tradition* I (1976), 5-17.

Barter, Geraldine, *A Critically Annotated Bibliography of Works Published and Unpublished Relating to the Culture of French Newfoundlanders*. St. John's: Memorial University of Newfoundland, 1977.

Barter, Geraldine, "The Folktale and Children in the Tradition of French Newfoundlanders". *Canadian Folklore canadien* I, 1-2 (1979), 5-11.

Bauman, Richard, "Verbal Art as Performance". *American Anthropologist* LXVII (1975), 290-311.

Bauman, Richard et Joel Sherzer, eds., *Explorations in the Ethnography of Speaking*. New York: Cambridge University Press, 1974.

Baughman, Ernest W., *Type and Motif Index of the Folktales of England and North America*. The Hague: Mouton, 1966.

Ben-Amos, Dan, "Toward a Definition of Folklore in Context". In *Toward New Perspectives in Folklore*, Américo Paredes and Richard Bauman, eds. (*Journal of American Folklore* LXXXIV (1971), 3-15; and in a separate volume, Austin, 1972.

Ben-Amos, Dan and Kenneth S. Goldstein, eds., *Folklore. Performance and Communication*. The Hague: Mouton, 1975.

Bernier, Hélène, *La Fille aux mains coupées (conte-type 706)*. Québec: Presses de l'Université Laval, 1971. Les Archives de Folklore 12.

Biays, Pierre. "Un village terreneuvien: Cap-St. Georges". *Cahiers de Géographie* I (1952), 5-29.

Brékilien, Yann, *La vie quotidienne des paysans bretons (au XIXe siècle)*. Paris: Hachette, 1966.

Brosnan, R. P. Michael, *Pioneer History of St. George's Diocese, Newfoundland*. Toronto: Mission Press, 1948.

Carrière, Joseph Médard, *Tales from the French Folk-Lore of Missouri*, Chicago and Evanston: Northwestern University, 1937.

Carrière, Joseph Médard, "The Present State of French Folklore Studies in North America". *Southern Folklore Quarterly* X (1946), 219-226.

Chiasson Père Anselme, *Chéticamp. Histoire et Traditions acadiennes*. Moncton: Éditions des Aboiteaux, 1961.

Chiasson, Père Anselme, *Les Légendes des îles de la Madeleine*. Moncton: Éditions des Aboiteaux, 1969.

Claudel, Calvin, "Les contes populaires de la Louisiane". *Comptes Rendus de l'Athénée louisianais* (March 1955), 15-23.

Cosquin, Emmanuel, *Contes populaires de Lorraine*. 2 vols. Paris: Vieweg, 1887.

Dauzat, Albert, *Dictionnaire des noms de famille et prénoms de France*. Paris: Larousse, 1951.

Dégh, Linda, *Folktales and Society: Story-Telling in a Hungarian Peasant Community*. Bloomington and London: Indiana University Press, 1969.

Delarue, Paul, ed., *Contes merveilleux des Provinces de France*. 7 vols. Paris: 1953-56.

Delarue, Paul, *Le Conte populaire français*. Vol. I. Paris: Érasme, 1957.

Delarue, Paul and Marie-Louise Tenèze, *Le Conte populaire français*. Vol. II. Paris: Maisonneuve & Larose, 1964.

Dorrance, Ward Allison, *The Survival of French in the Old Sainte Genevieve District*, University of Missouri, 1935.

Dorson, Richard M., *Negro Folktales in Michigan*. Cambridge: Harvard University Press, 1956.

Dorson, Richard M., "Oral Styles of American Folk Narrators". In *Folklore in Action: Essays in Honor of MacEdward Leach*, ed. Horace P. Beck. Publications of the American Folklore Society, Bibliographical and Special Series, Vol. XIV. Philadelphia: The American Folklore Society, Inc., 1962, 77-100.

Doucet, Alain, *La littérature orale de la Baie Sainte-Marie*. Mavillette, Nova Scotia, 1965 and 1977.

Drouillet, Jean, *Folklore du Nivernais et du Morvan*. 7 vols. Vol. 1, La Charité-sur-Loire, Thoreau, 1959; vols. 2-7, M. Bernadat, 1961-74.

Dundes, Alan, *The Study of Folklore*. Englewood Cliffs, New Jersey: Prentice-Hall, Inc., 1965.

Dundes, Alan, *Interpreting Folklore*. Bloomington and London: Indiana University Press, 1980.

Dupont, Jean-Claude, *Le légendaire de la Beauce*. Québec: Garneau, 1974.

Dupont, Jean-Claude, *Contes de bûcherons*. Montréal: Les Quinze, 1976.

Dupont, Jean-Claude & Jacques Mathieu, eds., *Héritage de la Francophonie Canadienne—traditions orales.* Québec: Presses de l'Université Laval, 1986.

Fabre, Daniel and Jacques Lacroix, *La tradition orale du conte occitan.* 2 vols. Paris: Presses Universitaires de France, 1973, 1974.

Finnegan, Ruth, *Limba Stories and Story-Telling.* Oxford: The Clarendon Press, 1967.

Finnegan, Ruth, *Oral Poetry: Its Nature, Significance and Social Context.* Cambridge: Cambridge University Press, 1977.

Fortier, Alcée, *Louisiana Folk Tales, in French Dialect and English Translations.* Memoirs of the American Folklore Society, vol. II. Boston and New York: Houghton, Mifflin, 1895.

Fouché, P., *Traité de prononciation française.* Paris: 1956.

Fowke, Edith, *Folktales of French Canada.* Toronto: NC Press Ltd., 1979.

Gobineau, comte Arthur de, *Voyage à Terre-Neuve.* Paris: Hachette, 1861; reprinted, Montréal: Éditions du Jour, 1972.

Goffman, Erving, *The Presentation of Self in Everyday Life.* New York: Doubleday Anchor, 1959.

Goldstein, Kenneth S., *A Guide for Field Workers in Folklore.* Hatboro, Pennsylvania: Folklore Associates, Inc., 1964.

Goldstein, Kenneth S., ed., *Canadian Folklore Perspectives.* St. John's: Memorial University of Newfoundland, 1978.

Goldstein, Kenneth S. and N. V. Rosenberg, eds., *Folklore Studies in Honour of Herbert Halpert.* St. John's: Memorial University of Newfoundland, 1980.

Grammont, M., *Traité pratique de prononciation française.* Paris: 1933.

Grosvenor, Melville Bell, "'White Mist' Cruises to Wreck-Haunted St. Pierre and Miquelon". *National Geographic* CXXXII, 3 (1967), 378-419.

Haiding, K., *Von der Gebärdensprache der Märchenerzähler.* Helsinki: FF Communications No. 155, 1955.

Hélias, Pierre Jakez, *Le cheval d'orgueil. Mémoires d'un breton du pays bigouden.* Paris: Plon, 1975.

Hélias, Pierre Jakez, *Les autres et les miens.* Paris: Plon, 1977.

Hanlon, Catherine, "Census of Black Duck Brook, 1874-1921". Unpublished MS., C.E.F.T., Memorial University of Newfoundland, 1975.

Hayes, Francis C., "Gestos o Ademanes Folkloricos". *Folklore Americas* XI, 2 (1951), 15-21.

Hayes, Francis C., "Guía por el que recoge ademanes o gestos". *Folklore Americas* XIX, 1, (1959), 1-6.

Hayes, Francis C., "Gestures: A Working Bibliography". *Southern Folklore Quarterly* XXI, 4 (1957), 218-317.

Hymes, Dell, "Introduction: Toward Ethnographies of Communication". In John J. Gumperz and Dell Hymes, eds., *The Ethnography of Communication (American Anthropologist* LXVI, 6 (1964)), 1-34.

Hymes Dell, "Breakthrough into Performance". In Dan Ben-Amos and Kenneth S. Goldstein, eds., *Folklore. Performance and Communication,* 11-94.

Ives, Edward D., "Lumbercamp Singing and the Two Traditions". *Canadian Folk Music Journal* 5 (1977), 17-23.

Jacobs, Melville, *The Content and Style of an Oral Literature.* Chicago: University of Chicago Press, 1959.

Jansen, William Hugh, "Classifying Performance in the Study of Verbal Folklore". In *Studies in Folklore, in Honor of Distinguished Service Professor Stith Thompson,* ed. W. Edson Richmond. Bloomington: Indiana University Publications, Folklore Series 9, 1957, 110-118.

Joisten, Charles, *Contes populaires de l'Ariège*. Paris: Maisonneuve & Larose, 1965. Coll. Documentaire de Folklore de Tous les Pays, 7.

Joisten, Charles, *Contes populaires du Dauphiné*. 2 vols. Grenoble: Musée dauphinois, 1971.

Jolicoeur, Catherine, *Le Vaisseau Fantôme. Légende étiologique*. Québec: Presses de l'Université Laval, 1970. Les Archives de Folklore 11.

Jolicoeur, Catherine, *Les Plus Belles Légendes Acadiennes*. Montréal and Paris: Stanké, 1981.

Juneau, Marcel, *La Jument qui crotte de l'argent*. Québec: Presses de l'Université Laval, 1976.

King, Ruth, "Communities of the Cape St. George Area of the Port-au-Port Peninsula, 1874-1911". Unpublished MS, C.E.F.T., Memorial University of Newfoundland, 1975.

Labrie, Vivian, "Le Sabre de Lumière et de Vertu de Sagesse: Anatomie d'une Remémoration". *Canadian Folklore canadien* I, 1-2 (1979), 37-70.

Labrie, Vivian, *Précis de Transcription de Documents d'Archives Orales*. Québec: Institut Québécois de Recherche sur la Culture, 1982.

Lacourcière, Luc, "The Present State of French-Canadian Folklore Studies". *Journal of American Folklore* LXXIV, 294 (1961), 373-382.

Lacourcière, Luc, "Les Transplantations Fabuleuses. Conte-type 660". *Cahiers d'Histoire* 22 (1970), 194-204.

Lacourcière, Luc, "Les Échanges avantageux (Conte-type 1655)". *Cahiers des Dix* 35 (1970), 227-250.

Lacourcière, Luc, "Le ruban qui rend fort (Conte-type 590)". *Cahiers des Dix* 36 (1971), 235-297.

Lacourcière, Luc, "Un pacte avec le diable (Conte-type 361)". *Cahiers des Dix* 37 (1972), 275-294.

La Follette, James E., *Étude linguistique de quatre contes folkloriques du Canada français*. Québec: Presses de l'Université Laval, 1969. Les Archives de Folklore 9.

Laforte, Conrad, *Menteries drôles et merveilleuses. Contes traditionnels du Saguenay*. Montréal: Les Quinze, 1978.

Lamarre, Nicole, "Kinship and Inheritance Patterns in a French Newfoundland Village". *Recherches sociologiques* XII, 3 (1971), 345-359.

Laport, George, *Les contes populaires wallons*. FF Communications No. 101, Helsinki, 1932.

Legaré, Clément. *Contes populaires de la Mauricie*. Montréal: Fides, 1978.

Legaré, Clément., *La bête à sept têtes et autres contes de la Mauricie*. Montréal: Les Quinze, 1980.

Lemieux, Germain, *Placide-Eustache. Sources et Parallèles du conte-type 938*. Québec: Presses de l'Université Laval, 1970. Les Archives de Folklore 10.

Lemieux, Germain, *Les Jongleurs du Billochet. Conteurs et contes franco-ontariens*. Montréal: Bellarmin, 1972.

Lemieux, Germain, *Les Vieux m'ont conté*. 30 vols. Montréal: Bellarmin, 1973-

Lord, Albert B., *The Singer of Tales*. Cambridge: Harvard University Press, 1960.

Luzel, François-Marie, *Contes populaires de la Basse-Bretagne*. 3 vols. Paris: Maisonneuve, 1887. Coll. Littératures populaires de toutes les nations, XIV-XVI.

Maillet, Antonine, *Rabelais et les traditions populaires en Acadie*. Québec: Presses de l'Université Laval, 1971. Les Archives de Folklore 13.

Maranda, Elli Köngäs, "French-Canadian Folklore Scholarship: An Overview". In *Canadian Folklore Perspectives*, Kenneth S. Goldstein, ed. St. John's: Memorial University of Newfoundland, 1978, 21-37.

Marin, Louis, *Les contes traditionnels en Lorraine*. Paris: 1964.

Martinet, A., *La prononciation du français contemporain*. Paris: 1945.

Massignon, Geneviève, *Les Parlers français d'Acadie*. 2 vols. Paris: Klincksieck, 1962.

Massignon, Geneviève, *Folktales of France*. Chicago: University of Chicago Press, 1968. Coll. Folktales of the World, ed. Richard M. Dorson.

Matthews, Ralph, *"There's No Better Place Than Here": Social Change in Three Newfoundland Communities*. Toronto: Peter Martin Associates, 1976.

Mélanges en l'honneur de Luc Lacourcière. Folklore français d'Amérique. Under the direction of Jean-Claude Dupont, Ottawa. Leméac, 1978.

Morandière, Charles de la, *Histoire de la pêche française de la morue dans l'Amérique septentrionale*. 3 vols. Paris: Maisonneuve & Larose, 1962, 1966.

Morison, Samuel Eliot, *The European Discovery of America: The Northern Voyages*. New York: Oxford University Press, 1971.

Moulis, Adelin, *Contes merveilleux des Pyrénées (comté de Foix)*. Verniolle, Eds. de l'Auteur, 1976.

Newcomb, Horace, *TV: The Most Popular Art*. New York: Doubleday Anchor, 1974.

Nord 7, Contes et Légendes (Quebec), 1977.

Paddock, Harold J., *Languages in Newfoundland and Labrador* (second version). St. John's: Memorial University of Newfoundland, Department of Linguistics, 1982.

Parsons, Elsie Clews, *Folk-Lore of the Antilles, French and English*. New York: vols. I and II, Stechert & Co.; vol. III, The American Folklore Society, 1933-43. Memoirs of the American Folklore Society, vol. XXVI.

Posen, I. Sheldon, "'Just One More Before you Go': Singing and Coaxing in an Irish/Québécois Community". Unpublished paper, Folklore Studies Association of Canada, Saskatoon, 1979.

Recher, Jean, *Le grand métier. Journal d'un capitaine de pêche de Fécamp*. Paris: Plon, 1977.

Récits et contes populaires. Coll. dirigée by Jean Cuisenier. Paris: Gallimard, 1978-

Roy, Carmen, *Littérature orale en Gaspésie*. Ottawa: National Museum of Canada, 1962 (1955).

Roy, Carmen, *Saint-Pierre et Miquelon. Une mission folklorique aux îles*. Ottawa: National Museum of Canada, 1966.

Sandor, Istvan, "Dramaturgy of Tale-Telling". *Acta Ethnographica* XVI. Budapest: 1967, 305-338.

Saucier, Corinne L., *Traditions de la Paroisse des Avoyelles en Louisiane*. Philadelphia: American Folklore Society, 1956.

Saucier, Corinne L., *Folktales of French Louisiana*. Bâton Rouge: 1972 (1962).

Schmitz, Nancy, *La Mensongère (conte-type 710)*. Québec: Presses de l'Université Laval, 1972. Les Archives de Folklore 14.

Sébillot, Paul, *Contes populaires de la Haute Bretagne*. Paris: Charpentier, 1880.

Sébillot, Paul. *Contes des paysans et des pêcheurs*. Paris: Charpentier, 1881.

Sébillot, Paul. *Contes des marins*. Paris: Charpentier, 1882.

Sébillot, Paul, *Littérature orale de la Haute Bretagne*. Paris: Maisonneuve, 1881. Coll. Littératures populaires de toutes les nations, I.

Sébillot, Paul, *Le Folk-lore des pêcheurs*. Paris: Maisonneuve & Larose, 1901. Coll. Littératures populaires de toutes les nations, XLIII.

Stoker, John T., "Spoken French in Newfoundland". *Culture* XXV (1964), 349-359.

Taft, Michael, "The Itinerant Movie Man and His Impact on the Folk Culture of the Outports of Newfoundland". *Culture & Tradition* I (1976), 107-119.

Tenèze, Marie-Louise, *Le Conte populaire français*. Vol. III. Paris: Maisonneuve & Larose, 1976.

Tenèze, Marie-Louise, *Le Conte populaire français*. Vol. IV., pt. 1. Paris: Maisonneuve & Larose, 1985.

Thomas, Gerald, "Some Examples of *Blason populaire* from the French Tradition of Western Newfoundland". *RLS Regional Language Studies...Newfoundland* 7 (1976), 29-33.

Thomas, Gerald, "A Tradition Under Pressure: Folk Narratives of the French Minority of the Port-au-Port Peninsula, Newfoundland (Canada)". *Studia Fennica* 20, *Folk Narrative Research*. Helsinki: 1976, 192-201.

Thomas, Gerald, "Contexte, fonction et style d'un genre de littérature orale: *Le Rouban d'Varture*, un conte merveilleux franco-terreneuvien". *Nord* 7, *Contes et Légendes* (1977), 65-83.

Thomas, Gerald, "The Wild and the Tame: Animals in the Folklore of French Newfoundlanders". *Culture & Tradition* II (1977), 65-74.

Thomas, Gerald, "Le Centre d'Études Franco-Terreneuviennes et la culture tradionnelle des Franco-Terreneuviens". In *Archives et Recherches régionales au Canada français*. Ottawa: CRCCF, 1977, 3-12.

Thomas, Gerald, "Les études de folklore et d'histoire orale chez les Franco-Terreneuviens". In *Folklore and Oral History*, ed. Neil V. Rosenberg. St. John's: Memorial University of Newfoundland, 1978, 63-72.

Thomas, Gerald, "The French Spoken on the Port-au-Port Peninsula of Newfoundland". In *Languages in Newfoundland and Labrador*, ed. Paddock, 42-61.

Thomas, Gerald, "L'état actuel de la recherche sur le conte populaire chez les Franco-Terreneuviens". In *Mélanges en l'honneur de Luc Lacourcière: Folklore français d'Amérique*, ed. Jean-Claude Dupont. Ottawa: Leméac, 1978, 421-430.

Thomas, Gerald, "Le Centre d'Études Franco-Terreneuviennes: Bilan des activités, axes de développement". *Terre-Neuve* II, 3 (1978), 3-7.

Thomas, Gerald, "The Folktale and Folktale Style in the Tradition of French Newfoundlanders". *Canadian Folklore canadien* I, 1-2 (1979), 71-78.

Thomas, Gerald, "Other Worlds: The Folktale and Soap Opera in Newfoundland's French Tradition". In *Folklore Studies in Honour of Herbert Halpert*, ed. K. S. Goldstein & N. V. Rosenberg, 343-351.

Thomas, Gerald, "Effets réciproques entre conteur et assistance dans un contexte narratif franco-terreneuvien". *Culture & Tradition* V (1980), 33-42.

Thomas, Gerald, "'Le Conte du Renard Rouge': Conte Merveilleux Franco-Terreneuvien". *The Livyere* No. 1 (Summer 1981), 8-11.

Thomas, Gerald, "'Le Conte de la Main Coupée', conte franco-terreneuvien de Cap-St-Georges". *The Livyere* I, 2 (Fall 1981), 6-8.

Thomas, Gerald, "Two Folktales from Marche's Point, Port-au-Port Peninsula". *The Livyere* I, 3-4 (Winter-Spring 1982) 6-7.

Thomas, Gerald, "Cornelius Rouzes (1926-1981), violoneux, chanteur, raconteur franco-terreneuvien". *The Livyere* I, 3-4 (Winter-Spring 1982), 8-11.

Thomas, Gerald, "'Le Conte de l'Épée d'Or': Conte Merveilleux Franco-Terreneuvien". *The Livyere* II, 1 (August-October 1982), 6-9.

Thomas, Gerald, "Some Acadian Family Names in Western Newfoundland". *Onomastica Canadiana* 62 (Dec. 1982), 23-34.

Thomas, Gerald, "Les *devinailles* de Guillaume Robin ou l'apprentissage du professeur". In *En r'montant la tradition. Hommage au père Anselme Chiasson*, ed. Ronald Labelle & Lauraine Léger. Moncton: Les Éditions d'Acadie, 1982, 195-210.

Thomas, Gerald, "Public and Private Storytelling Situations in Franco-Newfoundland Tradition." *Arv. Scandinavian Yearbook of Folklore*, 1980, vol. 36 (Uppsala: The Royal Gustavus Adolphus Academy and Stockholm: Almqvist and Wiksell International, 1982), 175-181.

Thomas, Gerald, "Emile Benoit, Franco-Newfoundland Storyteller: Individual and Ethnic Identity." *Papers of the 8th ISFNR Congress*, 1984, Vol. IV, eds., Reimund Kvideland & Torunn Selberg, Bergen, 1985, 287-298.

Thomas, Gerald, "Noms de lieux et de lieux-dits associés aux Franco-Terreneuviens de la presqu'île de Port-au-Port." In *450 Ans de Noms de Lieux Français en Amérique du Nord*, Québec: Les Publications du Québec, 1986, 259-275.

Thomas, Gerald, "Albert 'Ding-Ding' Simon: A Tall Tale Teller From Newfoundland's French Tradition." *Newfoundland Studies*, 3, 2 (1987), 227-250.

Thomas, Gerald, "The Folktale in a Changing World: The French Newfoundland Experience." *Proceedings of the International and Interdisciplinary Congress on Dimensions of the Marvellous*, Oslo (June 1986), Vol. I, 345-360.

Thomas, Gerald, "French Family Names on the Port-au-Port Peninsula, Newfoundland." *Onomastica Canadiana* 68, 1 (June 1986), 21-22.

Thomas, Gerald, "Problèmes de transcription du texte narratif folklorique dans un contexte franco-terreneuvien." In *Le Conte*, eds. Pierre Léon & Paul Perron, Ottawa: Didier, 1987, 37-48.

Thompson, Stith, *The Folktale*. New York: Holt, Rinehart and Winston, 1946.

Thompson, Stith, *Motif-Index of Folk-Literature*. 6 vols. Bloomington: Indiana University Press, 1955-58.

Van Daele, H., *Phonétique du Français moderne*. Paris: 1927.

Van Gennep, Arnold, *Manuel de Folklore français contemporain*. Vols. I, III and IV. Paris: Picard, 1937-58.

Van Gennep, Arnold. *La Formation des Légendes*. Paris: Flammarion, 1910.

Van Gennep, Arnold, *Le Folklore du Dauphiné (Isère)*. 2 vols. Paris: Maisonneuve & Larose, 1932-33. Coll. Littératures populaires de Toutes les Nations, Nouvelle Série, vol. II-III.

Van Gennep, Arnold, *Le Folklore de la Bourgogne (Côte d'Or)*. Gap: Impr. L. Jean, 1934. Contributions au Folklore des Provinces de France, I.

Van Gennep, Arnold, *Le Folklore de la Flandre et du Hainaut français (dépt. du Nord)*. 2 vols. Paris: Maisonneuve & Larose, 1935. Contributions au Folklore des Provinces de France, II, III.

Van Gennep, Arnold, *Le Folklore de l'Auvergne et du Velay*. Paris: Maisonneuve & Larose, 1942. Contributions au Folklore des Provinces de France, V.

Von Sydow, C.W., *Selected Papers on Folklore*. Copenhagen: Rosenkilde and Bagger, 1948.

White, Thomas W., "Les Acadiens de Terre-Neuve". Moncton, New Brunswick: *L'Évangéline*, Nos. of 26 and 28 February, 4, 11, 18 and 25 March, 1, 8, 15 April and 6 May 1948.

XVI

INDEX

C

Cabot, John 21
Canada 21, 23, 145, 194, 247
— Federal Government 36
— French 153, 200, 217, 266
Cancale 26
Cap de Latte 22
Cape Bonavista 21, 22
Cape Breton Island 11, 25, 27, 90
Cape Norman 11, 22, 23, 25
Cape Ray 11, 22, 23
Cape St. George 12, 13, 22, 26, 27, 32, 33, 35, 36, 43, 45, 58, 59, 61, 62, 115, 133, 135, 144, 182, 191
Cape St. John 23
Carrière, Joseph-Médard 15, 143n
Cartier, Jacques 22
Ça Vient du Tchoeur/It Comes from the Heart 275
Census 32, 33, 36, 37n, 39n
Centre d'Etudes Franco-Terreneuviennes (CEFT) 10, 39n, 56n, 143n, 144, 148, 158, 162, 163, 168, 177, 183, 191, 200, 247, 267
Chaisson, Julien 116, 120, 121, 123, 263
Chaisson, Monica 61, 62
Chaisson, Narcisse 116, 121, 227
Châteauneuf 26
Chéticamp 24, 91
Chiasson, Fr. Anselme 15
Church 12, 33-35, 104, 107, 133
Clam Bank Cove 36, 60, 93
Claudel, Calvin 15
Coaxing 57, 61-63, 65-68, 70n, 158, 205
Codroy Valley 11, 34
Commission on Bilingualism & Biculturalism 36
Confederation 36, 114
Conte 59
Context 46, 50, 52, 54, 57, 60, 61, 67, 72, 79, 89, 241, 272
Contextualist 14, 15, 137
— functionalist 14, 15, 137
Conversation (in tales) 128, 158, 188
Cooperation (in tales) 73, 74, 79, 158, 205
Costard, Joséphine (Josie Lacosta) 16n, 158

D

Degras (De Grau) 12, 22, 31, 32, 133
Delarue, Paul 16, 76, 143n, 145, 162, 163, 183, 263
Delivery (Speed of) 71, 72, 123, 126, 138
Denys, Jean 21
Desplanques, Marie-Annick 9
Deserters 11, 30
Devil 107-110, 120, 131
Dialogue 50, 136, 188, 193
Dieppe 21

Disguise 122
Dol 26
Double-entendre 79
Drama 226, 262
Dubourdieu, Summerest 91
Duffenais, Adéline 91
Duffenais, Isabell (née Dubourdieu) 91
Dupont, Jean-Claude 15
Dynamism 79, 127

E

Elasticity 131, 264
Emile's Dream 90, 106, 273
England 11, 21, 31
English 11, 12, 23, 24, 31, 34-36, 44, 52, 58, 60, 82, 86, 91, 116, 124, 129, 160, 205, 222, 265, 267, 268, 273
Exclamations 73,791
Excuses 65
Explanations 75,791, 167

F

Fairy tale 16n
Family names 22, 24, 25, 27, 38n
Fieldwork 13, 44, 60, 67
Figgy Duff 106
Folk festivals 90, 106
Folk religion 107
Folktale 13-15, 20, 35, 41, 50, 51, 54, 57, 59, 69, 77, 85, 128, 133, 149-217, 219-275
Formulas 51, 53, 55n, 76, 23, 194
— closing 51, 53, 81, 123, 124, 158, 167, 177, 185, 188, 227
— opening 51, 53, 79, 80, 123, 124, 185
— internal 51, 80, 125
— rhymed 52
Formulaic expressions 52, 70, 75
— speech 79, 134
Fortier, Alcée 15
Fort La Latte 22
Fortune Bay 34
France 11, 16, 21-25, 30-33, 90, 162, 163, 167, 169, 183, 194, 200, 210, 217, 227, 242, 263, 268
Franco-Newfoundland 21, 30, 44, 51, 53, 57, 60, 61, 79, 85, 114, 126, 129, 173, 177, 182, 200, 205, 227
French 11-13, 24, 26, 30-32, 36, 37, 52, 58-60, 77, 116, 120, 129, 133, 168, 173, 205, 273
— culture 36, 37, 133
— fishermen 11, 30, 133
— language, dialect 15, 21, 34, 37, 44, 66, 84, 86, 137-143, 160
— Newfoundlanders 12, 13, 16, 21, 26, 27, 30, 34-36, 42, 43, 47-49, 52, 54, 87, 89-91, 107, 108, 133, 134, 136, 141, 148, 153, 162, 185, 196, 200, 210, 222, 227, 241, 263, 265
— Shore 11, 21-25, 28, 30-32

123, 138
Suspense 51

T

Teasing 62, 73, 79
— reprimand 76, 158, 176, 182
Television 13, 14, 16, 35, 42-44, 49, 51, 61,
67-69, 71, 87, 90, 106
Tenèze, Marie-Louise 16, 147, 162, 163
Tension 167
Text 14, 15, 46, 48, 53, 127, 128, 136-138
— analysis 48, 52
— transcriptions 128, 137-142, 143n
Textual fidelity 15, 53, 81, 136, 173
— style 46, 123
Thareau, Anne 9
Theatre 15, 53, 134
Thomas, Mireille 9
Thompson, Stith 16, 147, 148, 266
Three Turn Tune 106
Tickle Harbour 106
Tourout, Jack 116, 121, 227
Transcriptions, Original French 277-358

U

U.S.A. 34
Utrecht, Treaty of 11, 22

V

Veillée 13, 35, 41-44, 46, 47, 49-51, 53, 62,
63, 67, 71, 73, 75, 79, 89, 90, 113, 114,
118, 136
Vocal effects 129
Voice 123, 188
Von Sydow, Carl 72

W

West Coast (of Newfoundland) 11, 20-23,
31, 33, 36, 54n, 133, 267
West Indies 23
"We Three" 144
White (Leblanc), Thomas W. 24
Winterhouses (Maisons-d'Hiver) 12, 22, 27,
31, 34, 35, 133
Wonderful Grand Band 106
Woods, Frank (Francis Dubois) 30, 31

Canada's Atlantic Folklore-Folklife Series

Awarded the Canadian Historical Association
Regional History\Certificate of Merit

Haulin' Rope and Gaff
Songs and Poetry of the
Newfoundland Seal Fishery
Shannon Ryan/Larry Small

Below the Bridge
Helen Porter

More Than 50%
Hilda Chaulk Murray

Little Nord Easter
Victor Butler/Wilf Wareham, Editor

Maritime Folk Songs
Helen Creighton

The Winds Softly Sigh
R.F. Sparkes

fish & brewis, toutens and tales
Len Margaret

Forty-Eight Days Adrift
Captain Job Barbour

On Sloping Ground
Reminiscences of Outport Like in
Notre Dame Bay
Aubrey Tizzard

Tall Ships and Master Mariners
R. Cunningham/R. Mabee

Come and I will Sing You
Genevieve Lehr, Editor

Rattles and Steadies
Memoirs of a Gander River Man
Gary Saunders

The Last Stronghold
Scottish Gaelic Traditions in
Newfoundland
Margaret Bennett

Cape Breton Lives
A Book from Cape Breton's
Magazine
Ronald Caplan, Editor

Miners of Wabana
The Story of the Iron Ore
Workers of Bell Island
Gail Weir

Community and Process
Studies in Newfoundland Folklore
Gerald Thomas/J.D.A. Widdowson,
Editors

www.ingramcontent.com/pod-product-compliance
Lightning Source LLC
LaVergne TN
LVHW051449080426
835509LV00017B/1710